**SOUTH-WESTERN**
CENGAGE Learning

*PFIN*
Lawrence J. Gitman
Michael D. Joehnk
Randall S. Billingsley

VP Editorial Director: Jack W. Calhoun

Publisher/Director 4LTR Press: Neil Marquardt

Publisher: Joe Sabatino

Executive Editor: Mike Reynolds

Product Development Manager 4LTR Press:
Steve Joos

Senior Developmental Editor: Laura Ansara

Developmental Editor: Mike Guendelsberger

Senior Editorial Assistant: Adele Scholtz

Executive Brand Marketing Manager:
Robin Lucas

Senior Marketing Communications Manager:
Jim Overly

Marketing Manager: Nathan Anderson

Marketing Coordinator: Suellen Ruttkay

Director, Content and Media Production:
Barbara Fuller-Jacobsen

Project Manager 4LTR Press: Clara Goosman

Content Project Manager: Emily Nesheim

Media Editor: Scott Fidler

Senior Frontlist Buyer: Kevin Kluck

Production Service: Elm Street Publishing
Services & Integra Software Services Pvt. Ltd.

Senior Art Director: Michelle Kunkler

Cover and Internal Designer: Ramsdell Design

Cover Image: © Microstocker (William Howell)/
Dreamstime.com

Senior Rights Acquisitions Manager, Text:
Mardell Glinski Schultz

Text Permissions Researcher: Elaine Kosta

Senior Rights Acquisitions Manager, Images:
Deanna Ettinger

Images Permissions Researcher:
Susan Van Etten

**Exam***View*® is a registered trademark of eInstruction Corp. Windows is a registered trademark of the Microsoft Corporation used herein under license. Macintosh and Power Macintosh are registered trademarks of Apple Computer, Inc. used herein under license.

© 2011 Cengage Learning. All Rights Reserved.

Library of Congress Control Number: 2010920346

Student Edition package ISBN-13: 978-0-538-74365-5
Student Edition package ISBN-10: 0-538-74365-4
Student Edition ISBN-13: 978-0-538-74366-2
Student Edition ISBN-10: 0-538-74366-2

**South-Western Cengage Learning**
5191 Natorp Boulevard
Mason, OH 45040
USA

Cengage Learning products are represented in Canada by Nelson Education, Ltd.

For your course and learning solutions, visit **www.cengage.com.**

Purchase any of our products at your local college store or at our preferred online store **www.CengageBrain.com.**

Printed in the United States of America
1 2 3 4 5 6 7 14 13 12 11 10

# BRIEF CONTENTS

# CONTENTS

©JAIMIE DUPLASS/SHUTTERSTOCK

©MICHAEL SHAKE/SHUTTERSTOCK

© SHIPOV OLEG/SHUTTERSTOCK

# ABOUT THE AUTHORS

**LAWRENCE J. GITMAN** is an emeritus professor of finance at San Diego State University. He received his bachelor's degree from Purdue University, his M.B.A. from the University of Dayton, and his Ph.D. from the University of Cincinnati. Professor Gitman is a prolific textbook author and has more than 50 articles appearing in *Financial Management, The Financial Review,* the *Journal of Financial Planning,* the *Journal of Risk and Insurance,* the *Financial Services Review,* the *Journal of Financial Research, Financial Practice and Education,* the *Journal of Financial Education,* and other scholarly publications.

His major textbooks include *The Future of Business,* Sixth Edition, and *The Future of Business: The Essentials,* Fourth Edition, both of which are co-authored with Carl McDaniel; and *Fundamentals of Investing,* Eleventh Edition, which is co-authored with Michael D. Joehnk and Scott B. Smart. Gitman and Joehnk also wrote *Investment Fundamentals: A Guide to Becoming a Knowledgeable Investor,* which was selected as one of 1988's ten best personal finance books by *Money* magazine; *Principles of Managerial Finance,* Fifth Brief Edition; *Principles of Managerial Finance,* Twelfth Edition; *Foundations of Managerial Finance,* Fourth Edition; and *Introduction to Finance,* co-authored with Jeff Madura.

An active member of numerous professional organizations, Professor Gitman is past president of the Academy of Financial Services, the San Diego Chapter of the Financial Executives Institute, the Midwest Finance Association, and the FMA National Honor Society. In addition, he is a Certified Financial Planner® (CFP®). Gitman formerly served as a director on the CFP® Board of Governors, as vice-president–financial education for the Financial Management Association, and as director of the San Diego MIT Enterprise Forum. He has two grown children and lives with his wife in La Jolla, California, where he is an avid bicyclist.

**MICHAEL D. JOEHNK** is an emeritus professor of finance at Arizona State University. In addition to his academic appointments at ASU, Professor Joehnk spent a year (1999) as a visiting professor of finance at the University of Otago in New Zealand. He received his bachelor's and Ph.D. degrees from the University of Arizona and his M.B.A. from Arizona State University. A Chartered Financial Analyst (CFA), he has served

as a member of the Candidate Curriculum Committee and of the Council of Examiners of the Institute of Chartered Financial Analysts. He has also served as a director of the Phoenix Society of Financial Analysts and as secretary-treasurer of the Western Finance Association, and he was elected to two terms as a vice-president of the Financial Management Association. Professor Joehnk is the author or co-author of some 50 articles, five books, and numerous monographs. His articles have appeared in *Financial Management,* the *Journal of Finance,* the *Journal of Bank Research,* the *Journal of Portfolio Management,* the *Journal of Consumer Affairs,* the *Journal of Financial and Quantitative Analysis,* the *AAII Journal,* the *Journal of Financial Research,* the *Bell Journal of Economics,* the *Daily Bond Buyer, Financial Planner,* and other publications.

In addition to co-authoring several books with Lawrence J. Gitman, Professor Joehnk was the author of a highly successful paperback trade book, *Investing for Safety's Sake.* Furthermore, Dr. Joehnk was the editor of *Institutional Asset Allocation,* which was sponsored by the Institute of Chartered Financial Analysts and published by Dow Jones–Irwin. He also was a contributor to the *Handbook for Fixed Income Securities* and to *Investing and Risk Management,* Volume 1 of the Library of Investment Banking. Additionally, he served a six-year term as executive co-editor of the *Journal of Financial Research.* He and his wife live in Flagstaff, Arizona, where they enjoy hiking and other activities in the nearby mountains and canyons.

**RANDALL S. BILLINGSLEY** is a finance professor at Virginia Tech. He received his bachelor's degree in economics from Texas Tech University and received both an M.S. in economics and a Ph.D. in finance from Texas A&M University. Professor Billingsley holds the Chartered Financial Analyst (CFA), Financial Risk Manager (FRM), and Certified Rate of Return Analyst (CRRA) professional designations. An award-winning teacher at the undergraduate and graduate levels, his research, consulting, and teaching focus on investment analysis and issues relevant to practicing financial advisors. Formerly a vice president at the Association for Investment Management and Research (now the CFA Institute), Professor Billingsley's published equity valuation case study of

Merck & Company was assigned reading in the CFA curriculum for several years. In 2006, the Wharton School published his book, *Understanding Arbitrage: An Intuitive Approach to Financial Analysis*. In addition, his research has been published in refereed journals that include the *Journal of Portfolio Management*, the *Journal of Banking and Finance*, *Financial Management*, the *Journal of Financial Research*, and the *Journal of Futures Markets*. Professor Billingsley advises the Student-Managed Endowment for Educational Development (SEED) at Virginia Tech, which manages an equity portfolio of about $4.6 million on behalf of the Virginia Tech Foundation.

Professor Billingsley's consulting to date has focused on two areas of expertise. First, he has acted extensively as an expert witness on financial issues. Second, he has taught seminars and published materials that prepare investment professionals for the CFA examinations. This has afforded him the opportunity to explore and discuss the relationships among diverse areas of investment analysis. His consulting endeavors have taken him across the United States and to Canada, Europe, and Asia. A primary goal of Professor Billingsley's consulting is to apply the findings of academic financial research to practical investment decision making and personal financial planning.

# FOUNDATIONS OF FINANCIAL PLANNING

# 1

# UNDERSTANDING THE FINANCIAL PLANNING PROCESS

## LEARNING GOALS

**LG1** Identify the benefits of using personal financial planning techniques to manage your finances. (p. 3)

**LG2** Describe the personal financial planning process and define your goals. (p. 5)

**LG3** Explain the life cycle of financial plans, the role they play in achieving your financial goals, how to deal with special planning concerns, and the use of professional financial planners. (p. 11)

**LG4** Examine the economic environment's influence on personal financial planning. (p. 17)

**LG5** Evaluate the impact of age, education, and geographic location on personal income. (p. 20)

**LG6** Understand the importance of career choices and their relationship to personal financial planning. (p. 20)

## LG1 The Rewards of Sound Financial Planning

What does living "the good life" mean to you? Does it mean having the flexibility to pursue your dreams and goals in life? Is it owning a home in a certain part of town, starting a company, being debt free, driving a particular type of car, taking luxury vacations, or having a large investment portfolio? Today's complex, fast-paced world offers a bewildering array of choices. Rapidly changing economic, political, technological, and social environments make it increasingly difficult to develop solid financial strategies that are guaranteed to improve your lifestyle. Moreover, the recent financial crisis dramatizes the need to plan for financial contingencies. No matter how you define it, the good life requires sound planning to turn financial goals into reality.

The best way to achieve financial objectives is through *personal financial planning,* which helps us define our financial goals and develop appropriate strategies to reach them. We cannot depend on employee or government benefits—such as steady salary increases or adequate funding from employer-paid pensions or Social Security—to retire comfortably. Creating flexible plans and regularly revising them is the key to building a sound financial future. Successful financial planning also brings rewards that include greater flexibility, an improved standard of living, wise spending habits, and increased wealth. Of course, planning alone does not guarantee success; but having an effective, consistent plan can help you use your resources wisely. Careful financial planning increases the chance that your financial goals will be achieved and that you will have sufficient flexibility to handle such contingencies as illness, job loss, and even financial crises.

The goal of this book is to remove the mystery from the personal financial planning process and replace it with the tools you need to take charge of your personal finances and your life. To organize this process, the text is divided into six parts as follows.

- **Part 1:** Foundations of Financial Planning
- **Part 2:** Managing Basic Assets
- **Part 3:** Managing Credit
- **Part 4:** Managing Insurance Needs
- **Part 5:** Managing Investments
- **Part 6:** Retirement and Estate Planning

©CHRISTINEG/DREAMSTIME.COM

Each part explains a different aspect of personal financial planning, as shown in Exhibit 1.1. This organizational scheme revolves around financial decision making that's firmly based on an operational set of financial plans. We believe that sound financial planning enables individuals to make decisions that will yield their desired results.

**standard of living**
The necessities, comforts, and luxuries enjoyed or desired by an individual or family.

## Improving Your Standard of Living

With personal financial planning we learn to acquire, use, and control our financial resources more efficiently. It allows us to gain more enjoyment from our income and thus to improve our **standard of living**—the necessities, comforts, and luxuries we have or desire.

Americans view standards of living, and what constitute necessities or luxuries, differently depending on their level of affluence. For example, 45% of Americans consider a second or vacation home the ultimate symbol of affluence, while others see taking two or more annual vacations or living in an exclusive neighborhood as an indicator of wealth.

So our quality of life is closely tied to our standard of living. Although other factors—geographic location, public facilities, local cost of living, pollution, traffic, and population density—also affect quality of life, wealth is commonly viewed as a key determinant. Material items such as a house, car, and clothing as well as money available for health care, education, art, music, travel, and entertainment all contribute to our quality of life. Of course, many so-called wealthy people live "plain" lives, choosing to save, invest, or support philanthropic organizations with their money rather than indulge themselves with luxuries.

One trend with a profound effect on our standard of living is the *two-income family.* What was relatively rare in the early 1970s has become commonplace today, and the incomes of millions of families have risen sharply as a result. About 75% of married adults state that they and their mate share all their money, while some partners admit to having a secret stash of cash. Two incomes buy more, but they also require greater responsibility to manage the money wisely.

**4ltrpress.cengage.com**

**Exhibit 1.1    Organizational Planning Model**

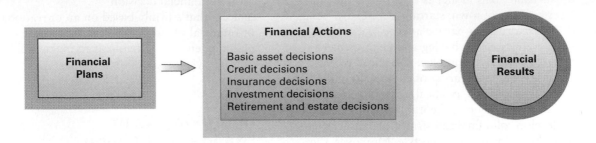

This text emphasizes making financial decisions regarding assets, credit, insurance, investments, and retirement and estates.

**Financial Plans** → **Financial Actions**
- Basic asset decisions
- Credit decisions
- Insurance decisions
- Investment decisions
- Retirement and estate decisions

→ **Financial Results**

© KAREN HERMANN/ISTOCKPHOTO

**average propensity to consume** The percentage of each dollar of income, on average, that a person spends for current needs rather than savings.

# Spending Money Wisely

Using money wisely is a major benefit of financial planning. Whatever your income, you can either spend it now or save some of it for the future. Determining your current and future spending patterns is an important part of personal money management. The goal, of course, is to spend your money so that you get the most satisfaction from each dollar.

## Current Needs

Your current spending level is based on the necessities of life and your **average propensity to consume**, which is the percentage of each dollar of income, on average, that is spent for current needs rather than savings. A minimum level of spending would allow you to obtain only the necessities of life: food, clothing, and shelter. Although the quantity and type of food, clothing, and shelter purchased may differ among individuals depending on their wealth, we all need these items to survive.

Some people with high average propensities to consume earn low incomes and spend a large portion of it for basic necessities. On the other hand, individuals earning large amounts quite often have low average propensities to consume, in part because the cost of necessities represents only a small portion of their income.

Still, two people with significantly different incomes could have the same average propensity to consume because of differences in their standard of living. The person making more money may believe it is essential to buy better-quality items or more items and will thus, on average, spend the same percentage of each dollar of income as the person making far less. This chapter's *Money in Action* feature reveals some of our attitudes toward acquiring and keeping wealth and its relationship to happiness.

## Future Needs

In any carefully developed financial plan, you should set aside a portion of current income for deferred, or future, spending. Placing these funds in various savings and investment vehicles allows you to generate a return on your funds until you need them. For example, you may want to build up a retirement fund to maintain a desirable standard of living in your later years. Instead of spending the money now, you defer actual spending until the future when you retire. Nearly 35% of Americans say retirement planning is their most pressing financial concern. Other examples of deferred spending include saving for a child's education, a primary residence or vacation home, a major acquisition (such as a car or home entertainment center), or even a vacation.

The portion of current income we commit to future

©PRESSMASTER/DREAMSTIME.COM

# MONEY IN ACTION

## Money and Happiness

Can money really buy happiness? Surely there is some link between money and happiness. But perhaps the better question is how you can transform your hard-earned money into the "good life," as you define it. Happiness researchers conclude that money can help you find happiness, but only if you have realistic expectations about what money can and cannot do for you.

We believe that a little bit more money will make us happier. But the more money you make, the more you want. And research shows that the more you get, the less happy it makes you. Since World War II, inflation-adjusted income has nearly tripled and the size of new homes has more than doubled. Yet polls show that the wealthiest Americans aren't any happier than those with less money. After basic human needs are met, more money doesn't seem to add much happiness. For example, a recent poll shows the happiness curve flattens out at an annual income of about $50,000. So making $100,000 a year will not make you twice as happy as when you only made $50,000. Simply put, we overestimate how much more money will add to happiness. In order to feel happy and secure, Americans need enough money to retire, to buy some of the things they want, and to cope with possible financial setbacks.

There is a tendency to compare ourselves with the family next door. The American journalist H. L. Mencken once remarked that the happy man earns $100 more than his wife's sister's husband. Happiness researchers find that how you compare to others has a bigger effect on your happiness than the absolute amount of money you make.

If you want to understand how money can make you happier, you must understand what makes people happy in general. A recent University of Chicago poll shows that people with five or more close friends are 50% more likely to consider themselves "very happy" than those with fewer friends. Even more important to your happiness is your "significant other." And being actively engaged affects happiness more than acquiring things. Humans are addicted to challenges. Indeed, we are often happier while working toward a goal than when we actually reach it.

So what do happy people do differently? They don't waste time stewing over unpleasant things. While they focus on interpreting life positively, they don't let the successes of others bother them. They just don't compare themselves with others. Happy people say that they spend less and appreciate what they have more.

Source: Adapted from David Futrelle, "Can Money Buy Happiness?" http://money.cnn.com/magazines/moneymag/moneymag_archive/2006/08/01/8382225/index.htm, accessed April 2009.

© KATIV/ISTOCKPHOTO

---

needs depends on how much we earn and also on our average propensity to consume. About 45% of affluent Americans say they need at least $2.5 million to feel rich. The more we earn and the less we devote to current spending, the more we can commit to meeting future needs. In any case, some portion of current income should be set aside regularly for future use. This practice creates good saving habits.

## Accumulating Wealth

In addition to using current income to pay for everyday living expenses, we often spend it to acquire assets such as cars, a home, or stocks and bonds. Our assets largely determine how wealthy we are. Personal financial planning plays a critical role in the accumulation of wealth by directing our financial resources to the most productive areas.

One's **wealth** depends on the total value of all the items that the individual owns. Wealth consists of financial and tangible assets. **Financial assets** are intangible, paper assets, such as savings accounts and securities (stocks, bonds, mutual funds, and so forth). They are *earning assets* that are held for the returns they promise. **Tangible assets**, in contrast, are physical assets, such as real estate and automobiles. These assets can be held for either consumption (e.g., your home, car, artwork, or jewelry) or investment purposes (e.g.,

a duplex purchased for rental income). In general, the goal of most people is to accumulate as much wealth as possible while maintaining current consumption at a level that provides a desired standard of living. To see how you compare with the typical American in financial terms, check out the statistics in Exhibit 1.2.

## LG2 The Personal Financial Planning Process

Many people erroneously assume that personal financial planning is only for the wealthy. However, nothing could be further from the truth. Whether you have a lot of money or not enough, you still need personal financial planning. If you have enough money, planning can help you spend and invest it wisely. If your income seems inadequate, taking steps to plan your financial activities will lead to an improved lifestyle. **Personal financial planning**

**wealth** The total value of all items owned by an individual, such as savings accounts, stocks, bonds, home, and automobiles.

**financial assets** Intangible assets, such as savings accounts and securities, that are acquired for some promised future return.

**tangible assets** Physical assets, such as real estate and automobiles, that can be held for either consumption or investment purposes.

**personal financial planning** A systematic process that considers important elements of an individual's financial affairs in order to fulfill financial goals.

## Exhibit 1.2   The Average American, Financially Speaking

This financial snapshot of the "average American" can give you an idea of where you stand in terms of income, net worth, and other measures. It should help you set some goals for the future.

| | Income and Assets |
|---|---|
| **What Do We Earn?** (*average*) | |
| All families | $   84,300 |
| Self-employed | 191,800 |
| Retired | 48,700 |
| **What Are We Worth?** (*average*) | |
| All families | $   556,300 |
| Self-employed | 1,961,300 |
| Retired | 543,100 |
| **Home Ownership** (*median*) | |
| Value of primary residence | $200,000 |
| Mortgage on primary residence | 107,000 |
| **How Much Savings Do We Have?** (*median*) | |
| Mutual funds | $   56,000 |
| Individual stocks | 17,000 |
| Bonds | 80,000 |
| Bank accounts/CDs | 24,000 |
| Retirement accounts | 45,000 |

*Source:* Adapted from Brian K. Bucks, Arthur B. Kennickell, Traci L. Mach, and Kevin B. Moore, "Changes in U.S. Family Finances from 2004 to 2007: Evidence from the Survey of Consumer Finances," *Federal Reserve Bulletin,* Board of Governors of the Federal Reserve System, Washington, DC, vol. 95 (February 2009), pp. A1–A55, http://www.federalreserve.gov/pubs/oss/oss2/2007/scf2007home.html, accessed April 2009.

is a systematic process that considers the important elements of an individual's financial affairs and is aimed at fulfilling his or her financial goals.

Everyone—including recent college graduates, young married couples, and others—needs to develop a personal financial plan. Knowing what you need to accomplish financially, and how you intend to do it, gives you an edge over someone who merely reacts to financial events as they unfold.

## Steps in the Financial Planning Process

If you take a closer look at financial planning, you'll see that the process translates personal financial goals into specific financial plans, which then help you implement those plans through financial strategies. The financial planning process involves the six steps shown in Exhibit 1.3. As you can see, the financial planning process runs full circle. You start with financial goals, formulate and implement financial plans

 *Everyone—including recent college graduates, young married couples, and others—needs to develop a personal financial plan.*

Just think of the example provided by the recent financial crisis. Do you think that a financial plan would have helped in weathering the financial storm?

and strategies to reach them, monitor and control progress toward goals through budgets, and use financial statements to evaluate the plan and budget results. This leads you back to redefining your goals so that

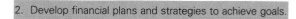

## Exhibit 1.3 The Six-Step Financial Planning Process

The financial planning process translates personal financial goals into specific financial plans and strategies, implements them, and then uses budgets and financial statements to monitor, evaluate, and revise plans and strategies as needed. This process typically involves the six steps shown in sequence here.

1. Define financial goals.

2. Develop financial plans and strategies to achieve goals.

3. Implement financial plans and strategies.

4. Periodically develop and implement budgets to monitor and control progress toward goals.

5. Use financial statements to evaluate results of plans and budgets, taking corrective action as required.

6. Redefine goals and revise plans and strategies as personal circumstances change.

they better meet your current needs and to revising your financial plans and strategies accordingly.

Let's now look at how goal setting fits into the planning process. In Chapters 2 and 3, we'll consider other information essential to creating your financial plans: personal financial statements, budgets, and taxes.

### Defining Your Financial Goals

**Financial goals** are the results that an individual wants to attain. Examples include buying a home, building a college fund, and achieving financial independence. What are your financial goals? Have you spelled them out? It's impossible to effectively manage your financial resources without financial goals. We

need to know where we are going, in a financial sense, to effectively meet the major financial events in our lives. Your financial goals or preferences must be stated in monetary terms because money, and the satisfaction it can foster, is an integral part of financial planning.

### The Role of Money

About 80% of Americans believe that money is power, and about 75% say that it is freedom. **Money** is the medium of exchange used to measure value in financial

**financial goals** Results that an individual wants to attain, such as buying a home, building a college fund, or achieving financial independence.

**money** The medium of exchange used as a measure of value in financial transactions.

### FINANCIAL ROAD SIGN

**GETTING YOUR FINANCIAL ACT TOGETHER**
Will this be the year you finally straighten out your finances? Here are five important things you can do to get your financial act together.

1. Start keeping good financial records.
2. Put together a realistic budget that you can live with.
3. Save for a specific goal by paying yourself first.
4. Begin saving for retirement.
5. Set up an emergency fund.

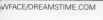

**utility** The amount of satisfaction received from purchasing certain types or quantities of goods and services.

transactions. It would be difficult to set specific personal financial goals and to measure progress toward achieving them without the standard unit of exchange provided by the dollar. Money, as we know it today, is the key consideration in establishing financial goals. Yet it's not money, as such, that most people want. Rather, we want the **utility**, which is the amount of satisfaction received from buying certain types or quantities of goods and services, that money makes possible. People may choose one item over another because of a special feature that provides additional utility. The added utility may result from the actual usefulness of the special feature or from the "status" it's expected to provide or both. Regardless, people receive varying levels of satisfaction from similar items, and their satisfaction isn't necessarily related to the cost of the items. We therefore need to consider utility along with cost when evaluating alternative qualities of life, spending patterns, and forms of wealth accumulation.

### Go to Smart Sites

Is getting the lowest price important to you? Where can you search for the best prices? Whenever you see "*Go to Smart Sites*" in this chapter, visit **4ltrpress .cengage.com** for help finding answers online. ●

### The Psychology of Money

Money and its utility are not only economic concepts; they're also closely linked to the psychological concepts of values, emotion, and personality. Your personal value system—the important ideals and beliefs that guide your life—will also shape your attitude toward money and wealth accumulation. If you place a high value on family life, you may choose a career that offers regular hours and less stress or choose an employer who offers flextime rather than a higher-paying position that requires travel and lots of overtime. You may have plenty of money but choose to live frugally and do things yourself rather than hire someone to do them for you. Or if status and image are important to you, you may spend a high proportion of your current income on acquiring luxuries. Financial goals and decisions should be consistent with your personal values. You can formulate financial plans that provide the greatest personal satisfaction and quality of life by identifying your values.

Money is a primary motivator of personal behavior because it has a strong effect on self-image. Each person's unique personality and emotional makeup

determine the importance and role of money in his or her life. You should become aware of your own attitudes toward money because they are the basis of your "money personality" and money management style. Check out the Bonus Exhibits at 4ltrpress.cengage.com to explore your attitude toward money.

Some questions to ask yourself include: How important is money to you? Why? What types of spending give you satisfaction? Are you a risk taker? Do you need large financial reserves to feel secure? Knowing the answers to these questions is a prerequisite to developing realistic and effective financial goals and plans. Trade-offs between current and future benefits are strongly affected by values, emotions, and personality. Effective financial plans are both economically and psychologically sound. They must not only consider your wants, needs, and financial resources but must also realistically reflect your personality and emotional reactions to money.

## Money and Relationships

The average couple spend between 250 and 700 hours planning their wedding, and they spend an average of about $20,000 on the big day. But with all the hoopla surrounding the wedding day, many couples overlook one of the most important aspects of marriage: financial compatibility. Money can be one of the most emotional issues in any relationship, including that with a partner, your parents, or children. Most people are uncomfortable talking about money matters and avoid such discussions, even with their partners. However, differing opinions on how to spend money may threaten the stability of a marriage or cause arguments between parents and children. Learning to communicate with your partner about money is a critical step in developing effective financial plans.

The best way to resolve money disputes is to be aware of your partner's financial style, keep the lines of communication open, and be willing to compromise. It's highly unlikely that you can change your partner's style (or your own, for that matter), but you can work out your differences. Financial planning is an especially important part of the conflict resolution process. To gain a better understanding of your differences, work together to establish a set of financial goals that takes into account each person's needs and values.

## Types of Financial Goals

Financial goals cover a wide range of financial aspirations: controlling living expenses, meeting retirement needs, setting up a savings and investment program, and minimizing your taxes. Other important financial goals include having enough money to live as well as possible, being financially independent, sending children to college, and providing for retirement.

Financial goals should be defined as specifically as possible. Saying that you want to save money next year is not a specific goal. How much do you want to save, and for what purpose? A goal such as "save 10% of my take-home pay each month to start an investment program" states clearly what you want to do and why.

Because they are the basis of your financial plans, your goals should be realistic and attainable. If you set a savings goal too high—for example, 25% of your take-home pay when your basic living expenses already account for 85% of it—then your goal is unattainable and there's no way to meet it. But if savings goals are set too low, you may not accumulate enough for a meaningful investment program. If your goals are unrealistic, they'll put the basic integrity of your financial plan at risk and be a source of ongoing financial frustration.

It's important to involve your immediate family in the goal-setting process. When family members "buy into" the goals, it eliminates the potential for future conflicts and improves the family's chances for financial success. After defining and approving your goals, you can prepare appropriate cash budgets. Finally, you should assign priorities and a time frame to financial goals. Are they short-term goals for the next year, or are they intermediate or long-term goals that will not be achieved for

many more years? For example, saving for a vacation might be a medium-priority short-term goal, whereas buying a larger home may be a high-priority intermediate goal and purchasing a vacation home a low-priority long-term goal. Normally, long-term financial goals are set first, followed by a series of corresponding short-term and intermediate goals.

**goal dates** Target dates in the future when certain financial objectives are expected to be completed.

## Putting Target Dates on Financial Goals

Financial goals are most effective when they are set with goal dates. **Goal dates** are target points in the future when you expect to have achieved or completed certain financial objectives. They may serve as progress checkpoints toward some longer-term financial goals and/or as deadlines for others. One goal may be to purchase a boat in 2015 (the goal date), another to accumulate a net worth of $200,000 by 2026. In the latter case, goal dates of 2016 and 2021 could be set for attaining a net worth of $10,000 and $110,000, respectively.

### Long-Term Goals

Long-term financial goals should indicate wants and desires for a period covering about 6 years out to the next 30 or 40 years. Although it's difficult to pinpoint exactly what you will want 30 years from now, it's useful to establish some tentative long-term financial goals. However, you should recognize that long-term goals will change over time and that you'll need to revise them accordingly. If the goals seem too ambitious, you'll want to make them more realistic. If they're too conservative, you'll want to adjust them to a level that encourages you to make financially responsible decisions rather than squander surplus funds.

### Short-Term Goals and Intermediate Goals

Short-term financial goals are set each year and cover a 12-month period. They include making substantial, regular contributions to savings or investments in order to accumulate your desired net worth. Intermediate goals bridge the gap between short- and long-term goals; and of course, both intermediate and short-term goals should be consistent with your long-term goals. Short-term goals become the key input for the cash budget, a tool used to plan for short-term income and expenses. To define your short-term goals, consider your immediate goals, expected income for the year, and long-term goals. Short-term planning should also include establishing an emergency fund with 3 to 6 months' worth of income. This special savings account serves as a safety reserve in case of financial emergencies such as a temporary loss of income.

Set financial goals carefully and realistically, as they form the basis for your personal financial plans. Each goal should be clearly defined and have a priority, time frame, and cost estimate.

## Personal Financial Goals

Name(s) __Bob and Cathy Case__    Date __December 27, 2010__

### Short-Term Goals (1 year or less)

| Goal | Priority | Target Date | Cost Estimate |
|------|----------|-------------|---------------|
| Buy new tires and brakes for Ford Focus | High | Feb. 2011 | $ 500 |
| Buy career clothes for Andrea | High | May 2011 | 1,200 |
| Take Colorado ski trip | Medium | Mar. 2011 | 1,800 |
| Replace stereo components | Low | Sept. 2011 | 1,100 |
| Buy new work clothes for Tim | Medium | June 2011 | 750 |
| | | | |
| | | | |
| | | | |

### Intermediate Goals (2 to 5 years)

| Goal | Priority | Target Date | Cost Estimate |
|------|----------|-------------|---------------|
| Start family | High | 2013 | – |
| Repay all loans except mortgage | High | 2014 | $ 7,500 |
| Trade Focus and buy larger car | High | 2014 | 10,500 |
| Buy new bedroom furniture | Low | 2015 | 4,000 |
| Take 2-week Hawaiian vacation | Medium | 2012–13 | 5,000 |
| Review insurance needs | High | 2013 | – |
| Accumulate $100,000 net worth | High | 2015 | – |

### Long-Term Goals (6+ years)

| Goal | Priority | Target Date | Cost Estimate |
|------|----------|-------------|---------------|
| Begin college fund | High | 2016 | ? /year |
| Diversify/increase investment portfolio | High | 2017 | Varies |
| Buy larger home | High | 2019 | $ 250,000 |
| Take European vacation | Low | 2018 | $ 10,000 |
| Retire from jobs | High | 2043 | ? |
| Increase college fund contributions | High | 2018 | – |

© KEITH WEBBER JR./ISTOCKPHOTO

Unless you attain your short-term goals, you probably won't achieve your intermediate or long-term goals. It's tempting to let the desire to spend now take priority over the need to save for the future. But by making some short-term sacrifices now, you're more likely to have a comfortable future. Worksheet 1.1 is a convenient way to summarize your personal financial goals. It groups them by time frame (short-term, intermediate, or long-term) and lists a priority for each goal (high, medium, or low), a target date to reach the goal, and an estimated cost.

We have filled out the form showing the goals that Bob and Cathy Case set in December 2010. The Case's were married in 2007, own a condominium in a Midwestern suburb, and have no children. Because Bob and Cathy are 28 and 26 years old, respectively, they have set their longest-term financial goal 33 years from now, when they want to retire. Bob has just completed his fifth year as a marketing representative for a large auto products manufacturer. Cathy, a former elementary school teacher, finished her MBA in May 2009 and began working at a local advertising agency. Bob and Cathy love to travel and ski. They plan to start a family in a few years, but for now they want to develop some degree of financial stability and independence. Their goals include purchasing assets (clothes, stereo, furniture, and car), reducing debt, reviewing insurance, increasing savings, and planning for retirement.

## LG3 From Goals to Plans: A Lifetime of Planning

How will you achieve the financial goals you set for yourself? The answer, of course, lies in the financial plans you establish. Financial plans provide the roadmap for achieving your financial goals. The six-step financial planning process (introduced in Exhibit 1.3) results in separate yet interrelated components covering all the important financial elements in your life. Some elements deal with the more immediate aspects of money management, such as preparing a budget to help manage spending. Others focus on acquiring major assets, controlling borrowing, reducing financial risk, providing for emergency funds and future wealth accumulation, taking advantage of and managing employer-sponsored benefits, deferring and minimizing taxes, providing for financial security when you stop working, and ensuring an orderly and cost-effective transfer of assets to your heirs.

> **{ Financial plans provide the roadmap for achieving your financial goals. }**

In addition to discussing your financial goals and attitudes toward money with your partner, you must allocate responsibility for money management tasks and decisions. Many couples make major decisions jointly and divide routine financial decision making on the basis of expertise and interest. Others, such as Beth and Jack Norris, believe it is important for their entire family to work together

as a team to manage the family finances. They hold family financial meetings once every few months to help their children understand how the household money is spent.

## The Life Cycle of Financial Plans

Financial planning is a dynamic process. As you move through different stages of your life, your needs and goals will change. Yet certain financial goals are important regardless of age. Having extra resources to fall back on in an economic downturn or period of unemployment should be a priority whether you are 25, 45, or 65. Some changes—a new job, marriage, children, moving to a new area—may be part of your original plan.

©REEFER/DREAMSTIME.COM

More often than not, you'll face unexpected "financial shocks" during your life: loss of a job, a car accident, divorce or death of a spouse, a long illness, or the need to support adult children or aging parents. With careful planning, you can get through tough times and prosper in good times. You need to plan ahead and take steps to weather life's financial storms. For example, setting up an emergency fund or reducing monthly expenses will help protect you and your family financially if a setback occurs.

As we move from childhood to retirement age, we traditionally go through different life stages. Exhibit 1.4 illustrates the various components of a typical *personal financial planning life cycle* as they relate to these different life stages. This exhibit presents the organizing framework of the entire financial planning process. We will refer to it throughout the book—as we suggest that you do for the rest of your life. As we pass from one stage of maturation to the next, our patterns of income, home ownership, and debt also change. From early childhood, when we rely on our parents for support, to early adulthood, when we hold our first jobs and start our families, we can see a noticeable change in income patterns. For example, those in the 45–64 age group tend to have higher income than those younger than age 45. Thus, as our emphasis in life changes, so do the kinds of financial plans we need to pursue.

**Exhibit 1.4** **The Personal Financial Planning Life Cycle**

As you move through life and your income patterns change, you'll typically have to pursue a variety of financial plans. For instance, after graduating from college your focus will be on buying a car and a house, and you'll be concerned about health and automobile insurance to protect against loss.

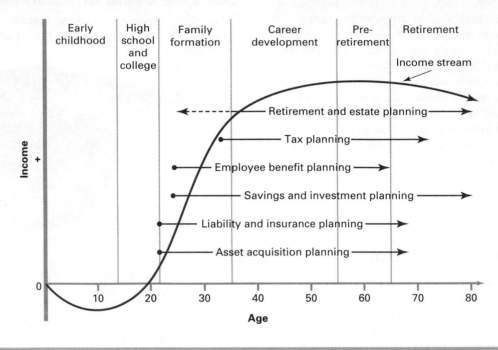

## Plans to Achieve Your Financial Goals

Today new career strategies—planned and unplanned job changes, or several different careers over a lifetime, for example—are common and may require that financial plans be revised. Many young people focus on their careers and building a financial base before marrying and having children. The families of women who interrupt their careers to stay home with their children, whether for 6 months or 6 years, will experience periods of reduced income. A divorce, a spouse's death, or remarriage can also drastically change your financial circumstances. Many people in their 30s, 40s, and 50s find themselves in the "sandwich generation," supporting their elderly parents while still raising their own children and paying for college. And some people must cope with reduced income due to jobs lost because of corporate downsizing or early retirement.

## Plans to Achieve Your Financial Goals

Financial goals can range from short-term goals, such as saving for a new sound system, to long-term goals, such as saving enough to start your own business. Reaching your particular goals requires different types of financial planning.

### Asset Acquisition Planning

One of the first categories of financial planning we typically encounter is asset acquisition. We accumulate *assets*—things we own—throughout our lives. These include *liquid assets* (cash, savings accounts, and money market funds) used to pay everyday expenses, *investments* (stocks, bonds, and mutual funds) acquired to earn a return on our money, *personal property* (movable property such as automobiles, household furnishings, appliances, clothing, jewelry, home electronics, and similar items), and *real property* (immovable property; land and anything fixed to it, such as a house). Chapters 4 and 5 focus on important considerations for managing liquid assets and other major assets such as automobiles and housing.

### Liability and Insurance Planning

Another category of financial planning is liability planning. A *liability* is something we owe, which is measured by the amount of debt we incur. We create liabilities by borrowing money. By the time most of us graduate from college, we have debts of some sort or another: e.g., education loans, car loans, credit card balances, and so on. Our borrowing needs typically increase as we acquire assets like a home, furnishings, and appliances. Whatever the source of credit, such transactions have one thing in common: *the debt must be repaid at some future time.* How we manage our debt burden is just as important as how we manage our assets. Managing credit effectively requires careful planning, which is covered in Chapters 6 and 7.

Obtaining adequate *insurance coverage* is also essential. Like borrowing money, obtaining insurance is generally something that's introduced relatively early in our life cycle (usually early in the family formation stage). Insurance is a way to reduce financial risk and protect both income (life, health, and disability insurance) and assets (property and liability insurance). Most consumers regard insurance as absolutely essential—and for good reason. One serious illness or accident can wipe out everything you have accumulated over many years of hard work. But having the wrong amount of insurance can be costly. We'll examine how to manage your insurance needs in Chapters 8, 9, and 10.

## Savings and Investment Planning

As your income begins to increase, so does the importance of savings and investment planning. Initially, people save to establish an emergency fund for meeting unexpected expenses. Eventually, however, they devote greater attention to investing excess income as a means of accumulating wealth, either for major expenditures such as a child's college education or for retirement. Individuals build wealth through savings and the subsequent investing of funds in various investment vehicles: common or preferred stocks, government or corporate bonds, mutual funds, real estate, and so on. The higher the returns on the investment of excess funds, the greater the wealth they accumulate.

Exhibit 1.5 shows the impact of alternative rates of return on accumulated wealth. The graph shows that if you had $1,000 today and could keep it invested at 8%, then you would accumulate a

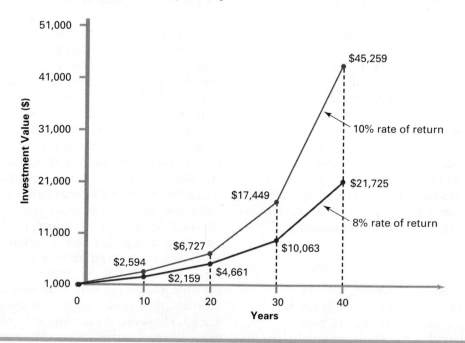

© PAKHNYUSHCYY/DREAMSTIME.COM

### Exhibit 1.5    How a $1,000 Investment Grows over Time

Eight or 10 percent: What's the big deal? The deal is more than twice the money over a 40-year period! Through the power of compound interest, a higher return means dramatically more money as time goes on.

considerable sum of money over time. For example, at the end of 40 years, you'd have $21,725 from your original $1,000. Earning a higher rate of return has even greater rewards. Some might assume that earning, say, 2 percentage points more (i.e., 10% rather than 8%) would not matter a great deal. But it certainly would! Observe that if you could earn 10% over the 40 years then you'd accumulate $45,259, or more than twice as much as you'd accumulate at 8%. This powerful observation applies not only to seemingly modest difference in rates of return over time. For as we'll explore in Part 5 on managing investments, apparently small differences in various investment management fees can also translate into significant differences in net investment returns over long periods of time. The length of time you keep your money invested is just as important as the rate of return you earn on your investments. You can accumulate more than twice as much capital by investing for 40 rather than 30 years with either rate (8% or 10%) of return. This is the magic of compound interest, which explains why it's so important to create strong savings and investment habits early in life. We'll examine compounding more fully in Chapter 2, savings in Chapter 4, and investments in Chapters 11, 12, and 13.

### Employee Benefit Planning
Your employer may offer a wide variety of employee benefit plans, especially if you work for a large firm. These could include life, health, and disability insurance; tuition reimbursement programs for continuing education; pension, profit-sharing, and 401(k) retirement plans; flexible spending accounts for child care and health care expenses; sick leave, personal time, and vacation days; and other miscellaneous benefits such as employee discounts and subsidized cafeterias or parking.

Managing your employee benefit plans and coordinating them with your other plans is an important part of the overall financial planning process. Especially in today's volatile labor market, you can no longer assume that you'll be working at the same company for many years. If you change jobs, your new company may not offer the same benefits. So your personal financial plans should include contingency plans to replace employer-provided benefits as required. We'll discuss employee benefits in greater detail in Chapters 2 (planning); 3 (taxes); 8, 9, and 10 (insurance); and 14 (retirement).

### Tax Planning
Despite all the talk about tax reform, our tax code remains highly complex. Income can be taxed as active (ordinary), portfolio (investment), passive, tax-free, or tax-deferred. Then there are tax shelters,

© IQONCEPT/SHUTTERSTOCK

which use various aspects of the tax code (such as depreciation expenses) to legitimately reduce an investor's tax liability. Tax planning considers all these factors and more. It involves looking at your current and projected earnings and then developing strategies that will defer and minimize taxes. Tax plans are closely tied to investment plans and will often specify certain investment strategies. Although tax planning is most common among individuals with high incomes, people with lower incomes can also obtain sizable savings. We'll examine taxes and tax planning in Chapter 3.

### Retirement and Estate Planning
While you're still working, you should be managing your finances to attain those goals you feel are important after you retire. These might include maintaining your standard of living, extensive travel, visiting children, frequent dining at better restaurants, and perhaps a vacation home or boat. Retirement planning should begin long before you retire. As a rule, most people don't start thinking about retirement until well into their 40s or 50s. This is unfortunate, because it usually results in a substantially reduced level of retirement income. The sooner you start, the better off you'll be. Take, for instance, the IRA (individual retirement account), whereby certain wage earners were allowed to invest up to $6,000 per year in 2009. If you start investing for retirement at age 40, and put only $2,000 per year in an IRA earning 5% for 25 years, then your account will grow to $95,454 at age 65. However, if you start your retirement program 10 years earlier (at age 30), your IRA will grow

to a whopping $180,641 at age 65. Although you're investing only $20,000 more ($2,000 per year for an extra 10 years), your IRA will nearly double in size. We'll look at IRAs and other aspects of retirement planning in Chapter 14.

Accumulating assets to enjoy in retirement is only part of the long-term financial planning process. As people grow older, they must also consider how they can most effectively pass their wealth on to their heirs, an activity known as *estate planning*. We'll examine this complex subject—which includes such topics as wills, trusts, and the effects of gift and estate taxes—in Chapter 15.

## Special Planning Concerns

Students may not think that they need to spend much time on financial planning—not yet, anyway. However, the sooner you start, the better prepared you'll be to adapt your plans to changing personal circumstances. Such changes include changing or losing a job, relocating to a new state, getting married, having children, being in a serious accident, getting a chronic illness, losing a spouse through divorce or death, retiring, or taking responsibility for dependent parents. These and other stressful events are "financial shocks" that require reevaluation of your financial goals and plans.

 **Go to Smart Sites**

The Genworth Center for Financial Learning Web site provides links to other Web sites that will help you plan for changing life situations, with planning tools, online courses, and advice geared to different life stages. ●

### Managing Two Incomes

As a general rule, partners in two-income households need to approach discussions on financial matters with an open mind and be willing to compromise. Spouses need to decide together how to allocate income to household expenses, family financial goals, and personal spending goals. Will you use a second income to meet basic expenses, afford a more luxurious lifestyle, save for a special vacation, or invest in retirement accounts? You may need to try several money management strategies to find the one that works best for you. Some couples place all income into a single joint account. Others have each spouse contribute *equal* amounts into a joint account to pay bills, but retain individual discretion over remaining income. Still others contribute a *proportional* share of each income to finance joint expenses and goals. In any case, both spouses should have money of their own to spend without accountability.

For an example of managing two incomes, see Worksheet 2.5 in Chapter 2, or get it online at 4ltrpress.cengage.com.

### Managing Employee Benefits

If you hold a full-time job, then your employer probably provides various employee benefits, ranging from health and life insurance to pension plans. These are valuable benefits, which can have a major financial impact on family income. Most American families depend solely on employer-sponsored group plans for their health insurance coverage and also for a big piece of their life insurance coverage and retirement needs.

Today's well-defined employee benefits packages cover a full spectrum of benefits that may include:

- Health and life insurance
- Disability insurance
- Long-term care insurance
- Pension and profit-sharing plans
- Supplemental retirement programs, such as 401(k) plans
- Dental and vision care
- Child care, elder care, and educational assistance programs
- Subsidized employee food services

Each company's benefit package is different. Some companies and industries are known for generous benefit plans; others offer far less attractive packages. In general, large firms can afford more benefits than small ones can. Because employee benefits can increase your total compensation by 30% or more, you should thoroughly investigate your employee benefits to choose those appropriate for your personal situation. Be sure to coordinate your benefits with your partner's to avoid paying for duplicate coverage. Companies change their benefit packages often and today are shifting more costs to employees. Although an employer may pay for some benefits in full, typically employees pay for part of the cost of group health insurance, supplemental life insurance, long-term care insurance, and participation in voluntary retirement programs.

Due to the prevalence of two-income families and an increasingly diverse workforce, many employers today are replacing traditional programs, where the company sets the type and amount of benefits, with **flexible-benefit (cafeteria) plans**. In flexible-benefit programs, the employer allocates a certain amount of money to each employee and then lets the employee "spend" that money for benefits that suit

**flexible-benefit (cafeteria) plans** The employer allocates a certain amount of money to each employee and then lets the employee "spend" that money for benefits that suit his or her age, marital status, number of dependent children, and level of income.

his or her age, marital status, number of dependent children, level of income, and so on. These plans usually cover everything from child care to retirement benefits, offer several levels of health and life insurance coverage, and have some limits on the minimum and maximum amounts of coverage. Within these constraints, you can select the benefits that do you the most good. In some plans, you can even take part of the benefits in the form of more take-home pay or extra vacation time!

## FINANCIAL ROAD SIGN

### PLANNING FOR CRITICAL LIFE EVENTS

Just like you, financial plans go through stages. Financial plans must adapt to changes over your lifetime. *Here are some more critical life events* that may make you reconsider and possibly revise an existing financial plan.

1. *Marriage:* Finances must be merged and there may be a need for life insurance.
2. *Children:* It's time to start a college saving plan and revise your budget accordingly. A will is needed that makes provisions for guardianship if both parents die while the children are minors.
3. *Divorce:* Financial plans based on two incomes are no longer applicable. Revised plans must reflect any property settlements, alimony, and/or child support.
4. *Death of a parent:* The estate must be settled and help in managing a possible inheritance may be needed.
5. *Retirement:* During retirement you will try to preserve your capital and will rely on the income generated by your investments. While investment risk should be reduced greatly, it has not been eliminated because inflation risk must be managed.

### Managing Your Finances in Tough Economic Times

Tough economic times can be due to broad macroeconomic trends like a recession, or they can be brought on by more personal, local developments. The effects of recessions and financial crises divide people into three groups: (1) those who are directly and severely hurt through job loss, (2) those who are marginally hurt by reduced income, and (3) those who are not directly hurt. If you are in either of the first two groups, you must make significant lifestyle changes to reduce spending. Even if you are in the last group, a recession affects you indirectly. For example, retirement accounts typically drop in value and financial plans must be revised. And everyone's expectations are at least temporarily affected, which causes most people to be more cautious about their expenditures during a recession or crisis.

The financial crisis of 2008 and 2009 was a macroeconomic challenge of historic global proportions. It drove home the benefits of having a sound financial plan—and dramatized the cost of not having one. The precipitous decline in stock and home prices and the many people laid off from their jobs made everyone think a lot more about financial planning in general and how to survive a financial crisis in particular. Although we all hope that such broad crises will be rare, it is important to plan for a possible recurrence. All of the financial planning principles explained in this book remained valid during the recent global financial crisis and should continue to serve us well in any future similar situations. But the breadth of the recent crisis posed some special planning issues.

So how do you best plan to survive a broad-based financial crisis? First, you remind yourself of the key principles of financial planning presented in this book:

- Spend less than you earn.
- Keep investing so your money continues to work toward your goals.
- Know where you are and plan for the unexpected. You cannot know where you are financially unless you carefully—and frequently—update your family's budget. And it is important to set aside money for an emergency fund. As discussed earlier in this chapter, you should set aside enough cash to last between 3 and 6 months.

Second, don't panic when financial markets crash! This means that you shouldn't try to time the market by buying when the experts say it's at a low or by selling when they say it's at a high. Continue to invest for the long-term but keep in mind how close you are to achieving your financial objectives. For example, if you pull all of your money out of the stock market when it has fallen, you will not be positioned to take advantage of its eventual recovery. Recessions and financial crises can be challenging. A financial plan that considers such contingencies will help you weather the storm.

## Using Professional Financial Planners

Most financial planners fall into one of two categories based on how they get paid: commissions or fees. *Commission-based planners* earn commissions on the financial products they sell, whereas *fee-only planners* charge fees based on the complexity of the plan they prepare. Many financial planners take a hybrid approach and charge fees and collect commissions on products they sell, offering lower fees if you make product transactions through them. For a guide to some of the different planning designations, see the Chapter 1 Bonus Exhibits at 4ltrpress.cengage.com.

## LG4 The Planning Environment

Financial planning takes place in a dynamic economic environment created by the actions of government, business, and consumers. Your purchase, saving, investment, and retirement plans and decisions are influenced by both the present and future states of the economy. Understanding the economic environment will allow you to make better financial decisions.

Consider that a strong economy can lead to high returns in the stock market, which in turn can positively affect your investment and retirement programs. The economy also affects the interest rates you pay on your mortgage and credit cards as well as those you earn on savings accounts and bonds. Periods of high inflation can lead to rapid price increases that make it difficult to make ends meet. Here we look at two important aspects of the planning environment: the major financial planning players and the economy.

### The Players

The financial planning environment contains various interrelated groups of players, each attempting to fulfill certain goals. Although their objectives are not necessarily incompatible, they do impose some constraints on one another. There are three vital groups: government, business, and consumers. Exhibit 1.6 shows the relationships among these groups.

#### Government

Federal, state, and local governments provide us with many essential public goods and services, such as police and fire protection, national defense, highways, public education, and health care. The federal government plays a major role in regulating economic activity. Government is also a customer of business and an employer of consumers, so it's a source of revenue for business and of wages for consumers. The two major constraints from the

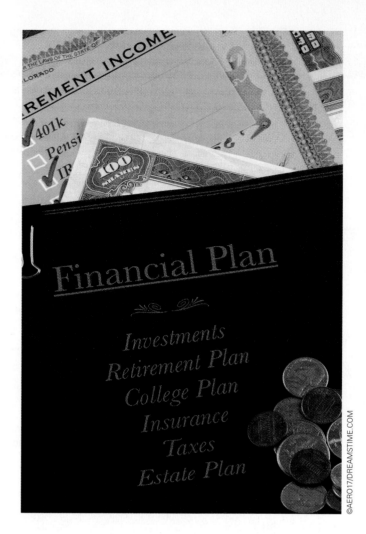

perspective of personal financial planning are taxation and regulation.

#### Business

As Exhibit 1.6 shows, business provides consumers with goods and services and in return receives payment in the form of money. Firms must hire labor and use land and financial capital (economists call these *factors of production*) to produce these goods and services. In return, firms pay out wages, rents, interest, and profits to the various factors of production. Thus, businesses are an important part of the circular flow of income that sustains our free enterprise system. In general, they create a competitive environment in which consumers may select from an array of goods and services. All businesses are limited in some way by federal, state, and local laws.

#### Consumers

The consumer is the central player in the financial planning environment. Consumer choices ultimately determine the kinds of goods and services that businesses will provide. The consumer's choice of whether to spend or save also has a direct impact on present and future circular flows of money. Cutbacks

**Exhibit 1.6** | **The Financial Planning Environment**

Government, business, and consumers are the major players in our economic system. They all interact with one another to produce the environment in which we carry out our financial plans.

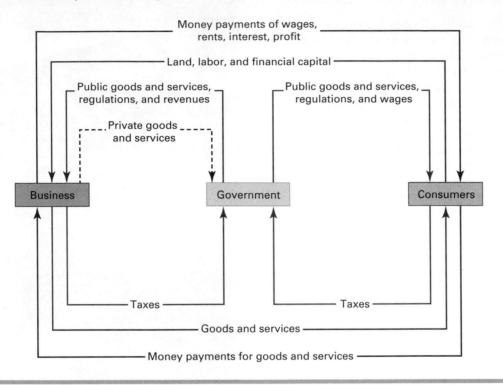

in consumer spending are usually associated with a decline in economic activity, whereas increases in consumer spending help the economy to recover.

## The Economy

Our economy is influenced by interactions among government, business, and consumers as well as by world economic conditions. Through specific policy decisions, the government's goal is to manage the economy to provide economic stability and a high level of employment. Government decisions have a major impact on the economic and financial planning environment. The federal government's *monetary policy*—programs for controlling the amount of money in circulation (the money supply)—is used to stimulate or moderate economic growth. For example, increases in the money supply tend to lower interest rates. This typically leads to a higher level of consumer and business borrowing and spending that increases overall economic activity. The reverse is also true. Reducing the money supply raises interest rates, which reduces consumer and business borrowing and spending and thus slows economic activity.

The government's other principal tool for managing the economy is *fiscal policy*—its programs of spending and taxation. Increased spending for social services, education, defense, and other programs stimulates the economy, while decreased spending slows economic activity. Increasing taxes, on the other hand, gives businesses and individuals less to spend and, as a result, negatively affects economic activity. Conversely, decreasing taxes stimulates the economy. The importance of fiscal policy is illustrated by the government's massive spending to stimulate the U.S. economy in 2008 and 2009 as the way to address the prevailing financial crisis.

### Economic Cycles

Although the government uses monetary and fiscal policy to manage the economy and provide economic stability, the level of economic activity changes constantly. The upward and downward movement creates *economic cycles* (also called *business cycles*). These cycles vary in length and in how high or low the economy moves. An economic cycle typically contains four stages: *expansion, recession, depression,* and *recovery.*

Exhibit 1.7 shows how each of these stages relates to employment and production levels, which are two important indicators of economic activity. The stronger the economy, the higher the levels of employment and production. Eventually a period of economic **expansion** will peak and begin moving downward, becoming a **recession** when the decline lasts more than 6 months. A **depression** occurs when a recession worsens to the point where economic growth is almost at a standstill or even negative. The **recovery** phase, with increasing levels of employment and production, follows either a recession or a depression. For about 75 years, the government has been reasonably successful in keeping the economy out of a depression, although we have experienced periods of rapid expansion and high inflation followed by periods of deep recession. And

©LIVIU TOADER/SHUTTERSTOCK

**expansion** The phase of the economic cycle when levels of employment and production are high and the economy is growing, generally accompanied by rising prices for goods and services.

**recession** The phase of the economic cycle when levels of employment and production fall and the growth of the economy slows.

**depression** The phase of the economic cycle when levels of employment and production are low and economic growth is at a virtual standstill or even negative.

**recovery** The phase of the economic cycle when levels of employment and production are improving and the economy is growing.

## Exhibit 1.7 The Economic Cycle

The economy goes through various stages over time, although real depressions are extremely rare. These stages tend to be cyclical and directly affect the levels of employment and production.

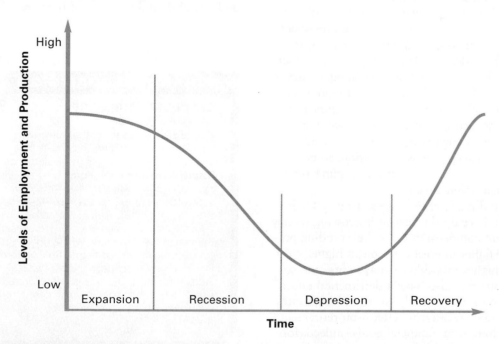

**inflation** A state of the economy in which the general price level is increasing.

**consumer price index (CPI)** A measure of inflation based on changes in the cost of consumer goods and services.

**purchasing power** The amount of goods and services each dollar buys at a given time.

some would argue that the financial crisis of 2008 and 2009 came close to precipitating a depression.

### Inflation, Prices, and Planning

As we've discussed, our economy is based on the exchange of goods and services between businesses and their customers—consumers, government, and other businesses—for a medium of exchange called money. The mechanism that facilitates this exchange is a system of *prices*. Technically speaking, the price of something is *the amount of money the seller is willing to accept in exchange for a given quantity of some good or service*—for instance, $3 for a pound of meat or $10 for an hour of work. The economy is said to be experiencing a period of **inflation** when the general level of prices *increases* over time. The most common measure of inflation, the **consumer price index (CPI)**, is based on changes in the cost of consumer goods and services. At times, the rate of inflation has been substantial. In 1980, for instance, prices went up by a whopping 13.6%. Fortunately, inflation has dropped dramatically in this country, and the annual rate of inflation has remained below 5% every year since 1983, except in 1990 when it was 5.4%. Since 2000, the rate of inflation has ranged between 1.6% and 3.8%.

Inflation is of vital concern to financial planning. It affects not only what we pay for our goods and services but also what we earn in our jobs. Inflation tends to give an illusion of something that doesn't exist. That is, though we seem to be making more money, we really aren't. As prices rise, we need more income because our **purchasing power**—the amount of goods and services each dollar buys at a given time—declines. For example, assume that you earned $45,000 in 2007 and received annual raises so that your salary was $48,000 by 2010. That represents an annual growth rate of 2.2%. However, if inflation averaged 2.8% per year then your purchasing power would have decreased, even though your income rose: you'd need $48,887 just to keep pace with inflation. So be sure to look at what you earn in terms of its purchasing power, not just in absolute dollars.

Inflation also directly affects interest rates. High rates of inflation drive up the cost of borrowing money as lenders demand compensation for their eroding purchasing power. Higher interest rates mean higher mortgage payments, higher monthly car payments, and so on. High inflation rates also have a detrimental effect on stock and bond prices. Finally, sustained high rates of inflation can have devastating effects on retirement plans and other long-term financial goals. Indeed, for many people they can put such goals out of reach.

©YURI ARCURS/SHUTTERSTOCK

## LG5, LG6 What Determines Your Personal Income?

An obvious and important factor in determining how well we live is the amount of income we earn. In the absence of any inheritance or similar financial windfall, your income will largely depend on such factors as your age, marital status, education, geographic location, and choice of career. Making a lot of money isn't easy, but it can be done! A high level of income—whether derived from your job, your own business, or your investments—is within your reach if you have the dedication, commitment to hard work, and a well-thought-out set of financial plans. The data

---

**FINANCIAL ROAD SIGN**  $$$

**CALCULATE THE COST OF THAT MOVE**
Before saying yes to that out-of-town job offer, take a minute to consult the various online cost-of-living calculators at Homefair.com, **http://www.homefair.com**. They will give you a feel for how your dollar will stretch in your new city compared with your old one. The site also offers guides to housing, schools, and other useful information.

If you are a homeowner, or are considering buying a home and want to know where you'll get the most house for your money, go to **http://hpci.coldwellbanker.com/**. Home Price Comparison Index provides a relocation price index for hundreds of areas in the United States. You can use it to find out what it would cost to buy a home or to decide whether your standard of living will go up or down if you move.

## Exhibit 1.8 How Age and Education Affect Annual Income

The amount of money you earn is closely tied to your age and education. Generally, the closer you are to middle age (45–65) and the more education you have, the greater your income will be.

### Annual Income (Head of Household)

| Age | Average Income |
| --- | --- |
| Less than 35 | $ 51,700 |
| 35–44 | 83,700 |
| 45–54 | 112,400 |
| 55–64 | 111,200 |
| 65–74 | 92,500 |
| 75 or more | 45,700 |

| Education | Average Income |
| --- | --- |
| No high school diploma | $ 31,300 |
| High school diploma | 51,500 |
| Some college | 68,100 |
| College degree | 143,800 |

*Source:* Adapted from Brian K. Bucks, Arthur B. Kennickell, Traci L. Mach, and Kevin B. Moore, "Changes in U.S. Family Finances from 2004 to 2007: Evidence from the Survey of Consumer Finances," *Federal Reserve Bulletin,* Board of Governors of the Federal Reserve System, Washington, DC, vol. 95 (February 2009), pp. A1–A55, http://www.federalreserve.gov/pubs/oss/oss2/2007/scf2007home.html, accessed April 2009.

in Exhibit 1.8 show how income changes with age and education. For example, people with low incomes typically fall into the very young or very old age groups. Heads of households who have more formal education earn higher annual incomes than do those with lesser degrees.

{ *Your income will largely depend on such factors as your age, marital status, education, geographic location, and choice of career.* }

## Where You Live

Geographic factors can also affect your earning power. Salaries vary regionally, tending to be higher in the Northeast and West than in the South. Typically, your salary will also be higher if you live in a large metropolitan area rather than a small town or rural area. Such factors as economic conditions, labor supply, and industrial base also affect salary levels in different areas. Living costs also vary considerably throughout the country. You'd earn more in Los Angeles than in Memphis, Tennessee, but your salary would probably not go as far due to the much higher cost of living in Los Angeles.

## Your Career

A critical determinant of your lifetime earnings is your career. The career you choose is closely related to your level of education and your particular skills, interests, lifestyle preferences, and personal values. Social, demographic, economic, and technological trends also influence your decision as to what fields offer the best opportunities for your future. It's not a prerequisite for many types of careers (e.g., sales, service, and certain types of manufacturing and clerical work), but a formal education generally leads to greater decision-making responsibility—and consequently increased income potential—within a career. Exhibit 1.9 presents a list of average salaries for various careers.

### Go to Smart Sites

One of the first steps in the job-search process is to assess your personality. Link to the Keirsey Temperament Sorter®-11 as a starting point. ●

## Planning Your Career

Career planning and personal financial planning are closely related activities, so the decisions you make in one

## Exhibit 1.9 Representative Salaries for Selected Careers

Professional and managerial workers, who typically have a college degree, tend to earn the highest salaries.

| Career | Average Annual Salary |
|--------|----------------------|
| Accountants and auditors | $ 65,840 |
| Architects and engineers | 71,430 |
| Computer programmer | 73,470 |
| Family and general practice physicians | 161,490 |
| Financial analyst | 84,780 |
| Human resources manager | 103,920 |
| Lawyer | 124,750 |
| Paralegal | 48,790 |
| Pharmacist | 104,260 |
| Police officer | 52,810 |
| Psychologist | 90,460 |
| Registered nurse | 65,130 |
| Teacher, elementary school | 52,240 |

*Source:* "News, Occupational Employment and Wages, 2008," *Occupational Outlook Handbook,* May 2009, United States Department of Labor, Bureau of Labor Statistics, http://www.bls.gov/oes, accessed May 2009.

area affect the other. Like financial planning, career planning is a lifelong process that includes short- and long-term goals. Since your career goals are likely to change several times, you should not expect to stay in one field, or to remain with one company, for your whole life.

 **Go to Smart Sites**

The U.S. News & World Report Career Center has material on a variety of career topics ranging from internships and résumés to the hottest careers and benefits. ●

The average American starting a career today can expect to have at least ten jobs with five or more employers, and many of us will have three, four, or even more careers during our lifetimes. Some of these changes will be based on personal decisions; others may result from layoffs or corporate downsizing. For example, a branch manager for a regional bank who feels that bank mergers have reduced her job prospects in banking may buy a quick-print franchise and become her own boss. Job security is practically a thing of the past, and corporate loyalty has given way to a more self-directed career approach that requires new career strategies.

Through careful career planning, you can improve your work situation to gain greater personal and professional satisfaction. Some of the steps are similar to the financial planning process described earlier.

● Identify your interests, skills, needs, and values.
● Set specific long- and short-term career goals.
● Develop and use an action plan to achieve those goals.
● Review and revise your career plans as your situation changes.

A personal portfolio of skills, both general and technical, will protect your earning power during economic downturns and advance it during prosperous times. Employers need flexible, adaptable workers as companies restructure and pare down their operations. It's important to keep your skills current with on-the-job training programs and continuing education.

Good job-hunting skills will serve you well throughout your career. Learn how to research new career opportunities and investigate potential jobs, taking advantage of online resources as well as traditional ones. Develop a broad base of career resources, starting with your college placement office, the public library, and personal contacts such as family and friends. Know how to market your qualifications to your advantage in your résumé and cover letters, on the phone, and in person during a job interview.

# FINANCIAL PLANNING EXERCISES

**LG1** 1. How can using personal financial planning tools help you improve your financial situation? Describe changes you can make in at least three areas.

**LG2, 3** 2. *Use Worksheet 1.1.* Fill out Worksheet 1.1, "Summary of Personal Financial Goals," with goals reflecting your current situation and your expected life situation in 5 and 10 years. Discuss the reasons for the changes in your goals and how you'll need to adapt your financial plans as a result.

**LG2** 3. Recommend three financial goals and related activities for someone in each of the following circumstances:
   a. Junior in college
   b. 25-year-old computer programmer who plans to earn an MBA degree
   c. Couple in their 30s with two children, ages 3 and 6
   d. Divorced 45-year-old man with a 15-year-old child and a 75-year-old father who is ill

**LG4** 4. Summarize current and projected trends in the economy with regard to GDP growth, unemployment, and inflation. How should you use this information to make personal financial and career planning decisions?

**LG6** 5. Assume that you graduated from college with a major in marketing and took a job with a large consumer products company. After 3 years, you are laid off when the company downsizes. Describe the steps you'd take to "repackage" yourself for another field.

# 2

# DEVELOPING YOUR FINANCIAL STATEMENTS AND PLANS

## LG1 Mapping Out Your Financial Future

On your journey to financial security, you need navigational tools to guide you to your destination: namely, the fulfillment of your financial goals. Operating without a plan is like traveling without a road map. Financial plans, financial statements, and budgets provide direction by helping you work toward specific financial goals. *Financial plans* are the roadmaps that show you the way, whereas *personal financial statements* let you know where you stand financially. *Budgets,* detailed short-term financial forecasts that compare estimated income with estimated expenses, allow you to monitor and control expenses and purchases in a manner that is consistent with your financial plans. All three tools provide control by bringing the various dimensions of your personal financial affairs into focus.

## The Role of Financial Statements in Financial Planning

Before you can set realistic goals, develop your financial plans, or effectively manage your money, you must take stock of your current financial situation. You'll also need tools to monitor your progress. **Personal financial statements** are planning tools that provide an up-to-date evaluation of your financial well-being, help you identify potential financial problems, and help you make better-informed financial decisions. They measure your financial condition so you can establish realistic financial goals and evaluate your progress toward those goals. Knowing how to prepare and interpret personal financial statements is a cornerstone of personal financial planning.

> *Knowing how to prepare and interpret personal financial statements is a cornerstone of personal financial planning.*

The **balance sheet** describes your financial position—the assets you hold, less the debts you owe, equal your net worth (general level of wealth)—at a *given point in time.* In contrast, the **income and expense statement** measures financial performance *over* time. **Budgets,** another type of financial report, are *forward* looking, and allow you to monitor and control spending because they are based on expected income and expenses. Exhibit 2.1 summarizes the various financial statements and reports and their relationship to each other in the personal financial planning process. Note that *financial plans* provide direction to annual budgets.

## LG2 The Balance Sheet: How Much Are You Worth Today?

Preparing a personal *balance sheet,* or *statement of financial position,* helps you get a handle on your financial well-being. Think of a balance sheet as a snapshot taken of your financial position on one day out of the year.

A balance sheet has three parts that, taken together, summarize your financial picture:

- **Assets:** What you own
- **Liabilities, or debts:** What you owe
- **Net worth:** The difference between your assets and liabilities

The accounting relationship among these three categories is called the *balance sheet equation* and is expressed as follows:

$$\text{Total assets} = \text{Total liabilities} + \text{Net worth}$$

or

$$\text{Net worth} = \text{Total assets} - \text{Total liabilities}$$

Let's now look at the components of each section of the balance sheet.

## Assets: The Things You Own

**Assets** are the items you own. An item is classified as an asset regardless of whether it was purchased for cash or financed with debt. A useful way to group assets is on the basis of their underlying characteristics and uses. This results in four broad categories: liquid assets, investments, real property, and personal property.

**personal financial statements** *Balance sheets* and *income and expense statements* that serve as planning tools that are essential to developing and monitoring personal financial plans.

**balance sheet** A financial statement that describes a person's financial position at a *given point* in time.

**income and expense statement** A financial statement that measures financial performance *over* time.

**budget** A detailed financial report that looks *forward,* based on expected income and expenses.

**assets** Items that one owns.

## Exhibit 2.1  The Interlocking Network of Financial Plans and Statements

Personal financial planning involves a network of financial reports that link future goals and plans with actual results. Such a network provides direction, control, and feedback.

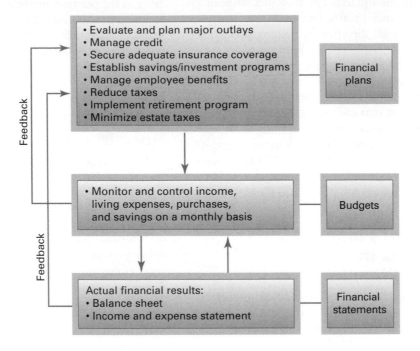

- Evaluate and plan major outlays
- Manage credit
- Secure adequate insurance coverage
- Establish savings/investment programs
- Manage employee benefits
- Reduce taxes
- Implement retirement program
- Minimize estate taxes

Financial plans

- Monitor and control income, living expenses, purchases, and savings on a monthly basis

Budgets

Actual financial results:
- Balance sheet
- Income and expense statement

Financial statements

Feedback

Feedback

**liquid assets** Assets that are held in the form of cash or can readily be converted to cash with little or no loss in value.

**investments** Assets such as stocks, bonds, mutual funds, and real estate that are acquired in order to earn a return rather than provide a service.

- **Liquid assets:** Low-risk financial assets held in the form of cash or instruments that can readily be converted to cash with little or no loss in value. Cash on hand or in a checking or savings account, money market deposit accounts, money market mutual funds, or certificates of deposit that mature within 1 year are all examples of liquid assets.

- **Investments:** Assets acquired to earn a return rather than provide a service. These assets are mostly intangible *financial assets* (stocks, bonds, mutual funds, and other types of securities), typically acquired to achieve long-term personal financial goals. Business ownership, the cash value of life insurance and pensions, retirement funds such as IRAs and 401(k) plans, and other investment vehicles such as commodities, financial futures, and options represent still other forms of investment assets.

©DENISE KAPPA/SHUTTERSTOCK

- **Real and personal property:** Tangible assets that we use in our everyday lives. **Real property** refers to immovable property: land and anything fixed to it, such as a house. Real property generally has a relatively long life and high cost, and it may *appreciate*, or increase in value. **Personal property** is movable property, such as automobiles, recreational equipment, household furnishings, and similar items. The first section of Worksheet 2.1 lists some of the typical assets you'd find on a personal balance sheet.

All assets, regardless of category, are recorded on the balance sheet at their current **fair market value**, which may differ considerably from their original purchase price. Fair market value is either the actual value of the asset (such as money in a checking account) or the price for which the asset can reasonably be expected to sell in the open market (as with a used car or a home). Under generally accepted accounting principles (GAAP), the accounting profession's guiding rules, assets appear on a company's balance sheet at *cost*, not *fair market value*.

## Liabilities: The Money You Owe

**Liabilities** represent an individual's or family's debts. They could result from department store charges, bank credit card charges, installment loans, or mortgages on housing and other real estate. A liability, regardless of its source, is something that you owe and must repay in the future.

Liabilities are generally classified according to maturity.

- **Current, or short-term, liabilities:** Any debt currently owed and due within 1 year of the date of the balance sheet. Examples include charges for consumable goods, utility bills, rent, insurance premiums, taxes, medical bills, repair bills, and total **open account credit obligations**—the outstanding balances against established credit lines (usually through credit card purchases).
- **Long-term liabilities:** Debt due 1 year or more from the date of the balance sheet. These liabilities typically

include real estate mortgages, most consumer installment loans, education loans, and margin loans used to purchase securities.

Although most loans will fall into the category of long-term liabilities, *any loans, or any portion thereof, that come due within a year should be shown as current liabilities*. Examples of short-term loans include a 6-month, single-payment bank loan and a 9-month consumer installment loan for a refrigerator. Regardless of the type of loan, *only the latest outstanding loan balance should be shown as a liability on the balance sheet*, because at any given time it is the balance still due—not the initial loan balance—that matters. Another important and closely-related point is that *only the principal portion of a loan or mortgage should be listed as a liability on the balance sheet*. You'll find the most common categories of liabilities on Worksheet 2.1.

## Net Worth: A Measure of Your Financial Worth

Now that you've listed what you own and what you owe, you can calculate your **net worth**, the amount of actual wealth or **equity** that an individual or family has in its owned assets. It represents the amount of money you'd have left after selling all your owned assets at their estimated fair market values and paying off all your liabilities (assuming there are no transaction costs). Rearranging this equation, we see that net worth equals total assets minus total liabilities. If net worth is less than zero, the family is *technically insolvent*. Although this form of **insolvency**

©KUTLAEV DMITRY/SHUTTERSTOCK

A balance sheet is set up to show what you own on one side (your assets) and how you paid for them on the other (debt or net worth). As you can see, the Cases have more assets than liabilities.

**BALANCE SHEET**

Name(s) _Bob and Cathy Case_   Date _December 31, 2010_

| ASSETS | | | LIABILITIES AND NET WORTH | | |
|---|---|---|---|---|---|
| **Liquid Assets** | | | **Current Liabilities** | | |
| Cash on hand | $ 90 | | Utilities | $ 120 | |
| In checking | 575 | | Rent | | |
| Savings accounts | 760 | | Insurance premiums | | |
| Money market funds and deposits | 800 | | Taxes | | |
| | | | Medical/dental bills | 75 | |
| Certificates of deposit | | | Repair bills | | |
| **Total Liquid Assets** | | $ 2,225 | Bank credit card balances | 395 | |
| | | | Dept. store credit card balances | 145 | |
| **Investments** | | | Travel and entertainment card balances | 125 | |
| Stocks | $ 1,250 | | Gas and other credit card balances | | |
| Bonds          Corp. | 1,000 | | | | |
| Certificates of deposit | | | Bank line of credit balances | | |
| Mutual funds | 1,500 | | Other current liabilities | 45 | |
| Real estate | | | **Total Current Liabilities** | | $ 905 |
| Retirement funds, IRA | 2,000 | | | | |
| Other | | | **Long-Term Liabilities** | | |
| **Total Investments** | | $ 5,750 | Primary residence mortgage | $160,000 | |
| **Real Property** | | | Second home mortgage | | |
| Primary residence | $185,000 | | Real estate investment mortgage | | |
| Second home | | | Auto loans | 4,250 | |
| Other | | | Appliance/furniture loans | 800 | |
| **Total Real Property** | | $ 185,000 | Home improvement loans | | |
| | | | Single-payment loans | | |
| **Personal Property** | | | Education loans | 3,800 | |
| Auto(s): '07 Toyota Corolla | $ 12,000 | | Margin loans used to purchase securities | | |
| Auto(s): '05 Ford Focus | 8,300 | | Other long-term loans (from parents) | 4,000 | |
| Recreational vehicles | | | **Total Long-Term Liabilities** | | $ 172,850 |
| Household furnishings | 3,700 | | | | |
| Jewelry and artwork | 1,500 | | **(II) Total Liabilities** | | $ 172,850 |
| Other | | | | | |
| Other | | | | | |
| **Total Personal Property** | | $ 25,500 | **Net Worth [(I) – (II)]** | | $ 45,625 |
| **(I) Total Assets** | | $218,475 | **Total Liabilities and Net Worth** | | $ 218,475 |

doesn't mean that the family will end up in bankruptcy proceedings, it likely shows insufficient financial planning. Net worth typically increases over the life cycle of an individual or family, as Exhibit 2.2 illustrates.

## Go to Smart Sites

What's the fair market value of your car? The personal watercraft your uncle gave you? Whenever you see *"Go to Smart Sites"* in this chapter, visit **4ltrpress** .cengage.com for online resources. ●

## Balance Sheet Format and Preparation

You should prepare your personal balance sheet at least once a year,

preferably every 3 to 6 months. Here's how to do it, using the categories in Worksheet 2.1 as a guide:

1. **List your assets at their fair market value as of the date you are preparing the balance sheet.** You'll find the fair market value of liquid and investment assets on checking and savings account records and investment account statements. Estimate the values of homes and cars using published sources of information, such as advertisements for comparable homes and the *Kelley Blue Book* for used car values (see www.kbb.com).
2. **List all current and long-term liabilities.** Show all outstanding charges, *even if you haven't received the bill,* as current liabilities on the balance sheet.
3. **Calculate net worth.** Subtract your total liabilities from your total assets. This is your net worth, which reflects the equity you have in your total assets.

## A Balance Sheet for Bob and Cathy Case

What can you learn from a balance sheet? Let's examine a hypothetical balance sheet as of

### Exhibit 2.2    Median Net Worth by Age

Net worth starts to build in the less-than-35 age bracket and continues to climb, peaking at around the 55–64 age bracket. It starts to decline once a person retires and begins to use assets to meet living expenses, usually around the age of 65.

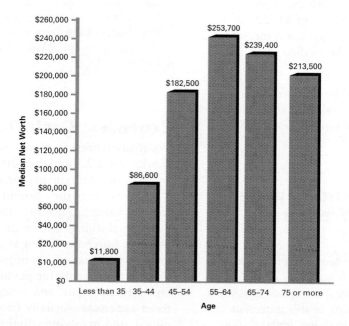

*Source:* Adapted from Brian K. Bucks, Arthur B. Kennickell, Traci L. Mach, and Kevin B. Moore, "Changes in U.S. Family Finances from 2004 to 2007: Evidence from the Survey of Consumer Finances," *Federal Reserve Bulletin*, Board of Governors of the Federal Reserve System, Washington, D.C., vol. 95 (February 2009), pp. A1–A55, http://www.federalreserve.gov/pubs/oss/oss2/2007/scf2007home.html, accessed April 2009.

**cash basis** A method of preparing financial statements in which only transactions involving actual cash receipts or actual cash outlays are recorded.

**income** Earnings received as wages, salaries, bonuses, commissions, interest and dividends, or proceeds from the sale of assets.

**expenses** Money spent on living expenses and to pay taxes, purchase assets, or repay debt.

**fixed expenses** Contractual, predetermined expenses involving equal payments each period.

December 31, 2010, prepared for Bob and Cathy Case, the young couple (ages 28 and 26) we met in Chapter 1 (see Worksheet 2.1). Here's what this financial statement tells us about the Cases' financial condition.

● **Assets:** Given their ages, the Cases' asset position looks quite good. Their dominant asset is their townhouse. They also have $5,750 in investments, which include retirement funds, and appear to have adequate liquid assets to meet their bill payments and cover small, unexpected expenses.

● **Liabilities:** The Cases' primary liability is the $160,000 mortgage on their townhouse. Their equity, or actual ownership interest, in the townhouse is approximately $25,000 ($185,000 market value minus $160,000 outstanding mortgage loan). Their current liabilities are $905, with other debts of $12,850 representing auto, furniture, and education loans as well as a loan from their parents to help with the down payment on their home.

● **Net worth:** The Cases' net worth ($218,475 in total assets minus total liabilities of $172,850) is $45,625—considering their ages, a respectable amount that is well above the median shown in Exhibit 2.2.

Comparing the Cases' total liabilities to their total assets gives a more realistic view of their current wealth position than merely looking at just assets or just liabilities.

## LG3 The Income and Expense Statement: What We Earn and Where It Goes

When confronted with a lack of funds, the first question people ask themselves is, "Where does all the money go?" Preparing an *income and expense statement* would answer this question. Think of this statement as a motion picture that not only shows actual results over time but also lets you compare them with budgeted financial goals.

The income and expense statement has three major parts: *income, expenses,* and *cash surplus* (or

*deficit*). A cash surplus (or deficit) is merely the difference between income and expenses. The statement is prepared on a **cash basis**, which means that *only transactions involving actual cash receipts or actual cash outlays are recorded.* The term *cash* is used in this case to include not only coin and currency but also checks and debit card transactions drawn against checking and certain types of savings accounts. Income and expense patterns change over the individual's or family's life cycle.

### Income: Cash In

Common sources of **income** include earnings received as wages, salaries, self-employment income, bonuses, and commissions; interest and dividends received from savings and investments; and proceeds from the sale of assets such as stocks and bonds or an auto. Other income items include pension, annuity, and social Security income; rent received from leased assets; alimony and child support; scholarships or grants; tax refunds; and miscellaneous types of income. Worksheet 2.2, Bob and Cathy Case's Income and Expense Statement, has general categories for recording income. Note also that the proper figure to use is *gross* wages, salaries, and commissions, which constitute the amount of income you receive from your employer *before* taxes and other payroll deductions.

 *Go to Smart Sites*

For current surveys and trends on consumer spending, check out the Consumer Expenditure Survey at the Department of Labor's Bureau of Labor Statistics. ●

### Expenses: Cash Out

**Expenses** represent money used for outlays. Worksheet 2.2, Bob and Cathy Case's Income and Expense Statement, categorizes them by the types of benefits they provide: (1) living expenses (such as housing, utilities, food, transportation, medical, clothing, and insurance), (2) tax payments, (3) asset purchases (such as autos, stereos, furniture, appliances, and loan payments on them), and (4) other payments for personal care, recreation and entertainment, and other expenses. Some are **fixed expenses**—usually contractual, predetermined, and involving equal payments each period (typically each month). Examples include mortgage and installment loan payments, insurance premiums, and cable TV fees. Others (such as food, clothing, utilities, entertainment, and medical expenses) are

The income and expense statement essentially shows what you earned, how you spent your money, and how much you were left with (or, if you spent more than you took in, how much you went "in the hole").

## INCOME AND EXPENSE STATEMENT

Name(s) _Bob and Cathy Case_

For the _Year_ _____ Ended _December 31, 2010_

### INCOME

| | | | |
|---|---|---|---|
| Wages and salaries | Name: Bob Case | $ | 55,000 |
| | Name: Cathy Case | | 15,450 |
| | Name: | | |
| Self-employment income | | | |
| Bonuses and commissions | Bob-sales commissions | | 2,495 |
| Investment income | Interest received | | 55 |
| | Dividends received | | 40 |
| | Rents received | | |
| | Sale of securities | | |
| | Other | | |
| Pensions and annuities | | | |
| Other income | | | |
| | **(I) Total Income** | $ | 73,040 |

### EXPENSES

| | | | |
|---|---|---|---|
| Housing | Rent/mortgage payment (include insurance and taxes, if applicable) | $ | 11,820 |
| | Repairs, maintenance, improvements | | 1,050 |
| Utilities | Gas, electric, water | | 1,750 |
| | Phone | | 480 |
| | Cable TV and other | | 240 |
| Food | Groceries | | 2,425 |
| | Dining out | | 3,400 |
| Transportation | Auto loan payments | | 2,520 |
| | License plates, fees, etc. | | 250 |
| | Gas, oil, repairs, tires, maintenance | | 2,015 |
| Medical | Health, major medical, disability insurance (payroll deductions or not provided by employer) | | 2,069 |
| | Doctor, dentist, hospital, medicines | | 305 |
| Clothing | Clothes, shoes, and accessories | | 1,700 |
| Insurance | Homeowner's (if not covered by mortgage payment) | | 1,320 |
| | Life (not provided by employer) | | 1,260 |
| | Auto | | 1,935 |
| Taxes | Income and social security | | 15,430 |
| | Property (if not included in mortgage) | | 2,040 |
| Appliances, furniture, and other major purchases | Loan payments | | 800 |
| | Purchases and repairs | | 450 |
| Personal care | Laundry, cosmetics, hair care | | 700 |
| Recreation and entertainment | Vacations | | 2,000 |
| | Other recreation and entertainment | | 2,630 |
| Other items | Tuition and books: Cathy | | 1,400 |
| | Gifts | | 215 |
| | Loan payments: Education loans | | 900 |
| | Loan payments: Parents | | 600 |
| | **(II) Total Expenses** | $ | 61,704 |
| | **CASH SURPLUS (OR DEFICIT) [(I) − (II)]** | $ | 11,336 |

**variable expenses**
Expenses involving payment amounts that change from one time period to the next.

**cash surplus** An excess amount of income over expenses that results in *increased* net worth.

**cash deficit** An excess amount of expenses over income, resulting in insufficient funds as well as in *decreased* net worth.

**variable expenses,** because their amounts change from one time period to the next.

Exhibit 2.3 shows the average annual expenses by major category as a percentage of after-tax income. It's a useful benchmark to see how you compare with national averages. However, your own expenses will vary according to your age, lifestyle, and where you live. For example, it costs considerably more to buy a home in San Francisco than in Indianapolis. Similarly, if you live in the suburbs, your commuting expenses will be higher than those of city dwellers.

## Cash Surplus (or Deficit)

The third component of the income and expense statement shows the net result of the period's financial activities. Subtracting total expenses from total income gives you the cash surplus (or deficit) for the period. At a glance, you can see how you did financially over the period. A positive figure indicates that expenses were less than income, resulting in a **cash surplus**. A value of zero indicates that expenses were exactly equal to income for the period, while a negative value means that your expenses exceeded income and you have a **cash deficit**.

## Preparing the Income and Expense Statement

As shown in Worksheet 2.2, the income and expense statement is dated to define the period covered. To prepare the statement, follow these steps.

1. **Record your income from all sources for the chosen period.**
2. **Establish meaningful expense categories.** Those shown on Worksheet 2.2 are a good starting point.

| Exhibit 2.3 | How We Spend Our Income |
| --- | --- |

Just three categories account for almost two-thirds of a household's after-tax income: food, housing, and transportation.

- Food–12.6%
- Housing–33.8%
- Apparel and services–3.9%
- Transportation–17.6%
- Entertainment–4.9%
- Health care–5.7%
- Pensions/Social Security–10.2%
- Life and personal insurance–0.7%
- Other–10.6%

*Source:* "Consumer Expenditures in 2006," Washington, D.C.: U.S. Department of Labor, Bureau of Labor Statistics, Report 1010, October 2008, p. 4.

3. **Subtract total expenses from total income to get the cash surplus (a positive number) or deficit (a negative number).** This "bottom line" summarizes the *net cash flow* resulting from your financial activities during the period.

Finally, when making your list of expenses for the year, remember to include the amount of income tax and Social Security taxes withheld from your paycheck as well as any other payroll deductions (health insurance, savings plans, retirement and pension contributions, and professional/union dues). These deductions (from gross wages, salaries, bonuses, and commissions) represent personal expenses, even if they don't involve a direct cash payment. You might be shocked when listing what's taken out of your paycheck. Even if you're in a fairly low federal income tax bracket, your paycheck could easily be reduced by more than 25% for taxes alone.

## An Income and Expense Statement for Bob and Cathy Case

Bob and Cathy Case's balance sheet in Worksheet 2.1 shows us their financial condition as of December 31, 2010. Their income and expense statement for the year ending December 31, 2010, in Worksheet 2.2, was prepared using the background material presented earlier, along with the Cases' balance sheet. This statement shows how cash flowed into and out of their "pockets":

- **Income:** Total income for the year ending December 31, 2010, is $73,040. Bob's wages clearly represent the family's chief source of income, although Cathy has finished her MBA and will now be making a major contribution. Other sources of income include $55 in interest on their savings accounts and bond investments and $40 in dividends from their common stock holdings.

- **Expenses:** Total expenses for the year of $61,704 include their home mortgage, food, auto loan, clothing, and income and Social Security taxes. Other sizable expenses during the year include home repairs and improvements, gas and electricity, auto license and operating expenses, insurance, tuition, and education loan payments.

- **Cash surplus:** The Cases end the year with a cash surplus of $11,336 (total income of $73,040 minus total expenses of $61,704). The Cases can use their surplus to increase savings, invest in stocks, bonds, or other vehicles, or make payments on some outstanding debts. If they had a cash deficit, the Cases would have to withdraw savings, liquidate investments, or borrow an amount equal to the deficit to meet their financial commitments (that is, to "make ends meet"). With their surplus of $11,336, the Cases have made a positive contribution to their net worth.

## LG4 Using Your Personal Financial Statements

Whether you're just starting out and have a minimal net worth or are further along the path toward achieving your goals, your balance sheet and income and expense statement provide insight into your current financial status. You now have the information you need to examine your financial position, monitor your financial activities, and track the progress you're making toward your financial goals. Let's now look at ways to help you create better personal financial statements and analyze them to better understand your financial situation.

## Keeping Good Records

Although recordkeeping doesn't rank high on most "to do" lists, a good recordkeeping system helps you manage and control your personal financial affairs. It's best to prepare your personal financial statements at least once each year, ideally when drawing up your budget. Many people update their financial statements every 3 or 6 months. You may want to keep a *ledger*, or financial record book, to summarize all your financial transactions. The ledger has sections for assets, liabilities, sources of income, and expenses; these sections contain separate accounts for each item.

## Organizing Your Records

Your system doesn't have to be fancy to be effective. Start by taking an inventory. Make a list of everything you own and owe. Check it at least once a year to make sure it's up-to-date and to review your financial progress. Then, record transactions manually in your ledger or with financial planning software. You'll want to set up separate files for tax-planning records, with one for income (paycheck stubs, interest on savings accounts, and so on) and another for deductions, as well as for individual mutual fund and brokerage account records.

# Tracking Financial Progress: Ratio Analysis

Each time you prepare your financial statements, you should analyze them to see how well you're doing on your financial goals. For example, with an income and expense statement, you can compare actual financial results with budgeted figures to make sure that your spending is under control. Likewise, comparing a set of financial plans with a balance sheet will reveal whether you're meeting your savings and investment goals, reducing your debt, or building up a retirement reserve. You can compare current performance with historical performance to find out if your financial situation is improving or getting worse.

Calculating certain financial ratios can help you evaluate your financial performance over time. What's more, if you apply for a loan, the lender probably will look at these ratios to judge your ability to carry additional debt. Four important money management ratios are (1) solvency ratio, (2) liquidity ratio, (3) savings ratio, and (4) debt service ratio. The first two are associated primarily with the balance sheet; the last two relate primarily to the income and expense statement. Exhibit 2.4 defines these ratios and illustrates their calculation for Bob and Cathy Case.

## Balance Sheet Ratios

When evaluating your balance sheet, you should be most concerned with your net worth at a given time. The **solvency ratio** shows, as a percentage, your degree of exposure to insolvency, or how much "cushion" you have as a protection against insolvency. Bob and Cathy's solvency ratio is 20.9%, which means that they could withstand about a 21% decline in the market value of their assets before they would be insolvent. Consider that the stock market, as measured by the S&P 500 index, fell about 37% during the financial crisis of 2008. Also, the average home's value fell about 18% during that crisis year, as measured by the S&P/Case-Shiller U.S. National Home Price Index. The low value of Bob and Cathy's solvency ratio suggests that they should consider improving it in the future to better manage a potential decline in the value of their assets.

Although the solvency ratio indicates the potential to withstand financial problems, it does not deal directly with the ability to pay current debts. This issue is addressed with the **liquidity ratio**, which shows how long you could continue to pay current debts (any

---

### Exhibit 2.4  Ratios for Personal Financial Statement Analysis

| Ratio | Formula | 2010 Calculation for the Cases |
|---|---|---|
| Solvency ratio | $\dfrac{\text{Total net worth}}{\text{Total assets}}$ | $\dfrac{\$45,625}{\$218,475} = 0.209$, or 20.9% |
| Liquidity ratio | $\dfrac{\text{Total liquid assets}}{\text{Total current debts}}$ | $\dfrac{\$2,225}{\$17,545^{(a)}} = 0.1268$, or 12.68% |
| Savings ratio | $\dfrac{\text{Cash surplus}}{\text{Income after taxes}}$ | $\dfrac{\$11,336}{\$73,040 - \$15,430} = \dfrac{\$11,336}{\$57,610} = 0.197$, or 19.7% |
| Debt service ratio | $\dfrac{\text{Total monthly loan payments}}{\text{Monthly gross (before-tax) income}}$ | $\dfrac{\$1,387^{(b)}}{\$6,807^{(c)}} = 0.204$, or 20.4% |

(a) You'll find the Cases' total liquid assets ($2,225) and total current liabilities ($905) on Worksheet 2.1. The total current debt totals $17,545: current liabilities of $905 (from Worksheet 2.1) plus loan payments due within 1 year of $16,640 (from Worksheet 2.2). Note that loan payments due within 1 year consist of $11,820 in mortgage payments, $2,520 in auto loan payments, $800 in furniture loan payments, $900 in education loan payments, and $600 in loan payments to parents.

(b) On an *annual* basis, the Cases' debt obligations total $16,640 ($11,820 in mortgage payments, $2,520 in auto loan payments, $800 in furniture loan payments, $900 in education loan payments, and $600 in loan payments to parents; all from Worksheet 2.2). The Cases' total *monthly* loan payments are about $1,387 ($16,640 ÷ 12 months).

(c) Dividing the Cases' *annual* gross income (also found in Worksheet 2.2) of $73,040 by 12 equals $6,087 per month.

---

bills or charges that must be paid *within 1 year*) with existing liquid assets in the event of income loss.

The calculated liquidity ratio indicates that the Cases can cover only about 13% of their existing 1-year debt obligations with their current liquid assets. In other words, they have about 1½ months of coverage (a month is one-twelfth, or 8.3%, of a year). If an unexpected event cut off their income, their liquid reserves would quickly be exhausted. Although there's no hard-and-fast rule for what this ratio should be, it seems too low for the Cases. They should consider strengthening it along with their solvency ratio. They should be able to add to their cash surpluses now that Cathy is working full-time.

The amount of liquid reserves will vary with your personal circumstances and "comfort level." Another useful liquidity guideline is to have a reserve fund equal to 3 to 6 months of after-tax income available to cover living expenses. The Cases' after-tax income for 2010 was $4,801 per month ([$73,040 total income − $15,430 income and Social Security taxes] ÷ 12). Therefore, this guideline suggests they should have between $14,403 and $28,806 in total liquid assets—considerably more than the $2,225 on their latest balance sheet. In troubled economic times, you may want to keep 6 months or more of income in this fund as protection in case you lose your job.

### Income and Expense Statement Ratios

When evaluating your income and expense statement, you should be concerned with the bottom line, which shows the cash surplus (or deficit) resulting from the period's activities. You can relate the cash surplus (or deficit) to income by calculating a **savings ratio**, which is done most effectively with after-tax income.

Bob and Cathy saved about 20% of their after-tax income, which is on the high side (American families, on average, save about 5% to 8%). How much to save is a personal choice.

Although maintaining an adequate level of savings is obviously important to personal financial planning, so is the ability to pay debts promptly. In fact, debt payments have a higher priority. The **debt service ratio** allows you to make sure you can comfortably meet your debt obligations. This ratio excludes current liabilities and considers only mortgage, installment, and personal loan obligations.

Monthly loan payments account for about 20% of Bob and Cathy's monthly gross income. This relatively low debt service ratio indicates that the Cases should have little difficulty in meeting their monthly loan payments. In your financial planning, try to keep your debt service ratio somewhere under 35% or so, because that's generally viewed as a manageable level

of debt. Of course, the lower the debt service ratio, the easier it is to meet loan payments as they come due.

## LG5 Cash In and Cash Out: Preparing and Using Budgets

Many of us avoid budgeting as if it were the plague. Yet preparing, analyzing, and monitoring your personal budget are essential steps for successful personal financial planning.

> *Preparing, analyzing, and monitoring your personal budget are essential steps for successful personal financial planning.*

After defining your short-term financial goals, you can prepare a cash budget for the coming year. Recall that a *budget* is a short-term financial planning report that helps you achieve your short-term financial goals. A cash budget is a valuable money management tool that helps you:

1. Maintain the necessary information to monitor and control your finances
2. Decide how to allocate your income to reach your financial goals
3. Implement a system of disciplined spending—as opposed to just existing from one paycheck to the next
4. Reduce needless spending so you can increase the funds allocated to savings and investments
5. Achieve your long-term financial goals

Just as your goals will change over your lifetime, so too will your budget as your financial situation becomes more complex. Typically, the number of income and expense categories increases as you accumulate more assets and debts and have more family responsibilities. For most people this process does not become simpler until retirement.

### The Budgeting Process

Like the income and expense statement, *a budget should be prepared on a cash basis*; thus, we call this document a **cash budget** because it deals with estimated cash receipts and cash expenses, including savings and investments, that are expected to occur in the coming year.

The cash budget preparation process has three stages: estimating income, estimating expenses, and finalizing the cash budget. When you're estimating income and expenses, take into account any anticipated changes in the cost of living and their impact on your budget components. If your income is fixed—not expected to change over the budgetary period—increases in various expense items will probably decrease the purchasing power of your income. Worksheet 2.3, the Cases' "Annual Cash Budget by Month," has separate sections to record income (cash receipts) and expenses (cash expenses) and lists the most common categories for each.

## Estimating Income

The first step in preparing your cash budget is to estimate your income for the coming year. Include all income expected for the year: year: the take-home pay of both spouses, expected bonuses or commissions, pension or annuity income, and investment income—interest, dividend, rental, and asset (particularly security) sale income. Unlike the income and expense statement, in the cash budget you should use *take-home pay* (rather than gross income). Your cash budget focuses on those areas that you can control—and most people have limited control over things like taxes withheld, contributions to company insurance and pension plans, and the like. In effect, take-home pay represents the amount of *disposable income* you receive from your employer.

## Worksheet 2.3  The Cases' Annual Cash Budget by Month

The Cases' annual cash budget shows several months in which substantial cash deficits are expected to occur; they can use this information to develop plans for covering those monthly shortfalls.

### ANNUAL CASH BUDGET BY MONTH

Name(s) Bob and Cathy Case

For the Year _____ Ended December 31, 2011

| INCOME | Jan. | Feb. | Mar. | April | May | June | July | Aug. | Sep. | Oct. | Nov. | Dec. | Total for the Year |
|---|---|---|---|---|---|---|---|---|---|---|---|---|---|
| Take-home pay | $4,775 | $4,775 | $4,775 | $4,965 | $4,965 | $5,140 | $5,140 | $5,140 | $5,140 | $5,140 | $5,140 | $5,140 | $60,235 |
| Bonuses and commissions | | | | | | 1,350 | | | | | | 1,300 | 2,650 |
| Pensions and annuities | | | | | | | | | | | | | |
| Investment income | | | 50 | | | 50 | | | 50 | | | 50 | 200 |
| Other income | | | | | | | | | | | | | |
| (I) Total Income | $4,775 | $4,775 | $4,825 | $4,965 | $4,965 | $6,540 | $5,140 | $5,140 | $5,190 | $5,140 | $5,140 | $6,490 | $63,085 |
| **EXPENSES** | | | | | | | | | | | | | |
| Housing (rent/mtge., repairs) | $1,185 | $1,485 | $1,185 | $1,185 | $1,185 | $1,185 | $1,185 | $1,185 | $1,185 | $1,185 | $1,185 | $1,185 | $14,520 |
| Utilities (phone, elec., gas, water) | 245 | 245 | 245 | 175 | 180 | 205 | 230 | 245 | 205 | 195 | 230 | 250 | 2,650 |
| Food (home and away) | 696 | 696 | 696 | 696 | 696 | 696 | 696 | 696 | 696 | 696 | 696 | 696 | 8,352 |
| Transportation (auto/public) | 370 | 620 | 370 | 355 | 370 | 370 | 575 | 370 | 370 | 450 | 370 | 370 | 4,960 |
| Medical/dental, incl. insurance | 30 | 30 | 30 | 30 | 30 | 45 | 30 | 30 | 30 | 30 | 30 | 30 | 375 |
| Clothing | 150 | 150 | 470 | 200 | 200 | 200 | 300 | 500 | 200 | 300 | 300 | 300 | 3,270 |
| Insurance (life, auto, home) | | | | 660 | 1,598 | | | | | 660 | 1,598 | | 4,516 |
| Taxes (property) | | 550 | | | | | | | 550 | | | | 1,100 |
| Appliances, furniture, and other (purchases/loans) | 60 | 60 | 60 | 60 | 60 | 60 | 60 | 60 | 60 | 60 | 60 | 60 | 720 |
| Personal care | 100 | 100 | 100 | 100 | 100 | 100 | 100 | 100 | 100 | 100 | 100 | 100 | 1,200 |
| Recreation and entertainment | 250 | 300 | 3,200 | 200 | 200 | 300 | 300 | 200 | 200 | 200 | 200 | 2,050 | 7,600 |
| Savings and investments | 575 | 575 | 575 | 575 | 575 | 575 | 575 | 575 | 575 | 575 | 575 | 575 | 6,900 |
| Other expenses | 135 | 250 | 235 | 135 | 410 | 180 | 135 | 285 | 245 | 135 | 605 | 385 | 3,135 |
| Fun money | 230 | 230 | 230 | 130 | 230 | 230 | 230 | 230 | 230 | 230 | 230 | 230 | 2,660 |
| (II) Total Expenses | $4,026 | $5,291 | $7,396 | $4,501 | $5,834 | $4,146 | $4,416 | $5,026 | $4,096 | $4,816 | $6,179 | $6,231 | $61,958 |
| CASH SURPLUS (OR DEFICIT) [(I) − (II)] | $749 | $(516) | $(2,571) | $464 | $(869) | $2,394 | $724 | $114 | $1,094 | $324 | $(1,039) | $259 | $1,127 |
| CUMULATIVE CASH SURPLUS (OR DEFICIT) | $749 | $233 | $(2,338) | $(1,874) | $(2,743) | $(349) | $375 | $489 | $1,583 | $1,907 | $868 | $1,127 | $1,127 |

### Estimating Expenses

The second step in the cash budgeting process is by far the most difficult: preparing a schedule of estimated expenses for the coming year. This is commonly done using actual expenses from previous years (as found on income and expense statements and in supporting information for those periods), along with predetermined short-term financial goals.

Whether or not you have historical information, when preparing your budget *be aware of your expenditure patterns and how you spend money.* After tracking your expenses over several months, study your spending habits to see if you are doing things that should be eliminated. For example, you may become aware that you are going to the ATM too often or using credit cards too freely. You'll probably find it easier to budget expenses if you group them into several general categories rather than trying to estimate each item. Worksheet 2.3 is an example of one such grouping scheme, patterned after the categories used in the income and expense statement.

Don't forget an allowance for "fun money," which family members can spend as they wish. This gives each person some financial independence and helps form a healthy family budget relationship.

### Finalizing the Cash Budget

After estimating income and expenses, finalize your budget by comparing projected income to projected expenses. Show the difference in the third section as a surplus or deficit. In a *balanced budget,* the total income for the year equals or exceeds total expenses. If you find that you have a deficit at year end, you'll have to go *back and adjust your expenses.* If you have several months of large surpluses, you should be able to cover any shortfall in a later month, as explained later. Budget preparation is complete once all monthly deficits are resolved and the total annual budget balances. The nearby *Money in Action* box shows how you can track your money using several useful free software programs.

## Dealing with Deficits

Even if the annual budget balances, in certain months expenses may exceed income, causing a monthly budget deficit. Likewise, a budget surplus occurs when income in some months exceeds expenses. Two remedies exist:

- Shift expenses from months with budget deficits to months with surpluses (or, alternatively, transfer income, if possible, from months with surpluses to those with deficits).

- Use savings, investments, or borrowing to cover temporary deficits.

Because the budget balances for the year, the need for funds to cover shortages is only temporary. In months with budget surpluses, you should return funds taken from savings or investments or repay loans. Either remedy is feasible for curing a monthly budget deficit in a balanced annual budget, although the second is probably more practical.

What can you do if your budget shows an *annual budget deficit* even after you've made a few expense adjustments? Here you have three options, as follows.

- **Liquidate enough savings and investments or borrow enough to meet the total budget shortfall for the year.** Obviously, this option is not preferred, because it violates the objective of budgeting: to set expenses at a level that allows you to enjoy a reasonable standard of living *and* progress toward achieving your long-term goals.

- **Cut low-priority expenses from the budget.** This option is clearly preferable to the first one. It balances the budget without using external funding sources by eliminating expenses associated with your least important short-term goals, such as flexible or discretionary expenses for nonessential items (e.g., recreation, entertainment, and some types of clothing).

# MONEY IN ACTION

## Tracking Your Money Online – And for Free!

There's plenty of software to help you track your spending, income, and investments. While much of it is reasonably priced, it's hard to beat some outstanding free online money tracking programs. Their cost is currently limited to the time spent setting them up, which can take up to several hours. Here is a sample of programs that provide the details of your finances with the convenience of Web access.

| | Mint.com | QuickenOnline.com | Moneycenter.yodlee.com | Wesabe.com |
|---|---|---|---|---|
| **Coverage** | Bank accounts, loans, credit cards, and investments. | Bank accounts, loans, credit cards, and investments. | Bank accounts, loans, credit cards, frequent flyer miles, real estate, and investments. | Bank accounts and credit cards. |
| **Strength** | Shows asset allocation and rates of return. Graphical displays helpful. | Influence of well-developed Quicken software shows—deep customer support. *Money* magazine's "pick" of the group. | Captures many account types. | Stores user names and passwords on personal computer–not the site's server. |
| **Limitation** | Advertising integrated with information you get. | Can't synchronize the online program with Quicken software. Detailed investment analysis relies on the software. | Needed information is harder to find. | Can't currently track investments. Emphasis on exchange of member ideas may not be appealing to all users. |

- **Increase income.** Finding a higher-paying job or perhaps a second, part-time job is the most difficult option; it takes more planning and may result in significant lifestyle changes. However, people who can't liquidate savings or investments or borrow funds to cover necessary expenses may have to choose this route to balance their budgets.

## A Cash Budget for Bob and Cathy Case

Using their short-term financial goals (Worksheet 1.1 in Chapter 1) and past financial statements (Worksheets 2.1 and 2.2), Bob and Cathy Case have prepared their cash budget for the 2011 calendar year. Worksheet 2.3 shows the Cases' estimated total 2011 annual income and expenses by month as well as the monthly and annual cash surplus or deficit.

The Cases list their total 2011 income of $63,085 by source for each month. By using take-home pay, they eliminate the need to show income-based taxes, Social Security payments, and other

payroll deductions as expenses. The take-home pay reflects Bob's and Cathy's expected salary increases.

In estimating annual expenses for 2011, the Cases anticipate a small amount of inflation and have factored some price increases into their expense projections. They have also allocated $6,900 to savings and investments, a wise budgeting strategy, and included an amount for fun money to be divided between them.

During their budgeting session, Bob and Cathy discovered that their first estimate resulted in expenses of $63,299, compared with their estimated income of $63,085. To eliminate the $214 deficit in order to balance their budget and to allow for unexpected expenses, Bob and Cathy made these decisions:

- Omit some low-priority goals: spend less on stereo components, take a shorter Hawaiian vacation instead of the Colorado ski trip shown in Worksheet 1.1.

- Reschedule some of the loan repayment to their parents.
- Reduce their fun money slightly.

These reductions lower Bob and Cathy's total scheduled expenses to $61,958, giving them a surplus of $1,127 ($63,085 − $61,958) and more than balancing the budget on an annual basis. Of course, the Cases can reduce other discretionary expenses to further increase the budget surplus and have a cushion for unexpected expenses.

The Case's final step is to analyze monthly surpluses and deficits and determine whether to use savings, investments, or borrowing to cover monthly shortfalls. The bottom line of their annual cash budget lists the cumulative, or running, totals of monthly cash surpluses and deficits. Despite their $1,127 year-end cumulative cash surplus, they have cumulative deficits in March, April, May, and June primarily because of their March Hawaiian vacation and insurance payments. To help cover these deficits, Bob and Cathy have arranged an interest-free loan from their parents. If they had dipped into savings to finance the deficits, they would have lost some interest earnings, included as income. They could also delay clothing and recreation and entertainment expenses until later in the year to reduce the deficits more quickly. If they weren't able to obtain funds to cover the deficits, they would have to reduce expenses further or increase income. At year end, they should use their surplus to increase savings or investments or to repay part of a loan.

## Using Your Budgets

In the final analysis, a cash budget has value only if (1) you use it and (2) you keep careful records of actual income and expenses. These records show whether you are staying within your budget limits.

At the beginning of each month, record the budgeted amount for each category and enter income received and money spent on the appropriate pages. At month-end, total each account and calculate the surplus or deficit. Except for certain income accounts (such as salary) and fixed expense accounts such as mortgage or loan payments, most categories will end the month with a positive or negative variance, indicating a cash surplus or deficit. You can then transfer your total spending by category to a **budget control schedule** that compares actual income and expenses with the various budget categories and shows the variances.

**budget control schedule** A summary that shows how actual income and expenses compare with the various budget categories and where variances (surpluses or deficits) exist.

The budget control schedule provides important feedback on how the actual cash flow is stacking up relative to the forecasted cash budget. If the variances are significant enough and/or continue month after month, the Cases should consider altering either their spending habits or their cash budget.

**BUDGET CONTROL SCHEDULE**

Name(s) Bob and Cathy Case

For the 3 _____  Months Ended March 31, 2011

| | Month: January | | | | Month: February | | | | Month: March | | | |
|---|---|---|---|---|---|---|---|---|---|---|---|---|
| **INCOME** | Budgeted Amount (1) | Actual (2) | Monthly Variance (3) | Year-to-Date Variance (4) | Budgeted Amount (5) | Actual (6) | Monthly Variance (7) | Year-to-Date Variance (8) | Budgeted Amount (9) | Actual (10) | Monthly Variance (11) | Year-to-Date Variance (12) |
| Take-home pay | $4,775 | $4,792 | $ 17 | $ 17 | $4,775 | $4,792 | $ 17 | $ 34 | $4,775 | $4,792 | $ 17 | $ 51 |
| Bonuses and commissions | | | | | | | | | | | | |
| Pensions and annuities | | | | | | | | | | | | |
| Investment income | | | | | | | | | 50 | 46 | (4) | (4) |
| Other income | | | | | | | | | | | | |
| (I) Total Income | $4,775 | $4,792 | $ 17 | $ 17 | $4,775 | $4,792 | $ 17 | $ 34 | $ 4,825 | $ 4,838 | $ 13 | $ 47 |
| **EXPENSES** | | | | | | | | | | | | |
| Housing (rent/mtge, repairs) | $ 1,185 | $1,185 | $ 0 | $ 0 | $ 1,485 | $1,485 | $ 0 | $ 0 | $ 1,185 | $1,185 | $ 0 | $ 0 |
| Utilities (phone, elec., gas, water) | 245 | 237 | (8) | (8) | 245 | 252 | 7 | (1) | 245 | 228 | (17) | (18) |
| Food (home and away) | 696 | 680 | (16) | (16) | 696 | 669 | (27) | (43) | 696 | 571 | (125) | (168) |
| Transportation (auto/public) | 370 | 385 | 15 | 15 | 620 | 601 | (19) | (4) | 370 | 310 | (60) | (64) |
| Medical/dental, incl. insurance | 30 | 0 | (30) | (30) | 30 | 45 | 15 | (15) | 30 | 0 | (30) | (45) |
| Clothing | 150 | 190 | 40 | 40 | 150 | 135 | (15) | 25 | 470 | 445 | (25) | 0 |
| Insurance (life, auto, home) | | | | | | | | | | | | |
| Taxes (property) | | | 0 | 0 | 550 | 550 | 0 | 0 | 0 | 0 | | 0 |
| Appliances, furniture, and other (purchases/loans) | 60 | 60 | 0 | 0 | 60 | 60 | 0 | 0 | 60 | 60 | 0 | 0 |
| Personal care | 100 | 85 | (15) | (15) | 100 | 120 | 20 | 5 | 100 | 75 | (25) | (20) |
| Recreation and entertainment | 250 | 210 | (40) | (40) | 300 | 290 | (10) | (50) | 3,200 | 3,285 | 85 | 35 |
| Savings and investments | 575 | 575 | 0 | 0 | 575 | 575 | 0 | 0 | 575 | 575 | 0 | 0 |
| Other expenses | 135 | 118 | (17) | (17) | 250 | 245 | (5) | (22) | 235 | 200 | (35) | (57) |
| Fun money | 230 | 200 | (30) | (30) | 230 | 225 | (5) | (35) | 230 | 230 | 0 | (35) |
| (II) Total Expenses | $ 4,026 | $3,925 | $ (101) | $ (101) | $ 5,291 | $5,252 | $ (39) | $(140) | $ 7,396 | $7,164 | $(232) | $(372) |
| **CASH SURPLUS (OR DEFICIT) [(I) − (II)]** | $ 749 | $ 867 | $ 118 | $ 118 | $ (516) | $ (460) | $ 56 | $ 174 | $(2,571) | $(2,326) | $ 245 | $ 419 |
| **CUMULATIVE CASH SURPLUS (OR DEFICIT)** | $ 749 | $ 867 | $ | $ 118 | $ 233 | $ 407 | $ | $ 174 | $(2,338) | $ (1,919) | $ | $ 419 |

Key: Col. (3) = Col. (2) − Col. (1); Col. (7) = Col. (6) − Col. (5); Col. (11) = Col. (10) − Col. (9); Col. (4) = Col. (3); Col. (8) = Col. (4) + Col. (7); Col. (12) = Col. (8) + Col. (11).

This monthly comparison makes it easy to identify major budget categories where income falls far short of—or spending far exceeds—desired levels (variances of 5% to 10% or more). After pinpointing these areas, you can take corrective action to keep your budget on course. Don't just look at the size of the variances. Analyze them, particularly the larger ones, to discover *why* they occurred. Only in exceptional situations should you finance budget adjustments by using savings and investments or by borrowing.

Looking at the Cases' budget control schedule for January, February, and March 2011, on Worksheet 2.4, you can see that actual income and expense levels are reasonably close to their targets and have a positive variance for the months shown (their surpluses exceed the budgeted surplus amounts). The biggest variances were in food and transportation expenses, but neither was far off the mark. Thus, for the first 3 months of the year, the Cases seem to be doing a good job of controlling their income and expenses. In fact, by cutting discretionary spending they have achieved a cumulative cash surplus of $419 for the year-to-date variance.

## LG6 The Time Value of Money: Putting a Dollar Value on Financial Goals

Assume that one of your financial goals is to buy your first home in 6 years. Your first question is how much do you want to spend on that home. Let's say you've done some "window shopping" and feel that, taking future inflation into consideration, you can buy a nice condominium for about $200,000 in 6 years. Of course, you won't need the full amount, but assuming that you'll make a 20% down payment of $40,000 (.20 × $200,000 = $40,000) and pay $5,000 in closing costs, you need $45,000. You now have a fairly well-defined long-term financial goal: *To accumulate $45,000 in 6 years to buy a home costing about $200,000.*

The next question is how to get all that money. You can easily estimate how much to save or invest each year if you know your goal and what you expect to earn on your savings or investments. In this case, if you have to start from scratch (that is, if nothing has already been saved) and estimate that you can earn about 5% on your money, you'll have to save or invest about $6,616 per year for each of the next 6 years to accumulate $45,000 over that time. Now you have another vital piece of information: *You know what you must do over the next 6 years to reach your financial goal.*

How did we arrive at the $6,616 figure? We used a concept called the **time value of money**, the idea that a dollar today is worth more than a dollar received in the future. With time value concepts, we can correctly compare dollar values occurring at different points in time. As long as you can earn a positive rate of return (interest rate) on your investments (ignoring taxes and other behavioral factors), in a strict financial sense you should always prefer to receive equal amounts of money sooner rather than later. The two key time value concepts, future value and present value, are discussed separately next. (*Note:* The time value discussions and demonstrations initially rely on the use of financial tables. As an alternative, Appendix E explains how to use financial calculators, which determine the interest factors internally to conveniently make time value calculations. The calculator keystrokes for each calculation are shown in the text margin near the related discussion.)

### Future Value

To calculate how much to save to buy the $200,000 condominium, we used **future value**, the value to which an amount today will grow if it earns a specific rate of interest over a given period. Assume,

for example, that you make annual deposits of $2,000 into a savings account that pays 5% interest per year. At the end of 20 years, your deposits would total $40,000 (20 × $2,000). If you made no withdrawals, your account balance would have increased to $66,132! This growth in value occurs not only because of earning interest but also because of **compounding**—the interest earned each year is left in the account and becomes part of the balance (or principal) on which interest is earned in subsequent years.

**time value of money** The concept that a dollar today is worth more than a dollar received in the future.

**future value** The value to which an amount today will grow if it earns a specific rate of interest over a given period.

**compounding** When interest earned each year is left in the account and becomes part of the balance (or principal) on which interest is earned in subsequent years.

### Future Value of a Single Amount

To demonstrate future value, let's return to the goal of accumulating $45,000 for a down payment to buy a home in 6 years. The correct way to approach this problem is to use the *future value* concept. For instance, if you can invest $100 today at 5%, you will have $105 in a year. You will earn $5 on your investment (.05 × $100 = $5) and get your original $100 back. Once you know the length of time and rate of return involved, you can find the

©TATIANA POPOVA/SHUTTERSTOCK

future value of any investment by using the following simple formula:

**Future value = Amount invested × Future value factor**

Tables of future value factors simplify the computations in this formula (see Appendix A). The table is easy to use; simply find the factor that corresponds to a given year and interest rate. Referring to Appendix A, you will find the future value factor for a 6-year investment earning 5% is 1.340 (the factor that lies at the intersection of 6 years and 5%).

Returning to the problem at hand, let's say you already have accumulated $5,000 toward the purchase of a new home. To find the future value of that investment in 6 years earning 5%, you can use the preceding formula as follows:

**Future value = $5,000 × 1.340 = $6,700**

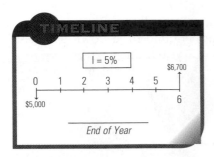

In 6 years, then, you will have $6,700 if you invest the $5,000 at 5%. Because you feel you are going to need $45,000, you are still $38,300 short of your goal.

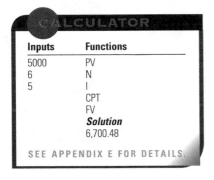

### Future Value of an Annuity

How are you going to accumulate the additional $38,300? You'll again use the future value concept, but this time you'll use the *future value annuity factor*. An **annuity** is a fixed sum of money that occurs annually; for example, a deposit of $1,000 per year for each of the next 5 years, with payment to be made at the end of each year. To find out how much you need to save each year in order to accumulate a given amount, use this equation:

$$\text{Yearly savings} = \frac{\text{Amount of money desired}}{\text{Future value annuity factor}}$$

When dealing with an annuity you need to use a different table of factors, such as that in Appendix B. Note that it's very much like the table of future value factors and, in fact, is used in exactly the same way: the proper future value annuity factor is the one that corresponds to a given year *and* interest rate. For example,

you'll find in Appendix B that the future value annuity factor for 6 years and 5% is 6.802. Using this factor in the previous equation, you can find out how much to save each year to accumulate $38,300 in 6 years, given a 5% rate of return, as follows:

**Yearly savings = $38,300 / 6.802 = $5,630.70**

You'll need to save about $5,630.70 a year to reach your goal. Note in this example that you must add $5,630.70 each year to the $5,000 you initially invested in order to build up a pool of $45,000 in 6 years. At a 5% rate of return, the $5,630.70 per year will grow to $38,300 and the $5,000 will grow to $6,700, so in 6 years you'll have

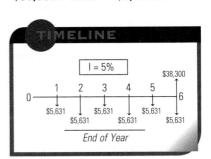

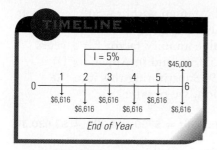

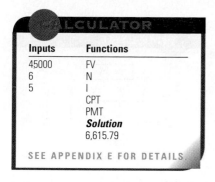

| Inputs | Functions |
|--------|-----------|
| 45000 | FV |
| 6 | N |
| 5 | I |
| | CPT |
| | PMT |
| | **Solution** |
| | 6,615.79 |

SEE APPENDIX E FOR DETAILS.

$38,300 + $6,700 = $45,000.

How much, you may ask, would you need to save each year if you didn't have the $5,000 to start with? In this case, your goal would still be the same (to accumulate $45,000 in 6 years), but because you'd be starting from scratch, the full $45,000 would need to come from yearly savings. Assuming you can still earn 5% over the 6-year period, you can use the same future value annuity factor (6.802) and compute the amount of yearly savings as follows:

**Yearly savings = $45,000 / 6.802 = $6,615.70**

or approximately $6,616. Note that this amount corresponds to the $6,616 figure cited at the beginning of this section.

## Present Value

Lucky you! You've just won $100,000 in your state lottery. You want to spend part of it now, but because you're 30 years old, you also want to use part of it for your retirement fund. Your goal is to accumulate $300,000 in the fund by the time you're age 55 (25 years from now). How much do you need to invest if you estimate that you can earn 5% annually on your investments during the next 25 years?

Using **present value**, the value today of an amount to be received in the future, you can calculate the answer. It represents the amount you'd have to invest today at a given interest rate over the specified time period to accumulate the future amount. The process of

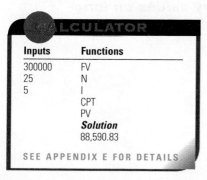

| Inputs | Functions |
|--------|-----------|
| 300000 | FV |
| 25 | N |
| 5 | I |
| | CPT |
| | PV |
| | **Solution** |
| | 88,590.83 |

SEE APPENDIX E FOR DETAILS.

finding present value is called **discounting**, which is the inverse of *compounding* to find future value.

### Present Value of a Single Amount

Assuming you wish to create the retirement fund (future value) by making a single lump-sum deposit today, you can use this formula to find the amount you need to deposit:

**Present value = Future value × Present value factor**

Tables of present value factors make this calculation easy (see Appendix C). First, find the present value factor for a 25-year investment at a 5% discount rate (the factor that lies at the intersection of 25 years and 5%) in Appendix C; it is 0.295. Then, substitute the future value of $300,000 and the present value factor of 0.295 into the formula as follows:

**Present value = $300,000 × 0.295 = $88,500**

The $88,500 is the amount you'd have to deposit today into an account paying 5% annual interest in order to accumulate $300,000 at the end of 25 years.

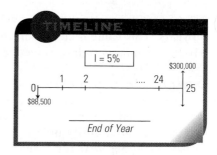

### Present Value of an Annuity

You can also use present value techniques to determine how much you can withdraw from your retirement fund each year over a specified time horizon. This calls for the *present value annuity factor*. Assume that at age 55 you wish to begin making equal annual withdrawals over the next 30 years from your $300,000 retirement fund. At first, you might think you could withdraw $10,000 per year ($300,000/30 years). However, the funds still on deposit would continue to earn 5% annual interest. To find the amount of the equal annual withdrawal, you again need to consider the time value of money. Specifically, you would use this formula:

$$\text{Annual withdrawal} = \frac{\text{Initial deposit}}{\text{Present value annuity factor}}$$

**present value** The value today of an amount to be received in the future; it's the amount that would have to be invested today at a given interest rate over a specified time period to accumulate the future amount.

**discounting** The process of finding present value; the inverse of *compounding* to find future value.

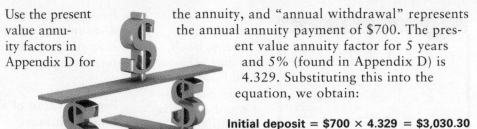

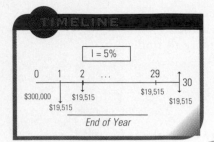

I = 5%

0    1    2    ...    29    30

$300,000    $19,515    $19,515    $19,515

$19,515

*End of Year*

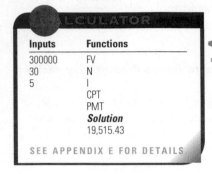

**CALCULATOR**

| Inputs | Functions |
|--------|-----------|
| 300000 | FV |
| 30 | N |
| 5 | I |
| | CPT |
| | PMT |
| | **Solution** |
| | 19,515.43 |

SEE APPENDIX E FOR DETAILS.

Use the present value annuity factors in Appendix D for this calculation. Substituting the $300,000 initial deposit and the present value annuity factor for 30 years and 5% of 15.373 (from Appendix D) into the preceding equation, we get:

$$\text{Annual withdrawal} = \frac{\$300,000}{15.373} = \$19,514.73$$

Therefore, you can withdraw $19,514.73 each year for 30 years. This value is clearly much larger than the $10,000 annual withdrawal mentioned earlier.

### Other Applications of Present Value

You can also use present value techniques to analyze investments. Suppose you have an opportunity to purchase an annuity investment that promises to pay $700 per year for 5 years. You know that you'll receive a total of $3,500 ($700 × 5 years) over the 5-year period. However, you wish to earn a minimum annual return of 5% on your investments. What's the most you should pay for this annuity today? You can answer this question by rearranging the terms in the formula to get:

Initial deposit = Annual withdrawal × **Present value annuity factor**

Adapting the equation to this situation, "initial deposit" represents the maximum price to pay for

the annuity, and "annual withdrawal" represents the annual annuity payment of $700. The present value annuity factor for 5 years and 5% (found in Appendix D) is 4.329. Substituting this into the equation, we obtain:

**Initial deposit = $700 × 4.329 = $3,030.30**

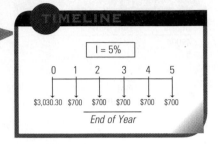

I = 5%

0    1    2    3    4    5

$3,030.30    $700    $700    $700    $700    $700

*End of Year*

**CALCULATOR**

| Inputs | Functions |
|--------|-----------|
| 700 | PMT |
| 5 | N |
| 5 | I |
| | CPT |
| | PV |
| | **Solution** |
| | 3,030.63 |

SEE APPENDIX E FOR DETAILS.

The most you should pay for the $700, 5-year annuity, given your 5% annual return, is about $3,030. At this price, you'd earn 5% on the investment.

Using the present value concept, you can easily determine the present value of a sum to be received in the future, equal annual future withdrawals available from an initial deposit, and the initial deposit that would generate a given stream of equal annual withdrawals. These procedures, like future value concepts, allow you to place monetary values on long-term financial goals.

{ *Future and present value concepts allow you to place monetary values on long-term financial goals.* }

# FINANCIAL PLANNING EXERCISES

**LG2, 3**

1. Michael Vaughn is preparing his balance sheet and income and expense statement for the year ending June 30, 2010. He is having difficulty classifying six items and asks for your help. Which, if any, of the following transactions are assets, liabilities, income, or expense items?
   a. Michael rents a house for $950 a month.
   b. On June 21, 2010, Michael bought diamond earrings for his wife and charged them using his Visa card. The earrings cost $600, but he hasn't yet received the bill.
   c. Michael borrowed $2,000 from his parents last fall, but so far he has made no payments to them.
   d. Michael makes monthly payments of $120 on an installment loan; about half of it is interest, and the balance is repayment of principal. He has 20 payments left, totaling $2,400.
   e. Michael paid $2,800 in taxes during the year and is due a tax refund of $450, which he hasn't yet received.
   f. Michael invested $1,800 in some common stock.

**LG5**

2. Harvey and Marlyn Elliott are preparing their 2011 cash budget. Help the Elliotts reconcile the following differences, giving reasons to support your answers:
   a. Their only source of income is Harvey's salary, which amounts to $5,000 a month before taxes. Marlyn wants to show the $5,000 as their monthly income, whereas Harvey argues that his take-home pay of $3,917 is the correct value to show.
   b. Marlyn wants to make a provision for *fun money*, an idea that Harvey cannot understand. He asks, "Why do we need fun money when everything is provided for in the budget?"

**LG6**

3. Use future or present value techniques to solve the following problems:
   a. If you inherited $25,000 today and invested all of it in a security that paid a 7% rate of return, how much would you have in 25 years?
   b. If the average new home costs $210,000 today, how much will it cost in 10 years if the price increases by 5% each year?
   c. You think that in 15 years it will cost $212,000 to provide your child with a 4-year college education. Will you have enough if you take $70,000 *today* and invest it for the next 15 years at 5%?
   d. If you can earn 5%, how much will you have to save *each year* if you want to retire in 35 years with $1 million?

**LG6**

4. Carl Wilfred wishes to have $400,000 in a retirement fund 20 years from now. He can create the retirement fund by making a single lump-sum deposit today.
   a. If upon retirement in 20 years Carl plans to invest $400,000 in a fund that earns 5%, what is the maximum annual withdrawal he can make over the following 15 years?
   b. How much would Carl need to have on deposit at retirement to annually withdraw $35,000 over the 15 years if the retirement fund earns 8%?
   c. To achieve his annual withdrawal goal of $35,000 calculated in part **b**, how much more than the amount calculated in part **a** must Carl deposit today in an investment earning 5% annual interest?

## LEARNING GOALS

**LG1** Discuss the basic principles of income taxes and determine your filing status. (p. 47)

**LG2** Describe the sources of gross income and adjustments to income, differentiate between standard and itemized deductions and exemptions, and calculate taxable income. (p. 50)

**LG3** Prepare a basic tax return using the appropriate tax forms and rate schedules. (p. 54)

**LG4** Explain who needs to pay estimated taxes, when to file or amend your return, and how to handle an audit. (p. 62)

**LG5** Know where to get help with your taxes and how software can streamline tax return preparation. (p. 62)

**LG6** Implement an effective tax planning strategy. (p. 66)

# **LG1** Understanding Federal Income Tax Principles

**Taxes** are dues we pay for membership in our society; they're the cost of living in this country. Federal, state, and local tax receipts fund government activities and a wide variety of public services, from national defense to local libraries. Administering and enforcing federal tax laws is the responsibility of the IRS, a part of the U.S. Department of Treasury.

Because federal income tax is generally the largest tax you'll pay, you are wise to make tax planning an important part of personal financial planning. A typical American family

> **Because federal income tax is generally the largest tax you'll pay, you are wise to make tax planning an important part of personal financial planning.**

currently pays *more than one-third of its gross income in taxes:* federal income and Social Security taxes as well as numerous state and local income, sales, and property taxes. You should make tax planning a year-round activity and always consider tax consequences when preparing and revising your financial plans and making major financial decisions.

The overriding objective of tax planning is simple: *to maximize the amount of money you keep by minimizing the amount of taxes you pay.* As long as it's done honestly and within the tax codes, there is nothing immoral, illegal, or unethical about trying to minimize your tax bill. Here we concentrate on *income taxes paid by individuals*—particularly the federal income tax, the

largest and most important tax for most taxpayers. To give you a good understanding of your future tax situation, we use a mid-career couple to demonstrate the key aspects of individual taxation.

**taxes** The dues paid for membership in our society; the cost of living in this country.

### Go to Smart Sites

How long does the average American have to work this year to pay federal, state, and local taxes? Find this year's date of "Tax Freedom Day" at the Tax Foundation Web site. You'll also find information there about tax policy, tax rates, tax collections, and the economics of taxation. Whenever you see "*Go to Smart Sites*" in this chapter, visit 4ltrpress.cengage .com for help finding answers online. ●

In addition to federal income tax, there are other forms of taxes to contend with—for example, federal self-employment taxes and state and local sales, income, property, and license taxes. Thus, a person saving to purchase a new automobile costing $25,000 should realize that the state and local sales taxes, as well as the cost of license plates and registration, may add 10% or more to the total cost of the car.

Here we present key tax concepts and show how they apply to common situations. The tax tables, calculations, and sample tax returns presented in this chapter are based on the tax laws applicable to the calendar year 2008. The 2009 tax laws were being finalized at the time this book was being revised. We present the 2008 treatment because in 2009 there was a one-year only financial crisis–related tax credit that is not representative of normal tax treatments. *Although tax rates and other provisions will change, the basic procedures will remain the same.*

**Chapter 3 • Preparing Your Taxes**

# The Economics of Income Taxes

**Income taxes** are the major source of revenue for the federal government. Personal income taxes are scaled on progressive rates. To illustrate how this **progressive tax structure** works, we'll use the following data for *single taxpayers* filing 2008 returns:

| Taxable Income | Tax Rate |
|---|---|
| $1 to $8,025 | 10% |
| $8,026 to $32,550 | 15% |
| $32,551 to $78,850 | 25% |
| $78,851 to $164,550 | 28% |
| $164,551 to $357,700 | 33% |
| Over $357,701 | 35% |

Of course, any nontaxable income can be viewed as being in the 0% tax bracket. As taxable income moves from a lower to a higher bracket, the higher rate applies *only to the additional taxable income in that bracket* and not to the entire taxable income. For example, consider two single brothers Will and Robert, whose taxable incomes are $45,000 and $90,000, respectively (see table below).

Note that Will pays the 25% rate only on that portion of the $45,000 in taxable income that exceeds $32,550. Due to this kind of progressive scale, the more money you make, the progressively more you pay in taxes: although Robert's taxable income is twice that of Will's, his income tax is about 2½ times higher than his brother's.

The tax rate for each bracket—10%, 15%, 25%, 28%, 33%, and 35%—is called the **marginal tax rate**, or the rate applied to the next dollar of taxable income. When you relate the tax liability to the level of taxable income earned, the tax rate, called the **average tax rate**, drops considerably. Will's average tax rate, calculated by dividing the tax liability by taxable income, is about 16.9% ($7,595/$45,000). Robert's average tax rate is about 21.3% ($19,179/$90,000). Clearly, taxes are still progressive, and the average size of the bite is not as bad as the stated tax rate might suggest.

## Your Filing Status

The taxes you pay depend in part on your *filing status*, which is based on your marital status and family situation on the last day of your tax year (usually December 31). There are five different filing status categories.

- **Single taxpayers:** Unmarried or legally separated from their spouses by either a separation or final divorce decree.

- **Married filing jointly:** Married couples who combine their income and allowable deductions and file one tax return.

- **Married filing separately:** Each spouse files his or her own return, reporting only his or her income, deductions, and exemptions.

- **Head of household:** A taxpayer who is unmarried or considered unmarried and pays more than half of the cost of keeping up a home for himself or herself and an eligible dependent child or relative.

- **Qualifying widow or widower with dependent child:** A person whose spouse died within 2 years of the tax year (for example, in 2006 or 2007 for the 2008 tax year) and who supports a dependent child may use joint return tax rates and is eligible for the highest standard deduction.

| Name | Taxable Income | Tax Calculation | Tax Liability |
|---|---|---|---|
| Will | $45,000 | = [($45,000 − $32,550) × 0.25]<br>+ [$32,550 − $8,025) × 0.15]<br>+ [$8,025 × 0.10]<br>= $3,113 + $3,679 + $803 = | $7,595 |
| Robert | $90,000 | = [($90,000 − $78,850) × 0.28]<br>+ [($78,850 − $32,550) × 0.25]<br>+ [($32,550 − $8,025) × 0.15]<br>+ [($8,025 × 0.10]<br>= $3,122 + $11,575 + $3,679 + $803 = | $19,179 |

©LAYLAND MASUDA/SHUTTERSTOCK

Every individual or married couple who earns a specified level of income is required to file a tax return. For example, for those under 65, a single person who earned more than $8,950 and a married couple with a combined income of more than $17,900 must file a tax return (for 2008). Like the personal tax rates, these minimums are adjusted annually based on the annual rate of inflation. Regardless, even if your income falls below the current minimum level and you had any income tax withheld during the year, you must file a tax return in order to receive a refund of the income tax withheld.

## Your Take-Home Pay

Most of us actually pay taxes as we earn income throughout the year. Under this *pay-as-you-go* system, your employer withholds (deducts) a portion of your income every pay period and sends it to the IRS to be credited to your own tax account. Self-employed persons must also prepay their taxes by forwarding part of their income to the IRS at four dates each year (referred to as quarterly estimated

tax payments). After the close of the taxable year, you calculate the actual taxes you owe and file your tax return. When you file, you receive full credit for the amount of taxes withheld (including estimated tax payments) from your income during the year and either (1) receive a refund from the IRS (if too much tax was withheld from your paycheck and/or prepaid in estimated taxes) or (2) have to pay additional taxes (if the amount withheld/prepaid didn't cover your tax liability). Your employer normally withholds funds not only for federal income taxes but also for FICA (Social Security) taxes and, if applicable, state and local income taxes (which may be deductible on federal returns). Other payroll deductions include life and health insurance, savings plans, retirement programs, professional or union dues, and charitable contributions—all of which lower your take-home pay. Your *take-home pay* is what you're left with after subtracting the amount withheld from your *gross earnings*.

### Federal Withholding Taxes

The amount of **federal withholding taxes** deducted from your gross earnings each pay period depends on both the level of your earnings and the number of withholding allowances you have claimed on a form called a *W-4*, which you must complete for your employer. Withholding allowances reduce the amount of taxes withheld from your income. A taxpayer is entitled to one allowance for himself or herself, one for a nonworking spouse (if filing jointly), and one for each dependent claimed (children or parents being supported mainly by the taxpayers). In addition, you may qualify for a *special allowance* or *additional withholding allowances* under certain circumstances. Taxpayers may have to change their withholding allowances during the tax year if their employment or marital status changes.

### FICA and Other Withholding Taxes

All employed workers (except certain federal employees) have to pay a combined old-age, survivor's, disability, and hospital insurance tax under provisions of the **Federal Insurance Contributions Act (FICA)**. Known more commonly as the **Social Security tax**, it is paid equally by employer and employee. In 2008, the total Social Security tax rate was 15.3%, allocating 12.4% to Social Security

**federal withholding taxes** Taxes—based on the level of earnings and the number of withholding allowances claimed—that an employer deducts from the employee's gross earnings each pay period.

**Federal Insurance Contributions Act (FICA) or Social Security tax** The law establishing the combined old-age, survivor's, disability, and hospital insurance tax levied on both employer and employee.

**taxable income** The amount of income subject to taxes; it is calculated by subtracting adjustments, the larger of itemized or standard deductions, and exemptions from gross income.

**gross income** The total of all of a taxpayer's income (before any adjustments, deductions, or exemptions) subject to federal taxes; it includes active, portfolio, and passive income.

and 2.9% to Medicare. The 12.4% applies only to the first $102,000 of an employee's earnings (this number rises with national average wages), whereas the Medicare component is paid on all earnings. In 2008, the employer and employee each pay 7.65% (i.e., half of the 15.3% rate); self-employed persons pay the full 15.3% tax and can deduct 50% of it on their tax returns.

Most states have their own income taxes, which differ from state to state. Some cities assess income taxes as well. These state and local income taxes will also be withheld from earnings. They are deductible on federal returns, but deductibility of federal taxes on the state or local return depends on state and local laws.

 **It's Taxable Income That Matters**

Calculating your income taxes is a complex process involving several steps and many computations. Exhibit 3.1 depicts the procedure to compute your **taxable income** and total tax liability owed. It looks simple enough—just subtract certain adjustments from your gross income to get your adjusted gross income; then subtract either the standard deduction or your itemized deductions and your total personal exemptions to get taxable income; and finally, compute your taxes, subtract any tax credits from that amount, and add any other taxes to it to get your total tax liability. This isn't as easy as it sounds, however! As we'll see, some problems can arise in defining what you may subtract.

- Gains from the sale of assets
- Income from pensions and annuities
- Income from rents and partnerships
- Prizes, lottery, and gambling winnings

In addition to these sources of income, others, such as child-support payments and municipal bond interest, are considered *tax exempt* and as such are excluded—totally or partially—from gross income.

### Three Kinds of Income
Individual income falls into one of three basic categories:

- **Active income:** Income *earned* on the job, such as wages and salaries, bonuses and tips; most other forms of *noninvestment* income, including pension income and alimony
- **Portfolio income:** Earnings (interest, dividends, and capital gains [profits on the sale of investments]) generated from most types of investment holdings; includes savings accounts, stocks, bonds, mutual funds, options, and futures
- **Passive income:** A special category that includes income derived from real estate, limited partnerships, and other forms of tax shelters

These categories limit the amount of deductions and write-offs that taxpayers can take. Specifically, the amount of allowable, deductible expenses associated with portfolio and passive income *is limited to the amount of income derived from these two sources.* For deduction purposes, you cannot combine portfolio and passive income with each other or with active income. *Investment-related expenses can be used only with portfolio income,* and with a few exceptions, *passive investment expenses can be used only to offset the income from passive investments.* All the other allowances and deductions we'll describe later

> **Calculating your income taxes is a complex process involving several steps and many computations.**

### Gross Income
**Gross income** essentially includes any and all income subject to federal taxes. Here are some common forms of gross income:

- Wages and salaries
- Bonuses, commissions, and tips
- Interest and dividends received
- Alimony received
- Business and farm income

are written off against the total amount of *active* income the taxpayer generates.

### Capital Gains
Technically, a *capital gain* occurs whenever an asset (such as a stock, a bond, or real estate) is sold for more than its original cost. So, if you purchased stock for $50 per share and sold it for $60, you'd have a capital gain of $10 per share.

Capital gains are taxed at different rates, depending on the holding period. Exhibit 3.2 shows the

**Exhibit 3.1  Calculating Your Taxable Income and Total Tax Liability Owed**

To find taxable income, you must first subtract all adjustments to gross income and then subtract deductions and personal exemptions. Your total tax liability owed includes tax on this taxable income amount, less any tax credits, plus other taxes owed.

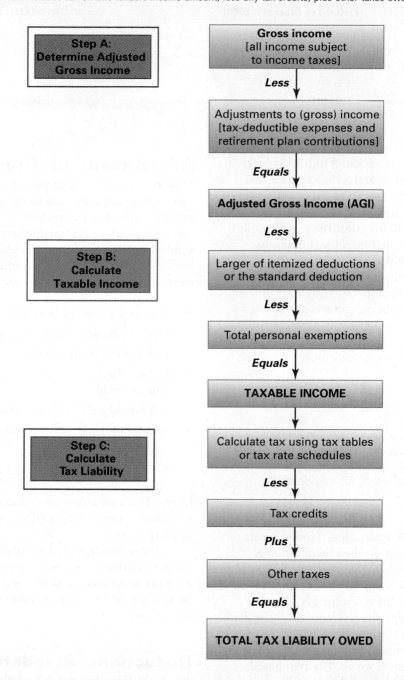

**Step A:**
**Determine Adjusted Gross Income**

**Gross income**
[all income subject to income taxes]

*Less*

Adjustments to (gross) income [tax-deductible expenses and retirement plan contributions]

*Equals*

**Adjusted Gross Income (AGI)**

*Less*

**Step B:**
**Calculate Taxable Income**

Larger of itemized deductions or the standard deduction

*Less*

Total personal exemptions

*Equals*

**TAXABLE INCOME**

**Step C:**
**Calculate Tax Liability**

Calculate tax using tax tables or tax rate schedules

*Less*

Tax credits

*Plus*

Other taxes

*Equals*

**TOTAL TAX LIABILITY OWED**

different holding periods and applicable tax rates based on the 2008 tax brackets.

Although there are no limits on the amount of capital gains taxpayers can generate, the IRS imposes some restrictions on the amount of capital losses (only on the sale of income-producing assets) taxpayers can take in a given year. Specifically, a taxpayer can write off capital losses, dollar for dollar, against any capital gains. After that, he or she can write off a maximum of $3,000 in additional capital losses against active income. Thus, if

Exhibit 3.2 Capital Gains Tax Categories as of 2008

Capital gains tax rates are as low as 5% or 15% for holding periods over 12 months, depending on the tax bracket (year 2008).

| Holding | Period Tax Brackets (2008) | Tax on Capital Gains |
|---|---|---|
| Less than 12 months | All (10%, 15%, 25%, 28%, 33%, and 35%) | Same as ordinary income |
| Over 12 months | 10%, 15% | 0% |
| | 25%, 28%, 33%, 35% | 15% |

**adjustments to (gross) income** Allowable deductions from gross income, including certain employee, personal retirement, insurance, and support expenses.

**adjusted gross income (AGI)** The amount of income remaining after subtracting all allowable adjustments to income from gross income.

a taxpayer had $10,000 in capital gains and $18,000 in capital losses in 2008, only $13,000 could be written off on 2008 taxes: $10,000 against the capital gains generated in 2008 and another $3,000 against active income. The remainder—$5,000 in this case—will have to be written off in later years, in the same order as just indicated: first against any capital gains and then up to $3,000 against active income.

 **Go to Smart Sites**

The IRS's Web site features a section on *Capital Gains and Losses* that will help you learn about tax treatment of securities sales. It's just one of many tax guides you'll find at the site's *Tax Guide for Investors.* ●

**SELLING YOUR HOME: A SPECIAL CASE.** Homeowners receive special tax treatment on the sale of a home. Single taxpayers can exclude from income the first $250,000 of gain ($500,000 for married taxpayers) on the sale of a principal residence. To qualify, the taxpayer must own and occupy the residence as a principal residence for at least 2 of the 5 years prior to the sale. For example, the Holtzmans (married taxpayers) just sold their principal residence, which they purchased 4 years earlier for $325,000, for $475,000. They may exclude their $150,000 gain ($475,000 − $325,000) from their income because they occupied the residence for more than 2 years, and the gain is less than $500,000.

This exclusion is available on only one sale every 2 years. A loss on the sale of a principal residence is not deductible. Generally speaking, this law is quite favorable to homeowners.

## Adjustments to (Gross) Income

Now that you've totaled your gross income, you can deduct your **adjustments to (gross) income**. These are allowable deductions from gross income, including certain employee, personal retirement, insurance, and support expenses. Most of these deductions are non-business in nature. Here are some items that can be treated as adjustments to income:

- Educator expenses (limited)
- Higher education tuition costs (limited)
- IRA contributions (limited)
- Self-employment taxes paid (limited to 50% of amount paid)
- Self-employed health insurance payments
- Penalty on early withdrawal of savings
- Alimony paid
- Moving expenses (some limits)

(*Note*: The limitations on deductions for self-directed retirement plans, such as IRAs and SEPs, are discussed in Chapter 14.)

After subtracting the total of all allowable adjustments to income from your gross income, you're left with **adjusted gross income (AGI)**. AGI is an important value, because it's used to calculate limits for certain itemized deductions.

## Deductions: Standard or Itemized?

As we see from Exhibit 3.1, the next step in calculating your taxes is to subtract allowable deductions from your AGI. This may be the most complex part of the tax preparation process. You have two options: take the *standard deduction*, a fixed amount that depends on your filing status, or list your *itemized deductions* (specified tax-deductible personal expenses). Obviously, you should use the method that results in larger allowable deductions.

## Standard Deduction

Instead of itemizing personal deductions, a taxpayer can take the **standard deduction**, a blanket deduction that includes the various deductible expenses that taxpayers normally incur. People whose total itemized deductions are too small take the standard deduction, which varies depending on the taxpayer's filing status (single, married filing jointly, and so on), age (65 or older), and vision (blind). In 2008, the standard deduction ranged from $5,450 to $15,100. For single filers it is $5,450, and for married people filing jointly it is $10,900. Those over 65 and those who are blind are eligible for a higher standard deduction. Each year the standard deduction amounts are adjusted annually for changes in the cost of living.

### FINANCIAL ROAD SIGN

**COMMONLY OVERLOOKED TAX DEDUCTIONS**

Often taxpayers miss deductions that would reduce their tax liability. Here are some you might overlook:

- Investment losses and charitable contributions carried from prior years.
- Cost of safe deposit box if used for investments or business.
- Professional organization dues.
- Points paid on mortgage or refinancing.
- Financial management fees paid to your broker to manage your portfolio.
- Personal property taxes on the value of your vehicles (in some states).
- Noncash contributions of clothing, furniture, and the like to Goodwill, a clothing bank, or a church.
- Unreimbursed job-related expenses.
- Health insurance premiums of self-employed people in a profitable business, subject to certain limits.
- Certain types of clean-fuel or hybrid cars may give you a tax credit as large as $3,400.
- Up to $4,000 in college tuition for family members if your AGI falls within certain limits.

## Itemized Deductions

**Itemized deductions** allow taxpayers to reduce their AGI by the amount of their allowable personal expenditures. Some of the more common ones allowed by the IRS include:

- Medical and dental expenses (*in excess* of 7.5% of AGI)
- State, local, and foreign income and property taxes; state and local personal property taxes
- Residential mortgage interest and investment interest (limited)
- Charitable contributions (limited to 50%, 30%, or 20% of AGI depending on certain factors)

- Casualty and theft losses (in excess of 10% of AGI; reduced by $100 per loss)
- Job and other expenses (in excess of 2% of AGI)
- Moving expenses (some restrictions; also deductible for those who don't itemize)

Taxpayers with an AGI over a specified amount, which is adjusted upward annually, lose part of their itemized deductions. In 2008, the level of AGI at which the phaseout began was $79,975 for married taxpayers filing separately and $159,950 for single people and for married persons filing jointly. This limitation applies to certain categories of deductions, such as other types of taxes, home mortgage interest, and charitable contributions. Medical expenses, casualty and theft losses, and investment interest are exempt from this limit on deductions; the amount of the total reduction in itemized deductions cannot be more than 80% of the total deductions to which the limitation applies. The reduction in itemized deductions, which is scheduled to be completely eliminated by 2010, effectively raises the tax rate slightly.

### Choosing the Best Option

Your decision to take the standard deduction or itemize deductions may change over time. Taxpayers who find they've chosen the wrong option and paid too much may recalculate their tax using the other method and file an *amended return (Form 1040X)* to claim a refund for the difference. For example, suppose that you computed and paid your taxes, which amounted to $2,450, using the standard deduction. A few months later you find that had you itemized your deductions, your taxes would have been only $1,950. Using the appropriate forms, you can file for a $500 refund ($2,450 − $1,950). To avoid having to file an amended return, it is best to estimate your deductions using both the standard and itemized deduction amounts and choose the one that results in lower taxes.

## Exemptions

Deductions from AGI based on the number of persons supported by the taxpayer's income are called **exemptions**. A taxpayer can claim an exemption for himself or herself, his or her spouse, and any *dependents*—children or other relatives earning less than a stipulated level of income ($3,500 in 2008)—for whom the *taxpayer provides more than half* of their total support. This income limitation is waived for dependent children under the age of 24 (at the end

**standard deduction**
A blanket deduction that depends on the taxpayer's filing status, age, and vision and can be taken by a taxpayer whose total itemized deductions are too small.

**itemized deductions**
Personal expenditures that can be deducted from AGI when determining taxable income.

**exemptions**
Deductions from AGI based on the number of persons supported by the taxpayer's income.

©MONKEY BUSINESS IMAGES/SHUTTERSTOCK

of the calendar year) who are full-time students. So a college student, for example, could earn $8,000 and still be claimed as an exemption by her parents as long as all other dependency requirements are met. In 2008, each exemption claimed was worth $3,500, an amount tied to the cost of living and adjusted annually. By 2010, exemptions will be phased out and eliminated altogether for taxpayers with high levels of AGI.

A personal exemption can be claimed only once. If a child is *eligible* to be claimed as an exemption by her parents, then she doesn't have the choice of using a personal exemption on her own tax return regardless of whether the parents use her exemption. In 2008, a family of four could take total exemptions of $14,000—that is, 4 × $3,500. Subtracting the amount claimed for itemized deductions (or the standard deduction) and exemptions from AGI results in the amount of *taxable income*, which is the basis on which taxes are calculated. A taxpayer who makes $50,000 a year may have only, say, $30,000 in taxable income after adjustments, deductions, and exemptions. It is the *lower*, taxable income figure that determines how much tax an individual must pay.

## LG3 Calculating and Filing Your Taxes

To calculate the amount of taxable income, we consider: (1) tax rates, (2) tax credits, (3) tax forms and schedules, and (4) the procedures for determining tax liability.

### Tax Rates

To find the amount of *taxable income* we subtract itemized deductions (or the standard deduction for non-itemizers) *and* personal exemptions from AGI. *Both itemizers and non-itemizers* use this procedure,

which is a key calculation in determining your tax liability. It is *reported taxable income* that determines the amount of income subject to federal income taxes. Once you know the amount of your taxable income, you can refer to *tax rate tables* or *tax rate schedules* (if taxable income is greater than $100,000) to find the amount of taxes you owe.

Tax rates vary not only with the amount of reported taxable income but also with filing status. Thus, different tax rate schedules apply to each filing category; two schedules are shown in Exhibit 3.3. The vast majority of taxpayers fall into the first three brackets and are subject to tax rates of either 10%, 15%, or 25%.

To see how the tax rates in Exhibit 3.3 work, consider two single taxpayers: one has taxable income of $12,500; the other, $35,600. Here's how we would calculate their respective tax liabilities:

- For taxable income of $12,500: $803 + [($12,500 − $8,025) × 0.15] = $803 + $671 = $1,474
- For taxable income of $35,600: $4,481 + [($35,600 − $32,550) × 0.25] = $4,481 + $763 = $5,244

The income of $12,500 is partially taxed at the 10% rate and partially taxed at the 15% rate. The first $8,025 of the $35,600 is taxed at 10%, the next $24,525 at 15%, and the remaining $3,050 at 25%. Keep in mind that taxpayers use the same procedures at this point whether they itemize or not. To show how the amount of tax liability will vary with the level of taxable income, Exhibit 3.4 lists the taxes due on a range of taxable incomes, from $1,500 to $357,700, for individual and joint returns.

Returning to our example involving the taxpayer with an income of $35,600, we see that this individual had an average tax rate of 14.7% ($5,244/$35,600), which is considerably less than the stated tax rate of 25%. Actually, the 25% represents the taxpayer's *marginal tax rate*—the rate at which the next dollar of taxable income is taxed. Notice in our calculations that the marginal 25% tax rate applies only to that portion of the single person's income that exceeds $32,550, or $3,050 in this example.

Some taxpayers are subject to the *alternative minimum tax (AMT)*, currently 26% of the first $175,000 and 28% of the excess. A taxpayer's tax liability is the higher of the AMT or the regular tax. The AMT is designed to ensure that high-income taxpayers with many deductions and tax shelter investments that provide attractive tax write-offs are paying their fair share of taxes. The AMT includes in taxable income certain types of deductions otherwise allowed, such as state and local income and property taxes, miscellaneous itemized deductions, unreimbursed medical expenses, and depreciation. Therefore, taxpayers with moderate levels of taxable income, including those living in

**Exhibit 3.3   Sample Tax Rate Schedules**

Tax rates levied on personal income vary with the amount of reported taxable income and the taxpayer's filing status.

# 2008 Tax Rate Schedules

**Schedule X—If your filing status is Single**

| If your taxable income is: Over— | But not over— | The tax is: | of the amount over— |
|---|---|---|---|
| $0 | $8,025 | ......... 10% | $0 |
| 8,025 | 32,550 | $802.50 + 15% | 8,025 |
| 32,550 | 78,850 | 4,481.25 + 25% | 32,550 |
| 78,850 | 164,550 | 16,056.25 + 28% | 78,850 |
| 164,550 | 357,700 | 40,052.25 + 33% | 164,550 |
| 357,700 | ......... | 103,791.75 + 35% | 357,700 |

**Schedule Y-1—If your filing status is Married filing jointly or Qualifying widow(er)**

| If your taxable income is: Over— | But not over— | The tax is: | of the amount over— |
|---|---|---|---|
| $0 | $16,050 | ......... 10% | $0 |
| 16,050 | 65,100 | $1,605.00 + 15% | 16,050 |
| 65,100 | 131,450 | 8,962.50 + 25% | 65,100 |
| 131,450 | 200,300 | 25,550.00 + 28% | 131,450 |
| 200,300 | 357,700 | 44,828.00 + 33% | 200,300 |
| 357,700 | ......... | 96,770.00 + 35% | 357,700 |

*Source:* Internal Revenue Service.

states with high tax rates and self-employed persons with depreciation deductions, may be subject to the AMT calculation and additional tax.

**tax credits**
Deductions from a taxpayer's tax liability that directly reduce his or her *taxes due* rather than *taxable income.*

## Tax Credits

After determining the amount of taxes you owe, some taxpayers are allowed to take certain deductions, known as **tax credits**, directly from it. A tax credit is much more valuable than a deduction or an exemption because it directly reduces, dollar for dollar, the amount of *taxes due*, whereas a deduction or an exemption merely reduces the amount of *taxable income.* An often-used tax credit is for *child and dependent care expenses.* This credit is based on the amount spent for dependent care while a taxpayer (and spouse, if married) works or goes

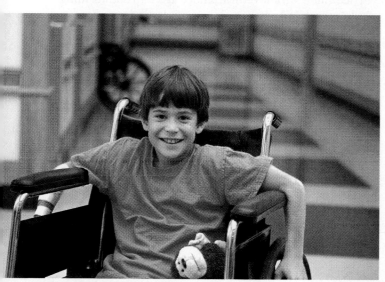

©SONYA ETCHISON/SHUTTERSTOCK

## Exhibit 3.4 Taxable Income and the Amount of Income Taxes Due (2008)

Given the progressive tax structure used in this country, it follows that the larger your income, the more you can expect to pay in taxes.

| Taxable Income | Taxes Due (rounded) Individual Returns | Joint Returns |
|---|---|---|
| $ 1,500 | $ 150[a] | $ 150[a] |
| 8,000 | 800[a] | 800[a] |
| 15,000 | 1,849[b] | 1,500[a] |
| 30,000 | 4,099[b] | 3,697[b] |
| 60,000 | 11,344[c] | 8,197[b] |
| 100,000 | 21,978[d] | 17,687[c] |
| 180,000 | 45,150[e] | 39,144[d] |
| 360,000 | 104,596[f] | 97,575[f] |

[a] Income is taxed at 10%.
[b] 15% tax rate now applies.
[c] 25% tax rate now applies.
[d] 28% tax rate now applies.
[e] 33% tax rate now applies.
[f] 35% tax rate now applies.

to school. An *adoption tax credit* of up to $11,650 is available for the qualifying costs of adopting a child under age 18. Other common tax credits include: credit for the elderly or the disabled, foreign tax credit, credit for prior year minimum tax, mortgage interest credit, and credit for a qualified electric vehicle. To receive any of these credits, the taxpayer must file a return, along with a separate schedule in support of the tax credit claimed.

### Go to Smart Sites

Need a tax form or instructions on how to fill it out? At the IRS Web site you can download tax forms, instructions, IRS publications, and regulations. Once there, you can also click on "More Online Tools" to access the IRS withholding calculator—you can use it to make sure you aren't having too much or too little withheld from your paycheck. ●

## Tax Forms and Schedules

The IRS requires taxpayers to file their returns using specified tax forms. These forms and various instruction booklets on how to prepare them are available to taxpayers free of charge. Generally, all persons who filed tax returns in the previous year are automatically sent a booklet containing tax forms and instructions for preparing returns for the current year. Inside the

booklet is a form that can be used to obtain additional tax forms for filing various tax-related returns and information. Check out the Bonus Exhibits at 4ltrpress.cengage.com for a list of commonly used tax forms and schedules.

### Variations of Form 1040

All individuals use some variation of Form 1040 to file their tax returns. *Form 1040EZ* is a simple, one-page form. You qualify to use this form if you are single or married filing a joint return; under age 65 (both if filing jointly); not blind; do not claim any dependents; have taxable income of less than $100,000 from only wages, salaries, tips, or taxable scholarships or grants; have interest income of less than $1,500; and do not claim any adjustments to income, itemize deductions, or claim any tax credits. Worksheet 3.1 shows the Form 1040EZ filed in 2008 by Akira Takyama, a full-time graduate student at Yourstate University. His sources of income include a $13,000 scholarship, of which $4,900 was used for room and board; $7,600 earned from part-time and summer jobs; and $50 interest earned on a savings account deposit. Because scholarships used for tuition and fees are not taxed, he should include as income only the portion used for room and board. He had a total of $475 withheld for federal income taxes during the year. Although Akira would also complete a Salaries & Wages Report form, it is omitted for simplicity because it only lists the $4,900 of his scholarship

Form 1040EZ is easy to use, and most of the instructions are printed on the form itself. Akira Takyama qualifies to use it because he is single, under age 65, not blind, and meets its income and deduction restrictions.

TAKYAMA 07 03 2009 10:38 AM

Department of the Treasury—Internal Revenue Service

**Form 1040EZ**

**Income Tax Return for Single and Joint Filers With No Dependents** (99) **2008**

OMB No. 1545-0074

**Label**
(See page 9.)
**Use the IRS label.**
Otherwise, please print or type.

| | |
|---|---|
| Your first name and initial | Last name |
| Akira | Takyama |

**Your social security number**
123-45-6789

Spouse's social security number

Home address (number and street). If you have a P.O. box, see page 9.
1000 State University Drive

Apt. no. 201-B

▲ You **must** enter your SSN(s) above. ▲

City, town or post office, state, and ZIP code. If you have a foreign address, see page 9.
Anytown, Anystate          10001

Checking a box below will not change your tax or refund.

**Presidential Election Campaign** (page 9) ▶

Check here if you, or your spouse if a joint return, want $3 to go to this fund  ▶  ☒ **You**    ☐ **Spouse**

**Income**

**Attach Form(s) W-2 here.**
Enclose, but do not attach, any payment.

| | | | |
|---|---|---|---|
| 1 | Wages, salaries, and tips. This should be shown in box 1 of your Form(s) W-2. Attach your Form(s) W-2.    SCH 4,900 | 1 | 12,500 00 |
| 2 | Taxable interest. If the total is over $1,500, you cannot use Form 1040EZ. | 2 | 50 00 |
| 3 | Unemployment compensation and Alaska Permanent Fund dividends (see page 11). | 3 | |
| 4 | Add lines 1, 2, and 3. This is your **adjusted gross income.** | 4 | 12,550 00 |
| 5 | If someone can claim you (or your spouse if a joint return) as a dependent, check the applicable box(es) below and enter the amount from the worksheet on back.  ☐ **You**    ☐ **Spouse**  If no one can claim you (or your spouse if a joint return), enter $8,950 if **Single**; $17,900 if **married filing jointly.** See back for explanation | 5 | 8,950 00 |
| 6 | Subtract line 5 from line 4. If line 5 is larger than line 4, enter -0-. This is your **taxable income.** ▶ | 6 | 3,600 00 |

**Payments and tax**

| | | | |
|---|---|---|---|
| 7 | Federal income tax withheld from box 2 of your Form(s) W-2. | 7 | 495 00 |
| 8a | **Earned income credit (EIC)** (see page 12).    NO | 8a | |
| b | Nontaxable combat pay election.    8b | | |
| 9 | Recovery rebate credit (see worksheet on pages 17 and 18). | 9 | |
| 10 | Add lines 7 and 8a. These are your **total payments.** ▶ | 10 | 495 00 |
| 11 | **Tax.** Use the amount on **line 6 above** to find your tax in the tax table on pages 24–32 of the booklet. Then, enter the tax from the table on this line. | 11a | 363 00 |

**Refund**

Have it directly deposited! See page 18 and fill in 12b, 12c and 12b cf Form 8888

| | | | |
|---|---|---|---|
| 12a | If line 10 is larger than line 11, subtract line 11 from line 10. This is your **refund.** ▶ If From 8888 is attached, click here ▶ ☐ | 12a | 132 00 |
| ▶ b | Routing number |  | ▶ c Type: ☐ Checking  ☐ Savings |
| ▶ d | Account number | | |

**Amount you owe**

| | | | |
|---|---|---|---|
| 13 | If line 11 is larger than line 10, subtract line 10 from line 11. This is the **amount you owe.** For details on how to pay, see page 20. ▶ | 13 | |

**Third party designee**

Do you want to allow another person to discuss this return with the IRS (see page 20)?  ☐ **Yes.** Complete the following.  ☐ **No**

Designee's name ▶ _____   Phone no. ▶ _____

Personal identification number (PIN) ▶ _____

**Sign here**

Joint return? See page 6. Keep a copy for your records.

Under penalties of perjury, I declare that I have examined this return, and to the best of my knowledge and belief, it is true, correct, and accurately lists all amounts and sources of income I received during the tax year. Declaration of preparer (other than the taxpayer) is based on all information of which the preparer has any knowledge.

| Your signature | Date | Your occupation | Daytime phone number |
|---|---|---|---|
| Akira Takyama | 4/14/09 | Student | |
| Spouse's signature. If a joint return, **both** must sign. | Date | Spouse's occupation | |

**Paid preparer's use only**

| Preparer's signature ▶ | Date | Check if self-employed ☐ | Preparer's SSN or PTIN |
|---|---|---|---|
| Firm's name (or yours if self-employed), address, and ZIP code ▶ | | | EIN  Phone no. |

For Disclosure, Privacy Act, and Paperwork Reduction Act Notice, see page 37.

Form **1040EZ** (2008)

that went toward his room and board, his part-time income of $7,600, and the details of his withholdings.

To use *Form 1040A*, a two-page form, your income must be less than $100,000 and be derived only from specified sources. Using this form, you may deduct certain IRA contributions and claim certain tax credits, but you cannot itemize your deductions. If your income is over $100,000 or you itemize deductions, you must use the standard *Form 1040* along with any applicable schedules.

Despite detailed instructions that accompany the tax forms, taxpayers still make a lot of mistakes when filling them out. Common errors include missing information and arithmetic errors. So check and recheck your forms *before submitting them to the IRS.*

## The 2008 Tax Return of Thomas and Emily Trimble

Let's now put all the pieces of the tax preparation puzzle together to see how Thomas and Emily Trimble calculate and file their income taxes. The Trimbles own their own home and are both 35 years old. Married for 11 years, they have three children—Doug (age 9), William (age 7), and Abbie (age 3). Thomas is a manager for an insurance company headquartered in their hometown. Emily has 1½ years of college and works part-time as a sales clerk in a retail store. During 2008, Thomas' salary totaled $60,415 while Emily earned $9,750. Thomas' employer withheld taxes of $6,260, and Emily's withheld $1,150. During the year, the Trimbles earned $800 interest on their joint savings account and realized $1,250 in capital gains on the sale of securities they had owned for 11 months. In addition, Thomas kept the books for his brother's

©TIEGO JORGE DE SILVA ESTIMA/SHUTTERSTOCK

car dealership, from which he netted $5,800 during the year. Because no taxes were withheld from any of their outside income, during the year they made estimated tax payments totaling $1,000. The Trimble records indicate they had $14,713 of potential itemized deductions during the

year. Finally, the Trimbles plan to contribute $4,000 to Emily's traditional IRA account. Beginning in 2009, the Trimbles plan to switch Emily's account to a Roth IRA (see Chapter 14).

### Finding the Trimbles' Tax Liability: Form 1040

Looking at the Trimbles' 2008 tax return (Worksheet 3.2), we can get a feel for the basic calculations required in the preparation of a Form 1040. Although we don't include the supporting schedules here, we illustrate the basic calculations they require. The Trimbles have detailed records of their income and expenses, which they use not only for tax purposes but as an important input to their budgeting process. Using this information, the Trimbles intend to prepare their 2008 tax return so that their total tax liability is as low as possible. Like most married couples, the Trimbles file a *joint return.*

**GROSS INCOME.** The Trimbles' gross income in 2008 amounted to $78,015—the amount shown as "total income" on line 22 of their tax return. They have both active income and portfolio income, as follows:

| ACTIVE INCOME | |
| --- | --- |
| Thomas' earnings | $60,415 |
| Emily's earnings | 9,750 |
| Thomas' business income (net) | 5,800 |
| Total active income | $75,965 |

| PORTFOLIO INCOME | |
| --- | --- |
| Interest from savings account | $ 800 |
| Capital gains realized* | 1,250 |
| Total portfolio income | $ 2,050 |
| Total income ($75,965 + $2,050) | $78,015 |

\* Because this gain was realized on stock held for less than 12 months, the full amount is taxable as ordinary income.

They have no investment expenses to offset their portfolio income, so they'll be liable for taxes on the full amount of portfolio income. Although they have interest income, the Trimbles don't have to file Schedule B (for interest and dividend income) with the Form 1040, because the interest is less than $1,500 and they earned no dividends. (If they receive dividends on stock in the future, they will have to complete a Qualified Dividends and Capital Gains Tax Worksheet, provided in the Form 1040 instruction booklet. Qualified dividends are taxed at the lower capital gains rates.) In addition, Thomas will have

Because they itemize deductions, the Trimbles use standard Form 1040 to file their tax return. When filed with the IRS, their return will include not only Form 1040 but also other schedules and forms detailing many of their expenses and deductions.

**Form 1040**

Department of the Treasury—Internal Revenue Service

**U.S. Individual Income Tax Return**  **2008**  (99)  IRS Use Only—Do not write or staple in this space.

For the year Jan. 1–Dec. 31, 2008, or other tax year beginning _____, 2008, ending _____, 20___

OMB No. 1545-0074

**Label** (See instructions on page 14.) Use the IRS label. Otherwise, please print or type.

Your first name and initial: Thomas B.  Last name: Trimble

Your social security number: 123 45 6789

If a joint return, spouse's first name and initial: Emily R.  Last name: Trimble

Spouse's social security number: 987 65 4321

Home address (number and street). If you have a P.O. box, see page 14.: 1234 Success Circle  Apt. no.

▲ You **must** enter your SSN(s) above. ▲

City, town or post office, state, and ZIP code. If you have a foreign address, see page 14.: Anytown, Anystate 10001

**Presidential Election Campaign** ▶ Check here if you, or your spouse if filing jointly, want $3 to go to this fund (see page ▶ ☑ You ☑ Spouse

Checking a box below will not change your tax or refund.

**Filing Status**

Check only one box.

- 1 ☐ Single
- 2 ☑ Married filing jointly (even if only one had income)
- 3 ☐ Married filing separately. Enter spouse's SSN above and full name here. ▶
- 4 ☐ Head of household (with qualifying person). (See page 15.) If the qualifying person is a child but not your dependent, enter this child's name here. ▶
- 5 ☐ Qualifying widow(er) with dependent child (see page 16)

**Exemptions**

- 6a ☐ Yourself. If someone can claim you as a dependent, **do not** check box 6a
- b ☐ Spouse

Boxes checked on 6a and 6b

- c Dependents:

| (1) First name   Last name | (2) Dependent's social security number | (3) Dependent's relationship to you | (4) ☑ if qualifying child for child tax credit (see page 17) |
|---|---|---|---|
| Douglas E. Trimble | 065 01 2347 | son | ☑ |
| William T. Trimble | 012 34 5678 | son | ☑ |
| Abbie S. Trimble | 034 65 1234 | daughter | ☑ |
| | | | ☐ |

If more than four dependents, see page 17.

No. of children on 6c who:
• lived with you
• did not live with you due to divorce or separation (see page 18)
Dependents on 6c not entered above

Add numbers on lines above ▶ 5

- d Total number of exemptions claimed

**Income**

Attach Form(s) W-2 here. Also attach Forms W-2G and 1099-R if tax was withheld.

If you did not get a W-2, see page 21.

Enclose, but do not attach, any payment. Also, please use Form 1040-V.

| | | | |
|---|---|---|---|
| 7 | Wages, salaries, tips, etc. Attach Form(s) W-2 | 7 | 70,165 00 |
| 8a | **Taxable** interest. Attach Schedule B if required | 8a | 800 00 |
| b | **Tax-exempt** interest. **Do not** include on line 8a  8b | | |
| 9a | Ordinary dividends. Attach Schedule B if required | 9a | |
| b | Qualified dividends (see page 21)  9b | | |
| 10 | Taxable refunds, credits, or offsets of state and local income taxes (see page 22) | 10 | |
| 11 | Alimony received | 11 | |
| 12 | Business income or (loss). Attach Schedule C or C-EZ | 12 | 5,800 00 |
| 13 | Capital gain or (loss). Attach Schedule D if required. If not required, check here ▶ ☐ | 13 | 1,250 00 |
| 14 | Other gains or (losses). Attach Form 4797 | 14 | |
| 15a | IRA distributions  15a ___ b Taxable amount (see page 23) | 15b | |
| 16a | Pensions and annuities  16a ___ b Taxable amount (see page 24) | 16b | |
| 17 | Rental real estate, royalties, partnerships, S corporations, trusts, etc. Attach Schedule E | 17 | |
| 18 | Farm income or (loss). Attach Schedule F | 18 | |
| 19 | Unemployment compensation | 19 | |
| 20a | Social security benefits  20a ___ b Taxable amount (see page 26) | 20b | |
| 21 | Other income. List type and amount (see page 28) _____ | 21 | |
| 22 | Add the amounts in the far right column for lines 7 through 21. This is your **total income** ▶ | 22 | 78,015 00 |

**Adjusted Gross Income**

| | | | |
|---|---|---|---|
| 23 | Educator expenses (see page 28)  23 | | |
| 24 | Certain business expenses of reservists, performing artists, and fee-basis government officials. Attach Form 2106 or 2106-EZ  24 | | |
| 25 | Health savings account deduction. Attach Form 8889  25 | | |
| 26 | Moving expenses. Attach Form 3903  26 | | |
| 27 | One-half of self-employment tax. Attach Schedule SE  27  443 70 | | |
| 28 | Self-employed SEP, SIMPLE, and qualified plans  28 | | |
| 29 | Self-employed health insurance deduction (see page 29)  29 | | |
| 30 | Penalty on early withdrawal of savings  30 | | |
| 31a | Alimony paid  b Recipient's SSN ▶ _____  31a | | |
| 32 | IRA deduction (see page 30)  32  4,000 00 | | |
| 33 | Student loan interest deduction (see page 33)  33 | | |
| 34 | Tuition and fees deduction. Attach Form 8917  34 | | |
| 35 | Domestic production activities deduction. Attach Form 8903  35 | | |
| 36 | Add lines 23 through 31a and 32 through 35 | 36 | 4,443 70 |
| 37 | Subtract line 36 from line 22. This is your **adjusted gross income** ▶ | 37 | 73,571 30 |

For Disclosure, Privacy Act, and Paperwork Reduction Act Notice, see page 88.  Cat. No. 11320B  Form **1040** (2008)

Form 1040 (2008)                                                                                                    Page **2**

| | | | | | |
|---|---|---|---|---|---|
| **Tax and Credits** | 38 | Amount from line 37 (adjusted gross income) . . . . . . . . . . | **38** | 73,571 | 30 |

39a  Check if: ☐ **You** were born before January 2, 1944, ☐ Blind. ☐ **Spouse** was born before January 2, 1944, ☐ Blind. **Total boxes** checked ▶ **39a** ☐

b  If your spouse itemizes on a separate return or you were a dual-status alien, see page 35 and check here ▶**39b** ☐

c  Check if standard deduction includes real estate taxes or disaster lose (see page 34) ▶**39c** ☐

**Standard Deduction for—**

• People who checked any box on line 39a, 39b or 39c **or** who can be claimed as a dependent, see page 34.

• All others:

Single or Married filing separately, $5,450

Married filing Jointly or Qualifing widow(er). $10,900

Head of household $8,000

| | | | | |
|---|---|---|---|---|
| 40 | **Itemized deductions** (from Schedule A) **or** your **standard deduction** (see left margin) . | **40** | 11,978 | 57 |
| 41 | Subtract line 40 from line 38 . . . . . . . . . . . . . . | **41** | 61,592 | 73 |
| 42 | If line 38 is over $119,975, or you provided housing to a Midwestern displaced individual , see page 36. Otherwise, multiply $3,500 by the total number of exemptions claimed on line 6d | **42** | 17,500 | 00 |
| 43 | **Taxable income.** Subtract line 42 from line 41. If line 42 is more than line 41, enter -0- | **43** | 44,092 | 73 |
| 44 | **Tax** (see page 36). Check if any tax is from: **a** ☐ Form(s) 8814 **b** ☐ Form 4972 . . | **44** | 5,811 | 26 |
| 45 | **Alternative minimum tax** (see page 39). Attach Form 6251 . . . . . | **45** | 0 | |
| 46 | Add lines 44 and 45 . . . . . . . . . . . . . . ▶ | **46** | 5,811 | 26 |
| 47 | Foreign tax credit. Attach Form 1116 if required . . | **47** | | |
| 48 | Credit for child and dependent care expenses. Attach Form 2441 | **48** | | |
| 49 | Credit for the elderly or the disabled. Attach Schedule R . | **49** | | |
| 50 | Education credits. Attach Form 8863 . . . . . | **50** | | |
| 51 | Retirement savings contributions credit. Attach Form 8880 . | **51** | | |
| 52 | Child tax credit (see page 42). Attach Form 8901 if required · | **52** | 3,000 | 00 |
| 53 | Credits from Form **a** ☐ 8859 **b** ☐ 8336 **c** ☐ 5695 | **53** | | |
| 54 | Other credits from Form **a** ☐ 3800 **b** ☐ 8801 **c** ☐ | **54** | | |
| 55 | Add lines 47 through 54. These are your **total credits** . . . . | **55** | 3,000 | 00 |
| 56 | Subtract line 55 from line 46. If line 55 is more than line 46, enter -0- . . ▶ | **56** | 2,811 | 26 |

| **Other Taxes** | | | | | |
|---|---|---|---|---|---|
| | 57 | Self-employment tax. Attach Schedule SE . . . . . | **57** | | |
| | 58 | Unreported social security and Medicare tax from From: **a** ☐ 4137 **b** ☐ 8919 . . | **58** | 887 | 40 |
| | 59 | Additional tax on IRAs, other qualified retirement plans, etc. Attach Form 5329 if required . | **59** | | |
| | 60 | Additional taxes: **a** ☐ AEIC payments **b** ☐ Household employment taxes. Attach Schedule H | **60** | | |
| | 61 | Add lines 56 through 62. This is your **total tax** . . . . . . . . ▶ | **61** | 3,698 | 66 |

| **Payments** | | | | | | | |
|---|---|---|---|---|---|---|---|
| | 62 | Federal income tax withheld from Forms W-2 and 1099 . | **62** | 7,410 | 00 | | |
| | 63 | 2008 estimated tax payments and amount applied from 2007 return | **63** | 1,000 | 00 | | |

If you have a qualifying child, attach Schedule EIC.

| | | | | | | |
|---|---|---|---|---|---|---|
| 64a | **Earned income credit (EIC)** . . . . . . | **64a** | | | | |
| b | Nontaxable combat pay election ▶ | **64b** | | | | |
| 65 | Excess social security and tier 1 RRTA tax withheld (see page 61) | **65** | | | | |
| 66 | Additional child tax credit. Attach Form 8812 . . . . | **66** | | | | |
| 67 | Amount paid with request for extension to file (see page 61) | **67** | | | | |
| 68 | Credit from Form: **a** ☐ 2439 **b** ☐ 4136 **c** ☐ 8801 **d** ☐ 8885 | **68** | | | | |
| 69 | First-time homebuyer cerdit. Attach Form 5405 | **69** | | | | |
| 70 | Recovery rebate cerdit (See worksheet on pages 62 and 63) . | **70** | | | | |
| 71 | Add lines 62 through 70. These are your **total payments** . . . . . . ▶ | **71** | 8,410 | 00 | | |

| **Refund** | | | | | |
|---|---|---|---|---|---|
| | 72 | If line 71 is more than line 61, subtract line 61 from line 71. This is the amount you **overpaid** | **72** | 4,711 | 34 |

Direct deposit? See page 63 and fill in 73b, 73c, and 73d, or Form 8888 ▶

| | | | | |
|---|---|---|---|---|
| 73a | Amount of line 72 you want **refunded to you**  If Form 8888 is attached, check here ▶ ☐ | **73a** | 4,711 | 34 |
| b | Routing number ▷ **c** Type: ☐ Checking ☐ Savings | | | |
| d | Account number | | | |
| 74 | Amount of line 72 you want **applied to your 2009 estimated tax** ▶ | **74** | | |

| **Amount You Owe** | | | | |
|---|---|---|---|---|
| | 75 | **Amount you owe.** Subtract line 71 from line 61. For details on how to pay, see page 65 ▶ | **75** | |
| | 76 | Estimated tax penalty (see page 65) . . . . . . | **76** | |

**Third Party Designee**

Do you want to allow another person to discuss this return with the IRS (see page 66)? ☐ **Yes.** Complete the following. ☐ **No**

Designee's name ▶                    Phone no. ▶ (    )                    Personal identification number (PIN) ▶ ☐☐☐☐☐

**Sign Here**

Joint return? See page 15. Keep a copy for your records.

Under penalties of perjury, I declare that I have examined this return and accompanying schedules and statements, and to the best of my knowledge and belief, they are true, correct, and complete. Declaration of preparer (other than taxpayer) is based on all information of which preparer has any knowledge.

| Your signature | Date | Your occupation | Daytime phone number |
|---|---|---|---|
| Thomas B. Trimble | 4/10/09 | Manager | (555) 555-1234 |
| Spouse's signature. If a joint return, **both** must sign. | Date | Spouse's occupation | |
| Emily A. Trimble | 4/10/09 | Sales Clerk | |

**Paid Preparer's Use Only**

| Preparer's signature ▶ | Date | Check if self-employed ☐ | Preparer's SSN or PTIN |
|---|---|---|---|
| Firm's name (or yours if self-employed), address, and ZIP code ▶ | | EIN | |
| | | Phone no. (    ) | |

Form **1040** (2008)

to file Schedule C, detailing the income earned and expenses incurred in his bookkeeping business, and Schedule D to report capital gains income.

**ADJUSTMENTS TO GROSS INCOME.** The Trimbles have only two adjustments to income: Emily's IRA contribution and 50% of the self-employment tax on Thomas' net business income. Since Emily isn't covered by a retirement plan and since Thomas' and her combined modified AGI is below $159,000, they can deduct her entire $4,000 maximum contribution to an IRA account even though Thomas is already covered by a company-sponsored retirement program (see Chapter 14). Thomas' self-employment tax will be 15.3% of his $5,800 net business income, and he will be able to deduct one-half that amount—$443.70 [(0.153 × $5,800) ÷ 2]—on line 27.

**ADJUSTED GROSS INCOME.** After deducting the $443.70 self-employment tax and Thomas' $4,000 IRA contribution from their gross income, the Trimbles are left with an AGI of $73,571.30, as reported on line 37.

**ITEMIZED DEDUCTIONS OR STANDARD DEDUCTION?** The Trimbles are filing a joint return, and neither is over age 65 or blind; so according to the box on page 2 of Form 1040, they are entitled to a standard deduction of $10,900. However, they want to evaluate their itemized deductions before deciding which type of deduction to take—obviously they'll take the highest deduction, because it will result in the lowest amount of taxable income and keep their tax liability to a minimum. Their preliminary paperwork resulted in the following deductions:

©KAREN ROACH/SHUTTERSTOCK

| | |
|---|---:|
| Medical and dental expenses | $ 1,223 |
| State income and property taxes paid | 2,560 |
| Mortgage interest | 7,893 |
| Charitable contributions | 475 |
| Job and other expenses | 2,522 |
| Total | $14,673 |

The taxes, mortgage interest, and charitable contributions are deductible in full; so at the minimum, the Trimbles will have itemized deductions amounting to $10,928 ($2,560 + $7,893 + $475). However, to be deductible, the medical and dental expenses and job and other expenses must exceed stipulated minimum levels of AGI—only that portion exceeding the specified minimum levels of AGI can be included as part of their itemized deductions. For medical and dental expenses the minimum is 7.5% of AGI, and

for job and other expenses it is 2% of AGI. Because 7.5% of the Trimbles' AGI is $5,517.85 (0.075 × $73,571.30), they fall short of the minimum and cannot deduct any medical and dental expenses. In contrast, because 2% of the Trimbles' AGI is $1,471.43 (0.02 × $73,571.30), they can deduct any job and other expenses exceeding that amount, or $2,522 − $1,471.43 = $1,050.57. Adding that amount to their other allowable deductions ($10,928) results in total itemized deductions of $11,978.57. This amount exceeds the standard deduction of $10,900 by nearly $1,079, or almost 10%, so the Trimbles should strongly consider itemizing their deductions. They would enter the details of these deductions on Schedule A and attach it to their Form 1040. (The total amount of the Trimbles' itemized deductions is listed on line 40 of Form 1040.)

The Trimbles are entitled to claim two exemptions for themselves and another three for their three dependent children, for a total of five (see line 6d). Because each exemption is worth $3,500, they receive a total personal exemption of $17,500 (5 × $3,500), which is the amount listed on line 42 of their Form 1040.

**THE TRIMBLES' TAXABLE INCOME AND TAX LIABILITY.** Taxable income is found by subtracting itemized deductions and personal exemptions from AGI. In the Trimbles' case, taxable income amounts to $73,571.30 − $11,978.57 − $17,500 = $44,092.73, as shown on line 43. Given this information, the Trimbles can now refer to the tax rate schedule (like the one in Exhibit 3.3) to find their appropriate tax rate and, ultimately, the amount of taxes they'll have to pay. (Because the Trimbles' taxable income is less than $100,000, they could use the *tax tables* [not shown] to find their tax. For clarity and convenience, we use the schedules here.) As we can see, the Trimbles' $44,092.73 in taxable income places them in the 15% marginal tax bracket. Using the schedule in Exhibit 3.3, they calculate their tax as follows: $1,605 + [0.15 × ($44,092.73 − $16,051)] = $5,811.26. They enter this amount on line 44.

The Trimbles also qualify for the child tax credit: $1,000 for each child under age 17. They enter $3,000 on lines 52 and 55 and subtract that amount from the tax on line 46, entering $2,811.26 on line 57. In addition, the Trimbles owe self-employment (Social Security) tax on Thomas' $5,800 net business income. This will increase their tax liability by $887.40 (0.153 × $5,800) and would be reported on Schedule SE and entered on line 58 of Form 1040. (Recall that the Trimbles deducted 50% of this amount, or $443.70, on line 27 as an adjustment to income.) The Trimbles enter their total tax liability on line 61: $3,698.66 ($2,811.26 + $887.40).

**DO THEY GET A TAX REFUND?** Because the total amount of taxes withheld of $7,410 ($6,260 from Thomas' salary and $1,150 from Emily's wages)

shown on line 62 plus estimated tax payments of $1,000 shown on line 63 total $8,410 as shown on line 71, the Trimbles' total tax payments exceed their tax liability. As a result, they are entitled to a refund of $4,711.34: the $8,410 withholding less their $3,698.66 tax liability. (About 65% of all taxpayers receive refunds each year.) Instead of paying the IRS, they'll be getting money back. (Generally, it takes 1 to 2 months after a tax return has been filed to receive a refund check.)

All the Trimbles have to do now is sign and date their completed Form 1040 and send it, along with any supporting forms and schedules, to the nearest IRS district office on or before April 15, 2009.

One reason for the Trimbles' large refund was the child tax credit. With such a sizable refund, the Trimbles may want to stop making estimated tax payments because their combined withholding more than covers the amount of taxes they owe. Another option is to change their withholding to reduce the amount withheld.

Note that if total tax payments had been less than the Trimbles' tax liability, they would have owed the IRS money—the amount owed is found by subtracting total tax payments made from the tax liability. If they owed money, they would include a check in the amount due with Form 1040 when filing their tax return.

## LG4, LG5  Other Filing Considerations

Other considerations related to tax filing include the need to pay estimated taxes, file for extensions, or amend the return; the possibility of a tax audit; and whether to use a tax preparation service or computer software to assist you in preparing your return.

## Estimates, Extensions, and Amendments

Like Thomas Trimble, who provided accounting services to his brother's business, you may have income that's not subject to withholding. You may need to file a declaration of estimated taxes with your return and to pay quarterly taxes. Or perhaps you are unable to meet the normal April 15 filing deadline or need to correct a previously filed return. Let's look at the procedures for handling these situations.

### Estimated Taxes
Because federal withholding taxes are regularly taken only from employment income, such as that paid in the form of wages or salaries, the IRS requires certain

people to pay **estimated taxes** on income earned from other sources. Estimated tax payments are most commonly required of investors, consultants, lawyers, business owners, and various other professionals who are likely to receive income that is not subject to withholding.

The declaration of estimated taxes (Form 1040-ES) is normally filed with the tax return. Estimated taxes must be paid in four installments on April 15, June 15, and September 15 of the current year, and January 15 of the following year. Failure to estimate and pay these taxes in accordance with IRS guidelines can result in a penalty levied by the IRS.

 **Go to Smart Sites**

It's easy to file and pay your taxes online, as you'll learn when you explore the federal government's Pay1040 Web site. ●

### April 15: Filing Deadline

As we've seen from the Trimble family example, at the end of each tax year those taxpayers required to file a return must determine the amount of their *tax liability*—the amount of taxes they owe due to the past year's activities. The tax year corresponds to the calendar year and covers the period January 1 through December 31. Taxpayers may file their returns any time after the end of the tax year and *must* file no later than April 15 of the year immediately following the tax year (or by the first business day after that date if it falls on a weekend or federal holiday). If you have a computer, an Internet connection, and tax preparation software, you can probably use the IRS's *e-file* and *e-pay* to file your return and pay your taxes electronically either by using a credit card or by authorizing

©THE SUPE87/SHUTTERSTOCK

an electronic withdrawal from your checking or savings account. You can use an "Authorized *e-file* Provider," who may charge a fee to file for you, or do it yourself using commercial tax preparation software.

Depending on whether the total of taxes withheld and any estimated tax payments is greater or less than the computed tax liability, the taxpayer either receives a refund or must pay additional taxes. Taxpayers can pay their taxes using a credit card; however, because the IRS cannot pay credit card companies an issuing fee, taxpayers must call a special provider and pay a service charge to arrange for the payment.

### Filing Extensions and Amended Returns

It's possible to receive an extension of time for filing your federal tax return. You can apply for an automatic 6-month **filing extension**, which makes the due date October 15, simply by submitting Form 4868. In filing for an extension, however, the taxpayer must estimate the taxes due and remit that amount with the application. The extension does *not* give taxpayers more time to pay their taxes.

After filing a return, you may discover that you overlooked some income or a major deduction or made a mistake, so you paid too little or too much in taxes. You can easily correct this by filing an **amended return** (Form 1040X) showing the corrected amount of income or deductions and the amount of taxes you should have paid, along with the amount of any tax refund or additional taxes owed. You generally have 3 years from the date you file your original return or 2 years from the date you paid the taxes, whichever is later, to file an amended return.

### Audited Returns

Because taxpayers themselves provide the key information and fill out the necessary tax forms, the IRS has no proof that taxes have been correctly calculated. In addition to returns that stand out in some way and warrant further investigation, the IRS also randomly selects some returns for a **tax audit**—an examination to validate the return's accuracy. The odds of being audited are actually quite low; the IRS audits fewer than 2% of returns. However, higher-income earners tend to have a greater chance of being audited. The outcome of an audit is not always additional tax owed to the IRS. In fact, about 5% of all audits result in a refund to the

**estimated taxes** Tax payments required on income not subject to withholding that are paid in four installments.

**filing extension** An extension of time beyond the April 15 deadline during which taxpayers, with the approval of the IRS, can file their returns without incurring penalties.

**amended return** A tax return filed to adjust for information received after the filing date of the taxpayer's original return or to correct errors.

**tax audit** An examination by the IRS to validate the accuracy of a given tax return.

taxpayer, and in 15% of all audits the IRS finds that returns are correctly prepared.

Typically, audits question (1) whether all income received has been properly reported and (2) if the deductions claimed are legitimate and the correct amount. The IRS can take as many as 3 years—and in some cases, 6 years—from the date of filing to audit your return, so you should retain records and receipts used in preparing returns for about 7 years. Severe financial penalties, even prison sentences, can result from violating tax laws.

In sum, you should take advantage of all legitimate deductions to minimize your tax liability, but you must also be sure to properly report all items of income and expense as required by the Internal Revenue Code.

## Tax Preparation Services: Getting Help on Your Returns

Many people with simple tax situations prepare their own tax returns. Some taxpayers with quite complicated financial affairs may also invest their time in preparing their own returns. The IRS offers many informational publications with step-by-step instructions to help you prepare your tax return. You can order them directly from the IRS by mail, download them from the IRS Web site (http://www.irs.gov), or order them by calling the IRS toll-free number (1-800-829-3676 or special local numbers in some areas). An excellent (and free) comprehensive tax preparation reference book is IRS *Publication 17, Your Federal Income Tax*. Other IRS information services are *TeleTax*, which provides recorded phone messages on selected tax topics via a toll-free number (1-800-829-4477), and FaxBack, which will fax many forms and instructions to you when you call 1-703-368-9694.

### Help from the IRS
The IRS, in addition to issuing various publications for use in preparing tax returns, also provides direct assistance to taxpayers. The IRS will compute taxes for those whose taxable income is less than $100,000 and who do not itemize deductions. Persons who use this IRS service must fill in certain data, sign and date the return, and send it to the IRS on or before April 15 of the year immediately following the tax year. The IRS attempts to calculate taxes to result in the "smallest" tax bite. It then sends taxpayers a refund, if their withholding exceeds their tax liability, or a bill, if their tax liability is greater than the amount of withholding. People who either fail to qualify for or do not want to use this total tax preparation service can still obtain IRS assistance in preparing their returns from a toll-free service. Consult your telephone directory for the toll-free number of the IRS office closest to you.

### Private Tax Preparers
More than half of all taxpayers prefer to use professional *tax preparation services* to improve accuracy and minimize their tax liability as much as possible. The fees charged by professional tax preparers can range from at least $100 for very simple returns to $1,000 or more for complicated returns. You can select from the following types of tax preparation services:

- **National and local tax services:** These include national services such as H&R Block and independent local firms. These services are best for taxpayers with relatively common types of income and expenditures.

- **Certified Public Accountants (CPAs):** Tax professionals who prepare returns and can advise taxpayers on planning.

- **Enrolled Agents (EAs):** Federally licensed individual tax practitioners who have passed a difficult, 2-day, IRS-administered exam. They are fully qualified to handle tax preparation at various levels of complexity.

- **Tax attorneys:** Lawyers who specialize in tax planning.

The *Money in Action* box in this chapter will help you find the right preparer for your needs.

# MONEY IN ACTION

## Finding the Right Tax Preparer for You

You are legally responsible for your tax returns even if someone else prepared them. Thus, it's important to choose the right person or firm to prepare them for you. The first step is deciding why you need a tax preparer. Most people look for speed, accuracy, advice on general tax strategy advice, or the management of a complex tax situation.

There are four types of tax preparers:

- Nonlicensed preparers are best for straightforward returns because they have minimal training. Be sure they operate year-round and that they stand by their work. They're usually less expensive.

- CPAs provide ongoing tax advice and can suggest tax-saving strategies.

- Enrolled agents (EAs) are licensed by the IRS. They specialize in preparing returns and offering tax advice for individuals. Fees to use an EA are usually about one-third lower than CPA fees.

- Tax attorneys are best for those who have complex tax situations that could result in legal issues. Examples include the complicated sale of a small business, not filing taxes in the past, or estate and trust tax issues.

If your primary concern is getting uncomplicated taxes done quickly, one of the national tax organizations like H&R Block or Jackson Hewitt is worth considering. However, most of the time CPAs or EAs provide much more personal service than the franchises for not much more money. If you have a complex tax situation, keep in mind that CPAs and EAs specialize. Look for a professional who has experience and expertise in your areas of concern.

Any tax preparer should guarantee the accuracy of his or her work on your return, be willing to amend the tax return if he or she made a mistake on it, and be willing to assist you in an IRS audit—although not necessarily for free.

After deciding which type of tax preparer is right for you, ask for referrals from your lawyer, financial planner, and friends. Then talk with these people to make sure you would be comfortable showing them your personal financial records. Most reputable preparers will ask to see your receipts and will ask you multiple questions to determine the appropriateness of your taking various expenses, deductions, and other items. Depending on the complexity of your return and the chosen type of tax preparer, you should expect to pay from $150 to $450.

Sources: Adapted from William Perez, "How to Find a Tax Preparer," http://taxes .about.com/od/findataxpreparer/ht/taxpreparer.htm, accessed July 2009; "Read This Before Choosing a Tax Preparer," IRS Tax Tip 2009-07, http://www.irs.gov/newsroom/ article/0,,id=120129,00.html, accessed July 2009.

Always check your own completed tax returns carefully before signing them. Remember that *taxpayers themselves must accept primary responsibility for the accuracy of their returns.* The IRS requires professional tax preparers to sign each return as the preparer, enter their own Social Security number and address, and give the taxpayer a copy of the return being filed. Tax preparers with the necessary hardware and software can electronically file their clients' tax returns so that eligible taxpayers can more quickly receive refunds.

There's no guarantee that your professional tax preparer will correctly determine your tax liability. Even the best preparers may not have all the answers at their fingertips. In a recent *Money* magazine annual tax return test, none of the 45 experienced tax preparers who were contacted prepared the tax return for a fictional family correctly; and only 24% of them calculated a tax liability that was within $1,000 of the correct amount. To reduce the chance of error, you should become familiar with the basic tax principles and regulations, check all documents (such as *W-2s* and *1099s*) for accuracy, maintain good communication with your tax preparer, and request an explanation of any entries on your tax return that you don't understand.

## Computer-Based Tax Returns

Many people use their personal computers to help with tax planning and preparing tax returns. Several good tax software packages will save hours when you're filling out the forms and schedules involved in filing tax returns. The programs often identify tax-saving opportunities you might otherwise miss. These computer programs aren't for everyone, however. Simple returns, like the 1040EZ, don't require them. And for complex returns, there's no substitute for the skill and expertise of a tax accountant or attorney. Tax preparation software will be most helpful for taxpayers who itemize deductions but don't need tax advice.

There are two general kinds of software: tax planning and tax preparation. Planning programs such as Quicken let you experiment with different strategies to see their effects on the amount of taxes you must pay. The other category of tax software focuses on helping you complete and file your tax return. These programs take much of the tedium out of tax preparation, reducing the time you spend from days to hours. If you file the long Form 1040 and some supporting forms, invest in the stock market, own real estate, or have foreign income or a home-based business, you'll probably benefit from using tax preparation programs.

The two major software players are Intuit's TurboTax and Block Financial Software's TaxCut, both available for either Windows or Macintosh. TurboTax even has a Web-based version that lets you work on your returns from any computer. Both major companies also offer an add-on program that accurately assigns fair market value to the household items most commonly donated to charity. Both programs feature a clean interface and guide you through the steps in preparing your return by asking you the questions that apply to your situation. In addition to the primary tax-form preparation section, they include extensive resources and links to additional Web references, video clips to make tricky concepts easier to understand, tax planning questionnaires, deduction finders, and more. They may warn you if a number you've typed looks incorrect. The basic version of each program costs approximately $40 for the regular CD-ROM. State tax return packages cost more. Both TurboTax and TaxCut guarantee their calculations and will pay any penalties you incur due to program errors.

The IRS recently introduced "fill-in forms," which allow you to enter information while the form is displayed on your computer by Adobe Acrobat Reader (free software readily available on the Web). After entering the requested information, you can print out the completed form. Fill-in forms give you a cleaner, crisper printout for your records and for filing with the IRS. Unlike tax preparation software, these fill-in forms have no computational capabilities, so you must do all your calculations before starting. In addition, you should be ready to enter all the data at once, because Acrobat Reader doesn't save your completed forms. These forms are labeled "Fill-in forms" at the IRS Web site.

## LG6 Effective Tax Planning

*Tax planning* is a key ingredient of your overall personal financial planning. The overriding objective of effective tax planning is to maximize total after-tax income by reducing, shifting, and deferring taxes to as low a level as legally possible. By all means, don't confuse tax avoidance with tax evasion, which includes such illegal activities as omitting income or overstating deductions. **Tax evasion**, in effect, involves a failure to accurately report income or deductions and, in extreme cases, a failure to pay taxes altogether. Persons found guilty of tax evasion are subject to severe financial penalties and even prison terms. **Tax avoidance**, in contrast, focuses on reducing taxes in ways that are legal and compatible with the intent of Congress.

> *The overriding objective of effective tax planning is to maximize total after-tax income by reducing, shifting, and deferring taxes to as low a level as legally possible.*

## Fundamental Objectives of Tax Planning

Tax planning basically involves the use of various investment vehicles, retirement programs, and estate distribution procedures to (1) reduce, (2) shift, and (3) defer taxes. You can *reduce* taxes, for instance, by using techniques that create tax deductions or credits, or that receive preferential tax treatment—such as investments that produce depreciation (such as real estate) or that generate tax-free income (such as municipal bonds). You can *shift* taxes by using gifts or trusts to transfer some of your income to other family members who are in lower tax brackets and to whom you intend to provide some level of support anyway, such as a retired, elderly parent.

The idea behind *deferring* taxes is to reduce or eliminate your taxes today by postponing them to some time in the future when you may be in a lower tax bracket. Perhaps more important, *deferring taxes gives you use of the money that would otherwise go to taxes*—thereby allowing you to invest it to make even more money. Deferring taxes is usually done through various types of retirement plans, such as IRAs, or by investing in certain

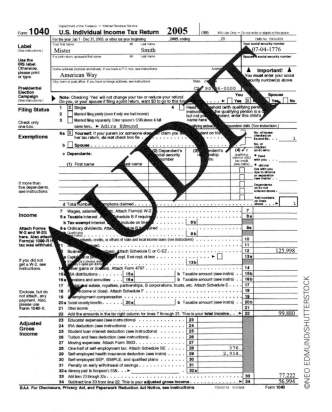

types of annuities, variable life insurance policies, or even Series EE bonds (U.S. savings bonds).

The fundamentals of tax planning include making sure that you take all the deductions to which you're entitled and also take full advantage of the various tax provisions that will minimize your tax liability. Thus comprehensive tax planning is an ongoing activity with both an immediate and a long-term perspective. Tax planning is closely interrelated with many financial planning activities, including investment, retirement, and estate planning.

## Some Popular Tax Strategies

Many tax strategies are fairly simple and straightforward and can be used by the average middle-income taxpayer. You certainly don't have to be in the top income bracket to enjoy the benefits of many tax-saving ideas and procedures. For example, the interest income on Series EE bonds is free from state income tax, and the holder can elect to delay payment of federal taxes until (1) the year the bonds are redeemed for cash or (2) the year in which they finally mature, whichever occurs first. This feature makes Series EE bonds an excellent vehicle for earning tax-deferred income.

There are other strategies that can cut your tax bill. Accelerating or bunching deductions into a single year may permit itemizing deductions. Shifting income from one year to another is one way to cut your tax liability. If you expect to be in the same or a higher income tax bracket this year than you will be next year, defer income until next year and shift expenses to this year so you can accelerate your deductions and reduce taxes this year.

### Maximizing Deductions

Review a comprehensive list of possible deductions for ideas, because even small deductions can add up to big tax savings. Accelerate or bunch deductions into one tax year if this allows you to itemize rather than take the standard deduction. For example, make your fourth-quarter estimated state tax payment before December 31 rather than on January 15 to deduct it in the current taxable year. Group miscellaneous expenses—and schedule unreimbursed elective medical procedures—to fall into one tax year so that they exceed the required "floor" for deductions (2% of AGI for miscellaneous expenses; 7.5% of AGI for medical expenses). Increase discretionary deductions such as charitable contributions.

### Income Shifting

One way of reducing income taxes is to use a technique known as **income shifting**. Here the taxpayer shifts a portion of his or her income, and thus taxes, to relatives in lower tax brackets. This can be done by creating trusts or custodial accounts or by making outright gifts of income-producing property to family members. For instance, parents with $125,000 of

taxable income (28% marginal tax rate) and $18,000 in corporate bonds paying $2,000 in annual interest might give the bonds to their 15-year-old child—with the understanding that such income is to be used ultimately for the child's college education. The $2,000 would then belong to the child, who would probably be assumed to be able to pay $110 (0.10 × [$2,000 − $900 minimum standard deduction for a dependent]) in taxes on this income, and the parents' taxable income would be reduced by $2,000, reducing their taxes by $560 (0.28 × $2,000).

Unfortunately, this strategy is not as simple as it might seem. A number of restrictions surround this strategy for children under 19, so it's possible to employ such techniques with older children (and presumably with other older relatives, such as elderly parents). Parents also need to recognize that shifting assets into a child's name to save taxes could affect the amount of college financial aid for which the child qualifies. Additional tax implications of gifts to dependents are discussed in Chapter 15.

### Tax-Free and Tax-Deferred Income

Some investments provide tax-free income; in most cases, however, the tax on the income is only deferred (or delayed) to a later day. Although there aren't many forms of tax-free investments left today, probably the best example would be the *interest* income earned on *municipal bonds*. Such income is free from federal income tax and possibly state income taxes. (Tax-free municipal bonds are discussed in Chapter 12.) Income that is **tax deferred**, in contrast, only delays the payment of taxes to a future date. Until that time arrives, however, tax-deferred investment vehicles allow you to *accumulate tax-free earnings*. This results in much higher savings than would occur in a taxed account. A good example of tax-deferred income would be income earned in a *traditional IRA*. See Chapter 14 for a detailed discussion of this and other similar arrangements.

Most any wage earner can open an IRA and contribute up to $5,000 (or possibly $6,000, depending on an age qualification) each year to the account (in 2008). *All the income you earn in your IRA accumulates tax free.* This is a *tax-deferred* investment, so you'll eventually have to pay taxes on these earnings, but not until you start drawing down your account. In addition to IRAs, tax-deferred income can also be obtained from other types of pension and retirement plans and annuities. See Chapter 14 for more information on these financial products and strategies.

income shifting A technique used to reduce taxes in which a taxpayer shifts a portion of income to relatives in lower tax brackets.

tax deferred Income that is not subject to taxes immediately but that will later be subject to taxes.

# FINANCIAL PLANNING EXERCISES

**LG2, 3**

1. Beverly Jones is 24 years old and single, lives in an apartment, and has no dependents. Last year she earned $45,000 as a sales assistant for Precision Business Instruments; $3,910 of her wages was withheld for federal income taxes. In addition, she had interest income of $142. Estimate her taxable income, tax liability, and tax refund or tax owed.

**LG2**

2. Jennifer Morris received the items and amounts of income shown in the chart to the right during 2008. Help her calculate (a) her gross income and (b) that portion (dollar amount) of her income that is tax exempt.

| | |
|---|---|
| Salary | $33,500 |
| Dividends | 800 |
| Gift from mother | 500 |
| Child support from ex-husband | 3,600 |
| Interest on savings account | 250 |
| Rent | 900 |
| Loan from bank | 2,000 |
| Interest on state government bonds | 300 |

**LG2**

3. If Barbara Guarin is single and in the 28% tax bracket, calculate the tax associated with each of the following transactions. (Use the IRS regulations for capital gains in effect in 2008.)

a. She sold stock for $1,200 that she purchased for $1,000 5 months earlier.
b. She sold bonds for $4,000 that she purchased for $3,000 3 years earlier.
c. She sold stock for $1,000 that she purchased for $1,500 15 months earlier.

**LG3**

4. *Use Worksheets 3.1 and 3.2.*
Daniel Chen graduated from college in 2008 and began work as a systems analyst in July 2008. He is preparing to file his income tax return for 2008 and has collected the financial information shown in the table to the right for calendar year 2008.

| | |
|---|---|
| Tuition, scholarships, and grants | $ 5,750 |
| Scholarship, room, and board | 1,850 |
| Salary | 30,250 |
| Interest income | 185 |
| Deductible expenses, total | 3,000 |
| Income taxes withheld | 2,600 |

a. Prepare Daniel's 2008 tax return, using a $5,450 standard deduction, a personal exemption of $3,500, and the tax rates given in Exhibit 3.3. Which tax form should Daniel use, and why?
b. Prepare Daniel's 2008 tax return using the data in part **a** along with the following information:

| | |
|---|---|
| IRA contribution | $5,000 |
| Cash dividends received | 150 |

Which tax form should he use in this case? Why?

**LG4**

5. Kathleen and Sean Madden have been notified that they are being audited. What should they do to prepare for the audit?

# PART 2

# MANAGING BASIC ASSETS

# 4

# MANAGING YOUR CASH AND SAVINGS

## LEARNING GOALS

**LG1** Understand the role of cash management in the personal financial planning process. (p. 71)

**LG2** Describe today's financial services marketplace, both depository and nondepository financial institutions. (p. 72)

**LG3** Select the checking, savings, electronic banking, and other bank services that meet your needs. (p. 74)

**LG4** Open and use a checking account. (p. 80)

**LG5** Calculate the interest earned on your money using compound interest and future value techniques. (p. 84)

**LG6** Develop a savings strategy that incorporates a variety of savings plans. (p. 84)

## 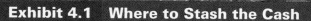LG1 The Role of Cash Management in Personal Financial Planning

Establishing good financial habits involves managing cash as well as other types of assets. In this chapter, we focus our attention on **cash management**—the routine, day-to-day administration of cash and near-cash resources, also known as *liquid assets*. These assets are considered liquid because they're either held in cash or can be readily converted into cash with little or no loss in value.

In addition to cash, there are several other kinds of liquid assets, including checking accounts, savings accounts, money market deposit accounts, money market mutual funds, and other short-term investment vehicles. Exhibit 4.1 briefly describes some popular types of liquid assets and the representative rates of return they earned in the spring of 2009. As a rule, near-term needs are met using cash on hand, and unplanned or future needs are met using some type of savings or short-term investment vehicle.

In personal financial planning, efficient cash management ensures adequate funds for both household use and an effective savings program. A good way to keep your spending in line is to make all household transactions (even fun money or weekly cash allowances) using a

**cash management** The routine, day-to-day administration of cash and near-cash resources, also known as *liquid assets*, by an individual or family.

### Exhibit 4.1  Where to Stash the Cash

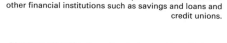

The wide variety of liquid assets available meets just about any savings or short-term investment need. Rates vary considerably both by type of asset and point in time, so shop around for the best interest rate.

Pocket money; the coin and currency in one's possession. — **0% Cash**

A substitute for cash. Offered by commercial banks and other financial institutions such as savings and loans and credit unions. — **0–0.58% Checking account**

Money is available at any time but cannot be withdrawn by check. Offered by banks and other financial institutions. — **1.30–1.80% Savings account**

Requires a fairly large (typically $1,000 or more) account (MMDA) minimum deposit. Offers check-writing privileges. — **0.40–1.79% Money market deposit**

Savings vehicle that is actually a mutual fund (not offered by banks, S&Ls, and other depository institutions). Like an MMDA, it also offers check-writing privileges. — **1.10% Money market mutual fund**

A savings instrument where funds are left on deposit for a stipulated period (1 week to 1 year or more); imposes a penalty for withdrawing funds early. Market yields vary by size and maturity; no check-writing privileges. — **0.81–2.68% Certificate of deposit (CD)**

Short-term, highly marketable security issued by the U.S. Treasury (originally issued with maturities of 13 and 26 weeks); smallest denomination is $1,000. — **0.15% U.S. Treasury bill (T-bill)**

Issued at a discount from face value by the U.S.Treasury; rate of interest is tied to U.S. Treasury securities. Long a popular savings vehicle (widely used with payroll deduction plans). Matures to face value in approximately 5 years; sold in denominations of $50 and more. — **0.70% U.S. savings bond (EE)**

**Percent** (0, 1, 2, 3, 4, 5, 6)

tightly controlled *checking account*. Write checks only at certain times of the week or month and, just as important, avoid carrying your checkbook (or debit card) when you might be tempted to spend money for unplanned purchases. If you're going shopping, set a maximum spending limit beforehand—an amount consistent with your cash budget. This system not only helps you avoid frivolous, impulsive expenditures but also documents how and where you spend your money.

> { In personal financial planning, efficient cash management ensures adequate funds for both household use and an effective savings program. }

Another aspect of cash management is establishing an ongoing savings program, which is an important part of personal financial planning. Savings are not only a cushion against financial emergencies but also a way to accumulate funds to meet future financial goals. You may want to put money aside so that you can go back to school in a few years to earn a graduate degree, or buy a new home, or take a vacation. Savings will help you meet these specific financial objectives.

## LG2 Today's Financial Services Marketplace

Beth White hasn't been inside her bank in years. Her company deposits her salary into her checking account each month, and she regularly does all her banking from her home computer: with the click of a mouse, she can check her account balances, pay her bills, even search for the best rates on savings instruments. And by making a few simple entries, she is able to withdraw money from her U.S. bank account using an automated teller machine (ATM) in London!

The financial services industry continues to evolve, thanks in large part to advanced technology and changing regulations. Today, consumers can now choose from many different types of financial institutions, all competing for their business. No longer must you go to one place for your checking account, another for credit cards or loans, and yet another for brokerage services. Instead, financial institutions are expanding services and competitively pricing their products by bundling different accounts. For example,

if you have $25,000 worth of funds in several Bank of America accounts, you're eligible for reduced or zero-cost commissions on stock trades, free checking, free bill-pay, a credit card, and free ATM debit card transactions. And online banking allows you to easily access all of these services.

The *financial services industry* as we know it today comprises all institutions that market various kinds of *financial products* (such as checking and savings accounts, credit cards, loans and mortgages, insurance, and mutual funds) and *financial services* (such as financial planning, securities brokerage, tax filing and planning, estate planning, real estate, trusts, and retirement). What 20–25 years ago were several distinct (though somewhat related) industries is now, in essence, one industry in which firms are differentiated more by organizational structure than by name or product offerings.

## Types of Financial Institutions

Financial institutions can be classified into two broad groups—depository and nondepository—based on whether or not they accept deposits as traditional banks.

 **Go to Smart Sites**

To help you decide if Internet banks are for you, research them online at Kiplinger. Whenever you see "*Go to Smart Sites*" in this chapter, visit 4ltrpress.cengage.com for help finding answers online. ●

### Depository Financial Institutions
The vast majority of financial transactions take place at *depository financial institutions*—commercial banks (both brick-and-mortar and Internet), savings and loan associations (S&Ls), savings banks, and credit unions. Although they're regulated by different agencies, depository financial institutions are commonly referred to as "banks" because of their similar products and services. What sets these institutions apart from others is their ability to accept deposits; most people use them for their checking and savings account needs. These depository financial institutions are briefly described in Exhibit 4.2.

### Nondepository Financial Institutions
Other types of financial institutions that offer banking services, *but don't accept deposits like traditional banks*, are considered *nondepository institutions*. Today you can hold a credit card issued by a stock brokerage firm or have an account with a mutual fund that allows you to write a limited number of checks.

© PHOTODISC/GETTY IMAGES FROM V96 MY MONEY

## How Safe Is Your Money?

Almost all commercial banks, S&Ls, savings banks, and credit unions are federally insured by U.S. government agencies. The few that are not federally insured usually obtain insurance through either a state-chartered or private insurance agency. Most experts believe that these privately insured institutions have less protection against loss than those that are federally insured. Exhibit 4.3 lists the insuring agencies and the maximum insurance amounts provided under the various federal deposit insurance programs.

**Deposit insurance** protects the funds you have on deposit at banks and other depository institutions against institutional failure. In effect, the insuring agency stands behind the financial institution and guarantees the safety of your deposits up to a specified maximum amount. The ordinary amount covered per depositor by federal insurance is $100,000, *which was temporarily increased to $250,000 during the financial crisis of 2009.* This

**deposit insurance**
A type of insurance that protects funds on deposit against failure of the institution; can be insured by the FDIC and the NCUA.

**Internet bank** An online commercial bank.

**share draft account**
An account offered by credit unions that is similar to interest-paying checking accounts offered by other financial institutions.

---

## Exhibit 4.2 Depository Financial Institutions

Depository financial institutions differ from their nonbank counterparts, such as stock brokerages and mutual funds, in their ability to accept deposits. Most consumers use these institutions to meet their checking and savings account needs.

| Institution | Description |
|---|---|
| Commercial bank | Offers checking and savings accounts and a full range of financial products and services; the only institution that can offer *non-interest-paying checking accounts (demand deposits)*. The most popular of the depository financial institutions. Most are traditional *brick-and-mortar banks*, but **Internet banks**—online commercial banks—are growing in popularity because of their convenience, lower service fees, and higher interest paid on account balances. |
| Savings and loan association (S&L) | Channels the savings of depositors primarily into mortgage loans for purchasing and improving homes. Also offers many of the same checking, saving, and lending products as commercial banks. Often pays slightly higher interest on savings than do commercial banks. |
| Savings bank | Similar to S&Ls, but located primarily in the New England states. Most are *mutual* associations—their depositors are their owners and thus receive a portion of the profits in the form of interest on their savings. |
| Credit union | A nonprofit, member-owned financial cooperative that provides a full range of financial products and services to its *members*, who must belong to a common occupation, religious or fraternal order, or residential area. Generally small institutions when compared with commercial banks and S&Ls. Offer interest-paying checking accounts—called **share draft accounts**—and a variety of saving and lending programs. Because they are run to benefit their members, they pay higher interest on savings and charge lower rates on loans than do other depository financial institutions. |

**Exhibit 4.3   Federal Deposit Insurance Programs**

Insurance on checking and savings accounts at federally insured institutions covers up to $250,000. In 2009 this was increased temporarily from $100,000, which is in effect until 2014.

| Savings Institution | Insuring Agency | Basic Insurance Amounts |
|---|---|---|
| Commercial bank | Federal Deposit Insurance Corporation (FDIC) | $250,000/depositor through the Bank Insurance Fund (BIF) |
| Savings and loan association | Federal Deposit Insurance Corporation (FDIC) | $250,000/depositor through the Savings Association Insurance Fund (SAIF) |
| Savings bank | Federal Deposit Insurance Corporation (FDIC) | $250,000/depositor through the Bank Insurance Fund (BIF) |
| Credit union | National Credit Union Administration (NCUA) | $250,000/depositor through the National Credit Union Share Insurance Fund (NCUSIF) |

higher amount is expected to be in effect until at least 2014. The current discussion applies the new higher amount of $250,000 per depositor under federal insurance.

It's important to understand that deposit insurance is provided to the *depositor* rather than to a *deposit account*. Thus, the checking *and* savings accounts of each depositor are insured and, *as long as the maximum insurable amount is not exceeded,* the depositor can have any number of accounts and still be fully protected. This is an important feature to keep in mind because many people mistakenly believe that the maximum insurance applies to *each* of their accounts. For example, a depositor with a checking account balance of $15,000 at a branch office of First National Bank, an MMDA of $135,000 at First National Bank's main office, and a $50,000 CD issued by the same First National Bank is entirely covered by the FDIC's deposit insurance amount of $250,000 per depositor. If the CD were for $150,000, however, then the total for this depositor would be $300,000 and thus not entirely covered under the plan. However, purchasing the CD *from another bank*, which also provides $250,000 of deposit insurance, would fully protect all of this depositor's funds.

Now that banks are offering a greater variety of products, including mutual funds, it's important to remember that only deposit accounts, including certificates of deposit, are covered by deposit insurance. *Securities purchased through your bank are not protected by any form of deposit insurance.*

As a depositor, it's possible to increase your $250,000 of traditional deposit insurance if necessary by opening accounts in different depositor names at the same institution. For example, a married couple can obtain as much as $1,500,000 in coverage by setting up several accounts:

- One in the name of each spouse ($500,000 in coverage)
- A *joint* account in both names (good for another $500,000, which is $250,000 per account owner)
- *Separate trust or self-directed retirement (IRA, Keogh, etc.) accounts* in the name of each spouse (good for an additional $250,000 per spouse)

In this case each depositor name is treated as a separate legal entity, receiving full insurance coverage—the husband alone is considered one legal entity, the wife another, and the husband and wife as a couple a third. The trust and self-directed retirement accounts are also viewed as separate legal entities.

## LG3 A Full Menu of Cash Management Products

As a student on a tight budget, working his way through college, Bob Matheson knew how important it was to plan his saving and spending, and Bob wanted to make the correct decisions about managing his financial resources. By using a checking account comparison chart, like the one in Exhibit 4.4, Bob could compare information on daily balance requirements, service fees, interest rates, and the services his bank offers to college students and others.

## Exhibit 4.4 Checking Accounts Comparison Chart

Most banks offer a variety of checking account options, typically differentiated by minimum balances, fees, and other services.

### Representative Bank USA

| Features | College Checking | Custom Checking | Advantage Checking | Advantage Plus Checking |
|---|---|---|---|---|
| Minimum daily balance (to waive monthly service fee) | None | $750 in checking | $5,000 in checking | $7,500 combined balance |
| Monthly service fee | $5.95 | $9 with direct deposit | $11 without direct deposit; no fee with Homeowner's Option | $12 ($2 discount with direct deposit) |
| Interest | No | No | Yes | Yes |
| Online statements | Free | Free | Free | Free |
| Check safekeeping | Free | Free | Free | Free |
| Monthly check return | $3.00 | $3.00 | $3.00 | Free |
| ATM & check card | Free | Free | Free | Free |
| Bank by phone | Free automated calls | Free automated calls | Free automated calls | Free banker-assisted calls |
| Overdraft protection | Credit card | Credit card | Credit card, line of credit account, and select deposit accounts | Credit card, line of credit account, and select deposit accounts |
| Direct deposit advance service | Not available | Yes, with a direct deposit of $100 a month or more | Yes, with a direct deposit of $100 a month or more | Yes, with a direct deposit of $100 a month or more |

# Checking and Savings Accounts

People hold cash and other forms of liquid assets, such as checking and savings accounts, for the convenience they offer in making purchase transactions, meeting normal living expenses, and providing a safety net, or cushion, to meet unexpected expenses. Because of the federal *Truth-in-Savings Act of 1993*, all depository financial institutions must clearly disclose fees, interest rates, and terms—on both checking and savings accounts. In addition, banks must use a standard *annual percentage yield (APY)* formula that takes compounding (discussed later) into account when stating the interest paid on accounts. This makes it easier for consumers to compare each bank's offerings. The law also requires banks to pay interest on a customer's full daily or monthly average deposit balance, and strictly prohibit them from paying interest on only the lowest daily balance or paying no interest if the account balance falls below the minimum balance for just 1 day. In addition, banks must notify customers 30 days in advance before lowering rates on deposit accounts or certificates of deposit.

## Checking Accounts

A checking account held at a financial institution is known as a **demand deposit**, meaning that the bank must permit these funds to be withdrawn whenever the account holder demands. You put money into your checking account by *depositing* funds; you withdraw it by *writing a check, using a debit card,* or *making a cash withdrawal.* As long as you have sufficient funds in your account, the bank, when presented with a valid check or an electronic debit, must immediately pay the amount indicated by deducting it from your account.

*Regular checking* is the most common type of checking account. Traditionally, it pays no interest, and any service charges can be waived if you maintain a minimum balance (usually between $500 and $1,500),

**demand deposit** An account held at a financial institution from which funds can be withdrawn on demand by the account holder; same as a *checking account.*

**time deposit** A savings deposit at a financial institution; remains on deposit for a longer time than a demand deposit.

**negotiable order of withdrawal (NOW) account** A checking account on which the financial institution pays interest; NOWs have no legal minimum balance.

**money market deposit account (MMDA)** A federally insured savings account, offered by banks and other depository institutions, that competes with money market mutual funds.

**money market mutual fund (MMMF)** A mutual fund that pools the funds of many small investors and purchases high-return, short-term marketable securities.

**asset management account (AMA)** A comprehensive deposit account, offered primarily by brokerage houses and mutual funds.

though many banks are moving away from such minimum balance requirements. Technically, only commercial banks can offer non-interest-paying regular checking accounts. Savings banks, S&Ls, and credit unions also offer checking accounts; but these accounts, which must pay interest, are called *NOW (negotiable order of withdrawal) accounts* or, in the case of credit unions, *share draft accounts.*

## Savings Accounts

A savings account is another form of liquid asset available at commercial banks, S&Ls, savings banks, credit unions, and other types of financial institutions. Savings deposits are referred to as **time deposits**, since they are expected to remain on deposit for longer periods of time than demand deposits. Because savings deposits earn higher rates of interest, they are typically preferable to checking accounts when the depositor's goal is to accumulate money for a future expenditure or to maintain balances for meeting unexpected expenses. Most banks pay higher interest rates on larger savings account balances. For example, a bank might pay 2.00% on balances up to $2,500, 2.50% on balances between $2,500 and $10,000, and 2.75% on balances of more than $10,000. In addition to withdrawal policies and deposit insurance, the stated interest rate and the method of calculating interest paid on savings accounts are important considerations when choosing the financial institution in which to place your savings.

## Interest-Paying Checking Accounts

Depositors can choose from NOW accounts, money market deposit accounts, and money market mutual funds.

**NOW ACCOUNTS. Negotiable order of withdrawal (NOW) accounts** are checking accounts on which the financial institution pays interest. There is no legal minimum balance for a NOW, but many institutions impose their own requirement, often between $500 and $1,000. Some pay interest on any balance in the account, but most institutions pay a higher rate of interest for balances above a specified amount.

**MONEY MARKET DEPOSIT ACCOUNTS. Money market deposit accounts (MMDAs)** are offered at banks and other depository institutions and compete with money market mutual funds for deposits. MMDAs are popular with savers and investors because of their convenience and safety and because deposits in MMDAs (unlike those in money funds) are *federally insured*. Most banks require a minimum MMDA balance of $1,000 or more.

Depositors can use check-writing privileges or ATMs to access MMDA accounts. They receive a limited number (usually six) of free monthly checks and transfers but pay a fee on additional transactions. Although this reduces the flexibility of these accounts, most depositors view MMDAs as savings and and as such, do not consider these restrictions a serious obstacle. Moreover, MMDAs pay the highest interest rate of any bank account on which checks can be written.

**MONEY MARKET MUTUAL FUNDS.** Money market mutual funds have become the most successful type of mutual fund ever offered. A **money market mutual fund (MMMF)** pools the funds of many small investors to purchase high-return, short-term marketable securities offered by the U.S. Treasury, major corporations, large commercial banks, and various government organizations. (Mutual funds are discussed in detail in Chapter 13.)

MMMFs have historically paid interest at rates of 1% to 3% above those paid on regular savings accounts. Moreover, investors have instant access to their funds through check-writing privileges, although these must be written for a stipulated minimum amount (often $500). The checks look like, and are treated like, any other check drawn on a demand deposit account. And as with all interest-bearing checking accounts, you continue to earn interest on your money while the checks make their way through the banking system.

## Asset Management Accounts

Perhaps the best example of a banking service offered by a nondepository financial institution is the **asset management account (AMA)**, or *central asset account*. The AMA is a comprehensive deposit account that combines checking, investing, and borrowing activities and is offered primarily by brokerage houses and mutual funds. AMAs appeal to investors because they can consolidate most of their financial transactions at one institution and on one account statement.

A typical AMA account includes an MMDA with unlimited free checking, a Visa or MasterCard debit card, use of ATMs, and brokerage and loan accounts. Annual fees and account charges, such as a per-transaction charge for ATM withdrawals, vary; so it pays to shop around. Their distinguishing feature is that they automatically "sweep" excess balances—for example, amounts over $500—into a higher-return MMMF daily or weekly. When the account holder needs funds to purchase securities or cover checks written on the MMDA, the funds are transferred back to the MMDA. And if the amount of securities purchased or checks presented for payment exceeds the account balance, the needed funds are supplied automatically through a loan.

Although AMAs are an attractive alternative to a traditional bank account, they do have some drawbacks. For example, compared with banks, there are fewer "branch" locations. However, AMAs are typically affiliated with ATM networks, making it easy to withdraw funds. Yet ATM transactions are more costly; checks can take longer to clear; and some bank services may not be offered. Moreover, AMAs are not covered by deposit insurance, although these deposits are protected by the *Securities Investor Protection Corporation* and the firm's private insurance.

## Electronic Banking Services

The fastest-changing area in cash management today is *electronic banking services*. Whether you're using an ATM or checking your account balance online, electronic banking services make managing your money easier and more convenient. Electronic funds transfer systems allow you to conduct many types of banking business at any hour of the day or night.

### Electronic Funds Transfer Systems

**Electronic funds transfer systems (EFTSs)** allow depositors to conduct a variety of different types of bank transactions at any hour of the day or night, by using the latest telecommunications and computer technology to electronically transfer funds into and out of their accounts. For example, your employer may use an EFTS to electronically transfer your pay from the firm's bank account directly into your personal bank account at the same or a different bank. This eliminates the employer's need to prepare and process checks and the employee's need to deposit them. Electronic transfer systems make possible such services as debit cards and ATMs, preauthorized deposits and payments, bank-by-phone accounts, and online banking.

### DEBIT CARDS AND AUTOMATED TELLER MACHINES.
This form of EFTS uses specially-coded plastic cards, called **debit cards**, to transfer funds from the customer's bank account (a debit) to the recipient's account. A debit card may be used to make purchases at any place of business set up with the point-of-sale terminals required to accept debit card payments. The personal identification number (PIN) issued with your debit card verifies that you are authorized to access the account.

Visa and MasterCard issue debit cards linked to your checking account that give you even more flexibility. In addition to using the card to purchase goods and services, you can use it at ATMs, which have become a popular way to make banking transactions. **Automated teller machines (ATMs)** are remote computer terminals that customers of a bank or other depository institution can use to make deposits, withdrawals, and other transactions such as loan payments or transfers between accounts—24 hours a day, 7 days a week. Most banks have ATMs outside their offices, and some place freestanding ATMs in shopping malls, airports, and grocery stores; at colleges and universities; and in other high-traffic areas to enhance their competitive position. If your bank belongs to an EFTS network, such as Cirrus, Star, or Interlink, you can get cash from the ATM of any bank in the United States or overseas that is a member of that network. (In fact, the easiest way to get foreign currency when you travel overseas is through an ATM on your bank's network! It also gives you the best exchange rate for your dollar.) Many banks charge a per-transaction fee of $1 to $4 for using the ATM of another bank, and some also charge when you use your ATM card to pay certain merchants. However, to be more competitive some banks now reimburse the fees associated with using the ATMs of other banks.

Debit card use is increasing because these cards are convenient both *for retailers*, who don't have to

**electronic funds transfer systems (EFTSs)** Systems using the latest telecommunications and computer technology to electronically transfer funds into and out of customers' accounts.

**debit cards** Specially coded plastic cards used to transfer funds from a customer's bank account to the recipient's account to pay for goods or services.

**automated teller machine (ATM)** A remote computer terminal that customers of depository institutions can use to make basic transactions 24 hours a day, 7 days a week.

© SVITLANA10/SHUTTERSTOCK

worry about bounced checks, and *for consumers*, who don't have to write checks. These cards are so popular, in fact, that the total dollar volume of purchases made using Visa's branded debit cards actually surpassed their credit-card purchases in 2008. Indeed, the convenience of debit cards may be their biggest drawback: i.e., *they make it very easy to overspend*. To avoid such problems, make sure you record all debit card purchases immediately in your checkbook ledger and deduct them from your checkbook balance. Also be aware that if there's a problem with a purchase, you can't stop payment—an action you could take if you had paid by check or credit card.

**PREAUTHORIZED DEPOSITS AND PAYMENTS.** Two related EFTS services are *preauthorized deposits and payments*. They allow you to receive automatic deposits or make payments that occur regularly. For example, you can arrange to have your paycheck or monthly pension or Social Security benefits deposited directly into your account. Regular, fixed-amount payments, such as mortgage and consumer loan payments or monthly retirement fund contributions, can be preauthorized to be made automatically from your account. You can also preauthorize regular payments of varying amounts such as monthly utility bills.

**BANK-BY-PHONE ACCOUNTS.** Bank customers can make various types of transactions by telephone, either by calling a customer service operator who handles the transaction or by using the keypad on a touch-tone telephone to instruct the bank's computer. After the customer

provides a secret code to access the account, the system provides the appropriate prompts to perform various transactions, such as obtaining an account balance, finding out what checks have cleared, transferring funds to other accounts, and dispatching payments to participating merchants. To encourage banking by phone, many banks today charge no fee on basic account transactions or allow a limited number of free transactions per month. However, online banking options are replacing bank-by-phone accounts.

**Online Banking and Bill Payment Services**

The Pew Internet & American Life Project recently found that nearly 45% of Internet users rely on some form of *online banking* services. This percentage has grown steadily as banks make online services easier to use and as people become more comfortable using the Internet for financial transactions. Many individuals do little more than check their balances, but more than half use the Internet to transfer funds as well. Today, most banks aggressively compete for your online banking business; and it's in their best financial interests to do so. A recent study showed that the cost of a full-service teller transaction is about $1.00, an ATM transaction is about 30 cents, and an Internet transaction is less than 1 cent.

> **{** *Nearly 45% of Internet users rely on some form of online banking services.* **}**

Although a computer-based bank-at-home system doesn't replace the use of an ATM to obtain cash or deposit money, it can save both time and postage when you're paying bills. Other benefits include convenience and the potential to earn higher interest rates and pay lower fees. While some banks still charge an average of $5 a month for online banking services, it's free at most banks. But online banking doesn't always live up to its promises. You can't make cash deposits, checks may get lost in the mail, and you don't know when the funds will reach your account. The nearby *Money in Action* provides more information to help you decide if online banking is right for you.

## Regulation of EFTS Services

The federal *Electronic Fund Transfer Act of 1978* describes your rights and responsibilities as an EFTS user. Under this law, you cannot stop payment on a defective or questionable purchase, although individual banks and state laws often have more lenient provisions. If there's an error, you must notify the bank within 60 days of its occurrence. The bank must then investigate and advise you of the results within 10 days. The bank can then take up to 45

**FINANCIAL ROAD SIGN**

**TIPS FOR SAFE ONLINE BANKING**

- *The all-important security "s" in Web-site URLs.* Web-site URLs starting with "https://" are more secure than Web-site URLs starting with "http://". This is particularly important when you are entering passwords and PINs. Security icons such as a padlock do not guarantee complete security because they can be reproduced by those seeking to deceive you.
- *Passwords and user IDs.* Passwords and user IDs should be a combination of upper and lower case letters, numbers, and symbols, and be at least 8 characters in length. NEVER provide your passwords in response to any e-mail requests information about your account!
- *Safe access points.* Avoid accessing your bank accounts at an Internet café or public places like an airport. Your session is just too easy to intercept.

*Source:* Adapted from http://www.419legal.org/blog/2009/04/16/scam-alert-online-banking-safety-guidelines/, accessed May 2009.

# MONEY IN ACTION

## Pros and Cons of Online Banking

**Pros:**

The convenience of online banking is hard to beat:

- *Bank balances verification.* You no longer have to wait to get your monthly statement. Just sign in to your online account and verify your bank account balance whenever you want.
- *Download transactions.* Most banks allow you to download your banking transactions into financial software like Quicken. Debit- and credit-card charges will show up, which simplifies record keeping.
- *Online bill payment.* It is easier and cheaper to pay online than to mail a paper check. Many banks offer free bill-pay services, which reduces the number of paper checks and stamps you need to buy. You can automate some payments, which is great for charges like cable, electric, and the like.
- *Funds transfer.* It is often free or nearly free to transfer funds between your eligible bank accounts and even your accounts at other U.S. financial institutions.

**Cons:**

But online banking does have its downside:

- *Threat of identity theft.* Security precautions, like those noted in the preceding *Financial Road Sign,* must be taken to protect your private information.
- *Not all businesses accept electronic payments.* Make sure that the businesses you deal with accept online payments well before you need to make a payment. Lack of coordination could lead to late charges. If you choose to pay bills online, make sure that recipients are capable of processing electronic payments. Always remember to print out a hard copy of all online transactions in case there is an error.
- *Web-site crashes.* All Web sites occasionally crash or go down for scheduled maintenance. Keep your bank's phone number handy in case you cannot access a needed account.
- *Fees.* Although many banks offer online services for free, some do not. It is essential to review any and all possible fees before you start using your online account.

more days to investigate the error but must return the disputed money to your account until the issue is resolved.

If you fail to notify the bank of an error within 60 days, the bank has no obligation under federal law to conduct an investigation or return your money. You must notify the bank immediately about the theft, loss, or unauthorized use of your EFTS card. Notification within 2 business days after you discover the card missing limits your loss to $50. After 2 business days, you may lose up to $500 (but never more than the amount that was withdrawn by the thief). If you don't report the loss within 60 days after your periodic statement was mailed, you can lose all the money in your account. When reporting

©JASON STITT/SHUTTERSTOCK

errors or unauthorized transactions, it's best to notify your bank by telephone and follow up with a letter; then keep a copy of the letter in your file. These safeguards not withstanding, *your best protection is to carefully guard the PIN used to access your accounts.* Don't write the PIN on your EFTS card, and be sure to check your statements for possible errors or unauthorized transactions.

## Other Bank Services

In addition to the services described earlier in this chapter, many banks offer other types of money management services, such as safe-deposit boxes and trust services.

- **Safe-deposit boxes:** A *safe-deposit box* is a rented drawer in a bank's vault. Boxes can be rented for $40–$85 per year (or more), depending on their size. When you rent a box, you receive one key to it, and the bank keeps another key. The box can be opened only when both keys are used.

This arrangement protects items in the box from theft and serves as an excellent storage place for jewelry, contracts, stock certificates, titles, and other important documents. Keeping valuables in a safe-deposit box may also reduce your homeowner's insurance by eliminating the "riders" that are often needed to cover such items.

- **Trust services:** Bank trust departments provide investment and estate planning advice. They manage and administer the investments in a trust account or from an estate.

## LG4 Maintaining a Checking Account

By the time David Renquist started college, he had a thriving car-detailing business that earned him several hundred dollars per week. Some customers paid him in advance, some paid after the fact, and some forgot to pay at all. But by depositing each check or cash payment into his checking account, David was able to keep track of his earnings without complicated bookkeeping. A checking account

©DIGITALVISION (CD PERSONAL FINANCE)

is one of the most useful cash management tools you can have. It's a safe and convenient way to hold money and streamline point-of-sale purchases, debt payments, and other basic transactions. You can have regular or interest-paying checking accounts at commercial banks, S&Ls, savings banks, credit unions, and even brokerage houses through asset management accounts. For convenience, we'll focus on commercial bank checking accounts, although our discussion also applies to checking accounts maintained at other types of financial institutions.

## Opening and Using Your Checking Account

Factors that typically influence the choice of where to maintain a checking account are convenience, services, and cost. Many people choose a bank based solely on convenience factors: location, business hours, number of drive-thru windows, and number and location of branch offices and ATMs. Ease of access is obviously an important consideration because most people prefer to bank near home or work. But in addition to convenience and safety, you should also consider the interest rates the bank offers, types of accounts (including special accounts that combine such features as credit cards, free checks, and reduced fees), structure and level of fees and charges, and quality of customer service.

### The Cost of a Checking Account

Bank service charges have increased sharply for a variety of reasons, including the growth of interest-bearing checking accounts. Today few, if any, banks and other depository institutions allow unlimited free check-writing privileges. Most banks levy monthly and per-check fees when your checking account balance drops below a required minimum, and some may charge for checking no matter how large a balance you carry.

Some banks are moving away from minimum balance requirements, but it is still common to be required to maintain a minimum balance of $500 to $1,000 or more to avoid service charges. Although some banks use the *average monthly* balance in an account to determine whether to levy a service charge, most use the *daily* balance procedure. This means that if your account should happen to fall just $1 below the minimum balance *just once* during the month, you'll be hit with the full service charge— even if your average balance is three times the minimum requirement. Service charges take two forms: (1) a base service charge of, say, $7.50 a month, and (2) additional charges of, say, 25 cents for each check you write and 10 cents for each ATM or bank-by-phone transaction.

In addition to the service charges on checking accounts, banks have increased most other check-related charges and raised the minimum balances required for free checking and waivers of specified fees. The average charge on a returned check is between $25 and $30, and stop-payment orders typically cost $20 to $35. Some banks charge fees for ATM or bank-by-phone transactions that exceed a specified number. Most also charge for using the ATM of another bank that is not a member of the same network. It's not surprising that smart consumers use cost as the single most important variable when choosing where to set up a checking account.

### Individual or Joint Account?

Two people wishing to open a checking account may do so in one of three ways:

1. They can each open individual checking accounts (on which the other cannot write checks).

2. They can open a joint account that requires both signatures on all checks.

3. They can open a joint account that allows either one to write checks (the most common type of joint account).

**checkbook ledger**
A booklet, provided with a supply of checks, used to maintain accurate records of all checking account transactions.

One advantage of the joint account over two individual accounts is lower service charges. In addition, the account has rights of survivorship: for a married couple, this means that if one spouse dies, the surviving spouse, after fulfilling a specified legal requirement, can draw checks on the account. If account owners are treated as tenants in common rather than having rights of survivorship, then survivor gets only his or her share of the account. Thus, when you're opening a joint account, be sure to specify the rights you prefer.

### General Checking Account Procedures

After you select the bank that meets your needs, it's a simple matter to open an account. The application form asks for basic personal information such as name, date of birth, Social Security number, address, phone, and place of employment. You'll also have to provide identification, sign signature cards, and make an initial deposit. The bank will give you a supply of checks to use until your personalized checks arrive.

After opening a checking account, follow these basic procedures:

- Always write checks in ink.

- Include the name of the person being paid, the date, and the amount of the check—written in both numerals and words for accuracy.

- Sign the check the same way as on the signature card you filled out when opening the account.

- Note the check's purpose on the check—usually on the line provided in the lower left corner. This information is helpful for both budgeting and tax purposes.

*Make sure to enter all checking account transactions*—checks written, deposits, point-of-sale debit purchases, ATM transactions, and preauthorized automatic payments and deposits—in the **checkbook ledger** provided with your supply of checks. Then, *subtract* the amount of each check, debit card purchase, ATM cash withdrawal, or payment, and *add* the amount of each deposit to the previous balance to keep track of your current account balance. Good transaction records and an accurate balance prevent overdrawing the account.

### FINANCIAL ROAD SIGN

**CHOOSING A NEW BANK**
If you're looking for a new bank, here are some important factors to consider:

- *Convenient location and online services.* Find a bank that is conveniently located *and* has online services because such banks tend to pay more competitive savings rates.

- *Fee-free checking and free money transfers.* "Free checking" usually means that you aren't required to keep a minimum balance in your account and can write as many checks a month as you like. Also look for banks that let you transfer funds between different accounts for free.

- *Convenient ATMs.* The average fee for using the ATM of another bank is about $3, so look for a bank that has ATMs close to your work and/or home.

- *Don't forget to consider credit unions.* Credit unions are not-for-profit institutions that often provide better rates because they don't spend as much on advertising and marketing. However, with this benefit comes the cost of typically having fewer physical branches and ATMs than major bank networks. You can find credit unions in your area at www.findacreditunion.com and www.creditunion.coop.

- *Overdraft and FDIC protection.* Given that fees for bounced checks average about $30, it is important to know what the charges are and what kind of overdraft protection is offered. Also make sure that your deposits are insured by the FDIC.

- *Competitive interest rates.* Find out if the bank pays interest on your balance. You can shop for the most competitive rates in your zip code at www.bankingmyway.com.

*Source:* Adapted from Farnoosh Torabi, "Back to Basics: Choosing a New Bank," October 1, 2008, and "How to Choose the Best Checking Account," http://www.mainstreet.com/article/moneyinvesting/savings/back-basics-choosing-new-bank; posted February 24, 2009, accessed May 2009.

Prepare a deposit slip with each deposit (such slips are generally included with your checks and also available at your bank) listing the currency, coins, and checks being deposited. List checks by the *transit ID number* printed on the check, usually at the top right. Also properly endorse all checks that you're depositing. To protect against possible loss of endorsed checks, it's common to use a special endorsement, such as "Pay to the order of XYZ Bank," or a restrictive endorsement, such as "For deposit only." When depositing checks, you may encounter a delay in funds' availability due to the time required for them to clear. To avoid overdrawing your account, know your bank's "hold" policy on deposits—as a rule, it generally takes between 1 and 5 business days for funds to become available.

### Overdrafts

When a check is written for an amount greater than the current account balance, the result is an **overdraft**. If the overdraft is proven to be intentional, the bank can initiate legal proceedings against the account holder. The action taken by a bank on an overdraft depends on the strength of its relationship with the account holder and the amount involved. In the vast majority of cases, the bank simply stamps the overdrawn check with the words "insufficient balance (or funds)" and returns it to the party to whom it was written. This is often called a "bounced check." The account holder is notified of this action, and the holder's bank deducts a penalty fee of as much as $20 to $25 or more from his checking account. The depositor of a "bad check" may also be charged as much as $15 to $20 by her bank, which explains why merchants typically charge bad check writers $15 to $25 per bounced check, and often refuse to accept future checks from them.

When you have a strong relationship with your bank or arrange **overdraft protection**, the bank will pay a check that overdraws the account. In cases where overdraft protection has not been prearranged but the bank pays the check, the account holder is usually notified by the bank and charged a penalty fee for the inconvenience. However, the check does not bounce, and the check writer's creditworthiness is not damaged.

There are several ways to arrange overdraft protection. Many banks offer an overdraft line of credit, which automatically extends a loan to cover the amount of an overdraft. In most cases, however, the loans are made only in specified increments, such as $50 or $100, and interest (or a fee) is levied against the loan amount, not the actual amount of the overdraft. This can be an expensive form of protection, particularly if you do not promptly repay the loan.

Another way to cover overdrafts is with an *automatic transfer program,* which automatically transfers funds from your savings account into your checking account in the event of an overdraft. Under this program, some banks charge both an annual fee and a fee on each transfer. Of course, *the best form of overdraft protection is to employ good cash management techniques and regularly balance your checking account.*

### Stopping Payment

Occasionally it's necessary to **stop payment** on a check if it was issued as part of a contract that was not carried out, or because a good or service paid for by check is found to be faulty (note that some states prohibit you from stopping payment on faulty goods or services). To stop payment on a check, you must notify the bank and fill out a form indicating the check number and date, amount, and the name of the party to whom it was written. You can initiate stop-payment orders online or by phone. Once you place a stop-payment order, the bank refuses payment on the affected check, and the check will be rejected if another bank presents it in the check-clearing process. Banks typically charge a fee ranging from $20 to $35 per check to stop payment. There's one big exception to all this and that is, *if your checks or checkbook are lost or stolen, there's no need to stop payment on them* because you have no personal liability. Stopping payment in this case only incurs expense; it doesn't change your personal liability.

## Monthly Statements

Once a month, your bank provides a statement—an itemized listing of all transactions in your checking account (checks written, ATM transactions, debit purchases, automatic payments, and deposits made). Also included are bank service charges and interest earned (see William R. Torgeson's May 2010 bank statement in Exhibit 4.5). Some banks include your original canceled checks with your bank statement, although most are abandoning this practice as we move closer to a "paperless society." Banks that don't return canceled checks will provide photocopies of them on request, generally for a fee. Many banks now let you view canceled checks online, free of

## Exhibit 4.5 A Bank Statement

Each month, you receive a statement from your bank or depository financial institution that summarizes the month's transactions and shows your latest account balance. This sample statement for May 2010 for William R. Torgeson not only shows the checks that have been paid, but it also lists all ATM transactions, point-of-sale transactions using his ATM card (the Interlink payments at Lucky Stores), and direct payroll deposits.

```
        YOUR BANK                          #240
        P.O. BOX 516   ANY CITY, USA    90000-0000

        WILLIAM R. TORGESON
        1765 SHERIDAN DRIVE                    N          CALL (800) 222-0000
        YOUR CITY, STATE 12091                 21         24 HOURS/DAY, 7 DAYS/WEEK
                                                          FOR ASSISTANCE WITH
                                                          YOUR ACCOUNT.

  PAGE 1 OF 1        THIS STATEMENT COVERS: 4/30/2010 THROUGH 5/29/2010

  PREMIUM           SUMMARY
  ACCOUNT
                    PREVIOUS BALANCE         473.68   MINIMUM BALANCE    21.78
  0123-45678        DEPOSITS               1,302.83+
                    WITHDRAWALS            1,689.02-
                    SERVICE CHARGES            7.50-
                    DIRECT DEPOSIT DISCOUNT    1.00+

                    NEW BALANCE               80.99
```

| CHECKS AND WITHDRAWALS | CHECK | DATE PAID | AMOUNT | CHECK | DATE PAID | AMOUNT |
|---|---|---|---|---|---|---|
| | 203 | 5/01 | 10.00 | 213 | 5/08 | 40.00 |
| | 204 | 4/30 | 15.00 | 214 | 5/09 | 9.58 |
| | 205 | 5/10 | 635.00 | 215 | 5/20 | 66.18 |
| | 206 | 5/08 | 25.00 | 216 | 5/20 | 64.92 |
| | 207 | 5/07 | 19.00 | 217 | 5/21 | 25.03 |
| | 208 | 5/07 | 50.00 | 218 | 5/21 | 37.98 |
| | 209 | 5/08 | 15.00 | 219 | 5/22 | 35.00 |
| | 210 | 5/10 | 83.00 | 220 | 5/22 | 105.00 |
| | 211 | 5/10 | 10.00 | 222* | 5/22 | 100.00 |
| | 212 | 5/08 | 70.00 | 223 | 5/21 | 40.00 |
| | | | | 224 | 5/29 | 40.82 |

| ATM TRANSACTIONS | | DATE PAID | AMOUNT |
|---|---|---|---|
| | PREMIUM ACCOUNT FEE LESS $1.00 DISCOUNT | 4/30 | 6.50 |
| | INTERLINK PURCHASE #572921 ON 04/30 AT LUCKY STORE NO 043 | 5/01 | 50.00 |
| | WITHDRAWAL #08108 AT 00165A ON 05/04 | 5/06 | 20.00 |
| | INTERLINK PURCHASE #807409 ON 05/11 AT LUCKY STORE NO 056 | 5/13 | 12.51 |
| | WITHDRAWAL #01015 AT 00240C ON 05/17 | 5/17 | 20.00 |
| | WITHDRAWAL #04792 AT 00167C ON 05/20 | 5/20 | 20.00 |
| | WITHDRAWAL #04386 AT 00240D ON 05/21 | 5/21 | 40.00 |
| | INTERLINK PURCHASE #880318 ON 05/28 AT LUCKY STORE #043 | 5/29 | 30.00 |

| DEPOSITS | | DATE POSTED | AMOUNT |
|---|---|---|---|
| | AVS RNT CAR SYST PAYROLL G2 000000035382 | 5/03 | 618.69 |
| | AVS RNT CAR SYST PAYROLL G2 000000035382 | 5/17 | 83.39 |
| | AVS RNT CAR SYST PAYROLL G2 000000035382 | 5/17 | 600.75 |

```
  ATM           00165A: 249 PRIMROSE RD, ANY CITY, USA
  LOCATIONS USED 00240C: 490 BROADWAY, ANY CITY, USA
                00167C: 1145 BROADWAY, ANY CITY, USA
                00240D: 490 BROADWAY, ANY CITY, USA
```

charge. It's important to review your monthly bank statement to verify the accuracy of your account records and to reconcile any differences between the statement balance and the balance shown in your checkbook ledger. The monthly statement is also a valuable source of information for your tax records.

## Account Reconciliation

You should reconcile your bank account as soon as possible after receiving your monthly statement. The **account reconciliation** process, or *balancing the checkbook,* can uncover errors in recording checks or deposits, in addition or subtraction, and, occasionally, in the bank's processing of a check. It can also help you avoid overdrafts by forcing you to verify your account balance monthly. Assuming that neither you nor the bank has made any errors, discrepancies between your checkbook ledger account balance and your bank statement can be attributed to one of four factors.

1. Checks that you've written, ATM withdrawals, debit purchases, or other automatic payments subtracted from your checkbook balance haven't yet been received and processed by your bank and therefore remain outstanding.

2. Deposits that you've made and added to your checkbook balance haven't yet been credited to your account.

3. Any service (activity) charges levied on your account by the bank haven't yet been deducted from your checkbook balance.

4. Interest earned on your account (if it's a NOW or an MMDA account) hasn't yet been added to your checkbook balance.

For a list of the steps to reconcile your checkbook each month, see "Make that Checkbook Balance" in the Bonus Exhibits section of 4ltrpress.cengage.com. The reverse side of your bank statement usually provides a form for reconciling your account, along with step-by-step instructions. As an illustration, Worksheet 4.1 includes an account reconciliation form that William Torgeson completed for the month of May 2010, using the reconciliation procedures described in the online exhibit "Make that Checkbook Balance." You can use this form to reconcile either regular or interest-paying checking accounts such as NOWs or MMDAs.

## Special Types of Checks

In some circumstances, sellers of goods or services may not accept personal checks because they can't be absolutely sure that the check is good. This is common for large purchases or when the buyer's bank is not located in the same area where the purchase is being made. A form of check that guarantees payment may be required instead; these include: cashier's checks, traveler's checks, or certified checks.

- **Cashier's check:** Anyone can buy a **cashier's check** from a bank. These checks are often used by people who don't have checking accounts. They can be purchased for the face amount of the check plus a service fee of about $5, although occasionally they're issued at no charge to bank customers. The bank issues a check payable to a third party and drawn on itself, not you—the best assurance you can give that the check is good.

- **Traveler's check:** Some large financial organizations—such as Citibank, American Express, MasterCard, Visa, and Bank of America—issue **traveler's checks**, which can be purchased at commercial banks and most other financial institutions. They typically come in denominations ranging from $20 to $100, and any amount—in multiples of $20 to $100—can be purchased at a time. A fee of about 1.5% is charged on their purchase, which is often waived for good customers. Properly endorsed and countersigned traveler's checks are accepted by most U.S. businesses and can be exchanged for local currencies in most parts of the world. Because they're insured against loss or theft, they provide a safe, convenient, and popular form of money for travel.

- **Certified check:** A **certified check** is a personal check that the bank certifies, with a stamp, to guarantee that the funds are available. The bank immediately deducts the amount of the check from your account. There's normally a charge of $10 to $15 or more for this service.

## LG5, LG6 Establishing a Savings Program

An estimated 75% of American households have some money put away in savings, making it clear that most of us understand the value of saving for the future. The act of saving is a deliberate, well-thought-out activity designed to preserve the value

William Torgeson used this form to reconcile his checking account for the month of May 2010. Because line A equals line B, he has fully reconciled the difference between the $80.99 bank statement balance and his $339.44 checkbook balance. Accounts should be reconciled each month—as soon as possible after receiving the bank statement.

---

### CHECKING ACCOUNT RECONCILIATION

For the Month of ___May___ , 20 _10_

Accountholder Name(s) ___William Torgeson___

Type of Account ___Regular Checking___

---

1. Ending balance shown on bank statement _____   $ 80.99

*Add* up checks and withdrawals still outstanding:

| Check Number or Date | Amount | Check Number or Date | Amount |
|---|---|---|---|
| 221 | $ 81.55 | | $ |
| 225 | 196.50 | | |
| Lucky—5/28 | 25.00 | | |
| ATM—5/29 | 40.00 | | |
| | | | |
| | | | |
| | | | |
| | | | |
| | | | |
| | | | |
| | TOTAL $ 343.05 | | |

2. Deduct total checks/withdrawals still outstanding from bank balance _____   − $ 343.05

*Add* up deposits still outstanding:

| Date | Amount | Date | Amount |
|---|---|---|---|
| 5/29/09 | $ 595.00 | | |
| | | | |
| | | | |
| | TOTAL $ 595.00 | | |

3. *Add* total deposits still outstanding to bank balance _____   + $ 595.00

**A** **Adjusted Bank Balance (1 − 2 + 3)** _____   $ 332.94

4. Ending balance shown in checkbook _____   $ 339.44

5. Deduct any bank service charges for the period _(−$ 7.50 + $ 1.00)_   − $ 6.50

6. Add interest earned for the period _____   + $ 0

**B** **New Checkbook Balance (4 − 5 + 6)** _____   $ 332.94

*Note:* Your account is reconciled when line A equals line B.

of money, ensure liquidity, and earn a competitive rate of return. Almost by definition, *smart savers are smart investors.* They regard saving as more than putting loose change into a piggy bank; rather, they recognize the importance of saving and know that savings must be managed as astutely as any security. After all, what we normally think of as "savings" is really a form of investing—albeit in short-term, highly liquid low-risk investment. Establishing and maintaining an ongoing savings program is a vital element of personal financial planning. To get the most from your savings, however, you must understand your options and how different savings vehicles pay interest.

## Starting Your Savings Program

Careful financial planning dictates that you hold a portion of your assets to meet liquidity needs and accumulate wealth. Although opinions differ as to how much you should keep as liquid reserves, the consensus is that most families should have an amount equal to 3 to 6 months of after-tax income. Therefore, if you take home $3,000 a month, you should have between $9,000 and $18,000 in liquid reserves. If your employer has a strong salary continuation program covering extended periods of illness, or if you have a sizable line of credit available, then the lower figure is probably adequate. If you lack one or both of these, however, the larger amount is more appropriate.

A specific savings plan should be developed to accumulate funds. Saving should be a priority item in your budget, not something that occurs only when income happens to exceed expenditures. Some people manage this by arranging to have savings directly withheld from their paychecks. Not only do direct deposit arrangements help your savings effort, they also enable your funds to earn interest sooner. Or you can transfer funds on a regular basis to other financial institutions, such as commercial banks, savings and loans, savings banks, credit unions, and even mutual funds. But the key to success is to establish a *regular* pattern of saving.

You must also decide which savings vehicles best meet your needs. Many savers prefer to keep their emergency funds in a regular savings or money market deposit account at an institution with federal deposit insurance. Although these accounts are safe, convenient, and highly liquid, they tend to pay relatively low rates of interest. Other important considerations include your risk preference, the length of time you can leave your money on deposit, and the level of current and anticipated interest rates.

Suppose that 1 year from now you plan to use $5,000 of your savings to make the down payment on a new car, and you expect interest rates to drop during that period. In such a case, you might want to lock in today's higher rate by purchasing a 1-year certificate of deposit (CD). On the other hand, if you're unsure about when you'll actually need the funds or believe that interest rates will rise, you may be better off with an MMDA or MMMF because their rates change with market conditions, and you can access your funds at any time without penalty.

Many financial planning experts recommend keeping a minimum of 10% to 25% of your investment portfolio in savings-type instruments, in addition to the 3 to 6 months of liquid reserves noted earlier. Thus, someone with $50,000 in investments should probably have a minimum of $5,000 to $12,500—and possibly more—in short-term vehicles such as MMDAs, MMMFs, or CDs. At times, the amount invested in short-term vehicles could far exceed the recommended minimum, approaching 50% or more of the portfolio. This generally depends on expected interest rate movements. If interest rates are relatively high and you expect them to fall, you would invest in long-term vehicles in order to lock in the attractive interest rates. On the other hand, if rates are relatively low and you expect them to rise, you might invest in short-term vehicles so that you can more quickly reinvest when rates do rise.

 **The key to success is to establish a regular pattern of saving.**

You should make it a practice to set aside an amount you can comfortably afford *each month,* even if it's only $50 to $100. (Keep in mind that $100 monthly deposits earning 4% interest will grow to more than $36,500 in 20 years.) For a listing of 10 strategies you can use to increase your savings and build a nest egg, check out the Bonus Exhibits at 4ltrpress.cengage.com.

## Earning Interest on Your Money

Interest earned is the reward for putting your money in a savings account or short-term investment vehicle, and it's important for you to understand how that interest is earned. But unfortunately, even in the relatively simple world of savings, not all interest rates are created equal.

## The Effects of Compounding

Interest can be earned in one of two ways. First, some short-term investments are sold on a *discount basis.* This means the security is sold for a price that's lower than its redemption value; the difference between the purchase price and redemption value is the amount of interest earned on the investment. Treasury bills, for instance, are issued on a discount basis. Another way to earn interest on short-term investments is by *direct payment,* which occurs when interest is applied to a regular savings account. That is, the amount of interest earned is added to the amount invested, so at maturity, you get your money back plus whatever you earned in interest. Although this is a relatively simple process, determining the actual rate of return can be complicated.

The first complication is in the method used to determine the amount and rate of **compound interest** earned annually. You've probably read or seen advertisements by banks or other depository institutions declaring that they pay daily, rather than annual, interest. Consider an example to understand what this means. Assume that you invest $1,000 in a savings account advertised as paying annual **simple interest** at a rate of 5%; that means the interest is paid only on the initial amount of the deposit. Thus, if you leave the $1,000 on deposit for 1 year, you'll earn $50 in interest, and the account balance will total $1,050 at year's end. In this case, the **nominal (stated) rate of interest** is 5%. In contrast, the **effective rate of interest** is the annual rate of return that's *actually earned* (or *charged*) during the period the funds are held (or borrowed). You can calculate it with the following formula:

$$\text{Effective rate of interest} = \frac{\text{Amount of interest earned during the year}}{\text{Amount of money invested or deposited}}$$

In our example, because $50 was earned during the year on an investment of $1,000, the effective rate is $50/$1,000 or 5%, which is the same as the nominal rate of interest. (Notice in the preceding formula that it's interest earned during the *year* that matters; if you wanted to calculate the effective rate of interest on an account held for 6 months, you'd double the amount of interest earned.)

But suppose you can invest your funds elsewhere at a 5% rate, *compounded semiannually.* Because interest is applied to your account at midyear, you'll earn *interest on interest* for the last 6 months of the year, thereby increasing the total interest earned for the year. The actual dollar earnings are determined as follows:

**First 6 months' interest** = $1,000 × 0.05 × 6/12 = **$25.00**
**Second 6 months' interest** = $1,025 × 0.05 × 6/12 = **$25.63**
**Total annual interest**                **$50.63**

Interest is generated on a larger investment in the second half of the year because the amount of money on deposit has increased by the amount of interest earned in the first half ($25). Although the nominal rate on this account is still 5%, the effective rate is 5.06% ($50.63/$1,000). As you may have guessed, *the more frequently interest is compounded, the greater the effective rate for any given nominal rate.* Exhibit 4.6 shows these relationships for a sample of interest rates and compounding periods. Note that with a 7% nominal rate, daily compounding adds one-fourth of a percent to the total return—not a trivial amount.

## Compound Interest Equals Future Value

Compound interest is the same as the *future value* concept introduced in Chapter 2. You can use the procedures described there to find out how much an investment or deposit will grow over time at a compounded rate

**compound interest** When interest earned in each subsequent period is determined by applying the *nominal (stated) rate of interest* to the sum of the initial deposit and the interest earned in each prior period.

**simple interest** Interest that is paid only on the initial amount of the deposit.

**nominal (stated) rate of interest** The promised rate of interest paid on a savings deposit or charged on a loan.

**effective rate of interest** The annual rate of return that is *actually earned* (or *charged*) during the period the funds are held (or borrowed).

Exhibit 4.6   The Magic of Compounding

The effective rate of interest you earn on a savings account will exceed the nominal (stated) rate of interest if interest is compounded more than once a year (as are most savings and interest-paying accounts).

| Nominal Rate | Effective Rate | | | | |
|---|---|---|---|---|---|
| | Annually | Semiannually | Quarterly | Monthly | Daily |
| 3% | 3.00% | 3.02% | 3.03% | 3.04% | 3.05% |
| 4 | 4.00 | 4.04 | 4.06 | 4.07 | 4.08 |
| 5 | 5.00 | 5.06 | 5.09 | 5.12 | 5.13 |
| 6 | 6.00 | 6.09 | 6.14 | 6.17 | 6.18 |
| 7 | 7.00 | 7.12 | 7.19 | 7.23 | 7.25 |
| 8 | 8.00 | 8.16 | 8.24 | 8.30 | 8.33 |
| 9 | 9.00 | 9.20 | 9.31 | 9.38 | 9.42 |
| 10 | 10.00 | 10.25 | 10.38 | 10.47 | 10.52 |
| 11 | 11.00 | 11.30 | 11.46 | 11.57 | 11.62 |
| 12 | 12.00 | 12.36 | 12.55 | 12.68 | 12.74 |

**certificate of deposit (CD)** A type of savings instrument issued by certain financial institutions in exchange for a deposit; typically requires a minimum deposit and has a maturity ranging from 7 days to as long as 7 or more years.

of interest. For example, using the future value formula and the future value factor from Appendix A (see Chapter 2), you can find out how much $1,000 will be worth in 4 years if it's deposited into a savings account that pays 5% interest, compounded annually:

**Future value = Amount deposited × Future value factor**
= **$1,000 × 1.216**
= **$1,216**

**CALCULATOR**

| Inputs | Functions |
|---|---|
| 1000 | PV |
| 4 | N |
| 5 | I |
| | CPT |
| | FV |
| | *Solution* |
| | 1,215.51 |

SEE APPENDIX E FOR DETAILS.

You can use the same basic procedure to find the future value of an *annuity,* except you'd use the future value annuity factor from Appendix B (see Chapter 2). For instance, if you put $1,000 a year into a savings account that pays 5% per year compounded annually, in 4 years you will have:

**Future value = Amount deposited yearly
× Future value annuity factor**
= **$1,000 × 4.310**
= **$4,310**

### Go to Smart Sites

If you're not satisfied with the CD rate at your local bank, go to Bankrate.com. There you'll find not only the highest rates on CDs nationwide but also the checking and savings account fees at banks in your city. ●

## A Variety of Ways to Save

During the past decade or so there has been a huge growth of savings and short-term investment vehicles, particularly for people of modest means. Today, investors can choose from savings accounts, money market deposit accounts, money market mutual funds, NOW accounts, certificates of deposit, U.S. Treasury bills, Series EE bonds, Series I Savings bonds, and asset management accounts. We examined several of these savings vehicles earlier in this chapter. Let's now look at the four remaining types of deposits and securities.

### Certificates of Deposit

**Certificates of deposit (CDs)** differ from the savings instruments discussed earlier in that CD funds (except for CDs purchased through brokerage firms) must remain on deposit for a specified period (from 7 days to as long as 7 or more years). Although it's possible to withdraw funds prior to maturity, an interest penalty usually makes withdrawal somewhat costly. The bank or other depository institution is free to charge whatever penalty it likes, but most require you to forfeit some interest. Banks, S&Ls, and other depository institutions can offer any rate and maturity CD they wish. As a result, a wide variety of CDs are offered by most banks, depository institutions, and other financial institutions such as brokerage firms. Most pay higher rates for larger deposits and longer periods of time. CDs are convenient to buy and hold because they offer attractive and highly competitive yields, plus federal deposit insurance protection.

### Go to Smart Sites

At the T-bill page of Treasury Direct's Web site, you can learn about T-bills and then buy them online. ●

### U.S. Treasury Bills

The **U.S. Treasury bill (T-bill)** is considered the ultimate safe haven for savings and investments. T-bills are issued by the U.S. Treasury as part of its ongoing process of funding the national debt. They are sold on a discount basis in minimum denominations of $1,000 and are issued with 1-month (4-week), 3-month (13-week), 6-month (26-week), or 1-year (52-week) maturities. The bills are auctioned off every Monday. Backed by the full faith and credit of the U.S. government, T-bills pay an attractive and safe return that is free from state and local income taxes.

T-bills are almost as liquid as cash because they can be sold at any time (in a very active secondary market) with no interest penalty. However, should you have to sell before maturity, you may lose some money on your investment if interest rates have risen, and you'll have to pay a broker's fee. Treasury bills pay interest on a *discount basis* and thus are different from other savings or short-term investment vehicles—that is, their interest is equal to the difference between the purchase price paid and their stated value at maturity. For example, if you paid $980 for a bill that will be worth $1,000 at maturity, you'll earn $20 in interest ($1,000 − $980).

An individual investor may purchase T-bills directly by participating in the weekly Treasury auctions or indirectly through a commercial bank or a securities dealer who buys bills for investors on a commission basis. T-bills may now be purchased over the Internet (www.treasurydirect.gov) or by using a touch-tone phone (call 800-722-2678 and follow the interactive menu to complete transactions).

### Series EE Bonds
Although they are issued by the U.S. Treasury on a discount basis and are free of state and local

**U.S. Treasury bill (T-bill)** A short-term (3-, 6-, or 12-month maturity) debt instrument issued at a discount by the U.S. Treasury in the ongoing process of funding the national debt.

©JOHN CLARK/SHUTTERSTOCK

income taxes, **Series EE bonds** are quite different from T-bills. Savings bonds are *accrual-type securities,* which means that interest is paid when they're cashed in or before maturity, rather than periodically during their lives. Also known as "Patriot Bonds," in honor of September 11, 2001—Series EE bonds are backed by the full faith and credit of the U.S. government and can be replaced without charge in case of loss, theft, or destruction. You can purchase them at banks or other depository institutions, or through payroll deduction plans. Issued in denominations from $50 through $10,000, their purchase price is a uniform 50% of the face amount (thus a $100 bond will cost $50 and be worth $100 at maturity).

Series EE savings bonds earn interest at a fixed rate for 30 years. Their long life lets investors use them for truly long-term goals like education and retirement. The higher the rate of interest being paid, the shorter the time it takes for the bond to accrue from its discounted purchase price to its maturity value. Bonds can be redeemed any time after the first 12 months, although redeeming EE bonds in less than 5 years results in a penalty of the last 3 months of interest earned. The interest rate is set every 6 months in May and November and changes with prevailing Treasury security market yields. EE bonds increase in value every month and the stipulated interest rate is compounded semiannually.

In addition to being exempt from state and local taxes, Series EE bonds give their holders an appealing tax twist: *Savers need not report interest earned on their federal tax returns until the bonds are redeemed.* A second attractive tax feature—available to qualified bond holders—allows partial or complete tax avoidance of EE bond earnings when proceeds are used to pay education expenses, such as college tuition, for the bond purchaser, a spouse, or another IRS-defined dependent.

## I Savings Bonds

**I savings bonds** are similar to Series EE bonds in several ways. For starters, both are issued by the U.S. Treasury, they're both accrual-type securities, and interest on both of them compounds semi-annually over a 30-year period. And like Series EE bonds, I savings bonds' interest remains exempt from state and local income taxes but does face state and local estate, inheritance, gift, and other

©MOSHIMOCHI/SHUTTERSTOCK

excise taxes. In addition, interest earnings are subject to federal income tax but may be excluded when used to finance education, with some limitations.

There are some major differences between the two savings vehicles, however. For one, I bonds are available in smaller denominations (between $25 and $5,000), and while Series EE bonds are sold at a discount, I bonds are sold at face value. I savings bonds also differ from Series EE bonds in that their annual interest rate combines a fixed rate that remains the same for the life of the bond with a semi-annual inflation rate that changes with the Consumer Price Index for all Urban Consumers (CPI-U). In contrast, the rate on Series EE bonds is based on the 6-month averages of 5-year Treasury security market yields. Thus, *the key difference between Series EE bonds and I bonds is that I bond returns are adjusted for inflation.* Note in particular that the earnings rate cannot go below zero and that the value of I bonds cannot drop below their redemption value.

# FINANCIAL PLANNING EXERCISES

**LG3**

1. Suppose that someone stole your ATM card and withdrew $650 from your checking account. How much money could you lose (according to federal legislation) if you reported the stolen card to the bank: (a) the day the card was stolen, (b) 6 days after the theft, (c) 75 days after receiving your periodic statement?

**LG2, 3, 4**

2. You're getting married and are unhappy with your present bank. Discuss your strategy for choosing a new bank and opening an account. Consider the factors that are important to you in selecting a bank—such as the type and ownership of new accounts and bank fees and charges.

**LG4**

3. Determine the annual net cost of these checking accounts:
   a. Monthly fee $5, check-processing fee of 25 cents, average of 19 checks written per month
   b. Annual interest of 2.5% paid if balance exceeds $750, $8 monthly fee if account falls below minimum balance, average monthly balance $815, account falls below $750 during 4 months

**LG5, 6**

4. If you put $5,000 in a savings account that pays interest at the rate of 4%, compounded annually, how much will you have in 5 years? (*Hint:* Use the *future value* formula.) How much interest will you earn during the 5 years? If you put $5,000 *each* year into a savings account that pays interest at the rate of 4% a year, how much would you have after 5 years?

**LG6**

5. Describe some of the short-term investment vehicles that can be used to manage your cash resources. What factors would you focus on if you were concerned that the 2009 financial crisis will lead to a significant increase in inflation?

# 5

# MAKING AUTOMOBILE AND HOUSING DECISIONS

## LEARNING GOALS

**LG1** Implement a plan to research and select a new or used automobile. (p. 93)

**LG2** Decide whether to buy or lease a car. (p. 98)

**LG3** Identify housing alternatives, assess the rental option, and perform a rent-or-buy analysis. (p. 101)

**LG4** Evaluate the benefits and costs of homeownership and estimate how much you can afford for a home. (p. 104)

**LG5** Describe the home-buying process. (p. 110)

**LG6** Choose mortgage financing that meets your needs. (p. 113)

## LG1 Buying an Automobile

Buying an automobile is probably the first major expenditure many of us make. The car purchase is second only to housing in the amount of money the typical consumer spends. Because you'll buy a car many times during your life—most people buy one every 2 to 5 years—a systematic approach to selecting and financing a vehicle can mean significant savings. Before making any major purchase—whether it's a car, house, or large appliance—consider some basic guidelines to wise purchasing decisions.

- *Research* your purchase thoroughly, considering not only the market but also your personal needs.

- *Select* the best item for your needs.

- *Buy* the item after negotiating the best price and arranging financing on favorable terms. Be sure you understand all the terms of the sale before signing any contracts.

- *Maintain* your purchase and make necessary repairs promptly.

Exhibit 5.1 summarizes the steps in the new car-buying process.

## Choosing a Car

Hybrid, diesel, or gas? Sport utility vehicle (SUV) or pickup truck? Sedan, convertible, or coupe? Car buyers today have more choices than ever before, so being an informed buyer is more important than ever. A good place to start your research is by tapping into the many available sources of information about cars, their prices, features, and reliability. Industry resources include

---

### Exhibit 5.1  10 Steps to Buying a New Car

These 10 steps summarize the car-buying process discussed in this chapter.

1. Research which car best meets your needs and determine how much you can afford to spend on it. Choose the best way to pay for your new car—cash, financing, or lease. Consult your insurance agent to learn the annual premium on various cars.

2. Check Web sites like Edmunds.com and TV and newspapers for incentives and rebates on the car you would like to buy. This could include a cash rebate or low-cost financing.

3. Decide on a price based on dealer's cost for the car and options, plus a markup for the dealer's profit, minus rebates and incentives.

4. Find the exact car for you in terms of size, performance, safety, and styling. Choose at least three "target cars" to consider buying. Get online quotes from multiple car dealers.

5. Test-drive the car—and the car salesman. Test-drive the car at least once, both on local streets and on highways. Determine if the car salesman is someone you want to do business with. Is he relaxed, open, and responsive to your questions?

6. If you are trading in your old car, you will not likely get as high a price as if you sold it yourself. Look up your car's trade-in value at Edmunds.com or kbb.com. Solicit bids from several dealers.

7. Negotiate the lowest price by getting bids from at least three dealers. Hold firm on your target price before closing the deal.

8. Close the deal after looking not just at the cost of the car but also the related expenses. Consider the sales tax and various fees. Get the saleperson to fax you a worksheet and invoice before you go to the dealership.

9. Review and sign the paperwork. If you have a worksheet for the deal, the contract should match it. Make sure the numbers match and there are no additional charges or fees.

10. Inspect the car for scratches and dents. If anything is missing—like floor mats, for example—ask for a "Due Bill" that states it in writing.

*Source:* Adapted from Philip Read, "10 Steps to Buying a New Car," http://www.edmunds.com/advice/buying, accessed May 2009.

©ANDREY ARMYAGOV/SHUTTERSTOCK

# MONEY IN ACTION

## Online Ways to Save Money When Buying a New Car

### Determining a Fair Price

You need the invoice price for the vehicle you're interested in to determine its fair price. There are two excellent places to get invoice prices online. The site **www.fightingchance.com** sells a package for $39.95 that includes invoice pricing information and data on current dealer inventories and special deals. Seem a bit pricey? Not if the information saves you several thousand dollars!

### Using the Competition to Get the Best Price

After you estimate a fair price for the vehicle, get several free quotes online. The following Web sites allow you to submit a free quote request: **http://www.invoicedealers.com, http://www.carbuyingtips.com, http://www.autos.yahoo.com/newcars, http://www.autos.com, http://www.edmunds.com, http://www.myride.com,** and **http://www.carsdirect.com**. When contacted, tell the dealer that you only want the best price on the car now and that you will deal with financing later.

### Getting Financing

In order to get the best financing rate, you should know your credit score before you shop. Your credit score can be obtained from **http://www.freecreditreport.com, http://www.equifax.com,** or **http://www.truecredit.com**. It will be used to determine the interest rate on your new car loan.

### Determining a Realistic Trade-in Value

The Kelley Blue Book Web site, **http://www.kbb.com**, allows you to estimate the trade-in and private resale value of your old car. Trading in your old car is easier but generally does not generate as much as when you sell it on your own. *Remember that the taxable amount of your new car purchase is reduced by the trade-in value of your old car, which reduces your sales tax.*

### Negotiating the Final Purchase Price

Compare all of your price quotes. Contact each of the other dealers and ask if they can beat the lowest quote. Contact the dealer with the lowest price and close the deal. Then negotiate the trade-in value of your old car if you aren't selling it on your own. You should negotiate your financing only after you have agreed on a fair trade-in value or have decided to sell your old car yourself.

*Source:* Adapted from http://www.carbuyingtips.com/buyingnewcar.htm, accessed May 2009. Reprinted with permission.

---

manufacturers' brochures and dealer personnel. Car magazines, such as *Car and Driver, Motor Trend,* and *Road and Track,* and consumer magazines, such as *Consumer Reports* and *Consumer Guide,* regularly compare and rate cars. In addition, *Consumer Reports* and *Kiplinger's Personal Finance* magazine publish annual buying guides that include comparative statistics and ratings on most domestic and foreign cars.

The Internet has made it especially easy to do your homework before ever setting foot in a dealer's showroom. It's so easy today to visit one of the many

> { *The Internet has made it especially easy to do your homework before ever setting foot in a dealer's showroom.* }

comprehensive Web sites for car shoppers, where you'll find pricing and model information, as well as links to other useful sites. Don't forget the Web sites of the automobile companies themselves; for example, Ford Motor Company is online at **http://www.ford.com,** Toyota is at **http://www.toyota.com,** and so on. This chapter's *Money in Action* box feature explores the online world of car buying.

 **Go to Smart Sites**

With Edmunds.com's auto loan calculators, you can evaluate auto financing options and check rates to find the lowest auto loan rates in your area. Whenever you see "*Go to Smart Sites*" in this chapter, visit 4ltrpress.cengage.com for help finding answers online. ●

## Affordability

Before shopping for a car, determine how much you can afford to spend. You'll need to calculate two numbers—unless you plan to pay cash for the entire cost of the car.

● **Amount of down payment:** This money will likely come from savings, so be sure not to deplete your emergency fund.

● **Size of the monthly loan payment you can afford:** Carefully consider the amount of money you have available and the amount you can afford to spend, along with your basic transportation needs. Don't forget to include insurance. And remember: your monthly car payment should be no more than 20% of your monthly net income.

## Crunching the Numbers

You can also use the down payment and monthly payment amounts to calculate the total amount you can afford for a car. For example, suppose you have $3,000 for a down payment, you can pay $500 a month, and your bank is offering 4-year (48-month) car loans at 6% annual (6%/12 = 0.5%, monthly) interest. How much of a loan can you afford? Using a financial calculator and the keystrokes shown in the margin, you'll find that you can take out a loan of about $21,300. Add that to the $3,000 down payment, and you'll be able to afford a car costing $24,300.

### CALCULATOR

| Inputs | Functions |
|--------|-----------|
| 48 | N |
| .5 | I |
| 500 | PMT |
| | CPT |
| | PV |
| | *Solution* |
| | 21,290.16 |

SEE APPENDIX E FOR DETAILS.

### Operating Costs

The out-of-pocket cost of operating an automobile includes not only car payments but also insurance, license, fuel, oil, tires, and other operating and maintenance outlays. Some of these costs are *fixed* regardless of how much you drive; others are *variable*, depending on the number of miles you drive. The biggest fixed cost is likely to be the *installment payments* associated with the loan (or lease) used to acquire the car; the biggest variable cost will probably be fuel.

Another significant cost is **depreciation**, which is the loss in value that occurs over the period of ownership. In effect, depreciation is the difference between the price you paid for the car and what you can sell it for. If you paid $20,000 for an automobile that can be sold 3 years later for $14,000, the car will cost you $6,000 in depreciation. Although depreciation may not be a recurring out-of-pocket cost, it's an important operating expense that shouldn't be overlooked.

### Gas, Diesel, or Hybrid?

One thing that's becoming increasingly important in car buying is the type of fuel you prefer to use in your car. If you're a "green" who's concerned about the environmental impact of the fuel your car uses, you may be interested

©MICHAEL SHAKE/SHUTTERSTOCK

only in a hybrid car. In this case, price differences may not matter. Although you'll want to consider fuel economy when car shopping, comparable gas-fueled, internal combustion engines and diesel-powered cars tend to have similar fuel economy. Generally, diesels are a bit noisier, have less acceleration but more power, and have longer engine lives than do traditional gas-powered cars.

*Hybrids*, which blend gas and battery power, have experienced rapid sales growth due to high gas prices, improved technology and availability, and greater public awareness of environmental issues. Although they're more economical and less polluting than gas- and diesel-powered vehicles, hybrids do have some disadvantages: high cost of battery replacement, more sluggish acceleration, generally higher repair costs, and typically higher initial purchase price. It's important to consider the differences between the costs and performance of differently fueled vehicles and decide on the vehicle you want before shopping for a specific new or used car.

### New, Used, or "Nearly New"?

One decision you must make is whether to buy a new, used, or "nearly new" car. If you can't afford to buy a new car, the decision is made for you. Some people who can afford to buy a new car choose to buy a used car so they can have a better model—a used luxury car such as a BMW, Lexus, or Mercedes—rather than a less-expensive brand of new car, such as a Ford. With the increasing popularity of used cars, car dealers are trying to dispel the negative image associated with buying a used, or "pre-owned," car. See the Bonus Exhibit, "Buying a Used Car: Getting a Lemon or Lemonade?" at 4ltrpress.cengage.com for some sound advice.

Once you know what you want, shop at these places.

- **Franchise dealerships:** Offer the latest-model used cars, provide financing, and will negotiate on price.

- **Superstores:** AutoNation, CarMax, and similar dealers offer no-haggle pricing and a large selection. They certify their cars and may offer a limited short-term warranty.

- **Independent used car lots:** Usually offer older (4 to 6 year old) cars and have lower overhead than franchise dealers. No industry standards, so be sure to check with the Better Business Bureau before buying.

**depreciation** The loss in the value of an asset such as an automobile that occurs over its period of ownership; calculated as the difference between the price initially paid and the subsequent sale price.

- **Private individuals:** Generally cost less because there's no dealer overhead; may have maintenance records. Be sure seller has title to car.

### Size, Body Style, and Features

Your first consideration should be what type of car you need. More than one style category may work for you. For example, a family of five can buy a mid-size or full-size sedan, station wagon, minivan, or compact or full-size SUV. When considering size, body style, and features, think about your needs, likes, and dislikes as well as the cost. In most cases there's a direct relationship between size and cost: In general, the larger the car, the more expensive it will be to purchase and to operate. Also consider performance, handling, appearance, fuel economy, reliability, repair problems, and the resale value of the car. And don't try to adapt your needs to fit the car you want—a two-passenger sports car may not be appropriate if you need the car for business or if you have children.

By listing all of the options you want before shopping for a new car, you can avoid paying for features you really don't need. Literally hundreds of options, ranging in price from a few dollars up to $2,000 or more, are available, including automatic transmission, a bigger engine, air conditioning, high-performance brakes, a CD or iPod/MP3 player, clock, power windows, power seats, electric door locks, leather seats, navigation systems, a rear window defroster, and special suspension. Some appearance-related options are two-tone or metallic paint, electric sunroof, special tires, sport wheels, and various interior and exterior trim packages. On new cars, window stickers detail each option and its price; in contrast, you're usually on your own with used cars.

### Other Considerations

Here are some other considerations regarding affordability:

- **Trading in or selling your existing car:** Although trading in is convenient, it's generally more financially advantageous to sell your old car outright. If you're willing to take the time, you can usually sell your car for more than the wholesale price typically offered by a dealer on a trade-in.

- **Fuel economy:** The *Environmental Protection Agency (EPA) mileage ratings* are especially useful on new vehicles, which carry a sticker indicating the number of miles per gallon each model is expected to get for both city and highway driving.

- **Safety features:** Government regulations ensure that these features are likely to be similar in new cars, but older used cars may not have some features such as side-impact airbags. And don't forget to include the cost of *auto insurance*.

## The Purchase Transaction

Once you've determined what you can afford to spend and the features you desire, you're ready to begin car shopping. If you plan to buy a new car, visit all dealers with cars that meet your requirements. Look the cars over and ask questions—but don't make any offers until you've found two or three cars with the desired features that are priced within your budget. Also, if you can be flexible about the model and options you want, you can sometimes negotiate a better deal than if you're determined to have a particular model and options. Be sure to do some comparison shopping, because a dealer selling the same brand as another may give you a better deal. And watch out for something called *lowballing,* where the salesperson quotes a low price to get you to make an offer, and then negotiates the price upward prior to your signing the sales contract. Exhibit 5.2 lists some other factors to consider once you begin looking at cars.

### Negotiating Price

Choosing among various makes, models, and options can make comparisons difficult. The price you pay for a car, whether new or used, can consequently vary widely. The more you narrow your choices to a particular car, the easier it is to get price quotes from dealers to make an "apples to apples" comparison.

The "sticker price" on a new car represents the manufacturer's *suggested retail price* for that particular car with its listed options. This price means very little. The key to negotiating a good price is knowing the *dealer's cost* for the car. The easiest and quickest way to find the dealer's invoice cost is going to the Edmunds (http://www.edmunds.com) or Kelley Blue

©JOHN DE BORD/SHUTTERSTOCK

## Exhibit 5.2 Finding the Best Car for You

**Start your examination of a car with an inspection of key points.** Don't overlook the obvious:

- *How easy is it to get people and things into and out of the car?*
  Do the doors open easily?
  Is the trunk large enough for your needs?
  Does the car offer a pass-through or fold-down rear seat for larger items?

- Comfort and visibility:
  Are the seats comfortable?
  Can you adjust the driver's seat and steering wheel properly?
  What are the car's blind spots for a person of your height?
  Can you see all the gauges clearly?
  Can you reach the controls for the radio, CD player, heater, air conditioner, and other features easily while driving?
  Does it have the options you want?

**Then take the car for a test drive.**

- Set aside at least 20 minutes and drive it on highways and local roads.

- To test acceleration, merge into traffic getting onto the freeway and try passing another car.

- If possible, drive home and make sure the car fits into your garage—especially if you're interested in a larger SUV or truck!

- For a used car, test the heater and air conditioner. Then turn the fan off and listen for any unusual engine noises.

- Check out overall handling. Parallel park, make a U-turn, brake hard, and so on. Do the gears shift smoothly? If testing a standard transmission, try to determine if the clutch is engaging too high or too low, which might indicate excessive wear or a problem.

**As soon as you return to the car lot, take notes on how well the car handled and how comfortable you felt driving it.** This is especially important if you are testing several cars.

---

Book (http://www.kbb.com) Web sites. Try to negotiate the lowest acceptable markup above dealer invoice (3% to 4% for cars priced under $20,000; 6% to 7% for higher-priced models), then push for a firm quote, and make it clear that you are comparison shopping.

If you want to avoid negotiating entirely, you can buy your car through a buying service, either by phone or over the Internet. These include independent companies—such as AutoVantage, Autobytel, AutoWeb, and Nationwide Auto Brokers—or services offered through credit unions, motor clubs, and discount warehouses such as Costco. Buying services work in a variety of ways. They may have an arrangement with a network of dealers to sell cars at a predetermined price above invoice, provide you with competitive bids from several local dealers, find the car you want and negotiate the price with the dealer, or place an order with the factory for a made-to-order car. The price for these services ranges from about $50 for a Costco membership to as much as $600, and results vary. You'll get a good price through a service—although you can't assume that it will be the best price.

It's best not to discuss your plan to finance the purchase or the value of your trade-in until you've settled the question of price. These should be separate issues. Salespeople will typically want to find out how much you can afford monthly and then offer financing deals with payments close to that amount. In the case of trade-ins, the dealer might offer you a good price for your old car and raise the price of the new car to compensate. The dealer may offer financing terms that sound attractive, but be sure to compare them with the cost of bank loans. Sometimes dealers increase the price of the car to make up for a low interest rate, or attractive financing may apply only to certain models. If you're interested in dealer financing, make sure the monthly payment quoted by the dealer's finance manager is just for the loan. Often financing charges include unneeded extras such as credit life insurance, accident insurance, an extended warranty, or a service package.

Manufacturers and dealers often offer buyers special incentives, such as rebates and cut-rate financing, particularly when car sales are slow. In some cases, you may have a choice between a rebate and low-cost financing. To determine which is the better deal, calculate the difference between the monthly payments on a market-rate bank loan and the special dealer loan for the same term.

Multiply the payment difference by the loan maturity, in months, and compare it with the rebate. For example, assume the dealer offers either a $1,000 rebate or a 4% interest rate on a $10,000, 4-year loan. Your monthly payments would be $226 with dealer financing and $244 on a 8% bank loan with similar terms. The payment savings over the life of the loan are $864 ($18 per month × 48 months), which is less than the $1,000 rebate. So in this case you would be better off with the rebate.

### Closing the Deal

Whether you're buying a new or used car, to make a legally binding offer you must sign a **sales contract** that specifies the offering price and all the conditions of your offer. The sales contract also specifies whether the offer includes a trade-in. If it does, the offering price will include both the payment amount and the trade-in allowance. Because this agreement contractually binds you to purchase the car at the offering price, be sure that you want and can afford the car before signing the agreement. You may be required to include a deposit of around $200 or more with the contract to show that you're making an offer in good faith.

Once the dealer accepts your offer, you complete the purchase transaction and take delivery of the car. If you're not paying cash for the car, you can arrange financing through the dealer, at your bank, a credit union, or a consumer finance company. The key aspects of these types of installment loans, which can be quickly negotiated if your credit is good, are discussed in Chapter 7.

### LG2 Leasing a Car

Don't worry about temperamental engines or transmissions—just get a new car every few years using a leasing arrangement. Put a small amount down, make easy payments. No wonder leasing is popular, accounting for nearly 20% of all new vehicles delivered. When

you **lease**, you (the lessee) receive the use of a car in exchange for monthly lease payments over a specified period of time, usually 2 to 4 years. Leasing appeals to a wide range of car owners, even though the total cost of leasing is generally more than buying a car with a loan, and at the end of the lease you have nothing. The car—and the money you paid to rent it—is gone. So why do so many car buyers lease their cars? Reasons include rising new car prices, the nondeductibility of consumer loan interest, lower monthly payments, driving a more expensive car for the same monthly payment, and minimizing the down payment to preserve cash.

With all the advertisements promising low monthly lease payments, it's easy to focus on only the payment. Unlike a loan purchase, with a lease you're paying not for the whole car but only for its use during a specified period. Leasing is a more complex arrangement than borrowing money to buy a car. Until you understand how leasing works, and compare lease terms with bank financing, you won't know if leasing is the right choice for you.

## The Leasing Process

The first step is the same for leasing as it is for purchasing: research car types and brands, comparison shop at several dealers, and find the car you want at the best price. Don't ask the dealer about leasing or any financing incentives until *after* you've negotiated the final price. Then compare the lease terms offered by the dealer to those of at least one independent leasing firm. As with a purchase, try to negotiate lower lease payments—a payment reduction of $20 a month saves nearly $1,000 on a 4-year lease. And don't reveal what you can afford to pay per month; doing so can lead you to a poor lease deal.

The vast majority of car lessees choose the **closed-end lease**, often called the *walk-away lease*, because at the end of its term you simply turn in the car and walk away, assuming that you have neither exceeded the preset mileage limit nor abused the car. Under the less popular **open-end (or finance) lease**, if the car is worth less than the estimated **residual value**—the remaining value of the car at the end of the lease term—then you must pay the difference. These leases are used primarily for commercial business leasing.

A commonly cited benefit of leasing is the absence of a down payment. However, today most leases require a "capital cost reduction," which is a type of down payment that lowers the potential depreciation and therefore your monthly lease payments.

Given the one-time, up-front capital cost reduction payment, the size of the monthly lease payment is based on four variables:

1. The **capitalized cost** of the car (the price of the car you are leasing)

2. The forecast *residual value* of the car at the end of the lease
3. The **money factor,** or financing rate on the lease (similar to the interest rate on a loan)
4. The *lease term*

Terminating a lease early is often difficult and costly, so be reasonably certain that you can keep the car for the full lease term. The lease contract should outline any costs and additional fees associated with early termination. Early termination clauses also apply to cars that are stolen or totaled in an accident. Some leases require "gap insurance" to cover the lost lease payments that would result from early termination caused by one of these events.

Under most leases, you are responsible for insuring and maintaining the car. Also, be aware that at the end of the lease, you are obligated to pay for any "unreasonable wear and tear." A good lease contract should clearly define what is considered unreasonable. In addition, most leases require the lessee to pay a disposition fee of about $150 to $250 when the car is returned.

The annual mileage allowance—typically, about 10,000 to 15,000 miles per year for the lease term—is another important lease consideration. Usually the lessee must pay between 10 and 25 cents per mile for any miles over the limit. For example, if the lease allows 15,000 miles per year, and you put 50,000 miles on a car over the three year term of the lease, you'd exceed the limit by 5,000 miles (3 × 15,000 = 45,000 < 50,000) and at 20 cents per mile, be liable for .20 × 5,000 = $1,000. Clearly, if you expect to exceed the allowable mileage, you would be wise to negotiate a more favorable rate for extra miles before signing the lease contract.

Most auto leases include a **purchase option** (either a fixed price, the market price at the end of the lease term, or the residual value of the car) that specifies the price at which the lessee can buy the car at the end of the lease term. A lower residual results in a lower purchase price but raises monthly payments.

## The Lease versus Purchase Analysis

To decide whether it is less costly to lease rather than purchase a car, you need to perform a *lease versus purchase analysis* to compare the total cost of leasing to the total cost of purchasing a car over equal periods. In

©SHELLYAGAMI-PHOTOAR/SHUTTERSTOCK

this analysis, the purchase is assumed to be financed with an installment loan over the same period as the lease.

For example, assume that Elaine Hodges is considering either leasing or purchasing a new Toyota Prius costing $22,000. The 4-year, closed-end lease she is considering requires a $2,200 down payment (capital cost reduction), a $500 security deposit, and monthly payments of $350, including sales tax. If she purchases the car, she will make a $3,500 down payment and finance the balance with a 4-year, 7% loan requiring monthly payments of $443. She will also have to pay 5% sales tax ($1,100) on the purchase, and she expects the car to have a residual value of $12,100 at the end of 4 years. After filling in Worksheet 5.1, Elaine concludes that purchasing is better because its *total cost* of $14,324 is $5,108 less than the $19,432 total cost of leasing—even though the monthly lease payment is $93 lower. Clearly, all else being equal, the least costly alternative is preferred.

## When the Lease Ends

At the end of the lease, you'll be faced with a major decision. Should you return the car and walk away, or should you buy the car? If you turn in the car and move on to a new model,

**money factor** The financing rate on a lease; similar to the interest rate on a loan.

**purchase option** A price specified in a lease at which the lessee can buy the car at the end of the lease term.

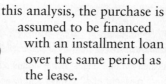

### FINANCIAL ROAD SIGN

**SHOULD YOU BUY OR LEASE YOUR NEXT CAR?**
Leasing is tempting: little or no money up front and lower monthly payments. But when the lease ends, you need to get another car. It's more expensive initially to buy, but at the end of the loan period you own the car. Here are the key factors to consider:

**ADVANTAGES OF LEASING**
• Better car for less money
• A new car every few years
• No trade-in hassles at the end of the lease

**ADVANTAGES OF BUYING**
• When interest rates are low, owning makes more financial sense than leasing
• No mileage penalty
• Increased flexibility—you can sell the car whenever you want

This worksheet illustrates Elaine Hodges' lease versus purchase analysis for a new Toyota Prius costing $22,000. The 4-year closed-end lease requires an initial payment of $2,700 ($2,200 down payment + $500 security deposit) and monthly payments of $350. Purchasing requires a $3,500 down payment, sales tax of 5% ($1,100), and 48 monthly payments of $443. The trade-in value of the new car at the end of 4 years is estimated to be $12,100. *Because the total cost of leasing of $19,432 is greater than the $14,324 total cost of purchasing, Elaine should purchase rather than lease the car.*

## AUTOMOBILE LEASE VERSUS PURCHASE ANALYSIS*

Name  Elaine Hodges                               Date  April: 7, 2011

| Item Description | | Amount |
|---|---|---|
| **LEASE** | | |
| 1 | Initial payment: | |
| | a. Down payment (capital cost reduction): | $ 2,200.00 |
| | b. Security deposit: | 500.00   $ 2,700.00 |
| 2 | Term of lease and loan (years)* | 4 |
| 3 | Term of lease and loan (months) (Item 2 × 12) | 48 |
| 4 | Monthly lease payment | $ 350.00 |
| 5 | Total payments over term of lease (Item 3 × Item 4) | $ 16,800.00 |
| 6 | Interest rate earned on savings (in decimal form) | 0.040 |
| 7 | Opportunity cost of initial payment (Item 1 × Item 2 × Item 6) | $ 432.00 |
| 8 | Payment/refund for market value adjustment at end of lease ($0 for closed-end leases) and/or estimated end-of-term charges | $ 0.00 |
| **9** | **Total cost of leasing (Item 1a + Item 5 + Item 7 + Item 8)** | $ 19,432.00 |
| **PURCHASE** | | |
| 10 | Purchase price | $ 22,000.00 |
| 11 | Down payment | $ 3,500.00 |
| 12 | Sales tax rate (in decimal form) | 0.050 |
| 13 | Sales tax (Item 10 × Item 12) | $ 1,100.00 |
| 14 | Monthly loan payment (Terms: _18,500.00_, _48_ months, _7_ %) | $ 443.01 |
| 15 | Total payments over term of loan (Item 3 × Item 14) | $ 21,264.27 |
| 16 | Opportunity cost of down payment (Item 2 × Item 6 × Item 11) | $ 560.00 |
| 17 | Estimated value of car at end of loan | $ 12,100.00 |
| **18** | **Total cost of purchasing (Item 11 + Item 13 + Item 15 + Item 16 − Item 17)** | $ 14,324.27 |

## DECISION

If the value of Item 9 is less than the value of Item 18, leasing is preferred; otherwise the *purchase alternative is preferred.*

*Note: This form is based on assumed equal terms (periods) for a lease and for an installment loan to finance the purchase.

you may be hit with "excess wear and damage" and "excess mileage" charges and disposition fees. If you can't return the car without high repair charges or greatly exceeded mileage allowances, you may come out ahead by buying the car. Whether the purchase option makes sense depends on the residual value. Sometimes, with popular cars, the residual value in your lease agreement is below the car's trade-in value. Buying the car then makes sense. Even if you want a different car, you can exercise the purchase option and sell the car on the open market and net the difference, which could be $1,000 or more. If the reverse is true, and the residual is higher than the price of a comparable used car, just let the lease expire.

## LG3 Meeting Housing Needs: Buy or Rent?

Knowing when to buy your first home is not always clear-cut. There are many factors to consider before taking on such a large financial responsibility. In the remainder of this chapter, we'll explore some of these factors and discuss how to approach the home-buying process.

Because you have your own unique set of likes and dislikes, the best way to start your search for housing is to list your preferences and classify them according to whether their satisfaction is essential, desirable, or merely a "plus." This exercise is important for three reasons. First, it screens out housing that doesn't meet your minimum requirements. Second, it helps you recognize that you may have to make trade-offs because seldom will you find a single home that meets all your needs. Third, it will help you focus on those needs for which you are willing and able to pay.

From early 2001 through 2006, home prices in the United States rose rapidly. The median nominal sales price of existing single-family homes rose from $141,437 to $245,842. In the third quarter of 2006, existing home prices started dropping and fell to a median price of $180,100 by the end of 2008. As of the first quarter of 2009, U.S. home prices had dropped for nine consecutive quarters and had fallen an average of about 22% since the market peak in 2006. Prices had fallen because the real estate bubble had popped and the finanical crisis of 2008-09 had vastly depressed home sales. This period of recession was characterized by high unemployment, low consumer confidence, and tighter credit. Indeed, about 1 in 7 American homeowners had *negative equity* in their homes, meaning they owed more on their mortgage than their homes were worth.

## What Type of Housing Meets Your Needs?

Homeownership in America has always been viewed as a highly desirable financial objective—which explains in part why we have such a high ownership rate in this country. Indeed, in early 2009, the homeownership rate in the United States was nearly 70%. As a potential homeowner, one of the first decisions you'll have to make is the type of housing unit that meets your needs. Several of the following may be suitable.

- **Single-family homes:** These are the most popular choice. They can be stand-alone homes on their own legally defined lots or *row houses* or *townhouses* that share a common wall. As a rule, single-family homes offer buyers privacy, prestige, pride of ownership, and maximum property control.

- **Condominiums:** The term **condominium**, or **condo,** describes a form of ownership rather than a type of building. Condominiums can be apartments, townhouses, or cluster housing. The condominium buyer receives title to an individual residential unit and joint ownership of common areas and facilities such as lobbies, swimming pools, lakes, and tennis courts. Buyers arrange their own mortgages and pay their own taxes for their units. They are assessed a monthly *homeowner's fee* for their proportionate share of common facility maintenance costs. Many home buyers are attracted to condominiums because they don't want the responsibility of maintaining and caring for a large property. The bonus exhibit, "Condo Buyer's Checklist," at 4ltrpress.cengage .com, lists some of the key things to check before buying a condominium.

- **Cooperative apartments:** In a **cooperative apartment**, or **co-op,** building, each tenant owns a share of the nonprofit corporation that owns the building. Residents lease their units from the corporation and pay a monthly assessment in proportion to ownership shares, based on the space they occupy. These assessments cover the cost of services, maintenance, taxes, and the mortgage on the entire building and are subject to change, depending on the actual costs of operating the building and the actions of the board of directors, which determines the corporation's policies.

**condominium (condo)** A form of direct ownership of an individual unit in a multiunit project in which lobbies, swimming pools, and other common areas and facilities are jointly owned by all property owners in the project.

**cooperative apartment (co-op)** An apartment in a building in which each tenant owns a share of the nonprofit corporation that owns the building.

- **Rental units:** Some individuals and families choose to *rent* or *lease* their place of residence rather than own it. They may be just starting out and have limited funds for housing, they may be uncertain as to where they want to live, or they just may prefer renting. Rental units range from duplexes, fourplexes, and even single-family homes to large, high-rise apartment complexes containing several hundred units. Renting does come with restrictions, however. For example, you may not be allowed to have a pet or make changes to the unit's appearance.

## The Rent-or-Buy Decision

Many people choose to rent rather than buy their home. For example, young adults usually rent for one or more of the following reasons: (1) they don't have the funds for a down payment and closing costs, (2) they're unsettled in their jobs and family status, (3) they don't want the additional responsibilities associated with homeownership, or (4) they believe they can afford a nicer home later by renting now because housing market conditions or mortgage rates are currently unattractive. The economics of renting or buying a place to live depends on three main factors: (1) housing prices and mortgage interest rates, (2) tax write-offs for homeowners, and (3) the expected increase or decrease in home values over time.

To choose the lowest-cost alternative, compare the cost of renting with the cost of buying, as illustrated by the rent-or-buy analysis in Worksheet 5.2. Note that because the interest deduction nearly always exceeds the amount of the standard deduction ($5,700 for single and $11,400 for married filing jointly in 2009), the form assumes that the taxpayer will itemize deductions. Suppose that you must decide between renting an apartment for $850 a month or buying a similar-sized, $150,000 condominium. Purchasing the condo involves a $30,000 down payment; taking out a $120,000, 6%, 30-year mortgage with monthly mortgage payments of $719; $4,500 in closing costs; and property taxes, insurance, and maintenance. With renting, the only costs are the $850 monthly rental payment

and an annual renter's insurance premium of $600. Assume that you're in the 25% ordinary income tax bracket and that you'll itemize deductions if you purchase the home. Substituting the appropriate values into Worksheet 5.2 and making the required calculations results in the total cost of each alternative.

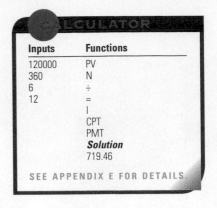

The cost of renting in part A of Worksheet 5.2 is simply the annual rent (monthly rent multiplied by 12) plus the annual renter's insurance premium of $600, all of which results in a total annual cost of $10,800. The annual cost of buying in part B includes mortgage payments, property taxes, homeowner's insurance, annual maintenance, and closing costs to arrive at total costs of $14,964 in Item 6. Then, subtract the portion of the mortgage payment going to pay off the loan balance because it's not part of the interest cost. Subtract the tax savings derived from interest and property taxes to arrive at Item 11, which is the after-tax cost of homeownership of $10,980. But as a homeowner, you also enjoy the benefits of appreciation. Assuming a modest 2% inflation in the value of the home reduces the annual cost to $7,980. Thus, buying is better than renting because the total cost of renting is $2,860 ($10,840 − $7,980) a year more than the total cost of buying.

It's important not to base the rent-or-buy decision solely on the numbers. Your personal needs and the general condition of the housing market are also important considerations. If you think you may want to move to a different city in a few years or if you're worried about job security, renting may make sense even if the numbers favor buying. Think of this as the intangible value of flexibility. Further, for some people, factors such as the need for privacy, the desire to personalize one's home,

©ANDRESR/SHUTTERSTOCK

With this procedure for making the rent-or-buy decision, you should *rent* if the total cost of renting is less than the total cost of buying or *buy* if the total cost of renting is more than the total cost of buying. In this example, the rental option requires monthly payments of $850. The purchase option is a $150,000 condo, financed with a $30,000 down payment and a $120,000, 6%, 30-year mortgage, with additional closing costs of $4,500.

## RENT-OR-BUY ANALYSIS

### A. COST OF RENTING

1. Annual rental costs
   (12 × monthly rental rate of $ ___850___)                                              $ ___10,200___

2. Renter's insurance                                                                      ___600___

3. Opportunity cost of security deposit: $ _1,000_ × after-tax savings rate _0.040_        ___40___

   Total cost of renting (line A.1 + line A.2 + line A.3)                                   $ ___10,840___

### B. COST OF BUYING

1. Annual mortgage payments (Terms: $_120,000.00_, _360_ months, _6_%)   $ _8,634_
   (12 × monthly mortgage payment of $ _719_ )

2. Property taxes                                                          ___3,000___
   (_2.0_% of price of home)

3. Homeowner's insurance                                                  ___750___
   (_0.5_% of price of home)

4. Maintenance                                                            ___1,200___
   (_0.8_% of price of home)

5. After-tax cost of interest on down payment and closing costs           ___1,380___
   ($_34,500_ × _4.0_ % after-tax rate of return)

6. Total costs (sum of lines B.1 through B.5)                             $ ___14,964___

Less:

7. Principal reduction in loan balance (see note below)      $ _1,434_

8. Tax savings due to interest deductions*                   ___1,800___
   (Interest portion of mortgage payments $__7,200_ × tax rate of _25_%)

9. Tax savings due to property tax deductions*               ___750___
   (line B.2 × tax rate of _25_ %)

10. Total deductions (sum of lines B.7 through B.9)                       ___3,984___

11. Annual after-tax cost of homeownership                   $ ___10,980___
    (line B.6 − line B.10)

12. Estimated annual appreciation in value of home                       ___3,000___
    (_2_ % of price of home)
    Total cost of buying (line B.11 − line B.12)                         $ ___7,980___

*Note:* Find monthly mortgage payments using a calculator or from Exhibit 5.5. An easy way to approximate the portion of the annual loan payment that goes to interest (line B.8) is to multiply the interest rate by the size of the loan (in this case, $120,000 × 0.06 = $7,200). To find the principal reduction in the loan balance (line B.7), simply subtract the amount that goes to interest from total annual mortgage payments ($8,634 − $7,200 = $1,434).
*Tax-shelter items.

and the personal satisfaction gained from homeownership outweigh the financial considerations. In some housing markets, a relative surplus of rental properties causes the cost of renting to be lower than the cost of owning a comparable house or condominium. You should look at the rent-or-buy decision over a timeline of several years, using different assumptions regarding rent increases, mortgage rates, home appreciation rates in the area, and the rate of return you can earn on the funds you could invest (if you rent) rather than use toward a down payment on a house (if you buy).

## LG4 How Much Housing Can You Afford?

Buying a home obviously involves a lot of careful planning and analysis. Not only must you decide on the kind of home you want (its location, number of bedrooms, and other features), you must also consider its cost, what kind of mortgage to get, how large a monthly payment you can afford, what kind of homeowner's insurance coverage to have, and so forth.

Sound financial planning dictates caution when buying a home or any other major item. Spending too much for a home or automobile can have a detrimental effect not only on your budget and lifestyle but also on your savings and investment plans and possibly even your retirement plans. Knowing how much housing you can afford goes a long way toward helping you achieve balanced financial goals.

## Benefits of Owning a Home

Homeownership offers the security and peace of mind derived from living in one's own home and the feeling of permanence and sense of stability. This so-called psychological reward is not the only reason people enjoy owning their home. There are also some significant financial payoffs from homeownership.

- **Tax shelter:** As noted in Chapter 3, you can deduct both mortgage interest and property taxes when calculating your federal and, in most states, state income taxes, thereby reducing your taxable income and thus your tax liability. The only requirement is that you itemize your deductions. This tax break is so good that people who have never itemized usually begin doing so after they buy their first house.

- **Inflation hedge:** Homeownership offers not only a place to live, but it also represents an investment that provides a valuable inflation hedge. That's because homes generally appreciate in value at a rate equal to or greater than the rate of inflation. For example, from 2001 through 2006, a home became one of the best investments you could make, generating a far better return than stocks, bonds, or mutual funds. Indeed, many people bought homes simply for their investment potential. More subdued expectations in the wake of the financial crisis of 2009 are that housing prices will roughly keep pace with the rate of inflation for the foreseeable future.

## The Cost of Homeownership

Although there definitely are some strong emotional and financial reasons for owning a home, there's still the question of whether you can afford to own one. There are two important aspects to consider when it comes to affordability: (1) you must be able to come up with the down payment and other closing costs, and (2) you must be able to meet the cash-flow requirements associated with monthly mortgage payments and other home maintenance expenses. In particular, there are five types of costs to consider: the down payment, points and closing costs, mortgage payments, property taxes and insurance, and maintenance and operating expenses.

> { *There definitely are some strong emotional and financial reasons for owning a home.* }

### The Down Payment

The first major hurdle is the **down payment**. Most buyers finance a major part of the purchase price of the home, but they're required by lenders to invest money of their own, called *equity*. The actual amount of down payment required varies among lenders, mortgage types, and properties. To determine the amount of down payment required in specific instances, lenders use the **loan-to-value ratio**, which specifies the

©COUPERFIELD/SHUTTERSTOCK

maximum percentage of the value of a property that the lender is willing to loan. For example, if the loan-to-value ratio is 80%, the buyer will have to come up with a down payment equal to the remaining 20%.

Generally, first-time home buyers must spend several years accumulating enough money to afford the down payment and other costs associated with a home purchase. You can best accumulate these funds if you plan ahead, using future value techniques to determine the monthly or annual savings necessary to have a stated amount by a specified future date. A detailed demonstration of this process is included in Chapter 11 (see Worksheet 11.1, part B). A disciplined savings program is the best way to obtain the funds needed to come up with the down payment and other closing costs on a home.

If you don't have enough savings to cover the down payment and closing costs, you can consider several other sources. The Federal National Mortgage Association ("Fannie Mae") has programs to help buyers who have limited cash for a down payment and closing costs. The "Fannie 3/2" Program is available from local lenders to limit required down payments for qualified buyers. "Fannie 97" helps the home buyer who can handle monthly mortgage payments but doesn't have cash for the down payment. It requires only a 3% down payment from the borrower's own funds, and the borrower needs to have only 1 month's mortgage payment in cash savings, or reserves, after closing. Programs have also developed to help banks liquidate homes owned by Fannie Mae because of the foreclosures resulting from the financial crisis of 2009. The HomePath Mortgage Financing program is available from local and national lenders. Borrowers who meet certain income criteria may qualify for a 97% loan-to-value mortgage and may obtain their down payment from a gift, grant or loan from a nonprofit organization, state or local government, or employer. The HomePath Renovation Mortgage Financing program is a comparable program available only on homes that will be a primary residence that are in need of light renovations.

As a rule, when the down payment is less than 20%, the lender will require the buyer to obtain **private mortgage insurance (PMI),** which protects the lender from loss if the borrower defaults on the loan. Usually PMI covers the lender's risk above 80% of the house price. Thus, with a 10% down payment, the mortgage will be a 90% loan, and mortgage insurance will cover 10% of the home's price. The cost of mortgage insurance can be included in your monthly payment, and the average cost ranges from about $40 to $70 per month. Under federal law, PMI on most loans made on or after July 29, 1999, ends automatically once the mortgage is paid down to 78% of the original value of the house.

### Go to Smart Sites

To find out how much more house you could afford with private mortgage insurance, visit the Mortgage Insurance Companies of America. ●

## Points and Closing Costs

A second hurdle to homeownership relates to mortgage points and closing costs. **Mortgage points** are fees charged by lenders at the time they grant a mortgage loan. Points are like interest in that they are a charge for borrowing money. They're related to the lender's supply of loanable funds and the demand for mortgages; the greater the demand relative to the supply, the more points you can expect to pay. One point equals 1% of the amount borrowed. Thus, if you borrow $100,000 and loan fees equal 3 points, the amount of money you'll pay in points is $100,000 \times 0.03 = $3,000$.

Lenders typically use points as an alternative way of charging interest on their loans. They can vary the interest rate along with the number of points they charge to create loans with comparable effective rates. For example, a lender might be willing to give you a 5% rather than an 6% mortgage if you're willing to pay more points; that is, you choose between an 6% mortgage rate with 1 point or a 5% mortgage rate with 3 points. If you choose the 5% loan, you'll pay a lot more *at closing* (although the amount of interest paid *over the life of the mortgage* may be considerably less).

Points increase the *effective rate of interest* or APR on a mortgage. The amount you pay in points and

**private mortgage insurance (PMI)** An insurance policy that protects the mortgage lender from loss in the event the borrower defaults on the loan; typically required by lenders when the down payment is less than 20%.

**mortgage points** Fees (one point equals 1% of the amount borrowed) charged by lenders at the time they grant a mortgage loan; they are related to the lender's supply of loanable funds and the demand for mortgages.

©FEVERPITCH/SHUTTERSTOCK

**closing costs** All expenses (including mortgage points) that borrowers ordinarily pay when a mortgage loan is closed and they receive title to the purchased property.

the length of time you hold a mortgage determine the increase in the effective interest rate. For example, on an 8%, 30-year, fixed-rate mortgage, each point increases the annual percentage rate by about 0.11% if the loan is held for 30 years or 0.17% if held 15 years. You pay the same amount in points regardless of how long you keep your home. So, the longer you hold the mortgage, the longer the period over which you amortize the points and the smaller the effect of the points on the effective annual interest rate.

According to IRS rulings, the points paid on a mortgage at the time a home is originally purchased are usually considered immediately tax deductible. However, the same points are *not* considered immediately tax deductible if they're incurred when *refinancing* a mortgage; in this case, the amount paid in points must be written off (*amortized*) over the life of the new mortgage loan.

**Closing costs** are all expenses that borrowers ordinarily pay when a mortgage loan is closed and they receive title to the purchased property. Closing costs are like down payments: they represent money

you must come up with *at the time you buy the house*. Closing costs are made up of such items as loan application and loan origination fees, mortgage points, title search and insurance fees, attorneys' fees, appraisal fees, and other miscellaneous fees. Exhibit 5.3 provides a list of these fees and shows that they can total 50% or more of the down payment amount. For example, as can be seen in the exhibit, with a 10% down payment on a $200,000 home, the closing costs are about 56% of the down payment, or $11,130.

## Mortgage Payments

The monthly mortgage payment is determined using a standard but fairly detailed formula. Each mortgage payment is made up partly of principal repayment on the loan and partly of interest charges on the loan. However, as Exhibit 5.4 shows, for most of the life of the mortgage the vast majority of each monthly payment goes to *interest*. The loan illustrated in the exhibit is a $100,000, 30-year, 5% mortgage with monthly payments of $536.82, for a total of $6,441.84 per year. Note that it is not until the 16th year of this 30-year mortgage that the principal portion of the monthly loan payment exceeds the amount that goes to interest.

## Exhibit 5.3 | Closing Costs: The Hidden Costs of Buying a Home

The closing costs on a home mortgage loan can be substantial—as much as 5% to 7% of the price of the home. Except for the real estate commission (generally paid by the seller), the buyer incurs the biggest share of the closing costs and must pay them—in addition to the down payment—when the loan is closed and title to the property is conveyed.

| | Size of Down Payment | |
| Item | 20% | 10% |
| --- | --- | --- |
| Loan application fee | $ 300 | $ 300 |
| Loan origination fee | 1,600 | 1,800 |
| Points | 4,160 | 5,400 |
| Mortgage and homeowner's insurance | — | 675 |
| Title search and insurance | 665 | 665 |
| Attorneys' fees | 400 | 400 |
| Appraisal fees | 425 | 425 |
| Home inspection | 350 | 350 |
| Mortgage tax | 665 | 725 |
| Filing fees | 80 | 80 |
| Credit reports | 35 | 35 |
| Miscellaneous | 200 | 200 |
| Total closing costs | $9,530 | $11,130 |

*Note:* Typical closing costs for a $200,000 home—2.6 points charged with 20% down, 3 points with 10% down. Actual amounts will vary by lender and location.

## Exhibit 5.4 Typical Principal and Interest Payment Patterns on a Mortgage Loan

For most of the life of a mortgage loan, the vast majority of each monthly payment goes to interest and only a small portion goes toward principal repayment. Over the 30-year life of the 5%, $100,000 mortgage illustrated here, the homeowner will pay about $93,255 in interest.

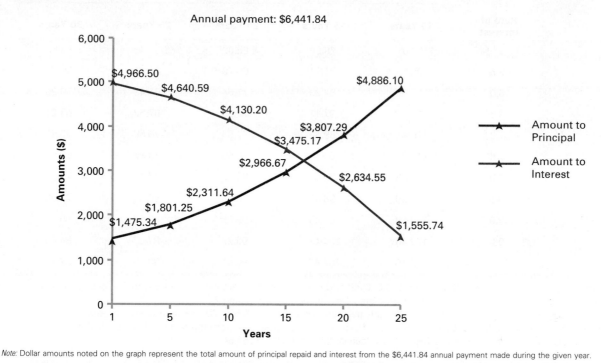

Annual payment: $6,441.84

*Note:* Dollar amounts noted on the graph represent the total amount of principal repaid and interest from the $6,441.84 annual payment made during the given year.

In practice, most mortgage lenders and realtors use their calculator to obtain monthly payments. Some of them still use *comprehensive mortgage payment tables*, which provide monthly payments for virtually any combination of loan size, interest rate, and maturity. Exhibit 5.5 provides an excerpt from one such comprehensive mortgage payment table (with values rounded to the nearest cent). It lists the *monthly payments* associated with a $10,000, fixed-rate loan for selected maturities of 10 to 30 years and for various interest rates ranging from 5% to 10%. This table can be used to find the monthly payment for a loan of any size. For example, suppose you'd like to find the monthly loan payment on a $180,000, 6%, 30-year mortgage.

| Inputs | Functions |
|--------|-----------|
| 180000 | PV |
| 360 | N |
| 6 | ÷ |
| 12 | = |
| | I |
| | CPT |
| | PMT |
| | **Solution** |
| | 1,079.19 |

CALCULATOR

SEE APPENDIX E FOR DETAILS.

To do so, simply divide the amount of the loan ($180,000) by $10,000 and then multiply this factor (18.0) by the payment amount shown in Exhibit 5.5 for a 6%, 30-year loan ($59.96):

**$180,000/$10,000 = 18.0 and 18.0 × $59.96 = $1,079.28**

The resulting monthly mortgage payment is thus $1,079.28. The calculator keystrokes shown in the margin can be used with a financial calculator to more easily and precisely calculate mortgage payments. Note that the mortgage payment of $1,079.19 is a more precise figure than the value above calculated using the table.

**AFFORDABILITY RATIOS.** The key issue regarding mortgage payments is *affordability*: How large a monthly mortgage payment can you afford, given your budget? This amount determines how much you can borrow to finance the purchase of a home.

To obtain a mortgage, a potential borrower must be "qualified"— i.e., demonstrate that he or she has adequate income and an acceptable credit record to reliably make scheduled loan payments. Federal and private mortgage insurers and institutional mortgage investors

The monthly loan payments on a mortgage vary not only by the amount of the loan, but also by the rate of interest and loan maturity.

| Rate of Interest | Loan Maturity | | | | |
|---|---|---|---|---|---|
| | 10 Years | 15 Years | 20 Years | 25 Years | 30 Years |
| 5.0% | $106.07 | $ 79.08 | $ 66.00 | $ 58.46 | $ 53.68 |
| 5.5 | 108.53 | 81.71 | 68.79 | 61.41 | 56.79 |
| 6.0 | 111.02 | 84.39 | 71.64 | 64.43 | 59.96 |
| 6.5 | 113.55 | 87.11 | 74.56 | 67.52 | 63.21 |
| 7.0 | 116.11 | 89.88 | 77.53 | 70.68 | 66.53 |
| 7.5 | 118.71 | 92.71 | 80.56 | 73.90 | 69.93 |
| 8.0 | 121.33 | 95.57 | 83.65 | 77.19 | 73.38 |
| 8.5 | 123.99 | 98.48 | 86.79 | 80.53 | 76.90 |
| 9.0 | 126.68 | 101.43 | 89.98 | 83.92 | 80.47 |
| 9.5 | 129.40 | 104.43 | 93.22 | 87.37 | 84.09 |
| 10.0 | 132.16 | 107.47 | 96.51 | 90.88 | 87.76 |

*Instructions:* (1) Divide amount of the loan by $10,000; (2) find the loan payment amount in the table for the specific interest rate and maturity; and (3) multiply the amount from step 1 by the amount from step 2.

*Example:* Using the steps just described, the monthly payment for a $98,000, 5.5%, 30-year loan would be determined as: (1) $98,000/$10,000 = 9.8; (2) the payment associated with a 5.5%, 30-year loan, from the table, is $56.79; (3) the monthly payment required to repay a $98,000, 5.5%, 30-year loan is 9.8 × $56.79 = $556.54.

**PITI** Acronym that refers to a mortgage payment including stipulated portions of *principal, interest,* property *taxes,* and homeowner's *insurance.*

**property taxes** Taxes levied by local governments on the *assessed value* of real estate for the purpose of funding schools, law enforcement, and other local services.

have certain standards they expect borrowers to meet to reduce the borrower's risk of default.

The most important affordability guidelines relate both *monthly mortgage payments and total monthly installment loan payments* (including the monthly mortgage payment and monthly payments on auto, furniture, and other consumer installment loans) *to monthly borrower gross income.* Customary ratios for a *conventional mortgage* stipulate that monthly mortgage payments cannot exceed 25% to 30% of the borrower's monthly *gross* (before-tax) income, and the borrower's total monthly installment loan payments (including the mortgage payment) cannot exceed 33% to 38% of monthly gross income. Because both conditions stipulate a range, the lender has some leeway in choosing the most appropriate ratio for a particular loan applicant.

Let's look at how these affordability ratios work. Assume that your monthly gross income is $4,500.

Applying the lower end of the ranges (that is, 25% and 33%), we see that this income level supports mortgage payments of $1,125 a month ($4,500 × 0.25 = $1,125) *so long as total monthly installment loan payments do not exceed $1,485 ($4,500 × 0.33 = $1,485).* If your nonmortgage monthly installment loan payments exceeded $360 (the difference between $1,485 and $1,125), then your mortgage payment would have to be reduced accordingly, or other installment loan payments would have to be reduced or paid off.

**Property Taxes and Insurance**

The standard mortgage payment often includes property taxes and homeowner's insurance. The mortgage payment therefore consists of *principal, interest,* property *taxes,* and homeowner's *insurance* (or **PITI** for short). Actually, that portion of the loan payment that goes for taxes and insurance is paid into an *escrow account,* where it accumulates until the lender pays property taxes and homeowner insurance premiums are due.

Because they're local taxes levied to fund schools, law enforcement, and other local services, the level of **property taxes** differs from one community to another. In addition, within a given community, individual property taxes will vary according to the *assessed value* of the real estate—the larger and/or more expensive the home, the higher the property taxes, and vice versa. As a rule, annual property taxes vary from less than .5% to more than 2% of a home's approximate market value. Thus the property taxes on a $100,000 home could vary from about $500 to more than $2,000 a year, depending on location and geographic area.

The other component of the monthly mortgage payment is **homeowner's insurance.** Its cost varies with such factors as the age of the house, location, materials used in construction, and geographic area. Homeowner's insurance is required by mortgage lenders and covers only the replacement value of the home and its contents, not the land. Annual insurance costs usually amount to approximately 0.25% to 0.5% of the home's market value, or from $500 to $1,000 for a $200,000 house.

### Maintenance and Operating Expenses

In addition to monthly mortgage payments, homeowners will incur periodic maintenance and operating expenses. Maintenance costs should be anticipated even on new homes. Painting, mechanical and plumbing repairs, and lawn maintenance, for example, are inescapable facts of homeownership. Such costs are likely to be greater for larger, older homes. Thus, although a large, established home may have an attractive purchase price, a new, smaller home may be a better buy in view of its lower maintenance and operating costs. Also consider the cost of operating the home, specifically the cost of utilities such as electricity, gas, water,

and sewage. These costs have skyrocketed over the past 20 years and today are a large part of homeownership costs, so obtain estimates of utilities when evaluating a home for purchase.

**homeowner's insurance** Insurance that is required by mortgage lenders and covers the replacement value of a home and its contents.

## Performing a Home Affordability Analysis

Worksheet 5.3 helps you determine the maximum price for a home purchase based on your monthly income and down payment amount after meeting estimated closing costs. In our example, the Ursula and Ernest Schmidt family has a combined annual income of $75,200 and savings of $30,000 for a down payment and closing costs. They estimate monthly property taxes and homeowner's insurance at $375 and expect the mortgage lender to use a 28% monthly mortgage payment affordability ratio, to lend at an average interest rate of 6% on a 30-year (360-month) mortgage, and to require a 10% minimum down payment. The Schmidts' analysis shows they can afford to purchase a home for about $201,000.

Worksheet 5.3 walks us through the steps the Schmidt family took to reach this conclusion. The maximum purchase price is determined from two perspectives: the maximum based on monthly income and the maximum based on the minimum acceptable down payment. The lower of the two estimates determines the maximum purchase price. Based on their monthly income and the 28% affordability ratio, their monthly payment could be $1,755 ($6,267 × 0.28), shown as Item 4. After deducting taxes and insurance, the maximum monthly mortgage payment amount is $1,380 (Item 6). We can use the calculator keystrokes shown in the margin or the table in Exhibit 5.5 to find the Schmidts' maximum loan. The calculator indicates a maximum purchase price of $230,172.43, which is more precise than the approximation provided using Exhibit 5.5. Using Exhibit 5.5, a $10,000 loan for 30 years at 6% would result in a monthly payment of $59.96, as indicated in Item 9. Now, find out how much of a loan a payment of $1,380 would support:

| Inputs | Functions |
|--------|-----------|
| 1380 | PMT |
| 360 | N |
| 6 | ÷ |
| 12 | = |
| | I |
| | CPT |
| | PV |
| | **Solution** |
| | 230,172.43 |

CALCULATOR

SEE APPENDIX E FOR DETAILS

$$\$10,000 \times \$1,380/\$59.96 = \$230,153.44$$

By using the following variables in the home affordability analysis form, the Schmidts' estimate a maximum home purchase price of $201,000: their combined annual income of $75,200; the $30,000 available for a down payment and paying all closing costs; estimated monthly property taxes and homeowner's insurance of $375; the lender's 28% monthly mortgage payment affordability ratio; an average interest rate of 6% and expected loan maturity of 30 years; and a minimum down payment of 10%.

## HOME AFFORDABILITY ANALYSIS*

Name _Ursula and Ernest Schmidt_          Date _August 14, 2011_

| Item | Description | Amount |
|------|-------------|--------|
| 1 | Amount of annual income | $ 75,200 |
| 2 | Monthly income (Item 1 ÷ 12) | $ 6,267 |
| 3 | Lender's affordability ratio (in decimal form) | 0.28 |
| 4 | Maximum monthly mortgage payment (PITI) (Item 2 × Item 3) | $ 1,755 |
| 5 | Estimated monthly prop tax and homeowner's insurance payment | $ 375 |
| 6 | Maximum monthly loan payment (Item 4 − Item 5) | $ 1,380 |
| 7 | Approximate average interest rate on loan | 6 % |
| 8 | Planned loan maturity (years) | 30 |
| 9 | Mortgage payment per $10,000 (using Item 7 and Item 8 and Table of Monthly Mortgage Payments in Exhibit 5.11) | $ 59.96 |
| 10 | Maximum loan based on monthly income ($10,000 × Item 6 ÷ Item 9) | $ 230,000.00 |
| 11 | Funds available for making a down payment and paying closing costs | $ 30,000 |
| 12 | Funds available for making a down payment (Item 11 × .67) | $ 20,100 |
| 13 | Maximum purchase price based on available monthly income (Item 10 + Item 12) | $ 250,100 |
| 14 | Minimum acceptable down payment (in decimal form) | 0.10 |
| 15 | Maximum purchase price based on down payment (Item 12 ÷ Item 14) | $ 201,000 |
| 16 | Maximum home purchase price (lower of Item 13 and Item 15) | $ 201,000 |

*Note: This analysis assumes that one-third of the funds available for making the down payment and paying closing costs are used to meet closing costs and that the remaining two-thirds are available for a down payment. This means that closing costs will represent an amount equal to 50% of the down payment.

With a down payment of $30,000 and monthly income of $6,267, the Schmidt family can afford a home costing $250,100 (Item 13). The Schmidts then look at the maximum purchase price based on their $30,000 down payment, or $150,000 (Item 15). Their maximum home purchase price is the lower of Items 13 and 15, or $201,000 (Item 16) and is limited by the amount available for a down payment.

## LG5 The Home-Buying Process

Buying a home requires time, effort, and money. You'll want to educate yourself about available properties and prevailing prices by doing a systematic search and

 *Buying a home requires time, effort, and money.*

careful analysis. You'll also need a basic understanding of the role of a real estate agent, the mortgage application process, the real estate sales contract, and other documents required to close a deal.

## Shop the Market First

Most people who shop the housing market rely on real estate agents for information, access to properties, and advice. Today, even with homes, it's becoming commonplace to shop via the Internet, visiting various real estate sites to learn about available properties. Going online, you can specify preferences such as location, price, and size, and obtain descriptions and color photos of all properties that meet your needs.

As noted earlier, you must begin your home search project by figuring out what *you* require for your particular lifestyle needs—in terms of living space, style, and other special features. The property's location, neighborhood, and school district are usually important considerations as well. It's helpful to divide your list into *necessary* features, such as the number of bedrooms and baths, and *optional*—but desirable—features, such as fireplaces, whirlpool tubs, and so on. And of course, an affordability analysis is a critical part of the housing search.

Keep an open mind as you start looking. You may find that you like a house that's far different from what you first thought you wanted. For example, you may begin your search looking for a one-story, contemporary ranch house with a pool, but fall in love with a two-story colonial with wonderful landscaping, no pool, and all the other features you want. Be flexible and look at a variety of homes in your price range. This can be invaluable in helping to define your wants and needs more clearly.

### Real Estate Short Sales

The bursting of the real estate bubble associated with the financial crisis of 2008-09 increased the use of real estate short sales. A **real estate short sale** is the sale of property in which *the proceeds are less than the balance owed on the mortgage* used to secure the property. This procedure is an effort by a mortgage lender to come to terms with homeowners who are about to default or are defaulting on their mortgage loans. A broker's price opinion or an appraisal is obtained to estimate the probable selling price of the property for the purposes of the short sale. The short sale typically occurs to prevent home foreclosure by finding the most economic means for the mortgage lender to recover as much of the loan balance owed on the property as possible. In contrast, in a **foreclosure** the borrower typically cannot make scheduled mortgage payments and the lender repossesses the property in an effort to recover the loan balance owed. Mortgage holders will agree to a short sale only if it believes that the proceeds generated by the sale will produce a smaller loss than foreclosing on the property. A real estate short sale may consequently be viewed as a negotiated effort to mitigate the losses of the mortgage lender.

While a short sale can reduce a lender's losses, *it can also be beneficial for the homeowner.* A real estate short sale will avoid having a foreclosure appear on the homeowner's credit history. Short sales should also help homeowners manage the costs that got them into trouble in the first place. Finally, a short sale is usually faster and cheaper for the homeowner than a foreclosure.

## Using an Agent

Real estate agents are professionals who are in daily contact with the housing market. Once you describe your needs to an agent, he or she can begin to search for appropriate properties. Your agent will also help you negotiate with the seller, obtain satisfactory financing, and, although not empowered to give explicit legal advice, prepare the real estate sales contract. Most real estate firms belong to a local **Multiple Listing Service (MLS)**, a comprehensive

### FINANCIAL ROAD SIGN

**TOP HOME REMODELING PROJECT PAYBACKS**

The National Association of Realtors found that the value of home remodeling projects declined by only about half as much as home prices during the recent financial crisis. While it's best to expect that you will not get all of your money back from home improvements when you sell your home, keep in mind that you will likely enjoy the improvements until that time and will probably recover most of the money. Here's a list of the top remodeling projects in terms of the percentage of the investment recovered at the sale of the home.

| Project | Cost Recovered |
|---|---|
| 1. Upscale fiber cement siding | 86.7% |
| 2. Midrange wood deck | 81.1% |
| 3. Midrange vinyl siding | 80.7% |
| 4. Upscale foam-backed vinyl | 80.4% |
| 5. Midrange minor kitchen remodel | 79.5% |

*Source:* Adapted from G. M. Filsko, "2008 Cost vs. Value Report: Still Many Happy Returns for Home Rehabs," *Realtor*, December 2008, http://www.realtor.org/rmohome_and_design/articles/2008/0812_costvsvalue_2008, accessed May 2009.

listing, updated daily, of properties for sale in a given community or metropolitan area. A brief description of each property and its asking price are included; many of which are accompanied by photos of the property.

Buyers should remember that *agents typically are employed by sellers*. Unless you've agreed to pay a fee to a sales agent to act as a buyer's agent, a realtor's primary responsibility, by law, is to sell listed properties at the highest possible prices. Agents are paid only if they make a sale, so some might pressure you to "sign now or miss the chance of a lifetime." But most agents will listen to your needs and work to match you with the right property and under terms that will benefit both you and the seller. Good agents recognize that their interests are best served when all parties to a transaction are satisfied.

Real estate commissions generally range from 5% to 6% for new homes and 6% to 7% for previously occupied homes or *resales*. It may be possible to negotiate a lower commission with your agent or to find a discount broker, or one who charges a flat fee. Commissions are paid only by the seller, but because the price of a home is often inflated by the size of the real estate commission, the buyer probably absorbs some or even all of the commission.

## Prequalifying and Applying for a Mortgage

Before beginning your home search, you may want to meet with one or more mortgage lenders to prearrange a mortgage loan. **Prequalification** can work to your advantage in several ways. You'll know ahead of time the specific mortgage amount that you qualify for—subject, of course, to changes in rates and terms—and can focus your search on homes within an affordable price range. Prequalification also provides estimates of the required down payment and closing costs for different types of mortgages. It identifies in advance any problems, such as credit report

errors, that might arise from your application and allows you time to correct them. Finally, prequalification enhances your bargaining power with the sellers of a house by letting them know that the deal won't fall through because you can't afford the property or obtain suitable financing. And since you will have already gone through the mortgage application process, the time required to close the sale should be relatively short.

## The Real Estate Sales Contract

After selecting a home to buy, you must enter into a sales contract. State laws generally specify that to be enforceable in court, real estate buy-sell agreements must be in writing and contain certain information, including (1) the names of buyers and sellers, (2) a description of the property sufficient for positive identification, (3) specific price and other terms, and (4) usually the signatures of the buyers and sellers. Real estate sales transactions often take weeks and sometimes months to complete. Contract requirements help keep the facts straight and reduce the chance for misunderstanding, misrepresentation, or fraud.

Although these requirements fulfill the minimums necessary for court enforcement, in practice real estate sales contracts usually contain several other contractual clauses relating to earnest money deposits, contingencies, personal property, and closing costs. An **earnest money deposit** is the money you pledge to show good faith when you make an offer. If, after signing a sales contract, you withdraw from the transaction without a valid reason, you may forfeit this deposit. A valid reason for withdrawal would be stated in the contract as a contingency clause. With a **contingency clause**, you can condition your agreement to buy on such factors as the availability of financing, a satisfactory termite inspection or other physical inspection of the property, or the advice of a lawyer or real estate expert.

## Closing the Deal

After you obtain financing and your loan is approved, the closing process begins. The **Real Estate Settlement Procedures Act (RESPA)** governs closings on owner-occupied houses, condominiums, and apartment buildings of four units or fewer. This act reduced closing costs by prohibiting kickbacks made to real estate agents and others from lenders or title insurance companies. It also requires clear, advance disclosure of all closing costs to home buyers. Exhibit 5.6 provides some tips to help you sail through the home buying process in general and the closing process in particular.

## Exhibit 5.6 Avoiding Common Home-Buying Mistakes

Keeping in mind the following pitfalls will improve your chances of becoming a happy, successful homeowner:

1. **Say no to "no money down" seminars.** Many of these seminar "experts" most likely never bought or sold a piece of real estate in their lives but are getting rich off the backs of suckers.

2. **Stay away from bad agents.** Interview your agent and ask hard questions. Make sure that he or she is experienced. Consider signing a buyer's broker agreement, which gives both you and the broker responsibilities and reasonable performance expectations.

3. **Don't wipe out your savings.** While it makes sense to put down the largest down payment you can afford, it is important to keep your emergency reserves intact, hold money for closing costs, and set aside funds to handle possible repairs and future maintenance. You don't want to be putting such extras on your credit card!

4. **Rely on professional advice.** Pay attention to what your agent or mortgage broker tells you. Look up information on the Internet, read real estate books, and ask for a second opinion. Lawyers and accountants are excellent resources.

5. **Avoid exotic financing.** One of the biggest lessons of the recent financial crisis is that real estate prices don't always go up. And what you don't know about your mortgage can hurt you! Don't sign off on your mortgage until you understand every detail. Terms like indexes, margins, caps, and negative amortization should make you nervous.

6. **Pick the right neighborhood.** You've heard that the three most important factors in valuing real estate are location, location, and location. This is no joke. Drive through a neighborhood, ask the police department about crime statistics, and talk to neighbors before you buy.

7. **Stay away from the most expensive home in the neighborhood.** While having the largest and most expensive home in the neighborhood might be appealing, it doesn't bode well for resale value. If you need three bedrooms, don't consider a five-bedroom that looks good but costs more and meets your needs less.

8. **Don't pass up the home inspection.** Home inspections are not a waste of time and money. Qualified home inspectors can find problems that most of us would miss.

9. **Don't change the financial picture before closing.** Just because your offer was accepted by the seller doesn't mean that you need to stay in buying mode. While waiting for loan funding, there is no need to buy a new car to match that new home. Your excellent credit report does not give you free rein to buy whatever you want. Borrowing too much more at this time could adversely affect the funding of a mortgage.

10. **Plunging into debt after closing.** After you become a homeowner, you'll be offered many deals on a home equity loan. Although it may be tempting to pull out all your equity and use this new-found money to buy all sorts of new toys, you should stick to a reasonable financial plan. More sources of debt should not cause you to ignore the need to cover the contingency of losing a job or setting aside money to meet an emergency.

*Source:* Adapted from Elizabeth Weintraub, "Top 10 Ways to Lose Your Home," http://homebuying.about.com/od/buyingahome/tp/072007LoseHome.htm, accessed May 2009. Used with permission of About, Inc., which can be found online at www.about.com. All rights reserved.

## LG6 Financing the Transaction

Earlier in this chapter, we saw that mortgage terms can dramatically affect the amount you can afford to spend on a home. The success of a real estate transaction often hinges on obtaining a mortgage with favorable terms. A **mortgage loan** is secured by the property: If the borrower defaults, the lender has the legal right to liquidate the property to recover the funds it is owed. Before you obtain such a loan, it's helpful to understand the sources and types of mortgages and their underlying economics.

### Sources of Mortgage Loans

The major sources of home mortgages today are commercial banks, thrift institutions, and mortgage bankers or brokers. Commercial banks are also an important source of *interim construction loans*, providing short-term financing during the construction phase for individuals who are building or remodeling a home. After the home is completed, the homeowner obtains *permanent financing*, in the form of a standard mortgage loan, and then uses the proceeds from it to repay the construction loan.

Another way to obtain a mortgage loan is through a mortgage banker or mortgage broker. Both solicit borrowers, originate loans, and place them with traditional mortgage lenders as well as life insurance companies and pension funds.

**mortgage loan** A loan secured by the property: If the borrower defaults, the lender has the legal right to liquidate the property to recover the funds it is owed.

**mortgage banker**
A firm that solicits borrowers, originates primarily government-insured and government-guaranteed loans, and places them with mortgage lenders; often uses its own money to initially fund mortgages it later resells.

**mortgage broker** A firm that solicits borrowers, originates primarily conventional loans, and places them with mortgage lenders; the broker merely takes loan applications and then finds lenders willing to grant the mortgage loans under the desired terms.

**fixed-rate mortgage**
The traditional type of mortgage in which both the rate of interest and the monthly mortgage payment are fixed over the full term of the loan.

Whereas **mortgage bankers** often use their own money to initially fund mortgages they later resell, **mortgage brokers** take loan applications and then seek lenders willing to grant the mortgage loans under the desired terms. Most brokers also have ongoing relationships with different lenders, thereby increasing your chances of finding a loan even if you don't qualify at a commercial bank or thrift institution. Brokers can often simplify the financing process by cutting through red tape, negotiating more favorable terms, and reducing the amount of time to close the loan. Mortgage brokers earn their income from commissions and origination fees paid by the lender, costs that are typically passed on to the borrower in the points charged on a loan. See Chapter 5's Bonus Exhibits section of 4ltrpress.cengage.com for advice on finding a good mortgage broker.

Shopping for the best mortgage rate and terms has become a lot easier thanks to the Internet. Many sites allow you to search for the best fixed-rate or adjustable-rate mortgage in your area. HSH Associates, a mortgage consulting firm with a Web site at **http://www.hsh.com,** lists mortgages offered by banks, mortgage companies, and brokerage firms across the country, along with information on prevailing interest rates, terms, and points. Bankrate, **http://www.bankrate.com,** and similar sites also offer mortgage comparisons.

 **Go to Smart Sites**

American Loan Search provides a list of online mortgage lenders in your area when you enter your state. The site also has a rate search engine to help you find a lender with the rate you want. ●

## Types of Mortgage Loans

For our purposes here, we'll group mortgages in two catagories, based on: (1) terms of payment and (2) whether they're conventional, insured, or guaranteed.

There are literally dozens of different types of home mortgages from which to choose. The most common types of mortgage loans made today are fixed-rate and adjustable-rate mortgages.

### Fixed-Rate Mortgages

The **fixed-rate mortgage** still accounts for a large portion of all home mortgages. Both the rate of interest and the monthly mortgage payment are fixed over the full term of the loan. The most common type of fixed-rate mortgage is the *30-year fixed-rate* loan, although *10- and 15-year loans* are becoming more popular as homeowners recognize the advantages of paying off their loan over a shorter period of time. Because of the risks that the lender assumes with a 30-year loan, it's usually the most expensive form of home financing.

Becoming especially popular is the *15-year fixed-rate* loan. Its chief appeal is that it is repaid twice as fast (15 years versus 30) and yet the monthly

©GERRY BOUGHAN/SHUTTERSTOCK

payments don't increase all that much. To pay off a loan in less time, the homeowner must pay more each month, but monthly payments don't have to be doubled to pay off the loan in half the time; rather, the monthly payment on a 15-year loan is generally only about 20–30% larger than the payment on a 30-year loan. The following table shows the difference in monthly payment and total interest paid for 30- and 15-year fixed-rate mortgages. In both cases the purchaser borrows $160,000 at a 5% fixed rate of interest:

| Term of Loan | Regular Monthly Payment | Total Interest Paid over Life of Loan |
|---|---|---|
| 30 years | $ 858.91 | $149,209.25 |
| 15 years | $1,265.27 | $ 67,748.56 |

Perhaps the most startling feature is the substantial difference in the total amount of interest paid over the term of the loan. Note in the example above that you can save *over $81,000* just by financing your home with a 15-year mortgage rather than over the traditional 30 years! And keep in mind this savings is possible even though monthly payments differ by only about $406.

## Adjustable-Rate Mortgages (ARMs)

Another popular form of home loan is the **adjustable-rate mortgage (ARM).** In this case, the rate of interest, and therefore the size of the monthly payment, is adjusted based on market interest rate movements. The mortgage interest rate is linked to a specific *interest rate index* and is adjusted at specific intervals (usually once or twice a year) based on changes in the index. When the index moves up, so does the interest rate on the mortgage and, in turn, the size of the monthly mortgage payment increases. The new interest rate and monthly mortgage payment remain in effect until the next adjustment date.

The term of an ARM can be 15 or 30 years. Because the size of the monthly payments will vary with interest rates, there's no way to tell what your future payments will be. However, because the borrower assumes most or all of the interest rate risk in these mortgages, the *initial rate of interest* on an adjustable-rate mortgage is normally well below—typically by 2 to 3 percentage points—the rate of a standard 30-year fixed-rate loan. Of course, whether the borrower actually ends up paying less interest depends on the behavior of market interest rates during the term of the loan.

**FEATURES OF ARMS.** It's important for home buyers to understand the basic features of an ARM:

- **Adjustment period:** Although the period of time between rate changes is typically 6 months to 1 year, adjustment periods can range from 3 months to 3 years, or more.

- **Index rate:** A baseline rate that captures the movement in interest rates, usually tied to 6-month U.S. Treasury securities, 6-month CDs, or the average cost of funds to savings institutions.

- **Margin:** The percentage points a lender *adds to the index* to determine the rate of interest on an ARM, usually a fixed amount over the life of the loan.

- **Interest rate caps:** Limits the amount the interest rate can increase over a given period. *Periodic caps* limit interest rate increases from one adjustment to the next (typically lenders cap annual rate adjustments at 1 to 2 percentage points), and *overall caps* limit the interest rate increase over the life of the loan (lifetime interest rate caps are typically set at 5 to 8 percentage points). Many ARMs have both periodic and overall interest rate caps.

- **Payment caps:** Limits on monthly payment increases that may result from a rate adjustment—usually a percentage of the previous payment. If your ARM has a 5% payment cap, your monthly payments can increase no more than 5% from one year to the next—regardless of what happens to interest rates.

**adjustable-rate mortgage (ARM)** A mortgage on which the rate of interest, and therefore the size of the monthly payment, is adjusted based on market interest rate movements.

**adjustment period** On an adjustable-rate mortgage, the period of time between rate or payment changes.

**index rate** On an adjustable-rate mortgage, the baseline index rate that captures interest rate movements.

**margin** On an adjustable-rate mortgage, the percentage points a lender adds to the *index rate* to determine the rate of interest.

**interest rate cap** On an adjustable-rate mortgage, the limit on the amount that the interest rate can increase each adjustment period and over the life of the loan.

**payment cap** On an adjustable-rate mortgage, the limit on the monthly payment increase that may result from a rate adjustment.

| CALCULATOR | |
|---|---|
| Inputs | Functions |
| 100000 | PV |
| 360 | N |
| 6.5 | ÷ |
| 12 | = |
| | I |
| | CPT |
| | PV |
| | **Solution** |
| | 632.07 |

SEE APPENDIX E FOR DETAILS.

**negative amortization** When the principal balance on a mortgage loan increases because the monthly loan payment is lower than the amount of monthly interest being charged; some ARMs are subject to this undesirable condition.

**convertible ARM** An adjustable-rate mortgage loan that allows borrowers to convert from an adjustable-rate to a fixed-rate loan, usually at any time between the 13th and the 60th month.

**two-step ARM** An adjustable-rate mortgage with just two interest rates: one for the first 5 to 7 years of the loan, and a higher one for the remaining term of the loan.

**interest-only mortgage** A mortgage that requires the borrower to pay only interest; typically used to finance the purchase of more expensive properties.

**graduated-payment mortgage** A mortgage that starts with unusually low payments that rise over several years to a fixed payment.

Because most ARMs are 30-year loans (360 payments), you can determine the initial monthly payment in the same manner as for any other 30-year mortgage. For example, for an $100,000 loan at 6.5% (4.5% index rate + 2% margin), we can use a calculator as shown in the margin or Exhibit 5.5 to find the first-year monthly payments of $632.07. Assuming a 1-year adjustment period, if the index rate rises to 5.5%, then the interest rate for the second year will be 7.5% (5.5% + 2% = 7.5%). The size of the monthly payment for the next 12 months will then be adjusted upward to about $697.83. This process is repeated each year thereafter until the loan matures.

**BEWARE OF NEGATIVE AMORTIZATION.** Some ARMs are subject to **negative amortization**—that is, there's actually an increase in the principal balance of the loan resulting from *monthly loan payments that are lower than the amount of monthly interest being charged.* In other words, you could end up with a larger mortgage balance on the next anniversary of your loan than on the previous one. This occurs when the payment is intentionally set below the interest charge, or when the ARM has interest rates that are adjusted monthly—with monthly payments that adjust annually. In the latter case, when rates are rising on these loans, the current monthly payment can be less than the interest being charged, and the difference is added to the principal, thereby increasing the size of the loan. When considering an ARM, be sure to learn whether negative amortization could occur. Generally, loans without the potential for negative amortization are available although they tend to have slightly higher initial rates and interest rate caps.

Here are a couple of other types of ARMs lenders may sometimes offer:

- **Convertible ARMs** allow borrowers to convert from an adjustable-rate to a fixed-rate loan during a specified time period, usually any time between the 13th and 60th month. Although these loans seldom provide the lowest initial rate, they allow the borrower to convert to a fixed-rate loan if interest rates decline. A conversion fee of about $500 is typical, and the fixed rate is normally set at 0.25% to 0.5% above the going rate on fixed-rate loans at the time you convert.

- **Two-step ARMs** have just two interest rates, the first for an initial period of 5 to 7 years and a higher one for the remaining term of the loan.

## Fixed or Adjustable Rate?

Fixed-rate mortgages are popular with home buyers who plan to stay in their homes for at least 5 to 7 years and want to know what their payments will be. Of course, the current level of interest rates and your expectations about future interest rates will influence your choice of a fixed-rate or adjustable-rate mortgage. When the average interest rate on a 30-year mortgage loan is high, people often choose adjustable-rate mortgages to avoid being locked into prevailing high rates. In sharp contrast, when interest rates are low, many home buyers opt for fixed-rate mortgages to lock in these attractive rates. In such situations, many homeowners with adjustable-rate mortgages will often refinance them with fixed-rate loans to take advantage of the favorable fixed rates.

## Other Mortgage Payment Options

In addition to standard fixed-rate and adjustable-rate mortgage loans, some lenders offer variations designed to help first-time home buyers.

- **Interest-only mortgages** are loans requiring the borrower to pay only the interest portion of the loan. Rather than amortizing the loan with equal monthly payments, the borrower merely pays the accrued interest each month—the option to pay interest only lasts for a specified period, often 5 to 10 years, after which time all future loan payments will also include principal. These mortgages allow the borrower to make lower payments (early on in the life of the loan) that are still fully tax deductible. Most interest-only mortgages are offered as ARMs.

- **Graduated-payment mortgages** are loans offering low payments for the first few years, gradually increasing until year 3 or 5, and then remaining fixed. The low initial payments appeal to people who are just starting out and expect their income to rise. If this doesn't occur, however, it could result in a higher debt load than the borrower can handle.

- **Growing-equity mortgages** are fixed-rate mortgages with payments that increase over a specific period. The extra funds are applied to the principal, so a conventional 30-year loan can be paid off in about 20 years.

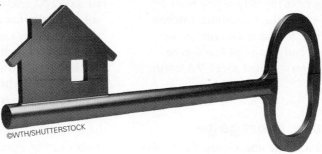
©WTH/SHUTTERSTOCK

- **Biweekly mortgages** are loans on which payments equal to half of a regular monthly payment are made every 2 weeks rather than once a month. Because you make 26 payments (52 weeks ÷ 2), which is the equivalent of 13 monthly payments, the principal balance declines faster, and you pay less interest over the life of the loan.

- **Buydowns** are a type of seller financing sometimes offered on new homes. A builder, for example, arranges for mortgage financing with a financial institution at interest rates well below market rates; to illustrate, a builder may offer 5% financing when the market rate of interest is around 6% or 6.5%. Be carefull though, because the reduced rate may only be good for a short period, or the buyer may actually end up paying for the reduced interest in the form of a higher purchase price.

### Conventional, Insured, and Guaranteed Loans

A **conventional mortgage** is a mortgage offered by a lender who assumes all the risk of loss. To protect themselves, lenders usually require a down payment of at least 20% of the value of the mortgaged property. For lower down payments, the lender usually requires *private mortgage insurance (PMI)*, as described earlier in the chapter. High borrower equity greatly reduces the likelihood of default on a mortgage and subsequent loss to the lender. However, a high down payment requirement makes home buying more difficult for many families and individuals.

The **FHA mortgage insurance** program helps people buy homes even when they have very little money available for a down payment and closing costs; these are known as *insured loans*. As of summer 2009, the up-front mortgage insurance premium for a 15- or 30-year mortgage was 1.5% of the loan amount—paid by the borrower at closing or included in the mortgage—plus another 0.5% annual renewal premium, paid monthly. Home buyers who want a 15-year mortgage and make a down payment greater than 10% of the purchase price only pay the up-front fee. The FHA agrees to reimburse lenders for losses up to a specified maximum amount if the buyer defaults. The minimum required down payment on an FHA loan is 3% of the sales price. The interest rate on an FHA loan is generally about 0.5% to 1% lower than that on conventional fixed-rate loans. The affordability ratios that are used to qualify applicants for these loans are typically less stringent than those used for conventional loans.

Guaranteed loans are similar to insured loans, but better—if you qualify. **VA loan guarantees** are provided by the U.S. Veterans Administration to lenders who make qualified mortgage loans to eligible veterans of the U.S. Armed Forces and their unmarried surviving spouses. This program, however, does not require lenders or veterans to pay a premium for the guarantee. In many instances, an eligible veteran must pay only closing costs; in effect, under such a program, a veteran can buy a home with no down payment. (This can be done *only once* with a VA loan.) The mortgage loan—subject to a maximum of about $417,000 for a no-money-down loan (as of summer 2009)—can amount to as much as 100% of a purchased property's appraised value. It is important to note that there are some regional differences in VA loan requirements. VA loans include a funding fee of about 2.15% on first-time, no-down-payment loans for regular military members (the fee is lower if the down payment is 10% or more). The VA sets the maximum interest rate, which (as with FHA loans) is usually about 0.5% *below* the rate on conventional fixed-rate loans. To qualify, the veteran must meet VA credit guidelines.

## Refinancing Your Mortgage

After you've purchased a home and closed the transaction, interest rates on similar loans may drop. If rates drop by 1% to 2% or more, then you should consider the economics of refinancing after carefully comparing the terms of the old and new mortgages, the anticipated number of years you expect to remain in the home, any prepayment penalty on the old mortgage, and the closing costs associated with the new mortgage.

Worksheet 5.4 provides a form for analyzing the impact of refinancing. The data for the D'Angelo family's analysis is shown. Their original $80,000, 10-year-old, 8% mortgage has a current balance

of $70,180 and monthly payments of $587 for 20 more years. If they refinance the $70,180 balance at the prevailing rate of 5%, then over the remaining 20-year life of the current mortgage, the monthly payment would drop to $463. The D'Angelos plan to live in their house for at least 5 more years. They won't have to pay a penalty for prepaying their current mortgage, and closing and other costs associated with the new mortgage are $2,400 after taxes. Substituting these values into Worksheet 5.4 reveals (in Item 7) that it will take the D'Angelos 26 months to break even with the new mortgage. Because 26 months is considerably less than their anticipated minimum 5 years (60 months) in the home, *the economics easily support refinancing their mortgage under the specified terms*. Most families decide to refinance in order to lower their monthly mortgage payments—it is after all, almost like getting a raise in pay! In such cases, the analysis is relatively simple: determine how long it will take for the monthly savings to equal any closing costs (as spelled out in Worksheet 5.4).

**Worksheet 5.4   Mortgage Refinancing Analysis for the D'Angelo Family**

Using this form, the D'Angelos find that—by refinancing the $70,180 balance on their 10-year-old, $80,000, 8%, 30-year mortgage (which has no prepayment penalty and requires payments of $587 per month) with a 5%, 20-year mortgage requiring $463 monthly payments and $2,400 in total after-tax closing costs—it will take 26 months to break even. Because the D'Angelos plan to stay in their home for at least 60 more months, the refinancing is easily justified.

### MORTGAGE REFINANCING ANALYSIS

Name  Ray and Carmen D'Angelo                     Date  October 8, 2011

| Item | Description | | Amount |
|---|---|---|---|
| 1 | Current monthly payment (Terms: $ 80,000, 8%, 30 years ) | | $ 587 |
| 2 | New monthly payment (Terms: $ 70,180, 5%, 20 years ) | | 463 |
| 3 | Monthly savings, pretax (Item 1 − Item 2) | | $ 124 |
| 4 | Tax on monthly savings [Item 3 × tax rate ( 25 %)] | | 31 |
| 5 | Monthly savings, after-tax (Item 3 − Item 4) | | $ 93 |
| 6 | Costs to refinance: | | |
| | a. Prepayment penalty | $ 0 | |
| | b. Total closing costs (after-tax) | 2,400 | |
| | c. Total refinancing costs (Item 6a + Item 6b) | | $ 2,400 |
| 7 | Months to break even (Item 6c ÷ Item 5) | | 26 |

# FINANCIAL PLANNING EXERCISES

**LG1, 2**

1. Beverly Cooper has just graduated from college and needs to buy a car to commute to work. She estimates that she can afford to pay about $450 per month for a loan or lease and has about $2,000 in savings to use for a down payment. Develop a plan to guide her through her first car-buying experience, including researching car type, deciding whether to buy a new or used car, negotiating the price and terms, and financing the transaction.

**LG2**

2. *Use Worksheet 5.1.* Art Winkler is trying to decide whether to lease or purchase a new car costing $18,000. If he leases, he'll have to pay a $600 security deposit and monthly payments of $425 over the 36-month term of the closed-end lease. On the other hand, if he buys the car, then he'll have to make a $2,400 down payment and will finance the balance with a 36-month loan requiring monthly payments of $515; he'll also have to pay a 6% sales tax ($1,080) on the purchase price, and he expects the car to have a residual value of $6,500 at the end of 3 years. Use the automobile lease versus purchase analysis form in Worksheet 5.1 to find the total cost of both the lease and the purchase and then recommend the best strategy for Art.

**LG4**

3. Using the maximum ratios for a conventional mortgage, how big a monthly payment could the Burton family afford if their gross (before-tax) monthly income amounted to $4,000? Would it make any difference if they were already making monthly installment loan payments totaling $750 on two car loans?

**LG4**

4. Find the *monthly* mortgage payments on the following mortgage loans using either your calculator or the table in Exhibit 5.5:
   a. $80,000 at 6.5% for 30 years
   b. $105,000 at 5.5% for 20 years
   c. $95,000 at 5% for 15 years

**LG3, 4**

5. *Use Worksheet 5.2.* Rosa Ramirez is currently renting an apartment for $725 per month and paying $275 annually for renter's insurance. She just found a small townhouse she can buy for $185,000. She has enough cash for a $10,000 down payment and $4,000 in closing costs. Rosa estimated the following costs as a percentage of the home's price: property taxes, 2.5%; homeowner's insurance, 0.5%; and maintenance, 0.7%. She is in the 25% tax bracket. Using Worksheet 5.2, calculate the cost of each alternative and recommend the least costly option—rent or buy—for Rosa.

**LG6**

6. *Use Worksheet 5.4.* Lin Wong purchased a condominium 4 years ago for $180,000, paying $1,250 per month on her $162,000, 8%, 25-year mortgage. The current loan balance is $152,401. Recently, interest rates dropped sharply, causing Lin to consider refinancing her condo at the prevailing rate of 6%. She expects to remain in the condo for at least 4 more years and has found a lender that will make a 6%, 21-year, $152,401 loan, requiring monthly payments of $1,065. Although there is no prepayment penalty on her current mortgage, Lin will have to pay $1,500 in closing costs on the new mortgage. She is in the 15% tax bracket. Based on this information, use the mortgage refinancing analysis form in Worksheet 5.4 to determine whether she should refinance her mortgage under the specified terms.

> "Overall, I enjoy the textbook and feel that **you have made it as easy as possible to succeed in this course by providing numerous study aids online.**"
>
> – Ben Larkins, Student at Middle Tennessee State University

# GET ONLINE

HE DID

Discover your **PFIN** online experience at **CengageBrain.com**.

You'll find everything you need to succeed in your class.

- Smart Sites
- Money Online Exercises
- Bonus Exhibits
- Concept Checks
- Quizzes
- Flash Cards
- Crossword Puzzles
- Interactive Worksheets
- Kiplinger Personal Finance Videos
- eBook
- And More!

©VICTORIA VISUALS/SHUTTERSTOCK

# 6

# USING CREDIT

## LEARNING GOALS

**LG1** Describe the reasons for using consumer credit and identify its benefits and problems. (p. 123)

**LG2** Develop a plan to establish a strong credit history. (p. 123)

**LG3** Distinguish among the different forms of open account credit. (p. 129)

**LG4** Apply for, obtain, and manage open forms of credit. (p. 134)

**LG5** Choose the right credit cards and recognize their advantages and disadvantages. (p. 140)

**LG6** Avoid credit problems, protect yourself against credit card fraud, and understand the personal bankruptcy process. (p. 140)

## LG1, LG2 The Basic Concepts of Credit

It's so easy—just slide that credit card through the reader and you can get gas for your car, buy a laptop at Staples, or furnish an apartment. It happens *several hundred million times a day* across the United States. Credit, in fact, has become an entrenched part of our everyday lives, and we as consumers use it in one form or another to purchase just about every type of good or service imaginable. Indeed, because of the ready availability and widespread use of credit, our economy is often called a "credit economy." And for good reason: by 2009, individuals in this country had run up almost *$2.56 trillion dollars* in consumer debt—and that *excludes* home mortgages.

Consumer credit is important in the personal financial planning process because of the impact it can have on (1) attaining financial goals and (2) cash budgets. For one thing, various forms of consumer credit can help you reach your financial objectives by enabling you to acquire some of the more expensive items in a systematic fashion, without throwing your whole budget into disarray. But there's another side to consumer credit: it has to be paid back! Unless credit is used intelligently, the "buy now, pay later" attitude can quickly turn an otherwise orderly budget into a budgetary nightmare and lead to some serious problems—even bankruptcy!

Whatever their age group, people tend to borrow for several major reasons.

- **To avoid paying cash for large outlays.** Rather than pay cash for large purchases such as houses and cars, most people borrow part of the purchase price and then repay the loan on some scheduled basis. Spreading payments over time makes big-ticket items more affordable, and consumers get the use of an expensive asset right away.

- **To meet a financial emergency.** For example, people may need to borrow to cover living expenses during a period of unemployment or to purchase plane tickets to visit a sick relative.

- **For convenience.** Merchants as well as banks offer a variety of charge accounts and credit cards that allow consumers to charge just about anything—from gas or clothes and stereos to doctor and dental bills and even college tuition. Further, in many places—restaurants, for instance—using a credit card is far easier than writing a check.

- **For investment purposes.** As we'll see in Chapter 11, it's relatively easy for an investor to partially finance the purchase of many different kinds of investments with borrowed funds. In fact, on the New York Stock Exchange, *margin loans*, as they're called, amounted to nearly $184 billion in the spring of 2009.

> { *It's so easy—just slide that credit card through the reader and you can get gas for your car, buy a laptop at Staples, or furnish an apartment.* }

## Why We Use Credit

People typically use credit as a way to pay for goods and services that cost more than they can afford to take from their current income. This is particularly true for those in the 25–44 age group, who simply have not had time to accumulate the liquid assets required to pay cash outright for major purchases and expenditures. As people begin to approach their mid-40s, however, their savings and investments start to build up, and their debt loads tend to decline—which is really not too surprising when you consider that the median household net worth for those in the 45–54 age group is *about 80% more* than for those aged 35 to 44.

## Improper Uses of Credit

Many people use consumer credit to live beyond their means. For some people, overspending becomes a way of life, and it is perhaps the biggest danger in borrowing—especially because it's so easy to do. And nowhere did that become more apparent than in the wake of *the credit crisis of 2007–2009*. Indeed, as credit became more readily available and easier to obtain, it also became increasingly clear that many consumers were, in fact, severely overusing it. Whether or not the consumer deserved the credit was really not an issue—the only thing that seemed to matter was that it was there for the taking! All this resulted in a credit meltdown unlike

©JASON STITT/SHUTTERSTOCK

# MONEY IN ACTION

## The Credit Meltdown of 2007–2009

In 2007, several broad economic trends conspired to push the United States into a severe economic crisis that lasted well into 2009. Although its effects were not evenly distributed, the crisis became global in scope. The causes of the crisis include a collapse of housing prices, U.S. monetary policy that made the cost of money extremely low and leverage very attractive, and a rise in the delinquencies on subprime mortgages (extended to higher-risk borrowers) that caused severe losses for financial institutions. Some argue that the deregulation of the U.S. financial sector made conditions ripe for the crisis. Also during the years leading up to the crisis, United States consumption was high and savings rates were low, which meant there were more funds to invest. The low cost of credit had encouraged massive investments in housing in the 2000s, which created bubble prices that were financed aggressively by mortgages that were too often extended to unqualified buyers. The high level of mortgage financing was greeted with increased creation of mortgage-backed securities (MBS), which are bonds that package mortgages and pass through the payments to investors. The value of the MBS were dependent on the mortgage payments and the prices of the underlying houses. Thus, when housing prices started slumping in 2006, the financial institutions that had invested heavily in MBS started reporting significant losses. These deep losses in the financial sector reduced their ability and willingness to loan money.

The downturn in the U.S. economy made it much more difficult for both consumers and businesses to borrow money. Homeowners' equity in their homes decreased, which reduced their ability to borrow. Consumers with reduced home equity are viewed as greater credit risks. The diminished profits prospect for businesses during the financial crisis made it harder for them to borrow money as well. This reduced ability to borrow made businesses cut back on their activities, which increased unemployment and fed the crisis further. Reduced credit availability caused a significant decline in consumer spending, which typically accounts for about two-thirds of economic activity in the United States. All lenders became pickier. Credit standards tightened and loan amounts and access dropped to a trickle—all of which only exacerbated the economic turndown.

*Sources:* Louis Uchitelle, "Pain Spreads As Credit Vise Grows Tighter," *The New York Times,* September 18, 2008, http://www.nytimes.com/2008/09/19/business/economy/19econ.html, accessed June 2009; Dean Baker, "It's Not the Credit Crisis, Damn It!" *The American Prospect,* http://www.prospect.org/csnc/blogs/beat_the_press_archive?month=11&year=2008&base_name=its_not_the_credit_crisis_damn, November 29, 2008, accessed June 2009; and "Declaration of G20," http://georgewbush-whitehouse.archives.gov/news/releases/2008/11/20081115-1.html, accessed June 2009.

anything this country had ever seen. This chapter's *Money in Action* feature focuses on the credit meltdown and discusses some of its causes and effects.

Fact is, once hooked on "plastic," people use their credit cards to make even routine purchases and all too often don't realize they have overextended themselves until it's too late. Overspenders simply won't admit that they're spending too much. As far as they're concerned, they can afford to buy all those things because, after all, they still have their credit cards and can still afford to pay the minimum amounts each month. Unfortunately, such spending eventually leads to mounting bills. And by making only the minimum payment, borrowers pay a huge price in the long run. Look at Exhibit 6.1, which shows the amount of time and interest charges required to repay credit card balances if you make only minimum payments of 3% of the outstanding balance. For example, if you carry a

## Exhibit 6.1  Minimum Payments Mean Maximum Years

Paying off credit card balances at the minimum monthly amount required by the card issuer will take a long time and cost you a great deal of interest, as this table demonstrates. *The calculations here are based on a minimum 3% payment and 15% annual interest rate.*

| Original Balance | Years to Repay | Interest Paid | Total Interest Paid as Percentage of Original Balance |
|---|---|---|---|
| $5,000 | 16.4 | $3,434 | 68.7% |
| 4,000 | 15.4 | 2,720 | 68.0 |
| 3,000 | 14.0 | 2,005 | 66.8 |
| 2,000 | 12.1 | 1,291 | 64.5 |
| 1,000 | 8.8 | 577 | 57.7 |

$3,000 balance—which is about *one-third* the national average—on a card that charges 15.0% annually, it would take you 14 years to retire the debt, and your interest charges would total some $2,000—*or more than 66% of the original balance!*

Some cards offer even lower minimum payments of just 2% of the outstanding balance. Although such small payments may seem like a good deal, clearly they don't work to your advantage and only increase the time and amount of interest required to repay the debt. Indeed, by making minimum 2% payments, it would take *more than 32 years* to pay off a $5,000 balance on a credit card that carries a 15% rate of interest. In contrast, that same $5,000 balance could be paid off in *just 16.4 years* if you had made 3% minimum payments. Just think, making an additional 1% payment can save you nearly 16 years of interest! That's why the federal banking regulators recently issued new guidelines stating that minimum monthly credit card payments should now cover at least 1% of the outstanding balance, plus all monthly finance charges and any other fees.

The best way to steer clear of future repayment shock is to avoid using your credit card in the following situations:

**(1)** to meet basic living expenses;
**(2)** to make impulse purchases, especially expensive ones; and
**(3)** to purchase nondurable (short-lived) goods and services.

Except in situations where credit cards are used occasionally for convenience, or where payments on recurring credit purchases are built into the monthly budget, a good rule to remember when considering the use of credit is that *the product purchased on credit should outlive the payments.*

Unfortunately, people who overspend eventually arrive at the point where they must choose to either become delinquent in their payments or sacrifice necessities, such as food and clothing. If payment obligations aren't met, the consequences are likely to be a damaged credit rating, lawsuits, or even personal bankruptcy. The Bonus Exhibit, "Some Credit Danger Signs," at 4ltrpress.cengage.com, lists some common signals that indicate it may be time to stop buying on credit. *Ignoring the telltale signs that you are overspending can only lead to more serious problems.*

## Establishing Credit

The willingness of lenders to extend credit depends on their assessment of your creditworthiness—that is, your ability to promptly repay the debt. Lenders look at various factors in making this decision, such as your present earnings and net worth. Equally important,

they look at your current debt position and your credit history. Thus, it's worth your while to do what you can to build a strong credit rating.

### First Steps in Establishing Credit

First, open checking and savings accounts. They signal stability to lenders and indicate that you handle your financial affairs in a businesslike way. Second, use credit: open one or two charge accounts and use them periodically, even if you prefer paying cash. You might pay an annual fee or interest on some (or all) of your account balances, but in the process, you'll build a record of being a reliable credit customer. Third, obtain a small loan, even if you don't need one. If you don't actually need the money, put it in a liquid investment, such as a money market account or certificate of deposit. The interest you earn should offset some of the interest expense on the loan; you can view the difference as a cost of building good credit. You should repay the loan promptly, perhaps even *a little* ahead of schedule, to minimize the difference in interest rates. Keep in mind that your ability to obtain a large loan in the future will depend, in part, on how you managed smaller ones in the past.

**debt safety ratio**
The proportion of total monthly consumer credit obligations to monthly take-home pay.

## Build a Strong Credit History

From a financial perspective, maintaining a strong credit history is just as important as developing a solid employment record! Don't take credit lightly, and don't assume that getting the loan or the credit card is the toughest part. It's not. That's just the first step; servicing it (i.e., making payments) in a prompt and timely fashion—month in and month out—is the really tough part of the consumer credit process. And in many respects, it's the most important element of consumer credit because it determines your creditworthiness. By using credit wisely and repaying it on time, you're establishing a *credit history* that tells lenders you're a dependable, reliable, and responsible borrower. When you take on credit, you have an *obligation* to live up to the terms of the loan, including how and when the credit will be repaid.

If you foresee difficulty in meeting a monthly payment, let the lender know. Usually arrangements can be made to help you through the situation. This is especially true with installment loans that require fixed monthly payments. Don't just skip a payment, because that's going to put your account into a *late status until you make up the missed payment.* Instead, try to work out an extension with your lender. Here's what you do. Explain the situation to the loan officer and ask for an extension of one (or two) months on your loan. In

©BRIAN A. JACKSON/SHUTTERSTOCK

most cases, so long as this hasn't occurred before, the extension is almost automatically granted. The maturity of the loan is formally extended for a month (or two), and the extra interest of carrying the loan for another month (or two) is either added to the loan balance or, more commonly, paid at the time the extension is granted (such an extension fee generally amounts to a fraction of the normal monthly payment). Then, in a month or two, you pick up where you left off and resume your normal monthly payments on the loan. This is the most sensible way of making it through those rough times because it doesn't harm your credit record. Just don't do it too often.

## How Much Credit Can You Stand?

Sound financial planning dictates that you need to have a good idea of how much credit you can comfortably tolerate. The easiest way to avoid repayment problems and ensure that your borrowing won't place an undue strain on your monthly budget is to *limit the use of credit to your ability to repay the debt!* A useful guideline (and one widely used by lenders) is to make sure your monthly repayment burden doesn't exceed 20% of your monthly *take-home pay*. Most experts, however, regard the 20% figure as the *maximum* debt burden and strongly recommend **debt safety ratios** closer to 15% or 10%—perhaps even lower if you plan on applying for a new mortgage in the near future. Note that the monthly repayment burden here *does include* payments on your credit cards, but it *excludes* your monthly mortgage obligation.

### Go to Smart Sites

The American Bankers Association provides helpful information about shopping for credit and managing debt at its consumer education site. Whenever you see "*Go to Smart Sites*" in this chapter, visit 4ltrpress.cengage.com for help finding answers online. ●

To illustrate, consider someone who takes home $2,500 a month. Using a 20% ratio, she should have monthly consumer credit payments of no more than $500—that is, $2,500 × .20 = $500. This is the maximum amount of her monthly disposable income that she should need to pay off both personal loans and other forms of consumer credit (such as credit cards and education loans). This, of course, is not the maximum amount of consumer credit she can have outstanding—in fact, her total consumer indebtedness can, and likely would, be considerably larger. The key factor is that with her income level, her *payments* on this type of debt should not exceed $500 a month. Exhibit 6.2 provides a summary of low (10%), manageable (15%), and maximum (20%) monthly credit payments for various income levels. Obviously, *the lower the debt safety ratio, the better shape you're in, credit-wise, and the easier it should be for you to service your outstanding consumer debt.*

You can compute the debt safety ratio as follows:

$$\text{Debt safety ratio} = \frac{\text{Total monthly consumer credit payments}}{\text{Monthly take-home pay}}$$

This measure is the focus of Worksheet 6.1, which you can use for keeping close tabs on your own debt safety ratio. It shows the impact that each new loan you take out, or credit card you sign up for, can have on this important measure of creditworthiness. Consider, for example, Charles and Angie Packard. As seen in Worksheet 6.1, they have five outstanding consumer loans, plus they're carrying

balances on three credit cards. All totaled, these eight obligations require monthly payments of almost $740, which accounts for about one-fifth of their combined take-home pay and gives them a debt safety ratio of 18%. And note toward the bottom of the worksheet that if the Packards want to lower this ratio to, say, 15%, then they'll either have to reduce their monthly payments to $615 or increase their take-home pay to at least $4,927 a month.

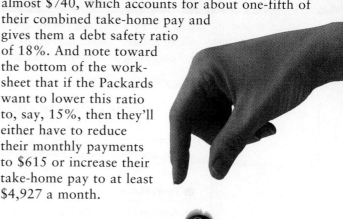

©RYASICK PHOTOGRAPHY/SHUTTERSTOCK

## Exhibit 6.2   Credit Guidelines Based on Ability to Repay

According to the debt safety ratio, the amount of consumer credit you should have outstanding depends on the monhtly payments you can afford to make.

| Monthly Take-Home Pay | Monthly Consumer Credit Payments | | |
| --- | --- | --- | --- |
| | *Low* Debt Safety Ratio (10%) | *Manageable* Debt Safety Ratio (15%) | *Maximum* Debt Safety Ratio (20%) |
| $1,000 | $100 | $150 | $ 200 |
| $1,250 | $125 | $188 | $ 250 |
| $1,500 | $150 | $225 | $ 300 |
| $2,000 | $200 | $300 | $ 400 |
| $2,500 | $250 | $375 | $ 500 |
| $3,000 | $300 | $450 | $ 600 |
| $3,500 | $350 | $525 | $ 700 |
| $4,000 | $400 | $600 | $ 800 |
| $5,000 | $500 | $750 | $1,000 |

A worksheet like this one will help a household stay on top of their monthly credit card and consumer loan payments, as well as their *debt safety ratio*—an important measure of creditworthiness. The key here is to keep the debt safety ratio as low as (reasonably) possible, something that can be done by keeping monthly loan payments in line with monthly take-home pay.

### MONTHLY CONSUMER LOAN PAYMENTS & DEBT SAFETY RATIO

**Name** Charles & Angie Packard          **Date** June 21, 2010

| ■ Type of Loan* | Lender | Current Monthly (or Min.) Payment |
|---|---|---|
| • Auto and personal loans | 1. Ford Motor Credit | $ 360.00 |
| | 2. Bank of America | 115.00 |
| | 3. | |
| • Education loans | 1. U.S. Dept. of Education | 75.00 |
| | 2. | |
| • Overdraft protection line | 1. Bank of America | 30.00 |
| • Personal line of credit | | |
| • Credit cards | 1. Bank of America Visa | 28.00 |
| | 2. Fidelity MC | 31.00 |
| | 3. JC Penney | 28.00 |
| | 4. | |
| • Home equity line | 1. Bank of America | 72.00 |
| **TOTAL MONTHLY PAYMENTS** | | $ 739.00 |

*\*Note:* List only those loans that require regular monthly payments.

| ■ Monthly Take-Home Pay | 1. Charles | $ 1,855.00 |
|---|---|---|
| | 2. Angie | 2,250.00 |
| **TOTAL MONTHLY TAKE-HOME PAY** | | $ 4,105.00 |

■ **Debt Safety Ratio:**

$$\frac{\text{Total monthly payments}}{\text{Total monthly take-home pay}} \times 100 = \frac{\$\ 739.00}{\$4,105.00} \times 100 = \underline{18.0\ \%}$$

• ***Changes needed to reach a new debt safety ratio***

1. New (Target) debt safety ratio: 15.0 %

2. At current take-home pay of $ 4,105.00 , total monthly payments must equal:

Total monthly take-home pay × Target debt safety ratio**

$\$4,105.00 \times \underline{0.150} = \$\ \underline{615.75}$

**New Monthly Payments**

**OR**

3. With current monthly payments of $ 739.00 , total take-home pay must equal:

$$\frac{\text{Total monthly payments}}{\text{New (target) debt safety ratio}} \times 100 = \frac{\$\ 739.00}{0.150} = \$4,926.67$$

**New take-home pay**

*\*\*Note:* Enter debt safety ratio as a decimal (e.g., 15% = 0.15).

## LG3 Credit Cards and Other Types of Open Account Credit

**Open account credit** is a form of credit extended to a consumer in advance of any transactions. Typically, a retail outlet or bank agrees to allow the consumer to buy or borrow up to a specified amount on open account. Credit is extended as long as the consumer does not exceed the established **credit limit** and makes payments in accordance with the specified terms. Open account credit issued by a retail outlet, such as a department store or oil company, is usually applicable only in that establishment or one of its locations. In contrast, open account credit issued by banks, such as *MasterCard* and *Visa* accounts, can be used to make purchases at a wide variety of businesses. Having open account credit is a lot like having your own personal line of credit—it's there when you need it.

Open account credit generally is available from two broadly defined sources:

**(1)** financial institutions, and

**(2)** retail stores/merchants.

*Financial institutions* issue general-purpose credit cards, as well as secured and unsecured revolving lines of credit and overdraft protection lines. *Retail stores and merchants* make up the other major source of open account credit. They provide this service as a way to promote the sales of their products, and their principal form of credit is the charge (or credit) card. Together, there are over 1.5 billion bank credit cards and retail charge cards outstanding today. Let's now take a look at these two forms of credit, along with *debit cards* and *revolving lines of credit*.

### Bank Credit Cards

Probably the most popular form of open account credit is the **bank credit card**, issued by commercial banks and other financial institutions—Visa and MasterCard being the two dominant types. These cards allow their holders to charge purchases worldwide at literally millions of stores, restaurants, shops, and gas stations as well as at state and municipal governments, colleges and universities, medical groups, and mail-order houses—not to mention the Internet, where they've become the currency of choice. They can be used to pay for almost anything—groceries, doctor bills, college tuition, airline tickets, and car rentals. They can also be used to borrow money. In fact, by 2003, the amount of transactions completed with credit and debit cards actually surpassed those made with cash or check.

The recent financial crisis brought tougher credit standards and sharply reduced credit lines to the bank credit card business. Standards tend to tighten quickly in a crisis, and it can take several years before they move back to their pre-crisis levels. As a result, consumers are finding it harder to get new credit cards, and the limits on exisiting cards are often slashed. Many economists forecast that, this time, credit standards are likely to remain far more stringent than what existed prior to the crisis. Yet even in spite of all this, bank credit cards can still be of great convenience and value to consumers. But to get the most from them, individuals who use these cards should be thoroughly familiar with their basic features.

### Line of Credit

The **line of credit** provided to the holder of a bank credit card is set by the issuer. It's the maximum amount that the cardholder can owe at any given time. The size of the credit line depends on both the applicant's request and the results of the issuer's investigation of the applicant's credit and financial status. Lines of credit can reach $50,000 or more, but for the most part, they range from about $500 to $2,500. Although card issuers fully expect you to keep your credit within the specified limits, most won't take any real action until you extend your account balance by a certain percentage. For example, if you had a $1,000 credit limit, you probably wouldn't hear a thing from the card issuer until your outstanding balance exceeded, say, $1,200 (i.e., 20% above the $1,000 line of credit). On the other hand, don't count on getting off scot-free, because most card issuers assess *over-the-limit* fees whenever you go over your credit limit (more on this later).

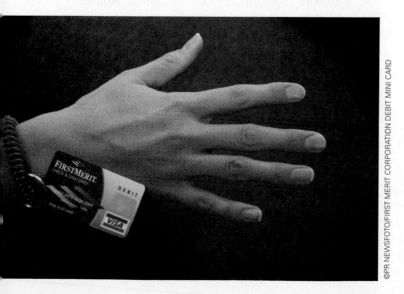

©PR NEWSFOTO/FIRST MERIT CORPORATION DEBIT MINI CARD

## Cash Advances

In addition to purchasing merchandise and services, the holder of a bank credit card can obtain a **cash advance** from any participating bank. Cash advances are loans on which interest begins to accrue immediately. They're transacted in the same way as merchandise purchases, except that they take place at a commercial bank or some other financial institution and involve the receipt of cash (or a check) instead of goods and services. Another way to get a cash advance is to use the "convenience checks" you receive from the card issuer to pay for purchases. You can even use your credit card to draw cash from an ATM, any time of the day or night. Usually, the size of the cash advance from an ATM is limited to some nominal amount (a common amount is $500 or less), although the amount you can obtain from the teller window at a bank is limited only by the unused credit in your account.

## Interest Charges

Generally speaking, *the interest rates on credit cards are higher than any other form of consumer credit.* With few exceptions, the average *annual rate of interest* charged on standard fixed-rate bank credit cards was around 13.5% in mid-2009, while the average rate on variable-rate cards was closer to 10.5%. You'll find that most bank cards have one rate for merchandise purchases and a much higher rate for cash advances. For example, the rate on merchandise purchases might be 12%, while the rate on cash advances could be 19% or 20%. And when shopping for a credit card, watch out for those *special low introductory rates* that many banks offer. Known as "teaser rates," they're usually only good for the first 6 to 12 months. Then, just as soon as the introductory period ends, so do the low interest rates.

Most of these cards have variable interest rates that are tied to an index that moves with market rates. The most popular is the prime or **base rate**: the rate a bank uses as a base for loans to individuals and small or midsize businesses. These cards adjust their interest rate monthly or quarterly and usually have minimum and maximum rates. To illustrate, consider a bank card whose terms are *prime plus 7.5%*, with a minimum of 10% and a maximum of 15.25%. If the prime rate is 3.25%, then the rate of interest charged on this card would be 3.25% + 7.5% = 10.75%. Given the widespread use of variable interest rates, bank cardholders should know that—just as falling rates bring down interest rates on credit cards—rising market rates are guaranteed to lead to much higher interest charges!

Bank credit card issuers must disclose interest costs and related information to consumers *before* extending credit. In the case of purchases of merchandise and services, the specified interest rate may not apply to charges until after the **grace period**. During this short period, usually 20 to 30 days, you have historically been able to pay your credit card bill in full and avoid any interest charges. However, once you carry a balance—that is, when you don't pay your card in full during the grace period—the interest rate is usually applied to any unpaid balances carried from previous periods as well as to any new purchases made. Interest on cash advances, in contrast, *begins the day the advance is taken out.*

## Then There Are Those Other Fees

Besides the interest charged on bank credit cards, there are a few other fees you should be aware of. To begin with, many (though not all) bank cards charge *annual fees* just for the "privilege" of being able to use the card. In most cases, the fee is around $25 to $40 a year, though it can amount to much more for prestige cards. As a rule, the larger the bank or S&L, the more likely it is to charge an annual fee for its credit cards. What's more, many issuers also charge a *transaction fee* for each (non-ATM) cash advance; this fee usually amounts to about $5 per cash advance *or* 3% of the amount obtained in the transaction, whichever is more.

Historically, card issuers have come up with many ways to squeeze additional revenue from you. These have included late-payment fees, over-the-limit charges, foreign transaction fees, and balance transfer fees. For example, if you're a bit late in making your payment then some banks will hit you with a late-payment fee, which is really a redundant charge because you're already paying interest on the unpaid balance. Similarly, if you happened to go over your credit limit then you'd be hit with a charge for that too (again, this is in addition to the interest you're already paying). Critics really dislike this fee because they maintain it's hard for cardholders to know when they've hit their credit ceilings. Some card issuers even went so far as to slap you with a fee for *not using your credit card*—one bank, for example, charged a $15 fee to customers (cardholders) who didn't use their credit cards in a 6-month period.

These onerous credit card issuer practices and extra fees led to the passage of the Credit Card Act of 2009. In the past, credit card companies could change interest rates and other aspects of the agreement without notice. They could even change terms retroactively such that they applied two months before you were notified. Among other things, the new law requires credit card companies to give 45 days notice before changing your agreement. Similarly, credit card companies previously could raise your interest rate if your credit report deteriorated or if you were late on even just one payment. The new law prohibits that, and allows credit card companies to apply a new interest rate only to new balances after you are 60 days delinquent in paying on your account. Importantly, your old balance can only be charged your old interest rate.

## Special Types of Bank Credit Cards

Bank credit cards sure aren't what they used to be. Today, in addition to standard, "plain vanilla" bank cards, you can obtain cards that offer rebates and special incentive programs, cards that are sponsored by nonprofit organizations, even credit cards aimed specifically at college students.

### Reward Cards

One of the fastest-growing segments of the bankcard market is the **reward (co-branded) credit card**, which combines features of a traditional bank credit card with an incentive: cash, merchandise rebates, airline tickets, or even investments. About half of credit cards are rebate cards, and new types are introduced almost every day. Here are some of the many incentive programs.

- **Frequent flyer programs.** In this program, the cardholder earns free frequent flyer miles for each dollar charged on his or her credit card. These frequent flyer miles can then be used with airline-affiliated programs for free tickets, first-class upgrades, and other travel-related benefits.

- **Automobile rebate programs.** Some credit cards allow the cardholder to earn annual rebates of up to 5% that can be used, up to specified limits, for new car purchases, leases, or auto maintenance programs. Indeed, most of the major car companies offer some kind of rewards-related credit card that can be used to buy a car or related items.

- **Other merchandise rebates.** An increasing number of companies are participating in bankcard reward programs, including, for example, Norwegian Cruise Line, Harrahs, NASCAR, Starbucks, and Marriott Hotels. Several regional phone companies even offer rebates on phone calls. (A good site for finding information about rebate card offers is **http://www.cardtrak.com**.)

Are rebate cards a good deal? Well, yes and no. To see if they make sense for you, evaluate these cards carefully by looking at your usage patterns and working out the annual cost of the cards before and after the rebate. Don't get so carried away with the gimmick that you lose sight of the total costs. Most incentive cards carry higher interest rates than regular bankcards do. These cards generally work best for those who can use the rebates, charge a lot, and who don't carry high monthly balances.

### Affinity Cards

"Credit cards with a cause" is the way to describe **affinity cards**. These cards are nothing more than standard Visa or MasterCards that are issued in conjunction with a sponsoring group—most commonly some type of charitable, political, or professional organization. So-named because of the bond between the sponsoring group and its members, affinity cards are sponsored by such nonprofit organizations as MADD, the American Wildlife Fund, AARP, and Special Olympics. In addition, they are issued by college and university alumni groups, labor organizations, religious and fraternal groups, and professional societies. So, why even bother with one of these cards? Well, unlike traditional bank cards, affinity cards make money for the group backing the card because the sponsoring groups receive a share of the profits. But to cover the money that goes to the sponsoring organization, the issuer/bank usually charges higher fees or higher interest rates. Even so, some may view these cards as a great way to contribute to a worthy cause. Others, however, may feel it makes more sense to use a traditional credit card and then write a check to their favorite charity.

### Secured Credit Cards

You may have seen the ads on TV where the announcer says that no matter how bad your credit, you can still qualify for one of their credit cards. The pitch may sound too good to be true; and in some respects, it is because there's a catch. Namely, the credit is "secured"—meaning you have to put up *collateral* in order to get the card! These are so-called **secured**, or **collateralized credit cards** where the amount of credit is determined by the amount of liquid collateral you're able to put up. These cards are targeted at people with no credit, or bad credit histories, who don't qualify for conventional credit cards. Issued as Visa or MasterCard, they're like any other credit card except for the collateral. To qualify, a customer must deposit a certain amount (usually $500 or more) into a 12- to 18-month certificate of deposit that the issuing bank holds as collateral. The cardholder then gets a credit line equal to the deposit. If the customer

**reward (co-branded) credit card** A bank credit card that combines features of a traditional bank credit card with an additional incentive, such as rebates and airline mileage.

**affinity cards** A standard bank credit card issued in conjunction with some charitable, political, or other nonprofit organization.

**secured (collateralized) credit cards** A type of credit card that's secured with some form of collateral, such as a bank CD.

defaults, the bank has the CD to cover its losses. By making payments on time, it's hoped that these cardholders will establish (or reestablish) a credit history that may qualify them for a conventional (unsecured) credit card. Secured credit cards normally carry annual fees and finance charges that are equal to, or greater than, those of regular credit cards.

### Student Credit Cards

Some large banks, through their Visa and MasterCard programs, have special credit cards that specifically target college students. These **student credit cards** often come packaged with special promotional programs that are meant to appeal to this segment of the market—such as free music, movie tickets, and the like. Except for these features, there's really nothing unusual about these cards or their terms. Most simply require that you be enrolled in a 2- or 4-year college or university and have some source of income, whatever that may be. In particular, they usually *do not require* any parental or guardian guarantees, nor do they require that you hold a full-time (or even a part-time) job. From the student's perspective, these cards not only offer convenience but are also great for building up a solid credit history. Just *remember to use them responsibly*—that's the way to get the most from these cards or any other form of credit, for that matter!

## Retail Charge Cards

**Retail charge cards** are issued by department stores, oil companies, car rental agencies, and so on. These cards are popular with merchants because they build consumer loyalty and enhance sales; consumers like them because they offer a convenient way to shop. These cards carry a preset credit limit—a line of credit—that varies with the creditworthiness of the cardholder. This form of credit is most common in department and clothing stores and other high-volume outlets, where customers are likely to make several purchases each month. Most large oil companies also offer charge cards that allow customers to buy gas and oil products, *but they're expected to pay for such purchases in full upon receipt of the monthly bill.* Interest on retail charge cards is typically fixed at 1.5% to 1.85% monthly, or about 18% to 22% per year—considerably more than what most bank cards charge.

## Debit Cards

It looks like a credit card, it works like a credit card, it even has the familiar MasterCard and Visa credit card markings. But it's not a *credit* card—rather, it's a *debit* card. Simply put, a **debit card** provides direct access to your checking account and, thus, *works like writing a check*. That is, when you use a debit card to make a purchase, the amount of the transaction is charged directly to your checking account. Using a debit card isn't the same thing as buying on credit; it may appear that you're charging it, but actually *you're paying with cash*. Accordingly, there are no finance charges to pay.

Debit cards are becoming very popular, especially with consumers who want the convenience of a credit card but not the high cost of interest that comes with them. In fact, in 2006, debit card use exceeded credit card use for the first time. This is no small feat given there are more than 50 billion credit/debit card transactions each year in the United States. Debit cards are accepted at most establishments displaying the Visa or MasterCard logo but function as an alternative to writing checks. If you use a debit card to make a purchase at a department store or restaurant, the transaction will show up on your next monthly *checking account* statement. Needless to say, to keep your records straight, you should enter debit card transactions directly into your checkbook ledger as they occur and treat them as withdrawals, or checks, by subtracting them from your checking account balance. Debit cards can also be used to gain access to your account through 24-hour teller machines or ATMs—which is the closest thing to a cash advance that these cards have to offer.

A big disadvantage of a debit card, of course, is that it doesn't provide a line of credit. In addition, it can cause overdraft problems if you fail to make the proper entries to your checking account or inadvertently use it when you think you're using a credit card. Also, some debit card issuers charge a transaction fee or a flat annual fee; and some *merchants* may even charge you just for using your debit card. On the plus side, a debit card enables you to avoid the potential credit problems and high costs of credit cards. Further, it's as convenient to use as a credit card—in fact, if convenience is the major reason you use a credit card, you might want to consider switching to a debit card for at least some transactions, especially at outlets such as gas stations that give discounts for cash purchases and consider a debit card to be as good as cash.

## Revolving Credit Lines

**Revolving lines of credit** are offered by banks, brokerage houses, and other financial institutions. These credit lines normally don't involve the use of credit cards. Rather, they're accessed by writing checks on regular checking accounts or specially designated credit line accounts. They are a form of open account credit and often represent a far better deal than credit cards, not only because they offer more credit but also because they can be a lot less expensive. And there may even be a tax advantage to using one of these other kinds of credit. These lines basically provide their users with ready access to borrowed money (that is, cash advances) through revolving lines of credit. The three major forms of open (non–credit card) credit are overdraft protection lines, unsecured personal lines of credit, and home equity credit lines.

### Overdraft Protection

An **overdraft protection line** is simply a line of credit linked to a checking account that enables a depositor to overdraw his or her checking account up to a pre-determined limit. These lines are usually set up with credit limits of $500 to $1,000, but they can be for as much as $10,000 or more. The consumer taps this line of credit by simply writing a check, and if that particular check happens to overdraw the account, the overdraft protection line will automatically advance funds in an amount necessary to put the account back in the black. In some cases, overdraft protection is provided by *linking the bank's credit card to your checking account*. These arrangements act like regular overdraft lines except that, when the account is overdrawn, the bank automatically taps your credit card line and transfers the money into your checking account. It's treated as a cash advance from your credit card, but the result is the same as a regular overdraft protection line; it automatically covers overdrawn checks.

If you're not careful, you can quickly exhaust this type of credit by writing a lot of overdraft checks. As with any line of credit, there's a limit to how much you can obtain. Be extremely careful with such a credit line and by all means, *don't take it as a license to routinely overdraw your account!* Doing so on a regular basis is a signal that you're probably mismanaging your cash and/or living beyond your budget. It's best to view an overdraft protection line strictly as an *emergency* source of credit—and any funds advanced should be repaid as quickly as possible.

### Unsecured Personal Lines

Another form of revolving credit is the **unsecured personal credit line**, which basically makes a line of credit available to an individual on an as-needed basis. In essence, it's a way of borrowing money from a bank, S&L, credit union, savings bank, or brokerage firm any time you wish and without going through all the hassle of setting up a new loan.

Here's how it works. Suppose you apply for and are approved for a personal line of credit at your bank. Once you've been approved and the credit line is established, you'll be issued *checks* that you can write against it. If you need a cash advance, all you need to do is write a check (against your credit line account) and deposit it into your checking account. Or, if you need the money to buy some big-ticket item—say, an expensive stereo system—you can just make the credit line check out to the dealer and, when it clears, it will be charged against your unsecured personal credit line as an advance. Personal lines of credit are usually set up for minimums of $2,000 to $5,000 and often amount to $25,000 or more. As with an overdraft protection line, once an advance is made, repayment is set up on a monthly installment basis. Depending on the amount outstanding, repayment is normally structured over a period of 2 to 5 years; to keep the monthly payments low, larger amounts of debt are usually given longer repayment periods.

Although these credit lines do offer attractive terms to the consumer, they come with their share of problems, perhaps the biggest of which is how easily the cash advances can be obtained. These lines also normally involve *substantial* amounts of credit and are nearly as easy to use as credit cards. This combination can have devastating effects on a family's budget if it leads to overspending or excessive reliance on credit. As such, systematic repayment of the debt should be built into the budget, and every effort should be made to ensure that using this kind of credit will not overly strain the family finances.

### Home Equity Credit Lines

Consider this: A couple buys a home for $285,000; some 10 years later, it's worth $365,000. The couple now has an asset worth $365,000 on which all they owe is the original mortgage, which may now have a balance of, say, $220,000. The couple clearly has built up a substantial amount of equity in their home: $365,000 – $220,000 = $145,000. But how can they tap that equity without having to sell their home? The answer is a **home equity credit line**. Such lines are much like unsecured personal credit lines except that they're *secured with a second mortgage on the home*. These lines of credit allow you to tap up to 100% (or more) of the equity in your home by merely writing a check. Although some banks and financial institutions allow their customers to borrow up to 100% of the *equity* in their homes—or, in some cases, even

**overdraft protection line** A line of credit linked to a checking account that allows a depositor to overdraw the account up to a specified amount.

**unsecured personal credit line** A line of credit made available to an individual on an as-needed basis.

**home equity credit line** A line of credit issued against the existing equity in a home.

@HANNAMARIAH/SHUTTERSTOCK

more—most lenders set their maximum credit lines at 75% to 80% of the *market value* of the home, which reduces the amount of money they'll lend.

Here's how these lines work. Recall the couple in our example that has built up equity of $145,000 in their home—equity against which they can borrow through a home equity credit line. Assuming they have a good credit record and using a 75% loan-to-market-value ratio, a bank would be willing to lend up to $273,750; that is, 75% of the value of the house is 0.75 × $365,000 = $273,750. Subtracting the $220,000 still due on the first mortgage, we see that our couple could qualify for a home equity credit line of $53,750. Note, in this case, that if the bank had been willing to lend the couple *100% of the equity* in their home, it would have given them a (much higher) credit line of $145,000, which is the difference between what the house is worth and what they still owe on it. Most lenders don't like to do this because it results in very large credit lines and, perhaps more important, it doesn't provide the lender with much of a cushion should the borrower default.

Home equity lines also have an attractive tax feature: the annual interest charges on such lines may be fully deductible for those who itemize. This is the only type of consumer loan that still qualifies for such tax treatment. According to the latest provisions of the tax code, a homeowner is allowed to *fully deduct the interest charges on home equity loans up to $100,000*, regardless of the original cost of the house or use of the proceeds. Indeed, the only restriction is that *the amount of total indebtedness on the house cannot exceed its fair market value*, which is highly unlikely because homeowners usually cannot borrow more than 75% to 80% of the home's market value anyway. In our preceding example, the homeowners could take out the full amount of their credit line ($53,750) and every dime they paid in interest would be tax deductible. If they paid, say, $3,225 in interest and if they were in

the 28% tax bracket, then this feature would reduce their tax liability by some $903 (i.e., $3,225 × 0.28)—assuming, of course, that they itemize their deductions.

Not only do home equity credit lines offer shelter from taxes, they're also among *the cheapest forms of consumer credit*. For example, while the average rate on standard credit cards in mid-2009 was about 13.5%, the average rate on home equity credit lines was 8.6%. To see what that can mean to you as a borrower, assume you have $10,000 in consumer debt outstanding. If you had borrowed that money through a standard consumer loan at 13.5%, then you'd pay interest of $1,350 per year—none of which would be tax deductible. Borrow the same amount through a home equity credit line at 8.6% and you'll pay only $860 in interest. And because that's all tax deductible, if you're in the 28% tax bracket, then after-tax cost to you would be $860 × (1 − 0.28) = $619.20.

Home equity credit lines are offered by a variety of financial institutions, from banks and S&Ls to major brokerage houses. All sorts of credit terms and credit lines are available, and most of them carry repayment periods of 10 to 15 years, or longer. Perhaps most startling, however, is the maximum amount of credit available under these lines—indeed, $100,000 figures are not at all unusual. And it's precisely because of the enormous amount of money available that this form of credit should be used with caution. *The fact that you have equity in your home does not necessarily imply that you have the cash flow necessary to service the debt that such a credit line imposes*. Remember, your home serves as the collateral on this line of credit, and if you can't repay the loan, you could lose it!

## LG4 Obtaining and Managing Open Forms of Credit

Consumers love to use their charge cards. In 2008, Visa and MasterCard handled about $6.7 trillion in transactions.

 *Consumers love to use their charge cards.*

For the sake of convenience, people often maintain several different kinds of open credit. Nearly every household, for example, uses 30-day charge accounts to pay their utility bills, phone bills, and so on. In addition, most families have one or more retail charge cards and a couple of bank cards; some people, in fact, may have as many as 15 to 20 cards, or more. And that's not all—families can also have revolving credit lines in the form of overdraft protection or a home equity line. When all these cards and lines are totaled together, a family conceivably can have tens of thousands of dollars of readily available credit. It's easy to see why consumer credit has become such a popular way of making relatively routine purchases.

## Opening an Account

What do retail charge cards, bank credit cards, and revolving lines of credit all have in common? *Answer:* They all require you to go through a formal credit application. Let's now look at how you'd go about obtaining open forms of credit, including the normal credit application, investigation, and decision process. We'll couch our discussion in terms of credit cards, but keep in mind that similar procedures apply to other revolving lines of credit as well.

### The Credit Application

With over 640 million credit cards in the hands of American consumers, you'd think that consumer credit is available to just about anyone. And it is—but you must apply for it. Applications are usually available at the store or bank involved. Sometimes they can be found at the businesses that accept these cards or obtained on request from the issuing companies. The type of information requested in a typical credit card application covers little more than personal/family matters, housing, employment and income, and existing charge accounts. Such information is intended to give the lender insight about the applicant's creditworthiness. In essence, the lender is trying to determine whether the applicant has the *character* and *capacity* to handle the debt in a prompt and timely manner.

### The Credit Investigation

Once the credit application has been completed and returned to the establishment issuing the card, or more commonly today, submitted online, it is subject to a **credit investigation**. The purpose is to evaluate the kind of credit risk you pose to the lender. So be sure to fill out your credit application carefully. Believe it or not, they really do look at those things. The key items lenders look at are how much money you make, how much debt you have outstanding and how well you handle it, and how stable you are (for example, your age, employment history, whether you own or rent a home, and so on). Obviously, the higher your income and the better your credit history, the greater the chances of having your credit application approved. During the investigation, the lender will verify much of the information you've provided—obviously, false or misleading information will almost certainly result in outright rejection of your application.

### The Credit Bureau

A **credit bureau** is a type of reporting agency that gathers and sells information about individual borrowers.

If, as is often the case, the lender doesn't know you personally, it must rely on a cost-effective way of verifying your employment and credit history. And that's where credit bureaues come into play, as they maintain basic credit files on current and potential borrowers.

Contrary to popular opinion, your credit file does *not* contain everything anyone would ever want to know about you—there's nothing on your lifestyle, friends, habits, or religious or political affiliations. Instead, most of the information is pretty dull stuff and covers such things as name, social security number, age, number of dependents, employment record and salary data, public records of bankruptcies, and the names of those who recently requested copies of your file.

Although one late credit card payment probably won't make much of a difference on an otherwise clean credit file, a definite pattern of delinquencies (consistently being 30 to 60 days late with your payments) or a personal bankruptcy certainly will. Unfortunately, poor credit traits will stick with you for a long time, because delinquencies remain on your credit file for as long as 7 years and bankruptcies for 10 years. An example of an actual credit bureau report (or at least a part of one) is provided in Exhibit 6.3.

Local credit bureaus are established and mutually owned by local merchants and banks. They collect and store credit information on people living within the community and make it available, for a fee, to members who request it. Local bureaus are linked together nationally through one of the "big three" national bureaus—TransUnion, Equifax Credit Information Services, and Experian—each of which provides the mechanism for obtaining credit information from almost any place in the United States. Traditionally, credit bureaus did little more than collect and provide credit information; they neither analyzed the information nor used it to make final credit decisions. In 2006, however, the three major credit bureaus announced that they had jointly developed a new credit-scoring system, called *VantageScore*, that would incorporate data from all three bureaus—Equifax, Experian, and TransUnion. Thus, for the first time, each of the three national bureaus began assigning uniform credit ratings to individual credit files—though they're still obligated to report other credit scores, such as the widely used FICO scores.

Credit bureaus in the past were heavily criticized because of the large numbers of reporting errors they made and their poor record in promptly and efficiently correcting these errors. Fortunately, things have changed dramatically in recent years as the major bureaus have taken a more consumer-oriented

**credit investigation** An investigation that involves contacting credit references or corresponding with a credit bureau to verify information on a credit application.

**credit bureau** An organization that collects and stores credit information about individual borrowers.

**Exhibit 6.3 An Example of a Credit Bureau Report**

Credit bureau reports have been revised and are now easier to understand. Notice that in addition to some basic information, the report deals strictly with credit information—including payment records, past-due status, and types of credit.

## Your Credit Report as of 04/09/2010

This Credit Report is available for you to view for 30 days. If you would like a current Credit Report, you may order another from MyEquifax.

ID # XXXXXXXXXXXX

• *Personal Data*

John Q. Public
2351 N 85th Ave
Phoenix, AZ 85037

Social Security Number:  022-22-2222
Date of Birth:  1/11/1960

• *Previous Address(es):*

133 Third Avenue
Phoenix, AZ 85037

• *Employment History*

Cendant Hospitality FR

| Location: | Employment Date: | Verified Date: |
|---|---|---|
| Phoenix, AZ | 2/1/1989 | 1/3/2001 |

Previous Employment(s):

SOFTWARE Support Hospitality Franch

| Location: | Employment Date: | Verified Date: |
|---|---|---|
| Atlanta, GA | 1/3/2001 | 1/3/2001 |

• *Public Records*

No bankruptcies on file
No liens on file
No foreclosures on file

• *Collection Accounts*

No collections on file.

• *Credit Information*

| Company Name | Account Number and Whose Account | Date Opened | Last Activity | Type of Account and Status | High Credit | Items as of Date Reported Terms Balance | | Past Due | Date Reported |
|---|---|---|---|---|---|---|---|---|---|
| Americredit Financial Services | 40404XXXX JOINT ACCOUNT | 03/1999 | 03/2010 | Installment REPOSSESSION | $16933 | $430 | $9077 | $128 | 2/2010 |

**Prior Paying History**
30 days past due 07 times; 60 days past due 05 times; 90+ days past due 03 times
INVOLUNTARY REPOSSESION AUTO

| | | | | | | | | | |
|---|---|---|---|---|---|---|---|---|---|
| Capital One | 41217414712BXXXX INDIVIDUAL ACCOUNT | 10/1997 | 01/2010 | Revolving PAYS AS AGREED | $777 | 15 | $514 | | 01/2010 |

**Prior Paying History**
30 days past due 02 times; 60 days past due 1 times; 90+ days past due 00 times
CREDIT CARD

| | | | | | | | | | |
|---|---|---|---|---|---|---|---|---|---|
| Desert Schools FCU | 423325003406XXXX INDIVIDUAL ACCOUNT | 07/1997 | 06/2007 | Revolving PAYS AS AGREED | $500 | | $0 | | 07/2007 |

**Prior Paying History**
30 days past due 02 times; 60 days past due 00 times; 90+ days past due 00 times
ACCOUNT PAID     CLOSED ACCOUNT

• *Credit Inquiries*

**Companies that Requested your Credit File**

04/09/2009 EFX Credit Profile Online
06/30/2009 Automotive
01/18/2008 Desert Schools Federal C.U.
07/02/2007 Time Life, Inc.

approach. Even so, you should ensure that your credit report accurately reflects your credit history. The best way to do that is to obtain a copy of your own credit report—by law, you're entitled to receive *a free copy of your credit report once a year* (to get yours, go to the Web site set up by the Federal Trade Commission at http://www.annualcreditreport.com)—and then go through it carefully. If you do find a mistake, let the credit bureau know immediately—and by all means, put it writing; *then request a copy of the corrected file to make sure that the mistake has been eliminated.* Most consumer advisors recommend that you review your credit files annually.

Here are the addresses, Web sites, and toll-free phone numbers for the three national credit bureaus:

- Equifax Credit Information Services
  P.O. Box 740241, Atlanta, GA 30374; **http://www.equifax.com** or phone 1-888-766-0008

- TransUnion LLC Consumer Disclosure Center
  P.O. Box 1000, Chester, PA 19022; **http://www.tuc.com** or phone 1-800-888-4213

- Experian (formerly TRW) National Consumer Assistance Center
  P.O. Box 2002, Allen, TX 75013; **http://www.experian.com** or phone 1-888-397-3742

## FINANCIAL ROAD SIGN

### KEEPING UP YOUR FICO SCORES

Raising your FICO score is a lot like losing weight: It takes time and there's no quick fix. But here are some tips you might want to follow to reach a high score:

- Pay your bills on time.
- If you've missed payments, get current and stay current.
- If you're having trouble making ends meet, contact your creditors and work out a payment plan.
- Keep credit card balances low.
- Pay off debt rather than move it around.
- Don't open new credit cards just to increase your available credit.
- Reestablish your credit history if you've had problems in the past.

*Source:* http://www.myfico.com, accessed June 2009. Copyright Notice: © 2002–2006 Fair Isaac Corporation. Copyright © Fair Isaac Corporation. Used with permission. Fair Isaac, myFICO, the Fair Isaac logos, and the Fair Isaac product and service names are trademarks or registered trademarks of Fair Isaac Corporation.

## The Credit Decision

Using the data provided by the credit applicant, along with any information obtained from the credit bureau, the store or bank must decide whether to grant credit. Very likely, some type of **credit scoring** scheme will be used to make the decision. An overall credit score is developed for you by assigning values to such factors as your annual income, whether you rent or own your home, number and types of credit cards you hold, level of your existing debts, whether you have savings accounts, and general credit references. Fifteen or 20 different factors or characteristics may be considered, and each characteristic receives a score based on some predetermined standard. For example, if you're 26 years old, single, earn $32,500 a year (on a job that you've had for only 2 years), and rent an apartment, you might receive the following scores:

| | | |
|---|---|---|
| 1. | Age (25–30) | 5 points |
| 2. | Marital status (single) | –2 points |
| 3. | Annual income ($30–35 thousand) | 12 points |
| 4. | Length of employment (2 years or less) | 4 points |
| 5. | Rent or own a home (rent) | 0 points |
| | | 19 points |

Similar scores would be assigned to another 10 to 15 factors and other things being equal, the stronger your personal traits or characteristics, the higher the score you'll receive. Statistical studies have shown that certain personal and financial traits can be used to determine your creditworthiness. Indeed, the whole credit scoring system is based on extensive statistical studies that identify the characteristics to look at and the scores to assign.

The biggest provider of credit scores is, by far, Fair Isaac & Co.—the firm that produces the widely used *FICO scores*. Unlike some credit score providers, *Fair Isaac uses only credit information in its calculations.* There's nothing in them about your age, marital status, salary, occupation, employment history, or where you live. Instead, FICO scores are derived from the following five major components, which are listed along with their respective weights: payment history (35%), amounts owed (30%), length of credit history (15%), new credit (10%), and types of credit used (10%). FICO scores, which are reported by all three of the major credit bureaus, range from a low of 300 to a max of 850. These scores are meant to be an indication of a borrower's credit risk; the higher the score, the lower the risk. While few, if any, credit decisions are based solely on FICO scores, you can be sure that higher scores are likely to result in lower interest rates on loans, and therefore, lower loan payments.

**credit scoring** A method of evaluating an applicant's creditworthiness by assigning values to such factors as income, existing debts, and credit references.

### Go to Smart Sites

To learn more about FICO scores—including what's in your FICO score, what's not in it, and what you can do to improve it—visit the Fair Isaac & Co. Web site. ●

# Computing Finance Charges

Because card issuers don't know in advance how much you'll charge on your account, they cannot specify the dollar amount of interest you will be charged. But they can—and must, according to the Truth in Lending Act— disclose the *rate of interest* they charge and their method of computing finance charges. This is the **annual percentage rate (APR)**, the true or actual rate of interest paid, which must include all fees and costs and be calculated as defined by law. Remember, it's your right as a consumer to know—and it is the lender's obligation to tell you—the dollar amount of charges (where applicable) and the APR on any financing you consider.

The amount of interest you pay for open credit depends partly on the method the lender uses to calculate the balances on which they apply finance charges. Most bank and retail charge card issuers use one of two variations of the **average daily balance (ADB) method**, which applies the interest rate to the average daily balance of the account over the billing period. The most common method (used by an estimated 95% of bankcard issuers) is the *average daily balance including new purchases*. An alternative is the ADB method that *excludes new purchases*. Balance calculations under each of these methods are as follows.

- **ADB including new purchases.** For each day in the billing cycle, take the outstanding balance, including new purchases, and subtract payments and credits, then divide by the number of days in the billing cycle.

- **ADB excluding new purchases.** Same as first method but *exclude* new purchases.

These different calculations can obviously affect a card's credit balance and therefore the amount of finance charges you'll have to pay. Also be aware that the finance charges on two cards with the same APR but different methods of calculating balances may differ dramatically. It's important to know the method your card issuer uses. As a rule, for active card users, the ADB procedure that *includes new purchases* will produce considerably more interest income for the issuer and in turn, is *far more expensive* from the cardholder's perspective.

## Crunching the Numbers

Let's look at an example of how to calculate balances and finance charges under the most popular method, *the average daily balance including new purchases.* Assume that you have a FirstBank Visa card with a monthly interest rate of 1.5%.

Your statement for the billing period extending from October 10, 2010, through November 10, 2010—a total of 31 days—shows that your beginning balance was $1,582, you made purchases of $750 on October 15 and $400 on October 22, and you made a $275 payment on November 6. Therefore, the outstanding balance for the first 5 days of the period (October 11 through 15) was $1,582; for the next 7 days (October 16 through 22), it was $2,332 ($1,582 + $750); for the next 15 days (October 23 through November 6), it was $2,732 ($2,332 + $400); and for the last 4 days, it was $2,457 ($2,732 less the $275 payment), all of which is summarized in Exhibit 6.4.

We can now calculate the average daily balance using the procedure shown in Exhibit 6.4. Note that the outstanding balances are weighted by the number of days that the balance existed and then averaged (divided) by the number of days in the billing period. By multiplying the average daily balance of $2,420.71 by the 1.5% interest rate, we get a finance charge of $36.31.

©FANTASISTA/SHUTTERSTOCK

## Exhibit 6.4   Finding the Average Daily Balance and Finance Charge

The average daily balance including new purchases is the method most widely used by credit card issuers to determine the monthly finance charge on an account.

| Number of Days (1) | Balance (2) | Calculation (1) × (2) (3) |
|---|---|---|
| 5 | $1,582 | $ 7,910 |
| 7 | $2,332 | 16,324 |
| 15 | $2,732 | 40,980 |
| 4 | $2,457 | 9,828 |
| Total      31 | | $75,042 |

Average daily balance = $\dfrac{\$75,042}{31}$ = $2,420.71

Finance charge: $2,420.71 × .015 = $36.31

## Managing Your Credit Cards

Congratulations! You have applied for and been granted a bank credit card, as well as a retail charge card from your favorite department store. You carefully reviewed the terms of the credit agreement and have at least a basic understanding of how finance charges are computed for each account. Now you must manage your accounts efficiently, using the monthly statements to help you make the required payments on time as well as to track purchases.

### The Statement

If you use a credit card, you'll receive monthly statements similar to the sample bank card statement in Exhibit 6.5, showing billing cycle and payment due dates, interest rate, minimum payment, and all account activity during the current period. (Retail charge cards have similar monthly statements, but without a section for cash advances.) The statement summarizes your account activity: the previous balance (the amount of credit outstanding at the beginning of the month—not to be confused with past-due, or late, payments); new charges made (four, in this case) during the past month; any finance charges (interest) on the unpaid balance; the preceding period's payment; any other credits (such as those for returns); and the new balance (previous balance plus new purchases and finance charges, less any payments and credits). You should review your statements every month. Save your receipts and use them to verify statement entries for purchases and returns *before* paying. If you find any errors or suspect fraudulent use of your card, first use the issuer's toll-free number to report any problems; then follow up *in writing* within 60 days of the postmark on the bill.

Although merchandise and cash transactions are separated on the statement, the finance charge in each case is calculated at the rate of 1.5% per month (18% annually). This procedure works fine for illustration, but it's a bit out of the ordinary because most card issuers charge a higher rate for cash advances than for purchases.

**minimum monthly payment** In open account credit, a minimum specified percentage of the new account balance that must be paid in order to remain current.

### Payments

Credit card users can avoid *future* finance charges by paying the total new balance shown on their statement each month. For example, if the $534.08 total new balance shown in Exhibit 6.5 is paid by the due date of September 21, 2010, then no additional finance charges will be incurred. (The cardholder, however, is still liable for the $4.40 in finance charges incurred to date.) If cardholders cannot pay the total new balance, they can pay any amount that is equal to or greater than the **minimum monthly payment** specified on the statement. If they do this, however, they will incur additional finance charges in the following months. Note that the account in Exhibit 6.5 has a minimum payment of 5% of the new balance, rounded to the nearest full dollar. As shown at the bottom of the statement, this month's minimum payment is $27.00 (i.e., $534.08 × 0.05 = $26.70 ≈ $27.00). This $27.00 includes a *principal payment of $22.60*; that is: $27.00–$4.40 (in interest charges) = $22.60. That's actually about 4.25% of the "new balance." If the new balance had been less than $200, the bank would have required a payment of $10 (which is the absolute minimum dollar payment) or of

## Exhibit 6.5 A Bank Credit Card Monthly Statement

Each month, a bank credit cardholder receives a statement that provides an itemized list of charges and credits as well as a summary of previous activity and finance charges.

Please detach the above portion and return it with your payment to insure proper credit.

# Bank Card Statement

Retain this statement for your records.

| Account Number | Name(s) | | |
|---|---|---|---|
| 123-XYZ-45678 | Mr. Ronald A. Prillaman<br>Mrs. Cynthia B. Prillaman | 8-24-10<br>Statement Date | 09-21-10<br>Payment Due Date |

### ACCOUNT ACTIVITY

| | | | FINANCE CHARGE CALCULATION | | |
|---|---|---|---|---|---|
| Previous Balance | 203.64 | Credit Status | Amounts Subject to Finance Charge | | This Month's Charge |
| Payments − | 119.89 | Your Credit Limit is: | A. *Average | | ENTIRE BAL. |
| Credits − | .00 | | Daily Balance 293.25 | 4.40 | 1.5%          18.00% |
| Subtotal | 83.75 | | B. *Cash Advance          .00 | .00 | Monthly        Nominal |
| New Transaction + | 445.93 | 2000.00 | C. *Loan Advance          .00 | .00 | Periodic       Annual |
| Finance Charge + | 4.40 | Your Available Credit is: | | | Rate           Rate |
| Late Charge + | .00 | | | 4.40 | 18.00% |
| NEW BALANCE | 534.08 | 1465.92 | *Finance Charges explained on reverse side | Finance Charge | Annual Percentage Rate |

Mail Billing Inquiries to: Post Office Box 7890, Van Niles, California, 85258, or call          800/000-0000
For Inquiries on Past Due Accounts, Overlimits or Credit Line Increase, call          800/000-0000

| Posted Mo./Day | Transaction Description or Merchant Name and Location | | Purchase Mo./Day | Bank Reference Number | Purchases/ Advances/Debits | Payments Credits |
|---|---|---|---|---|---|---|
| 8-08 | AMERICA WEST AIRLINES | LOS ANGELES | 07-25 | 850000008823395192 | 42.00 | |
| 8-13 | HACIENDA MOTORS | COSTA MESA | 08-05 | 015400018537022316 | 166.86 | |
| 8-15 | RICOS RESTAURANT | PALM SPRG | 08-10 | 114500018856161722 | 132.47 | |
| 8-12 | PAYMENT—THANK YOU | | 08-11 | 4501000182MD02139 | | 119.89 |
| 8-24 | RENEES RESTAURANT | NEWPORT | 08-13 | 114500068201632483 | 104.60 | |

Notice  See reverse side for important information

| MIN. PAYMENT: | 27.00 | NEW BALANCE: | 534.08 | | Total Debits 445.93 | Total Credits 119.89 |
|---|---|---|---|---|---|---|

the total new balance, if less than $10. Cardholders who fail to make the minimum payment are considered to be in default on their account, and the bank issuing the card can take whatever action it deems necessary.

### Go to Smart Sites

Use About.com's Credit Card Calculators to find out how interest rate changes affect your balance, if debt consolidation makes sense, and answers to similar questions. ●

## LG5, LG6 Using Credit Wisely

As we've discussed, credit cards and revolving lines of credit can simplify your life financially. Unfortunately, you can also get into real trouble with these forms of credit unless you use them wisely! That's why you should carefully shop around to choose the right credit cards for your personal situation, understand the advantages and disadvantages of credit cards, learn how to resolve credit problems, and know how to avoid the ultimate cost of credit abuse—bankruptcy.

## Shop Around for the Best Deal

They say it pays to shop around, and when it comes to credit cards, that's certainly true. With all the fees and high interest costs, it pays to get the best deal possible. So, where do you start? Most credit experts suggest the first thing you should do is step back and take a look at yourself. What kind of "spender" are you, and how do you pay your bills? The fact is, no single credit card is right for everyone. If you pay off your card balance each month, then you'll want a card that's different from the one that's right for someone who carries a credit balance from month to month and may only pay the minimum due. Regardless of which category you fall into, there are basically four card features to look for:

- Annual fees
- Rate of interest charged on account balance
- Length of the grace period
- Method of calculating balances

Now, if you normally pay your account balance in full each month, get a card with *no annual fees and a long grace period*. The rate of interest on the card is irrelevant because you don't carry account balances from month to month anyway. In sharp contrast, if you don't pay your account in full, then look for cards that charge *a low rate of interest on unpaid balances*. The length of the grace period isn't all that important here, but obviously, other things being equal, you're better off with low (or no) annual fees.

Sometimes, however, "other things aren't equal" and you have to decide between interest rates and annual fees. If you're not a big spender and don't build up big balances on your credit card, then *avoid* cards with annual fees and get one with as *low* a rate of interest as possible. (*Note:* This situation probably applies to most college students—or at least it should.) On the other hand, if you do carry big balances (say, $1,000 or more), then you'll probably be better off *paying an annual fee* (even a relatively high one) *to keep the rate of interest on the card as low as possible.*

The bottom line is: don't take the first credit card that comes along. Instead, get the one that's right for you. Learn as much as you can about the credit cards you've been offered or are considering. To do that, go to Web sites like www.bankrate.com; www.creditcards.com; or www.cardtrak.com, to mention just a few. These sites provide all sorts of information about fees, rates, credit terms, etc. on a wide array of different types of credit cards. Another alternative is to go to publications like *Money* magazine and *Kiplinger's Personal Finance*. These magazines regularly publish information about banks and other financial institutions that offer low-cost credit cards nationally, an example of which is shown in Exhibit 6.6.

## Avoiding Credit Problems

Unfortunately, as the volume of credit card purchases has grown, so has the level of credit card debt. As a result, it's not unusual to find people using credit cards

---

### Exhibit 6.6  Published Information about Bank Credit Card Terms

Information about low-cost credit cards is readily available in the financial media. Here's an example of what you can find online. Notice the report lists the *cards with the lowest rates* (probably best for people who regularly carry an account balance) and *no-fee cards with the lowest rates* (probably best for people who pay their accounts in full each month).

#### Low Interest Cards: *Best If You Carry a Balance*

| Issuer | Recent Rate (APR) | Cash Advance Rate/Fee | Annual Fee | Late/Over-Limit Fee | Grace Period |
|---|---|---|---|---|---|
| Fifth Third Bank | 3.25% V | 21.99% V/3.5% | $85 | $39/$39 | 20 days |

#### No-Fee Cards with the Lowest Rates: *Best If You Usually Pay the Balance Each Month*

| Issuer | Recent Rate (APR) | Cash Advance Rate/Fee | Annual Fee | Late/Over-Limit Fee | Grace Period |
|---|---|---|---|---|---|
| Redstone FCU | 7.00% V | 7.00% V/$0 | $0 | $20/$20 | 25 days |
| First Command Bank | 4.25% V | 4.25 V/$0 | $0 | $0/$0 | 30 days |
| RBC Bank | 6.74% V | 19.99 V/3.5% | $0 | $35/$35 | 21 days |

As of June 8, 2009; rates are adjustable. Banks sometimes offer lower introductory rates. "V" denotes variable rate. Data compiled from http://www.bankrate.com, accessed June 2009.

to solve cash-flow problems; even the most careful consumers occasionally find themselves with mounting credit card debt, especially after the year-end holiday buying season. The real problems occur when the situation is no longer temporary and the debt continues to increase. If overspending is not curtailed, then the size of the unpaid balance may seriously strain the budget. Essentially, people who let their credit balances build up are *mortgaging their future.* By using credit, they're actually committing a part of their future income to make payments on the debt. Unfortunately, the more income that has to go just to make payments on charge cards (and other forms of consumer credit), the less there is available for other purposes.

The best way to avoid credit problems is to be disciplined when using credit. Reduce the number of cards you carry, and don't rush to accept the tempting preapproved credit card offers that you may get in the mail. A wallet full of cards can work against you in two ways. Obviously, the ready availability of credit can tempt you to overspend and incur too much debt. But there's another, less obvious, danger: when you apply for a loan, lenders look at the *total amount* of credit you have available as well as at the outstanding balances on your credit cards. If you have a lot of unused credit capacity, it may be harder to get a loan because of lender concerns that you could become overextended. So think twice before accepting a new credit card. You really don't need three or four bankcards. Two is the most that financial advisors suggest you carry. And should you decide to start using a new card (because their offer was just too good to pass up), then *get rid of one of your old cards*—physically cut up the old card and inform the issuer in writing that you're canceling your account.

## Credit Card Fraud

Despite all the efforts of law enforcement officials, there are still people out there who are doing their best to rip you off! In fact, plastic has become the vehicle of choice among crooks. No doubt about it: credit card crime is big business, with annual losses in the United States estimated to run in the billions of dollars a year! Basically, "it's us against them," and the first thing you have to understand is that the credit card you're carrying around is a powerful piece of plastic. Be careful with it. To reduce your chances of being defrauded, here are some suggestions you should follow.

- Never, ever, give your account number to people or organizations *who call you.* No matter how legitimate it sounds.

- It's okay to give your account number over the phone (if you initiated the call) when ordering or purchasing something from a major catalog house, airline, hotel, and so on.

- Use the same precautions *when purchasing something over the Internet* with your credit card—don't do it *unless* you're dealing with a major retailer who uses state-of-the-art protection against fraud and thievery.

- When paying for something *by check*, don't put your Social Security or credit card account number on the check, and don't let the store clerk do it.

- Don't put your phone number or address (and certainly not your Social Security number) on credit/charge slips, even if the merchant asks for it—they're *not* entitled to it.

- When using your card to make a purchase, *always keep your eye on it*; if the clerk wants to make another imprint, ask for the first one and tear it up on the spot.

- Always draw a line on the credit slip through any blank spaces above the total.

- *Destroy* all old credit slips; and when you receive your monthly statement, be sure to *go over it promptly* to make sure there are no errors. If you find a mistake, call or send a letter immediately, detailing the error.

- If you lose a card or it's stolen, *report it to the card issuer immediately*—the most you're ever liable for with a lost or stolen card is $50 (per card), but if you report the loss *before* the card can be used, you won't be liable for any unauthorized charges.

- Destroy old cards or those you no longer use.

# Bankruptcy: Paying the Price for Credit Abuse

It certainly isn't an overstatement to say that during the 1980s and 1990s, *debt was in!* In fact, the explosion of debt that has occurred since 1980 is almost incomprehensible. The national debt rose from less than a trillion dollars when the 1980s began to about $11.3 trillion by mid-2009. Businesses also took on debt rapidly. Not to be outdone, consumers were using credit like there was no tomorrow. So it should come as no surprise that when you couple this heavy debt load with a serious economic recession like that in 2009, you have all the ingredients of a real financial crisis. And that's just what happened, as personal bankruptcies soared—indeed, in 2008 alone, more than 1.1 million people filed for **personal bankruptcy**.

When too many people are too heavily in debt, a recession (or some other economic reversal) can come along and push many of them over the edge. But let's face it, the recession is not the main culprit here; the only way a recession can push you over the edge is if you're already sitting on it! The real culprit is excess

> **The only way a recession can push you over the edge is if you're already sitting on it!**

debt. Some people simply abuse credit by taking on more than they can afford. Then, sooner or later, these debtors start missing payments and their credit rating begins to deteriorate. Unless corrective actions are taken, this is followed by repossession of property and, eventually, even bankruptcy. Two of the most widely used bankruptcy procedures (employed by well over 95% of those individuals who file for bankruptcy) are (1) the Wage Earner Plan, and (2) straight bankruptcy.

## Wage Earner Plan

The **Wage Earner Plan** (as defined in *Chapter 13* of the U.S. Bankruptcy Code) is a workout procedure involving some type of debt restructuring—usually by establishing a debt repayment schedule that's more compatible with the person's income. It may be a viable alternative for someone who has a steady source of income, not more than $1,010,650 in secured debt and $336,900 in unsecured debt, and a reasonably good chance of being able to repay the debts in 3 to 5 years. A majority of creditors must agree to the plan and interest charges, along with late-payment penalties, are waived for the repayment period. Creditors usually will go along with this plan because they stand to lose more in a straight bankruptcy.

## Straight Bankruptcy

**Straight bankruptcy**, which is allowed under *Chapter 7* of the bankruptcy code, can be viewed as a legal procedure that results in "wiping the slate clean and starting anew." *About 70% of those filing personal bankruptcy choose this route.* However, straight bankruptcy does not eliminate all the debtor's obligations, nor does the debtor necessarily lose all of his or her assets. For example, the debtor must make certain tax payments and keep up alimony and child-support payments but is allowed to retain certain payments from Social Security, retirement, veterans', and disability benefits. The debtor also may retain the equity in a home, a car, and some other personal assets. Minimum values are established by federal regulations, though state laws are generally much more generous regarding the amount the debtor is allowed to keep.

**personal bankruptcy** A form of legal recourse open to insolvent debtors, who may petition a court for protection from creditors and arrange for the orderly liquidation and distribution of their assets.

**Wage Earner Plan** An arrangement for scheduled debt repayment over future years that is an alternative to straight bankruptcy; used when a person has a steady source of income and there is a reasonable chance of repayment within 3 to 5 years.

**straight bankruptcy** A legal proceeding that results in "wiping the slate clean and starting anew"; most of a debtor's obligations are eliminated in an attempt to put the debtor's financial affairs in order.

# FINANCIAL PLANNING EXERCISES

**LG1**

1. After graduating from college last fall, Arlene Dukes took a job as a consumer credit analyst at a local bank. From her work reviewing credit applications, she realizes that she should begin establishing her own credit history. Describe for Arlene several steps she could take to begin building a strong credit record. Does the fact that she took out a student loan for her college education help or hurt her credit record?

**LG2**

2. Brian Southard has a monthly take-home pay of $1,685; he makes payments of $410 a month on his outstanding consumer credit (excluding the mortgage on his home). How would you characterize Brian's debt burden? What if his take-home pay were $850 a month and he had monthly credit payments of $150?

**LG2**

3. *Use Worksheet 6.1.* Beverly Smitham is evaluating her debt safety ratio. Her monthly take-home pay is $3,320. Each month, she pays $380 for an auto loan, $120 on a personal line of credit, $60 on a department store charge card, and $85 on her bank credit card. Complete Worksheet 6.1 by listing Beverly's outstanding debts, and then calculate her debt safety ratio. Given her current take-home pay, what is the maximum amount of monthly debt payments that Beverly can have if she wants her debt safety ratio to be 12.5%? Given her current monthly debt payment load, what would Beverly's take-home pay have to be if she wanted a 12.5% debt safety ratio?

**LG3**

4. Bill and Ethel Patterson have a home with an appraised value of $180,000 and a mortgage balance of only $90,000. Given that an S&L is willing to lend money at a loan-to-value ratio of 75%, how big a home equity credit line can Bill and Ethel obtain? How much, if any, of this line would qualify as tax-deductible interest if their house originally cost $100,000?

**LG4**

5. Parviz Sayyad recently graduated from college and is evaluating two credit cards. Card A has an annual fee of $75 and an interest rate of 9%. Card B has no annual fee and an interest rate of 16%. Assuming that Parviz intends to carry no balance and pay off his charges in full each month, which card represents the better deal? If Parviz expected to carry a significant balance from one month to the next, which card would be better? Explain.

# 7

# USING CONSUMER LOANS

©SLAVOLJUB PANTELIC/SHUTTERSTOCK

## LEARNING GOALS

**LG1** Know when to use consumer loans and be able to differentiate between the major types. (p. 146)

**LG2** Identify the various sources of consumer loans. (p. 146)

**LG3** Choose the best loans by comparing finance charges, maturity, collateral, and other loan terms. (p. 151)

**LG4** Describe the features of, and calculate the finance charges on, single-payment loans. (p. 153)

**LG5** Evaluate the benefits of an installment loan. (p. 159)

**LG6** Determine the costs of installment loans and analyze whether it is better to pay cash or take out a loan. (p.159)

## LG1, LG2 Basic Features of Consumer Loans

In previous chapters, we've discussed the different types of financial goals that individuals and families can set for themselves. These goals often involve large sums of money and may include such things as a college education or the purchase of a new car. One way to reach these goals is to systematically save the money. Another is to use a loan to at least partially finance the transaction. Consumer loans are important to the personal financial planning process because they can help you reach certain types of financial goals. The key, of course, is to successfully manage the credit by keeping both the amount of debt used and the debt-repayment burden *well within your budget*!

## Using Consumer Loans

As we saw in Chapter 6, using open or revolving credit can prove helpful to those who plan and live within their personal financial budgets. More important to the achievement of long-run personal financial goals, however, are *single-payment* and *installment loans*. These long-term liabilities are widely used to finance goods that are far too expensive to buy from current income, to help fund a college education, or to pay for certain types of nondurable items, such as expensive vacations.

off. Furthermore, no credit cards or checks are issued with this form of credit. Finally, whereas open account credit is used chiefly to make repeated purchases of relatively low-cost *goods and services*, consumer loans are used mainly to *borrow money* to pay for big-ticket items.

## Different Types of Loans

Although they can be used for just about any purpose imaginable, most consumer loans fall into one of the following categories.

- **Auto loans.** Financing a new car, truck, SUV, or minivan is the single most common reason for borrowing money through a consumer loan. Indeed, auto loans account for about 35% of all consumer credit outstanding. Generally speaking, about 80% to 90% of the cost of a new vehicle (somewhat less with used cars) can be financed with credit. The buyer must provide the rest through a *down payment*. The loan is *secured* with the auto, meaning that the vehicle serves as **collateral** for the loan and can be repossessed by the lender should the buyer fail to make payments. These loans generally have maturities ranging from 36 to 60 months.

- **Loans for other durable goods.** Consumer loans can also be used to finance other kinds of *costly durable goods,* such as furniture, home appliances, TVs, home computers, recreational vehicles, and even small airplanes and mobile homes. These loans are also secured by the items purchased and generally

> { *Using open or revolving credit can prove helpful to those who plan and live within their personal financial budgets.* }

They differ from open forms of credit in several ways, including the formality of their lending arrangements. That is, while open account credit results from a rather informal process, **consumer loans** are *formal, negotiated contracts* that specify both the terms for borrowing and the repayment schedule. Another difference is that an open line of credit can be used again and again, but consumer loans are one-shot transactions made for specific purposes. Because there's no revolving credit with a consumer loan, no more credit is available (from that particular loan) once it's paid

require some down payment. Maturities vary with the type of asset purchased: 9- to 12-month for less costly items, such as TVs and stereos, whereas 10- to 15-year loans are normal with mobile homes.

- **Education loans.** Getting a college education is another important reason for taking out a consumer loan. Such loans can be used to finance either undergraduate or graduate studies, and special government-subsidized loan programs are available to students and parents. We'll discuss student loans in more detail in the following section.

- **Personal loans.** These loans are typically used for nondurable expenditures, such as an expensive European vacation or to cover temporary cash shortfalls. Many personal loans are *unsecured,* which means there's no collateral with the loan other than the borrower's good name.

- **Consolidation loans.** This type of loan is used to straighten out an unhealthy credit situation, which often occurs when consumers overuse credit cards, credit lines, or consumer loans and can no longer promptly service the debt. By borrowing money from one source to pay off other forms of credit, borrowers can replace, say, five or six monthly payments that total $400 with one payment amounting to $250. *Consolidation loans are usually expensive, and people who use them must be careful to stop using credit cards and other forms of credit until they repay the loans. Otherwise, they may end up right back where they started.*

## Student Loans

Today, the annual cost of a college education ranges from about $10,000 to $12,000 at a state school to well over $35,000 or $40,000 at some private colleges. Many families, even those who started saving for college when their children were young, are faced with higher-than-expected bills. Fortunately, there are many types of financial aid programs available, including some federal programs, as well as state, private, and college-sponsored programs.

Certainly, paying for a college education is one of the most legitimate reasons for going into debt. Although you could borrow money for college through normal channels—that is, take out a regular consumer loan from your bank and use the proceeds to finance an education—there are better ways to go about getting education loans. That's because the federal government (and some state governments) have available several different types of subsidized educational loan programs. The federally sponsored programs are:

- Stafford loans (Direct and Federal Family Education Loans—FFEL)
- Perkins loans
- Parent Loans (PLUS)

The Stafford and Perkins loans have the best terms and are the foundation of the government's student loan program. In contrast, PLUS

©ANDRESR/SHUTTERSTOCK

(which stands for *Parent Loans for Undergraduate Students*) loans are *supplemental loans* for *undergraduate students* who demonstrate a need but, for one reason or another, don't qualify for Stafford or Perkins loans, or need more aid than they're receiving. Under this program, parents can take out loans to meet or supplement the costs of their children's college education, *up to the full cost of attendance.* Whereas Stafford and Perkins loans are made directly to students, PLUS loans are made to the parents or legal guardians of college students. Probably the best place to look for information about these and other programs is the Internet. For example, look up FASTWEB (which stands for *Financial Aid Search Through the WEB*). This site, which is free, not only provides details on all the major, and some of the not-so-major, student loan programs but also has a service that matches individuals with scholarships and loans, even going so far as to provide form letters to use in requesting more information. (The address for this Web site is **http://www.fastweb.com**.)

Let's look at the Stafford loan program to see how student loans work. There are two types of Stafford loans. In the subsidized loan program, the U.S. Department of Education pays interest while the student is in school and also during certain grace and deferment periods. In the unsubsidized program, the borrower is responsible for all interest, whether in or out of school. Stafford loans carry low, government-subsidized interest rates; most major banks as well as some of the bigger S&Ls and credit unions participate in the program. Actually, the loans are made directly by one of the participating banks or financial institutions, although the student has no direct contact with the lending institution. Instead, the whole process—and it really is quite simple—begins with a visit to the school's financial aid office, where a financial aid counselor will help you determine your eligibility. To be eligible, you must demonstrate a *financial need,* where the amount of your financial need is defined as the cost of attending school *less* the amount that can be paid by you or your family. Thus, in these programs, students are expected to contribute something to their educational expense regardless of their income. You must also be making *satisfactory progress in your academic program,* and you cannot be

in default on any other student loans. Each academic year, you'll have to fill out a Free Application for Federal Student Aid [FAFSA] statement to attest that these qualifications are being met (you can complete and submit the form on the Web at **http://www.fafsa.ed.gov**).

 **Go to Smart Sites**

To find advice on financing college (loans and scholarships) and helpful online calculators, check out The Princeton Review's financing section. Whenever you see "*Go to Smart Sites*" in this chapter, visit **4ltrpress.cengage.com** for help finding answers online. ●

**OBTAINING A STUDENT LOAN.** All you have to do to obtain a (Stafford) loan is complete a simple application form, which is then submitted to *your school's financial aid office*. You do *not* have to deal with the bank, and you won't be subject to credit checks—although with PLUS loans, the borrower (parent) may be subject to a credit judgment by the lender. The latest innovation in this procedure involves transmitting the application electronically to the necessary parties, thus reducing paperwork and speeding up the processing (see, for example, **http://www.staffordloan.com**).

Each program has specific loan limits. For example, with subsidized Stafford loans for *dependent* students, you can borrow up to $3,500 per academic year for first-year studies, $4,500 for the second year, and $7,500 per academic year thereafter, up to a maximum of $31,000 for undergraduate studies—you can obtain even more if you can show that you're no longer dependent on your parents; in other words, that you're an *independent* undergraduate student paying for your college education on your own. Graduate students can qualify for up to $6,000 per academic year for dependent students and $8,500 per academic year for independent students. The maximum for both undergraduate and graduate loans combined is $138,500 (or $224,000 for health professionals). And there's no limit on the *number* of loans you can have, only on the maximum dollar amount that you can receive annually from each program. Exhibit 7.1 compares the major loan provisions of the three federally sponsored student loan programs—Stafford, Perkins, and PLUS loans.

Each year, right on through graduate school, a student can take out a loan from one or more of these government programs. Over time, that can add up to a lot of loans, and a substantial amount of debt—all of which must be repaid. But here's another nice feature of these loans: *loan repayment doesn't begin until after you're out of school* (for the Stafford and Perkins programs only—repayment on PLUS loans normally begins within

---

## Exhibit 7.1 Federal Government Student Loan Programs at a Glance

More and more college students rely on loans subsidized by the federal government to finance all or part of their educations. There are three types of federally subsidized loan programs, the basic loan provisions of which are listed here. These loans all have low interest rates and provide various deferment options and extended repayment terms. (*Note: Loan rates and terms shown here are for the 2009–2010 school year.*)

| Loan Provisions | Type of Federal Loan Program | | |
| --- | --- | --- | --- |
| | **Stafford Loans*** | **Perkins Loans** | **PLUS Loans** |
| Borrower | Student | Student | Parent |
| Interest rate | 5.6% | 5% | 8.5% |
| Borrowing limits | *Dependent students:* $23,000 (undergrad); $65,000 (grad/professional) *Independent students:* $57,500 (undergrad) $65,000 (grad/professional) | $20,000 (undergrad) $40,000 (grad/professional) | *No total dollar limit:* Cost of attendance minus any other financial aid received |
| Loan fees | Up to 4% of loan amount | None | Up to 4% of loan amount |
| Loan term | 10–25 years | 10 years | 10 years |

*Data are for subsidized Stafford loans, and interest rates are as of mid-2009. Subsidized Stafford loans also have annual borrowing limits ranging from $3,500 for the freshman year for dependent students to $8,500 per year in grad/professional school for independent students; likewise, Perkins loans have annual limits of $4,000 per year of undergraduate study and $6,000 per year of graduate school.
*Source:* http://www.fastweb.com and http://www.staffordloan.com, accessed June 2009.

60 days of loan disbursement). In addition, except for PLUS loans, interest doesn't begin accruing until you get out of school. Once repayment begins, you start paying interest on the loans, which may be tax deductible, depending on your income.

Student loans are usually amortized with monthly (principal and interest) payments over a period of 5 to 10 years. To help you service the debt, if you have several student loans outstanding, then you can *consolidate* the loans, at a single blended rate, and extend the repayment period to as long as 20 years. You also can ask for either: (1) an *extended repayment* for a longer term of up to 30 years; (2) a *graduated repayment schedule*, which will give you low payments in the early years and then higher payments later on; or (3) an *income-contingent repayment plan*, with payments that fluctuate annually according to your income and debt levels. But no matter what you do, *take the repayment provisions seriously because defaults will be reported to credit bureaus and become a part of your credit file!* What's more, due to recent legislation, you can't get out of repaying your student loans by filing for bankruptcy: whether you file under Chapter 7 or Chapter 13, *student loans are no longer dischargeable in a bankruptcy proceeding.*

### Single Payment or Installment Payments
Consumer loans can also be broken into categories based on the type of repayment arrangement— single-payment or installment. **Single-payment loans** are made for a specified period, at the end of which time payment in full (principal plus interest) is due. They generally have maturities ranging from 30 days to a year, or so. Sometimes single-payment loans are made to finance purchases or pay bills when the cash to be used for repayment is known to be forthcoming in the near future; in this case, they serve as a form of **interim financing**. In other situations, single-payment loans are used by consumers who want to avoid being strapped with monthly installment payments.

**Installment loans**, in contrast, are repaid in a series of fixed, scheduled payments rather than in one lump sum. The payments are almost always set up on a monthly basis, with each installment made up partly of principal and partly of interest. For example, out of a $75 monthly payment, $50 might be credited to principal and the balance to interest. These loans are typically made to finance the purchase of a good or service for which current resources are inadequate. The repayment period can run from 6 months to 6 years or more. Installment loans have become a way of life for many consumers. They're popular because they provide a convenient way to "buy now and pay later."

### Fixed- or Variable-Rate Loans
Most consumer loans are made at fixed rates of interest—that is, the interest rate charged and the monthly payments remain the same over the life of the obligation. However, variable-rate loans are also being made with increasing frequency, especially on *longer-term installment loans*. As with an adjustable-rate home mortgage, the rate of interest charged on such loans changes periodically in keeping with prevailing market conditions. If market interest rates go up, the rate of interest on the loan goes up accordingly, as does the monthly loan payment. These loans have periodic adjustment dates (for example, monthly, quarterly, or semiannually), at which time the interest rate and monthly payment are adjusted as necessary. Once an adjustment is made, the new rate remains in effect until the next adjustment date (sometimes the payment amount remains the same, but the number of payments changes). Many variable-rate loans have caps on the maximum increase per adjustment period as well as over the life of the loan. Generally speaking, variable-rate loans are desirable *if interest rates are expected to fall* over the course of the loan. In contrast, fixed-rate loans are preferable *if interest rates are expected to rise.*

## Where Can You Get Consumer Loans?
Consumer loans can be obtained from a number of sources, including commercial banks, consumer finance companies, credit unions, S&Ls, sales finance companies, and life insurance companies—even brokerage firms, pawnshops, or friends and relatives. *Commercial banks* dominate the field and provide nearly half of all consumer loans. Second to banks are *consumer finance companies* and then *credit unions*. Together, about 75% of all consumer loans are originated by these three financial institutions!

### Commercial Banks
Because they offer various types of loans at attractive rates of interest, commercial banks are a popular source of consumer loans. One nice thing about commercial banks is that they typically charge lower rates than most other lenders, largely because they take only the best credit risks and are able to obtain relatively inexpensive funds from their depositors. The demand for their loans is generally high, and they can be selective in making consumer loans. Commercial banks usually lend only to customers with good credit ratings who can readily demonstrate an ability to repay a loan

**single-payment loan** A loan made for a specified period, at the end of which payment is due in full.

**interim financing** The use of a single-payment loan to finance a purchase or pay bills in situations where the funds to be used for repayment are known to be forthcoming in the near future.

**installment loan** A loan that is repaid in a series of fixed, scheduled payments rather than a lump sum.

**consumer finance company** A firm that makes secured and unsecured personal loans to qualified individuals; also called a *small loan company*.

**sales finance company** A firm that purchases notes drawn up by sellers of certain types of merchandise, typically big-ticket items.

**captive finance company** A sales finance company that is owned by a manufacturer of big-ticket merchandise. GMAC is a captive finance company.

**cash value (of life insurance)** An accumulation of savings in an insurance policy that can be used as a source of loan collateral.

according to the specified terms. They also give preference to loan applicants who are account holders. Although banks prefer to make loans secured by some type of collateral, they also make unsecured loans to their better customers.

### Consumer Finance Companies

Sometimes called *small loan companies*, **consumer finance companies** make secured and unsecured (signature) loans to qualified individuals. These companies do not accept deposits but obtain funds from their stockholders and through open market borrowing. Because they don't have the inexpensive sources of funds that banks and other deposit-type institutions do, their interest rates are generally quite high. Actual rates charged by consumer finance companies are regulated by interest-rate ceilings (or usury laws) set by the states in which they operate. The maximum allowable interest rate may vary with the size of the loan, and the state regulatory authorities may also limit the length of the repayment period. Loans made by consumer finance companies typically are for $5,000 or less and are secured by some type of collateral. These lenders specialize in small loans to high-risk borrowers. As such, they are quite costly, but they may be the only alternative for people with poor credit ratings.

 **Go to Smart Sites**

What does a consumer finance company like Household Finance offer its customers? Go to their site to check out the company's different credit cards and loans as well as its consumer education sections. ●

### Credit Unions

A credit union is a cooperative financial institution that is owned by the people ("members") who use its services. Only the members can obtain installment loans and other types of credit from these institutions, but credit unions can offer membership to just about anyone they want and not merely to certain groups of people. Because they are nonprofit organizations with minimal operating costs, credit unions charge relatively low rates on their loans. They make either unsecured or secured loans, depending on the size and type of loan requested. Generally speaking, membership in a

credit union provides the most attractive borrowing opportunities available because their interest rates and borrowing requirements are usually more favorable than other sources of consumer loans.

### Savings and Loan Associations

Savings and loan associations (as well as savings banks) primarily make mortgage loans. They aren't major players in the consumer loan field, but S&Ls are permitted to make loans on such consumer durables as automobiles, televisions, refrigerators, and other appliances. They can also make certain types of home improvement and mobile-home loans, as well as some personal and educational loans. Rates of interest on consumer loans at S&Ls are fairly close to the rates charged by commercial banks; if anything, they tend to be a bit more expensive. Like their banking counterparts, the rates charged at S&Ls will, in the final analysis, depend on such factors as type and purpose of the loan and the borrower's overall creditworthiness.

### Sales Finance Companies

Businesses that sell relatively expensive items—such as automobiles, furniture, and appliances—often provide installment financing to their customers. Because dealers can't afford to tie up their funds in installment contracts, they sell them to a **sales finance company**. This procedure is often called "selling paper" because the merchants are, in effect, selling their loans to a third party. When the sales finance company purchases these notes, customers are usually notified to make payments directly to it.

The largest sales finance organizations are the **captive finance companies** owned by the manufacturers of big-ticket items. Ford Motor Credit Corporation (FMCC) and General Electric Credit Corporation (GECC) are just two examples of captive finance companies that purchase the installment loans made by the dealers of their products. Most commercial banks also act as sales finance companies by buying paper from auto dealers and other businesses. The cost of financing through a sales finance company is generally higher than the rates charged by banks and S&Ls, particularly when you let the dealer do all the work in arranging the financing (dealers normally get a cut of the finance income, so it's obviously in their best interest to secure as high a rate as possible).

### Life Insurance Companies

Life insurance policyholders may be able to obtain loans from their insurance companies. That's because certain types of policies not only provide death benefits, but also have a savings function, so they can be used as collateral for loans. Life insurance companies are required by law to make loans against the **cash value**—the amount of accumulated savings—of certain types of life insurance policies. The rate of interest on this type of loan is stated in the policy and usually carries a variable rate that goes up and down with prevailing market conditions. Although you'll be charged interest for as long as the policy loan is outstanding, these loans don't have repayment dates—in other words, *you don't have to pay them back.* When you take out a loan against the cash value of your life insurance policy, you're really borrowing from yourself. Thus, the amount of the loan outstanding, plus any accrued interest, is deducted from the amount of coverage provided by the policy—*effectively lowering your insurance coverage.* The chief danger in life insurance loans is that they don't have a firm maturity date, so *borrowers may lack the motivation to repay them.*

this transaction fit into your financial plans?, and (2) does the required debt service on the loan fit into your monthly cash budget? Indeed, when *full consideration is given not only to the need for the asset or item in question, but also to the repayment of the ensuing debt,* sound credit management is the result. In contrast, if the expenditure in question will seriously jeopardize your financial plans or if repaying of the loan is likely to strain your cash budget, then you should definitely reconsider the purchase! Perhaps it can be postponed, or you can liquidate some other assets in order to come up with more down payment. Whatever route you choose, the key point is to make sure that the debt will be fully compatible with your financial plans and cash budget *before* the loan is taken out and the money spent.

## FINANCIAL ROAD SIGN

**POTENTIAL FOR DISASTER: LENDING TO FAMILY OR FRIENDS**

If you're faced with little or no alternative and must either lend or borrow money to/from a friend or family member, then do so carefully. Here are some guidelines to follow.

- *Lend only money you can afford to give away.* About 20% to 50% of these loans are never repaid.
- *Do it in a businesslike fashion.* Draw up a formal promissory note with specific terms.
- *Charge interest if the loan is not to be repaid quickly.* Set the rate at about what you'd earn with a savings account, but at less than prevailing loan rates.
- *Both parties must understand this is a loan, not a gift.* Be specific about repayment terms.

Bottom line: A loan to or from a friend or family member is far more than a run of the mill banking transaction: the interest is emotional, and the risks are the relationship itself!

## LG3 Managing Your Credit

Borrowing money to make major purchases—and, in general, using consumer loans—is a sound and perfectly legitimate way to conduct your financial affairs. From a financial planning perspective, you should ask yourself two questions when considering the use of a consumer loan: (1) does making

> **Borrowing money to make major purchases is a sound and perfectly legitimate way to conduct your financial affairs.**

## Shopping for Loans

Once you've decided to use credit, it's equally important that you shop around and evaluate the various costs and terms available. You may think the only thing you need do to make a sound credit decision is to determine which source offers the lowest finance charge. But this could not be farther from the truth—as we'll see below, finance charges are just one of the factors to consider when shopping for a loan. And as you'll learn from reading this chapter's *Money in Action* feature, you'll also want to steer clear of so-called predatory lenders—they definitely do not have your best interests at heart!

### Finance Charges

What's it going to cost me? That's one of the first things most people want to know when taking out a loan. And that's appropriate because borrowers should know what they'll have to pay to get the money. Lenders are required by law to clearly state all finance charges and other loan fees. Find out the effective (or true) *rate* of interest you'll

# MONEY IN ACTION

## Watch Out for Predatory Lenders!

Predatory lenders often engage in one or more of the following practices:

- Say that they are your only chance of getting a loan or owning a home.

- Ask you to sign loan documents that are blank or that contain untrue information. Common examples include overstating your income, misrepresenting the source of your down payment, and failing to fully disclose the details of your debts.

- The cost or loan terms at closing are different from what you agreed to.

- You are told that refinancing can solve your credit problems.

- Charge fees for unnecessary or nonexistent products and services.

- Pressure borrowers to accept higher-risk loans with balloon payments, interest-only payments, costly prepayment penalties, or negative amortization.

- Convince borrowers to refinance repeatedly when there is no benefit to the borrower.

You can avoid being a victim of predatory lending as follows:

- Read everything and ask prospective lenders questions.

- Do not sign anything that isn't completely clear. Have your loan agreement reviewed by an attorney before you sign it. Write "N/A" (not applicable) or cross through any blanks.

- Do not let a lender persuade you to borrow more money than you know you can afford to repay.

- Shop for a loan and compare costs.

*Source:* Adapted from U.S. Department of Housing and Urban Development, "Don't Be a Victim of Loan Fraud: Protect Yourself from Predatory Lenders," http://www.hud.gov/offices/hsg/sfh/buying/loanfraud.cfm, accessed June 2009.

---

have to pay on the loan as well as whether the loan carries a fixed or variable rate. In this regard, ask the lender what the *annual rate of interest* on the loan will be because it's easier (and far more relevant) to compare percentage rates on alternative borrowing arrangements than the dollar amount of the loan charges. This rate of interest, known as the *APR* (annual percentage rate), includes not only the basic cost of money but also any additional fees that might be required on the loan (APR is more fully discussed later). Also, if it's a variable-rate loan, find out what the interest rate is pegged to, how many "points" are added to the base rate, how often the loan rate can be changed, and if rate caps exist. Just as important is how the lender makes the periodic adjustments: will the *size* of the monthly payment change or the *number* of monthly payments?

### Loan Maturity

Try to make sure that the size and number of loan payments will fit comfortably into your spending and savings plans. As a rule, the cost of credit increases with the length of the repayment period. Thus, to lower your cost, you should consider shortening the loan maturity—but only to the point where doing so won't place an unnecessary strain on your cash flow. Although a shorter maturity may reduce the cost of the loan, it also increases the size of the monthly loan payment. Indeed, finding

©DAVID BRIMM/SHUTTERSTOCK

a monthly loan payment you'll be comfortable with is a critical dimension of sound credit management.

Altering the loan maturity is just one way of coming up with an affordable monthly payment; fortunately, there are scores of Web sites where you can quickly run through all sorts of alternatives to find the monthly payment that will best fit your monthly budget. (The "tools" section of most major financial services sites on the Internet have "calculators" that enable you to quickly and easily figure interest rates and monthly loan payments for all sorts of loans; generally, all you need to do is plug in a few key pieces of information—such as the interest rate and loan term—and then hit "calculate" and let computer do the rest. For example, go to the calculator page of **http://www.finaid.org** and try out their "Loan Payments Calculator.")

### Total Cost of the Transaction

When comparison shopping for credit, always look at the total cost of *both* the price of the item purchased *and* the price of the credit. Retailers often manipulate both sticker prices and interest rates, so you really won't know what kind of deal you're getting until you look at the total cost of the transaction. Along this line, comparing *monthly payments* is a good way to get a handle on total cost. It's a simple matter to compare total costs: *just add the amount put down on the purchase to the total of all the monthly loan payments*; other things being equal, the one with the lowest total is the one you should pick.

### Collateral

Make sure you know up front what collateral (if any) you'll have to pledge on the loan and what you stand to lose if you default on your payments. Actually, if it makes no difference to you and if it's not too inconvenient, using collateral often makes sense, as it may result in *lower* finance charges—perhaps half a percentage point or so.

### Other Loan Considerations

In addition to following the guidelines just described, here are some questions that you should also ask: Can you choose a *payment date* that will be compatible with your spending patterns? Can you obtain the loan *promptly and conveniently?* What are the charges for late payments, and are they reasonable? Will you receive a refund on credit charges if you prepay your loan, or are there prepayment penalties? Taking the time to look around for the best credit deal will pay off, not only in reducing the cost of such debt but also in keeping the burden of credit in line with your cash budget and financial plans. In the long run, you're the one who has the most to gain (or lose). Thus *you should see to it that the debt you undertake does, in fact, have the desired effects on your financial condition!* You're paying for the loan, so you might as well make the most of it!

---

### FINANCIAL ROAD SIGN

**NO PAYMENTS, NO INTEREST—WHAT A DEAL!**
Or is it? You've seen plenty of these offers, for everything from carpeting to cars. Buy now and don't pay a penny until a year or more in the future. Is there a catch? Probably! So before you jump into one of these arrangements, make sure you fully understand the terms.

- *Do you have to make a minimum monthly payment for a specified period to avoid interest?*
- *Are no payments of either principal or interest required until a future date?*
- *Will the purchase price be due in full when the payment moratorium ends?* Very often it is; and if you can't pay in full, the merchant may be able to charge you interest (often at a very high rate) starting from your purchase date.
- *When does the 0% interest rate period end?* Read the fine print. You're likely to discover that 0% is a teaser rate that jumps after a short initial period.

---

### Keeping Track of Your Consumer Debt

To stay abreast of your financial condition, it's a good idea to periodically take inventory of the consumer debt you have outstanding. Ideally, you should do this every 3 or 4 months but at least once a year. To take inventory of what you owe, simply list all your outstanding consumer debt. Include *everything except your home mortgage*—installment loans, student loans, single-payment loans, credit cards, revolving credit lines, overdraft protection lines, even home equity credit lines.

Worksheet 7.1 should be helpful in preparing a list of your debts. To use it, simply list the current monthly payment and the latest balance due for each type of consumer credit outstanding; then, total both columns to see how much you're paying each month and how large a debt load you have built up. Hopefully, when you've totaled all the numbers, you won't be surprised to learn just how much you really do owe.

An easy way to assess your debt position is to compute your *debt safety ratio* (we discussed this ratio in Chapter 6) by dividing the total monthly payments (*from the worksheet*) by your monthly take-home pay. If 20% or more of your take-home pay is going to monthly credit payments, then you're relying too heavily on credit, but if your debt safety ratio works out to 10% or less, you're in a strong credit position. *Keeping track of your credit and holding the amount of outstanding debt to a reasonable level is the surest way to maintain your creditworthiness.*

**LG4** ## Single-Payment Loans

Unlike most types of consumer loans, a single-payment loan is repaid in full with a single payment on a given due date. The payment usually consists of principal and all interest charges. Sometimes, however, interim interest payments must be made (for example, every quarter), in which case the payment at maturity is made up of principal plus any unpaid interest. Although installment loans are far more popular, single-payment loans still have their place in the consumer loan market.

Single-payment loans can be secured or unsecured and can be taken out for just about any purpose. They're perhaps most useful when the funds needed for a given purchase or transaction are temporarily unavailable but are expected to be forthcoming in the near future. By helping you cope with a temporary cash shortfall, these loans can serve as a form of interim financing until more permanent arrangements can be made.

### Important Loan Features

When applying for either a single-payment or installment loan, you must first submit a **loan application**, an example of which is shown in Exhibit 7.2. Basically, the

**loan application** An application that gives a lender information about the purpose of the loan as well as the applicant's financial condition.

Use a worksheet like this one to keep track of your outstanding credit along with your monthly debt service requirements. Such information is a major component of sound credit management.

### AN INVENTORY OF CONSUMER DEBT

Name _Jeremy & Karen van Sant_  Date _June 14, 2010_

| Type of Consumer Debt | Creditor | | Current Monthly Payment* | Latest Balance Due |
|---|---|---|---|---|
| Auto loans | 1. | Ford | $ 342.27 | $ 13,796.00 |
| | 2. | | | |
| | 3. | | | |
| Education loans | 1. | U.S. Dept of Education | 117.00 | 7,986.00 |
| | 2. | | | |
| Personal installment loans | 1. | Chase Bank | 183.00 | 5,727.00 |
| | 2. | Bank of America | 92.85 | 2,474.00 |
| Home improvement loan | | | | |
| Other installment loans | 1. | | | |
| | 2. | | | |
| Single-payment loans | 1. | | | |
| | 2. | | | |
| Credit cards (retail charge cards, bank cards, T&E cards, etc.) | 1. | MBNA Visa | 42.00 | 826.00 |
| | 2. | Amex Blue | 35.00 | 600.00 |
| | 3. | Sears | 40.00 | 1,600.00 |
| | 4. | | | |
| | 5. | | | |
| | 6. | | | |
| | 7. | | | |
| Overdraft protection line | Hilands Schools Credit Union | | 15.00 | 310.00 |
| Personal line of credit | | | | |
| Home equity credit line | Wells Fargo | | 97.00 | 9,700.00 |
| Loan on life insurance | | | | |
| Margin loan from broker | | | | |
| Other loans | 1. | Mom & Dad | | 2,500.00 |
| | 2. | | | |
| | 3. | | | |
| | Totals | | $ 964.12 | $ 45,519.00 |

$$\text{Debt safety ratio} = \frac{\text{Total monthly payments}}{\text{Monthly take-home pay}} \times 100 = \frac{\$ \ 964.12}{\$ \ 5,200.00} \times 100 = \underline{18.5\%}$$

*Leave the space blank if there is *no* monthly payment required on a loan (e.g., as with a single-payment or education loan).

loan application gives the lending institution information about the purpose of the loan, whether it will be secured or unsecured, and the applicant's financial condition. The loan officer uses this document, along with other information (such as a credit report from the local credit bureau and income verification) to determine whether you should be granted the loan. Here again, some type of *credit scoring* (as discussed in Chapter 6) may be used to make the decision. When applying for a loan, you should also consider various features of the debt, the three most important of which are loan collateral, loan maturity, and loan repayment.

**Exhibit 7.2   A Consumer Loan Credit Application**

A typical loan application, like this one, contains information about the persons applying for the loan, including source(s) of income, current debt load, and a brief record of employment.

## CONSUMER CREDIT APPLICATION

### LOAN INFORMATION

| Amount Requested $ | Purpose | Application Type ☐Individual ☐Joint |
|---|---|---|

### COLLATERAL INFORMATION

☐Motor Vehicle: Year____Make_____Model_____Miles_____
☐Personal Property   ☐Other (Describe)

### APPLICANT INFORMATION

| Name (Last, First,  M.I.) | | E-mail Address |
|---|---|---|
| Social Security  #  -  - | Date of Birth  /  / | ☐Married ☐Unmarried ☐Separated | # of Dependents |

### CO-APPLICANT INFORMATION

| Name (Last, First,  M.I.) | | E-mail Address |
|---|---|---|
| Social Security  #  -  - | Date of Birth  /  / | ☐Married ☐Unmarried ☐Separated | # of Dependents |

### APPLICANT RESIDENCE INFORMATION

| Address (Number, St,   and Apt. or  Lot # if applicable) | Telephone # |
|---|---|
| City, State, Zip Code | Time At Residence Years / Months / |
| Previous Address | Time At Residence Years / Months / |
| ☐Rent ☐Live with Parents ☐Own ☐Other_____ | Landlord or Mortgage  Holder Name: Phone #: | Monthly Payment $ |

### CO-APPLICANT RESIDENCE INFORMATION

| Address (Number, St,   and Apt. or  Lot # if applicable) | Telephone # |
|---|---|
| City, State, Zip Code | Time At Residence Years / Months / |
| Previous Address | Time At Residence Years / Months / |
| ☐Rent ☐Live with Parents ☐Own ☐Other_____ | Landlord or Mortgage  Holder Name: Phone #: | Monthly Payment $ |

### APPLICANT EMPLOYMENT INFORMATION

| Employer | Employer Telephone |
|---|---|
| Employer Address | Position |
| Gross Income: $ | ☐Weekly ☐Bi-weekly ☐Monthly | Time At Job Years / Months / |
| Other Income: $     Source | |
| Previous Employer &   location | Previous Emp.  Phone # |
| Position | Time At Job Years / Months / |

### CO-APPLICANT EMPLOYMENT

| Employer | Employer Telephone |
|---|---|
| Employer Address | Position |
| Gross Income: $ | ☐Weekly ☐Bi-weekly ☐Monthly | Time At Job Years / Months / |
| Other Income: $     Source | Alimony, Child support, or separate maintenance income need not be revealed if you do not wish to have it considered as a basis for repaying this obligation. |
| Previous Employer &   Location | Previous Emp.  Phone # |
| Position | Time At Job Years / Months / |

### APPLICANT CREDIT REFERENCES

| Creditor | Payment | Balance |
|---|---|---|
| | | |
| | | |
| | | |
| | | |

☐Checking   Bank Name_____ Acct#_____
☐Savings    Bank Name_____ Acct#_____

### CO-APPLICANT CREDIT REFERENCES

| Creditor | Payment | Balance |
|---|---|---|
| | | |
| | | |
| | | |
| | | |

☐Checking   Bank Name_____ Acct#_____
☐Savings    Bank Name_____ Acct#_____

### AUTHORIZATION AND SIGNATURES

By signing this application, you promise that all information provided is true and complete.  You also promise that you have revealed any pending lawsuits or unpaid judgements against you.  You intend the lender and/or assignee to rely upon these promises in deciding whether to extend credit to you.  You authorize a full investigation of your credit record and your employment history.  You also authorize the seller and/or assignee to release information about your credit experience with them.  You understand that the lender will retain this application whether or not it is approved.  I understand that if the application is for a secured loan additional information  may be required.

| Applicant Signature | Date | Co-Applicant Signature | Date |
|---|---|---|---|

## Loan Collateral

Most single-payment loans are secured by certain specified assets. For *collateral*, lenders prefer items they feel are readily marketable at a price that's high enough to cover the principal portion of the loan—for example, an automobile, jewelry, or stocks and bonds.

**lien** A legal claim permitting the lender, in case the borrower defaults, to liquidate the items serving as collateral to satisfy the obligation.

**chattel mortgage** A mortgage on personal property given as security for the payment of an obligation.

**collateral note** A legal note giving the lender the right to sell collateral if the borrower defaults on the obligation.

**prepayment penalty** An additional charge you may owe if you decide to pay off your loan prior to maturity.

**loan rollover** The process of paying off a loan by taking out another loan.

**loan disclosure statement** A document, which lenders are required to supply borrowers, that states both the dollar amount of finance charges and the APR applicable to a loan.

If a loan is obtained to purchase some personal asset, then that asset may be used to secure it. In most cases, lenders don't take physical possession of the collateral but instead file a **lien**, which is a legal claim that permits them to liquidate the collateral to satisfy the loan if the borrower defaults. If the borrowers maintain possession or title to *movable* property—such as cars, TVs, and jewelry—then the instrument that gives lenders title to the property in event of default is called a **chattel mortgage**. If lenders hold title to the collateral—or take possession of it, as is often the case with stocks and bonds—then the agreement giving them the right to sell these items in case of default is a **collateral note**.

### Loan Maturity

As indicated previously, the maturity (or term) on a single-payment loan is usually for a period of 1 year or less; it very rarely extends to 2 years or longer. When you request a single-payment loan, be sure that the term is long enough to allow you to obtain the funds for repaying the loans *but* not any longer than necessary. Don't stretch the maturity out too far as the amount of the finance charges paid will increase with time. Because the loan is retired in a single payment, the lender must be assured that you'll be able to repay it even if certain unexpected events occur in the future. So, the term of your single-payment loan must be reconciled with your budget as well as with your ability to pay.

### Loan Repayment

Repayment of a single-payment loan is expected at a single point in time: on its maturity date. Occasionally, the funds needed to repay this type of loan will be received prior to maturity. Depending on the lender, the borrower might be able to repay the loan early and thus reduce the finance charges. Many credit unions actually permit early repayment of these loans with *reduced* finance charges. However, commercial banks and other single-payment lenders may not accept early repayments or, if they do, may charge a **prepayment penalty** on them. This penalty normally amounts to a set percentage of the interest that would have been paid over the remaining life

of the loan. The Truth in Lending Act requires lenders to disclose in the loan agreement whether, and in what amount, prepayment penalties are charged on a single-payment loan.

Occasionally, an individual will borrow money using a single-payment loan and then discover that he or she is short of money when the loan comes due. Should this happen to you, don't just let the payment go past due; instead, *inform the lender in advance so that a partial payment, loan extension, or some other arrangement can be made*. Under such circumstances, the lender will often agree to a **loan rollover**, in which case the original loan is paid off by taking out another loan. The lender will usually require that all the interest and at least part of the principal be paid at the time of the rollover. So, if you originally borrowed $5,000 for 12 months, then the bank might be willing to lend you a lower amount like $3,500 for another 6 to 9 months as part of a loan rollover. In this case, you'll have to "pay down" $1,500 of the original loan, along with all interest due. However, you can expect the interest rate on a rollover loan to go up a bit; that's the price you pay for falling short on the first loan. Also, you should not expect to get more than one, or at the most two, loan rollovers—a bank's patience tends to grow short after a while!

## Finance Charges and the Annual Percentage Rate

As indicated in Chapter 6, lenders are required to disclose both the dollar amount of finance charges and the annual percentage rate (APR) of interest. A sample **loan disclosure statement** applicable to either a single-payment or installment loan can be seen in Exhibit 7.3.

### FINANCIAL ROAD SIGN

$$$

**KEEP THE LENDER'S PERSPECTIVE IN MIND**
What do lenders look for when reviewing loan applications and credit reports? Here are their top questions:

- Do you pay your bills on time?
- How much of your income is already committed to debt repayment?
- How much available credit do you already have, even if it's not currently being used?
- How stable and responsible are you? How long have you been with your employer and lived at the same address?
- Are there many recent inquiries on your credit report? (Lenders see this as a sign that you may be applying for a lot of credit.)

**Exhibit 7.3 A Loan Disclosure Statement**

The loan disclosure statement informs the borrower of all charges (finance and otherwise) associated with the loan and the annual percentage rate (APR). It also specifies the payment terms as well as the existence of any balloon payments.

# FEDERAL TRUTH IN LENDING DISCLOSURE STATEMENT

**Creditor: YOUR FAVORITE MORTGAGE CORPORATION**
**Borrower(s):**

Account Number: 1111111

| ANNUAL PERCENTAGE RATE | FINANCE CHARGE | Amount Financed | Total of Payments |
|---|---|---|---|
| The cost of your credit as a yearly rate | The dollar amount the credit will cost you | The amount of credit provided to you or on your behalf | The amount you will have paid after you have made all payments as scheduled |
| 7.337 % | $ 205,017.52 | $ 138,796.50 | $ 343,814.02 |

Your payment schedule will be:

| NUMBER OF PAYMENTS | AMOUNT OF PAYMENTS | WHEN PAYMENTS ARE DUE |
|---|---|---|
| 359 | $955.05 | Monthly beginning 09/01/10 |
| 1 | 951.07 | Monthly beginning 08/01/41 |

**Variable Rate:** If checked, your loan contains a variable rate feature. Disclosures about the variable rate feature have been provided to you earlier.

**Demand Feature:** If checked, this obligation has a demand feature.

**Insurance:** You may obtain property insurance from anyone you want that is acceptable to the creditor.

If checked, you can get insurance through Your Favorite Mortgage Corporation. You will pay $____ for 12 months hazard insurance coverage. You will pay $ ____ for 12 months flood insurance coverage.

**Security:** You are giving a security interest in property being purchased property located at **1234 118TH STREET, NW, WASHINGTON, DC 20009**
Assignment of brokerage account and pledge of securities Personal property: stocks and lease
Assignment of life insurance policy Other:
**Late Charges:** If a payment is late, you will be charged **5.000 %** of the payment.

**Prepayment:** If you pay off early, you may will not have to pay a penalty. You may will not be entitled to a refund of part of the finance charge.

**Assumption:** Someone buying your house may, subject to conditions, be allowed to cannot assume the remainder of the mortgage on the original terms.

See your contract documents for any additional information about nonpayment, default, any required repayment in full before the scheduled date, prepayment refunds and penalties and assumption policy.

<u>ACKNOWLEDGMENT</u>

By signing below you acknowledge that you have received a completed copy of this Federal Truth in Lending Statement prior to the execution *of* any closing documents.

_____
Borrower/Date of Acknowledgment

_____
Borrower/Date of Acknowledgment

Note that such a statement discloses not only interest costs but also other fees and expenses that may be tacked onto the loan. Although disclosures like this one allow you to compare the various borrowing alternatives, you still need to understand the methods used to compute finance charges because similar loans with the same *stated* interest rates may have different finance charges and APRs. The two basic procedures used to calculate the finance charges on single-payment loans are the *simple interest method* and the *discount method*.

## Simple Interest Method

Interest is charged only on the *actual loan balance outstanding* in the **simple interest method**. This method is commonly used on revolving credit lines and installment loans made by commercial banks, S&Ls, and credit unions. To see how it's applied

©GVICTORIA/DREAMSTIME.COM

to a single-payment loan, assume that you borrow $1,000 for two years at an 8% annual rate of interest. On a single-payment loan, the actual loan balance outstanding for the 2 years will be the full $1,000 because no principal payments will be made until this period ends. With simple interest, the finance charge, $F_s$, is obtained by multiplying the *principal* outstanding by the stated annual rate of interest and then multiplying this amount by the term of the loan:

$$F_s = P \times r \times t$$

where:

$F_s$ = finance charge calculated using simple interest method
$P$ = principal amount of loan
$r$ = stated annual rate of interest
$t$ = term of loan, as stated in years (for example, $t$ would equal 0.5 for a 6-month loan, 1.25 for a 15-month loan, and 2.0 for a 2-year loan).

Thus, substituting $1,000 for $P$, 0.08 for $r$, and 2 for $t$ in the equation, we see that the finance charge, $F_s$, on our $1,000, 2-year loan would be: $160 (i.e., $1,000 \times 0.08$ per year × 2 years). With this type of credit arrangement, the size of the loan repayment is found by adding the finance charges to the principal amount of the loan, so you'd have to make a payment of $1,000 + $160 = $1,160 at maturity to retire this debt. To calculate the true, or annual, percentage rate (APR) on this loan, the average annual finance charge is divided by the average loan balance outstanding, as follows:

$$APR = \frac{\text{Average annual finance charge}}{\text{Average loan balance outstanding}}$$

In this case, the average annual finance charge is found by dividing the total finance charge by the life of the loan (in years). In our example, the result is $80 ($160 ÷ 2). Because no principal payments are made on these loans, the outstanding loan balance is fixed at $1,000, as is the average loan balance. Dividing the $80 average annual finance charge by the $1,000 average loan balance, we obtain an APR of 8%. Note, the APR and the stated rate of interest are equivalent: they both equal 8%. *This will always be the case when the simple interest method is used to calculate finance charges, regardless of whether loans are single-payment or installment.*

## Discount Method

The **discount method** calculates total finance charges on the full principal amount of the loan, *which is then subtracted from the amount of the loan*. The difference between the amount of the loan and the finance charge is then disbursed (paid) to the borrower—in other words, finance charges are paid in advance and represent a discount from the principal portion of the loan. The finance charge on a single-payment loan using the discount method, $F_d$, is calculated in exactly the same way as for a simple interest loan:

$$F_d = F_s = P \times r \times t$$

Using the above formula, the finance charge, $F_d$, on the $1,000, 8%, 2-year, single-payment loan is (of course) the same $160 that we calculated earlier. But, in sharp contrast to simple interest loans, the loan repayment with a discount loan is based on the original principal amount of the loan, $P$. Thus, for the $1,000 loan, the borrower will receive $840 ($1,000 less $160) and in 2 years will be required to pay back $1,000.

To find the APR on this loan, substitute the appropriate values into the APR equation shown previously. But in this case, while the average annual finance charge is the same $80 ($160 ÷ 2), the borrower will receive only $840, which is the average amount of the loan. When these figures are used in the APR equation, we find the true rate for this 8% discount loan is closer to 9.52% ($80/$840). Clearly, the discount method yields a much higher APR on single-payment loans than does the simple interest method. The Bonus Exhibit "Finance Charges and APRs for a Single-Payment Loan ($1000 Loan for 2 Years at 8% Interest)," at 4ltrpress.cengage.com, contrasts the results from both methods for the single-payment loan example discussed here.

## LG5, LG6 Installment Loans

Installment loans (known as ILs for short) differ from single-payment loans in that they require the borrower to repay the debt in a series of installment payments (usually monthly) over the life of the loan. Installment loans have long been one of the most popular forms of consumer credit—right up there with credit cards! Much of this popularity is due to how conveniently the loan repayment is set up; not surprisingly, most people find it easier on their checkbooks to make a series of small payments rather than one big one.

### Go to Smart Sites

Find out about federal protection laws for borrowers and get tips on financing consumer loans at the Federal Trade Commission site. ●

**discount method** A method of calculating finance charges in which interest is computed and then subtracted from the principal, with the remainder being disbursed to the borrower.

## A Real Consumer Credit Workhorse

As a financing vehicle, installment loans can be used to finance just about any type of big-ticket item imaginable. New car loans are the dominant type of IL, but this form of credit is also used to finance home furnishings, appliances and entertainment centers, camper trailers and other recreational vehicles, and even expensive vacations. Also, more and more college students are turning to this type of credit as the way to finance their education. Not only can installment loans be used to finance all sorts of things, they can also be obtained at many locations. You'll find them at banks and other financial institutions as well as at major department stores and merchants that sell relatively expensive products. Go into a home appliance store to buy a high-priced stereo, and chances are you'll be able to arrange for IL financing right there on the spot. These loans can be taken out for just a few hundred dollars, or they can involve thousands of dollars—indeed, ILs of $25,000 or more are not that uncommon. In addition, installment loans can be set up with maturities as short as 6 months or as long as 7 to 10 years or even 15 years.

> **As a financing vehicle, installment loans can be used to finance just about anything.**

Most installment loans are secured with some kind of collateral—for example, the car or home entertainment center you purchased with the help of an IL usually serves as collateral on the loan. Even personal loans used to finance things like expensive vacations can be secured—in these cases, the collateral could be securities, CDs, or some other type of financial asset. One rapidly growing segment of this market is ILs secured by second mortgages. These so-called *home equity loans* are similar to the home equity credit lines discussed in Chapter 6, except they involve a set amount of money loaned over a set period of time (often as long as 15 years) rather than a revolving credit line from which you can borrow, repay, and reborrow. For example, if a borrower needs $25,000 to help pay for an expensive new boat, he can simply take out a loan in that amount and *secure it* with a second mortgage on his home. This loan would be like any other IL in the sense that it'll be repaid over a set period of time in monthly installments. Besides their highly competitive interest rates, a big attraction of *home equity loans* is that the interest paid on them usually can be taken as a tax deduction. Thus, borrowers get the double benefit of *low interest rates and tax deductibility*.

## Finance Charges, Monthly Payments, and the APR

Earlier, we discussed two ways of computing finance charges on single-payment loans. Here, we look at the two procedures—*simple and add-on interest*—that are normally used to compute finance charges and monthly payments on installment loans. To illustrate, we'll use an 8%, $1,000 installment loan that is to

be paid off in 12 monthly payments. As in the earlier illustration for single-payment loans, we assume that interest is the only component of the finance charge; there are no other fees and charges.

### Using Simple Interest

When simple interest is used with ILs, interest is charged only on the outstanding balance of the loan. Thus, as the loan principal declines with monthly payments, the amount of interest being charged also decreases. Because finance charges change each month, the procedure used to find the interest expense is mathematically complex. Fortunately, this isn't much of a problem in practice because of the widespread use of computers, handheld financial calculators (which we'll illustrate later), and preprinted finance tables—an example of which is provided in Exhibit 7.4 The

---

**Exhibit 7.4    A Table of Monthly Installment Loan Payments (to Repay a $1,000, Simple Interest Loan)**

You can use a table like this to find the monthly payments on a wide variety of simple interest installment loans. Although it's set up to show payments on a $1,000 loan, with a little modification you can easily use it with any size loan (the principal can be more or less than $1,000).

| Rate of Interest | Loan Maturity | | | | | | |
|---|---|---|---|---|---|---|---|
| | 6 Months | 12 Months | 18 Months | 24 Months | 36 Months | 48 Months | 60 Months |
| 6.0% | $169.60 | $86.07 | $58.23 | $44.32 | $30.42 | $23.49 | $19.33 |
| 6.5 | 169.84 | 86.30 | 58.46 | 44.55 | 30.65 | 23.71 | 19.57 |
| 7.0 | 170.09 | 86.53 | 58.68 | 44.77 | 30.88 | 23.95 | 19.80 |
| 7.5 | $170.33 | $86.76 | $58.92 | $45.00 | $31.11 | $24.18 | $20.05 |
| 8.0 | 170.58 | 86.99 | 59.15 | 45.23 | 31.34 | 24.42 | 20.28 |
| 8.5 | 170.82 | 87.22 | 59.37 | 45.46 | 31.57 | 24.65 | 20.52 |
| 9.0 | 171.07 | 87.46 | 59.60 | 45.69 | 31.80 | 24.89 | 20.76 |
| 9.5 | 171.32 | 87.69 | 59.83 | 45.92 | 32.04 | 25.13 | 21.01 |
| 10.0 | 171.56 | 87.92 | 60.06 | 46.15 | 32.27 | 25.37 | 21.25 |
| 11.0 | 172.05 | 88.50 | 60.64 | 46.73 | 32.86 | 25.97 | 21.87 |
| 12.0 | 172.50 | 88.85 | 60.99 | 47.08 | 33.22 | 26.34 | 22.25 |
| 13.0 | 173.04 | 89.32 | 61.45 | 47.55 | 33.70 | 26.83 | 22.76 |
| 14.0 | 173.54 | 89.79 | 61.92 | 48.02 | 34.18 | 27.33 | 23.27 |
| 15.0 | 174.03 | 90.26 | 62.39 | 48.49 | 34.67 | 27.84 | 23.79 |
| 16.0 | 174.53 | 90.74 | 62.86 | 48.97 | 35.16 | 28.35 | 24.32 |
| 17.0 | 175.03 | 91.21 | 63.34 | 49.45 | 35.66 | 28.86 | 24.86 |
| 18.0 | 175.53 | 91.68 | 63.81 | 49.93 | 36.16 | 29.38 | 25.40 |

---

tables show the *monthly payment* that would be required to retire an installment loan carrying a given simple rate of interest with a given term to maturity. Because these tables (sometimes referred to as *amortization schedules*) have interest charges built right into them, the monthly payments shown cover both principal and interest.

Notice that the loan payments shown in Exhibit 7.4 cover a variety of interest rates (from 6% to 18%) and loan maturities (from 6 to 60 months). The values in the table represent the monthly payments required to retire a $1,000 loan. Although it's assumed that you're borrowing $1,000, you can use the table with any size loan. For example, if you're looking at a $5,000 loan, just multiply the monthly loan payment from the table by 5; or, if you have a $500 loan, multiply the loan payment by 0.5. In many respects, this table is just like the mortgage loan payment schedule introduced in Chapter 5, except we use much shorter loan maturities here than with mortgages.

©FEDOROV OLEKSIY/SHUTTERSTOCK

Here's how to use the table in Exhibit 7.4. Suppose we want to find the monthly payment required on our $1,000, 8%, 12-month loan. Looking under the 12-month column and across from the 8% rate of interest, we find a value of $86.99; that is the monthly payment it will take to pay off the $1,000 loan in 12 months. When we multiply the monthly payments ($86.99) by the term of the loan in months (12), the result is total payments of $86.99 × 12 = $1,043.88. The difference between the total payments on the loan and the principal portion represents the *finance charges on the loan*—in this case, $1,043.88 − $1,000 = interest charges of $43.88 in interest charges.

From each monthly payment (of $86.99), a certain portion goes to interest and the balance is used to reduce the principal. Because the principal balance declines with each payment, the amount that goes to interest also *decreases* while the amount that goes to principal *increases*.

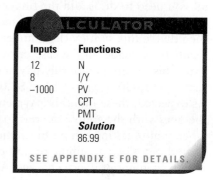

| Inputs | Functions |
|---|---|
| 12 | N |
| 8 | I/Y |
| −1000 | PV |
| | CPT |
| | PMT |
| | *Solution* |
| | 86.99 |

SEE APPENDIX E FOR DETAILS.

> **add-on method** A method of calculating interest by computing finance charges on the original loan balance and then adding the interest to that balance.

## Calculator Keystrokes

Instead of using a table like the one in Exhibit 7.4, you could just as easily have used a handheld financial calculator to *find the monthly payments on an IL*. Here's what you'd do. First, set the payments per year (P/Y) key to 12 to put the calculator in a monthly payment mode. Now, to find the monthly payment needed to pay off an 8%, 12-month, $1,000 installment loan, use the keystrokes shown, where

> N = length of the loan, *in months*
> I/Y = the *annual* rate of interest being charged on the loan
> PV = the amount of the loan, entered as a *negative* number

As seen, to pay off this IL, you'll have to make payments of $86.99 per month for the next 12 months.

### Add-on Method

Some installment loans, particularly those obtained directly from retail merchants or made at finance companies and the like, are made using the **add-on method**. Add-on loans are very expensive. Indeed, they generally rank as one of the most costly forms of consumer credit, with APRs that are often well above the rates charged even on many credit cards. With add-on interest, the finance charges are calculated using the *original* balance of the loan; this amount (the total finance charges) is then added on to the original loan balance to determine the total amount to be repaid. The amount of finance charges on an add-on loan can be found by using the familiar simple interest formula:

$$F_s = P \times r \times t$$

Given the $1,000 loan we've been using for illustrative purposes, the finance charges on an 8%, 1-year add-on loan would be

$$F_s = \$1{,}000 \times 0.08 \times 1 = \$80$$

Compared to the finance charges for the same loan on a simple interest basis ($43.88), *the add-on loan is a lot more expensive.* Keep in mind that both of these loans would be quoted as "8%" loans. Thus, you may think you're getting an 8% loan, but looks can be deceiving—especially when you're dealing with add-on interest!

To find the monthly payments on an add-on loan, all you need to do is add the finance charge ($80) to the *original* principal amount of the loan ($1,000) and then divide this sum by the number of monthly payments to be made. In the case of our $1,000, 1-year loan, this results in monthly payments of $90.00; that is: ($1,000 + $80) / 12 = $1,080 / 12 = $90.00 As expected, these monthly payments are higher than the ones with the simple interest loan ($86.99). So, when you're taking out an installment loan, be sure to find out whether simple or add-on interest is being used to compute finance charges. And if it's add-on, you might want to consider looking elsewhere for the loan.

Because the actual rate of interest with an add-on loan is considerably higher than the stated rate, we must determine the loan's APR. That can easily be done with a financial calculator, as shown next. As you can see, the APR on this 8% add-on loan is more like 14.45%. Clearly, when viewed from an APR perspective, the add-on loan is an expensive form of

financing! This is because when add-on interest is applied to an installment loan, the interest included in each payment is charged on the *initial principal* even though the outstanding loan balance is reduced as installment payments are made. A summary of comparative finance charges and APRs for simple interest and add-on interest methods is presented in Exhibit 7.5.

Federal banking regulations require that the exact APR (accurate to the nearest 0.25%) must be disclosed to borrowers. And note that not only interest but also any other fees required to obtain a loan are considered part of the finance charges and must be included in the computation of APR.

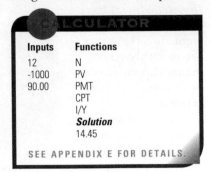

| Inputs | Functions |
|---|---|
| 12 | N |
| -1000 | PV |
| 90.00 | PMT |
| | CPT |
| | I/Y |
| | *Solution* |
| | 14.45 |

SEE APPENDIX E FOR DETAILS.

## Prepayment Penalties

Another type of finance charge that's often found in installment loan contracts is the *prepayment penalty*, which is an additional charge you may owe if you decide to pay off your loan prior to maturity. When you pay off a loan early, you may find that you owe quite a bit more than expected, especially if the lender uses the **rule of 78s** (or **sum-of-the-digits method**) to calculate the amount of interest paid and the principal balance to date. You might think that paying off a $1,000, 8%, 1-year loan at the end of 6 months would mean that you've paid about half of the principal and owe somewhere around $500 to the lender. Well, that's just not so with a loan that uses the rule of 78s! This method charges more interest in the early months of the loan on the theory that the borrower has use of more money in the loan's early stages and so should pay more finance charges in the early months and progressively less later. There's nothing wrong with that, of course; it's how all loans operate. But what's wrong is that *the rule of 78s front-loads an inordinate amount of interest charges to the early months of the loan, thereby producing a much higher principal balance than you'd normally expect* (remember: the more of the loan payment that goes to interest, the less that goes to principal).

## Buy on Time or Pay Cash?

When buying a big-ticket item, you often have little choice but to take out a loan—the item being purchased is just so expensive that you can't afford to

---

### Calculator Keystrokes

Here's how you *find the APR on an add-in IL* using a financial calculator. First, make sure the payments per year (P/Y) key is set to 12 so that the calculator is in the monthly payment mode. Then, to find the APR on a $1,000, 12-month, 8% add-on IL, use the following keystrokes, where

> N = length of the loan, in months
> PV = size of the loan, entered as a negative number
> PMT = size of the monthly IL payments

You'll find that the APR on the 8% add-on loan is a whopping 14.45%!

## Exhibit 7.5 Comparative Finance Charges and APRs (Assumes a $1,000, 8%, 12-Month Installment Loan)

In sharp contrast to simple interest loans, the APR with add-on installment loans is much higher than the stated rate.

|  | Simple Interest | Add-on Interest |
|---|---|---|
| Stated rate on loan | 8% | 8% |
| Finance charges | $43.88 | $80.00 |
| Monthly payments | $86.99 | $90.00 |
| Total payments made | $1,043.88 | $1,080.00 |
| APR | 8% | 14.45% |

pay cash. And even if you do have the money, you may still be better off using something like an IL *if the cash purchase would end up severely depleting your liquid reserves*. But don't just automatically take out a loan. Rather, take the time to find out if, in fact, that is the best thing to do. Such a decision can easily be made by using Worksheet 7.2, which considers the cost of the loan relative to the after-tax earnings generated from having your money in some type of short-term investment. Here, it's assumed that the consumer has an adequate level of liquid reserves and that these reserves are being held in some type of savings account. (Obviously, if this is not the case, then there's little reason to go through the exercise because you have no choice but to borrow the money.) Essentially, it all boils down to this: *If it costs more to borrow the money than you can earn in interest, then withdraw the money from your savings to pay cash for the purchase; if not, you should probably take out a loan.*

Consider this situation: You're thinking about buying a second car (a nice, low-mileage used vehicle) but after the normal down payment, you still need to come up with $12,000. This balance can be taken care of in one of two ways: (1) you can take out a 36-month, 8% IL (with a monthly payment of $376.04), or (2) you can pay cash by drawing the money from a money fund (paying 4% interest today and for the foreseeable future). We can now run the numbers to decide whether to buy on time or pay cash—see Worksheet 7.2 for details. In this case, we assume the loan is a standard IL (where the interest does not qualify as a tax deduction) and that you're in the 28% tax bracket. The worksheet shows that by borrowing the money, you'll end up paying about $1,537 in interest (line

4), none of which is tax deductible. In contrast, by leaving your money on deposit in the money fund, you'll receive only $1,038 in interest, after taxes (see line 11). Taken together, we see the net cost of borrowing (line 12) is nearly $500—so you'll be paying $1,537 to earn only $1,038, which certainly doesn't make much sense! Clearly, it's far more cost-effective in this case to take the money from savings and pay cash for the car, because you'll save nearly $500.

Although $500 is a pretty convincing reason for avoiding a loan, sometimes the actual dollar spread between the cost of borrowing and interest earned is very small, perhaps only $100 or less. Being able to deduct the interest on a loan can lead to a relatively small spread, but it can also occur, for example, if the amount being financed is relatively small—say, you want $1,500 or $2,000 for a ski trip

©GH19/DREAMSTIME.COM

Using a worksheet like this, you can decide whether to buy on time or pay cash by comparing the after-tax cost of interest paid on a loan with the after-tax interest income lost by taking the money out of savings and using it to pay cash for the purchase.

### BUY ON TIME OR PAY CASH

Name _Jackson R. Hunt_                                                                Date _2/28/2010_

| ■ Cost of Borrowing | | |
|---|---|---|
| 1. Terms of the loan | | |
|     a. Amount of the loan | $ 12,000.00 | |
|     b. Length of the loan (in years) | 3.00 | |
|     c. Monthly payment | $ 376.04 | |
| 2. Total loan payments made (monthly loan payment × length of loan in months) $ _376.04_ per month _36_ months | | $ 13,537.44 |
| 3. Less: Principal amount of the loan | | $ 12,000.00 |
| 4. Total interest paid over life of loan (line 2 — 3) | | $ 1,537.44 |
| 5. Tax considerations:<br>• Is this a home equity loan (where interest expenses can be deducted from taxes)? . . . . . . . . . . . . . . . . . . . . . ☐ yes ☑ no<br>• Do you itemize deductions on your federal tax returns? ☑ yes ☐ no<br>• If you answered yes to BOTH questions, then proceed to line 6; if you answered no to *either one* or *both* of the questions, then proceed to *line 8* and use *line 4* as the after-tax interest cost of the loan. | | |
| 6. What federal tax bracket are you in? (use either 10, 15, 25, 28, 33, or 35%) | 28 % | |
| 7. Taxes saved due to interest deductions (line 4 × tax rate, from line 6: $_____ × _____%) | | $ 0.00 |
| 8. Total after-tax interest cost on the loan (line 4 − line 7) | | $ 1,537.44 |
| ■ Cost of Paying Cash | | |
| 9. Annual interest earned on savings (annual rate of interest earned on savings × amount of loan: _4_% × _12,000.00_ ) | | $ 480.00 |
| 10. Annual after-tax interest earnings (line 9 × [1 − tax rate] — e.g., 1 − 28% = 72%: $_480.00_ × _72_%) | | $ 346.00 |
| 11. Total after-tax interest earnings over life of loan (line 10 × line 1b: $_346.00_ × _3_ years) | | $ 1,038.00 |
| ■ Net Cost of Borrowing | | |
| 12. Difference in cost of borrowing vs. cost of paying cash (line 8 minus line 11) | | $ 499.44 |

BASIC DECISION RULE: *Pay cash* if line 12 is positive; *borrow the money* if line 12 is negative.

*Note:* For simplicity, compounding is ignored in calculating *both* the cost of interest and interest earnings.

to Colorado. In this case—and so long as the spread stays small enough—you may decide it's still worthwhile to borrow the money in order to maintain a higher level of liquidity. Although this decision is perfectly legitimate when very small spreads exist, it makes less sense as the gap starts to widen.

# FINANCIAL PLANNING EXERCISES

**LG3, 6**

1. Assume that you've been shopping for a new car and intend to finance part of it through an installment loan. The car you're looking for has a sticker price of $15,000. Excellent Autos has offered to sell it to you for $2,500 down and finance the balance with a loan that will require 48 monthly payments of $329.17; Hot Cars will sell you exactly the same vehicle for $3,000 down plus a 60-month loan for the balance, with monthly payments of $268.45. Which of these two finance packages is the better deal?

**LG5, 6**

2. Using the simple interest method, find the monthly payments on a $3,000 installment loan if the funds are borrowed for 24 months at an annual interest rate of 8%.

**LG4**

3. Find the finance charges on a 7.5%, 18-month, single-payment loan when interest is computed using the simple interest method. Find the finance charges on the same loan when interest is computed using the discount method. Determine the APR in each case.

**LG5, 6**

4. Assuming that interest is the only finance charge, how much interest would be paid on a $5,000 installment loan to be repaid in 36 monthly installments of $166.10? What is the APR on this loan?

**LG6**

5. *Use Worksheet 7.2:* Marie Herrera wants to buy a home entertainment center. Complete with a big-screen TV, DVD, and sound system, the unit would cost $4,500. Marie has over $15,000 in a money fund, so she can easily afford to pay cash for the whole thing (the fund is currently paying 5% interest, and Marie expects that yield to hold for the foreseeable future). To stimulate sales, the dealer is offering to finance the full cost of the unit with a 36-month installment loan at 9%, simple. Marie wants to know: Should she pay cash for the home entertainment center or buy it on time? (*Note:* Assume Marie is in the 28% tax bracket and that she itemizes deductions on her tax returns.) Briefly explain.

"It's easy to read, it outlines important topics, and it's relevant. Thanks for the good stuff on the website, I think it will **really help with tests**."

– Thomas Scholtes, Student at University of Maryland, College Park

# REVIEW HE DID

**PFIN** puts a multitude of study aids at your fingertips. After reading the chapters, check out these resources for further help:

- **Chapter in Review cards**, found in the back of your book, include all learning goal summaries, key terms, and definitions.

- **Online printable flash cards** give you additional ways to check your comprehension of personal finance key concepts.

Other great ways to help you study include **quizzes, interactive worksheets, flash cards, and an eBook.**

You can find it all at **CengageBrain.com**.

# PART 4

# MANAGING INSURANCE NEEDS

167

## LG1 Basic Insurance Concepts

As most people discover, life is full of unexpected events that can have far-reaching consequences. Your car is sideswiped on the highway and damaged beyond repair. A family member falls ill and can no longer work. A fire or other disaster destroys your home. Your spouse dies suddenly. Although most people don't like to think about possibilities like this, protecting yourself and your family against unforeseen events is part of sound financial planning. Insurance plays a central role in providing that protection. *Life insurance* helps replace lost income if premature death occurs, providing funds so that your loved ones can keep their home, maintain an acceptable lifestyle, pay for education, and meet other special needs. *Health insurance* covers medical costs when you get sick or become disabled. *Property insurance*, for example, reimburses you if your car or home are destroyed or damaged.

### Risk Avoidance

The simplest way to deal with risk is to avoid the act that creates it. For example, people who are afraid they might lose everything as a result of an automobile accident could avoid driving. Similarly, avid skydivers or bungee jumpers might want to choose another recreational activity. But **risk avoidance** has its costs. People who avoid driving experience considerable inconvenience, and the retired skydiver may suffer from stress-related health risks. Risk avoidance is attractive when the cost of avoidance is less than the cost of handling it some other way.

### Loss Prevention and Control

**Loss prevention** is any activity that reduces the chance that a loss will occur (such as driving

> **risk avoidance**
> Avoiding an act that would create a risk.
>
> **loss prevention**
> Any activity that reduces the probability that a loss will occur.
>
> **loss control** Any activity that lessens the severity of loss once it occurs.
>
> **risk assumption** The choice to accept and bear the risk of loss.

> { *Although most people don't like to think about possibilities like this, protecting yourself and your family against unforeseen events is part of sound financial planning.* }

All of these types of insurance are intended *to protect you and your dependents from the financial consequences of losing assets or income when an accident, illness, or death occurs.* By anticipating the potential risks to which your assets and income could be exposed and by weaving insurance protection into your financial plan, you lend a degree of certainty to your financial future. This chapter introduces important insurance concepts and then focuses on life insurance decisions.

## The Concept of Risk

In insurance terms, *risk* is the chance of economic loss. Whenever you and your family have a financial interest in something—your life, health, home, car, or business—there's a risk of financial loss. To protect against such losses, you must employ strategies such as risk avoidance, loss prevention and control, risk assumption, and insurance.

within the speed limit to lessen the chance of being in a car accident). **Loss control**, in contrast, is any activity that lessens the severity of loss once it occurs (such as wearing a safety belt or buying a car with air bags). Loss prevention and control should be important parts of all risk management programs.

### Risk Assumption

**Risk assumption** involves bearing the risk of loss. Risk assumption is an effective way to handle small exposures to loss when insurance is too expensive. For example, the risk of having your *PFIN* text stolen probably doesn't justify buying insurance. It's also a reasonable approach for dealing with very large uninsurable risks such as a nuclear holocaust. Unfortunately, people often assume risks, unaware of exposures to loss or thinking that their insurance policy offers adequate protection when it doesn't.

**insurance policy**
A contract between the insured and the insurer under which the insurer agrees to reimburse the insured for any losses suffered according to specified terms.

**underwriting** The process used by insurers to decide who can be insured and to determine applicable rates that will be charged for premiums.

## Insurance

An **insurance policy** is a contract between you (the insured) and an insurance company (the insurer) under which the insurance company agrees to reimburse you for any losses you suffer according to specified terms. From your perspective, *you are transferring your risk of loss to the insurance company.* You pay a relatively small *certain* amount (the insurance premium) in exchange for a promise from the insurance company that it will reimburse you if you suffer a covered loss.

Why are insurance companies willing to accept this risk? Simple. They combine the loss experiences of large numbers of people and use statistical information, called *actuarial data,* to estimate the risk—frequency and magnitude—of loss for the given population. They set and collect premiums, which they invest and use to pay out losses and expenses. If they pay out less than the sum of the premiums and the earnings on them, they make a profit.

## Underwriting Basics

Insurance companies take great pain in **underwriting,** deciding whom they will insure and the applicable premiums they will charge. Underwriters design rate-classification schedules so that people pay premiums that reflect their chance of loss. Through underwriting, insurance companies try to guard against *adverse selection,* which happens when only high-risk clients apply for and get insurance coverage. Insurers are always trying to improve their underwriting capabilities in order to set premium rates that will adequately protect policyholders and yet be attractive and reasonable. Because underwriting practices and standards also vary among insurance companies, you can often save money by shopping around for the company offering the most favorable underwriting policies for your specific characteristics and needs.

## LG2 Why Buy Life Insurance?

Life insurance planning is an important part of every successful financial plan. Its primary purpose is to *protect your dependents from financial loss in the event of your untimely death.* Life insurance protects the assets you've accumulated during your life and

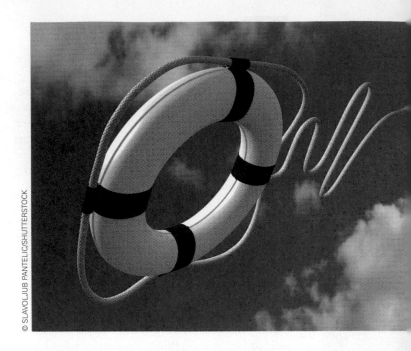

© SLAVOLJUB PANTELIC/SHUTTERSTOCK

provides funds to help your family reach important financial goals, even after you die.

{ *Life insurance planning is an important part of every successful financial plan.* }

## Benefits of Life Insurance

People don't like to talk about death or the things associated with it, so they often delay addressing their life insurance needs. Life insurance is intangible and its benefits typically occur after you die. The key benefits of life insurance include the following.

- **Financial protection for dependents.** If your family or loved ones depend on your income, will they be able to maintain their current lifestyle, stay in their home, or afford a college education after you die? The most important benefit of life insurance is providing financial protection for your dependents after your death.

- **Protection from creditors.** A life insurance policy can be structured so that death benefits are paid directly to a named beneficiary, so that creditors cannot claim the cash benefits from your life insurance policy.

- **Tax benefits.** Life insurance proceeds paid to your heirs, as a rule, aren't subject to state or federal income taxes, and under certain circumstances can pass to named beneficiaries free of any *estate* taxes.

- **Vehicle for savings.** Some types of life insurance policies can serve as a savings vehicle, particularly for those who are looking for safety of principal.

Just as with other other aspects of personal financial planning, life insurance decisions can be made easier by following a step-by-step approach. You will need answers to the following questions.

1. Do you need life insurance?
2. If so, how much life insurance do you need?
3. Which type of life insurance is best given your financial objectives?
4. What factors should be considered in making the final purchase decision?

## Do You Need Life Insurance?

In general, life insurance should be considered if you have dependents counting on you for financial support. Neither a single adult without children or other relatives to support nor a child typically needs life insurance. Life insurance requirements of married couples depend on their earning potential and assets—such as a house—that they want to protect. The need for life insurance increases with children because they will suffer the greatest financial hardship from the premature death of a parent. Even non-wage-earning parents often need life insurance to ensure that children are adequately cared for if the parent dies. As families accumulate assets, their life insurance requirements continue to change. Life changes, such as divorce, will also affect life insurance needs.

## LG3 How Much Life Insurance Is Right for You?

After confirming your need for life insurance, you must determine the appropriate amount of life insurance coverage to buy. You can use one of two methods to estimate how much insurance is needed: the *multiple-of-earnings method* and the *needs analysis method*.

The **multiple-of-earnings method** takes your gross annual earnings and multiplies it by some selected (often arbitrary) number to arrive at an estimate of adequate life insurance coverage. A rule of thumb used by many insurance agents is that your insurance coverage should equal 5 to 10 times your current income. For example, if you currently earn $70,000 a year, using the multiple-of-earnings method, you'd need between $350,000 and $700,000 of life insurance. Because the multiple-of-earnings method fails to consider your financial obligations and resources, it should be considered a rough approximation of life insurance needs.

The second, more detailed, approach is the **needs analysis method**. This method considers both the financial obligations and resources of the insured and involves the three steps shown in Exhibit 8.1 and described below.

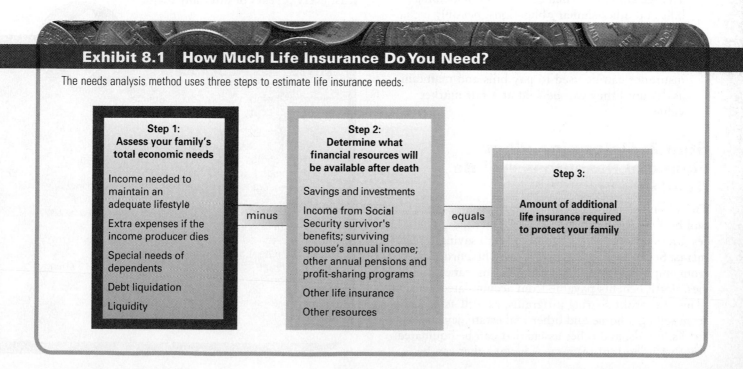

### Exhibit 8.1   How Much Life Insurance Do You Need?

The needs analysis method uses three steps to estimate life insurance needs.

**Step 1:**
**Assess your family's total economic needs**

Income needed to maintain an adequate lifestyle

Extra expenses if the income producer dies

Special needs of dependents

Debt liquidation

Liquidity

minus

**Step 2:**
**Determine what financial resources will be available after death**

Savings and investments

Income from Social Security survivor's benefits; surviving spouse's annual income; other annual pensions and profit-sharing programs

Other life insurance

Other resources

equals

**Step 3:**

**Amount of additional life insurance required to protect your family**

## Step 1: Assess Your Family's Total Economic Needs

The first step in needs analysis asks: *What financial resources will my survivors need should I die tomorrow?* The following five items guide answering this question.

1. **Income needed to maintain an adequate lifestyle.** If you died, how much money would your dependents need monthly in order to live a comfortable life? Estimate this amount by reviewing your family's current monthly budget, including expenses for housing costs, utilities, food, clothing, and medical and dental needs. Also consider other expenses such as property taxes, insurance, recreation and travel, and savings. Recognize that the amount needed may change over time.

2. **Extra expenses if the income producer dies.** These expenses include funeral costs and any expenses, such as child care and housekeeping, that might be incurred to replace services currently provided by the insured or surviving spouse, who must give up those responsibilities and find a job.

3. **Special needs of dependents.** In addition to daily economic needs, you may want to provide for special needs of your dependents, such as long-term nursing care for a disabled or chronically ill child, an emergency fund for unexpected financial burdens, or a college education fund for your children.

4. **Debt liquidation.** To leave the insured's family relatively debt free, it's necessary to determine the average amount needed to pay off outstanding bills and other similar obligations, possibly including the home mortgage.

5. **Liquidity.** If a high percentage of your wealth is in illiquid assets, the cash proceeds from life insurance can be used to pay bills and maintain assets until they can be sold at a fair market value.

## Step 2: Determine What Financial Resources Will Be Available after Death

The second step is to list all current resources that will be available for meeting economic needs. The resources typically include money from savings, investments, Social Security survivor's benefits, proceeds from employer-sponsored group life insurance policies, death benefits payable from accumulated pension plans and profit-sharing programs, as well as proceeds from selling a home and other real estate, jewelry, stocks, bonds, and other assets that can be liquidated. Another important resource is income that can be earned by the surviving spouse or children. After isolating these resources, reasonable estimates of their value should be made and totaled.

## Step 3: Subtract Resources from Needs to Calculate How Much Life Insurance You Require

Finally, subtract the total available resources (from Step 2) from the total economic needs (from Step 1). If available resources are greater than anticipated needs, then no additional life insurance is required. If the resources are less than the needs—as is the case in most families with children—then the difference is the amount of life insurance necessary to protect the family.

 **Go to Smart Sites**

Estimate the amount of life insurance your family needs for financial security with the Life Insurance Coverage Needs Analyzer in the Learning Center section of their Web site. Whenever you see *"Go to Smart Sites"* in this chapter, visit **4ltrpress.cengage.com** for help finding answers online. ●

The needs analysis method may seem complex, but insurance companies and Internet sites have software that can be used to quickly determine the insurance needs of individuals and families. Because *life insurance needs are not static,* you should review and adjust life insurance programs (as necessary) at least every 5 years or after any major

---

**FINANCIAL ROAD SIGN** $$$

**BUYING LIFE INSURANCE**
It is helpful to answer the following questions before you buy life insurance.

- Which policy benefits best meet the needs of my financial plan?
- Is term or cash-value insurance best for me?
- Have I compared similar policies from different companies to get the best value?
- Is the insurance company highly rated for financial stability?
- Do I understand the guarantees in my policy and the surrender penalties?
- Am I prepared to review my policy every few years and update it accordingly?
- What is the cost of replacing the insurance if I change my mind?

*Source:* Adapted from "Consumer Alert: Tips for Buying Life Insurance," National Association of Insurance Commissioners, http://www.naic.org/documents/consumer_alert_life_tips.pdf, accessed June 2009.

family changes occur, such as the birth of a child, the purchase of a home, or a job change.

### Needs Analysis in Action: The Klauder Family
We can demonstrate the needs analysis method by considering the hypothetical case of Harry and Denise Klauder. Harry Klauder is 37 and the primary breadwinner in the family; his currently earns $85,000 per year. Harry and his wife, Denise, use Worksheet 8.1. to estimate the amount of life insurance needed to provide for Denise and their two children, ages 6 and 8, if he should die.

### Financial Resources *Needed* after Death (Step 1)
Harry and Denise Klauder review their budget and decide that monthly living expenses for Denise and the two children would be about $3,500 in current dollars while the children are still living at home, or $42,000 annually. After both children leave home, Denise, now 35, will need a monthly income of $3,000—or $36,000 a year—until she retires at age 65. At that point, the Klauders estimate Denise's living expenses would fall to $2,750 a month, or $33,000 annually. The life expectancy of a woman Denise's age is 87 years, so the Klauders calculate that Denise will spend about 22 years in retirement. Therefore, as shown in the first section of the worksheet, the total income necessary for the Klauders' living expenses over the next 52 years is $1,878,000.

Although Denise previously worked as a stockbroker, they are concerned that her previous education may be somewhat outdated at that point, so they include $25,000 for Denise to update her education and skills. Harry and Denise also want to fund their children's college educations and decide to establish a college fund of $75,000 for this purpose. Last, they estimate final expenses (i.e., funeral costs and estate taxes) of $15,000.

The Klauders use credit sparingly, so their outstanding debts total $155,000 (a current mortgage balance of $150,000, an automobile loan $4,000, and miscellaneous charge account balances of $1,000).

All of these estimates are shown in the top half of Harry and Denise's insurance calculations in Worksheet 8.1. Note that $2,148,000 is the total amount of financial resources needed to meet their financial goals if Harry were to die.

### Financial Resources *Available* after Death (Step 2)
If Harry died, Denise would be eligible to receive **Social Security survivor's benefits** for both her children and herself. Social Security survivor's benefits, discussed in more detail in Chapter 14, are intended to provide basic, minimum support to families faced with the loss of the principal wage earner. Denise and Harry visit the Social Security Administration's Web site and estimate that Denise will receive approximately $3,200 a month, or $38,400 a year, in Social Security survivor's benefits for herself and the children until the youngest child graduates from high school in 12 years.

In the 18 years between the time the children leave home and Denise retires, the Klauders expect Denise to be employed full-time and earn about $35,000 after taxes. After Denise turns 65, she'd receive approximately $2,250 a month ($27,000 a year) from Harry's survivor's benefits, her own Social Security benefits, and her own retirement benefits. However, Denise will have some other resources available if Harry should die. The couple has saved $65,000 in a mutual fund, and Harry's employer provides a $100,000 life insurance policy for him. Adding these amounts to Denise's expected income means she'd have $1,849,800 in total resources available.

### Additional Life Insurance Needed (Step 3)
To determine the amount of life insurance the Klauders should buy for Harry, they subtract the total financial resources available ($1,849,800) from the total financial resources needed ($2,148,000) and get $298,200, so Harry should buy an additional $300,000 of life insurance to protect his family. Now the Klauders can begin to consider which type of policy is best.

 **Go to Smart Sites**

What's your life expectancy? Northwestern Mutual offers a quick and simple calculator that gives you a statistical estimate of how long you'll live. Link to their Web site and click on the Learning Center for *The Longevity Game.* ●

## Life Insurance Underwriting Considerations

Insurance companies use *underwriting* to determine whom they will insure and what they will charge for the coverage. It begins by asking potential insureds to complete an application designed to gather information for use in estimating the likelihood that the insured will die while the life insurance policy is in effect. Underwriters use life expectancy figures to look at overall longevity for various age groups and also consider specific factors related to the applicant's health, habits, and experiences. This information is used to determine whether to accept you and what premium to charge. For example, someone in excellent health is usually considered "preferred"

**Social Security survivor's benefits** Benefits under Social Security intended to provide basic, minimum support to families faced with the loss of a principal wage earner.

## LIFE INSURANCE NEEDS ANALYSIS METHOD

**Insured's Name** Harry and Denise Klauder      **Date** April 12, 2010

### Step 1: Financial resources needed after death

1. Annual living expenses and other needs:

| | | Period 1 | Period 2 | Period 3 | |
|---|---|---|---|---|---|
| a. | Monthly living expenses | $ 3,500 | $ 3,000 | $ 2,750 | |
| b. | Net yearly income needed (a × 12) | $ 42,000 | $ 36,000 | $ 33,000 | |
| c. | Number of years in time period | 12 | 18 | 22 | |
| d. | Total living need per time period (b × c) | $ 504,000 | $ 648,000 | $ 726,000 | |
| TOTAL LIVING EXPENSES (add line d for each period): | | | | | $ 1,878,000 |

2. Special needs

| | | | |
|---|---|---|---|
| a. | Spouse education fund | $ | 25,000 |
| b. | Children's college fund | $ | 75,000 |
| c. | Other needs | | 0 |
| 3. Final expenses (funeral, estate costs, etc.) | | $ | 15,000 |
| 4. Debt liquidation | | | |
| a. | House mortgage | $ 150,000 | |
| b. | Other loans | 5,000 | |
| c. | Total debt (4 a + 4 b) | $ | 155,000 |
| 5. Other financial needs | | | 0 |
| TOTAL FINANCIAL RESOURCES NEEDED (add right column) | | $ | 2,148,000 |

### Step 2: Financial resources available after death

1. Income

| | | Period 1 | Period 2 | Period 3 | |
|---|---|---|---|---|---|
| a. | Annual Social Security survivor's benefits | $ 38,400 | 0 | 0 | |
| b. | Surviving spouse's annual income | 0 | $ 35,000 | 0 | |
| c. | Other annual pensions and Social Security benefits | 0 | 0 | $ 27,000 | |
| d. | Annual income | $ 38,400 | $ 35,000 | $ 27,000 | |
| e. | Number of years in time period | 12 | 18 | 22 | |
| f. | Total period income (d × e) | $ 460,800 | $ 630,000 | $ 594,000 | |
| g. TOTAL INCOME | | | | | $ 1,684,800 |
| 2. | Savings and investments | | | | $ 65,000 |
| 3. | Other life insurance | | | | $ 100,000 |
| 4. | Other resources | | | | 0 |
| TOTAL FINANCIAL RESOURCES AVAILABLE (1g + 2 + 3 + 4) | | | | | $ 1,849,800 |

### Step 3: Additional Life Insurance needed

| | |
|---|---|
| Step 1: Total financial resources needed | $ 2,148,000 |
| Step 2: Total financial resources available | $ 1,849,800 |
| | |
| ADDITIONAL LIFE INSURANCE NEEDED | $ 298,200 |

and pays the lowest premium. Clearly, if you have any of the risks commonly considered in life insurance underwriting—such as obesity, heart disease, or a high-risk hobby or job—then it's important to shop carefully and compare the cost implications of different types of insurance policies and the underwriting standards used by different companies.

## LG4 What Kind of Policy Is Right for You?

After determining the amount of life insurance you need, your next step is to choose the correct type of insurance policy. Three major types of policies account for 90% to 95% of life insurance sales: term life, whole life, and universal life.

## Term Life Insurance

**Term life insurance**, which provides a specified amount of insurance protection for a set period, is the simplest type of insurance policy. If you die while the policy is in force, your beneficiaries will receive the full amount specified in your policy. Term insurance can be bought for many different time increments, such as 5 years, 10 years, even 30 years. Premiums typically can be paid annually, semiannually, or quarterly.

### Types of Term Insurance

The most common types of term insurance are *straight (or level) term* and *decreasing term*.

**STRAIGHT TERM.** A straight term life insurance policy is written for a set number of years during which the amount of coverage remains unchanged. The *annual premium* on a **straight term policy** can increase each year on an *annual renewable term policy* or remain level throughout the policy period on a *level premium term policy*. Exhibits 8.2 and 8.3 list representative annual premiums for annual renewable term and level premium term life policies, respectively. (*Note*: The premiums are for nonsmokers; clearly, rates for similar smoker policies would be higher in view of the greater risk and generally shorter life expectancies of smokers.) Annual renewable term policies aren't popular today. Because people now live longer, the rates for level premium term are now well below those on annual renewable term from year 1 on, so they're a better value.

**DECREASING TERM.** Because the death rate increases with each year of life, the premiums on annual renewable straight term policies for each successive period of coverage will also increase. As a result, some term policies *maintain a level premium* throughout all periods of coverage while *the amount of protection decreases*. Such a policy is called a **decreasing term policy** because the amount of protection decreases

**term life insurance** Insurance that provides only death benefits, for a specified period, and does not provide for the accumulation of cash value.

**straight term policy** A term insurance policy written for a given number of years, with coverage remaining unchanged throughout the effective period.

**decreasing term policy** A term insurance policy that *maintains a level premium* throughout all periods of coverage while *the amount of protection decreases*.

### Exhibit 8.2 Representative Annual Renewable Term Life Insurance Premiums: $100,000 Policy, Preferred Nonsmoker Rates

When you buy term life insurance, you're buying a product that provides life insurance coverage and nothing more. This table shows representative rates for several age categories and selected policy years; actual premiums increase every year. As you can see, females pay less than males for coverage, and premiums increase sharply with age.

| Policy Year | Age 25 | | Age 40 | | Age 60 | |
|---|---|---|---|---|---|---|
| | Male | Female | Male | Female | Male | Female |
| 1 | $ 130 | $ 119 | $ 148 | $ 139 | $ 366 | $ 252 |
| 5 | $ 169 | $ 147 | $ 252 | $ 219 | $ 927 | $ 562 |
| 10 | $ 218 | $ 187 | $ 426 | $ 368 | $ 1,702 | $ 1,080 |
| 15 | $ 196 | $ 176 | $ 647 | $ 507 | $ 2,666 | $ 1,313 |
| 20 | $ 279 | $ 259 | $1,258 | $1,054 | $ 4,574 | $ 2,989 |
| **Total Cost, 20 years** | $3,777 | $3,381 | $9,871 | $8,287 | $38,457 | $22,346 |

## Exhibit 8.3 Representative Level Premium Term Life Rates: $100,000 Preferred Nonsmoker Policy

This table shows representative annual premiums for $100,000 of level premium term life insurance. Although level premium costs less than annual renewable term for the same period, you must requalify at the end of each term to retain the low premium.

| Age | 5 Year Male/Female | 10 Year Male/Female | 15 Year Male/Female | 20 Year Male/Female |
|---|---|---|---|---|
| 25 | $102/$102 | $81/$75 | $89/$84 | $103/$95 |
| 35 | $102/$101 | $81/$75 | $90/$84 | $103/$95 |
| 40 | $121/$119 | $96/$89 | $111/$102 | $132/$113 |
| 50 | $176/$136 | $183/$142 | $237/$167 | $259/$195 |
| 60 | $358/$245 | $380/$259 | $475/$295 | $555/$394 |

**renewability**
A term life policy provision allowing the insured to renew the policy at the end of its term without having to show evidence of insurability.

over its life. Decreasing term is used when the amount of needed coverage declines over time. For example, a homeowner can match his life insurance coverage with the declining balance on his home mortgage. And families with young children can match coverage with the declining level of family income needed as their kids grow up and become independent.

The type and length of term policy you choose affects the amount of premiums you'll pay over time. The annual premium for a specified initial amount of coverage, say $250,000, would be lowest for straight term, higher for decreasing term, and highest for annual renewable term. The premium on decreasing term is higher than the premium on straight term because most major insurance companies don't offer decreasing term policies, so there is less competition between companies offering decreasing term policies and they can therefore charge high premiums.

### Advantages and Disadvantages of Term Life

One of the biggest advantages of term life is that its initial premiums are lower than other types of insurance, especially for younger people. Term life is an economical way to buy a large amount of life insurance protection over a relatively short period to cover needs that will disappear over time.

The main disadvantage, however, is that term insurance offers only temporary coverage. If you need more coverage when the policy expires, renewal can be a problem if you then have factors that make it difficult to qualify for insurance. Term policies that offer a **renewability** provision give you the option to renew

your policy at its expiration, even if you have become uninsurable due to an accident or other illness during the original policy period. Of course, the premium will increase to reflect the greater chance of death at

older ages. Renewable term policies are renewable at the end of each term until the insured reaches age 65 or 70.

Another option that overcomes some of the limitations of term insurance is a **convertibility** provision, which at stated times allows you to convert your term policy into a comparable whole life policy. A whole life policy, as we'll discuss next, provides lifelong protection, eliminating the need to continually renew your life insurance. Convertibility, which is standard on most term policies, is particularly useful if you need a large amount of relatively low-cost, short-term protection immediately but in the future expect to have greater income that will allow you to purchase permanent insurance.

One way to overcome the drawback of having to pay increased premiums at the end of each term is to purchase a longer term policy. Recently, the insurance industry has started offering 30-year straight term policies that lock in a set premium. For example, a 35-year-old man who qualifies for preferred rates could lock in a $250,000 death benefit for 30 years in a row and pay only a set premium of $360 a year. As with all insurance policies, however, before signing up make sure that the rate is fully locked in for the duration of the policy.

### Who Should Buy Term Insurance?

Because most young families on limited budgets have a high need for death protection, they should focus on guaranteed renewable and convertible term insurance. This will preserve financial resources for meeting immediate and future consumption and savings goals. Healthy older people with adequate financial resources may tend to use term policies to meet specific coverage needs.

# Whole Life Insurance

Unlike term insurance, **whole life insurance** provides permanant insurance coverage during an individual's entire life. In addition to death protection, whole life insurance has a *savings* feature, called **cash value**, that results from the investment earnings on paid-in insurance premiums. Thus, *whole life provides not only insurance coverage but also a modest return on your investment*. The savings rates on whole life policies are normally *fixed* and *guaranteed* to be more than a certain rate (say, 4% to 6%). Exhibit 8.4 illustrates how the cash value in a whole life policy builds up over time. Obviously, the longer the insured keeps the policy in force, the greater the cash value. Whole life can be purchased through several different payment plans, all providing for accumulation of cash values.

If a policyholder cancels his contract prior to death, then that portion of the assets set aside to provide payment for the death claim is available to

him. This right to a cash value is termed the policyholder's **nonforfeiture right**. By terminating their insurance contracts, policyholders forfeit their rights to death benefits.

### Types of Whole Life Policies

Three major types of whole life policies are available: continuous premium, limited payment, and single premium. To develop a sense for the costs of these policies, look at the representative rates shown in Exhibit 8.5.

**CONTINUOUS PREMIUM.** Under a *continuous premium whole life* policy—or *straight life,* as it's more commonly called—individuals pay a level premium each year until they either die or exercise a nonforfeiture right. The earlier in life the coverage is purchased, the lower the annual premium. Whole life should seldom be purchased by anyone simply because the annual premium will be lower now than if it's purchased later. Of the various whole life policies available, continuous premium/straight life offers the greatest amount of permanent death protection and the least amount of savings per premium dollar.

**LIMITED PAYMENT.** A *limited payment whole life* policy covers your entire life but the premium payment is based on a specified period—for example, 20 or 30 years during which you pay a level premium. For stipulated age policies such as those paid up at age 55 or 65, you pay premiums until you reach the stated age. In all cases, on completion of the scheduled payments, *the insurance remains in force at its face value for the rest of the insured's life.*

If lifelong death protection is the primary aim of the life insurance policy, then the insured should purchase continuous premium whole life instead of a limited payment policy. Because more continuous premium whole life insurance can be purchased with the same number of dollars as limited payment whole life, people who need whole life insurance are probably better off using straight life insurance to get the most for their life insurance dollars. Then, once their insurance needs are reduced, they can convert the policy to a smaller amount of paid-up life insurance. On the other hand, if people have life insurance already in force that is sufficient to protect

**convertibility** A term life policy provision allowing the insured to convert the policy to a comparable whole life policy.

**whole life insurance** Life insurance designed to offer ongoing insurance coverage over the course of an insured's entire life.

**cash value** The accumulated refundable value of an insurance policy; results from the investment earnings on paid-in insurance premiums.

**nonforfeiture right** A life insurance feature giving the whole life policyholder, upon policy cancellation, the portion of those assets that were set aside to provide payment for the future death claim.

Here is an example of the projected cash value for an actual $200,000 whole life policy issued by a major life insurer to a male, age 30. For *each year* of the illustration, the difference between the $200,000 death benefit and the projected cash value represents the *death protection* offered by the insurer.

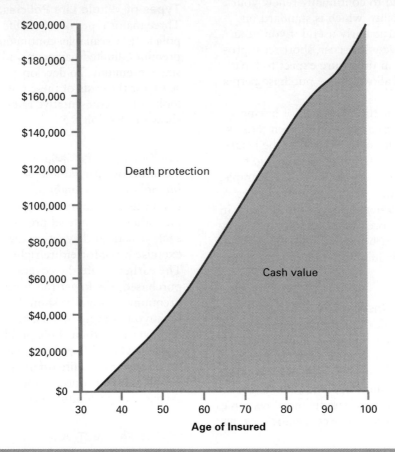

against income loss, then they can use limited payment policies as part of their savings or retirement plans.

**SINGLE PREMIUM.** *Single premium whole life insurance* is purchased with one cash premium payment at the inception of the contract, thus buying life insurance coverage for the rest of your life. Because of its investment attributes, single premium life insurance, or *SPLI* for short, has limited usefulness for most families but appeals to those looking for a *tax-sheltered investment vehicle.* Like any whole life insurance policy, interest/investment earnings within the policy are tax-deferred; however, any cash withdrawals or loans taken against the SPLI cash value before age 59½ are taxed as capital gains and subject to the 10% penalty for early withdrawal.

**Advantages and Disadvantages of Whole Life**
The most noteworthy advantage of whole life insurance is that premium payments contribute toward building an estate, regardless of how long the insured lives. And the insured can borrow against the policy or withdraw cash value when the need for insurance protection has expired. Another benefit (except for SPLI) is that individuals who need coverage can budget their premium payments over a relatively long period, thereby avoiding affordability and uninsurability problems. Also, earnings build up on a tax-sheltered basis, which means that the underlying cash value of the policy increases at a much faster rate than it otherwise would. Other valuable options include the ability to continue coverage after the policy lapses because premiums were not paid (nonforfeiture option) and the ability to revive an

Like any life insurance product, whole life is more expensive the older you are. Also, whole life is more costly than term because you're getting an investment/savings account, represented by the "total cash value" column, in addition to life insurance coverage. Of course, the actual amount of cash value will depend on the actual dividend rate, which is subject to change (up or down) based on current market conditions.

| Age | Annual Premium | | Premiums Paid through Year 20 | | Total Cash Value at Year 20* |
|---|---|---|---|---|---|
| | Male | Female | Male | Female | Male/Female |
| 25 | $ 988 | $ 941 | $19,760 | $18,820 | $ 30,894 |
| 30 | $1,233 | $1,188 | $24,460 | $23,760 | $ 38,971 |
| 35 | $1,473 | $1,438 | $29,460 | $28,760 | $ 46,223 |
| 40 | $1,833 | $1,788 | $36,660 | $35,760 | $ 55,980 |
| 50 | $2,816 | $2,666 | $55,425 | $52,425 | $ 76,225 |
| 60 | $4,291 | $3,899 | $85,820 | $77,980 | $112,765 |

*Guaranteed cash value plus annual dividends at the assumed annual rate of 6.8%.

older, favorably priced policy that has lapsed (policy reinstatement).

One disadvantage of whole life insurance is its cost. It provides less death protection per premium dollar than does term insurance. Compare the premiums paid for various whole life products with those of term insurance by comparing Exhibits 8.2, 8.3, and 8.5, and you can readily see how much more expensive whole life is than term life. Another frequently cited disadvantage of whole life is that its investment feature provides lower yields than many otherwise comparable vehicles. A *whole life policy should not be used to obtain maximum return on investment.* However, if a person wishes to combine a given amount of death protection for the entire life of the insured (or until the policy is terminated) with a savings plan that provides a *moderate* tax-sheltered rate of return, then whole life insurance may be a wise purchase.

One way to keep the cost of whole life down is to purchase *low-load whole life insurance,* which is sold directly by insurers to consumers, sometimes via a toll-free number or over the Internet, thereby eliminating sales agents and large commissions from the transaction. As a result, cash values of low-load policies grow much more quickly than traditional policies sold by agents.

### Who Should Buy Whole Life Insurance?

Some financial advisors recommend that you use cash-value insurance to cover your *permanent need*

© COMSTOCK IMAGES (RF)/GETTY IMAGES FROM FINANCIAL MATTERS

**universal life insurance** Permanent cash-value insurance that combines term insurance (death benefits) with a tax-sheltered savings/investment account that pays interest, usually at competitive money market rates.

*for insurance*—the amount your dependents will need regardless of the age at which you die. Such needs may include final expenses and either the survivor's retirement need (Period 3 in Worksheet 8.1) or additional insurance coverage, whichever is less. This amount is different for every person. Using these guidelines, the Klauders in our earlier example would need about $147,000 in whole life insurance (in Worksheet 8.1: $15,000 final expenses [Step 1, line 3] plus about $132,000 of Period 3 living expenses [Step 1, line 1d for Period 3 minus Step 2, line 1f for Period 3—$726,000 – $594,000]) and about another $151,000 in term life (in Worksheet 8.1: about $298,000 [Step 3] minus about $147,000 in permanent insurance just calculated). Limited payment whole life and single premium whole life policies should be purchased only when the primary goal is savings or additional tax-deferred investments and not protection against financial loss resulting from death.

## Universal Life Insurance

**Universal life insurance** is permanent cash-value insurance that combines term insurance, which provides death benefits, with a tax-sheltered savings/investment account that pays interest, usually at competitive money market rates. The death protection (or pure insurance) portion and the savings portion are identified separately in its premium. This is referred to as *unbundling*. Exhibit 8.6 shows representative annual outlays, premiums, and cash values for a $100,000 universal life policy.

With universal life, part of your premium pays administrative fees, and the remainder is put into the cash-value (savings) portion of the policy, where it earns a certain rate of return. This rate of earnings varies with market yields but is guaranteed to be more than some stipulated minimum rate (say, 4%). Then, each month the cost of 1 month's term insurance is withdrawn from the cash value to purchase the required death protection. As long as there's enough in the savings portion to buy death protection, the policy will stay in force. Should the cash value grow to an unusually large amount, the amount of insurance coverage must be increased in order for the policy to retain its favorable tax treatment (tax laws require that the death benefits in a universal life policy *must always exceed the cash value* by a stipulated amount).

Universal life policies enjoy the same favorable tax treatment as do other forms of whole life insurance: death benefits are tax free and, prior to the insured's death, amounts credited to the cash value (including investment earnings) accumulate on a tax-deferred basis. The insurance company sends the insured an annual statement summarizing the monthly credits of interest and deductions of expenses.

## Exhibit 8.6 Representative Universal Life Insurance Annual Outlays: $100,000 Policy, Preferred Nonsmoker Rates

Universal life premiums are lower than whole life and can vary over the policy's life. After deducting the cost of the death benefit and any administrative fees from your annual contribution, the rest goes into an accumulation account and builds at a variable rate—in this example, the current rate is 7.4%. However, the guaranteed rate is only 4% and so your actual cash value may be less.

| Age | Annual Outlay | | Premiums Paid through Year 20 | | Cash Surrender Value at Year 20* | |
|-----|------|--------|------|--------|------|--------|
|     | Male | Female | Male | Female | Male | Female |
| 25 | $2,419 | $2,358 | $ 8,380 | $ 7,160 | $ 6,091 | $ 5,048 |
| 30 | $2,505 | $2,425 | $10,100 | $ 8,500 | $ 8,137 | $ 6,176 |
| 35 | $2,644 | $2,534 | $12,880 | $10,680 | $11,235 | $ 8,453 |
| 40 | $2,841 | $2,682 | $16,820 | $13,640 | $15,107 | $11,399 |
| 50 | $1,469 | $1,146 | $29,380 | $22,920 | $25,168 | $20,074 |
| 60 | $2,598 | $1,992 | $51,960 | $39,840 | $36,638 | $32,633 |

*Based on an assumed annual rate of 7.4%.

## Advantages and Disadvantages of Universal Life

As with any insurance policy, universal life has its pros and cons. There are two principal advantages.

- **Flexibility.** The annual premium you pay can be increased or decreased from year to year, because the cost of the death protection *may be covered from either the annual premium or the accumulation account* (i.e., the cash value). If the accumulation account is adequate, you can use it to pay the annual premium. The death benefit also can be increased (subject to evidence of insurability) or decreased, and you can change from the level benefit type of policy to the cash value plus a stated amount of insurance.

- **Savings feature.** A universal life insurance policy credits cash value at the "current" rate of interest, and this *current* rate of interest may well be higher than the *guaranteed* minimum rate.

Universal life's flexibility in making premium payments, although an attractive feature, is also one of its two major drawbacks:

- **Changing premiums and protection levels.** A policyholder who economizes on premium payments in early years may find that premiums must be higher than originally planned in later policy years to keep the policy in force. Indeed, some policyholders expect their premiums to vanish once cash value builds to a certain level, but often the premiums never disappear or they reappear when interest rates fall.

- **Charges or fees.** Universal life carries heavy fees compared to other policy types. Most states require the insurance company to issue an annual disclosure statement spelling out premiums paid, all expenses and mortality costs, interest earned, and beginning and ending cash values.

 **Go to Smart Sites**

For more details about various life insurance products and policy types, turn to Insure.com's searchable database of over 3,000 articles on insurance topics. ●

### Who Should Buy Universal Life Insurance?

Universal life is a suitable choice if you're looking for a savings vehicle with greater potential returns than offered by a whole life policy. Its flexible nature makes it particularly useful for people anticipating changes, such as birth of a child, that require changes in death protection.

## Other Types of Life Insurance

Besides term, whole life, and universal life, you can buy several other types of life insurance products, including variable life insurance, group life, and other special-purpose life policies such as credit life, mortgage life, and industrial life insurance. These insurance products serve diverse needs.

### Variable Life Insurance

A **variable life insurance** policy goes further than whole and universal life policies in combining death benefits and savings. The policyholder decides how to invest the money in the savings (cash-value) component. The investment accounts are set up just like *mutual funds,* and most firms that offer variable life policies let you choose from a full menu of different types of funds. Variable life insurance does not guarantee a *minimum return.* And as the name implies, the amount of insurance coverage provided varies with the profits (and losses) generated in the investment account. Exhibit 8.7 demonstrates how two possible investment return scenarios would affect the cash value and death benefits of a variable life insurance policy for a 45-year-old, nonsmoking male over a 20-year period.

Variable life is more of an investment vehicle than a life insurance policy. If you want the benefits of higher investment returns, then you must also be willing to assume the risks of reduced insurance coverage. Therefore, *you should use extreme care when buying variable life insurance.*

### Group Life Insurance

Under **group life insurance**, one master policy is issued and each eligible group member receives a certificate of insurance. Group life is nearly always term insurance, and the premium is based on the group's characteristics as a whole rather than the characteristics of any specific individual. Employers often provide group life insurance as a fringe benefit for their employees. However, just about any type of group (e.g., a labor union, a professional association, an alumni organization) can secure a group life policy, as long as the insurance is only incidental to the reason for the group's existence.

Accounting for about one-third of all life insurance in the United States, group life insurance is one of the fastest-growing areas of insurance. Group life policies generally provide that individual members who leave the group may continue the coverage by converting their protection to individually issued whole life policies. It is important to note that conversion

## Exhibit 8.7 Representative Variable Life Insurance Values: $100,000 Policy, Preferred Nonsmoker, Male, Age 45

Variable life insurance pays a death benefit whose amount is tied to the policy's investment returns. The cash value created over the life of the policy is also related to investment returns. This table shows the effects of 6% and 12% annual returns over a 20-year period. Lower returns result in lower cash value and death benefits; higher returns result in higher cash value and death benefits.

| Policy Year | Total Premiums Paid | 6% Return | | 12% Return | |
| --- | --- | --- | --- | --- | --- |
| | | Cash Value | Death Benefit | Cash Value | Death Benefit |
| 1 | $ 1,575 | $ 995 | $100,995 | $ 1,064 | $101,064 |
| 5 | $ 8,705 | $ 5,244 | $105,244 | $ 5,705 | $105,705 |
| 10 | $19,810 | $10,592 | $110,592 | $15,365 | $115,365 |
| 15 | $33,986 | $15,093 | $115,093 | $27,688 | $127,688 |
| 20 | $52,079 | $17,080 | $117,080 | $43,912 | $143,912 |

**credit life insurance** Life insurance sold in conjunction with installment loans.

**mortgage life insurance** A term policy designed to pay off the mortgage balance in the event of the borrower's death.

**industrial life insurance (home service life insurance)** Whole life insurance issued in policies with relatively small face amounts, often $1,000 or less.

normally doesn't require evidence of insurability as long as it occurs within a specified period. Of course, after conversion, the individual pays all premiums. The availability of group coverage through employee benefit programs should be considered when developing a life insurance program. Because of its potentially temporary nature and relatively low benefit amount (often equal to about 1 year's salary), only in rare cases should a family rely solely on group life insurance to fulfill its primary income-protection requirements.

### Other Special-Purpose Life Policies

Use caution before buying one of the following types of life insurance.

- **Credit life insurance.** Banks, finance companies, and other lenders generally sell **credit life insurance** in conjunction with installment loans. Usually credit life is a term policy of less than 5 years, with a face value corresponding to the outstanding balance on the loan. Although liquidating debts on the death of a family breadwinner is often desirable, it's usually preferable to do so with term or whole life insurance because credit life is a very expensive form of life insurance.

- **Mortgage life insurance. Mortgage life insurance** is a term policy designed to pay off the mortgage balance on a home in the event of the borrower's death. As in the case of credit life, this need can usually be met less expensively by shopping the market for a suitable decreasing term policy.

- **Industrial life insurance.** Sometimes called **home service life insurance,** this whole life insurance is issued in policies with small face amounts, often $1,000 or less. Agents call on policyholders weekly or monthly to collect the premiums. Industrial life insurance costs much more per $1,000 of coverage than regular whole life policies, primarily because of its high marketing costs. Even so, some insurance authorities believe that industrial life insurance offers the only practical way to deliver coverage to low-income families.

## LG5 Buying Life Insurance

Once you have evaluated your personal financial needs and have become familiar with the basic life insurance options, you're ready to begin shopping for a life insurance policy. Exhibit 8.8 summarizes the major advantages and disadvantages of the most popular types of life insurance we've discussed in this chapter. The key activities involved in shopping for life insurance include: (1) comparing costs and features of competitive policies, (2) selecting a financially healthy insurance company, and (3) choosing a good agent.

### Compare Costs and Features

The costs of similar life insurance policies can vary considerably from company to company. Comparison shopping can save thousands of dollars over the life

## Exhibit 8.8 Major Advantages and Disadvantages of the Most Popular Types of Life Insurance

Major advantages and disadvantages of the most popular types of life insurance are summarized here. They should be considered when shopping for life insurance.

| Type of Policy | Advantages | Disadvantages |
|---|---|---|
| Term | Low initial premiums<br>Simple, easy to buy | Provides only temporary coverage for a set period<br>May have to pay higher premiums when policy is renewed |
| Whole life | Permanent coverage<br>Savings vehicle: cash value builds as premiums are paid<br>Some tax advantages on accumulated earnings | Cost: provides less death protection per premium dollar than term<br>Often provides lower yields than other investment vehicles<br>Sales commissions and marketing expenses can increase costs of fully loaded policy |
| Universal life | Permanent coverage<br>Flexible: lets insured adapt level of protection and cost of premiums<br>Savings vehicle: cash value builds at current rate of interest<br>Savings and death protection identified separately | Can be difficult to evaluate true cost at time of purchase; insurance carrier may levy costly fees and charges |
| Variable life | Investment vehicle: insured decides how cash value will be invested | Higher risk |

of a policy. For example, the total cost for a 10-year, $250,000, term life policy at preferred rates for a 25-year-old can range from $1,170 to more than $2,000. The Bonus Exhibit, "Major Insurance Rating Agencies," at 4ltpress.cengage.com, summarizes differences in the key features of various types of life insurance. If you have an unusual health problem or some other type of complication, spending time checking out several companies can really pay off.

don't compare a $100,000 term life policy from one company with a $150,000 universal life policy from another. Instead, *first decide how much and what kind of policy you want and then compare costs.* For similar cash-value policies, you may find it useful to compare interest-adjusted cost indexes that are often shown on policy illustrations.

It's easy to gather information that allows you to compare costs and features. Term life quote services,

{ ***The costs of similar life insurance policies can vary considerably from company to company.*** }

However, it's not enough, however, to look only at current rates. You'll also need to ask how long the rates are locked-in and to find out about guaranteed rates—the maximum you can be charged when you renew. A guaranteed policy may cost another $20 a year, but you won't be hit with unexpected rate increases later. Establish for how long you'll need the coverage, and then find the best rates for the total period; low premiums for a 5-year policy may jump when you renew for additional coverage. Also be sure you're getting the features you need, like the convertibility of term policies.

Finally, be sure the policies you are comparing *have similar provisions and amounts*. In other words,

available over the phone or on the Internet, can streamline the selection process by providing you, free of charge, with the names of several companies offering the lowest-cost policies based on your specifications. Probably the fastest-growing source of life insurance quotes and policies in recent years is the Internet. You can not only obtain quick, real-time quotes but also can buy insurance electronically. Buying on the Internet allows you to avoid dealing with insurance salespeople, and you can purchase the policies (usually term insurance only) on cost-effective terms. For example, one major life insurer offers discounts of up to 20% for term life policies purchased online. Of course, you'll still need a physical exam, but often the insurance company will send a qualified technician/nurse to your home or office to take a blood sample and other basic readings. E Financial (**http://www.efinancial.com**), Select Quote Insurance Services (**http://www.select quote.com**), Insure.com (**http://www.insure.com**), and Matrix Direct Insurance Services (**http://matrix direct.com**) maintain databases of life insurance policy costs for various companies and will also act as your agent to buy the policy if you wish. Insure.com and Matrix Direct provide quotes for both term insurance and whole life. Also, don't overlook companies that sell directly to the public or offer low-load policies, such as Ameritas, Lincoln Benefit, and USAA.

## FINANCIAL ROAD SIGN

### WHAT TO EXPECT FROM A LIFE INSURANCE MEDICAL EXAM

If you're buying life insurance—especially large policies—you'll often be asked to take a medical exam before the insurance company approves your policy. Here's what you should know before taking an exam.

- Don't misrepresent your medical history—insurance companies can track down your medical background through insurance industry information clearinghouses.
- A paramedical professional often conducts the exam, which can sometimes be done at your home or office.
- Samples of blood, urine, and saliva may be taken to test for the presence of HIV antibodies, cholesterol, diabetes, and other medical issues. Blood presssure, pulse, and physical measurements of height and weight are also taken.
- If you're buying larger policies or are older than 50, an EKG, X-rays, or even a treadmill test may be required.
- The test results will be used to determine your insurance premium rate. Whatever the outcome, your test results become part of the MIB Group's database, which is a clearinghouse of medical information shared by insurers. You can get one free report a year at **http://www.mib.com**.

*Source:* Adapted from Insure.com, "The Lowdown on Life Insurance Medical Exams," http://articles.moneycentral.msn.com/Insurance/InsureYourLife/TheLowdownOnLifeInsuranceMedicalExams.aspx, accessed June 2009.

## Select an Insurance Company

Selecting a life insurance company is an important part of shopping for life insurance. You want to be sure that the company will be around and have the assets to pay your beneficiaries. Factors to consider before making the final choice include the firm's reputation, financial history, commissions and other fees, and the specifics of their policy provisions. If you're choosing a company for a cash value life insurance policy, the company's investment performance and dividend history are also

important considerations. Unless there's a good reason to do otherwise, you should probably limit the companies you consider to those that have been doing business for 25 years or more and that have annual premium volume of more than $100 million. These criteria will rule out a lot of smaller firms, but there are still plenty of companies left to choose from. You may also find that one company is preferable for your term protection and another for your whole life needs.

Private rating agencies—A.M. Best, Fitch, Moody's, Standard & Poor's, and Weiss—have done much of the work for you. These agencies use publicly available financial data evaluate the insurance company's ability to pay future claims made by policyholders, known as their *claims paying ability*. The Bonus Exhibit, "Key Features of Various Types of Life Insurance" at 4ltrpress.cengage.com, provides detailed contact information for each of these agencies. The ratings agencies then give each insurance firm a "grade" based on their analysis of the firm's financial data. Most experts agree that it's wise to purchase life insurance only from insurance companies that are assigned ratings by at least two of the major rating agencies and are consistently rated in the top two or three categories (say, Aaa, Aa1, or Aa2 by Moody's) by each of the major agencies from which they received ratings. Most public libraries and insurance agents have these ratings, and each of the agencies mentioned above have an Internet presence where some insurance company ratings may be found.

## Choose an Agent

There's an old axiom in the life insurance business that life insurance is sold, not bought. Life insurance agents play a major role in most people's decision to buy life insurance. Unless you plan to buy all of your life insurance via the Internet, selecting a good life insurance agent is important because you'll be relying on him or her for guidance in making some important financial decisions.

When seeking a good life insurance agent, try to obtain recommendations from other professionals who work with agents. Bankers in trust departments, attorneys, and accountants who are specialists in estate planning are usually good sources. In contrast, be a bit wary of selecting an agent simply because of the agent's aggressiveness in soliciting your patronage.

Don't assume that just because agents are licensed they are competent and will serve your best interests. Consider an agent's formal and professional level of educational attainment. Does the agent have a college degree with a major in business or insurance? Does the agent have a professional designation, such as Chartered Life Underwriter (CLU), Chartered Financial Consultant (ChFC), or Certified Financial Planner® (CFP®)? These designations are awarded only to those who meet certain experience requirements and pass comprehensive examinations in such fields as life and health insurance, estate and pension planning, investments, and federal income tax law.

Observe how an agent reacts to your questions. Does the agent use fancy buzzwords and generic answers or really listen attentively and, after some thought, logically answer your questions? These and other personal characteristics should be considered. In most cases, you should talk with several agents and discuss the pros and cons of each agent with your spouse before committing yourself. Then, when you've decided, call and ask that agent to return for another visit.

 **Go to Smart Sites**

Looking for an insurance agent? Link to the site sponsored by the Independent Insurance Agents and Brokers of America, Inc. ●

## LG6 Key Features of Life Insurance Policies

A life insurance policy is a contract that spells out the policyholder's and the insurer's rights and obligations and policy features. There's no such thing as a standard life insurance

### FINANCIAL ROAD SIGN

**HOW TO UNDERSTAND INSURANCE ILLUSTRATIONS**
Life insurance agents often use illustrations to help sell life insurance products. They typically show financial projections for how a policy is expected to perform over time. It includes three elements: current and maximum premiums each year, total premiums paid up to that year, and each year's death benefits. However, these illustrations can be difficult to use when comparing different policies. Here's what to look for.

- *Interest Adjusted Net Cost (IANC).* All illustrations must include this index, which provides the cost per $1,000 for projected death benefits and policy cash value.
- *Payoff projections.* These numbers show the policy payout if current interest rates continue into the future. Always ask for a second illustration that shows what will happen if the rates drop by at least 2 percentage points.
- *National Association of Securities Dealers (NASD) license* (for variable insurance products). By law, only NASD-licensed agents can explain policy illustrations for these policies, which are considered an investment product.

*Sources:* Adapted from Ginger Applegarth, "Avoid the Insurance Illustration Trap," http://articles.moneycentral.msn.com/Insurance/AvoidRipoffs/AvoidTheInsuranceIllustrationTrap.aspx, accessed June 2009.

policy and policies can vary from state to state. Even so, certain elements are common in most life insurance contracts.

**beneficiary** A person who receives the death benefits of a life insurance policy after the insured's death.

## Life Insurance Contract Features

Key features found in most life insurance contracts are the beneficiary clause, settlement options, policy loans, premium payments, grace period, nonforfeiture options, policy reinstatement, and change of policy.

### Beneficiary Clause

The **beneficiary** is the person who will receive the death benefits of the policy on the insured's death. All life insurance policies should have one or more beneficiaries. An insured should name both a *primary beneficiary* and various *contingent beneficiaries*. The primary beneficiary receives the entire death benefit if he or she is surviving when the insured dies. If the primary beneficiary does not survive the insured, the insurer will distribute the death benefits to the contingent beneficiaries. If neither primary nor contingent beneficiaries are living at the death of the insured, then the death benefits pass to the insured's estate and are distributed by the probate court according to the insured's will or, if no will exists, according to state law.

The identification of named beneficiaries should be clear. For example, if a man designating his beneficiary as "my wife," later divorces and remarries, there could be a controversy as to which "wife" is entitled to the benefits. Obviously, you change your named beneficiary if circumstances, such as marital status, change. The person you name as a beneficiary can be changed at any time by notifying the insurance company as long as you didn't indicate an *irrevocable beneficiary* when you took out the policy.

### Settlement Options

Insurance companies generally offer several ways of paying life insurance policy death proceeds. The distribution method can either be permanently established by the policyholder before death or left up to the beneficiary when the policy proceeds are paid out.

● **Lump sum.** This is the most common settlement option, chosen by more than 95% of policyholders. The entire death benefit is paid in a single amount, allowing beneficiaries to use or invest the proceeds soon after death occurs.

● **Interest only.** The insurance company keeps policy proceeds for a specified time; the beneficiary

**policy loan** An advance, secured by the cash value of a whole life insurance policy, made by an insurer to the policyholder.

receives interest payments, usually at some guaranteed below-market rate. This option is used when there's no current need for the principal—for example, proceeds could be left on deposit until children go to college, with interest supplementing family income.

- **Fixed period.** The face amount of the policy, along with interest earned, is paid to the beneficiary over a fixed time period. For example, a 55-year-old beneficiary may need additional income until Social Security benefits start.

- **Fixed amount.** The beneficiary receives policy proceeds in regular payments of a fixed amount until the proceeds run out.

- **Life income.** The insurer guarantees to pay the beneficiary a certain amount for the rest of his or her life, based on the beneficiary's sex, age when benefits start, life expectancy, policy face value, and interest rate assumptions. This option appeals to beneficiaries who don't want to outlive the income from policy proceeds and so become dependent on others for support. An interesting variation of this settlement option is the *life-income-with-period-certain option*, which guarantees a specified number of payments that would pass to a secondary beneficiary if the original beneficiary dies before the period ends.

This chapter's *Money in Action* feature contains useful advice about filing a life insurance claim when the insured dies.

### Policy Loans

An advance made by a life insurance company to a policyholder against a whole life policy is called a **policy loan**. These loans are secured by the cash value of the life insurance policy. Although these loans do *not* have to be repaid, any balance plus interest on the loan remaining at the insured's death is *subtracted from the proceeds of the policy*. Typically, policies offer either a fixed-rate loan or a rate that varies with market interest rates on high-quality bonds. Policy loans should be used only if the insured's estate is large enough to cover the accompanying loss of death proceeds when the loan is not repaid. A word of caution: *Be careful*

© HJALMEIDA/DREAMSTIME.COM

*with these loans; unless certain conditions are met, the IRS may treat them as withdrawals, meaning they could be subject to tax penalties.*

### Premium Payments

All life insurance contracts specify when premiums, which are normally paid in advance, are due. Most insurers allow the policyholder to elect to pay premiums annually, semiannually, quarterly, or monthly, but typically charge a fee to those paying more often than annually.

### Grace Period

The *grace period* permits the policyholder to retain full death protection for a short period (usually 31 days) after missing a premium payment date. In other words, you won't lose your insurance protection just because you're a little late in making the premium payment.

### Nonforfeiture Options

As noted earlier, a *nonforfeiture option* pays a cash value life insurance policyholder the policy's cash value when a policy is terminated before its maturity. State laws require that all permanent whole, universal, or variable life policies contain a nonforfeiture provision. Rather than receiving the policy's cash value, insurance companies usually offer the following two options—*paid-up insurance* and *extended term insurance*.

- **Paid-up insurance.** The policyholder uses the cash value to buy a new, single premium policy with a lower face value. For example, a policy canceled after 10 years might have a cash value of $90.84 per $1,000 of face value, which will buy $236 of paid-up whole life insurance. This paid-up insurance is useful because the cash value would continue to grow from future interest earnings, even though the policyholder makes no further premium payments. This option is useful when a person's income and need for death protection decline but she still wants some coverage.

- **Extended term insurance.** The insured uses the accumulated cash value to buy a term life policy for the same face value as the lapsed policy and a coverage period determined by the amount of term

# MONEY IN ACTION

## Filing a Life Insurance Claim

Although no one likes to deal with paperwork immediately after a loved one's death, filing a life insurance claim should not be delayed. Life insurance proceeds can provide surviving family members with access to needed cash quickly.

- Never assume that the deceased didn't have life insurance. It's always a good idea to check with current and former employers to see if group life insurance was provided. The deceased's lawyer, banker, or accountant may know where the insured kept a life insurance policy. If all else fails, MIB's Policy Locator Service (http://www.policylocator.com) has over 170 million records on insurance applications processed during the last 13 years. The cost is around $75 and responses are usually received within ten business days.

- Obtain several copies of the death certificate. At least one copy should be certified, which will be submitted with the policy claim.

- Contact your insurance company or agent. A representative or your agent can provide the necessary forms and help you fill them out.

- Decide how you want the proceeds of the policy distributed. Options include paying a lump sum, paying principal and interest on a predetermined schedule, paying a guaranteed income for life that depends on the gender and age of the beneficiary at the time of the insured's death, and the payment of interest while the company holds the proceeds.

*Sources:* Adapted from "How Do I File a Life Insurance Claim," http://www.iii.org/individuals/life/help/fileaclaim/, accessed June 2009; Thomson Reuters, "Policy Locator Service from MIB Solutions Helps Attorneys Find Missing Life Insurance Policies," http://www.reuters.com/article/pressRelease/idUS125340+24-Mar-2009+PRN20090324, March 24, 2009, accessed June 2009.

protection the single premium payment buys at the insured's present age. This option usually goes into effect automatically if the policyholder quits paying premiums and gives no instructions to the insurer.

### Policy Reinstatement

As long as a whole life policy is under the reduced paid-up insurance option or the extended term insurance option, the policyholder may reinstate the original policy, usually within 3 to 5 years of its lapsing, by paying all back premiums plus interest at a stated rate and by providing evidence that he or she can pass a physical examination and meet any other insurability requirements. *Reinstatement* revives the original contractual relationship between the company and the policyholder. Before exercising a reinstatement option, a policyholder should determine whether buying a new policy is less costly.

### Change of Policy

Many life insurance contracts contain a provision that permits the insured to switch from one policy form to another. For instance, policyholders may decide they'd rather have policies that are paid up at age 65 rather than their current continuous premium whole life policies. A change-of-policy provision allows this change without penalty. When policyholders change from high- to lower-premium policies, they may need to prove insurability.

## Other Policy Features

Along with the key contractual features described earlier, here are some other policy features to consider.

**multiple indemnity clause** A clause in a life insurance policy that typically doubles or triples the policy's face amount if the insured dies in an accident.

- **Multiple indemnity clause.** Multiple indemnity clauses increase the face amount of the policy, most often doubling or tripling it, if the insured dies in an accident. This benefit is usually offered to the

© JOGGIE BOTMA/SHUTTERSTOCK

policyholder at a small additional cost. This coverage should be ignored as a source of funds when determining insurance needs because it offers no protection if the insured's death is due to illness.

- **Disability clause.** A **disability clause** may contain a waiver-of-premium benefit alone or coupled with disability income. A *waiver-of-premium benefit* excuses the payment of premiums on the life insurance policy if the insured becomes totally and permanently disabled prior to age 60 (or sometimes age 65). Under the *disability income portion,* the insured not only is granted a waiver of premium but also receives a monthly income equal to $5 or $10 per $1,000 of policy face value. Some insurers will continue these payments for the life of the insured; others terminate them at age 65. Disability riders for a waiver of premium and disability income protection are relatively inexpensive and can be added to most whole life policies but generally not to term policies.

- **Guaranteed purchase option.** The policyholder who has a **guaranteed purchase option** may purchase additional coverage at stipulated intervals without providing evidence of insurability. This option is frequently offered to buyers of a whole life policy who are under age 40. Increases in coverage usually can be purchased every 3, 4, or 5 years in sums equal to the amount of the original policy or $10,000, whichever is lower. This option should be attractive to individuals whose life insurance needs and ability to pay are expected to increase over a 5- to 15-year period.

- **Suicide clause.** Nearly all life insurance policies have a *suicide clause* that voids the contract if an insured commits suicide within a certain period, normally 2 years after the policy's inception. In these cases, the company simply returns the premiums that have been paid. If an insured commits suicide after this initial period has elapsed, the policy proceeds are paid regardless.

- **Exclusions.** Although all private insurance policies exclude some types of losses, life policies offer broad protection. Other than the suicide clause, the only common exclusions are aviation, war, and hazardous occupation or hobby. However, a company would rarely be able to modify the premium charged or coverage offered should the insured take up, say, Formula One racing or hang gliding *after* a policy is issued.

- **Participation.** In a **participating policy**, the policyholder is entitled to receive *policy dividends* reflecting the difference between the premiums that are charged and the amount of premium necessary to fund the actual mortality experience of the company. When the base premium schedule for participating policies is established, a company estimates what it believes its mortality and investment experience will be and then adds a generous margin of safety to these figures. The premiums charged the policyholder are based on these conservative estimates.

- **Living benefits.** Also called *accelerated benefits*, this feature allows the insured to receive a percentage of the death benefits from a whole or universal life policy prior to death. Some insurers offer this option at no charge to established policyholders if the insured suffers a terminal illness that is expected to result in death within a specified period (such as 6 months to a year) or needs an expensive treatment (such as an organ transplant) to survive. These benefits can also be added as a *living benefit rider* that pays a portion of a policy's death benefit in advance, usually about 2% per month, for long-term healthcare, such as nursing home expenses. This rider can add an extra 5% to 15% to the normal life insurance premium, and benefits are capped at some fixed percentage of the death benefit.

- **Viatical settlement.** Like a living benefits feature, this option allows a terminally ill insurance holder to receive a percentage of the insurance policy's death benefit for immediate use. But unlike the living benefits feature, this isn't handled through the insurance company but rather through a third-party investor. The insured sells an interest in the life insurance policy to the investor, who then becomes the policy's beneficiary, and then receives a cash amount from that investor—most commonly 60% of the policy value. After the insured dies, the investor receives the balance from the policy. Approach viatical settlements carefully because they mean giving up all future claims on the life insurance policy and can also affect a patient's Medicare eligibility in some cases. Note also that some viatical settlement companies—the firms that arrange the transfer between insureds and investors—have been scrutinized by government agencies for unethical practices.

# FINANCIAL PLANNING EXERCISES

**LG2, 3, 4**

1. *Use Worksheet 8.1.* Brett Hardesty, 43, is a recently divorced father of two children, ages 9 and 7. He currently earns $95,000 a year as an operations manager for a utility company. The divorce settlement requires him to pay $1,500 a month in child support and $400 a month in alimony to his ex-wife. She currently earns $25,000 a year as a preschool teacher. Brett is now renting an apartment, and the divorce settlement left him with about $100,000 in savings and retirement benefits. His employer provides a $75,000 life insurance policy. Brett's ex-wife is currently the beneficiary listed on the policy. What advice would you give to Brett? What factors should he consider in deciding whether to buy additional life insurance at this point in his life? If he does need additional life insurance, what type of policy or policies should he buy? Use Worksheet 8.1 to help answer these questions for Brett.

**LG4**

2. Using the premium schedules provided in Exhibits 8.2, 8.3, and 8.5, how much in *annual* premiums would a 25-year-old male have to pay for $100,000 of annual renewable term, level premium term, and whole life insurance? (Assume a 5-year term or period of coverage.) How much would a 25-year-old woman have to pay for the same coverage? Consider a 40-year-old male (or female): Using annual premiums, compare the cost of 10 years of coverage under annual renewable and level premium term options and whole life insurance coverage. Relate the advantages and disadvantages of each policy type to their price differences.

**LG2, 3, 4, 5**

3. Sofia and Carlos Ramirez are a dual-career couple who just had their first child. Carlos, age 29, already has a group life insurance policy, but Sofia's employer does not offer life insurance. A financial planner is recommending that the 25-year-old Sofia buy a $250,000 whole life policy with an annual premium of $1,670 (the policy has an assumed rate of earnings of 5% a year). Help Sofia evaluate this advice and decide on an appropriate course of action.

**LG2, 3, 4, 6**

4. While at lunch with a group of coworkers, one of your friends mentions that he plans to buy a variable life insurance policy because it provides a good annual return and is a good way to build savings for his 5-year-old's college education. Another colleague says that she's adding coverage through the group plan's additional insurance option. What advice would you give them?

# INSURING YOUR HEALTH

## LEARNING GOALS

**LG1** Discuss why having adequate health insurance is important and identify the factors contributing to the growing cost of health insurance. (p. 191)

**LG2** Differentiate among the major types of health insurance plans and identify major private and public health insurance providers and their programs. (p. 192)

**LG3** Analyze your own health insurance needs and explain how to shop for appropriate coverage. (p. 197)

**LG4** Explain the basic types of medical expenses covered by the policy provisions of health insurance plans. (p. 199)

**LG5** Assess the need for and features of long-term care insurance. (p. 205)

**LG6** Discuss the features of disability income insurance and how to determine your need for it. (p. 208)

## LG1 The Importance of Health Insurance Coverage

The next best thing to good health is a good health insurance plan. In recent years, the price of medical treatment has risen dramatically. The cost of a major illness can easily total tens (or even hundreds) of thousands of dollars in expense due to hospital, medical care, and loss of income. Health insurance helps you pay both routine and major medical care costs. Indeed, in 2007, about 60% of all U.S. personal bankruptcies were due to medical costs.

Despite the financial importance of health insurance, nearly 16% of the population under age of 65—about 49 million people—don't have

health insurance. Young adults between 18 and 24 are even less likely to have health insurance; nearly 70% of individuals in that age group are not covered by health insurance.

Exhibit 9.1 helps to explain why so many are uninsured; the cost of adequate health insurance increased an average of about 10% annually between 2000 and 2007—significantly faster than the 2.8% average annual inflation rate or the 3.2% average worker's annual wage growth during that same period. In 2007, the average annual premium for employer-sponsored plans was $4,479 for

single coverage and $12,106 for family coverage. During 2007, the average percentage of health care premiums paid by covered workers was

> **The next best thing to good health is a good health insurance plan.**

### Exhibit 9.1    Historical Trends in Health Insurance Costs

As the chart shows, the year-to-year percentage change for health insurance premiums has been much higher than both the inflation rate and average workers' earnings.

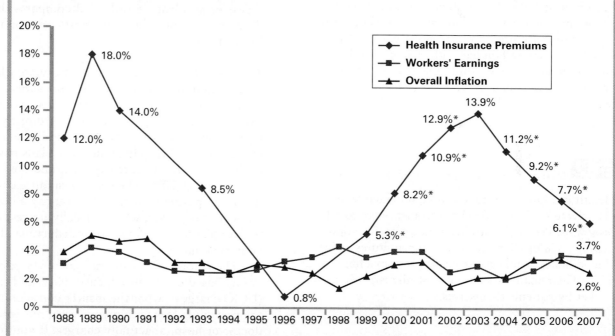

*Estimate is statistically different from estimate for the previous year shown (*p* < 0.05). No statistical tests are conducted for years prior to 1999.

*Note:* Data on premium increases reflect the cost of health insurance premiums for a family of four. The average premium increase is weighted by covered workers.

*Source:* Kaiser/HRET Survey of Employer-Sponsored Health Benefits, 1999–2007; KPMG Survey of Employer-Sponsored Health Benefits, 1993, 1996; Health Insurance Association of America (HIAA), 1988, 1989, 1990; Bureau of Labor Statistics, Consumer Price Index, U.S. City Average of Annual Inflation (April to April), 1988–2007; Bureau of Labor Statistics, Seasonally Adjusted Data from the Current Employment Statistics Survey, 1988–2007 (April to April).

© KURHAM

**group health insurance** Health insurance consisting of contracts written between a group, (employer, union, etc.) and the health care provider.

**indemnity (fee-for-service) plan** Health insurance plan in which the health care provider is separate from the insurer, who pays the provider or reimburses you for a specified percentage of expenses after a deductible amount has been met.

16% for single plans and 28% for family plans.

 **Go to Smart Sites**

You can learn more about the political, economic, and social factors affecting the cost and availability of health insurance from America's Health Insurance Plans Web site. Whenever you see "*Go to Smart Sites*" in this chapter, visit 4ltrpress.cengage.com. ●

Costly advances in medical technology, an aging U.S. population, and a poor demand-and-supply distribution of health care facilities and services have fueled rapidly rising health care costs. In addition, administrative costs, excessive paperwork, increased regulation, and insurance fraud are also contributing to rising health care costs.

It can be risky to go without adequate health insurance coverage. Concern over health care costs and the number of uninsured Americans has made health care reform a major priority of Congress and the administration. Policy solutions concerning the proper mix between government- and privately-run health insurance programs prompt vigorous debate. Clearly, becoming familiar with current health insurance options and issues should help you make better decisions as well as provide a useful perspective on the health care reform debate.

## LG2 Health Insurance Plans

Health insurance coverage can be obtained from (1) private sources and (2) government-sponsored programs. Private health insurance pays for approximately 35% of all medical care expenditures in the United States, while government programs fund about 45%. The remaining amount typically is paid out-of-pocket by patients themselves.

## Private Health Insurance Plans

Private companies sell a variety of health insurance plans to both groups and individuals. **Group health insurance** is a contract written between a group (such as an employer, union, credit union, or other organization) and the health care provider: a private insurance

company, Blue Cross/Blue Shield plan, or a managed care organization. Typically, group plans provide comprehensive medical expense coverage and may also offer prescription drug, dental, and vision care services.

If your employer has more than just a few employees, you'll probably have access to some type of group health plan. Due to today's high cost of health care, most employers require employees to pay part of the cost. Some groups self-insure, which means that they take responsibility for the full or partial payment of claims. Health insurance coverage can also be purchased on an individual basis directly from providers. To control rising costs, many employers underwrite employee health care coverage much the way insurers do. In addition, many employers are shifting a larger percentage of health care costs to employees. So be sure to compare group and individual policies before deciding which coverage to buy.

Most private health insurance plans fall into one of two categories: traditional *indemnity (fee-for-service) plans* and *managed care plans*, which include health maintenance organizations (HMOs), preferred provider organizations (PPOs), and similar plans. Both categories of plans cover, in somewhat different ways, the medical care costs arising from illness or accidents. Exhibit 9.2 compares the key differences among the three most common types of health plans.

### Traditional Indemnity (Fee-for-Service) Plans

With a traditional **indemnity (fee-for-service) plan**, the health care provider is separate from your insurer. Your insurer either pays the provider directly or reimburses your expenses when you submit claims for medical treatment. Typically, indemnity plans pay 80% of the eligible health care expenses, and the insured pays the other 20%. The health insurance company will begin paying its share after you pay a deductible amount of expenses, which typically ranges from $100 to over $2,000. The lower your deductible, the higher your premium.

The amount the insurance company pays is commonly based on the usual, customary, and reasonable (UCR) charges—what the insurer considers to be the prevailing fees within your area, not what your doctor or hospital actually charges. If your doctor charges more than the UCR, you may be responsible for the full amount of the excess. UCR charges vary significantly among insurers, so you should compare your doctor's fees with what a plan pays. Under many indemnity plans, physicians who accept the insurance agree to accept the UCR payments set by the insurer.

## Exhibit 9.2 How the Most Common Types of Health Plans Compare

This table highlights some of the key differences among the three most common types of health plans.

| Type | Choice of Service Providers | Premium Cost | Out-of-Pocket Costs | Annual Deductible |
|------|------------------------------|--------------|----------------------|--------------------|
| Indemnity | Yes | Low if high-deductible plan, high if low-deductible plan | Usually 20% of medical expenses plus deductible | Yes |
| HMO | No | Low | Low co-pay | No |
| PPO | Some | Higher than HMO | Low if using network providers, higher if provider is outside the network | No |

## Managed Care Plans

Today, employers are moving toward **managed care plans** under which subscribers/users contract with and make monthly payments directly to the organization that provides the health care service. Most major health insurance companies offer both indemnity and managed care plans. Managed care plan members receive comprehensive health care services from a designated group of doctors, hospitals, and other providers.

Under a managed care plan, the insured pays no deductibles and only a small fee, or co-payment, for office visits and medications. Most medical services—including preventive and routine care that indemnity plans may not cover—are fully covered when obtained from plan providers. Managed care plans include health maintenance organizations (HMOs), preferred provider organizations (PPOs), exclusive provider organizations (EPOs), and point-of-service (POS) plans.

## HEALTH MAINTENANCE ORGANIZATIONS. A health

maintenance organization (HMO) is an organization of hospitals, physicians, and other health care providers that provides comprehensive health care services to its members. HMO members pay a monthly fee that varies according to the number of people in their family. A co-payment of $5 to $30 is charged each time services are provided by the HMO or a prescription is filled. The services provided to HMO members include doctors' office visits, imaging and laboratory services, preventive care, health screenings, hospital inpatient care and surgery, maternity care, mental health care, and drug prescriptions. The advantages of HMO membership include a lack of deductibles, few or no exclusions, and not having to file insurance claims. The primary disadvantages are that HMO members can't always choose their physicians and they may face limitations on care outside of the geographic area of the HMO.

**managed care plan** A health care plan in which subscribers/users contract with the provider organization, which uses a designated group of providers meeting specific selection standards to furnish health care services for a monthly fee.

**health maintenance organization (HMO)** An organization of hospitals, physicians, and other health care providers who have joined to provide comprehensive health care services to its members, who pay a monthly fee.

**group HMO**
An HMO that provides health care services *from a central facility;* most prevalent in larger cities.

**individual practice association (IPA)**
A form of HMO in which subscribers receive services from physicians practicing *from their own offices and from community hospitals* affiliated with the IPA.

**preferred provider organization (PPO)**
A health provider that combines the characteristics of the IPA form of HMO with an indemnity plan to provide comprehensive health care services to its subscribers within a network of physicians and hospitals.

**exclusive provider organization (EPO)**
A managed care plan that is similar to a PPO, but reimburses members only when affiliated providers are used.

**point-of-service (POS) plan** A hybrid form of HMO that allows members to go outside the HMO network for care and reimburses them at a specified percentage of the cost.

**Blue Cross/Blue Shield plans** Prepaid hospital and medical expense plans under which health care services are provided to plan participants by member hospitals and physicians.

There are two main types of HMOs: group and individual practice associations. A **group HMO** employs a group of doctors to provide health care services to members *from a central facility.* Often, the group HMO's hospital facilities are located in the same facility. Group HMOs are most prevalent in larger cities.

An **individual practice association (IPA)** is the most popular type of HMO. IPA members receive medical care from individual physicians practicing *from their own offices and from community hospitals* that are affiliated with the IPA. As a member of an IPA, you have some choice of which doctors and hospitals to use.

**PREFERRED PROVIDER ORGANIZATIONS.** A **preferred provider organization (PPO)** is a managed care plan that has the characteristics of both an IPA and an indemnity plan. An insurance company or provider group contracts with a network of physicians and hospitals that agree to accept a negotiated fee for medical services provided to the PPO members. Unlike the HMO, however, a PPO also provides insurance coverage for medical services not provided by the PPO network, so you can choose to go to other doctors or hospitals. You will, however, pay a higher price for medical services provided by network doctors and hospitals.

**OTHER MANAGED CARE PLANS.** You may encounter two other forms of managed care plans. An **exclusive provider organization (EPO)** contracts with medical providers to offer services to members at reduced costs, but reimburses members only when affiliated providers are used. Plan members who use a nonaffiliated provider must bear the entire cost. The **point-of-service (POS) plan** is a hybrid form of HMO that allows members to go outside of the HMO network for care. Payment for nonaffiliated physician services is similar to indemnity plan payments: the plan pays a specified percentage of the cost after your medical costs reach an annual deductible.

### Blue Cross/Blue Shield Plans

In a technical sense, **Blue Cross/Blue Shield plans** are not insurance policies but rather prepaid hospital and medical expense plans. Today, there are over 35 independent local Blue Cross/Blue Shield organizations, all of them for-profit corporations.

Blue Cross contracts with hospitals that agree to provide specified hospital services to members of subscriber groups in exchange for a specified fee or payment. Blue Cross also contracts for surgical and medical services. Blue Cross serves as the intermediary between the groups that want these services and the physicians who contractually agree to provide them. Today, many Blue Cross and Blue Shield plans have combined to form one provider, and they compete for business with other private insurance companies. Blue Cross/Blue Shield payments for health care services are seldom made to the subscriber but rather directly to the participating hospital or physician.

## Government Health Insurance Plans

In addition to health insurance coverage provided by private sources, federal and state agencies provide health care coverage to eligible individuals. About 25% of the U.S. population is covered by some form of government health insurance program.

### The Possibility of National Health Care

The health care reform debate includes the possibility of a nationalized health insurance program in which health care would be placed under the control of the government. The goal of health care reform is to provide more people access to needed services at affordable rates. However, in nationalized programs like those in Canada and the United Kingdom, there is reportedly still some difficulty in obtaining health

# MONEY IN ACTION

## Health Care Reform and You

Health care reform implies changes in health care insurance. While specific changes continue to be debated, understanding how we got to this point provides a needed perspective on how health care reform is likely to affect you.

So what's broken? Cost–benefit analysis leaves the U.S. health care system looking anemic. The U.S. economy spends about 17 cents of every dollar on health care, which is about twice the average for other rich economies. So what do we get in return? Outcomes for infant mortality, life expectancy, and heart attack survival rates are all worse than the average for members of the Organization for Economic Cooperation and Development (OECD). And about 49 million citizens are not covered by health insurance. Health care in the United States is more expensive because of two significant economic distortions:

- *The cost of employer-provided health care insurance is tax-deductible.* This encourages overly generous programs in which true costs are hard to determine. Further, the uninsured still subsidize such plans through their tax payments. The tax deductibility of health care programs is estimated to cost the U.S. government at least $250 billion annually.

- *Most U.S. physicians are compensated on a fee-for-service basis.* This creates an incentive for excessive health care expenses that do not always lead to better outcomes. Although this problem is not unique to the United States, it is thought to be worse there than in any other rich country. Reducing unnecessarily expensive procedures and prescriptions could save from 10% to 30% on health care costs.

High health care costs hurt the United States in three important ways:

- *Taxpayer burdens are already high.* More than half of the U.S. population relies on the government for health care, which presses federal and state budgets.

- *Private insurance programs are costly for employers.* Consider that the cost of health insurance was instrumental in GM's downfall. And many small firms are being forced to give up funding employee health care insurance because of its cost.

- *High health care insurance premiums reduce workers' wages.*

So if the proposed health care reform is actually enacted, how might it affect you? In a few years, you probably won't have the same health insurance that you do now. Health insurance markets will likely be restructured. Currently, insurance firms are allowed to carry the healthiest patients and reject the sickest. Yet this unfairly burdens those firms who carry a lot of older and sicker people. In the near future, we are likely to see government-funded programs for risk pooling. The insurance industry may well accept this approach if it requires all citizens to purchase coverage. If you have been denied health insurance, there could be some good news. President Obama has strongly argued that no insurance plan should be able to deny coverage on the basis of preexisting conditions. If you currently have good private health insurance through your employer, then you are likely to be able to keep it and your physicians—at least in the short run. However, some argue that your employer could choose to replace it with a less expensive government plan. Although the exact nature of the changes continues to be debated, one thing is clear: health care reform is inevitable.

*Sources:* Adapted from "Health-Care Reform in America: This Is Going to Hurt," *The Economist,* June 25, 2009, http://www.economist.com/opinion/displaystory.cfm?story_id=13900898, accessed July 2009; "Reforming American Health Care: Heading for the Emergency Room," *The Economist,* June 25, 2009, http://www.economist.com/world/unitedstates/displaystory.cfm?story_id=13899647, accessed July 2009; Wendy Diller, "The Implications of Health-Care Reform," http://www.businessweek.com/investor/content/jul2008/pi20080725_983150.htm, July 25, 2008, accessed July 2009; "What You Need to Know about Health Care Reform," www.cnn.com/2009/HEALTH/06/18/ep.health.reform.basics/, June 18, 2009, accessed July 2009.

care. And some fear that removing health care from the free-market system will reduce its overall quality. This chapter's *Money in Action* provides an overview of the debate on health care reform in the United States. Notwithstanding the possibility of a national health care program, let's now take a look at some of the government health care plans that are currently in place and have been for some time.

## Medicare

**Medicare** is a health insurance program administered by the Social Security Administration. It's primarily designed to help persons 65 and over meet their health care costs, but it also covers many people under 65 who receive monthly Social Security disability benefits. Funds for Medicare benefits come from Social Security taxes paid by covered workers and their employers. Medicare provides basic hospital insurance, supplementary medical insurance, and prescription drug coverage.

- **Basic hospital insurance.** This coverage (commonly called *Part A*) provides inpatient hospital services such as room, board, and other customary inpatient service for the first 90 days of illness. A deductible is applied during the first 60 days of illness. Co-insurance provisions, applicable to days 61–90 of the hospital stay, can further reduce benefits. Medicare also covers all or part of the cost of up to 100 days in posthospital extended-care facilities that provide skilled care, such as nursing homes. However, it doesn't cover the most common types of nursing home care—intermediate

**Medicare** A health insurance plan administered by the federal government to help persons age 65 and over, and others receiving monthly Social Security disability benefits, to meet their health care costs.

**supplementary medical insurance (SMI)** A voluntary program under Medicare (commonly called *Part B*) that provides payments for services not covered under basic hospital insurance *(Part A)*.

**prescription drug coverage** A voluntary program under Medicare (commonly called *Part D)*, insurance that covers both brand-name and generic prescription drugs at participating pharmacies. Participants pay a monthly fee and a yearly deductible and must also pay part of the cost of prescriptions, including a co-payment or coinsurance.

**Medicaid** A state-run public assistance program that provides health insurance benefits only to those who are unable to pay for health care.

**workers' compensation insurance** Health insurance required by state and federal governments and paid nearly in full by employers in most states; it compensates workers for job-related illness or injury.

and custodial care. Medicare basic hospital insurance also covers some posthospital medical services such as intermittent nursing care, therapy, rehabilitation, and home health care. Medicare deductibles and coinsurance amounts are revised annually to reflect changing medical costs.

- **Supplementary medical insurance.** The **supplementary medical insurance (SMI)** program (commonly called *Part B*) covers the services of physicians and surgeons in addition to the costs of medical and health services such as imaging, laboratory tests, prosthetic devices, rental of medical equipment, and ambulance transportation. It also covers some home health services (such as in-home visits by a registered nurse) and limited psychiatric care. Unlike Medicare's basic hospital insurance, SMI is a *voluntary program* for which participants pay premiums, which are then matched with government funds. Anyone age 65 or over can enroll in SMI.

- **Prescription drug coverage.** The **prescription drug coverage** program (commonly called *Part D*) is insurance covering both brand-name and generic prescription drugs at participating pharmacies. It's intended to provide protection for people who have very high drug costs. All Medicare recipients are eligible for this coverage, regardless of their income and

resources, health status, or existing prescription expenses. There are several ways to obtain this coverage. Participants in this *voluntary program* pay a monthly fee and a yearly deductible, which was $295 in 2009. They also pay part of the cost of prescriptions, including a co-payment or coinsurance. The plan provides extra help—paying almost all prescription drug costs—for the 1 in 3 Medicare recipients who have limited income and resources.

Although Medicare pays for many health care expenses for the disabled and those over 65, there are still gaps in its coverage. Many Medicare enrollees buy private insurance policies to fill in these gaps.

## Medicaid

**Medicaid** is a state-run public assistance program that provides health insurance benefits only to those who are unable to pay for health care. Each state has its own Medicaid regulations, eligibility requirements, and covered medical services. Although Medicaid is primarily funded by each state, the federal government also contributes funds. More than 63 million people are covered by Medicaid.

### Workers' Compensation Insurance

**Workers' compensation insurance** is designed to compensate workers who are injured on the job or become ill through work-related causes. Although mandated by the federal government, each state is responsible for workers' compensation legislation and regulation. Specifics vary from state to state, but typical workers' compensation benefits include medical and rehabilitation expenses, disability income, and scheduled lump-sum amounts for death and certain injuries, such as dismemberment. Employers bear nearly the entire cost of workers' compensation

© ANDI BERGER/SHUTTERSTOCK

insurance in most states. Premiums are based on historical usage; employers who file the most claims pay the highest rates. Self-employed people are required to contribute to workers' compensation for themselves and their employees.

## LG3 Health Insurance Decisions

How can you systematically plan your health insurance purchases? As with other insurance decisions, you'll need to consider potential areas of loss, types of coverage and other resources available to you and your family, and any gaps in protection. Then you can choose a health insurance plan that's best for you.

### Evaluate Your Health Care Cost Risk

Most people need protection against two costs resulting from illness or accidents: (1) expenses for medical care and rehabilitation and (2) loss of income or household services. The cost of medical care can't be estimated easily; but in cases of long-term, serious illness, medical bills and related expenses can easily run into hundreds of thousands of dollars. An adequate amount of protection against these costs for most people would be at least $300,000 and, with a protracted illness or disability, as much as $1 million. In contrast, lost income is typically calculated as a percentage of your (or your spouse's) current monthly earnings, generally, 60% to 75%.

A good health insurance plan embodies more than financing medical expenses, lost income, and replacement services. It should incorporate other means of risk reduction such as risk avoidance, loss prevention and control, and risk assumption.

- **Risk avoidance.** Look for ways to avoid exposure to health care loss before it occurs. For example, people who don't take illegal drugs never have to worry about disability from overdose, people who refuse to ride on motorcycles avoid the high risk of injury, and people who don't smoke in bed will never doze off and start a fire in their house.

- **Loss prevention and control.** Accept responsibility for your own well-being and live a healthier lifestyle to prevent illness and reduce high medical costs. Smoking, alcohol and drug dependency, improper diet, inadequate sleep, and lack of regular exercise contribute to more than 60% of all diagnosed illnesses. Eliminating some or all of these factors from your lifestyle can reduce your chances of becoming ill. Similarly, following highway safety laws, not driving while intoxicated, and wearing a seat belt help prevent injury from car accidents.

- **Risk assumption.** Consider the health risks you're willing to retain. Some risks pose relatively small loss potential and you can budget for them rather than insure against them. For example, choosing insurance plans with deductibles and waiting periods is a form of risk assumption because it's more economical to pay small amounts from savings than to pay higher premiums to insure them.

### Determine Available Coverage and Resources

Some employers offering health insurance as an employee benefit offer only one plan and pay either all or part of the premiums. If you work for an employer who provides health insurance this way, you should evaluate the plan's benefits and costs to determine if additional coverage—either for yourself or your dependents—is necessary. Other employers offer their employees a choice among several types of health insurance plans during an open enrollment period each year.

Some employers offer employees a *flexible-benefit ("cafeteria") plan* that allows employees to choose fringe benefits. Typically, the menu of benefits includes more than one health insurance option as well as life insurance, disability income insurance, and other benefits. The employer specifies a set dollar amount it will provide, and employees choose a combination of benefits. If the employee wants or needs additional insurance benefits, most employers will deduct the additional cost of providing them from the employee's paycheck.

Some employers offer consumer-directed health plans that go one step beyond a flexible-benefit plan. These plans combine a high-deductible health insurance policy with a tax-free **health reimbursement account (HRA)**, a plan funded by employers for each participating employee. When the account balance is used up, you must pay the remaining deductible of the health insurance policy before insurance begins to pay. You can "roll over" the amount of unused money annually.

Another similar type of account is the **health savings account (HSA)**. The HSA is also a tax-free account, but the money is contributed by employees, employers, or both, for use in paying routine medical costs. An HSA is also combined with a high-deductible insurance policy to pay for catastrophic care in case of major accident or illness, and—as with an HRA—any unused money can be rolled over each year. If you change jobs, the money

**health reimbursement account (HRA)** An account into which employers place contributions that employees can use to pay for medical expenses. Usually combined with a high-deductible health insurance policy.

**health savings account (HSA)** A tax-free savings account—funded by employees, employer, or both—to spend on routine medical costs. Usually combined with a high deductible policy to pay for catastrophic care.

in your HSA belongs only to you and is yours to keep. In addition to the HSA and HRA, there are many other consumer-directed health plans.

If you are married and your spouse is employed, you should evaluate his or her benefit package before making any decisions. You may, for example, already be covered under your spouse's group health insurance plan or be able to purchase coverage for yourself and family members at a cheaper rate than through your own employer's plan.

Another important area of group coverage to consider is retiree benefits. Some companies provide health insurance to retirees, but most don't, so you probably shouldn't count on receiving employer-paid benefits once you retire. Know what your options are to ensure continued coverage for both you and your family after you retire. Medicare will cover basic medical expenses, but you'll probably need to supplement this coverage with one of the 12 standard Medigap plans, which are termed plans "A" through "L."

There are several other possible sources of health care coverage. Homeowner's and automobile insurance policies often contain limited amounts of medical expense protection. For example, your automobile policy may cover your medical expenses if you're involved in an auto accident regardless of whether you're in a car, on foot, or on a bicycle when the accident occurs. In addition to Social Security's Medicare program, various other government programs help pay medical expenses. For instance, medical care is provided for people who've served in the armed services and were honorably discharged. Public health programs exist to treat communicable diseases, handicapped children, and mental health disorders.

If you need or want to purchase additional medical insurance coverage on an individual basis, you can purchase a variety of indemnity and managed care plans from a private insurance company such as Aetna, CIGNA, and United Healthcare. You should buy health care plans from an insurance agent who will listen to your needs and provide well-thought-out responses to your questions. You should also research carriers and choose one that is rated highly by at least two of the major ratings agencies and that has a reputation for settling claims fairly and promptly. The National Committee for Quality Assurance (NCQA) is a nonprofit, unbiased organization that issues annual "report cards" that rate the service quality of various health plans.

## Choose a Health Insurance Plan

After familiarizing yourself with the different health insurance plans and providers and reviewing your needs, you must choose one or more plans to provide coverage. If you're employed, first review the various health insurance plans your company offers. If you can't get coverage from an employer, get plan descriptions and policy costs from several providers, including a group plan from a professional or trade organization, if available, for both indemnity and managed care plans. Then take your time and carefully read the plan materials to understand exactly what is covered, and at what cost. Next, review your past medical costs, estimate your future costs, and use them to see what your costs would be under various plans.

You'll have to ask yourself some difficult questions to decide whether you want an indemnity or a managed care plan and then to choose the particular plan:

### Go to Smart Sites

What grade did your health plan get on its quality "report card" this year? The National Committee for Quality Assurance (NCQA) can tell you. ●

● **How important is cost compared with having freedom of choice?** You may have to pay more to stay with your current doctor if he or she is not part of a managed care plan you're considering. Also, you have to decide if you can tolerate the managed care plan's approach to health care.

**FINANCIAL ROAD SIGN** $$$

**HOW TO CHOOSE A HEALTH INSURANCE PLAN**

- *Determine your needs.* Consider your current and planned use of health care. List the services that are most important to you and your family. Find out about dependents' coverage.
- *Compare benefits and coverage details.* If you are comparing plans, look at monthly premiums, deductibles, co-payments, co-insurance rates, and costs for using out-of-network providers. Consider the costs of preventive care, physical exams, and immunizations. Get the details on less traditional coverage for fertility services, mental health, and long-term care.
- *Limitations for preexisting conditions.* Find out if there are limitations for preexisting conditions or if there is a waiting period before being treated.
- *Appeals process.* Determine how the insurance company handles denied claims.
- *Key questions to ask.* Are my current health care providers part of this plan? Are referrals needed for specialist visits? Can I change doctors? Which hospitals can be used under the plan? Does an emergency-room visit need to be approved?

*Sources:* Adapted from "How to Choose a Health Insurance Plan," www.ehow .com/how_138961_choose-health-insurance.html, accessed July 2009, and U.S. Department of Health & Human Services, Agency for Healthcare Research and Quality, "Questions and Answers about Health Insurance, A Consumer Guide," http://www.ahrq.gov/consumer/insuranceqa/insuranceqa5.htm, accessed July 2009.

- **Will you be reimbursed if you choose a managed care plan and want to see an out-of-network provider?** For most people, the managed care route is cheaper, even if you visit a doctor only once a year because of indemnity plans' "reasonable charge" provisions.

- **What types of coverage do you need?** Everyone has different needs; one person may want a plan with good maternity and pediatric care whereas another may want outpatient mental health benefits. Make sure the plans you consider offer what you want.

- **How good is the managed care network?** Look at the participating doctors and hospitals to see how many of your providers are part of the plan. Check out the credentials of participating providers; a good sign is accreditation from the National Committee for Quality Assurance (NCQA). Are the providers' locations convenient for you? What preventive medical programs does it provide? Has membership grown? Talk to friends and associates to see what their experiences have been with the plan.

- **How old are you, and how is your health?** Many financial advisors recommend buying the lowest-cost plan—which may be an indemnity plan with a high deductible—if you're young and healthy.

After considering all of the coverages and resources available to you, isolate gaps in your health insurance coverage and determine how best to fill them. Doing this requires an understanding of the features, policy provisions, and coverage provided by various insurance carriers and policies. We'll discuss these in detail in the next section.

## LG4 Medical Expense Coverage and Policy Provisions

To evaluate different insurance plan options you should compare and contrast what they cover and how each plan's policy provisions may affect you and your family. By doing so, you can decide which health plan offers the best protection at the most reasonable cost. Worksheet 9.1 provides a convenient

> *To evaluate different insurance plan options you should compare and contrast what they cover and how each plan's policy provisions may affect you and your family.*

checklist for comparing the costs and benefits of competing health insurance plans.

## Types of Medical Expense Coverage

The medical services covered vary among health plans. You can purchase narrowly defined plans that cover only what you consider to be the most important medical services or, if you want the comfort of broader coverage and can afford it, you can purchase insurance that covers most or all of your health care needs. Here we describe the medical expenses most commonly covered by health insurance.

### Hospitalization

A *hospitalization insurance policy* reimburses you for the cost of your hospital stay. Hospitalization policies usually pay for a portion of: (1) the hospital's daily semiprivate room rate, which typically includes meals, nursing care, and other routine services and (2) the cost of ancillary services such as laboratory tests, imaging, and medications you receive while hospitalized. Many hospitalization plans also cover some outpatient and out-of-hospital services once you're discharged, such as in-home rehabilitation, diagnostic treatment, and preadmission testing. Some hospitalization plans merely pay a flat daily amount for each day the insured is in the hospital, regardless of actual charges. Most policies limit the number of days of hospitalization and a maximum dollar amount on ancillary services that they will reimburse.

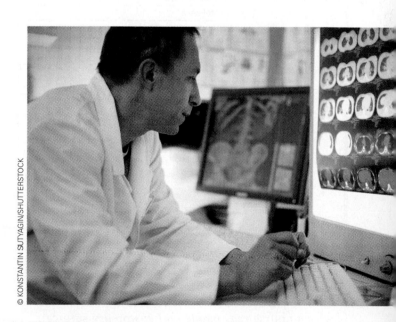

© KONSTANTIN SUTYAGIN/SHUTTERSTOCK

### Surgical Expenses

*Surgical expense insurance* covers the cost of surgery in or out of the hospital. Usually, surgical expense

Here is a convenient checklist that you can use to compare the costs and benefits of competing health care plans.

|  | Company 1 | Company 2 | Company 3 |
|---|---|---|---|
| **PLAN TYPE (HMO, PPO, etc.)** | | | |
| **COSTS** | | | |
| Premium per month | | | |
| Annual deductible: Per person/Per family | | | |
| Co-payment % after deductible | | | |
| Co-pay or % coinsurance per office visit | | | |
| Co-pay or % coinsurance for "wellness" care | | | |
| **COVERED MEDICAL SERVICES WITHIN NETWORK** | | | |
| Inpatient hospital services | | | |
| Outpatient surgery | | | |
| Physician visits (in the hospital) | | | |
| Office visits (provider) | | | |
| Skilled nursing care | | | |
| Medical tests and X-rays | | | |
| Prescription drugs | | | |
| Mental health care | | | |
| Drug and alcohol abuse treatment | | | |
| Home health care visits | | | |
| Rehabilitation facility care | | | |
| Physical therapy | | | |
| Speech therapy | | | |
| Hospice care | | | |
| Maternity care | | | |
| Chiropractic treatment | | | |
| Preventive care and checkups | | | |
| Well-baby care | | | |
| Dental care | | | |
| Other covered services | | | |
| **OTHER PROVISIONS** | | | |
| Out-of-network coverage | | | |
| Medical service limits, exclusions, or preexisting conditions | | | |
| Requirements for utilization review, preauthorization, or certification procedures | | | |

*Source:* Developed from information in *AHIP Guide to Health Insurance,* http://www.ahip.org/content/default.aspx?bc=41|329|351, accessed July 2009.

coverage is provided as part of a hospitalization insurance policy or as a rider to such a policy. Most plans reimburse *reasonable and customary* surgical expenses based on a survey of surgical costs during the previous year. They may also cover anesthesia, nonemergency treatment using imaging, and a limited allowance for diagnostic tests. Some plans still pay according to a *schedule of benefits*, reimbursing up to a fixed maximum for a particular surgical procedure. For example, the policy might state that you would receive no more than $1,500 for an appendectomy or $1,200 for diagnostic arthroscopic surgery on a knee. Scheduled benefits are often inadequate when compared with typical surgical costs.

Most elective cosmetic surgeries, such as a "nose job" or "tummy tuck," are typically excluded from reimbursement unless they are deemed a medical necessity.

### Physician Expenses

*Physicians expense insurance*, also called *regular medical expense insurance*, covers the cost of visits to a doctor's office or for a doctor's hospital visits, including consultation with a specialist. Also covered are imaging and laboratory tests performed outside of a hospital. Plans are offered on either a *reasonable and customary* or *scheduled benefit* basis. Sometimes, the first few visits with the physician for any single cause are excluded. This exclusion serves the same purpose as the deductible and waiting-period features found in other types of insurance. Often, these plans specify a maximum payment per visit as well as a maximum number of visits per injury or illness.

### Major Medical Insurance

**Major medical plans** provide broad coverage for nearly all types of medical expenses resulting from either illnesses or accidents. The amounts that can be collected under this coverage are relatively large, commonly lifetime limits of $500,000 or $1,000,000, and some policies have no limits at all. Because hospitalization, surgical, and physicians expense coverage meets the smaller medical costs, major medical is used to finance more catastrophic medical costs. Many people buy major medical with a high deductible to protect against a catastrophic illness.

### Comprehensive Major Medical Insurance

A **comprehensive major medical insurance** plan combines basic hospitalization, surgical, and physicians expense coverage with major medical protection into a single policy, usually with a low deductible. Comprehensive major medical insurance is often written under a group contract, although efforts have been taken to make this type of coverage available to individuals.

### Dental Services

*Dental insurance* covers necessary dental care and some dental injuries sustained through accidents. (Expenses for accidental damage to natural teeth are normally covered under standard surgical expense and major medical policies.) Covered services may include examinations, X-rays, dental cleanings, fillings, extractions, dentures, root canal therapy, orthodontics, and oral surgery. The maximum coverage under most dental policies is often low—$1,000 to $2,500 per patient—so these plans don't fully protect against high dental work costs.

The types of health plans discussed above are sufficient to meet the protection needs of most individuals and families. But insurance companies offer other options that provide limited protection against certain types of perils:

- *Accident policies* that pay a specified sum to an insured injured in a certain type of accident
- *Sickness policies*, sometimes called *dread disease policies*, that pay a specified sum for a named disease, such as cancer
- *Hospital income policies* that guarantee a specific daily, weekly, or monthly amount as long as the insured is hospitalized

Remember that sound insurance planning seldom dictates the purchase of such policies. The cost of purchasing these insurance options typically outweighs the limited coverage they provide. Accident and sickness policies, for example, usually cover only one type of accident or illness, and hospital income policies generally exclude illnesses that could result in extended hospitalization and health conditions existing at the time of purchase.

The problem with buying policies that cover only a certain type of accident, illness, or financial need is that major gaps in coverage will often occur. Financial loss can be just as great regardless of whether the insured falls down a flight of stairs or contracts cancer, lung disease, or heart disease. Most limited-peril policies should be used only to supplement a comprehensive insurance program if the coverage is not overlapping.

## Policy Provisions of Medical Expense Plans

To compare the health insurance plans offered by different insurers, evaluate whether they contain liberal or restrictive provisions. Generally, policy provisions can be divided into two groups: terms of payment and terms of coverage.

### Terms of Payment

Four provisions govern how much your health insurance plan will pay: (1) deductibles, (2) participation (coinsurance), (3) internal limits, and (4) coordination of benefits.

**DEDUCTIBLES.** Because major medical insurance plans are designed to supplement basic hospitalization, surgical, and physicians expense plans, those

**major medical plan** An insurance plan designed to supplement the basic coverage of hospitalization, surgical, and physicians expenses; used to finance more catastrophic medical costs.

**comprehensive major medical insurance** A health insurance plan that combines into a single policy the coverage for basic hospitalization, surgical, and physician expense along with major medical protection.

**deductible** The initial amount *not* covered by an insurance policy and thus the insured's responsibility; it's usually determined on a calendar-year basis or on a per-illness or per-accident basis.

**participation (coinsurance) clause** A provision in many health insurance policies stipulating that the insurer will pay some portion—say, 80% or 90%—of the amount of the covered loss in excess of the deductible.

**internal limits** A feature commonly found in health insurance policies that limits the amounts that will be paid for certain specified expenses, even if the claim does *not* exceed overall policy limits.

**coordination of benefits provision** A provision often included in health insurance policies to prevent the insured from collecting more than 100% of covered charges; it requires that benefit payments be coordinated if the insured is eligible for benefits under more than one policy.

offered under an indemnity (fee-for-service) plan often have a relatively large *deductible*, typically $500 or $1,000. The **deductible** represents the initial amount that's *not* covered by the policy and thus must be paid by the insured. Comprehensive major medical plans tend to offer lower deductibles, sometimes $100 or less. Most plans offer a calendar-year, all-inclusive deductible, which allows the insured to accumulate the deductible from more than one incident of use. Some plans also include a *carryover provision* whereby any part of the deductible that occurs during the final 3 months of the year (October, November, and December) can be applied to the current year's deductible and can *also* be applied to the following calendar year's deductible. In a few plans, the deductible is on a per-illness or per-accident basis. For example, if you were covered by this type of policy with a $1,000 deductible and suffered three separate accidents in one year, each requiring $1,000 of medical expenses, you wouldn't be eligible to collect any benefits from the major medical plan.

**PARTICIPATION (COINSURANCE).** A **participation**, or **coinsurance, clause** stipulates that the company will pay some portion—say, 80% or 90%—of the amount of the covered loss in excess of the deductible rather than the entire amount. Coinsurance helps reduce the possibility that policyholders will fake illness and discourages them from incurring unnecessary medical expenses. Many major medical plans also have a *stop-loss provision* that places a cap on the amount of participation required. Without a stop-loss provision, a $1 million medical bill could leave the insured responsible for, say, $200,000 of costs. Often such provisions limit the insured's participation to less than $10,000 and sometimes to as little as $2,000.

**INTERNAL LIMITS.** Most major medical policies are written with **internal limits** that control the amounts paid for certain specified expenses—even if the claim

*doesn't* exceed overall policy limits. Charges commonly subject to internal limits are hospital room and board, surgical fees, mental and nervous conditions, and nursing services. If an insured chooses an expensive physician or medical facility, then he or she is responsible for paying the portion of the charges that are above a "reasonable and customary" level or beyond a specified maximum amount. The following example shows how deductibles, coinsurance, and internal limits constrain the amount a company is obligated to pay under a major medical plan.

**MAJOR MEDICAL POLICY: AN EXAMPLE.** Assume that Rick Sizemore, a graduate student, has coverage under a major medical insurance policy that specifies a $500,000 lifetime limit of protection, a $1,000 deductible, an 80% coinsurance clause, internal limits of $350 per day on hospital room and board, and $6,000 as the maximum payable surgical fee. When Rick was hospitalized for 3 days to remove a small tumor, he incurred these costs:

| | |
|---|---|
| Hospitalization: 3 days at $500 a day | $ 1,500 |
| Surgical expense | 5,800 |
| Other covered medical expenses | 3,800 |
| Total medical expenses | $11,100 |

By the terms of the policy's co-insurance clause, the maximum the company must pay is 80% of the covered loss in excess of the deductible. Without internal limits, the company would pay $8,080 (0.80 × [$11,100 − $1,000]). The internal limits further restrict the payment. Even though 80% of the $500-per-day hospitalization charge is $400, the most the company would have to pay is $350 per day. Thus Rick, the insured, becomes liable for $50 per day for 3 days, or $150. The surgical expense is below the $6,000 internal limit, so the 80% coinsurance clause applies and the insurer will pay $4,640 (0.80 × $5,800). The company's total obligation is reduced to $7,930 ($8,080 − $150), and Rick must pay a total of $3,170 ($1,000 deductible + 0.20 [$11,100 − $1,000] coinsurance + $150 excess hospital room and board charges). This example shows that although major medical insurance can offer large amounts of reimbursement, the insured may still be responsible for substantial payments.

**COORDINATION OF BENEFITS.** Health insurance policies are not contracts of *indemnity*. This means that the insured party can collect multiple payments for the same illness or accident unless health insurance policies include a **coordination of benefits provision**. This clause prevents you from collecting more than 100% of covered charges by collecting benefits from more than one policy. For example, many private health insurance policies coordinate benefit provisions with medical benefits paid under workers' compensation. Others widely advertise that their policies will pay claims regardless of the policyholder's other coverage and, of course, often charge more per dollar of protection. Using policies with coordination of benefits clauses can help you prevent coverage overlaps and, ideally, reduce your premiums.

Considering the complexity of medical expense contracts, the various clauses limiting payments, and coordination of benefits with other policies, one might expect that insurers often pay only partial claims and sometimes completely deny claims. However, if you make a claim and don't receive satisfactory payment, don't give up. The Bonus Exhibit, "How to Get Paid on a Health Insurance Claim" at 4ltrpress.cengage.com, provides some guidelines on how you might go about getting your health insurance claims paid.

### Terms of Coverage

Several contract provisions affect a health insurance plan's value to you. Some important provisions address (1) the persons and places covered, (2) cancellation, (3) preexisting conditions, (4) pregnancy and abortion, (5) mental illness, (6) rehabilitation coverage, and (7) continuation of group coverage.

**PERSONS AND PLACES COVERED.** Some health insurance policies cover only the named insured; others offer protection to all family members. Of those that offer family coverage, some terminate benefits payable on behalf of children at age 18 and others continue them to age 24 as long as the child remains in school or is single. *If you are in this age group, then you or your parents should*

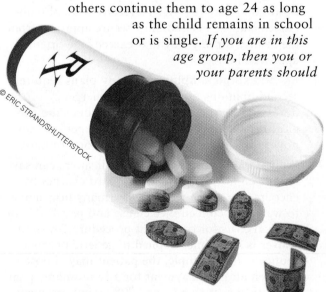

© ERIC STRAND/SHUTTERSTOCK

*check to see whether you are covered under your parents' policy.* If not, you can sometimes add such coverage by paying an additional premium. Some policies protect you only while you're in the United States or Canada; others offer worldwide coverage but exclude certain named countries.

**CANCELLATION.** Many health insurance policies are written to permit *cancellation* at the insurer's option at any time. Some policies explicitly state this; others don't. To protect yourself against premature cancellation, buy policies that specifically state that the insurer won't cancel coverage as long as premiums are paid.

**PREEXISTING CONDITIONS.** Most health insurance policies sold to individuals (as opposed to group/employer-sponsored plans) contain a **preexisting condition clause**. This means the policy might exclude coverage for any physical or mental problems you had at the time you bought it. In some policies, the exclusion is permanent; in others, it lasts only for the first year or two that the coverage is in force. Group insurance plans may also have preexisting condition clauses, but these tend to be less restrictive than those in individually written policies.

Employees who have recently left a job or retired are covered by the **Health Insurance Portability and Accountability Act**, or **HIPAA**. This federal law, implemented in 1996, is designed to protect people's ability to obtain continued health insurance after they leave a job or retire, even if they have a serious health problem. Under HIPAA, if you've already been covered by a health plan and you apply for new insurance, insurers cannot turn you down, charge you higher premiums, or enforce an exclusionary period because of your health status. HIPAA doesn't guarantee you group coverage, but it does protect your ability to buy individual health insurance even if you have a preexisting health condition.

**PREGNANCY AND ABORTION.** Many individual and group health insurance plans include special clauses for medical expenses incurred through pregnancy or abortion. Some liberal policies pay for all related expenses, including sick-leave pay during the final months of pregnancy, whereas others pay for medical expenses that result from pregnancy or abortion

**preexisting condition clause** A clause included in most individual health insurance policies permitting permanent or temporary exclusion of coverage for any physical or mental problems the insured had at the time the policy was purchased.

**Health Insurance Portability and Accountability Act (HIPAA)** Federal law that protects people's ability to obtain continued health insurance after they leave a job or retire, even if they have a serious health problem.

complications but not for routine procedure expenses. In the most restrictive cases, the policy offers no coverage for any costs of pregnancy or abortion.

**MENTAL ILLNESS.** Many health insurance plans omit or offer only reduced benefits for treatment of mental disorders. For example, a health insurance policy may offer hospitalization benefits that continue to pay as long as you remain hospitalized—except for mental illness. It may restrict payment for mental illness to one-half the normally provided payment amounts and for a period not to exceed 30 days. Unfortunately, mental illness is the number one sickness requiring long-term hospital care. Because coverage for mental illness is an important insurance protection, check your policies to learn how liberal—or how restrictive—they are regarding this feature.

**REHABILITATION COVERAGE.** Health insurance plans focus primarily on meeting reasonable and necessary medical expenses. But many policies also include *rehabilitation coverage* for counseling, occupational therapy, and even some educational or job training programs for insureds who are partially or totally disabled due to an illness or accident. This is a good feature to look for in major medical and disability income policies.

**CONTINUATION OF GROUP COVERAGE.** Under the *Consolidated Omnibus Budget Reconciliation Act (COBRA),* passed by Congress in 1986, an employee who leaves the insured group voluntarily or involuntarily (except in the case of "gross misconduct") may elect to continue coverage for up to 18 months by paying premiums to his or her former employer on time (up to 102% of the company cost). The employee retains all benefits previously available, except for disability income coverage.

Similar continuation coverage is available for retirees and their families for up to 18 months or until they become eligible for Medicare, whichever occurs first. An employee's dependents may be covered for up to 36 months under COBRA under special circumstances, such as divorce or death of the employee. After COBRA coverage expires, most states provide for conversion of the group coverage to an individual policy regardless of the insured's current health and without evidence of insurability.

## Cost Containment Provisions for Medical Expense Plans

Due to the ongoing inflation in medical costs, insurers and employers that sponsor medical expense plans try to control their costs. Cost containment provisions are included in almost all medical expense plans and include the following.

- **Preadmission certification.** This requires you to receive approval from your insurer before entering the hospital for a scheduled stay. Such approval is not normally required for emergency stays.

- **Continued stay review.** To receive normal reimbursement, the insured must secure approval from the insurer for any stay that exceeds the originally approved limits.

- **Second surgical opinions.** Many plans require second opinions on specific nonemergency procedures and, in their absence, may reduce the surgical benefits paid. Most surgical expense plans now fully reimburse the cost of second opinions.

- **Waiver of coinsurance.** Because insurers can save money on hospital room-and-board charges by encouraging outpatient surgery, many now agree to waive the coinsurance clause and pay 100% of surgical costs for outpatient procedures. A similar waiver is sometimes applied to generic pharmaceuticals. For example, the patient may choose between an 80% payment for a brand-name pharmaceutical costing $35 or 100% reimbursement for its $15 generic equivalent.

- **Limitation of insurer's responsibility.** Many policies also have provisions limiting the insurer's financial responsibility to reimbursing only for costs that are considered "reasonable and customary." This provision can sometimes place limitations on the type and place of medical care for which the insurer will pay.

## LG5 Long-Term Care Insurance

**Long-term care** involves the delivery of medical and personal care, other than hospitalization, to persons with chronic medical conditions in a nursing home, in an assisted-living community, or in the patient's home. Long-term care is expensive; for example, a year's stay in a private nursing home averages over $76,000 according to a 2008 cost-of-care survey by Genworth Financial. About 70% of 65-year-olds are expected to need long-term care at some time, and the average long-term stay is about 2½ years.

Consumers directly pay about 25% of long-term care costs and government programs such as Medicare and Medicaid cover less than half of the total cost for those meeting their strict eligibility requirements. Major medical insurance plans also exclude most of the costs related to long-term care. Fortunately, long-term care insurance policies are available that are indemnity policies that pay a fixed dollar amount for each day you receive specified care either in a nursing home or at home. The decision to buy long-term care insurance is an important part of health insurance and retirement financial planning.

insurance as an individual or through an employer-sponsored plan, however, it's important to evaluate policy provisions and costs.

> **long-term care** The delivery of medical and personal care, other than hospital care, to persons with chronic medical conditions resulting from either illness or frailty.

## Do You Need Long-Term Care Insurance?

The odds of needing more than a year of nursing home care before you reach age 65 are 1 in 33, and the expense of a prolonged nursing home stay can cause severe financial hardship. Answer the following questions to decide if you need long-term care insurance.

- **Do you have many assets to preserve for your dependents?** Because you must deplete most of your assets before Medicaid will pay for nursing home care, some financial advisors recommend that people over 65 whose net worth is more than $100,000 and income exceeds $50,000 a year consider long-term care insurance—*if* they can afford the premiums. The very wealthy, however, may prefer to self-insure.

- **Can you afford the premiums?** Premiums of many good-quality policies can be 5% to 7% of annual income or more. Such high premiums may cause more financial hardship than the cost of a potential nursing home stay. You may be better off investing the amount you'd spend in premiums; it would then be available for *any* future need, including long-term health care.

- **Is there a family history of disabling disease?** This factor increases your odds of needing long-term care. If there's a history of Alzheimer's,

> { *The decision to buy long-term care insurance is an important part of health insurance and retirement financial planning.* }

About 10 million individuals currently have long-term care insurance policies in force. Most individual long-term care products are purchased either through organizations like the American Association of Retired Persons (AARP) or directly from the more than 100 insurance companies that offer them. Employer-sponsored long-term care insurance is also growing in popularity. Usually, however, employees pay the full cost of premiums, although employer-sponsored plans can often cost less than purchasing long-term care on an individual basis. Whether you purchase long-term care

neurological disorders, or other potentially debilitating diseases, the need for long-term care insurance may increase.

- **What is your gender?** Women tend to live longer and are more likely to require long-term care. They're also the primary caregivers for other family members, which may mean that when they need care, help won't be available.

- **Do you have family who can care for you?** The availability of relatives or home health services to provide care can reduce the cost of long-term care.

## Long-Term Care Insurance Provisions and Costs

When purchasing long-term care insurance, it is important to evaluate and compare policy provisions, which are important factors in determining the premium for each policy. Exhibit 9.3 summarizes the typical provisions of policies offered by leading insurers. Let's take a closer look at the most important policy provisions to consider in purchasing long-term care insurance.

- **Type of care.** Some long-term care policies offer benefits only for nursing home care, whereas others pay only for services in the insured's home, such as skilled or unskilled nursing care, physical therapy, homemakers, and home health aides. Because it's hard to predict whether a person might need to be in a nursing home, most financial planners recommend policies covering both. Many of these policies focus on nursing home care, and any expenses for health care in the insured's home are covered in a rider to the basic policy. Many policies also cover assisted living, adult day care and other community care programs, alternative care, and respite care for the caregiver.

- **Eligibility requirements.** Some important *gatekeeper provisions* determine whether the insured will receive payment for claims. The most liberal policies state that the insured will qualify for benefits as long as his or her physician orders the care. A popular and much more restrictive provision pays only for long-term care that's medically necessary because of sickness or injury. One common gatekeeper provision requires the insured's inability to perform a given number of *activities of daily living (ADLs)* such as bathing, dressing, or eating. Some policies also provide care for cognitive impairment or when medically necessary and prescribed by the patient's physician. In the case of an Alzheimer's patient who remains physically healthy, inclusion of cognitive abilities as ADLs would be extremely important.

- **Services covered.** Most policies today cover several levels of service in state-licensed nursing homes: skilled, intermediate, and custodial care. *Skilled care* is needed when a patient requires constant attention from a medical professional, such as a physician or registered nurse. *Intermediate care* is provided when the patient needs medical attention or supervision but not the constant attention of a medical professional. *Custodial care* provides assistance in the normal activities of daily living but no medical attention or supervision; a physician or nurse may be on call, however. Most long-term care policies also cover home care services, such as skilled or unskilled nursing care, physical therapy, homemakers, and home health aides provided by

### Exhibit 9.3  Typical Provisions in Long-Term Care Insurance Policies

Long-term care insurers offer a wide range of provisions in their policies. A typical policy includes the following:

| | |
|---|---|
| **Services covered** | Skilled, intermediate, and custodial care; home health care; adult day care (often) |
| **Benefit eligibility** | Physician certification/medically necessary |
| **Daily benefit** | $100–$350/day, nursing home; $50–$150/day, home health care |
| **Benefit period** | 3–4 years |
| **Maximum benefit period** | 5 years; unlimited |
| **Waiting period** | 0–100 days |
| **Renewability** | Guaranteed |
| **Preexisting conditions** | Conditions existing 6–12 months prior to policy coverage |
| **Inflation protection** | Yes, for an additional premium |
| **Deductibility periods** | 0, 20, 30, 90, 100 days |
| **Alzheimer's disease coverage** | Yes |
| **Age limits for purchasing** | 40–84 |

state-licensed or Medicare-certified home health agencies.

- **Daily benefits.** Long-term care policies reimburse the insured for the cost of services incurred up to a daily maximum. For nursing home care policies, the daily maximums generally range from $100 to $350, depending on the amount of premium the insured is willing to pay. For combination nursing home and home care policies, the maximum home care benefit is normally half the nursing home maximum.

- **Benefit duration.** The maximum duration of benefits ranges from 1 year to the insured's lifetime. Lifetime coverage is expensive, however. Most financial planners recommend the purchase of a policy with a duration of 3 to 6 years to give the insured protection for a longer-than-average period of care.

- **Waiting period.** Even if the policy's eligibility requirements are met, the insured must pay long-term care expenses during the **waiting**, or **elimination, period.** Typical waiting periods are 90 to 100 days. Although premiums are much lower for policies with longer waiting periods, the insured must have liquid assets to cover his or her expenses during that period. An insured who is still requires care after the waiting period expires will begin to receive benefits for the duration of the policy as long as its eligibility requirements continue to be met.

### Go to Smart Sites

Want to learn more about disability income insurance? America's Health Insurance Plans offers a Guide to Disability Income Insurance.

- **Renewability.** Most long-term care insurance policies now include a **guaranteed renewability** provision to ensure continued coverage for your lifetime as long as you continue to pay the premiums. This clause does not ensure a level premium over time, however. Nearly all policies allow the insurer to raise premiums if the claims experience for your peer group of policyholders is unfavorable. Watch out for policies with an **optional renewability** clause because they are renewable *only at the insurer's option.*

- **Preexisting conditions.** Some policies include a *preexisting conditions clause,* similar to those explained earlier, ranging - from 6 to 12 months. On the other hand, other policies have no such clause, which effectively eliminates a potential source of possible claim disputes.

- **Inflation protection.** Many policies offer inflation protection riders that for an additional premium let you increase benefits by a flat amount, often 5%, per year. Others offer benefits linked to the rise in the consumer price index (CPI). Most policies discontinue inflation adjustments after either 10 or 20 years. Inflation protection riders can add between 25% and 40% to the basic premium for a long-term care insurance policy.

- **Premium levels.** Long-term care insurance is rather expensive, and premiums vary widely among insurance companies. For example, an average healthy 65-year-old male may pay about $2,998 per year for a policy that pays for 3 years' care at $150 per day for nursing home care with a 90-day waiting period and a 5% inflation rider. The same coverage may cost a 55-year-old male $1, 578 per year and a 79-year-old around $8,000 per year. Because of the significant rise in premium with age, some financial planners recommend buying long-term care insurance when you are fairly young. But keep in mind that, although the annual premiums are lower, you'll be paying for a lot longer time before you would likely need the benefits.

**waiting (elimination) period** The period after an insured meets the policy's eligibility requirements, during which he or she must pay expenses out-of-pocket; the waiting period expires, the insured begins to receive benefits.

**guaranteed renewability** Policy provision ensuring continued insurance coverage for the insured's lifetime as long as the premiums continue to be paid.

**optional renewability** Contractual clause allowing the insured to continue insurance *only at the insurer's option.*

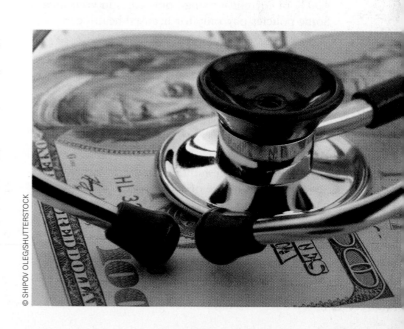

© SHIPOV OLEG/SHUTTERSTOCK

## How to Buy Long-Term Care Insurance

When buying long-term care insurance make sure the insurer is a financially sound company (based on ratings from the major ratings agencies) with a proven track record in this market segment. Here are some additional guidelines to help you choose the right policy.

- **Buy the policy when you're healthy.** Once you have a disease, such as Alzheimer's or multiple sclerosis, or have a stroke, you become uninsurable. So the best time to buy is when you're in your mid-50s or 60s.

- **Buy the right types of coverage—but don't buy more coverage than you need.** Your policy should cover skilled, intermediate, and custodial care as well as adult daycare centers and assisted living facilities. If you have access to family caregivers or home health services, opt for only nursing home coverage; if not, select a policy with generous home health care benefits. To reduce costs, increase the waiting period before benefits begin; the longer you can cover the costs yourself, the lower your premiums. You may also choose a shorter benefit payment period; 3 years is a popular choice, but the average nursing home stay is about 2½ years. Lifetime coverage increases the premium for a 65-year-old by as much as 40%.

- **Understand what the policy covers and when it pays benefits.** The amounts paid, benefit periods, and services covered vary among insurers. One rule of thumb is to buy a policy covering 80% to 100% of current nursing home costs in your area. Some policies pay only for licensed health care providers, whereas others include assistance with household chores. Know how the policy defines benefit eligibility.

## LG6 Disability Income Insurance

When a family member becomes sick for an extended period, the effect on the family goes beyond medical bills. The average chance of a person age 35 becoming disabled for 90 days or longer before age 65 is about 50%; this chance drops to about 32%—2½ times greater than the chance of death at that age—at age 55. Although most Americans have life insurance, few have taken steps to protect their family should a serious illness or accident prevent them from working for an extended period.

The best way to protect against the potentially devastating financial consequences of a health-related disability is with disability income insurance. **Disability income insurance** provides families with weekly or monthly payments to replace income when the insured is unable to work because of a covered illness, injury, or disease. Some companies also offer disability income protection for a spousal homemaker; such coverage helps pay for the services that the spouse would normally provide.

Almost all employers offer disability income insurance at attractive rates, but it is often voluntary and you may have to pay the entire premium yourself. Group coverage is usually a good buy because the premiums average $200 to $400 a year—about one-third less than the cost of comparable private coverage. Of course if you change jobs, you may lose the coverage. The benefits from a group plan in which you pay the premiums are tax free (unless paid through a flexible spending account).

Social Security offers disability income benefits, but you must be unable to do *any* job whatsoever to receive benefits. Benefits are payable only if your disability is expected to last at least 1 year (or to be fatal), and they don't begin until you've been disabled for at least 5 months. The actual amount paid is a percentage of your previous monthly earnings, with some statistical adjustments. The percentage is higher for people with low earnings. For example, a 35-year-old who was earning $20,000 annually and has dependents would receive about $1,300 per month

© ERWIN WODICKA/SHUTTERSTOCK

(about 78% of earnings); if he or she had earned $50,000, the amount would rise to about $2,250 per month (but only to 54% of earnings).

The need for disability income coverage is great. Although most workers receive some disability insurance benefits from their employer, in many cases, the group plan falls short and pays only about 60% of salary for a limited period. The first step in considering disability income insurance is to determine the dollar amount your family would need (typically monthly) if an earner becomes disabled. Then you can buy the coverage you need or supplement existing coverage if necessary.

## Estimating Your Disability Insurance Needs

The main purpose of disability income insurance is to replace all (or most) of the income—that is, earnings—that would be lost if you became disabled and physically unable to hold a job. In essence, it should enable you to maintain a standard of living at or near your present level. To help decide how much disability income insurance is right for you, use Worksheet 9.2 to estimate your monthly disability benefit needs. Here is all you have to do.

1. **Calculate take-home pay.** Disability benefits are generally, but not always, tax-free, so you typically need to replace only your *take-home (after-tax) pay*. Benefits from employer-paid policies are fully or partially taxable. To estimate take-home pay, subtract income and Social Security taxes paid from your gross earned income (salary only). Divide this total by 12 to get your monthly take-home pay.

2. **Estimate the monthly amounts of disability benefits from government or employer programs.**
   a. *Social Security disability benefits.* Obtain an estimate of your benefits by calling 1-800-772-1213 for a *Personal Earnings and Benefit Estimate Statement.* An insurance agent may also have a computer program that can easily calculate it. The average Social Security disability benefit is about $1,793.00 per month for a wage earner with dependents.
   b. *Other government program disability benefits* for which you qualify (armed services, Veterans Administration, civil service, the Federal Employees Compensation Act, state workers' compensation systems). There are also special programs for railroad workers, longshoremen, and people with black-lung disease.
   c. *Company disability benefits.* Ask your company benefits supervisor to help you calculate company-provided benefits, including sick pay or wage continuation plans (these are essentially short-term disability income insurance) and plans formally designated as disability insurance. For each benefit your employer offers, check on its tax treatment.

## Worksheet 9.2 Estimating Disability Income Insurance Needs

Using a worksheet like this makes the job of estimating disability benefit insurance needs a lot easier.

### DISABILITY BENEFIT NEEDS

Name(s) _____ Date _____

1. Estimate current monthly *take-home* pay ..................................... $ _____
2. Estimate existing monthly benefits
   a. Social Security benefits ........................ $ _____
   b. Other government program benefits ........ _____
   c. Company disability benefits .................. _____
   d. Group disability policy benefits ............ _____
3. Total existing monthly disability benefits (2a + 2b + 2c + 2d) ....... $ _____
4. **Estimated monthly disability benefits needed ([1] – [3])** ............. $ _____

**d.** *Group disability policy benefits.* A private insurer provides the coverage, and you pay for it, often through payroll deduction.

3. **Add up your existing monthly disability benefits.**

4. **Subtract your existing monthly disability benefits from your current monthly take-home pay.** The result shows the estimated monthly disability benefits you'll need in order to maintain your present after-tax income. Note that investment income and spousal income (if the spouse is presently employed) are ignored because it's assumed this income will continue and is necessary to maintain your current standard of living. If your spouse is now unemployed but would enter the workforce if you ever became disabled, then his or her estimated monthly income (take-home pay) could be subtracted from item 4 of Worksheet 9.2 to determine your net monthly disability benefit needs.

## Disability Income Insurance Provisions and Costs

The scope and cost of your disability income coverage depend on its contractual provisions. Although disability income insurance policies can be complex, certain features are important: (1) definition of disability, (2) benefit amount and duration, (3) probationary period, (4) waiting period, (5) renewability, and (6) other provisions.

### Definition of Disability

Disability policies vary in the standards you must meet to receive

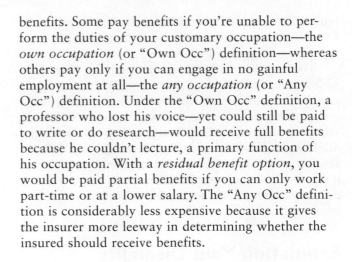

benefits. Some pay benefits if you're unable to perform the duties of your customary occupation—the *own occupation* (or "Own Occ") definition—whereas others pay only if you can engage in no gainful employment at all—the *any occupation* (or "Any Occ") definition. Under the "Own Occ" definition, a professor who lost his voice—yet could still be paid to write or do research—would receive full benefits because he couldn't lecture, a primary function of his occupation. With a *residual benefit option*, you would be paid partial benefits if you can only work part-time or at a lower salary. The "Any Occ" definition is considerably less expensive because it gives the insurer more leeway in determining whether the insured should receive benefits.

### Benefit Amount and Duration

Most individual disability income policies pay a flat monthly benefit, which is stated in the policy, whereas group plans pay a fixed percentage of gross income. In either case, insurers normally won't agree to amounts of more than 60% to 70% of the insured's gross income. Insurers won't issue policies for the full amount of gross income because this would give some people an incentive to fake a disability (for example, "bad back") and collect more in insurance benefits than they normally would receive as take-home pay.

Monthly benefits can be paid for a few months or a lifetime. If you're ensured a substantial pension, Social Security, or other benefits at retirement, then a policy that pays benefits until age 65 is adequate. Most people, however, will need to continue their occupations for many more years and should consider a policy offering lifetime benefits. Many policies offer benefits for periods as short as 2 or 5 years. Although these policies may be better than nothing, they don't protect against the major financial losses associated with long-term disabilities.

### Probationary Period

Both group and individual disability income policies are likely to include a probationary period, usually 7 to 30 days, which is a time delay from the date the policy is issued until benefit privileges are available. Any disability stemming from an illness, injury, or disease that occurs during the probationary period is *not* covered—even if it continues beyond this period. This feature keeps costs down.

### Waiting Period

The waiting, or elimination, period provisions in a disability income policy are similar to those discussed for long-term care insurance. Typical waiting periods range from 30 days to 1 year. If you have an adequate emergency fund to provide family income during the early months of disability, you can choose a longer waiting period and substantially reduce your premiums, as shown in Exhibit 9.4.

With most insurers, you can trade off an increase in the waiting period—say, from 30 days to 90 days—for an increase in the duration of benefits from 5 years to age 65. In fact, as Exhibit 9.5 shows, the premium charged by this insurer for a policy covering a 35-year-old male with a 30-day waiting period and 2-year benefit period ($698) is about the same as one charged for benefits payable to age 65 with a 6-month waiting period ($692). Accepting this type of trade-off usually makes sense because the primary purpose of insurance is to protect the insured against a catastrophic loss, not from smaller losses that are better handled through proper budgeting and saving.

### Renewability

Most individual disability income insurance is either *guaranteed renewable* or *noncancelable*. As with long-term care policies, guaranteed renewability ensures that you can renew the policy until you reach the age stated in the clause, usually age 65. Premiums can be raised over time if justified by the loss experience of all those in the same class (usually based on age, sex, and occupational category). Noncancelable policies offer guaranteed renewability, but they also guarantee that future premiums will remain the same as those stated in the policy at issuance. Because of this stable premium guarantee, noncancelable policies generally are more expensive than those with only a guaranteed renewability provision.

### Other Provisions

The purchasing power of income from a long-term disability policy that pays, say, $2,000 per month could be severely affected by inflation. In fact, a 3% inflation rate would reduce the purchasing power of this $2,000 benefit to less than $1,500 in 10 years. To counteract such a reduction, many insurers offer a *cost-of-living adjustment (COLA)*. With a COLA provision, the monthly benefit is adjusted upward each year, often in line with the CPI, although these annual adjustments are often capped at a given rate (say, 8%). Although some financial advisors suggest buying COLA riders, others feel the 10% to 25% additional premium is too much to pay given for it.

Although the COLA provision applies only once the insured is disabled, the *guaranteed insurability option (GIO)* can allow you to purchase additional disability income insurance in line with inflation increases while you're still healthy. Under the GIO, the price of this additional insurance is fixed at the contract's inception, and you don't have to prove insurability.

A *waiver of premium* is standard in disability income policies. If you're disabled for a minimum period, normally 60 or 90 days, then the insurer will waive any future premiums that come due while you remain disabled. In essence, the waiver of premium gives you additional disability income insurance in the amount of your regular premium payment.

*Remember that disability income insurance is just one part of your overall personal financial plan.* You'll need to find your own balance between cost and coverage.

## Exhibit 9.4    Representative Disability Income Insurance Premium Costs

The cost of disability income insurance varies with the terms of payment as well as the length of the waiting period. Because they have longer life expectancies, women pay substantially higher rates than men do. This table shows premiums for basic disability income coverage for a 35-year-old that pays $2,000 per month in benefits, with guaranteed premiums to age 65. Any additional features, such as inflation riders, cost more.

| Benefit Period | 2 Years | | 5 Years | | To Age 65 | | Lifetime | |
|---|---|---|---|---|---|---|---|---|
| Waiting Period | Male | Female | Male | Female | Male | Female | Male | Female |
| 30 days | $698 | $1,192 | $922 | $1,601 | $1,284 | $2,327 | $1,402 | $2,508 |
| 60 days | 539 | 983 | 715 | 1,145 | 986 | 1,674 | 1,086 | 1,821 |
| 90 days | 427 | 587 | 559 | 809 | 746 | 1,163 | 829 | 1,281 |
| 6 months | 386 | 514 | 514 | 728 | 692 | 1,067 | 774 | 1,183 |
| One year | 358 | 464 | 475 | 660 | 638 | 972 | 718 | 1,086 |

# FINANCIAL PLANNING EXERCISES

LG2, 3, 4

1. Michael Cheung was seriously injured in a snowboarding accident that broke both his legs and an arm. His medical expenses included five days of hospitalization at $900 a day, $6,200 in surgical fees, $4,300 in physician's fees (including time in the hospital and eight follow-up office visits), $520 in prescription medications, and $2,100 for physical therapy treatments. All of these charges fall within customary and reasonable payment amounts.
   a. If Michael had an indemnity plan that pays 80% of his charges with a $500 deductible and a $5,000 stop-loss provision, how much would he have to pay out-of-pocket?
   b. What would Michael's out-of-pocket expenses be if he belonged to an HMO with a $20 co-pay for office visits?
   c. Monthly premiums are $155 for the indemnity plan and $250 for the HMO. If he had no other medical expenses this year, which plan would have provided more cost-effective coverage for Michael? What other factors should be considered when deciding between the two plans?

LG2, 3, 4

2. *Use Worksheet 9.1.* Jessica Waverly, a recent college graduate, has decided to accept a job offer from a nonprofit organization. She'll earn $34,000 a year but will receive no employee health benefits. Jessica estimates that her monthly living expenses will be about $2,000 a month, including rent, food, transportation, and clothing. She has no health problems and expects to remain in good health in the near future. Using the Internet or other resources, gather information about three health insurance policies that Jessica could purchase on her own. Include at least one HMO. Use Worksheet 9.1 to compare the policies' features. Should Jessica buy health insurance? Why or why not? Assuming that she does decide to purchase health insurance, which of the three policies would you recommend and why?

LG6

3. *Use Worksheet 9.2.* Robert Terhune, a 35-year-old computer programmer, earns $72,000 a year. His monthly take-home pay is $3,750. His wife, Gwen, works part-time at their children's elementary school but receives no benefits. Under state law, Robert's employer contributes to a workers' compensation insurance fund that would provide $2,250 per month for 6 months if Robert were disabled and unable to work.
   a. Use Worksheet 9.2 to calculate Robert's disability insurance needs assuming that he won't qualify for Medicare under his Social Security benefits.
   b. Based on your answer in part **a**, what would you advise Robert about his need for additional disability income insurance? Discuss the type and size of disability income insurance coverage he should consider, including possible provisions he might want to include. What other factors should he take into account if he decides to purchase a policy?

LG5

4. Discuss the pros and cons of long-term care insurance. Does it make sense for anyone in your family right now? Why or why not? What factors might change this assessment in the future?

LG6

5. *Use Worksheet 9.2.* Do you need disability income insurance? Calculate your need using Worksheet 9.2. Discuss how you'd go about purchasing this coverage.

# 10 PROTECTING YOUR PROPERTY

## LEARNING GOALS

**LG1** Discuss the importance and basic principles of property insurance, including types of exposure, indemnity, and co-insurance. (p. 214)

**LG2** Identify the types of coverage provided by homeowner's insurance. (p. 217)

**LG3** Select the right homeowner's insurance policy for your needs. (p. 217)

**LG4** Analyze the coverage in a personal automobile policy (PAP) and choose the most cost-effective policy. (p. 223)

**LG5** Describe other types of property and liability insurance. (p. 229)

**LG6** Choose a property and liability insurance agent and company, and settle claims. (p. 230)

## LG1 Basic Principles of Property Insurance

Suppose that a severe storm destroyed your home. Could you afford to replace it? Most people couldn't. To protect yourself from this and other similar types of property loss, you need property insurance. What's more, every day you face some type of risk of negligence. For example, you might be distraught over a personal problem and unintentionally run a red light, seriously injuring a pedestrian. Could you pay for the medical and other costs? Because consequences like this and other potentially negligent acts could cause financial ruin, having appropriate liability insurance is essential.

Property and liability insurance should be as much a part of your personal financial plans as life and health insurance. Such coverage protects the assets you've already acquired and safeguards your progress toward financial goals. **Property insurance** guards against catastrophic losses of real and personal property caused by such perils as fire, theft, vandalism, windstorms, and other calamities. **Liability insurance** offers protection against the financial consequences that may arise from the insured's responsibility for property loss or personal injuries to others.

### Exposure to Property Loss

Most property insurance contracts define the property covered and name the **perils**—the causes of loss—for which the insured will be compensated in case of a claim against their policy. As a rule, most property insurance contracts impose two obligations on the property owner: (1) developing a complete inventory of the property being insured and (2) identifying the perils against which protection is desired. Some property contracts limit coverage by excluding certain types of property and perils, while others offer more comprehensive protection.

**PROPERTY INVENTORY.** Inventorying property is part of the financial planning process. It is especially important in the case of a total loss— if your home is burned by fire, for example. Because all property insurance companies require you to show *proof of loss* when making a claim, your personal property inventory, along with corresponding values, can provide this information. A comprehensive property inventory not only helps you settle a claim when a loss occurs but also serves as a useful guide for selecting the most appropriate coverage for your particular needs.

Most families have a home, household furnishings, clothing and personal belongings, lawn and garden equipment, and motor vehicles, all of which need to be insured. Fortunately, most homeowner's and automobile insurance policies provide coverage for these types of belongings. But many families also own such items as motorboats and trailers, various types of off-road vehicles, business property and inventories, jewelry, stamp or coin collections, furs, musical instruments, antiques, paintings, bonds, securities, and

> **Property and liability insurance should be as much a part of your personal financial plans as life and health insurance.**

Inefficient or inadequate insurance protection is at odds with the objectives of personal financial planning. It is consequently important to become familiar with the principles of property and liability insurance. Here we begin with a discussion of the basic principles of property and liability insurance.

### Types of Exposure

Most individuals face two basic types of exposure: physical loss of property and loss through liability.

other items of special value, such as cameras, golf clubs, electronic equipment, and personal computers. Coverage for these belongings (and those that accompany you when you travel) often require special types of insurance.

Many insurance companies have easy-to-complete personal property inventory forms available to help policyholders prepare inventories. A partial sample of one such form is shown in Exhibit 10.1. These inventory forms can be supplemented with photographs or videos

**Exhibit 10.1   A Personal Property Inventory Form**

Using a form like this will help you keep track of your personal property, including date of purchase, original purchase price, and replacement cost.

*Living Room*

**Stereo System**

| Brand | |
| Model | |
| Serial # | Date purchased |
| Purchase price $ | Replacement cost $ |

**Large Screen TV**

| Brand | |
| Model | |
| Serial # | Date purchased |
| Purchase price $ | Replacement cost $ |

**Compact Disc Player**

| Brand | |
| Model | |
| Serial # | Date purchased |
| Purchase price $ | Replacement cost $ |

**Home Theater System**

| Brand | |
| Model | |
| Serial # | Date purchased |
| Purchase price $ | Replacement cost $ |

**DVD Player**

| Brand | |
| Model | |
| Serial # | Date purchased |
| Purchase price $ | Replacement cost $ |

*Living Room*

| Article | Qty. | Date Purchased | Purchase Price | Replacement Cost |
|---|---|---|---|---|
| Air conditioners (window) | | | | |
| Blinds/shades | | | | |
| Bookcases | | | | |
| Books | | | | |
| Cabinets | | | | |
| Carpets/rugs | | | | |
| Chairs | | | | |
| Chests | | | | |
| Clocks | | | | |
| Couches/sofas | | | | |
| Curtains/draperies | | | | |
| Fireplace fixtures | | | | |
| Lamps/lighting fixtures | | | | |
| Mirrors | | | | |
| Pictures/paintings | | | | |
| CDs | | | | |
| Planters | | | | |
| Stereo equipment | | | | |
| Tables | | | | |
| Television sets | | | | |
| Other | | | | |
| Other | | | | |
| | | | | |
| | | | | |
| | | | | |

of household contents and belongings. *Every effort should be made to keep these documents in a safe place,* where they can't be destroyed—such as a bank safe-deposit box. You might also consider keeping a *duplicate copy* with a parent or trusted relative. Remember, you may need inventories and photographs to authenticate any property losses that may occur.

**IDENTIFYING PERILS.** Many people feel a false sense of security after buying insurance because they believe they're safeguarded against all contingencies. The fact is, however, that certain *perils* cannot be reasonably

insured. For example, most homeowner's or automobile insurance policies limit or exclude damage or loss caused by flood (remember Hurricane Katrina in New Orleans in 2005), earthquake, mudslides, mysterious disappearance, war, nuclear radiation, and ordinary wear and tear. In addition, property insurance contracts routinely limit coverage based on the location of the property, time of loss, persons involved, and types of hazards to which the property is exposed.

## Liability Exposures

We all encounter a variety of liability exposures daily. Driving a car, entertaining guests at home, or being

**negligence** Failing to act in a reasonable manner or to take necessary steps to protect others from harm.

**principle of indemnity** An insurance principle stating that an insured may not be compensated by the insurance company in an amount exceeding the insured's economic loss.

**actual cash value** A value assigned to an insured property that is determined by subtracting the amount of physical depreciation from its replacement cost.

**right of subrogation** The right of an insurer, who has paid an insured's claim, to request reimbursement from either the person who caused the loss or that person's insurer.

careless in performing professional duties are some common liability risks. Loss exposures result from **negligence**, which is failing to act in a reasonable manner or take necessary steps to protect others from harm. Even if you're never negligent and always prudent, someone might *believe* you are the cause of a loss and bring a costly lawsuit against you. Losing the judgment could cost you thousands—or even millions—of dollars, and possibly result in bankruptcy or financial ruin.

Fortunately, *liability insurance* protects you against losses resulting from these risks, *including the high legal fees* required to defend yourself against lawsuits. It's important to obtain adequate liability insurance through your homeowner's and automobile policies or through a separate umbrella policy.

© CHRISTINA RICHARDS/SHUTTERSTOCK

## Principle of Indemnity

The **principle of indemnity** states that the insured may not be compensated by the insurance company in an amount exceeding the insured's economic loss. Most property and liability insurance contracts are based on this principle—although, as noted in Chapters 8 and 9, this *principle does not apply to life and health insurance*. Several important concepts relate to the principle of indemnity.

### Actual Cash Value versus Replacement Cost

The principle of indemnity limits the amount an insured may collect to the **actual cash value** of the property: the replacement cost less the value of physical depreciation. Some insurers guarantee replacement cost without taking depreciation into account—for example, most homeowner's policies cover building losses on a replacement cost basis, if the proper type and amount of insurance is purchased. If an insured property is damaged and there is no replacement cost provision, then the insurer is obligated to pay no more than the property would cost new today (its replacement cost) less the amount of depreciation from wear and tear.

For example, assume that fire destroys two rooms of furniture that were 6 years old and had an estimated useful life of 10 years. The replacement cost is $5,000. Therefore, at the time of loss, the furniture was subject to an assumed physical depreciation of 60% (6 years ÷ 10 years)—in this case, $3,000. Because the actual cash value is estimated at $2,000 ($5,000 replacement cost minus $3,000 of depreciation), the maximum the insurer would have to pay is $2,000. Note that the original cost of the property has no bearing on the settlement.

### Subrogation

After an insurance company pays a claim, its **right of subrogation** allows it to request reimbursement from either the person who caused the loss or that person's insurance company. For example, if you're in an automobile accident in which the other party damages your car, you may collect the amount of the loss from your insurer or the at-fault party's insurer, but not from both. Clearly, collecting the full amount of the loss from both parties would violate the principle of indemnity by leaving you better off after the loss than before it. So if your insurer pays you and the other party is at fault, your insurance company can go after the responsible party to recover the amount it paid out to you.

### Other Insurance

Nearly all property and liability insurance contracts have an *other-insurance clause*, which normally states that if a person has more than one insurance policy on a property, each company is liable for only a pro-rated amount of the loss based on its proportion of the total insurance covering the property. Without this provision, insured persons could use duplicate property insurance policies to collect from multiple companies and actually profit from their losses.

## Co-insurance

**Co-insurance,** a provision commonly found in property insurance contracts, requires policyholders to buy insurance in an amount equal to a specified percentage of the replacement value of their property. The provision stipulates that if a property isn't properly covered, the property owner will become the "coinsurer" and bear part of the loss. If the policyholder has the stipulated amount of coverage (usually 80% of the value of the property), then the insurance company will reimburse for covered losses, dollar-for-dollar, up to the amount of the policy limits. Assume, for example, that Dave and Beth have a fire insurance policy on their $200,000 home with an 80% co-insurance clause. Further, assume that they ran short of money and decided to save by buying a $120,000 policy instead of $160,000 (80% of $200,000) as required by the co-insurance clause. If a loss occurred, then the company would be obligated to pay only 75% ($120,000/$160,000) of the loss, up to the amount of the policy limit. Thus, on damages of $40,000, the insurer would pay only $30,000 (75% of $40,000). Clearly, it is important to meet the requirements of the co-insurance clauses of your property insurance policies.

### Go to Smart Sites

For assistance on evaluating your insurance needs, go to the Insurance 101 Web site. Under Insurance Learning Center, click on Home or Auto Insurance for quotes and other useful information. Whenever you see "*Go to Smart Sites*" in this chapter, visit **4ltrpress.cengage.com.** ●

## LG2, LG3 Homeowner's Insurance

Homeowners can choose from four different forms (HO-1, HO-2, HO-3, and HO-8). Two other forms (HO-4 and HO-6) meet the needs of renters and owners of condominiums (see Exhibit 10.2). An HO-4 renter's policy offers essentially the same broad protection as an HO-2 homeowner's policy, but the coverage doesn't apply to the rented dwelling unit because the tenant usually doesn't own it.

All HO forms are divided into two sections. Section I applies to the dwelling, accompanying structures, and personal property of the insured. Section II deals with comprehensive coverage for personal liability and for medical payments to others. The scope of coverage under Section I is least with an HO-1 policy and greatest

with an HO-3 policy. HO-8 is a modified coverage policy for older homes, which is used to insure houses that have market values well below their cost to rebuild. The coverage in Section II is the same for all forms.

In the following paragraphs, we'll explain the important features of homeowner's forms HO-2 and HO-3, the most common policies. (As Exhibit 10.2 shows, HO-1 is a basic, seldom-used policy with relatively narrow coverage.) The key difference in coverage under the HO-2 and HO-3 forms is the number of perils against which protection applies.

## Perils Covered

Some property and liability insurance agreements, called **comprehensive policies,** cover all perils except those specifically excluded, whereas **named peril policies** name individual perils covered.

### Section I Perils

The perils against which the home and its contents are insured are shown in Exhibit 10.2. Coverage on household belongings is the same for the HO-2 and HO-3

**co-insurance** In property insurance, a provision requiring a policyholder to buy insurance in an amount equal to a specified percentage of the replacement value of their property.

**comprehensive policy** Property and liability insurance policy covering all perils unless they are specifically excluded.

**named peril policy** Property and liability insurance policy that individually names the perils covered.

**Exhibit 10.2    A Guide to Homeowner's Policies**

The amount of insurance coverage you receive depends on the type of homeowner's (HO) policy you buy. You can also obtain coverage if you're a renter or a condominium owner.

| Form | Coverages* | Covered perils |
|---|---|---|
| **Basic Form** (HO-1) | A—$15,000 minimum; B—10% of A; C—50% of A; D—10% of A; E—$100,000; F—$1,000 per person | Fire, smoke, lightning, windstorm, hail, volcanic eruption, explosion, glass breakage, aircraft, vehicles, riot or civil commotion, theft, vandalism or malicious mischief |
| **Broad Form** (HO-2) | Minimum varies; other coverages in same percentages or amounts except D—20% of A | Covers all basic-form risks plus weight of ice, snow, sleet; freezing; accidental discharge of water or steam; falling objects; accidental tearing, cracking, or burning of heating/ cooling/sprinkler system or appliance; damage from electrical current |
| **Special Form** (HO-3) | Minimum varies; other coverages in same percentages or amounts except D—20% of A | Dwelling and other structures covered against risks of direct physical loss to property except losses specifically excluded; personal property covered by same perils as HO-2 plus damage by glass or safety glazing material, which is part of a building, storm door, or storm window |
| **Renter's Form** (HO-4) | Coverages A and B—Not applicable C—Minimum varies by company D—20% of C E—$100,000 F—$1,000 per person | Covers same perils covered by HO-2 for personal property |
| **Condominium Form** (HO-6) | Coverage A—Minimum $1,000 B—Not applicable C—Minimum varies by company D—40% of C E—$100,000 F—$1,000 per person | Covers same perils covered by HO-2 for personal property |
| **Modified Coverage Form** (HO-8) | Same as HO-1, except losses are paid based on the amount required to repair or replace the property using common construction materials and methods | Same perils as HO-1, except theft coverage applies only to losses on the residence premises up to a maximum of $1,000; certain other coverage restrictions also apply |

\* Coverages:
A. Dwelling                    D. Loss of use
B. Other structures            E. Personal liability
C. Personal property           F. Medical payments to others

forms, but coverage on the house itself and other structures (for example, a detached garage) is comprehensive under HO-3 and a named peril in HO-2. Whether homeowners should buy an HO-2 or an HO-3 form depends primarily on how much they're willing to spend to secure the additional protection. The size of premiums for HO-2 and HO-3 policies can differ substantially among insurance companies and states. Buying an HO-1 is not recommended because of its more limited coverage.

Note in Exhibit 10.2 that the types of Section I perils covered include just about everything from fire and explosions to lightning and wind damage to theft and vandalism. Some perils are specifically excluded from most homeowner's contracts—in particular, *most policies (even HO-2 and HO-3 forms) exclude earthquakes and floods,* even if you live in an area where the risk of an earthquake or a flood is relatively high and the catastrophic nature of such events causes widespread and costly damage. Of course, you can obtain coverage for earthquakes and floods under a separate policy or a rider.

### Section II Perils

The coverage under Section II of the homeowner's contract is called *comprehensive personal liability coverage* because it offers protection against nearly any source of liability (major exclusions are noted later) resulting from *negligence.* It does not insure against other losses for which one may become liable, such as libel, slander, defamation of character, and contractual or intentional wrongdoing. For example, coverage would apply if you carelessly, but unintentionally, knocked someone down your stairs. If you purposely struck and injured another person, however, or harmed someone's reputation either orally or in writing, homeowner's liability coverage would not protect you.

Section II also provides a limited amount of medical coverage, irrespective of negligence or fault, for persons other than the homeowner's family in certain types of minor accidents on or off the insured's premises. This coverage helps homeowners to meet their moral obligations and helps deter possible lawsuits.

## Factors Affecting Home Insurance Costs

Several influences have an impact on premiums for home and property insurance.

- **Type of structure.** The construction materials used, the style, or age of your home affect the cost of insuring it. For example, a home built from brick costs less to insure than a similar home of wood, yet the reverse is true when it comes to earthquake insurance—brick homes are more expensive to insure.

- **Location of home.** Local crime rates, weather, and proximity to a fire hydrant all affect your home's insurance premium costs. If many claims are filed from your area, insurance premiums for all the homeowners there will be higher.

- **Other factors.** If you have a swimming pool, trampoline, large dog, or other potentially hazardous risk factors on your property, your homeowner's premiums will be higher. Deductibles and the type and amount of coverage also affect the cost.

## Property Covered

The homeowner's policy offers property protection under Section I for the dwelling unit, accompanying structures, and personal property of homeowners and their families. Coverage for certain types of loss also applies to lawns, trees, plants, and shrubs. However, the policy excludes structures on the premises used for business purposes (except incidentally), animals (pets or otherwise), and motorized vehicles not used in maintaining the premises (such as autos, motorcycles, golf carts, or snowmobiles). *Business inventory* (for example, goods held by an insured who is a traveling salesperson, or other goods held for sale) is not covered. Although the policy doesn't cover business inventory, it does cover *business property* (such as books, computers, copiers, office furniture, and supplies), typically up to a maximum of $2,500, while it is on the insured premises.

**personal property floater (PPF)**
An insurance endorsement or policy providing either blanket or scheduled coverage of expensive personal property not adequately covered in a standard homeowner's policy.

## Personal Property Floater

Because your homeowner's policy may not adequately protect your expensive personal property, you can either add the **personal property floater (PPF)** as an endorsement to your homeowner's policy or take out a separate floater policy. *The PPF provides either blanket or scheduled coverage of items not adequately covered in a standard homeowner's policy.* A *blanket,* or *unscheduled,* PPF provides the maximum protection available for virtually all the insured's personal property. *Scheduled PPFs* list the items to be covered and provide supplemental coverage under a homeowner's contract. This coverage is especially useful for expensive property, such as furs, jewelery, fine art, and collections, that is valued at more than coverage C limits (discussed later), and it includes loss, damage, and theft. For example, you should itemize a diamond ring valued at $7,500 because it's worth more than the standard $1,000 coverage C allowance for jewelry theft.

## Renter's Insurance: Don't Move In without It

If you live in an apartment (or some other type of rental unit), be aware that although the building you live in is likely to be fully insured, *your furnishings and other personal belongings are not.* As a renter

> *If you live in an apartment (or some other type of rental unit), be aware that although the building you live in is likely to be fully insured, your furnishings and other personal belongings are not.*

(or even the owner of a condominium unit), you need a special type of HO policy to obtain insurance coverage on your personal possessions.

Consider, for example, Leslie Brigham's predicament. She never got around to insuring her personal possessions in the apartment she rented in Chicago. One wintry night, a water pipe ruptured and the escaping water damaged her furniture, rugs, and other belongings. When the building owner refused to pay for the loss, Leslie hauled him into court—and lost. Why did she lose her case? Simple: *Unless a landlord can be proven negligent—and this one wasn't—he or she isn't responsible for a tenant's property.* The moral of this story is clear: once you've accumulated valuable personal belongings (from clothing and home furnishings to stereo equipment, TVs, computers, and DVD players), make sure they're adequately covered by insurance, even if you're only renting a place to live! Otherwise, you could risk losing everything you own.

Renter's insurance, Form HO-4, is a scaled-down version of homeowner's insurance that is available at reasonable rates. It covers the contents of a house, apartment, or cooperative unit but not the structure itself, against the same perils as Form HO-2. Owners of condominium units need Form HO-6; it's similar but includes a minimum of $1,000 in protection for any building alterations, additions, and decorations paid for by the policyholder. HO-4 and HO-6 policies include liability coverage and protect you at home and away. For example, if somebody is injured and sues you, the policy would pay for damages up to a specified limit, generally $100,000, although some insurers go as high as $500,000.

A standard renter's insurance policy covers furniture, carpets, appliances, clothing, and most other personal items for their cash value at the time of loss. Expect to pay around $200 to $250 a year for about $15,000 in coverage, depending on where you live. For maximum protection, you can pay about 10% more and buy *replacement-cost insurance*, which pays the actual cost of replacing articles with comparable ones. The standard renter's policy provides limited coverage of such valuables as jewelry, furs, and silverware, although some insurers pay up to $1,000 for the loss of watches, gems, and furs and up to $2,500 for silverware.

## Coverage: What Type, Who, and Where?

Homeowner's policies define the types of losses they cover and the persons and locations covered.

### Types of Losses Covered

There are three types of property-related losses when misfortune occurs:

1. Direct loss of property
2. Indirect loss occurring due to loss of damaged property
3. Additional expenses resulting from direct and indirect losses

Homeowner's insurance contracts offer compensation for each type of loss.

**SECTION I COVERAGE.** When a house is damaged by an insured peril, the insurance company will pay reasonable living expenses, such as the cost of renting alternative accommodations while the insured's home is being repaired or rebuilt. The insurer will also pay for damages caused by perils other than those mentioned in the policy if a named peril is determined to be the underlying cause of the loss. For example, if lightning (a covered peril) strikes a house while a family is away and knocks out power, causing $400 worth of food in the freezer and refrigerator to spoil, the loss will be paid even though temperature change (the direct cause) is not mentioned in the policy.

**SECTION II COVERAGE.** In addition to paying successfully pursued liability claims against an insured, a homeowner's policy covers (1) the cost of defending the insured, (2) reasonable expenses incurred by an insured in helping the insurance company's defense, and (3) the payment of court costs. This coverage applies even when the liability suit is found to be without merit.

## Persons Covered

A homeowner's policy covers the persons named in the policy and members of their families who are residents of the household. A person, such as a college student, can be a resident of the household even while temporarily living away from home. The college student's parents' homeowner's policy may cover their belongings at school—including such items as stereo equipment, TVs, personal computers, and microwave ovens, but there could be limits and exceptions to the coverage. The standard homeowner's contract also extends limited coverage to guests of the insured.

## Locations Covered

Most homeowner's policies offer coverage worldwide. For example, an insured's personal property is fully covered when lent to the next-door neighbor or kept in a hotel room in Outer Mongolia. The only exception is property left at a second home where coverage is reduced unless the loss occurs while the insured is residing there.

Homeowners and their families have liability protection for their negligent acts wherever they occur. Excluded are negligent acts involving certain types of motorized vehicles (such as large boats and aircraft) and those occurring in the course of employment or professional practice.

**replacement cost** The amount necessary to repair, rebuild, or replace an asset at today's prices.

## Limitations on Payment

Other factors that influence the amount an insurance company will pay for a loss include replacement-cost provisions, policy limits, and deductibles.

### Replacement Cost

The amount necessary to repair, rebuild, or replace an asset at today's prices is the **replacement cost**. When replacement-cost coverage is in effect, a homeowner's reimbursement for damage to a house or accompanying structures is based on the cost of repairing or replacing those structures, without taking any deductions for depreciation. Exhibit 10.3 illustrates a replacement-cost calculation for a 2,400-square-foot home with a two-car garage.

However, for homeowners to be eligible for reimbursement on a full replacement-cost basis, they must keep their homes insured for at least 80% of the amount it would cost to build them today, not including the value of the land. Because inflation could cause coverage to fall below the 80% requirement, at a small cost, homeowners can purchase an inflation protection rider that automatically adjusts the amount of coverage based on prevailing inflation rates. Without the rider, maximum compensation for losses would thus be based on a specified percentage of loss.

Even if a home is in an excellent state of repair, its market value may be lessened by functional obsolescence within the structure—for example, when a

### Exhibit 10.3   Calculating Replacement Cost

Here's a typical example of how an insurance company calculates replacement cost. It would take $256,000 to fully replace this home today.

| | |
|---|---|
| Dwelling cost: 2,400 sq. ft. at $85 per sq. ft. | $204,000 |
| Extra features: built-in appliances, mahogany cabinets, 3 ceiling fans | 10,600 |
| Porches, patios: screened and trellised patio | 3,700 |
| Two-car garage: 900 sq. ft. at $35 per sq. ft. | 31,500 |
| Other site improvements: driveway, storage, landscaping | 6,200 |
| Total replacement cost | $256,000 |

house that doesn't have enough electrical power to run a dishwasher, microwave, and hair dryer at the same time. The HO-8 homeowner's form (for older homes) was adopted in partial response to this problem. A 2,200-square-foot home in an older neighborhood might have a market value (excluding land) of $95,000, yet the replacement cost might be $160,000. The HO-8 policy solves this problem by covering property in full, up to the amount of the loss or up to the property's market value, whichever is less.

### Policy Limits

In Section I of the homeowner's policy, the amount of coverage on the dwelling unit (coverage A) establishes the amounts applicable to the accompanying structures (coverage B), the unscheduled personal property (coverage C), and the temporary living expenses (coverage D). Generally, the limits under coverage B, C, and D are 10%, 50%, and 10%–20%, respectively, of the amount of coverage under A.

For example, if a house is insured for $150,000, then the respective limits for coverage B, C, and D would be $15,000, $75,000, and $30,000 (that is, 10% of $150,000, 50% of $150,000, and 20% of $150,000). Each of these limits can be increased if it's considered insufficient to cover the exposure. Also, for a small reduction in premium, some companies will permit a homeowner to reduce coverage on unscheduled personal property to 40% of the amount on the dwelling unit.

Remember that homeowner's policies usually specify limits for certain types of personal property included under the coverage C category. These coverage limits are *within the total dollar amount* of coverage C and in no way act to increase that total. For example, the dollar limit for losses of money, bank notes, bullion, and related items is $200; securities, accounts, deeds, evidences of debt, manuscripts, passports, tickets, and stamps have a $1,000 limit. Loss from jewelry theft is limited to $1,000, and payment for theft of silverware, goldware, and pewterware has a $2,500 limit. Some policies also offer $5,000 coverage for home computer equipment. You can increase these limits by increasing coverage C.

In Section II, the personal liability coverage (coverage E) often tops out at $100,000, and the medical payments portion (coverage F) normally has a limit of $1,000 per person. Additional coverage included in Section II consists of claim expenses, such as court costs and attorney fees; first aid and medical expenses, including ambulance costs; and damage to others' property of up to $500 per occurrence.

Although these are the most common limits, most homeowners need additional protection, especially liability coverage. In these days of high damage awards by juries, a $100,000 liability limit may not be adequate. The cost to increase the liability limit with most companies is small. For example, the annual premium difference between a $100,000 personal liability limit and a $300,000 limit is likely to be only $50 to $100. You can also increase personal liability coverage by purchasing a personal liability umbrella policy.

### Deductibles

Each of the preceding limits on recovery constrains the maximum amount an insurance company must pay under the policy. *Deductibles*, which limit what a company must pay for small losses, help reduce insurance premiums by doing away with the frequent small loss claims that are proportionately more expensive to administer. The standard deductible in most states is $250 on the physical damage protection covered in Section I. However, choosing higher deductible amounts of $500 or $1,000 results in considerable premium savings—as much as 10% in some states. Deductibles don't apply to liability and medical payments coverage because insurers want to be notified of all claims in order to properly investigate and prepare adequate defenses for resulting lawsuits.

## Homeowner's Premiums

As you might expect, the size of insurance premiums vary widely depending on the insurance provider (company) and the location of the property (neighborhood/city/state). It pays to shop around! When you're shopping, be sure to clearly state the type of insurance you're looking for and to obtain and compare the cost, net of any discounts, offered by a number of agents or insurance companies. Remember, each type of property damage coverage is subject to a deductible of $250 or more.

Most people need to modify the basic package of coverage by adding an inflation rider and increasing the coverage on their homes to 100% of the replacement cost. Changing the contents protection from actual cash value to replacement cost and scheduling some items of expensive personal property may be desirable. Most insurance professionals also advise homeowners to increase their liability and medical payments limits. Each of these changes results in an additional premium charge.

And to reduce your total premium, you can increase the amount of your deductibles. Because it's better to budget for small losses than to insure against them, larger deductibles are a popular strategy. You may also qualify for discounts for deadbolt locks, monitored security systems, and other safety features, such as smoke alarms and sprinkler systems. Indeed, as explained in this chapter's *Money in Action* feature, there are a number of steps you can take to keep your homeowner's insurance affordable.

## LG4 Automobile Insurance

Automobiles also involve risk because damage to them or negligence in their use can result in significant loss. Fortunately, insurance can protect individuals against a big part of these costs. Automobile insurance includes several types of coverage packaged together. Here we begin by describing the major features of a private passenger automobile policy. Then, we'll briefly explain no-fault laws, followed by discussions of auto insurance premiums and financial responsibility laws.

### Types of Auto Insurance Coverage

The **personal automobile policy (PAP)** is a comprehensive automobile insurance policy designed to be easily understood by the "typical" insurance purchaser. Made up of six parts, the policy's first four parts identify the coverage provided.

● Part A: Liability coverage
● Part B: Medical payments coverage
● Part C: Uninsured motorists coverage
● Part D: Coverage for damage to your vehicle

Part E pertains to your duties and responsibilities if you're involved in an accident, and Part F defines basic provisions of the policy, including the policy coverage period and the right of termination.

You're almost sure to purchase liability, medical payments, and uninsured motorists protection, but you may *not* buy protection against damage to your automobile if it's an older vehicle of relatively little value. On the other hand, if your vehicle is leased or you have a loan against it, then you'll probably be required to have a specified amount of physical damage coverage—part D.

© EVGENY MURTOLA/SHUTTERSTOCK

Exhibit 10.4 illustrates how the four basic parts of a PAP might be displayed in a typical automobile insurance policy, and shows the premium for a 6-month period. Here we will take a closer look at the coverage provided by parts A through D.

### Part A: Liability Coverage

Most states require you to buy at least a minimum amount of liability insurance. Under the typical PAP, the insurer agrees to:

1. Pay damages for bodily injury and/or property damage for which you are legally responsible as a result of an automobile accident
2. Settle or defend any claim or suit asking for such damages

The provision for legal defense is important and could save thousands of dollars, even if you're not at fault in an automobile accident. Note, the policy doesn't cover defense of criminal charges against the insured due to an accident (such as a drunk driver who's involved in an accident). Part A also provides for certain supplemental payments (not restricted by the applicable policy limits) for expenses incurred in settling the claim, reimbursement of premiums for appeal bonds, bonds to release attachments of the insured's property, and bail bonds required as a result of an accident.

**POLICY LIMITS.** Although the insurance company provides both bodily injury and property damage liability insurance under part A, it typically sets *a dollar limit up to which it will pay for damages from any one accident*. Typical limits are $50,000, $100,000, $300,000, and $500,000. You'd be well advised to consider no less than $300,000 coverage in today's legal liability environment. Damage awards are increasing, and the insurer's duty to defend you *ends when the coverage limit has been exhausted*. It's easy to "exhaust" $50,000 or $100,000, leaving you to pay any additional costs above the policy limit. So be sure to purchase adequate coverage—*regardless of the minimum requirements in your state*. Otherwise, you place your personal assets at risk. As Exhibit 10.4 shows, the Carter family obtained fairly high coverage limits.

Some insurers make so-called *split limits* of liability coverage available, with the first amount in each combination the per-individual limit and the second, the per-accident limit. Some policy limit combinations for protecting individuals against claims made for **bodily injury liability losses** are $25,000/$50,000, $50,000/$100,000, $100,000/$300,000, $250,000/$500,000, and $500,000/$1,000,000. Because the

**personal automobile policy (PAP)** A comprehensive automobile insurance policy designed to be easily understood by the "typical" insurance purchaser.

**bodily injury liability losses** A PAP provision that protects the insured against claims made for bodily injury.

**Exhibit 10.4  The Four Parts of a Personal Automobile Policy (PAP)**

This automobile insurance statement for 6 months of coverage shows how the four major parts of a PAP might be incorporated. Notice that the premium for collision/comprehensive damage is relatively low because of the age and type of car (a 2005 Ford Taurus); these drivers also enjoyed a premium reduction of more than $130 for the 6 months due to having other insurance with the same provider, a car alarm system, and a good driving record.

**ANYSTATE INSURANCE COMPANIES**                                     **AUTO RENEWAL**

Anystate Automobile Insurance Company
1665 West Anywhere Drive
Yourtown, CO 80209                                                   2005 Ford Taurus

| POLICY NUMBER | PERIOD COVERED | DATE DUE | PLEASE PAY THIS AMOUNT |
|---|---|---|---|
| ABC-123-XYZ-456 | MAY 26 2010 to NOV 26 2010 | MAY 26 2010 | $392 |

1 H -1582    A

Carter, Michael S. & Beth R.
1643 Thunder Rd. #32
Yourtown, CO 80209

| Coverages and Limits | | | Premiums |
|---|---|---|---|
| Part A | A | Liability | |
| | | Bodily Injury 250,000/500,000 | $219 |
| | | Property Damage 100,000 | |
| Part B | M | Medical 5,000 | 14 |
| Part C | U | Uninsured Motor Vehicle | |
| | | Bodily Injury 100,000/300,000 | 27 |
| Part D | G | 500 Deductible Collision | 102 |
| | D-WG | 500 Deductible Comprehensive | 24 |
| | H | Emergency Road Service | 6 |
| **Amount Due** | | | **$392** |

Your premium has already been adjusted by the following:

**Premium Reductions**

| | |
|---|---|
| Multiple Line | 22 |
| Antitheft devices | 40 |
| Good driver | 70 |

*Your premium is based on the following ...*
*If not correct, contact your agent.*

2005 Ford Taurus SES Sedan
Serial number: 4 ABCD12M3NP456789

*Drivers of vehicle in your household ...*
There are no male or unmarried female
drivers under age 25.
Younger drivers included if rated on another
car insured with us.

*Ordinary use of vehicle ...*
To and from work or school, more than
100 miles weekly.
Driven more than 7,500 miles annually.
(National average is 10,000 miles
annually.)

*Source:* Adapted from a major automobile insurance company quote.

Carters purchased the $250,000/$500,000 policy limits, the maximum amount any one person negligently injured in an accident could receive from the insurance company would be $250,000. Further, the total amount the insurer would pay to all injured victims in one accident would not exceed $500,000. If a jury awarded a claimant $80,000, the defendant whose insurance policy limits were $50,000/$100,000 could be required to pay $30,000 out of his or her pocket ($80,000 award minus $50,000 paid by insurance). For the defendant, this could mean loss of home, cars, bank accounts, and other assets. In many states, if the value of these assets is too little to satisfy a claim, then defendant's wages may be garnished (taken by the court and used to satisfy the outstanding debt).

# MONEY IN ACTION

## Keeping Your Homeowner's Insurance Affordable

The first step to keeping homeowner's insurance premiums affordable is to shop around. Use the telephone and the Internet to contact major insurance companies and get an idea of price ranges. Also ask friends or colleagues about companies they have done business with and their reputations for good service. If a claim is filed, do they pay right away or do they stall? Do they have a local office and an agent with whom you can meet personally, or does the company operate from a distant city?

After choosing a company, you can further reduce your premiums by making certain decisions. If you have to choose between buying a new home or an older one, be aware that the older home may cost more to insure because of antiquated heating and plumbing systems. Newer homes are typically less susceptible to fire and other hazards, so they cost less to insure. The closer your home is to a fire station, the lower your premium will be. Frame and brick homes, because of their resistance to earthquake and wind damage (respectively), also reduce premiums. Avoiding areas that are prone to flooding—a peril that homeowner's insurance doesn't cover--saves several hundred dollars in flood insurance.

One way *not* to save money is to underinsure. It's imperative to get "guaranteed replacement-cost" coverage, not just actual cash value. Replacement cost will likely be higher than actual cash value because the cost to build is usually higher than the cost to buy. Don't scrimp on liability coverage either—it's important to be covered for damages if someone who's injured on your property sues you.

Consider the following specific ways to have the right coverage for reasonable premiums.

- *Maintain smoke and burglar alarms.* A burglar alarm can lower your homeowner's premiums by 5% or more and smoke alarms by 10% or more.

- *Increase your deductible.* Higher deductibles bring lower premiums. Although this means that you'll have to absorb the cost of smaller claims like broken windows or damage from leaky pipes, it's usually an economical decision.

- *Consolidate your insurance policies.* Many companies will give a discount of 10% or more if you have multiple policies with them. For example, keeping homeowner's, auto, and health insurance with the same insurance company could earn you a discount.

- *Review your policy annually and make comparisons.* Review your coverage and compare the cost of your coverage with that of other providers. Maybe your property has changed enough to warrant a premium reduction.

*Sources:* Adapted from Glenn Curtis, "Insurance Tips for Homeowners," http://www.investopedia.com/articles/pf/07/homeowners_insurance.asp, accessed July 2009; Insurance Information Institute, "12 Ways to Lower Your Homeowners Insurance Costs," http://www.pueblo.gsa.gov/cic_text/housing/12ways/12ways.htm, accessed July 2009.

---

The policy limits available to cover **property damage liability losses** are typically $10,000, $25,000, $50,000, and $100,000. In contrast to bodily injury liability limits, property damage limits are stated as a per-accident limit, without specifying limits applicable on a per-item or per-person basis.

**PERSONS INSURED.** Two basic definitions in the PAP determine who is covered under part A: insured person and covered auto. Essentially, an *insured person* includes you (the named insured) and any family member, any person using a covered auto, and any person or organization that may be held responsible for your actions. The *named insured* is the person named in the declarations page of the policy. The spouse of the person named is considered a named insured if he or she resides in the same household. Family members are persons related by blood, marriage, or adoption and residing in the same household. An unmarried college student living away from home usually is considered a family member. *Covered autos* are the vehicles shown in the declarations page of your PAP, autos acquired during the policy period, any trailer owned, and any auto or trailer used as a temporary substitute while your auto or trailer is being repaired or serviced. An automobile that you lease for an extended time can be included as a covered automobile.

The named insured and family members have part A liability coverage regardless of the automobile they are driving. However, for persons other than the named insured and family members to have liability coverage, they must be driving a covered auto.

> **property damage liability losses** A PAP provision that protects the insured against claims made for damage to property.

### Part B: Medical Payments Coverage

Medical payments coverage insures a covered individual for reasonable and necessary medical expenses incurred within 3 years of an automobile accident in an amount not to exceed the policy limits. It provides for reimbursement even if other sources of recovery, such as health or accident insurance, also make payments. What's more, in most states, the insurer reimburses the insured for medical payments even if the insured proves that another person was negligent in the accident and receives compensation from that party's liability insurer.

A person need not be occupying an automobile when the accidental injury occurs to be eligible for benefits. Injuries sustained as a pedestrian, or on a bicycle in a traffic accident, are also covered. (Motorcycle accidents are normally not covered.) Part B insurance also pays on an excess basis. For instance, if you're a passenger in a friend's automobile during an accident and suffer $8,000 in medical expenses, you can collect under his medical payments insurance up to his policy limits. Further, you can collect (up to the amount of your policy limits) from your insurer the amount exceeding what the other medical payments provide.

**POLICY LIMITS.** Medical payments insurance usually has per-person limits of $1,000, $2,000, $3,000, $5,000, or $10,000. Thus, an insurer could conceivably pay $60,000 or more in medical payments benefits for one accident involving a named insured and five passengers. Most families are advised to buy the $5,000 or $10,000 limit because even though they may have other health insurance available, they can't be sure their passengers are as well protected.

**PERSONS INSURED.** Coverage under an automobile medical payments insurance policy applies to the named insured and to family members who are injured while occupying an automobile (whether owned by the named insured or not) or when struck by an automobile or trailer of any type. Part B also applies to any other person occupying a covered automobile.

### Part C: Uninsured Motorists Coverage

**Uninsured motorists coverage** is available to meet the needs of "innocent" victims of accidents who are negligently injured by uninsured, underinsured, or hit-and-run motorists. Nearly all states require uninsured motorists insurance to be included in each liability insurance policy issued, but the coverage can be rejected in most of these states. Rejecting uninsured motorists coverage is not a good idea. Under uninsured motorists coverage, an insured is legally entitled to collect an amount equal to the sum that could have been collected from the negligent motorist's liability insurance, had such coverage been available, up to a maximum amount equal to the policy's stated *uninsured motorists limit*.

Three points must be proven to receive payment through uninsured motorists insurance: (1) another motorist must be at fault, (2) the motorist has no available insurance or is underinsured, and (3) damages were incurred. With uninsured motorists coverage, you can generally collect only for losses arising from bodily injury.

**POLICY LIMITS.** Because uninsured motorists insurance is fairly low in cost (usually around $50 to $75 per year), drivers should purchase at least its minimum available limits. The Carters purchased $100,000/$300,000 coverage for just $54 per year ($27 per 6 months).

**PERSONS INSURED.** Uninsured motorists protection covers the named insured, family members, and any other person occupying a covered auto.

**UNDERINSURED MOTORISTS COVERAGE.** In addition to *uninsured motorists*, in some states, for a small premium, you can obtain **underinsured motorists coverage**, which protects against damages caused by being in an accident with an underinsured motorist who is found liable. Underinsured motorists insurance has become increasingly popular and *can be purchased for both bodily injury and property damage*. If an at-fault driver causes more damage to you than the limit of her liability, your insurance company makes up the difference (up to the limits of your coverage) and then goes after the negligent driver for the deficiency. Clearly, if available in your state, you should consider purchasing this optional coverage.

### Part D: Coverage for Physical Damage to a Vehicle

This part of the PAP provides coverage for damage to your auto. The two basic types of coverage are collision and comprehensive (or "other than collision").

© SYLUMAGRAPHICA/SHUTTERSTOCK

**COLLISION INSURANCE. Collision insurance** is automobile insurance that pays for collision damage to an insured automobile *regardless of who is at fault*. The amount of insurance payable is the actual cash value of the loss in excess of your deductible. Remember that *actual cash value is defined as replacement cost less depreciation*. So, if a car is demolished, the insured is paid an amount equal to the car's depreciated value minus any deductible. Deductibles typically range between $50 and $1,000, and selecting a higher deductible, as did the Carters, will reduce your premium.

Lenders and lessors typically require collision insurance on cars they finance. In some cases, especially when the auto dealer is handling the financing, it will try to sell you this insurance. *Avoid buying automobile insurance from car dealers or finance companies*. It is best to buy such insurance from your regular insurance agent and include collision insurance as part of your full auto insurance policy (PAP). A full-time insurance agent is better able to assess and meet your insurance needs. The collision provision of your insurance policy often fully protects you, in a rental car, so be sure to check before purchasing supplemental collision insurance when renting a car.

 **Go to Smart Sites**

It's important to know what to do if you have a car accident. Smart Sites directs you to your legal rights and responsibilities in the event of an accident. ●

**COMPREHENSIVE AUTOMOBILE INSURANCE.**
**Comprehensive automobile insurance** protects against loss to an insured automobile caused by any peril (with a few exceptions) *other than collision*. The maximum compensation provided under this coverage is the actual cash value of the automobile. Coverage includes, but is not limited to, damage caused by fire, theft, glass breakage, falling objects, malicious mischief, vandalism, riot, and earthquake. The automobile insurance policy normally does *not* cover theft of personal property left in the insured vehicle, but rather it may be covered by the off-premises coverage of the homeowner's policy if the auto was locked when the theft occurred.

## No-Fault Automobile Insurance

**No-fault automobile insurance** is a system under which each insured party is compensated by his or her own company, regardless of which party caused the accident. In return, legal remedies and payments for pain and suffering are restricted. Under the concept of *pure*

no-fault insurance, the driver, passengers, and injured pedestrians are reimbursed by the insurer of the car for economic losses stemming from bodily injury. The insurer doesn't have to cover claims for losses to other motorists who are covered by their own policies.

Unfortunately, advocates of no-fault forget that the sole purpose of liability insurance is to protect the assets of the insured—not to pay losses, *per se*. State laws governing no-fault insurance vary widely, but most states provide from $2,000 to $10,000 in personal injury protection and restrict legal recovery for pain and suffering to cases where medical or economic losses exceed some threshold level, such as $500 or $1,000. In all states, recovery based on negligence is permitted for economic loss exceeding the amount payable by no-fault insurance.

## Automobile Insurance Premiums

The cost of car insurance depends on many things, including your age, where you live, the car you drive, your driving record, the coverage you have, and the amount of your deductible. Consequently, car insurance premiums—even for the same coverage—vary all over the map. You may think that auto insurance rates rise every year, but that's not always the case. While a survey by Insurance.com found a record 8% average increase in 2008, rates dropped an average of about 0.5% in early 2009.

### Factors Affecting Premiums

Factors that influence how auto insurance premiums are set include (1) rating territory, (2) amount of use the automobile receives, (3) personal characteristics of the driver, (4) type of automobile, and (5) insured's driving record.

● **Rating territory.** Rates are higher in geographic areas where accident rates, number of claims filed, and average cost of claims paid are higher. Rates reflect auto repair costs, hospital and medical expenses, jury awards, and theft and vandalism in the area. Even someone with a perfect driving record will be charged the going rate for the area where the automobile is garaged. Exhibit 10.5 gives some helpful tips for protecting your vehicle wherever you live. Some jurisdictions prohibit the use of rating territories, age, and sex

**collision insurance** Automobile insurance that pays for collision damage to an insured automobile *regardless of who is at fault.*

**comprehensive automobile insurance** Coverage that protects against loss to an insured automobile caused by any peril (with a few exceptions) *other than collision.*

**no-fault automobile insurance** Automobile insurance that reimburses the parties involved in an accident without regard to negligence.

15 miles to work and increase if your commute exceeds 15 miles each way.

- **Drivers' personal characteristics.** The insured's age, sex, and marital status can also affect automobile insurance premiums. Insurance companies base the premium differentials on the number of accidents involving certain age groups. For example, drivers aged 25 and under make up only about 15% of the total driving population but they are involved in nearly 30% of auto accidents and in 26% of all fatal accidents. Male drivers are involved in a larger percentage of fatal crashes, so unmarried males under age 30 (and married males under age 25) pay higher premiums than do older individuals. Females over age 24, as well as married females of any age, are exempt from the youthful operator classification and pay lower premiums.

- **Type of automobile.** Insurance companies charge higher rates for automobiles classified as intermediate-performance, high-performance, and sports vehicles and also for rear-engine models. Some states even rate four-door cars differently from two-door models. If you're thinking of buying, say, a Corvette or a Porsche, be prepared for some hefty insurance rates.

- **Driving record.** The driving records—traffic violations and accidents—of those insured and the people who live with them affect premium levels. More severe traffic convictions—driving under the influence of alcohol or drugs, leaving the scene of an accident, homicide or assault arising from the operation of a motor vehicle, and driving with a revoked or suspended driver's license—result in higher insurance premiums. Any conviction for a

factors because they believe these factors unfairly discriminate against the urban, the young, and the male.

- **Use of the automobile.** Rates are also lower if the insured automobile isn't usually driven to work or is driven less than 3 miles one way. Premiums rise slightly if you drive more than 3 but fewer than

## Exhibit 10.5   Prevent Auto Theft

You can help prevent your car from being stolen by taking the following precautions:

- Close the windows and lock your doors.
- Don't leave your vehicle registration and proof of insurance in your car. No personal identifying information should be left in your car.
- Park in well-lit, heavily traveled areas.
- Take any packages that are in plain sight with you.
- Invest in and install a good anti-theft device like a burglar alarm or a steering wheel lock.
- Never leave your car unattended with the motor running.
- When parking your car, turn the wheels sharply toward or away from the curb and set the emergency brake.
- Don't leave a spare key in the car. Thieves always know where to look.
- Etch the VIN (vehicle identification number) in the windows and on other major parts of your car, which makes it harder to resell the car or its major components.

*Sources:* Adapted from "Prevent Your Car from Being Stolen," http://www.insurance.com/article.aspx/Prevent_Your_Car_from_Being_Stolen/artid/101, March 6, 2007, accessed July 2009; "Protect Yourself from Auto Theft," http://www.allstate.com/tools-and-resources/theft.aspx, accessed July 2009.

moving traffic violation that results in the accumulation of points under a state point system also may incur a premium surcharge. In most states, accidents determined to be the insured's fault also incur points and a premium surcharge.

 **Go to Smart Sites**

Can you save money on your insurance by using a direct underwriter? Get a quote from Geico Direct and compare it with your current policies and premiums. ●

### Driving Down the Cost of Auto Insurance

One of the best ways to reduce the cost of auto insurance is to take advantage of the insurer's discounts, which can knock from 5% to 50% off your annual premium. The Bonus Exhibit, "Auto Insurance Discounts" available at 4ltrpress.cengage.com, summarizes some of the discounts offered by top auto insurance companies. Some give overall *safe-driving (accident-free) discounts*, and most give youthful operators lower rates if they've had *driver's training*. High school and college students may also receive *good-student discounts* for maintaining a B average or making the dean's list at their school.

> { *One of the best ways to reduce the cost of auto insurance is to take advantage of the insurer's discounts, which can knock from 5% to 50% off your annual premium.* }

Nearly all insurance companies give discounts to families with two or more automobiles insured by the same company (the *multicar discount*). Most insurers also offer discounts to owners who install *antitheft devices* in their cars. Likewise, some insurers offer *nonsmoker* and *nondrinker discounts*. Some insurers accept only persons who are educators or executives; others accept only government employees. Through more selective underwriting, these companies are able to reduce losses and operating expenses, which results in lower premiums.

Clearly, it's to your advantage to look for and use as many of these discounts as you can. Take another look at the auto insurance statement in Exhibit 10.4, and you'll see that the insured reduced his overall cost of coverage by 25% by qualifying for just three of the discounts (labeled "Premium Reductions"). Another effective way to drive down the cost of car insurance is to *raise your deductibles* (as discussed earlier in this chapter). For example, the premium difference between

a $100 deductible and a $500 deductible may be as much as 25% on collision coverage and 30% on comprehensive coverage; and a $1,000 deductible may save you as much as 50% on both collision and comprehensive coverage.

## Financial Responsibility Laws

Most states have **financial responsibility laws** whereby motorists *must buy a specified minimum amount of automobile liability insurance* or provide other proof of comparable financial responsibility. The required limits are low in most states—well below what you should carry. Financial responsibility laws fall into two categories. *Compulsory auto insurance laws* require motorists to show evidence of insurance coverage *before* receiving their license plates. Penalties for not having liability insurance include fines and suspension of your driver's license. The second category requires motorists to show evidence of their insurance coverage only *after* being involved in an accident. If they then fail to demonstrate compliance with the law, their registrations and driver's licenses are suspended.

> **financial responsibility laws** Laws requiring motorists to buy a specified minimum amount of automobile liability insurance or to provide other proof of comparable financial responsibility.

## **LG5** Other Property and Liability Insurance

Homeowner's and automobile insurance policies provide the basic protection needed by most families, but some need other more specialized types of insurance. Popular forms of other insurance include supplemental property insurance—earthquake, flood, and other forms of transportation—as well as the personal liability umbrella policy.

## Supplemental Property Insurance Coverage

Because homeowner's policies exclude certain types of damage, you may want to consider some of the following types of supplemental coverage.

- **Earthquake insurance.** In addition to California, areas in other states are also subject to this type of loss. Very few homeowners buy this coverage because these policies typically carry a 15% deductible on the replacement cost of a home damaged or destroyed by earthquake.

- **Flood insurance.** In 1968, the federal government established a subsidized flood insurance program in cooperation with private insurance agents, who can now sell this low-cost coverage to homeowners and tenants living in designated communities. The flood insurance program also encourages communities to initiate land-use controls to reduce future flood losses.

● **Other forms of transportation insurance.** In addition to automobiles, you can buy policies to insure other types of vehicles, such as mobile homes, recreational vehicles, or boats.

## Personal Liability Umbrella Policy

Persons with moderate to high levels of income and net worth may want to purchase a **personal liability umbrella policy**, which provides added liability coverage for homeowner's and automobile insurance. Umbrella policies often include limits of $1 million or more. Some also provide added amounts of coverage for a family's major medical insurance. The premiums are usually quite reasonable for the broad coverage offered—$150 to $300 a year for as much as $1 million in coverage. The insured party must already have relatively high liability limits ($100,000 to $300,000) on their homeowner's and auto coverage in order to purchase a personal liability umbrella policy.

## LG6 Buying Insurance and Settling Claims

The first step when buying property and liability insurance is to develop an inventory of exposures to loss and then arrange them from highest to lowest priority. Losses that lend themselves to insurance protection are those that seldom occur but are potentially substantial—for example, damage to a home and its contents or liability arising from a negligence claim. Somewhat less important, but still desirable, is insurance to cover losses that could disrupt a family's financial plans even if the losses might not result in insolvency. Such risks include physical damage to automobiles, boats, and other personal property of moderate value. Lowest-priority exposures can be covered by savings or from current income.

## Property and Liability Insurance Agents

A good property insurance agent can make the purchase process much easier. Most property insurance agents fall into either the captive or independent category. A

**captive agent** represents only one insurance company and is more or less an employee of that company. Allstate, Nationwide, and State Farm are major insurance companies that market their products through captive agents. In contrast, **independent agents** typically represent from 2 to 10 different insurance companies. These agents may place your coverage with any of the companies with whom they have an agency relationship. Some well-known companies that operate through independent agents include The Hartford, Unitrin Kemper, Chubb, and Travelers. Either type of agent can serve your needs well and should take the time to:

● Review your total property and liability insurance exposures

● Inventory property and identify exposures

● Determine appropriate covered perils, limits, deductibles, and floater policies

Because of large variations in premiums and services, it pays to comparison shop.

Property insurance agents who meet various experiential and educational requirements, including passing a series of written examinations, qualify for the *Chartered Property and Casualty Underwriter (CPCU)* or *Certified Insurance Counselor (CIC)* designation. Another alternative to consider is companies that sell directly to the consumer through an 800 number or online. Generally, their premiums are lower. Examples of direct sellers are Amica, Erie, Geico, and USAA.

## Property and Liability Insurance Companies

When selecting an agent, you should ask questions about the company, including its financial soundness, its claims-settlement practices, and the geographic range of its operations (this could be important if you're involved in an accident 1,000 miles from home). As with any form of insurance, you should check the company's ratings (see Chapter 8) and stick with those rated in the top categories. Friends and acquaintances often can provide insight into its claims settlement policy. Many insurance companies now have elaborate home pages on the Web containing basic information about the provider and its products, directions to local agents, or calculators to crunch the numbers and generate sample premiums.

## Settling Property and Liability Claims

Insurance companies typically settle claims promptly and fairly—especially life and healthcare claims. But in settling property and liability claims, there is often some claimant–insurer disagreement. Here, we'll review the claims settlement process, beginning with consideration of what you should do immediately following an accident.

## First Steps Following an Accident

After an accident, record the names, addresses, and phone numbers of all witnesses, drivers, occupants, and injured parties, along with the license numbers of the automobiles involved. Never leave the scene of an accident, even if the other party says it's OK. Immediately notify law enforcement officers and your insurance agent of the accident. Never discuss liability at the scene of an accident, or with anyone other than the police and your insurer. It's the duty of the police to assess the probability of a law violation and maintain order at the scene of an accident—not to make judgments about liability.

## Steps in Claims Settlement

If you're involved in an accident, one of the first things to decide is whether you want to file a claim. Most experts agree that unless it's a very minor or insignificant accident, the best course of action is to file a claim. Be aware, though, that if you've made several claims then your insurance company may decide to drop you after settling the current one. The claims settlement process typically involves these steps:

1. **Notice to your insurance company**. You must notify your insurance company that a loss (or potential for loss) has occurred. Timely notice is extremely important.
2. **Investigation**. Insurance company personnel may talk to witnesses or law enforcement officers and gather physical evidence to determine whether the claimed loss is covered by the policy, and they'll check to make sure that the date of the loss falls within the policy period. If you delay filing your claim, you hinder the insurer's ability to check the facts. All policies specify the period within which you must give notice. Failure to report can result in losing your right to collect.
3. **Proof of loss**. This proof requires you to give a sworn statement. You may have to show medical bills, submit an inventory, and certify the value of lost property (for example, a written inventory, photographs, and purchase receipts). You may also have to submit an employer statement of lost wages and, if possible, physical evidence of damage (e.g., X-rays if you claim a back injury; a broken window or pried door if you claim a break-in and theft at your home). After reviewing your proof of loss, the insurer may (1) pay you the amount you asked for, (2) offer you a lesser amount, or (3) deny that the company has any legal responsibility under the terms of your policy.

If the amount is disputed, most policies provide for some form of claims arbitration. You hire a third party, the company hires a third party, and these two arbitrators jointly select one more person. When any two of the three arbitrators reach agreement, their decision binds you and the company to their solution. When a company denies responsibility, you do not get the right of arbitration. In such cases, the company is saying the loss does not fall under the policy coverage. You must then either forget the claim or bring in an attorney or, perhaps, a public adjustor (discussed next).

> **claims adjustor** An insurance specialist who works for the insurance company, as an independent adjustor, or for an adjustment bureau, to investigate claims.

---

### FINANCIAL ROAD SIGN

#### WHAT TO DO WHEN A CLAIM IS DENIED

Fight back if your homeowner's or automobile insurance company refuses to pay all or part of a claim.

1. *Document everything.* Obtain written copies of police or fire department reports and outside appraisals, and take photos.
2. *Don't take no for an answer.* Complain to your insurer and ask for another review.
3. *File and follow up on your appeal promptly.* Some companies have a 1-year limit on challenges, starting with the date of the first decision.
4. *Go to your state's insurance department.* Insurers then have about 6 weeks to resolve a dispute.
5. *Don't bother filing a lawsuit for small claims.* State regulators can't force a solution. However, most lawyers won't handle lawsuits for relatively small amounts, typically less than about $2,000.

---

## Claims Adjustment

Usually the first person to call when you need to file a claim is your insurance agent. If your loss is relatively minor, the agent can quickly process it and, in fact, often gives you a check right on the spot. If your loss is more complex, your company will probably assign a claims adjustor to the case. A **claims adjustor** is an insurance specialist who works for the insurance company either as an independent adjustor or for an adjustment bureau. The adjustor investigates claims, looking out for the company's interests—which might very well be to keep you, its customer, satisfied. However, many claimants are out to collect all they can from insurance companies, which they think have "deep pockets." Thus adjustors walk a fine line: they must diligently question and investigate while at the same time offering service to minimize settlement delays and financial hardship. To promote your own interest in the claim, cooperate with your adjustor and answer inquiries honestly—keeping in mind that the insurance company writes the adjustor's paycheck.

# FINANCIAL PLANNING EXERCISES

**LG1**

1. Assume Donna Thurman had a homeowner's insurance policy with $100,000 of coverage on the dwelling. Would a 90% co-insurance clause be better than an 80% clause in such a policy? Give reasons to support your answer.

**LG2**

2. Last year Charles and Kathy Price bought a home with a dwelling replacement value of $250,000 and insured it (via an HO-3 policy) for $210,000. The policy reimburses for actual cash value and has a $500 deductible, standard limits for coverage C items, and no scheduled property. Recently, burglars broke into the house and stole a 2-year-old television set with a current replacement value of $600 and an estimated useful life of 8 years. They also took jewelry valued at $1,850 and silver flatware valued at $3,000.
   a. If the Prices' policy has an 80% co-insurance clause, do they have enough insurance?
   b. Assuming a 50% coverage C limit, calculate how much the Prices would receive if they filed a claim for the stolen items.
   c. What advice would you give the Prices about their homeowner's coverage?

**LG3**

3. Steve and Brenda Edwards, both graduate students, moved into an apartment near the university. Brenda wants to buy renter's insurance, but Steve thinks they don't need it because their furniture isn't worth much. Brenda points out that, among other things, they have some expensive computer and stereo equipment. To help the Edwardses resolve their dilemma, suggest a plan for deciding how much insurance to buy, and give them some ideas for finding a policy.

**LG4**

4. Alex Evans has a personal automobile policy (PAP) with coverage of $25,000/$50,000 for bodily injury liability, $25,000 for property damage liability, $5,000 for medical payments, and a $500 deductible for collision insurance. How much will his insurance cover in each of the following situations? Will he have any out-of-pocket costs?
   a. Alex loses control and skids on ice, running into a parked car and causing $3,785 damage to the unoccupied vehicle and $2,350 damage to his own car.
   b. Alex runs a stop sign and causes a serious auto accident, badly injuring two people. The injured parties win lawsuits against him for $30,000 each.
   c. Alex's wife borrows his car while hers is being repaired. She backs into a telephone pole and causes $450 damage to the car.

# PART 5

# MANAGING INVESTMENTS

# INVESTMENT PLANNING

## LEARNING GOALS

**LG1** Discuss the role that investing plays in the personal financial planning process and identify several different investment objectives. (p. 235)

**LG2** Distinguish between primary and secondary markets as well as between broker and dealer markets. (p. 240)

**LG3** Explain the process of buying and selling securities and recognize the different types of orders. (p. 244)

**LG4** Develop an appreciation of how various forms of investment information can lead to better investing skills and returns. (p. 249)

**LG5** Gain a basic understanding of the growing impact of the computer and the Internet on the field of investments. (p. 253)

**LG6** Describe an investment portfolio and how you'd go about developing and managing a portfolio of securities. (p. 256)

## LG1 The Objectives and Rewards of Investing

People invest their money for all sorts of reasons. Some do it as a way to accumulate the down payment on a new home; others do it as a way to supplement their income; still others invest to build up a nest egg for retirement. Actually, the term *investment* means different things to different people; that is, while millions of people *invest* regularly in securities like stocks, bonds, and mutual funds, others *speculate* in commodities or options. **Investing** is generally considered to take a long-term perspective and is viewed as a process of purchasing securities wherein stability of value and level of return are somewhat predictable. **Speculating**, on the other hand, is viewed as a short-term activity that involves the buying and selling of securities in which future value and expected return are highly uncertain. Think of an *investor* as someone who wears both a belt *and* suspenders, whereas a *speculator* wears neither.

If you're like most investors, at first you'll probably keep your funds in some type of savings vehicle (as described in Chapter 4). Once you have *sufficient savings*—for emergencies

the unexpected. For our purposes here, we'll assume that you're adequately insured and that the cost of insurance coverage is built into your family's monthly cash budget. Ample insurance and liquidity (cash and savings) with which to meet life's emergencies are two *investment prerequisites* that are absolutely essential to developing a successful investment program. Once these conditions are met, you're ready to start investing.

> **investing** The process of placing money in some medium such as stocks or bonds in the expectation of receiving some future benefit.

> **speculating** A form of investing in which future value and expected returns are highly uncertain.

## How Do I Get Started?

Contrary to what you may believe, there's really nothing magical about the topic of investments. The terminology may seem baffling at times, and some of the procedures and techniques may seem quite complicated. But don't let that mislead you into thinking there's no room for the small, individual investor. Nothing could be farther from the truth! As we'll see in this and the next two chapters, individual investors can choose from a wide array of securities and investment vehicles.

> ❰ *Contrary to what you may believe, there's really nothing magical about the topic of investments.* ❱

and other purposes—you can start building up a *pool of investable capital*. This often means making sacrifices and doing what you can to *live within your budget*. Granted, it's far easier to spend money than to save it, but if you're really serious about getting into investments, you'll have to accumulate the necessary capital! In addition to a savings and capital accumulation program, it's also important to have adequate *insurance coverage* to provide protection against

### Go to Smart Sites

With so many investing Web sites, how can you find what you need? Start with An Opinionated Guide to the Web's Best Investing Sites, for links to useful Web sites listed by category. An added benefit: most are free. Whenever you see *"Go to Smart Sites"* in this chapter, visit 4ltrpress .cengage.com for help finding answers online. ●

How, then, do you get started? First, you need some money—not a lot; $500 to $1,000 will do, although $4,000 or $5,000 would be better (and remember, this is *investment capital* we're talking about here—money you've accumulated above and beyond basic emergency savings). Besides the money, you need knowledge and know-how. Never invest in something you're not sure about—that's the quickest way to lose money. Instead, learn as much as you can about the market, different types of securities, and various trading strategies. Also try to stay current with major developments as they occur in the market; start following the stock market, interest rates, and developments in the bond market.

We strongly suggest that, after you've learned a few things about stocks and bonds, you set up a portfolio of securities on paper and make *paper trades* in and out of your portfolio, for 6 months to a year, to get a feel for what it's like to make (and lose) money in the market. Start out with an imaginary sum of, say, $50,000 (as long as you're going to dream, you might as well dream big). Then keep track of the stocks, bonds, and mutual funds you hold, record the number of shares bought and sold, dividends received, and so on. Throughout this exercise, be sure to use actual prices (as obtained from *The Wall Street Journal*, cnn.com, or your local newspaper) and keep it as realistic as possible. You might even want to use one of the *portfolio tracking* programs offered at such sites as **www.quicken.com** or **moneycentral.msn.com**. Eventually, you'll become familiar with the market and be comfortable with how things are done there. When that happens, you'll be ready to take the plunge.

As a beginning investor with limited funds, it's probably best to confine your investment activity to the basics. Stick to stocks, bonds, and mutual funds. Avoid getting fancy, and certainly don't try to make a killing every time you invest—that will only lead to frustration, disappointment, and very possibly, heavy losses. Further, *be patient*! Don't expect the price of the stock to double overnight, and don't panic when things don't work out as expected in the short run (after all, security prices do occasionally go down). Finally, remember that you don't need spectacular returns in order to make a lot of money in the market. Instead, be consistent and let the concept of compound interest work for you. While the type of security you invest in is a highly personal decision, you might want to seriously consider some sort of mutual fund as your first investment (see Chapter 13). They provide professional management and diversification that individual investors—especially those with limited resources—can rarely obtain on their own.

## The Role of Investing in Personal Financial Planning

Buy a car, build a house, enjoy a comfortable retirement—these are goals we'd all like to attain some day and, in many cases, they're the centerpieces of well-developed financial plans. As a rule, a financial goal such as building a house is not something we pay for out of our cash reserves. Instead, we must accumulate the funds over time, which is where investment planning and the act of investing enters into the personal financial planning process.

It all starts with an objective: a particular financial goal you'd like to achieve within a certain period of time. Take the case of the Colberts. Shortly after the birth of their first child, they decided to start a college education fund. After doing some rough calculations, they concluded they'd need to accumulate about $160,000 over the next 18 years to have enough money for their daughter's education. Simply by setting that objective, the Colberts created a well-defined, specific financial goal. The purpose is to meet their child's educational needs and the amount of money involved is $160,000 in 18 years.

### Coming Up with the Capital

So far, the Colberts know how much money they want to accumulate ($160,000) and how long they have to accumulate it (18 years). The only other thing they need to determine at this point is the *rate of return* they feel they can earn on their money. The Colberts know that the amount of money they'll have to put into their investment program largely depends on *how much they can earn from their investments*: the higher their rate of return, the less they'll have to put up. Let's say they feel comfortable using a 6% rate of return. That's a fairly conservative number—one that won't require them to put all or most of their money into high-risk investments—and they're reasonably certain they can reach that level of return, *on average*, over the long haul. It's important to use some care in coming up with a projected rate of return. Don't saddle yourself with an unreasonably high rate, since that will simply reduce the chance of reaching your targeted financial goal.

Now, there are two ways of coming up with the capital needed to reach a targeted sum of money: (1) you can make a lump-sum investment right up front and let that amount grow over time; or (2) you can set up a systematic savings plan and put away a certain amount of money each year. Worksheet 11.1 is designed to help you find the amount of investment capital you'll need to reach a given financial goal. It employs the *compound value* concept discussed in Chapter 2 and is based on a given financial target (of≈$160,000 – line 1) and a projected average rate of return on your investments (of 6% – line 2). You can use this worksheet to find either a required lump-sum investment (part A) or an amount that will have to be put away each year in a savings plan (part B). For our purposes here, we'll assume the Colberts have $7,500 to start with (this comes mostly from gifts their daughter received from her grandparents). Because they know they'll need a lot more than that to reach their target, the Colberts decide to use part B of the worksheet to find out how much they'll have to save annually.

The first thing to do is find the future value of the $7,500 initial investment. The question here is: How much will that initial lump-sum investment grow to over an 18-year period? Using the compound value concept and the appropriate "future value factor" (from Appendix A), we see in line 7 that this deposit will grow to some $21,408. But that's only about 13% of the target amount of $160,000. Indeed, by subtracting the terminal value of the initial investment (line 7) from our target (line 1), we find the amount that must be generated from some sort of annual savings plan—see line 8.

You can use a worksheet like this one to find out how much money you must come up with to reach a given financial goal. This worksheet is based on the same future value concepts we first introduced in Chapter 2.

### DETERMINING AMOUNT OF INVESTMENT CAPITAL

Financial goal: _To accumulate $160,000 in 18 years for the purpose of meeting the cost of daughter's college education._

| | | |
|---|---|---|
| 1. Targeted Financial Goal (see Note 1) | $ | 160,000 |
| 2. Projected Average Return on Investments | | 6% |
| **A. Finding a Lump Sum Investment:** | | |
| 3. Future Value Factor, from Appendix A<br>■ based on _____ years to target date and a projected<br>average return on investment of ___%___ | | 0.000 |
| 4. Required Lump Sum Investment<br>■ line 1 ÷ line 3 | $ | 0 |
| **B. Making a Series of Investments over Time:** | | |
| 5. Amount of Initial Investment, if any (see Note 2) | $ | 7,500 |
| 6. Future Value Factor, from Appendix A<br>■ based on __18__ years of target date and a projected average<br>return on investment of __6%__ | | 2.854 |
| 7. Terminal Value of Initial Investment<br>■ line 5 × line 6 | $ | 21,408 |
| 8. Balance to Come from Savings Plan<br>■ line 1 − line 7 | $ | 138,592 |
| 9. Future Value Annuity Factor, from Appendix B<br>■ based on __18__ years to target date and a projected average<br>return on investment of __6%__ | | 30.91 |
| 10. Series of Annual Investments Required over Time<br>■ line 8 ÷ line 9 | $ | 4,484.00 |

Note 1: The "targeted financial goal" is the amount of money you want to accumulate by some target date in the future.

Note 2: If you're starting from scratch—i.e., there is *no* initial investment—enter zero on line 5, *skip* lines 6 and 7, and then use the total targeted financial goal (from line 1) as the amount to be funded from a savings plan; now proceed with the rest of the worksheet.

**investment plan** A statement— preferably written— that specifies how investment capital will be invested to achieve a specified goal.

Again, using the appropriate future value factor (this time from Appendix B), we find that the Colberts will have to put away about $4,484 a year in order to reach their target of $160,000 in 18 years. That is, the $4,484 a year will grow to $138,592, and this amount plus $21,408 (the amount to which the initial $7,500 will grow) equals the Colberts' targeted financial goal of $160,000. As you might have suspected, the last few steps in the worksheet can just as easily be done on a good handheld calculator. That is, after determining the size of the nest egg (as in step 8), you can use a financial calculator to find the amount of money that must be put away each year to fund the nest egg.

| CALCULATOR | |
|---|---|
| **Inputs** | **Functions** |
| 18 | N |
| 6 | I/Y |
| −138,592 | FV |
| | CPT |
| | PMT |
| | *Solution* |
| | 4,484.36 |

SEE APPENDIX E FOR DETAILS.

## Calculator Keystrokes

You can use a financial calculator to *find the annual payments necessary to fund a target amount* by first putting the calculator in the *annual compounding* mode. Then, to determine the amount of money that must be put away each year, at a 6% rate of return, to accumulate $138,592 in 18 years, make the keystrokes shown here, where:

**N** = number of *years* in investment horizon

**I/Y** = expected average *annual* rate of return on investments

**FV** = the targeted amount of money you want to accumulate, entered as a *negative* number

The calculator should then display a value of $4,484.36, which is the amount of money that must be put away each year to reach the targeted amount of $138,592 in 18 years. (*Note:* The calculator keystrokes take you from steps 8 to 10 in Worksheet 11.1. You can also do steps 5 to 7 on the calculator by letting N = 18; I/Y = 6.0; and *PV* = −7,500; then solve for (CPT)FV. Try it—you should come up with a number fairly close to the amount shown on line 7 of Worksheet 11.1.)

### An Investment Plan Provides Direction

Now that the Colberts know how much they have to save each year, their next step is deciding how they'll save it. It's probably best to follow some type of *systematic savings plan*—for example, build a set amount of savings each month or quarter into the household budget and then stick with it. But whatever procedure is followed, keep in mind that all we're doing here is *accumulating the required investment capital*. That money still has to be put to work in some kind of investment program, and that's where an investment plan enters the picture. An **investment plan** is a simple—preferably written—statement explaining how the accumulated investment capital will be invested in order to reach the targeted goal. In the Colberts' case, their capital accumulation plan calls for a 6% rate of return as a target they feel they can achieve. Now they need to find a way to obtain that 6% return on their money—meaning they have to specify, in general terms at least, the kinds of investment vehicles they intend to use.

## What Are Your Investment Objectives?

Some people buy securities for the protection they provide from taxes. Others put money aside for that proverbial rainy day or, perhaps, to build up a nice retirement nest egg. *Your goals tend to set the tone for your investment program, and they play a major role in determining how conservative (or aggressive) you're likely to be in making investment decisions.* These goals provide a purpose for your investments. The most frequent investment objectives are to (1) enhance current income, (2) save for a major purchase, (3) accumulate funds for retirement, and (4) seek shelter from taxes.

## Current Income

The idea here is to put your money into investments that will enable you to supplement your income. In other words, it's for people who want to live off their investment income. A secure source of high current income, from dividends or interest, is the primary concern of such investors. Retired people, for example, often choose investments offering high current income—at low risk.

© ROB BYRON/SHUTTERSTOCK

## Major Expenditures

People often put money aside, sometimes for years, to save up enough to make just one major expenditure. Here are the most common ones:

- The down payment on a home
- Money for a child's college education
- Some capital for going into business
- An expensive (perhaps once-in-a-lifetime) vacation
- The purchase of a special, expensive item
- Funds for retirement (discussed in the next section)

Whatever your goal, the idea is to set your sights on something and then go about building your capital with that objective in mind. It sure makes the act of investing more pleasurable. Once you know about how much money you're going to need to attain one of these goals (following a procedure like the one illustrated in Worksheet 11.1), you can specify the types of investment vehicles you intend to use. For example, you might follow a low-risk approach by making a single lump-sum investment in a high-grade bond that matures the same year you'll need the funds; or you could follow a riskier investment plan that calls for investing a set amount of money over time in something like a growth-oriented mutual fund. Of course, for some purposes—such as the down payment on a home or a child's education—you'll probably want to accept a lot less risk than for others, because attaining these goals should not be jeopardized by the types of investment vehicles you choose to employ.

## Retirement

Accumulating funds for retirement is *the single most important reason for investing.* Too often, though, retirement planning occupies only a small amount of our time because we tend to rely too heavily on employers and Social Security for our retirement needs. As many people learn too late in life, that can be a serious mistake. A much better approach is to review the amounts of income you can realistically expect to receive from Social Security and your employee pension plan, and then decide, based on your retirement goals, *whether they'll be adequate to meet your needs.* You'll probably find that you'll have to supplement them through personal investing. (Retirement plans are discussed in Chapter 14.)

## Shelter from Taxes

As explained in Chapter 3, federal income taxes do not treat all sources of income equally. For example, if you own real estate, then you may be able to take depreciation deductions against certain other sources of income, thereby reducing the amount of your final taxable income. This tax write-off feature can make real estate an attractive investment vehicle for some investors, even though its pretax rate of return may not appear very high. The goal of sheltering income from taxes is a legitimate one that, for some investors, often goes hand in hand with the goals of saving for a major outlay or for retirement. Clearly, if you can avoid paying taxes on the income from an investment, then you will, all other things considered, have more funds available for reinvestment during the period.

# Different Ways to Invest

After establishing your investment objectives, you can use a variety of investment vehicles to fulfill those goals. In this section, we'll briefly describe various types of investmentss that are popular with (and widely used by) individual investors.

## Common Stock

*Common stocks* are a form of *equity*—each share of stock represents a fractional ownership position in a corporation. A share of stock entitles the holder to equal participation in the corporation's earnings and dividends, an equal vote, and an equal voice in management. From the investor's perspective, the return to stockholders comes from dividends and/or appreciation in share price. Common stock has no maturity date and, as a result, remains outstanding indefinitely (common stocks are discussed in Chapter 12).

## Bonds

In contrast to stocks, *bonds* are *liabilities*—they're IOUs of the issuer. Governments and corporations issue

securities markets
The marketplace in which stocks, bonds, and other financial instruments are traded.

bonds that pay a stated return, called *interest*. An individual who invests in a bond receives a stipulated interest income, typically paid every 6 months, plus the return of the principal (face) value of the bond at maturity. For example, if you purchased a $1,000 bond that paid 10% interest in semiannual installments, then you could expect to receive $50 every 6 months (that is, 10% x 0.5 years x $1,000) and at maturity recover the $1,000 face value of the bond. Of course, a bond can be bought or sold prior to maturity at a price that may differ from its face value because bond prices, like common stock prices, fluctuate in the marketplace (see Chapter 12).

### Preferreds and Convertibles

These are *hybrid securities* in that each has the characteristics of both stocks and bonds. *Preferred securities* are issued as stock and, as such, represent an equity position in a corporation. But unlike common stock, preferreds have a stated (fixed) dividend rate that is paid before the dividends to holders of common stock are paid. Like bonds, preferred stocks are usually purchased for the current income (dividends) they pay. A *convertible security*, in contrast, is a special type of fixed-income obligation (usually a bond) that carries a conversion feature permitting the investor to convert it into a specified number of shares of common stock. Thus convertible securities provide the fixed-income benefits (interest) of a bond while offering the price appreciation (capital gains) potential of common stock. (Convertibles are briefly discussed in Chapter 12.)

### Mutual Funds and Exchange Traded Funds

An organization that invests in and professionally manages a diversified portfolio of securities is called a *mutual fund*. A mutual fund sells shares to investors, who then become part owners of the fund's securities portfolio. Most mutual funds issue and repurchase shares at a price that reflects the underlying value of the portfolio at the time the transaction is made. Mutual funds have become popular with individual investors because they offer not only a wide variety of investment opportunities but also a full array of services that many investors find particularly appealing. *Exchange traded funds (ETFs)* are similar to mutual funds in that they, too, represent portfolios of securities. They are usually set up to track a basket or index of securities, like the S&P 500 or a particular sector, such as telecommunications or utility stocks. Whereas mutual funds can be bought or sold only at the end of the day, investors can trade ETFs throughout the trading day just like individual shares of stock. Further, ETFs provide more favorable tax treatment than mutual funds. (Mutual funds and ETFs are discussed in Chaper 13.)

### Real Estate

Investments in *real estate* can take many forms, ranging from speculating in raw land to limited-partnership shares in commercial property; there are even mutual funds that specialize in real estate. The returns on real estate come from rents, capital gains, and certain tax benefits. (Various types of real estate investments are discussed in Chapter 13.)

## LG2 Securities Markets

The term **securities markets** generally describes the arena where stocks, bonds, and other financial instruments are traded. Such markets can be physical places, but they can just as easily be *electronic networks* that allow buyers and sellers to come together to execute trades. Securities markets can be broken into two parts: capital markets and money markets. The *capital market* is where long-term securities like stocks and bonds are traded. The *money market* is the marketplace for short-term, low-risk credit instruments with maturities of 1 year or less; these include U.S. Treasury bills, commercial paper, and so on. Both types of markets provide the mechanism for bringing the buyers and sellers of securities together. Some of the more popular money market securities were discussed in Chapter 4; in this chapter we'll concentrate on the capital markets.

## Primary and Secondary Markets

In the *primary market*, new securities are sold to the public and one party to the transaction is always the issuer. In contrast, old (outstanding) securities are

© AL RUBLINETSKY/SHUTTERSTOCK

bought and sold in the *secondary market,* where the securities are "traded" between investors. A security is sold in the primary market just once, when it's originally issued by a corporation or a governmental body (e.g., a state or municipality). Subsequent transactions, in which securities are sold by one investor to another, take place in the secondary market.

### Primary Markets

When a corporation sells a new issue to the public, several financial institutions will participate in the transaction. To begin with, the corporation will probably use an *investment banking firm,* which specializes in *underwriting* (selling) new security issues. The investment banker will give the corporation advice on pricing and other aspects of the issue and will either sell the new security itself or arrange for a *selling group* to do so. The selling group is normally made up of several brokerage firms, each responsible for selling a certain portion of the new issue. On very large issues, the originating investment banker will bring in other underwriting firms and form an *underwriting syndicate* in order to spread the risks associated with underwriting and selling the new securities. A potential investor in a new issue must be given a **prospectus**, which is a document describing the firm and the issue. Certain federal agencies are responsible for ensuring that all the information included in a prospectus accurately represents the facts.

### Secondary Markets

The secondary markets permit investors to execute transactions among themselves; it's the marketplace where an investor can easily sell his or her holdings to someone else. Unlike primary market transactions, the secondary market does not generate cash for the underlying company (issuer). Included among the secondary markets are the various *securities exchanges,* in which the buyers and sellers of securities are brought together for the purpose of executing trades. Another major segment of the market is made up of those securities that are listed and traded on the *NASDAQ market,* which employs an all-electronic trading platform to execute trades. Finally, the *over-the-counter (OTC)* market deals in smaller, unlisted securities.

## Broker Markets and Dealer Markets

By far, the vast majority of trades made by small individual investors take place in the secondary market, so we'll focus on it for the rest of this chapter. When you look at the secondary market *on the basis of how securities are traded,* you'll find you can essentially divide the market into two segments: broker markets and dealer markets. Exhibit 11.1 shows the structure

of the secondary market in terms of broker or dealer markets. As you can see, the *broker market* consists of national and regional "securities exchanges," while the *dealer market* is made up of both the NASDAQ market and the OTC market.

**prospectus**
A document made available to prospective security buyers that describes the firm and a new security issue.

Probably *the biggest difference in these two markets is a technical point about how the trades are executed.* That is, when a trade occurs in a *broker market* (on one of the so-called securities exchanges), then the two sides to the transaction—the buyer and the seller—are brought together and the trade takes place at that point: Party A sells his securities directly to the buyer, Party B. In a sense, with the help of a *broker,* the securities change hands right there on the floor of the exchange. In contrast, when trades are made in one of the *dealer markets,* the buyer and seller are never brought together directly; instead, their buy/sell orders are executed separately through *securities dealers,* who act as *market makers.* Essentially, two separate trades are made: Party A sells his securities (in, say, the XYZ Corp.) to one dealer, and Party B buys her securities (in the same XYZ Corp.) from the same or another dealer. Thus, there is always a dealer (market maker) on one side of the transaction.

### Broker Markets

When you think of the stock market, if you're like most individual investors, then the first name to come to mind is the New York Stock Exchange (NYSE), which is the largest stock exchange in the United States. In 2007, the NYSE combined with Euronext, a combination of stock exchanges in Amsterdam, Brussels, Lisbon, and Paris. The combined entity, *NYSE Euronext,* operates six securities exchanges in seven countries. At the end of 2008, it had about 8,500 listed issues with a market capitalization of *$16.7 trillion.* Average daily trading volume was aproximately $153 billion in 2008. In 2008, the NYSE Euronext also acquired the American Stock Exchange (AMEX), which was formerly the second-largest U.S. exchange. The AMEX has less restrictive listing requirements than the NYSE, so the acquisition allowed the NYSE to broaden the types of companies falling under its umbrella. The NYSE Euronext entity is a part of the broker market—indeed, it's their biggest player! Trading on NYSE Euronext takes place on centralized trading floors.

The NYSE Group (NYSE for short), the U.S.-based part of NYSE Euronext, is the biggest securities exchange in the world. Known as "the big board," at year-end 2008, the NYSE's listed companies had a market value of some *$15 trillion.* The exchange, which has stringent listing requirements, includes about 93% of the

## Exhibit 11.1  Broker and Dealer Markets

On a typical trading day, the secondary market is a beehive of activity, where literally billions of shares change hands daily. This market consists of two parts, the broker market and the dealer market. As can be seen, each of these markets is made up of various exchanges and trading venues.

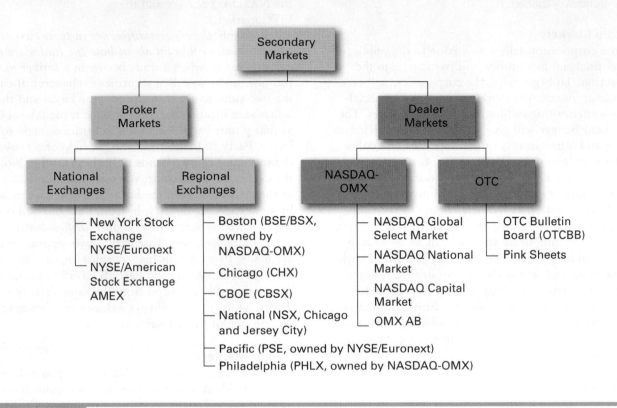

```
                          Secondary
                           Markets

         Broker                                Dealer
         Markets                               Markets

   National        Regional           NASDAQ-            OTC
   Exchanges       Exchanges          OMX

— New York Stock   — Boston (BSE/BSX,   — NASDAQ Global    — OTC Bulletin
  Exchange           owned by            Select Market       Board (OTCBB)
  NYSE/Euronext      NASDAQ-OMX)       — NASDAQ National  — Pink Sheets
— NYSE/American    — Chicago (CHX)       Market
  Stock Exchange   — CBOE (CBSX)       — NASDAQ Capital
  AMEX             — National (NSX,      Market
                     Chicago           — OMX AB
                     and Jersey City)
                   — Pacific (PSE, owned by NYSE/Euronext)
                   — Philadelphia (PHLX, owned by NASDAQ-OMX)
```

**bid price** The price at which one can sell a security.

**ask price** The price at which one can purchase a security.

firms in the Dow Jones Industrial Average and 82% of the firms in the S&P 500 index. As of the end of 2008, more than 2,400 firms from around the world listed their shares on the NYSE.

Besides the NYSE Euronext, a handful of *regional exchanges* are also part of the broker market. The number of securities listed on each of these exchanges typically ranges from about 100 to 500 companies. The best-known of these are the Boston, National, Pacific, and Philadelphia exchanges. These exchanges deal primarily in securities with local and regional appeal. To enhance their trading activity, regional exchanges often list securities that are also listed on the NYSE.

### Dealer Markets

A key feature of the dealer market is that, unlike the NYSE, it doesn't have centralized trading floors. Instead, it's made up of many market makers who are linked together via a mass telecommunications network. Each market maker is actually a securities dealer who makes a market in one or more securities by offering to either buy or sell them at stated bid/ask prices. (The **bid price** and **ask price** represent, respectively, the highest price offered to purchase a given security and the lowest price at which the security is offered for sale; in effect, an investor pays the ask price when *buying* securities and receives the bid price when *selling* them.) Consisting of both the NASDAQ and OTC markets, dealer markets account for about 40% of all shares traded in the U.S. market—with the NASDAQ accounting for the overwhelming majority of those trades.

The biggest dealer market, hands down, is made up of a select list of stocks that are listed and traded on the *National Association of Securities Dealers Automated Quotation System*, or *NASDAQ* for short. Founded in 1971, NASDAQ had its origins in the OTC market but today is considered *a totally separate entity that's no longer a part of the OTC market*. In fact, in 2006, the SEC formally recognized NASDAQ as a "listed exchange," giving it much the same stature and prestige as the NYSE. To be traded on NASDAQ, all stocks must have at least two market makers—although the bigger, more actively traded stocks (such as Cisco) will have many more than that. These dealers electronically post all their bid/ask prices so that when investors place (market) orders, they're immediately filled at the best available price. In 2008, NASDAQ combined its business with OMX AB, which owned and operated the largest securities market in northern Europe. It also acquired the Philadelphia and Boston stock exchanges. Across its markets, at the end of 2008, NASDAQ listed more than 3,800 companies listing from 38 countries.

NASDAQ sets various listing standards, the most comprehensive of which are for the 2,000 or so stocks traded on the *NASDAQ National Market (NNM)* and the roughly 1,000 stocks traded on the *NASDAQ Global Select Market* (created in 2006, this market is reserved for the biggest and bluest NASDAQ stocks). Stocks included on these two markets are all actively traded and, in general, have a *national following*. These securities are widely quoted, and the trades, all executed electronically, are just as efficient as they are on the floor of the NYSE. Indeed, just as the NYSE has its list of big-name players (like ExxonMobil, Wal-Mart, Pfizer, IBM, Coca-Cola, Home Depot, and UPS), so too does NASDAQ—including names like Microsoft, Intel, Cisco Systems, Dell, eBay, Google, and Apple. (The *NASDAQ Capital Market* is yet another NASDAQ market; it includes about 600 or 700 stocks that, for various reasons, aren't eligible for the NNM.)

The other part of the dealer market is made up of securities that trade in the *over-the-counter (OTC) market*. This market is separate from NASDAQ and includes mostly small companies that either can't or don't wish to comply with NASDAQ listing requirements. They trade on either the *OTC Bulletin Board*

*(OTCBB)* or in the so-called *Pink Sheets*. The OTCBB is an electronic quotation system that links the market makers who trade the shares of small companies. The Bulletin Board is regulated by the SEC, which requires (among other things) that all companies traded on this market file audited financial statements and comply with federal securities law. In sharp contrast, the OTC Pink Sheets represent the *unregulated* segment of the market, where the companies aren't even required to file with the SEC.

> **Securities and Exchange Commission (SEC)** An agency of the federal government that regulates the disclosure of information about securities and generally oversees the operation of the securities exchanges and markets.

## Foreign Securities Markets

In addition to those in the United States, more than 100 other countries worldwide have organized securities exchanges. Indeed, actively traded markets can be found not only in the major industrialized nations like Japan, Great Britain, Germany, and Canada but also in emerging economies. In terms of market capitalization (total market value of all shares traded), the NYSE Euronext is the biggest stock market in the world, followed by the Tokyo stock market and then the NASDAQ market. Other major exchanges are located in Sydney, Zurich, Hong Kong, Singapore, Rome, and Amsterdam. Besides these markets, you'll find developing markets all over the globe—from Argentina and Armenia to Egypt and Fiji; from Iceland, Israel, and Malaysia to New Zealand, Russia, and Zimbabwe.

## Regulating the Securities Markets

Several laws have been enacted to regulate the activities of various participants in the securities markets and to provide for adequate and accurate disclosure of information to potential and existing investors. State laws, regulating the sale of securities within state borders, typically establish procedures that apply to the sellers of securities doing business within the state. However, the most important and far-reaching securities laws are those enacted by the federal government:

- **Securities Act of 1933.** This act was passed by Congress to ensure full disclosure of information with respect to new security issues and to prevent a stock market collapse similar to the one that occurred during 1929–1932. The Act requires the issuer of a new security to file a registration statement containing information about the new issue with the **Securities and Exchange Commission (SEC)**, an agency of the U.S. government established to enforce federal securities laws.

- **Securities Exchange Act of 1934.** This act expanded the scope of federal regulation and formally established the SEC as the agency in charge of

**National Association of Securities Dealers (NASD)** An agency made up of brokers and dealers in over-the-counter securities that regulates OTC market operations.

**bull market** A market condition normally associated with investor optimism, economic recovery, and expansion; characterized by generally rising securities prices.

**bear market** A condition of the market typically associated with investor pessimism and economic slowdown; characterized by generally falling securities prices.

**stockbroker (account executive, financial consultant)** A person who buys and sells securities on behalf of clients and gives them investment advice and information.

the administration of federal securities laws. The act gives the SEC power to regulate organized securities exchanges and the OTC market by extending disclosure requirements to outstanding securities.

● **Investment Company Act of 1940.** This act protects those purchasing investment company (mutual fund) shares. It established rules and regulations for investment companies and formally authorized the SEC to regulate the companies' practices and procedures. It also prohibits investment companies from paying excessive fees to their advisors and from charging excessive commissions to purchasers of company shares.

● **The Sarbanes-Oxley Act of 2002.** The purpose of this act (known as "SOX") is to eliminate corporate fraud as related to accounting practices and other information released to investors. Among other things, SOX requires an annual evaluation of internal controls and procedures for financial reporting; it also requires the top executives of the corporation, as well as its auditors, to certify the accuracy of its financial statements and disclosures.

● **Other significant federal legislation.** The *Maloney Act of 1938* provided for the establishment of trade associations for the purpose of self-regulation within the securities industry. This act led to the creation of the **National Association of Securities Dealers (NASD)**, which is made up of all brokers and dealers who participate in the OTC market. The NASD is a self-regulatory organization that polices the activities of brokers and dealers to ensure that its standards are upheld. *The Securities Investor Protection Act of 1970* created the SIPC (Securities Investor Protection Corp.), an organization that protects investors against the financial failure of brokerage firms, much as the FDIC protects depositors against bank failures (we'll examine the SIPC later in this chapter).

## Bull Market or Bear?

The general condition of the market is termed as either *bullish* or *bearish*, depending on whether securities prices are rising or falling over extended periods.

Changing market conditions generally stem from changing investor attitudes, changes in economic activity, and certain governmental actions aimed at stimulating or slowing down the economy. Prices go *up* in **bull markets**; these favorable markets are normally associated with investor optimism, economic recovery, and growth. In contrast, prices go *down* in **bear markets**, which are normally associated with investor pessimism and economic slowdowns. These terms are used to describe conditions in the bond and other securities markets as well as the stock market. As a rule, investors can earn attractive rates of return during bull markets and only low (or negative) returns during bear markets. Exhibit 11.2 shows historical U.S. stock market performance going all the way back to 1825.

Look closely at the exhibit and you'll notice that over the past 50 years or so, stock market behavior has been generally bullish, reflecting the growth and prosperity of the economy (the market was up in 38 of the last 50 years). Since the Second World War, the longest bull market lasted 125 months—from November 1990 through March of 2000. This bull market is probably as well known for *how it ended* as it is for the returns it generated. That record-breaking bull market ended abruptly in the spring of 2000, when a nasty bear market took over. After recovering in October 2002, the market generally advanced until about October of 2007, when the full effects of the financial crisis started to become apparent. The loses continued through 2008 as the S&P 500 lost about 37%, but rose by about 40% between March and May of 2009.

## LG3 Making Transactions in the Securities Markets

In many respects, dealing in the securities markets almost seems like operating in another world, one with all kinds of unusual orders and strange-sounding transactions. Actually, making securities transactions is relatively simple once you understand the basics—in fact, you'll probably find it's no harder than using a checking account!

## Stockbrokers

**Stockbrokers** (or **account executives,** as they're also called) buy and sell securities for their customers. Although deeply ingrained in our language, the term *stockbroker* is really somewhat of a misnomer, as they help investors to buy and sell not only stocks but also bonds, convertibles, mutual funds, options, and many other types of securities. Brokers must be licensed by the exchanges and must abide by the strict ethical guidelines of the exchanges and the SEC. They work for brokerage

Exhibit 11.2

## Exhibit 11.2 · Historical Performance of U.S. Stocks as Measured by NYSE Returns

This graphical portrayal of U.S. stock market performance since 1825 shows that the high returns in recent years are quite uncommon. Forturnately, the recent low returns have also been rare in the historical record.

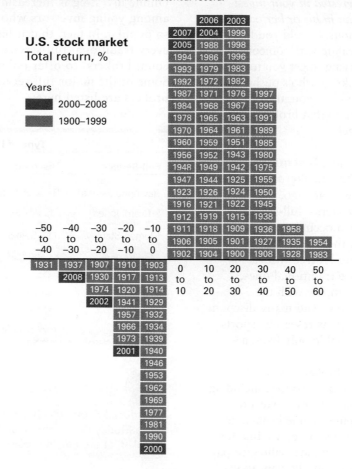

**U.S. stock market**
Total return, %

Years

- ■ 2000–2008
- ▨ 1900–1999

Positive returns:

| 0 to 10 | 10 to 20 | 20 to 30 | 30 to 40 | 40 to 50 | 50 to 60 |
|---|---|---|---|---|---|
| 2006 | 2003 | | | | |
| 2007 | 2004 | 1999 | | | |
| 2005 | 1988 | 1998 | | | |
| 1994 | 1986 | 1996 | | | |
| 1993 | 1979 | 1983 | | | |
| 1992 | 1972 | 1982 | | | |
| 1987 | 1971 | 1976 | 1997 | | |
| 1984 | 1968 | 1967 | 1995 | | |
| 1978 | 1965 | 1963 | 1991 | | |
| 1970 | 1964 | 1961 | 1989 | | |
| 1960 | 1959 | 1951 | 1985 | | |
| 1956 | 1952 | 1943 | 1980 | | |
| 1948 | 1949 | 1942 | 1975 | | |
| 1947 | 1944 | 1925 | 1955 | | |
| 1923 | 1926 | 1924 | 1950 | | |
| 1916 | 1921 | 1922 | 1945 | | |
| 1912 | 1919 | 1915 | 1938 | | |
| 1911 | 1918 | 1909 | 1936 | 1958 | |
| 1906 | 1905 | 1901 | 1927 | 1935 | 1954 |
| 1902 | 1904 | 1900 | 1908 | 1928 | 1933 |

Negative returns:

| -50 to -40 | -40 to -30 | -30 to -20 | -20 to -10 | -10 to 0 |
|---|---|---|---|---|
| 1931 | 1937 | 1907 | 1910 | 1903 |
| | 2008 | 1930 | 1917 | 1913 |
| | | 1974 | 1920 | 1914 |
| | | 2002 | 1941 | 1929 |
| | | | 1957 | 1932 |
| | | | 1966 | 1934 |
| | | | 1973 | 1939 |
| | | | 2001 | 1940 |
| | | | | 1946 |
| | | | | 1953 |
| | | | | 1962 |
| | | | | 1969 |
| | | | | 1977 |
| | | | | 1981 |
| | | | | 1990 |
| | | | | 2000 |

*Sources*: "U.S. Stockmarket Returns: Booms and Busts," http://www.economist.com/daily/chartgallery/displaystory.cfm?story_id=12811306, January 6, 2009, accessed July 2009. Based in part on data from Value Square Asset Management, "A New Historical Database of the NYSE 1815 to 1925: Performance and Predictability," Yale School of Management Working Paper, July 2000.

firms and in essence are there to execute the orders placed. As we saw earlier, procedures for executing orders in broker markets differ a bit from those in dealer markets; but you as an investor would never know the difference because you'd place your order in exactly the same way.

### Selecting a Broker

If you decide to start investing with a *full-service broker*, it's important to select someone *who understands your investment objectives and who can effectively help you pursue them.* If you choose a broker whose own disposition toward investing is similar to yours, then you should be able to avoid conflict and establish a solid working relationship. A good place to start the search is to ask friends, relatives, or business associates to recommend a broker. It's not important to know your

**full-service broker**
A broker who, in addition to executing clients' transactions, offers a full array of brokerage services.

**discount broker** A broker with low overhead who charges low commissions and offers little or no services to investors.

**online broker**
Typically a discount broker through which investors can execute trades electronically/online through a commercial service or on the Internet; also called *Internet broker* or *electronic broker*.

stockbroker socially because most, if not all, of your transactions/orders will probably be placed by phone. A broker should be far more than just a salesperson; *a good broker is someone who's more interested in your investments than in his or her own commissions.* Should you find you're dealing with someone who's always trying to get you to trade your stocks or who's pushing new investments on you, then by all means dump that broker and find a new one!

### Full-Service, Discount, and Online Brokers

Just a few years ago, there were three distinct types of brokers—full-service, discount, and online—and each occupied a well-defined market niche. Today, the lines between these three types of brokers are blurred. Most brokerage firms, even the more traditional ones, now offer online services to compete with the increasingly popular online firms. And many discount brokers now offer services, such as research reports for clients, that once were available only from a full-service broker.

The traditional **full-service broker** offers investors a wide array of brokerage services, including investment advice and information, trade executions, holding securities for safekeeping, online brokerage services, and margin loans. Such services are fine for investors who want such help—and are willing to pay for it. In contrast, investors who simply want to execute trades and aren't interested in obtaining all those brokerage services should consider either a *discount broker* or an *online broker*. **Discount brokers** tend to have low-overhead operations and offer fewer customer services than do full-service brokers. Transactions are initiated by calling a toll-free number—or visiting the broker's Web site—and placing the desired buy or sell order. The brokerage firm then executes the order at the best possible price and confirms the transaction details by phone, e-mail, or regular mail. Depending on the transaction size, *discount brokers can save investors from 30% to 80% of the commissions charged by full-service brokers.*

With the technology that's available to almost everyone today, it's not surprising that investors can just as easily trade securities online as on the phone. All you need is an **online broker** (also called *Internet* or *electronic brokers*) and you, too, can execute

trades electronically. The investor merely accesses the online broker's Web site to open an account, review the commission schedule, or see a demonstration of available transaction services and procedures. Confirmation of electronic trades can take as little as a few seconds, and most occur within a minute. Online investing is increasingly popular, particularly among young investors who enjoy surfing the Web—so popular, in fact, that it has prompted virtually every traditional full-service broker (and many discount brokers) to offer online trading to their clients. Some of the major full-service, discount, and online brokers are listed here:

| Type of Broker | | |
|---|---|---|
| **Full-Service** | **Discount** | **Online** |
| Raymond James | Bank of America | AccuTrade |
| Edward Jones | Charles Schwab | TD Ameritrade |
| Morgan Stanley | J.D. Seibert | E*Trade |
| Merrill Lynch | Muriel Siebert | Fidelity Brokerage Services |
| Wachovia/Wells Fargo | Vanguard Brokerage Services | Scottrade |
| UBS | York Securities | TD Waterhouse |

 **Go to Smart Sites**

Confused about which broker is right for you? Use The Motley Fool's checklist, 10 Ways to Size Up a Broker, at the Fool's Broker Center. ●

### Brokerage Fees

Brokerage firms receive commissions for executing buy and sell orders for their clients. These commissions are said to be *negotiated*, meaning they're not fixed. In practice, however, most firms have *established fee schedules* that they use with small transactions. Fees definitely do differ from one brokerage firm to another, and so it pays to shop around. If you're an "active trader," who generates a couple thousand dollars (or more) in annual commissions, then by all means try to negotiate a reduced commission schedule with your broker. Chances are, they'll probably agree to a deal with you: brokers much prefer active traders to buy-and-hold investors because traders generate a lot more commissions. Generally speaking, brokerage fees on a round lot of common stock will amount to roughly 1% to 2% of the transaction value.

Because there are so many discount brokers today, there is greater variation in fees charged and services offered. The way commissions are calculated also varies; some firms base them on the dollar value of the transaction, some on the number of shares, and some use both. Exhibit 11.3 ranks the best discount brokerage firms using criteria that include commissions. The firms with higher commissions generally offer more services; similarly, many discounters charge clients extra for their research services.

Security transactions can be made in either odd or round lots. An **odd lot** consists of fewer than 100 shares of stock, while a **round lot** represents a 100-share unit or multiples thereof. The sale of 400 shares of stock would be considered a round-lot transaction, but the purchase of 75 shares would be an odd-lot transaction; trading 250 shares of stock would involve two round lots and an odd lot. Because the purchase or sale of odd lots requires additional processing, an added fee—known as an *odd-lot differential*—is often tacked on to the normal commission charge, driving up the costs of these small trades. Indeed, the relatively high cost of an odd-lot trade is why it's best to deal in round lots whenever possible.

### Investor Protection

As a client, you're protected against the loss of securities or cash held by your broker by the **Securities Investor Protection Corporation (SIPC)**, a nonprofit corporation authorized by the Securities Investor Protection Act of 1970 to protect customer accounts against the financial failure of a brokerage firm. Although subject to SEC and congressional oversight, the SIPC is *not* an agency of the U.S. government.

SIPC insurance covers each account for up to $500,000 (of which up to $100,000 may be in cash balances held by the firm). Note, however, that SIPC insurance does not guarantee that the dollar value of the securities will be recovered. It ensures only that *the securities themselves will be returned.* So what happens if your broker gives you bad advice and you lose a lot of money on an investment? SIPC won't help you because it's not intended to insure you against bad investment advice, stock market risk, or broker fraud. If you do have a dispute with your broker, first discuss the situation with the managing officer at the branch where you do your business. If that doesn't help, then write or talk to the firm's compliance officer and contact the securities office in your home state. If you still aren't satisfied, you may have to take the case to **arbitration**, a process whereby you and your broker present the two sides of the argument before an arbitration panel, which then decides how the case will be resolved. If it's *binding* arbitration, and it usually is, then you have no choice but to accept the decision—you cannot go to court to appeal your case.

## Executing Trades

For most individual investors, a securities transaction involves placing a buy or sell order, usually by phone or on the Internet, and later receiving confirmation that the order has been completed. These investors have no idea what happens to their orders. In fact, a lot goes on—and very quickly—once the order is placed. It has to because on a typical day the NYSE alone executes *millions* of trades, and many more occur on the NASDAQ and the rest of the market. In most cases, if the investor places a market order (which we will explain later), then it should take *less than 2 minutes* to place, execute, and confirm a trade.

The process starts with a phone call to the broker, who then transmits the order via sophisticated telecommunications equipment to the stock exchange floor, the NASDAQ market, or the OTC Bulletin Board, where it's promptly executed. Confirmation that the order has been executed is transmitted to the originating broker and then to the customer. Once the trade takes place, the investor has three (business) days to "settle" his or her account with the broker—that is, to pay for the securities. Investors can also use their computers to execute online securities trades. In an online trade, your order goes from your computer to the broker's computer, which checks the type of order and confirms that it's in compliance with regulations. It is then transmitted to the exchange floor, or a NASDAQ (or OTC) dealer for execution. The time for the whole process, including a confirmation that's sent back to your computer, is usually less than a minute.

## Types of Orders

Investors may choose from several different kinds of orders when buying or selling securities. The type of order chosen normally depends on the investor's goals and expectations regarding the given transaction. The three basic types of orders are the market order, limit order, and stop-loss order.

**odd lot** A quantity of fewer than 100 shares of a stock.

**round lot** A quantity of 100 shares of stock or multiples thereof.

**Securities Investor Protection Corporation (SIPC)** A nonprofit corporation, created by Congress and subject to SEC and congressional oversight, that insures customer accounts against the financial failure of a brokerage firm.

**arbitration** A procedure used to settle disputes between a brokerage firm and its clients; both sides present their positions to a board of arbitration, which makes a final and often binding decision on the matter.

## Market Order

An order to buy or sell a security at the best price available at the time it's placed is a **market order**. It's usually the quickest way to have orders filled because market orders are executed as soon as they reach the trading floor. In fact, on small trades of less than a few thousand shares, it takes less than 10 seconds to fill a market order once it hits the trading floor! These orders are

## Exhibit 11.3  SmartMoney's 2009 Discount Broker Survey (Rated on a Scale of 5 Stars)

They say it pays to shop around, and that advice certainly applies when it comes to selecting a broker. Just look at the different commissions these brokers charge to execute essentially the same trade.

| | | | | SCORES | | | | |
|---|---|---|---|---|---|---|---|---|
| RANK* | BROKER | COMMENT | COMMISSION ($)** | MUTUAL FUNDS & INVESTMENT PRODUCTS | BANKING SERVICES | TRADING TOOLS† | RESEARCH | CUSTOMER SERVICE |
| 1 | E*TRADE www.etrade.com | Strength across the board notches top ranking for third straight year. | 9.99 | **** | ***** | ***** | ***** | ***** |
| 2 | Fidelity www.fidelity.com | Keeps No. 2 spot with robust product offerings and biggest mix of funds. | 10.95 | ***** | ***** | ***** | ***** | **** |
| 3 | Charles Schwab www.schwab.com | New, easy-to-use Web site, but takes time to prepare an online trade order. | 12.95 | ***** | **** | *** | ***** | ***** |
| 4 | TradeKing www.tradeking.com | Short on some product offerings; strong on customer service. | 4.95 | *** | ** | ***** | *** | ***** |
| 5 | TD Ameritrade www.tdameritrade.com | Large selection of trading tools. Missing some banking services. | 9.99 | ***** | ** | ***** | **** | *** |
| 6 | Muriel Siebert www.siebertnet.com | Top-ranked in customer service, though lacks robust research. | 14.95 | *** | *** | ***** | *** | ***** |
| 7 | Scottrade www.scottrade.com | Limited banking services. But filling a trade is fast and easy. | 7.00 | **** | * | **** | *** | **** |
| 8 | Firstrade www.firstrade.com | Large selection of products; small mix of research and trading tools. | 6.95 | **** | *** | *** | ** | *** |
| 9 | OptionsXpress www.optionsxpress.com | High marks for trading tools. Limited hours for phone-based customer service. | 9.95 | *** | ** | ***** | *** | ** |
| 10 | Banc of America www.baisidirect.com | $25,000 in bank linked to a brokerage account earns 360 free trades a year. | 14.00 | **** | **** | **** | *** | ** |
| 11 | Just2Trade www.just2trade.com | Newcomer to survey offers cheap trades but caters to experienced investors. | 2.50 | ** | ** | **** | *** | ** |
| 12 | WellsTrade www.wellstrade.com | Combined $25,000 in bank and brokerage earns 100 free trades a year. | 19.95 | *** | ***** | * | **** | *** |
| 13 | ShareBuilder www.sharebuilder.com | Jump three spots, after adding 300 mutual funds. Extra fees for research. | 9.95 | ** | *** | * | * | *** |
| 14 | WallStreet*E www.wallstreete.com | Still bare-bones on research; poor performance in customer service. | 9.99 | **** | *** | *** | * | * |
| 15 | Zecco Trading www.zecco.com | Faster customer service, but free trades now require $25,000 minimum balance. | 0.00 | ** | * | ** | * | *** |
| 16 | SogoTrade www.sogotrade.com | Lacking in mutual funds, bonds, and research. But filling a trade is faster. | 3.00 | * | * | ** | * | ** |

*Criteria are not equity weighted. **For clients with a brokerage balance of $50,000 making up to 20 trades per year." †Includes data from Gomez Inc.

Source: Roya Woverson and Neil Parmar, "SmartMoney's 2009 Broker Survey," in SmartMoney, http://www.smartmoney.com/investing/stocks/SmartMoney-2009-Broker-Survey/?page=8, May 19, 2009, accessed July 2009. SmartMoney Content © 2009 SmartMoney. Licensed for use by Cengage Learning. SmartMoney is a registered trademark of SmartMoney, a Joint Venture of Dow Jones & Company, Inc. & Hearst SM Partnership.

executed through a process that attempts to allow *buy orders* to be filled at the lowest price and *sell orders* at the highest, thereby providing the best possible deal to both the buyers and sellers of a security.

### Limit Order

An order to buy at a specified price (or lower), or sell at a specified price (or higher) is known as a **limit order**. The broker transmits a limit order to a *specialist* dealing in the given security on the floor of the exchange. The order is executed as soon as the specified market price is reached and all other such orders with precedence have been filled. For example, assume you place a limit order to buy 100 shares of a stock at a price of $20, even though the stock is currently selling at $20.50. Once the stock hits $20 and the specialist has cleared all similar orders received before yours, the specialist will execute the order. Although a limit order can be quite effective, it can also cost you money! If, for instance, you wish to buy at 20 or less and the stock price moves from its current $20.50 to $32 while you're waiting, your limit order will have caused you to forgo an opportunity to make a profit of $11.50 per share. Had you placed a market order, this profit would have been yours.

### Stop-Loss Order

An order to *sell a stock* when the market price reaches or drops below a specified level is called a **stop-loss**, or **stop order**. Used to protect the investor against rapid declines in stock prices, the stop order is placed on the specialist's book and activated when the stop price is reached. At that point, the stop order becomes a *market order* to sell. This means that the stock is offered for sale at the prevailing market price, which could be less than the price at which the order was initiated by the stop. For example, imagine that you own 100 shares of DEF, which is currently selling for $25. Because of the high uncertainty associated with the price movements of the stock, you decide to place a stop order to sell at $21. If the stock price drops to $21, your stop order is activated and the specialist will sell all your DEF stock at the best price available, which may be $18 or $19 a share. Of course, if the market price increases, or stays at or about $25 a share, nothing will have been lost by placing the stop-loss order.

## LG4 Becoming an Informed Investor

Face it: Some people know more about investing than others. As a result, they may use certain investment vehicles or tactics that aren't even in another investors' vocabulary. Investor know-how, in short, defines the playing field. It helps determine how well you'll meet your investment objectives. While being an informed

{ *Investor know-how defines the playing field. It helps determine how well you'll meet your investment objectives.* }

investor can't guarantee you success, it can help you avoid unnecessary losses—as happens all too often when people put their money into investment vehicles they don't fully understand. Thus, before making any major investment decision, thoroughly investigate the security and its merits. Formulate some basic expectations about its future performance and gain an understanding of the sources of

© ATANASIS/SHUTTERSTOCK

risk and return. This can usually be done by reading the popular financial press and referring to other print or Internet sources of investment information.

## Annual Stockholders' Reports

Every publicly traded corporation is required to provide its stockholders and other interested parties with **annual stockholders' reports**. These documents contain a wealth of information about the companies, including balance sheets, income statements, and other financial reports. They usually describe the firm's business activities, recent developments, and future plans and outlook. Financial ratios describing past performance are also included, along with other relevant statistics. In fact, annual reports offer a great deal of insight into the company's past, present, and future operations. You can obtain them for free directly from the companies, through a brokerage firm, or at most large libraries; and with today's technology, most companies are also posting their annual reports on the Internet, so now you can obtain them online.

Here are some suggestions to help you get the most information when reading an annual report:

- **Start with the highlights or selected financial data sections.** These provide a quick overview of performance by summarizing key information, such as the past 2 years' revenues, net income, assets, earnings per share (EPS), and dividends.

- **Read the chief executive's letter.** But read it with a careful eye, looking for euphemisms like "a slowing of growth" to describe a "drop in earnings."

- **Move on to the discussion of operations in management's discussion and analysis.** This section provides information on sales, earnings, debt, ongoing litigation, and so on.

- **Review the financial statements, including the notes.** These will tell you about the company's financial condition and performance.

- **Read the auditor's report.** Look for phrases like "*except for*" or "*subject to,*" as they mean just one thing: *there may be problems you need to understand.*

## The Financial Press

The most common source of financial news is the local newspaper. The newspapers in many larger cities often devote several pages to business news and information. Of course, big-city papers, like *The New York Times*, provide even more information. Other, more specific sources of financial news include *The Wall Street Journal*, *Barron's*, *Investor's Business Daily*, and the "Money" section of *USA Today*. These are all national publications that include articles on the behavior of the economy, the market, various industries, and individual companies. The most comprehensive and up-to-date coverage of financial news is provided Monday through Saturday by *The Wall Street Journal*. Other excellent sources of investment information include magazines, such as *Money*, *Forbes*, *Fortune*, *Business Week*, *Smart Money*, and *Kiplinger's Personal Finance*. The Internet has also become a major source of information for investors.

### Market Data

Usually presented in the form of averages, or indexes, *market data* describe the general behavior of the securities markets. The averages and indexes are based on the price movements of a select group of securities over an extended period. They're used to capture the overall performance of the market as a whole. You would want to follow one or more of these measures *to get a feel for how the market is doing over time* and, perhaps, an indication of what lies ahead. The absolute level of the index at a specific time (or on a given day) is far less important than *what's been happening to that index over a given period.* The most commonly cited market measures are those calculated by Dow Jones, Standard & Poor's, the New York Stock Exchange, and NASDAQ. These measures are all intended to track the behavior of the stock market, particularly NYSE stocks (Dow, S&P, and NYSE averages all follow stocks on the big board).

**DOW JONES INDUSTRIAL AVERAGES.** The grand-daddy of them all and probably the most widely followed measure of stock market performance is the **Dow Jones Industrial Average (DJIA)**. Actually, the Dow Jones averages, which began in 1896, are made up of four parts: (1) an industrial average, the DJIA, which is based on 30 stocks; (2) a transportation average based on 20 stocks; (3) a utility average based on 15 stocks; and (4) a composite average based on all 65 industrial, transportation, and utility stocks. Most of the stocks in the DJIA are picked from the NYSE; but a few NASDAQ stocks, such as Intel and Microsoft, are included. Although these stocks are intended to represent a cross section of companies, there's a strong bias toward blue chips, which is a major criticism of the Dow Jones Industrial Average. The Bonus Exhibit, "The Dow Jones Industrial Average" (available at 4ltrpress.cengage.com), lists the 30 stocks currently in the DJIA.

**STANDARD & POOR'S INDEXES.** The **Standard & Poor's (S&P) indexes** are similar to the Dow Jones averages in that both are used to capture the overall performance of the market. However, some important differences exist between the two measures. For one thing, the S&P uses a lot more stocks; the popular S&P 500 composite index is based on 500 different stocks, whereas the DJIA uses only 30. What's more, the S&P index is made up of all large NYSE stocks in addition to some major AMEX and NASDAQ stocks, so there are not only more issues in the S&P sample but also a greater breadth of representation. Finally, there are some technical differences in the mathematical procedures used to compute the two measures; the Dow Jones is an *average*, whereas the S&P is an *index*. Despite the technical differences, movements in these two measures are, in fact, *highly correlated*. Even so, the S&P has a much lower value than the DJIA—for example, in September 2009, the Dow stood at over 9,500, whereas the S&P index of 500 stocks was just over 1000. Now, this doesn't mean that the S&P consists of less valuable stocks; rather, the disparity is due solely to the different methods used to compute the measures. In addition to the S&P 500, two other widely-followed S&P indexes are the *MidCap 400* (made up of 400 medium-sized companies with market values ranging from about $750 million to $3.3 billion) and the *SmallCap 600* (consisting of companies with market caps of around $200 million to $1 billion).

**THE NYSE, NASDAQ, AND OTHER MARKET INDEXES.** The most widely followed exchange-based indexes are those of the New York Stock Exchange (NYSE) and NASDAQ. The **NYSE index** includes all the stocks listed on the "big board" and provides a measure of performance in that market. Behavior in the NASDAQ market is measured by several indexes, the most comprehensive of which is the *NASDAQ Composite index*, which is calculated using virtually all the stocks traded on NASDAQ. In addition, there's the *NASDAQ 100 index*, which tracks the price behavior of the biggest 100 (non-financial) firms traded on NASDAQ—companies like Microsoft, Intel, Oracle, Cisco, Staples, and

Dell. The NASDAQ Composite is often used as a benchmark in assessing the price behavior of *high-tech* stocks.

Besides these major indexes, there are a couple of other measures of market performance, one of which is the **Dow Jones Wilshire 5000 index**. It's estimated that the Wilshire index reflects the *total market value of 98%–99% of all publicly traded stocks in the United States*. In essence, it shows what's happening in the stock market as a whole—the dollar amount of market value added or lost as the market moves up and down. In this index, one point is worth $1 *billion* (versus about 1 cent in the DJIA). Another widely followed measure is the *Russell 2000*, which tracks the behavior of 2,000 relatively small companies and is widely considered to be a fairly accurate measure of the small-cap segment of the market.

### Industry Data

Local newspapers, *The Wall Street Journal*, *Barron's*, and various financial publications regularly contain articles and data about different industries. For example, Standard & Poor's *Industry Surveys* provides detailed descriptions and statistics for all the major industries; on a smaller scale, *Business Week* and other magazines regularly include indexes of industry performance and price levels.

### Stock Quotes

To see how price quotations work and what they mean, consider the quotes that appear daily (Monday–Saturday) in *The Wall Street Journal*. As we'll see, the quotations provide not only current prices but a great deal of additional information as well. A portion of the NYSE stock quotations from *The Wall Street Journal* is presented in Exhibit 11.4. (We'll look at stock quotes here, briefly discuss bond prices in Chapter 12, and then cover mutual fund quotes in Chapter 13.) Let's use the quotations for *Nike* stock, which trades under the symbol *NKE*, for purposes of illustration. These quotes are for July 24, 2009. A glance at the quotes shows that stocks, like most other securities, are given in dollars and cents.

**Standard & Poor's (S&P) indexes** Indexes compiled by Standard & Poor's that are similar to the DJIA but employ different computational methods and consist of far more stocks.

**NYSE index** An index of the performance of all stocks listed on the New York Stock Exchange.

**Dow Jones Wilshire 5000 index** An index of the total market value of the approximately 6,000–7,000 or so most actively traded stocks in the United States.

**Exhibit 11.4** **Listed Stock Quotes**

This list summarizes one day's trading activity and price quotes for a group of stocks traded on the New York Stock Exchange. Note that, in addition to the latest stock prices, a typical stock quote conveys an array of other information.

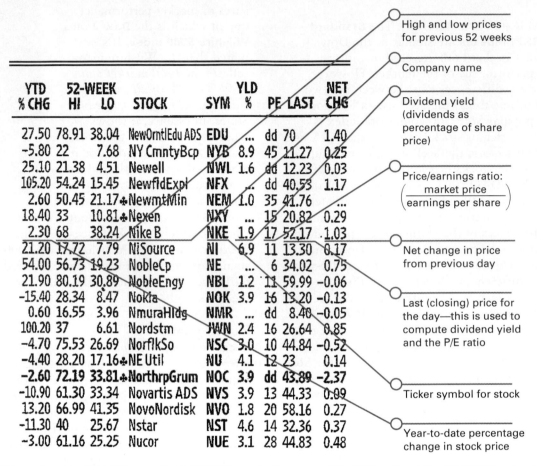

| YTD % CHG | 52-WEEK HI | LO | STOCK | SYM | YLD % | PE | LAST | NET CHG |
|---|---|---|---|---|---|---|---|---|
| 27.50 | 78.91 | 38.04 | NewOrntlEdu ADS | EDU | ... | dd | 70 | 1.40 |
| -5.80 | 22 | 7.68 | NY CmntyBcp | NYB | 8.9 | 45 | 11.27 | 0.25 |
| 25.10 | 21.38 | 4.51 | Newell | NWL | 1.6 | dd | 12.23 | 0.03 |
| 105.20 | 54.24 | 15.45 | NewfldExpl | NFX | ... | dd | 40.53 | 1.17 |
| 2.60 | 50.45 | 21.17✦ | NewmtMin | NEM | 1.0 | 35 | 41.76 | ... |
| 18.40 | 33 | 10.81✦ | Nexen | NXY | ... | 15 | 20.82 | 0.29 |
| 2.30 | 68 | 38.24 | Nike B | NKE | 1.9 | 17 | 52.17 | 1.03 |
| 21.20 | 17.72 | 7.79 | NiSource | NI | 6.9 | 11 | 13.30 | 0.17 |
| 54.00 | 56.73 | 19.23 | NobleCp | NE | ... | 6 | 34.02 | 0.75 |
| 21.90 | 80.19 | 30.89 | NobleEngy | NBL | 1.2 | 11 | 59.99 | -0.06 |
| -15.40 | 28.34 | 8.47 | Nokia | NOK | 3.9 | 16 | 13.20 | -0.13 |
| 0.60 | 16.55 | 3.96 | NmuraHldg | NMR | ... | dd | 8.40 | -0.05 |
| 100.20 | 37 | 6.61 | Nordstm | JWN | 2.4 | 16 | 26.64 | 0.85 |
| -4.70 | 75.53 | 26.69 | NorflkSo | NSC | 3.0 | 10 | 44.84 | -0.52 |
| -4.40 | 28.20 | 17.16✤ | NE Util | NU | 4.1 | 12 | 23 | 0.14 |
| -2.60 | 72.19 | 33.81✦ | NorthrpGrum | NOC | 3.9 | dd | 43.89 | -2.37 |
| -10.90 | 61.30 | 33.34 | Novartis ADS | NVS | 3.9 | 13 | 44.33 | 0.09 |
| 13.20 | 66.99 | 41.35 | NovoNordisk | NVO | 1.8 | 20 | 58.16 | 0.27 |
| -11.30 | 40 | 25.67 | Nstar | NST | 4.6 | 14 | 32.36 | 0.37 |
| -3.00 | 61.16 | 25.25 | Nucor | NUE | 3.1 | 28 | 44.83 | 0.48 |

High and low prices for previous 52 weeks

Company name

Dividend yield (dividends as percentage of share price)

Price/earnings ratio: $\frac{\text{market price}}{\text{earnings per share}}$

Net change in price from previous day

Last (closing) price for the day—this is used to compute dividend yield and the P/E ratio

Ticker symbol for stock

Year-to-date percentage change in stock price

Starting with the first column on the left (in Exhibit 11.4) and then working our way across, we see that the change in Nike's stock price for the year to date (YTD) is 2.30%. Over the past 52 weeks, Nike hit a high of $68 a share and a low of $38.24. Next is the company name, Nike B; the "B" after the company name indicates that it's *Nike's Class B common shares* that are listed and traded on the NYSE. Following that, we see that Nike's trading symbol is NKE. Its annual cash dividend yield is 1.9%, which is found by dividing the latest annual dividend by the indicated closing price. The next entry is the P/E ratio, which is the current market price divided by the per-share earnings for the most recent 12-month period (these are known as "trailing P/Es"); as can be seen, NKE is

trading at a P/E of 17 times earnings—a nice solid multiple. The last price is the closing price for the indicated quotation day, followed by the net change in Nike's price from the close of the prior trading day. We see that Nike's closing price (on the final trade of the day) was $52.17, which was $1.03 higher than the price at which the stock had ended the day before, when it closed at $51.14. Basically the same quotation system is used for NASDAQ *Global Market* and *National Market* shares. That's not the case, however, for small NASDAQ/OTC stocks, where you may get little more than the stock's name and symbol, share volume, closing price, and change in price; and even then, such information is provided for only a limited number of the larger companies.

## Advisory Services

Subscription advisory services provide information and recommendations on various industries and specific securities. The services normally cost from $50 to several hundred dollars a year, although you can usually review such material (for free) at your broker's office, at university and public libraries, or online. Probably the best-known investment advisory services are those provided by Standard & Poor's, Moody's Investors Service, and Value Line Investment Survey. An example of one of these reports is given in Exhibit 11.5. This two-page report, prepared by Standard & Poor's, presents a concise summary of a company's financial history, current finances, and future prospects; similar stock reports are also available from *Value Line* and Morningstar.

## LG5 Online Investing

The Internet today is a major force in the investing environment. It has opened the world of investing to individual investors, leveling the playing field and providing access to tools and market information formerly restricted to professionals. Not only can you trade all types of securities online, you can also find a wealth of information, from real-time stock quotes to securities analysts' research reports. So instead of weeding through mounds of paper, investors can quickly sort through vast databases to find appropriate investments, monitor their current investments, and make securities transactions—all without leaving their computers. However, online investing also carries risks. The Internet requires investors to exercise the same—and possibly more—caution as they would if they were getting information from and placing orders with a human broker. You don't have the safety net of a live broker suggesting that you rethink your trade. Online or off, the basic rules for smart investing are still the same: *know what you're buying, from whom, and at what level of risk.*

## Online Investor Services

The Internet offers a full array of online investor services, from up-to-the-minute stock quotes and research reports to charting services and portfolio tracking. When it comes to investing, you name it and you can probably find it online! Unfortunately, although many of these are truly high-quality sites offering valuable information, many others are pure garbage, so be careful when entering the world of online investing. Let's now review the kinds of investor services you can find online, starting with investor education sites.

## Investor Education

The Internet offers a wide array of tutorials, online classes, and articles to educate the novice investor. Even experienced investors will find sites that expand their investing knowledge. Although most good investment-oriented Web sites include many educational resources, here are a few good sites featuring *investment fundamentals*.

- *The Motley Fool* (**http://www.fool.com**) *Fool's School* has sections on fundamentals of investing, mutual fund investing, choosing a broker, investment strategies and styles, lively discussion boards, and more.
- Morningstar (**http://www.morningstar.com**) provides comprehensive information on stocks mutual funds, ETFs, and more.
- Zacks Investment Research (**http://www.zacks.com**) is an excellent starting place to learn what the Internet can offer investors.
- NASDAQ (**http://www.nasdaq.com**) has an Investor Resource section that helps with financial planning and choosing a broker.

## Investment Tools

Once you're familiar with the basics of investing, you can use the Internet to develop financial plans and set investment goals, find securities that meet your investment objectives, analyze potential investments, and organize your portfolio. Many of these tools, once used only by professional money managers, are free to anyone who wants to go online.

### FINANCIAL ROAD SIGN

**SUCCESSFUL ONLINE INVESTING**

Before submitting an online stock trade, follow these tips to protect yourself from common problems.

- Know how to place and confirm your order before you begin trading.
- Verify the stock symbol of the security you wish to buy (or sell).
- Use limit orders to obtain a specific desired price.
- Know what to do if you cannot access your online account. Most trading firms provide alternatives that include automated telephone trades, faxing an order, or talking with a broker over the telephone.
- Double-check orders for accuracy. Review the confirmation notice to make sure each trade was completed according to your instructions.

*Source:* "Tips for Online Investing: What You Need to Know about Trading in Fast-Moving Markets," U.S. Securities and Exchange Commission, http://www.sec.gov/investor/pubs/onlinetips.htm, accessed July 2009.

## Exhibit 11.5 An S&P Stock Report

An S&P report like this one provides a wealth of information about the operating results and financial condition of the company and is an invaluable source of information to investors.

Stock Report | August 1, 2009 | NYS Symbol: **NKE** | NKE is in the S&P 500

**STANDARD &POOR'S**

# NIKE Inc.

| **S&P Recommendation** BUY ★★★★☆ | Price $56.64 (as of Jul 31, 2009) | 12-Mo. Target Price $65.00 | Investment Style Large-Cap Growth |

UPDATE: PLEASE SEE THE ANALYST'S LATEST RESEARCH NOTE IN THE COMPANY NEWS SECTION

**GICS Sector** Consumer Discretionary
**Sub-Industry** Footwear

**Summary** NIKE is the world's leading designer and marketer of high-quality athletic footwear, athletic apparel, and accessories.

### Key Stock Statistics (Source S&P, Vickers, company reports)

| | | | | | | | |
|---|---|---|---|---|---|---|---|
| 52-Wk Range | $68.00–38.24 | S&P Oper. EPS 2010E | 3.90 | Market Capitalization(B) | $22.125 | Beta | 0.85 |
| Trailing 12-Month EPS | $3.03 | S&P Oper. EPS 2011E | NA | Yield (%) | 1.77 | S&P 3-Yr. Proj. EPS CAGR(%) | 6 |
| Trailing 12-Month P/E | 18.7 | P/E on S&P Oper. EPS 2010E | 14.5 | Dividend Rate/Share | $1.00 | S&P Credit Rating | A+ |
| $10K Invested 5 Yrs Ago | $16,764 | Common Shares Outstg. (M) | 485.9 | Institutional Ownership (%) | 89 | | |

### Price Performance

30-Week Mov. Avg. · · · 10-Week Mov. Avg. – – GAAP Earnings vs. Previous Year   Volume Above Avg. STARS
12-Mo. Target Price — Relative Strength   ▲ Up ▼ Down ▶ No Change   Below Avg.

Options: ASE, CBOE, P, Ph

Analysis prepared by **Marie Driscoll, CFA** on June 15, 2009, when the stock traded at **$56.61**.

### Highlights

➤ We project revenue growth of about 4% for FY 09 (May), on growth estimates of 15% for Asia/Pacific and 3% for the U.S. We see flat European sales slowing from a currency-charged 19% gain in FY 08. We see FY 10 sales growth of about 3%. We think NKE's broad geographic exposure, with more than 60% of sales outside the U.S., positions it well for growth, while mitigating risk overall. China is NKE's second largest market, with an estimated $1.5 billion in sales in FY 09.

➤ We see operating margins at 12.9% (down 20 bps) in FY 09, as NKE holds SG&A spending flat, reduces management layers and leverages support services globally. NKE is in the midst of a companywide restructuring expected to result in a 4% work force reduction, at a cost of $175 million to $225 million, which should benefit FY 10 profitability by a like amount. We see modest operating margin expansion in FY 10.

➤ NKE had $2.6 billion in cash and short-term investments at the end of February 2009 ($3.69/share net of debt), and generates strong free cash flow. We expect NKE to maintain its dividend while suspending its share buyback program as part of a cash conservation policy.

### Investment Rationale/Risk

➤ Over the past three years, NKE has more than doubled its quarterly dividend and repurchased nearly $3.3 billion worth of its shares. We see strong fundamentals and a dominant global brand with exceptional international growth opportunities supporting the share price. Moreover, NKE has launched key marketing and sales strategies that are designed to more closely align the company and sales with key markets. NKE entered the final quarter of FY 09 with future orders down 10% for the Nike brand (-2% excluding currency impact). Recent retail sales suggest sporting goods retailers enjoy more robust demand than other retailers, which should translate into increased wholesale orders in the FY 10 first half.

➤ Risks to our recommendation and target price include a severe economic slowdown domestically and a greater than expected moderation in consumer spending. International risks include economic weakness, supply disruptions, and unfavorable currency fluctuations.

➤ Our 12-month target price of $65 is equal to about 17X our FY 10 EPS estimate of $3.90, at the low end of the 14X to 26X range in which the stock has traded over the past five years.

### Qualitative Risk Assessment

| LOW | MEDIUM | HIGH |

Our risk assessment reflects what we see as NKE's strong financial and operating metrics, offset by an increasingly competitive global marketplace and prospects for slowing consumer spending in the U.S.

### Quantitative Evaluations

**S&P Quality Ranking**   A+

| D | C | B- | B | B+ | A- | A | A+ |

**Relative Strength Rank**   MODERATE

48

LOWEST = 1   HIGHEST = 99

### Revenue/Earnings Data

**Revenue (Million $)**

| | 1Q | 2Q | 3Q | 4Q | Year |
|---|---|---|---|---|---|
| 2009 | 5,432 | 4,590 | 4,441 | 4,713 | 19,176 |
| 2008 | 4,655 | 4,340 | 4,544 | 5,088 | 18,627 |
| 2007 | 4,194 | 3,822 | 3,927 | 4,383 | 16,326 |
| 2006 | 3,862 | 3,475 | 3,613 | 4,005 | 14,955 |
| 2005 | 3,562 | 3,148 | 3,308 | 3,721 | 13,740 |
| 2004 | 3,025 | 2,837 | 2,904 | 3,487 | 12,253 |

**Earnings Per Share ($)**

| | | | | | |
|---|---|---|---|---|---|
| 2009 | 1.03 | 0.80 | 0.50 | 0.70 | 3.03 |
| 2008 | 1.12 | 0.71 | 0.92 | 0.98 | 3.74 |
| 2007 | 0.74 | 0.64 | 0.68 | 0.86 | 2.93 |
| 2006 | 0.81 | 0.57 | 0.62 | 0.64 | 2.64 |
| 2005 | 0.61 | 0.49 | 0.51 | 0.65 | 2.24 |
| 2004 | 0.49 | 0.33 | 0.37 | 0.57 | 1.76 |

Fiscal year ended May 31. Next earnings report expected: Late September. EPS Estimates based on S&P Operating Earnings; historical GAAP earnings are as reported.

### Dividend Data (Dates: mm/dd Payment Date: mm/dd/yy)

| Amount ($) | Date Decl. | Ex-Div. Date | Stk. of Record | Payment Date |
|---|---|---|---|---|
| 0.230 | 08/11 | 09/04 | 09/08 | 10/01/08 |
| 0.250 | 11/21 | 12/04 | 12/08 | 01/05/09 |
| 0.250 | 02/12 | 03/05 | 03/09 | 04/01/09 |
| 0.250 | 05/12 | 06/04 | 06/08 | 07/01/09 |

Dividends have been paid since 1984. Source: Company reports.

**Please read the Required Disclosures and Analyst Certification on the last page of this report.**

The McGraw-Hill Companies

Exhibit 11.5  An S&P Stock Report *continued*

Stock Report | August 1, 2009 | NYS Symbol: **NKE**

# NIKE Inc.

**STANDARD & POOR'S**

## Quantitative Evaluations

**S&P Fair Value Rank**  3+

| 1 | 2 | **3** | 4 | 5 |

LOWEST                    HIGHEST

Based on S&P's proprietary quantitative model, stocks are ranked from most overvalued (1) to most undervalued (5).

**Fair Value Calculation**  $51.50

Analysis of the stock's current worth, based on S&P's proprietary quantitative model suggests that NKE is slightly overvalued by $5.14 or 9.1%.

**Investability Quotient Percentile**  | 99 |

LOWEST = 1                    HIGHEST = 100

NKE scored higher than 99% of all companies for which an S&P Report is available.

**Volatility**  | **LOW** | AVERAGE | HIGH |

**Technical Evaluation**  NEUTRAL

Since July, 2009, the technical indicators for NKE have been NEUTRAL.

**Insider Activity**  | UNFAVORABLE | **NEUTRAL** | FAVORABLE |

## Expanded Ratio Analysis

| | 2009 | 2008 | 2007 | 2006 |
|---|---|---|---|---|
| Price/Sales | 1.45 | 1.38 | 2.01 | 1.75 |
| Price/EBITDA | NA | 9.36 | 13.64 | 1.09 |
| Price/Pretax Income | 14.21 | 10.27 | 14.89 | 12.20 |
| P/E Ratio | 18.69 | 13.65 | 21.96 | 18.77 |
| Avg. Diluted Shares Outstg (M) | 490.7 | 504.1 | 509.9 | 527.6 |

Figures based on calendar year-end price

## Key Growth Rates and Averages

| Past Growth Rate (%) | 1 Year | 3 Years | 5 Years | 9 Years |
|---|---|---|---|---|
| Sales | 2.95 | 9.17 | 9.70 | 9.62 |
| Net Income | -21.06 | 4.40 | 11.01 | 11.62 |

| Ratio Analysis (Annual Avg.) | | | | |
|---|---|---|---|---|
| Net Margin (%) | 7.75 | 9.00 | 9.03 | 9.22 |
| % LT Debt to Capitalization | 4.77 | 3.37 | 4.19 | 7.86 |
| Return on Equity (%) | 18.00 | 21.92 | 22.47 | 24.06 |

## Company Financials  Fiscal Year Ended May 31

| Per Share Data ($) | 2009 | 2008 | 2007 | 2006 | 2005 | 2004 | 2003 | 2002 | 2001 | 2000 |
|---|---|---|---|---|---|---|---|---|---|---|
| Tangible Book Value | 16.54 | 13.51 | 12.93 | 11.23 | 9.77 | 8.14 | 7.22 | 6.39 | 5.77 | 5.05 |
| Cash Flow | NA | 4.36 | 3.51 | 3.17 | 2.72 | 2.22 | 1.83 | 3.51 | 1.44 | 1.37 |
| Earnings | 3.03 | 3.74 | 2.93 | 2.64 | 2.24 | 1.76 | 1.39 | 1.23 | 1.08 | 1.04 |
| S&P Core Earnings | 3.56 | 3.67 | 2.89 | 2.56 | 2.14 | 1.68 | 1.31 | 1.16 | 1.03 | NA |
| Dividends | 0.83 | 0.68 | 0.56 | 0.45 | 0.45 | 0.34 | 0.26 | 0.24 | 0.24 | 0.24 |
| Payout Ratio | 27% | 18% | 19% | 17% | 20% | 19% | 19% | 20% | 22% | 23% |
| Calendar Year | 2008 | 2007 | 2006 | 2005 | 2004 | 2003 | 2002 | 2001 | 2000 | 1999 |
| Prices:High | 70.60 | 67.93 | 50.60 | 45.77 | 46.22 | 34.27 | 32.14 | 30.03 | 28.50 | 33.47 |
| Prices:Low | 42.68 | 47.46 | 37.76 | 37.55 | 32.91 | 21.19 | 19.27 | 17.75 | 12.91 | 19.38 |
| P/E Ratio:High | 23 | 18 | 17 | 17 | 21 | 20 | 26 | 24 | 26 | 32 |
| P/E Ratio:Low | 14 | 13 | 13 | 14 | 15 | 12 | 16 | 14 | 12 | 19 |

| Income Statement Analysis (Million $) | | | | | | | | | | |
|---|---|---|---|---|---|---|---|---|---|---|
| Revenue | 19,176 | 18,627 | 16,326 | 14,955 | 13,740 | 12,253 | 10,697 | 9,893 | 9,489 | 8,995 |
| Operating Income | NA | 2,747 | 2,402 | 23,912 | 2,151 | 1,802 | 1,485 | 1,291 | 1,212 | 1,150 |
| Depreciation | 347 | 313 | 270 | 282 | 257 | 252 | 239 | 224 | 197 | 188 |
| Interest Expense | NA | 67.1 | Nil | Nil | 39.7 | 40.3 | 42.9 | 47.6 | 58.7 | 45.0 |
| Pretax Income | 1,957 | 2,503 | 2,200 | 2,142 | 1,860 | 1,450 | 1,123 | 2,035 | 921 | 919 |
| Effective Tax Rate | 24.0% | 24.8% | 32.2% | 35.0% | 34.9% | 34.8% | 34.1% | 17.2% | 36.0% | 37.0% |
| Net Income | 1,487 | 1,883 | 1,492 | 1,392 | 1,212 | 946 | 740 | 1,686 | 590 | 579 |
| S&P Core Earnings | 1,748 | 1,848 | 1,472 | 1,346 | 1,148 | 897 | 698 | 632 | 559 | NA |

| Balance Sheet & Other Financial Data (Million $) | | | | | | | | | | |
|---|---|---|---|---|---|---|---|---|---|---|
| Cash | 3,455 | 2,776 | 1,857 | 954 | 1,388 | 828 | 634 | 576 | 304 | 254 |
| Current Assets | NA | 8,839 | 8,077 | 7,359 | 6,351 | 5,512 | 4,680 | 4,158 | 3,625 | 3,596 |
| Total Assets | 13,250 | 12,443 | 10,688 | 9,870 | 8,794 | 7,892 | 6,714 | 6,443 | 5,820 | 5,857 |
| Current Liabilities | NA | 3,322 | 2,584 | 2,623 | 1,999 | 2,009 | 2,015 | 1,836 | 1,787 | 2,140 |
| Long Term Debt | 437 | 441 | Nil | Nil | 687 | 682 | 552 | 626 | 436 | 470 |
| Common Equity | 8,693 | 7,825 | 7,025 | 6,285 | 5,644 | 4,782 | 3,991 | 3,839 | 3,495 | 3,136 |
| Total Capital | 9,163 | 8,273 | 7,026 | 6,286 | 6,332 | 5,464 | 4,543 | 4,465 | 3,931 | 3,607 |
| Capital Expenditures | 456 | 449 | 314 | 334 | 257 | 214 | 186 | 283 | 318 | 420 |
| Cash Flow | NA | 2,196 | 1,761 | 1,674 | 1,469 | 1,198 | 979 | 1,909 | 787 | 767 |
| Current Ratio | 3.0 | 2.7 | 3.1 | 2.8 | 3.2 | 2.7 | 2.3 | 2.3 | 2.0 | 1.7 |
| % Long Term Debt of Capitalization | 4.8 | 5.3 | Nil | Nil | 10.9 | 12.5 | 12.1 | 14.0 | 11.1 | 13.0 |
| % Net Income of Revenue | 7.8 | 10.1 | 9.1 | 9.3 | 8.8 | 7.7 | 6.9 | 17.0 | 6.2 | 6.4 |
| % Return on Assets | 11.6 | 16.3 | 14.5 | 14.9 | 14.5 | 12.9 | 11.3 | 27.5 | 10.1 | 10.4 |
| % Return on Equity | 18.0 | 25.4 | 22.4 | 23.3 | 23.2 | 21.6 | 18.9 | 46.0 | 17.8 | 17.9 |

Data as orig reptd.; bef. results of disc opers/spec. items. Per share data adj. for stk. divs.; EPS diluted. E-Estimated. NA-Not Available. NM-Not Meaningful. NR-Not Ranked. UR-Under Review.

Source: Reprinted by permission of Standard & Poor's Financial Services LLC, a division of the McGraw-Hill Companies © 2009.

**portfolio** A collection of securities assembled for the purpose of meeting common investment goals.

**diversification** The process of choosing securities with dissimilar risk-return characteristics in order to create a portfolio that provides an acceptable level of return and an acceptable exposure to risk.

**INVESTMENT PLANNING.** Online calculators and worksheets can help you find answers to your financial planning and investing questions. With them, you can figure out how much to save each month for a particular goal, such as the down payment for your first home, a college education for your children, or to be able to retire by the time you reach 55. For example, Fidelity (**http://www.fidelity.com**) has a wide selection of planning tools that deal with such topics as investment growth, college planning, and retirement planning. One of the best sites for financial calculators is *Kiplinger's Personal Finance* (**http://www.kiplinger.com**). Go to their personal finance page, click on "Tools & Calculators," and you'll find over 100 calculators dealing with everything from stocks, bonds, and mutual funds to retirement planning, home buying, and taxes.

**INVESTMENT RESEARCH AND SCREENING.** One of the best investor services offered online is the ability to conduct high quality in-depth research on stocks, bonds, mutual funds, and other types of investment vehicles. Go to a site like **http://www.kiplinger.com**, click on "Investing," and you can obtain literally dozens of pages of financial and market information about a specific stock or mutual fund. Many of these sites have links back to the company itself, so with a few mouse clicks, you can obtain the company's annual report, detailed financial statements, and historical summaries of a full array of financial and market ratios. In addition, you'll also find various *online screening tools* that can be used to identify attractive and potentially rewarding investment vehicles. These tools, available at sites like Quicken, Morningstar, or MSN Money Central, enable you to quickly sort through huge databases of stocks and mutual funds to find those that meet specific characteristics, such as stocks with low or high P/E multiples, small market capitalizations, high dividend yields, specific revenue growth, and low debt-to-equity ratios. You answer a series of questions to specify the type of stock or fund you're looking for, performance criteria you desire, cost parameters, and so on. The screen then provides a list of stocks (or funds) that have met the standards you've set.

 **Go to Smart Sites**

Head to MSN MoneyCentral Investor to find good educational articles, research, interactive tools like Research Wizard, and a portfolio tracker. ●

**PORTFOLIO TRACKING.** Almost every investment-oriented Web site includes *portfolio tracking tools*. Simply enter the number of shares held, the purchase price, and the symbol for the stocks or mutual funds you wish to follow, and the tracker automatically updates the value of your portfolio in real time. What's more, you can usually click on one of the provided links and quickly obtain detailed information about each stock or mutual fund in your portfolio. Quicken.com, MSN MoneyCentral (**http://moneycentral.msn.com/investor**), and E*Trade (**http://www.etrade.com**) all have portfolio trackers that are easy to set up and use. For example, Quicken's tracker alerts you whenever an analyst changes the rating on one of your stocks or funds and tells you how well you're diversified among the major asset classes or sectors you hold.

## LG6 Managing Your Investment Holdings

Buying and selling securities is not difficult; the hard part is finding securities that will provide the kind of return you're looking for. Like most individual investors, in time you too will be buying, selling, and trading securities with ease. Eventually, your investment holdings will increase to the point where you're managing a whole portfolio of securities. In essence, a **portfolio** is a collection of investment vehicles assembled to meet a common investment goal. But a portfolio is far more than a collection of investments! It breathes life into your investment program, as it combines your personal and financial traits with your investment objectives to give some structure to your investments.

Seasoned investors often devote lots of attention to constructing diversified portfolios of securities. Such portfolios consist of stocks and bonds selected not only for their returns but also for their combined risk-return behavior. The idea behind **diversification** is that by combining securities with dissimilar risk-return characteristics, you can produce a portfolio of reduced risk and more predictable levels of return. In recent years, investment researchers have shown that you can achieve a noticeable reduction in risk simply by diversifying your investment holdings. For the small investor with a moderate amount of money to invest, this means that *investing in several securities rather than a single one should be beneficial*. The payoff from diversification comes in the form of reduced risk without a significant impact on return.

## Building a Portfolio of Securities

In developing a portfolio of investment holdings, it's assumed that diversification is a desirable investment attribute that leads to improved return and/or reduced risk. Again, as emphasized previously, holding a variety of investments is far more desirable than concentrating all your investments in a single security or industry. When you first start investing, you probably won't be able to do much, if any, diversifying because of insufficient investment capital. However, as you build up your investment funds, your opportunities for diversification will increase dramatically. Certainly, by the time you have $10,000 to $15,000 to invest, you should start to diversify your holdings. To get an idea of the kind of portfolio diversification employed by investors, look at the following numbers, which shows the types of investments held by *average individual investors:*

| Type of Investment Product | Percentage of Portfolio (June 2009) |
|---|---|
| Stocks and stock mutual funds | 57% |
| Bonds and bond mutual funds | 16% |
| Short-term investments (CDs, money market deposit accounts, etc.) | 27% |
| Total | 100% |

This portfolio reflects the results of monthly asset allocation surveys conducted by the *American Association of Individual Investors*; whether this is what your portfolio should look like depends on a number of factors, including your own needs and objectives.

### Investor Characteristics

To formulate an effective portfolio strategy, begin with an honest evaluation of your own financial condition and family situation. Pay particular attention to variables like these:

- Level and stability of income
- Family factors
- Investment horizon
- Net worth
- Investment experience and age
- Disposition toward risk

These are the variables that set the tone for your investments. They determine the kinds of investments you should consider and how long you can tie up your money. For your portfolio to work, it must be tailored to meet your personal financial needs. For example, the size and predictability of an investor's employment income has a significant bearing on portfolio strategy. An investor with a secure job is more likely to embark on a more aggressive investment program than is an investor with a less secure position. Income taxes also bear on the investment decision. The higher an investor's income, the more important the tax ramifications of an investment program become.

In addition, an individual's investment experience will influence the type of investment strategy employed. It's best to "get your feet wet" in the investment market by slipping into it slowly rather than leaping in head first. Investors who make risky initial investments often suffer heavy losses, damaging the long-run potential of their entire investment program. A cautiously developed investment program will likely provide far more favorable long-run results than an impulsive, risky one. Finally, investors should carefully consider risk. High-risk investments have not only high return potential but also high risk of loss. A good rule to remember is that *an investor's exposure to risk should never exceed his ability to bear that risk!*

### Investor Objectives

After developing a personal financial profile, the investor's next question is: "What do I want from my portfolio?" This seems like an easy question to answer. Ideally, we would all like to double our money every year by making low-risk investments. However, the realities of the highly competitive investment environment make this outcome unlikely, so the question must be answered more realistically. There's generally a trade-off between earning a high current income from an investment and obtaining significant capital appreciation from it. An investor must choose one or the other; it's hard to obtain both from a single investment vehicle. Of course, in a portfolio it's possible to have a *balance* of both income and growth (capital gains); but most often that involves "tilting" the portfolio in one direction (e.g., toward income) or the other (toward growth).

An investor's needs should determine which avenue to choose. For instance, a retired investor whose income depends partly on her portfolio will probably choose a lower-risk, current-income-oriented approach for financial survival. In contrast, a high-income, financially secure investor may be much more willing to take on risky investments in hopes of improving her net worth. Likewise, a young investor with a secure job may be less concerned about current income and more able to bear risk. This type of investor will likely be more capital gains oriented and may choose speculative investments.

## Asset Allocation and Portfolio Management

A portfolio must be built around an individual's needs, which in turn depend on income, family responsibilities, financial resources, age, retirement plans, and ability

**asset allocation** A plan for dividing a portfolio among different classes of securities in order to preserve capital by protecting the portfolio against negative market development.

to bear risk. These needs shape one's financial goals. But to create a portfolio geared to those goals, you need to develop an **asset allocation** strategy. Asset allocation centers on the question of *how to divide your portfolio among different types of securities*. For example, what portion of your portfolio will be devoted to short-term securities, to longer bonds and bond funds, and to common stocks and equity funds? The idea is to position your assets in such a way that you can protect your portfolio from negative developments in the market while still taking advantage of potential positive developments. There's overwhelming evidence that over the long run, *the total return on a portfolio is influenced far more by its asset allocation plan than by specific security selections*. Asset allocation deals in broad categories and *does not tell you which individual securities to buy or sell*. It might look something like this:

| Type of Investment | Asset Mix |
|---|---|
| Short-term securities | 5% |
| Longer bonds (7- to 10-year maturities) | 20% |
| Equity funds | 75% |
| Total portfolio | 100% |

- You're close to reaching a certain goal (such as saving for your child's college education).

Periodically, you may find it necessary to *rebalance* your portfolio—that is, to reallocate the assets in your portfolio. For example, suppose that your asset allocation plan calls for 75% equities but then the stock market falls and so stocks represent only 65% of your total portfolio value. If you're still bullish on the (long-term) market and if stocks are still appropriate for your portfolio, then you may view this as a good time to buy stocks and, in so doing, bring your portfolio back up to 75% in equities. But don't be too quick to rebalance every time your portfolio gets a little out of whack; you should allow for some variation in the percentages because market fluctuations will make it impossible to constantly maintain exact percentages. And don't forget to consider tax implicaitons and the costs from commissions or sales charges.

Portfolio management involves the buying, selling, and holding of various securities in order to meet a set of predetermined investment needs and objectives. To give you an idea of portfolio management in action, Exhibit 11.6 provides examples of four portfolios, each developed with a particular financial situation in mind. Notice that in each case the asset allocation strategies and portfolio structures change with the different financial objectives. The first one is the *newlywed couple*; in their late 20s, they earn $58,000 a year and spend

> *Over the long run,* **the total return on a portfolio is influenced far more by its asset allocation plan than by specific security selections.**

As you can see, all you're really doing here is deciding how to cut up the pie. You still have to decide which particular securities to invest in. Once you've decided that you want to put, say, 20% of your money into intermediate-term (7- to 10-year) bonds, your next step is to select those specific securities. For ideas on how to start your own portfolio, even if you don't have a lot of money, see this chapter's *Money in Action* feature.

After establishing your asset allocation strategy, you should check it regularly to make sure that your portfolio is still in line with your desired asset mix, and to see if that mix is still appropriate for your investment objectives. Here are some reasons to reevaluate your asset allocations.

- A major change in personal circumstances— marriage, birth of a child, loss of job, or family illness that changes your investment goals.

- The proportion of an asset rises or falls considerably and thereby changes your target allocation for that class by more than, say, 5%.

just about every cent. Next is the *two-income couple*; in their early 40s, they earn $115,000 a year and are concerned about college costs for their children, ages 17 and 12. Then there is the *single parent*; she is 34, has custody of her children, ages 7 and 4, and receives $40,000 a year in salary and child support. Finally, we have the *older couple*; in their mid-50s, they're planning for retirement in 10 years, when the husband will retire from his $95,000-a-year job.

## Keeping Track of Your Investments

Just as you need investment objectives to provide direction for your portfolio, so too do you need to *monitor* it by keeping track of what your investment holdings consist of, how they've performed over time, and whether they've lived up to your expectations. Sometimes investments fail to perform the way you thought they would. Their return may be well below what you'd like, or you may even have

# MONEY IN ACTION

## How to Build a Portfolio When You're Just Starting Out

After setting aside funds for emergencies and developing long-term goals and an investment strategy, you're now ready to start investing. If you have a limited amount of money to invest, it's best to start with a balanced mutual fund. You can invest in many of these funds with $1,000 or less. Mutual funds offering a mix of stocks and bonds enable you to diversify your assets with just one investment. Look for a fund with lower-than-average fees and a strong track record. This investment strategy is appropriate for those with limited knowledge of investing and/or little time to research and monitor their investments. The main disadvantage to this approach is that you don't control the asset mix.

If you are more risk tolerant and have a longer time horizon, then you might want to think about investing in a stock index fund, such as one that tracks the S&P 500. Because these funds are composed only of stocks, they're riskier than a balanced fund—but over time, you should be able to ride the market's ups and downs. You should still diversify your portfolio with additional assets, such as a bond fund, to minimize your risk. If you invest in individual stocks, consider participating in a dividend reinvestment plans (DRP), offered by about 1,000 companies. Under such plans, dividends are automatically reinvested in more shares, and you buy additional shares directly from the company—usually without a fee.

Whatever assets you choose, review your holdings regularly and rebalance your portfolio, even when it's doing well; some investment categories outperform others, so the asset allocation percentages shift. Rebalancing the portfolio involves buying or selling assets to bring them back to their original allocation. Also, try to invest regularly in your funds or stocks, every month or pay period if possible. Be patient and stick with your investment strategy, even if returns aren't as high as you'd like. With the market's volatility, you're bound to have down periods. Remember, you chose this plan for the long term, so being consistent should pay off over time.

*Sources:* Adapted from Walter Updegrave, "Stocks vs. Funds: Which is Right for You?" http://money.cnn.com/2009/06/28/pf/expert/stocks_funds.moneymag/index.htm, accessed November 2009; Katy Marquardt, "The Beauty of Balance," *Kiplinger's Personal Finance Magazine*, July 2006, p. 50; Joshua Kennon, "All About Dividends," http://beginnersinvest.about.com/od/dividendsdrips1/a/aa040904.htm, accessed November 2009.

---

### Exhibit 11.6    Four Model Portfolios

The type of portfolio you put together will depend on your financial and family situation as well as on your investment objectives. Clearly, what is right for one family may be totally inappropriate for another.

| Family Situation | Portfolio |
| --- | --- |
| **Newlywed couple** | 80% to 90% in common stocks, with three-quarters of that in mutual funds aiming for maximum capital gains and the rest in growth-and-income or equity-income funds |
| | 10% to 20% in a money market fund or other short-term money market securities |
| **Two-income couple** | 60% to 70% in common stocks, with three-quarters of that in blue chips or growth mutual funds and the rest in more aggressive issues or mutual funds aiming for maximum capital gains |
| | 25% to 30% in discount Treasury notes whose maturities correspond with the bills for college tuition |
| | 5% to 10% in money market funds or other short-term money market securities |
| **Single parent** | 50% to 60% in growth and income mutual funds |
| | 40% to 50% in money market funds or other short-term money market securities |
| **Older couple** | 60% to 70% in blue-chip common stocks, growth funds, or value funds |
| | 25% to 30% in municipal bonds or short- and intermediate-term discount bonds that will mature as the couple starts needing the money to live on |
| | 5% to 10% in CDs and money market funds |

suffered a loss. In either case, it may be time to sell the investments and put the money elsewhere. A monitoring system should allow you to identify such securities in your portfolio. It should also enable you to stay on top of the holdings that are performing to your satisfaction. Knowing when to sell and when to hold can significantly affect the amount of return you're able to generate from your investments.

You can use a tool like Worksheet 11.2 to keep an inventory of your investment holdings. All types of investments can be included on this worksheet—from stocks, bonds, and mutual funds to real estate and savings accounts. To see how it works, consider the investment portfolio that has been built up since 1987 by Barry and Susan Manley, a two-income couple in their early 50s. Worksheet 11.2 shows that as of December 2009, Barry and Susan hold common and preferred stock in five companies, one corporate bond, two mutual funds, some real estate, and a savings account. Using a worksheet like this in conjunction with an *online portfolio tracker* would give an investor plenty of information about the performance of his or her portfolio—the *worksheet* providing long-term information from the date of purchase of an asset, and the *online portfolio tracker* providing year-to-date or annual returns. Note that the Manley's earn almost $7,000 a year from their investments and that—thanks largely to their investments in a couple of stocks and stock funds—their holdings have grown from around $100,000 to more than $444,000! A report like this should be prepared at least once a year; when completed, it provides a quick overview of your investment holdings and lets you know where you stand at a given point in time.

## Worksheet 11.2 Keeping Tabs on Your Investment Holdings

A worksheet like this one will enable you to keep track of your investment holdings and to identify investments that aren't performing up to expectations.

### AN INVENTORY OF INVESTMENT HOLDINGS

Name(s): Barry & Susan Manley

Date: July 28, 2009

| Type of Investment | Description of Investment Vehicle | Date Purchased | Amount of Investment (Quote—$ Amount) | Amount of Income from Dividends, Interest, etc. | Latest Market Value (Quote—$ Amount) |
|---|---|---|---|---|---|
| Common stock | 250 shares - McDonald's | 12/7/1990 | $5.92 - $1,480 | $2,000 | 56.47 (now 1,000 shs) - $56,470 |
| Common stock | 300 shares - Disney | 10/20/1992 | $10.40 - $3,120 | $315 | $26.37 (now 900 shs) - $23,733 |
| Common stock | 400 shares - Pall Corp. | 4/12/1993 | $10.93 - $4,372 | $232 | $29.74 (now 400 shs) - $11,896 |
| Common stock | 150 shares - Intel | 8/11/1995 | $7.30 - $1,095 | $672 | $19.37 (now 1,200 shs) - $23,244 |
| | | | | | |
| Preferred stock | 100 shares - DuPont pf 4.5 | 1/26/1989 | $50.75 - $5,075 | $77.79 | $77.79 - $777.90 |
| | | | | | |
| Corporate bond | $5,000 Wal-Mart 7.55 - 30 | 2/15/2000 | $100 - $5,000 | $377.50 | $124.206 - $6,210.30 |
| | | | | | |
| Mutual fund | 1,300 shares - Vanguard Health Care | 6/16/1989 | $20.97 - $27,261 | $2,451.00 | $108.36 - $140,868.00 |
| Mutual fund | 725 shares - Clipper fund | 12/12/1992 | $17.72 - $12,850 | $617.77 | $46.31 - $33,574.75 |
| | | | | | |
| Real estate | four-plex at 1802 N. 75 Ave. | 9/16/1987 | $140,000 - $28,000 | N/A | (est) $250,000 - $138,000 |
| | | | | | |
| Savings | 1-year 1.5% CD at First National Bank | 7/28/2009 | N/A - $10,000 | $150 | N/A $10,000 |
| | Totals | | $98,253 | $6,893 | $444,774 |

Instructions: List number of shares of *common and preferred stock* purchased as part of the description of securities held; then put the price paid *per share* under the "Quote" column and total amount invested (number of shares × price per share) under the "$ Amount" column. Enter the principal (par) value of all bonds held in place of number of shares: "$ Amount" column for bonds = principal value of bonds purchased × quote (for example, $5,000 × .755 = $3,775). List *mutual funds* as you did for stock. For *real estate*, enter total market value of property under "Quote" column and amount actually invested (down payment and closing costs) under "$ Amount." Ignore the "Quote" column for *savings* vehicles. For "Amount of Income" column, list total amount received from dividends, interest, and so on (for example, dividends per share × number of shares held). Under "Latest Market Value," enter market price as of the date of this report. The latest market value for real estate is entered as an estimate of what the property would likely sell for (under "Quote") and the estimated amount of equity the investor has in the property (under "$ Amount").

# FINANCIAL PLANNING EXERCISES

**LG2** 1. Why do you suppose that large, well-known companies such as Oracle, Starbucks, and Nextel prefer to have their shares traded on the NASDAQ rather than on one of the major listed exchanges, such as the NYSE (for which they'd easily meet all listing requirements)? What's in it for them? What would they gain by switching over to the NYSE?

**LG3** 2. Suppose that Arthur Kessel places an order to buy 100 shares of Google. Explain how the order will be processed if it's a market order. Would it make any difference if it had been a limit order? Explain.

**LG4** 3. Using a resource like *The Wall Street Journal* or *Barron's* (either in print or online), find the latest values for each of the following market averages and indexes, and indicate how each has performed over the past 6 months:
   a. DJIA
   b. S&P 500
   c. NASDAQ Composite
   d. S&P MidCap 400
   e. Dow Jones Wilshire 5000
   f. Russell 2000

**LG4** 4. Using the stock quotations in Exhibit 11.4, find the 52-week high and low for Nucor's common. What is the stock's latest dividend yield? What was the closing price, and at what P/E ratio was the stock trading? Of the stocks listed in Exhibit 11.5, which had the highest price/earnings ratio and the biggest change in price? Which three stocks had the highest dividend yields, and which three had the highest closing prices?

**LG4** 5. Using the S&P report in Exhibit 11.5, find the following information as it pertains to Nike.
   a. What was the amount of revenues (i.e., sales) generated by the company in 2009?
   b. What were the latest annual dividends per share and dividend yield?
   c. What were the earnings (per share) projections for 2010?
   d. How many common shareholders were there?
   e. What were the book value per share and earnings per share in 2009?
   f. How much long-term debt did the company have in 2009?

# INVESTING IN STOCKS AND BONDS

## LG1, LG2 The Risks and Rewards of Investing

Most rational investors are motivated to buy or sell a security based on its expected (or anticipated) return: buy if the return looks good, sell if it doesn't. But a security's return is just part of the story; you can't consider the return on an investment without also looking at its *risk*—the chance that the actual return from an investment may differ from (i.e., fall short of) what was expected. Generally speaking, you'd expect riskier investments to provide higher levels of return.

> { *Most rational investors buy or sell a security based on its expected return— buy if the return looks good, sell if it doesn't.* }

Otherwise, what incentive is there for an investor to risk his or her capital? These two concepts (risk and return) are of vital concern to investors, so, before taking up the issue of investing in stocks and bonds, let's look more closely at the risks of investing and the various components of return. Equally important, we'll see how these two components can be used together to find potentially attractive investment vehicles.

## The Risks of Investing

Just about any type of investment is subject to some risk—some more than others. The basic types of investment risk are business risk, financial risk, market risk, purchasing power risk, interest rate risk, liquidity risk, and event risk. Other things being equal, you'd like to reduce your exposure to these risks as much as possible.

### Go to Smart Sites

What's your investment risk tolerance? Take a few quizzes at the Investor Education Fund site, and find out more about your risk profile and investing style. Link at **4ltrpress.cengage .com.** ●

### Business Risk

When investing in a company, you may have to accept the possibility that the firm will fail to maintain sales and profits, or even to stay in business. Such failure is due either to economic or industry factors or, as is more often the case, to poor management decisions. **Business risk**, in essence, represents the degree of uncertainty surrounding the firm's cash flows and its ability to meet operating expenses in a timely fashion.

### Financial Risk

**Financial risk** concerns the amount of debt used to finance the firm, as well as the possibility that the firm will not have sufficient cash flows to meet these obligations on time. Look to the company's balance sheet in order to get a handle on a firm's financial risk. As a rule, companies that have little or no long-term debt are fairly low in financial risk. This is particularly so if the company also has a healthy earnings picture as well. The problem with debt financing is that it creates principal and interest obligations that must be met regardless of how much profit the company is generating.

### Market Risk

**Market risk** results from the behavior of investors in the securities markets, which can lead to swings in security prices. These price changes can be due to underlying intrinsic factors, as well as changes in political and economic conditions or in investor tastes and preferences. Essentially, market risk is reflected in the *price volatility* of a security: the more volatile the price of a security, the greater its market risk.

### Purchasing Power Risk

Changes in the general level of prices within an economy produce **purchasing power risk**. In periods of rising prices (inflation), the purchasing power of the dollar declines. This means that a smaller quantity of goods and services can be purchased with a given number of dollars. In general, investments (like stocks or real estate) whose values tend to move with general price levels are

> **business risk** The degree of uncertainty associated with a firm's cash flows and with its subsequent ability to meet its operating expenses.
>
> **financial risk** A type of risk associated with the mix of debt and equity financing used by the issuing firm and its ability to meet its financial obligations.
>
> **market risk** A type of risk associated with the price volatility of a security.
>
> **purchasing power risk** A type of risk, resulting from possible changes in price levels, that can significantly affect investment returns.

most profitable during periods of rising prices, whereas investments (such as bonds) that provide fixed returns are preferred during periods of low or declining price levels.

### Interest Rate Risk

**Fixed-income securities**—which include notes, bonds, and preferred stocks, offer investors a fixed periodic return and, as such, are most affected by **interest rate risk**. As interest rates change, the prices of these securities fluctuate, decreasing with rising interest rates and increasing with falling rates. For example, the prices of fixed-income securities drop when interest rates increase, giving investors rates of return that are competitive with securities offering higher levels of interest income. Changes in interest rates are due to fluctuations in the supply of or demand for money.

### Liquidity Risk

The risk of not being able to liquidate (i.e., sell) an investment conveniently and at a reasonable price is called **liquidity (or marketability) risk**. In general, investment vehicles traded in *thin markets*, where supply and demand are small, tend to be less liquid than those traded in *broad markets*. However, to be liquid, an investment not only must be easily salable but also must be so *at a reasonable price*. Vehicles such as mutual funds, common stocks, and U.S. Treasury securities are generally highly liquid; others, such as raw land, are not.

### Event Risk

**Event risk** occurs when something substantial happens to a company and that event, in itself, has a sudden impact on the company's financial condition. It involves a largely (or totally) unexpected event that has a significant and usually immediate effect on the underlying value of an investment. A good example of event risk was the action by the Food and Drug Administration several years ago to halt the use of silicone breast implants. The share price of Dow Corning—the dominant producer of this product—was quickly affected (negatively) by this single event! Fortunately, event risk tends to be confined to specific companies, securities, or market segments.

## The Returns from Investing

Any investment vehicle—whether it's a share of stock, a bond, a piece of real estate, or a mutual fund—has just two basic sources of return: *current income* and

*capital gains*. Some investments offer only one source of return (for example, non-dividend-paying stocks provide only capital gains), but many others offer both income and capital gains, which together make up what's known as the *total return* from an investment. Of course, when both elements of return are present, the relative importance of each will vary among investments. For example, whereas current income is more important with bonds, capital gains are usually a larger portion of the total return from common stocks.

### Current Income

Current income is generally received with some degree of regularity over the course of the year. It may take the form of dividends on stock, interest from bonds, or rents from real estate. People who invest to obtain income look for investment vehicles that will provide regular and predictable patterns of income. Preferred stocks and bonds, which are expected to pay known amounts at specified times (e.g., quarterly or semi-annually), are usually viewed as good income investments.

### Capital Gains

The other type of return available from investments is capital appreciation (or growth), which is reflected as an increase in the market value of an investment vehicle. Capital gains occur when you're able to sell a security for more than you paid for it or when your security holdings go up in value. Investments that provide greater growth potential through capital appreciation normally have

© GEORGE ALLEN PENTON/SHUTTERSTOCK

lower levels of current income because the firm achieves its growth by reinvesting its earnings instead of paying dividends to the owners. Many common stocks, for example, are acquired for their capital gains potential.

### Earning Interest on Interest: Another Source of Return

When does an 8% investment end up yielding only 5%? Probably more often than you think! Obviously, it can happen when investment performance fails to live up to expectations. But it can also happen even when everything goes right. That is, so long as at least part of the return from an investment involves the periodic receipt of current income (such as dividends or interest payments), then that income must be *reinvested* at a given rate of return in order to achieve the yield you thought you had going into the investment. Consider an investor who buys an 8% U.S. Treasury bond and holds it to maturity, a period of 20 years. Each year the bondholder receives $80 in interest, and at maturity, the $1,000 in principal is repaid. There's no loss in capital, no default; everything is paid right on time. Yet this sure-fire investment ends up yielding

only 5%. Why? Because the investor failed to reinvest the annual interest payments he was receiving. By not plowing back all the investment earnings, the bondholder failed to earn any *interest on interest*.

Take a look at Exhibit 12.1. It shows the three elements of return for an 8%, 20-year

**FINANCIAL ROAD SIGN**

**ON THE ROAD TO EFFECTIVE INVESTING**
Here are some guidelines for getting the most from your investment capital.

1. Don't put it off—start investing early, not later.
2. Set reasonable savings goals and then do what's necessary to meet them.
3. Risk is unavoidable, so manage it wisely.
4. Diversify, diversify, diversify.
5. It's the long term that matters, not the short term.
6. Be patient: over time, the market rewards patience.
7. Avoid the temptation to time the markets: you'll only make your broker happy.

### Exhibit 12.1 Three Elements of Return for an 8%, 20-Year Bond

As seen here, the long-term return from an investment (in this case, a bond) is made up of three parts: recovery of capital, current income, and interest on interest; of the three components, interest on interest is particularly important, *especially for long-term investments.*

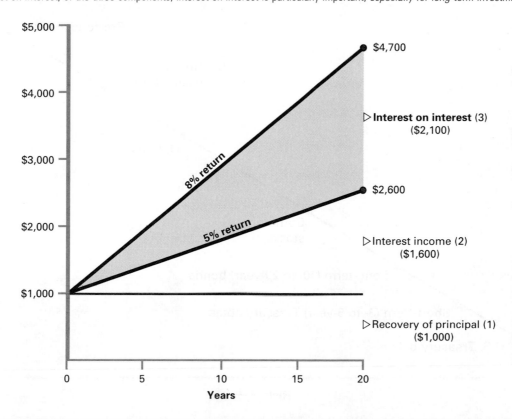

**risk-free rate of return** The rate of return on short-term government securities, such as Treasury bills, that is free from default risk.

bond: (1) the recovery of principal; (2) periodic interest income; and (3) the interest on interest earned from reinvesting the periodic interest payments. Note that because the bond was originally bought at par ($1,000), you start off with an 8% investment. *Where you end up depends on what you do with the profits (interest earnings) from this investment*. If you don't reinvest the interest income, then you'll end up on the 5% line.

You have to earn interest on interest from your investments in order to move to the 8% line. Specifically, because you started out with an 8% investment, *that's the rate of return you need to earn when reinvesting your income*. And keep in mind that even though we used a bond in our illustration, *this same concept applies to any type of long-term investment vehicle* as long as current income is part of an investment's return. This notion of earning interest on interest is what the market refers to as a *fully compounded rate of return*. The amount of interest

on interest embedded in a security's return depends in large part on the length of your investment horizon. That is, *long-term investments* (e.g., 20-year bonds) are subject to a lot more interest on interest than are short-term investments (e.g., 6-month T-bills or dividend-paying stocks that you hold for only 2 or 3 years).

## The Risk–Return Trade-off

The amount of risk associated with a given investment vehicle is directly related to its expected return. This universal rule of investing means that if you want a higher level of return, you'll probably have to accept greater exposure to risk. While higher risk generally is associated with higher levels of return, this relationship doesn't necessarily work in the opposite direction. That is, you can't invest in a high-risk security and expect to automatically earn a high rate of return. Unfortunately, it doesn't work that way—risk simply isn't that predictable!

Exhibit 12.2 generalizes the risk–return trade-off for some popular investment vehicles. Note that it's possible to receive a positive return for zero risk, such as at point A. This is referred to as the **risk-free rate of return**,

## Exhibit 12.2   The Risk–Return Relationship

For investments, there's generally a direct relationship between risk and return: the more risk you face, the greater the return you should expect from the investment.

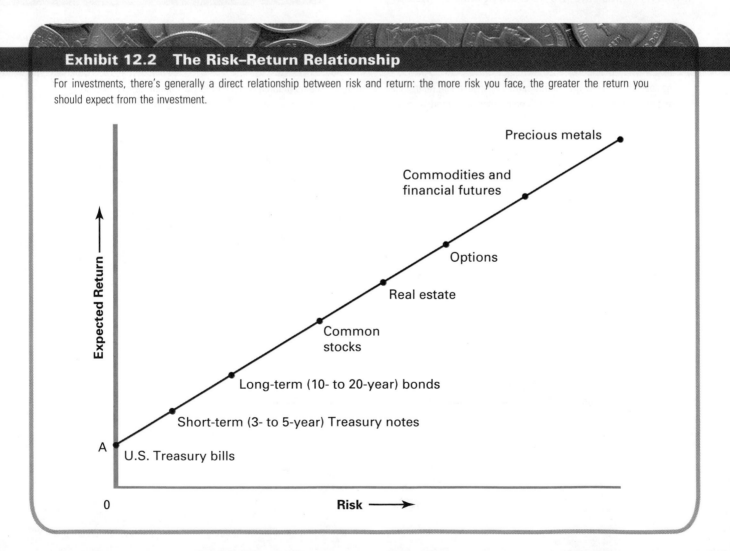

which is often measured by the return on a short-term government security, such as a 90-day Treasury bill.

## What Makes a Good Investment?

In keeping with the preceding risk–return discussion, it follows that the value of any investment depends on the amount of return it's expected to provide relative to the amount of perceived risk involved. And this applies to all types of investment vehicles, including stocks, bonds, or real estate and commodities. In this respect, they should all be treated the same.

### Future Return

In investments, it's the *expected future return on a security* that matters. Aside from the help they can provide in getting a handle on future income, *past returns are of little value to investors*—after all, it's not what the security did last year that matters, but rather what it's expected to do next year. To get an idea of the future return on an investment, we must *formulate expectations of its future current income and future capital appreciation.* As an illustration, assume you're thinking of buying some stock in Technology Applications Company, Inc. (TAC). After reviewing several financial reports, you've estimated the future dividends and price behavior of TAC as follows:

Expected average annual dividends,
2010–2012                                    $2.15 a share
Expected market price
of the stock, 2012                          $95.00 a share

Because the stock is now selling for $60 a share, the difference between its current and expected future market price ($95 − $60) represents the amount of *capital gains* you expect to receive over the next 3 years—in this case, $35 a share. The projected future price, along with expected average annual dividends, gives you an estimate of the stock's *future income stream;* what you need now is a way to measure *expected return.*

### Approximate Yield

Finding the exact rate of return on an investment involves a complex mathematical procedure—one that's hard to determine without using a handheld financial calculator (which we'll demonstrate shortly). There is, however, a fairly easy way to obtain a reasonably close estimation of expected return, and that is to compute an investment's *approximate yield.* Although this measure is only an approximation, it's useful when dealing with forecasted numbers (that are subject to some degree of uncertainty anyway). The measure considers not only current income and capital gains, but interest on interest as well. Hence, *approximate yield provides a measure of the fully compounded rate of return* from an investment. Finding the approximate yield on

an investment is shown in the equation below. If you briefly study the formula, you will see it's really not as formidable as it may first appear. All it does is relate (1) average current income and (2) average capital gains to the (3) average amount of the investment.

$$
\text{Approximate yield} = \frac{\text{Average annual current income} + \left[\dfrac{\text{Future price of investment} - \text{Current price of investment}}{\text{Number of years in investment period}}\right]}{\left[\dfrac{\text{Current price of investment} + \text{Future price of investment}}{2}\right]}
$$

$$
= \frac{CI + \left[\dfrac{FP - CP}{N}\right]}{\left[\dfrac{CP + FP}{2}\right]}
$$

where

$CI$ = average annual current income (amount you expect to receive annually from dividends, interest, or rent)
$FP$ = expected future price of investment
$CP$ = current market price of investment
$N$ = investment period (length of time, in years, that you expect to hold the investment)

### Crunching the Numbers

To illustrate, let's use the Technology Applications Company example again. Given the average current income (CI) fom annual dividends of $2.15, current stock price (CP) of $60, future stock price (FP) of $95, and an investment period (N) of 3 years (you expect to hold the stock from 2010 through 2012), you can use this equation to find the expected approximate yield on TAC as follows:

$$
\text{Approximate yield} = \frac{\$2.15 + \left[\dfrac{\$95 - \$60}{3}\right]}{\left[\dfrac{\$60 + \$95}{2}\right]}
$$

$$
= \frac{\$2.15 + \left[\dfrac{\$35}{3}\right]}{\left[\dfrac{\$155}{2}\right]}
$$

$$
= \frac{\$2.15 + \$11.67}{\$77.50} = \frac{\$13.82}{\$77.50}
$$

$$
= \underline{17.83\%}
$$

In this case, if your forecasts of annual dividends and capital gains hold up, an investment in Technology Applications Company should provide a return of around 17.83% per year.

Whether you should consider TAC a viable investment candidate depends on how this level of expected return stacks up to the amount of risk you must assume. Suppose you've decided the stock is moderately risky. To determine whether the expected rate of return on this investment will be satisfactory, you can compare it to some benchmark. One of the best is the rate of return you can expect from a *risk-free* security, such as a *U.S. Treasury bill*. The idea is that the return on a *risky* security should be greater than that available on a risk-free security. If, for example, U.S. T-bills are yielding 4% or 5%, then you'd want to receive considerably more—perhaps 10% to

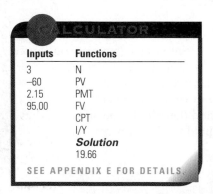

| Inputs | Functions |
|--------|-----------|
| 3 | N |
| −60 | PV |
| 2.15 | PMT |
| 95.00 | FV |
| | CPT |
| | I/Y |
| | *Solution* |
| | 19.66 |

SEE APPENDIX E FOR DETAILS.

## Calculator Keystrokes

You can easily find the *exact* return on this investment by using a handheld financial calculator. Here's what you do. First, put the calculator in the *annual compounding* mode. Then—to find the expected return on a stock that you buy at $60 a share, hold for 3 years (during which time you receive average annual dividends of $2.15 a share), and then sell at $95—use the keystrokes shown below, where:

N = number of *years* you hold the stock
PV = the price you pay for the stock (entered as a *negative* number)
PMT = *average* amount of dividends received *each year*
FV = the price you expect to receive when you *sell* the stock (in 3 years)

You'll notice there is a difference in the computed yield measures (17.83% with the approximate procedure versus 19.66% here). That's to be expected because one is only an approximate measure of performance, whereas this is exact measure.

12%—to justify your investment in a moderately risky security like TAC. In essence, the 10% to 12% is your **desired rate of return**: the minimum rate of return you feel you should receive in compensation for the amount of risk you must assume. *An investment should be considered acceptable only if it's expected to generate a rate of return that meets (or exceeds) your desired rate of return.* In the case of TAC, the stock *should be considered a viable investment candidate* because it more than provides the minimum or desired rate of return.

## LG3, LG4 Investing in Common Stock

Common stocks appeal to investors for a variety of reasons. To some, investing in stocks is a way to hit it big if the issue shoots up in price; to others, it's the level of current income they offer. The basic investment attribute of a share of common stock is that it enables the investor to participate in the profits of the firm. Every shareholder is, in effect, a part owner of the firm and, as such, is entitled to a piece of its profit. But this claim on income has limitations, for common stockholders are really the **residual owners** of the company, meaning they're entitled to dividend income and a prorated share of the company's earnings only after all of the firm's other obligations have been met.

> { *The basic investment attribute of a share of common stock is that it enables the investor to participate in the profits of the firm.* }

## Common Stocks as a Form of Investing

Given the nature of common stocks, if the market is strong then investors can generally expect to benefit from steady price appreciation. A good example is the performance in 1995, when the market, as measured by the Dow Jones Industrial Average (DJIA), went up more than 33%. Unfortunately, when markets falter, so do investor returns. Look at what happened over the 3-year period from early 2000 through late 2002, when the market (again, as measured by the DJIA) fell some 38%. Excluding dividends, that means a $100,000 investment would have declined in value to a little over $60,000.

Make no mistake, the market does have its bad days, and sometimes those bad days seem to go on for months. It may not always appear that way, but those bad days *really are the exception rather than the rule.* That was certainly the case over the 53-year period from 1956 through 2008, when the Dow went down (for the year) just 17 times. That's only about 32% of the time; the other 68%, the market was up—anywhere from around 2% on the year to nearly 40%! True, there's some risk and price volatility (even in good markets), but that's the price you have to pay for all the upside potential. Consider, for example, the behavior of the market from 1982 through early 2000. Starting in August 1982, when the Dow stood at 777, this market saw the DJIA climb nearly 11,000 points to reach a high of 11,723 in January 2000. Unfortunately, that all came to a screeching halt in early 2000, when each of the three major market measures peaked. Over the course of the next 32 months, through September 2002, these market measures fell flat on their collective faces. While the Dow recovered from 2003 through mid-2007, it fell big time from that point on through early 2009. In fact, it fell from about 14,000 in July 2007 to around 6,500 in March of 2009, with most of that loss occurring in 2008, when the Dow dropped by nearly 34%.

Take a look at Exhibit 12.3, which tracks the behavior of the DJIA and the NASDAQ Composite from 1999 to mid-2009, and you'll quickly get a feel for just how volatile this market was! That is, over this 10½ year period, the typical stock investor barely broke even, as the Dow fell nearly 200 points (or about 2.1%) while the NASDAQ fared even worse as it dropped some 525 points; in fact, had it not been for dividends, most investors would have actually lost money for the decade as a whole. Fortunately, that's something that doesn't happen very often!

### Issuers of Common Stock

Shares of common stock can be issued by any corporation in any line of business. All corporations have

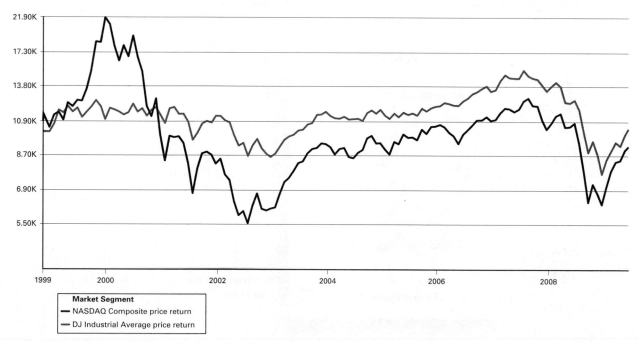

**Exhibit 12.3  Performance of Dow Jones Industrial Average and NASDAQ Composite, 1999 through mid-2009**

One of the greatest bull markets in history began on August 12, 1982, with the Dow at 777. It continued through the 1980s and into the 1990s, but it all ended in early 2000. The market went from a rip-snorting bull to a full-fledged bear in 2000, which lasted until 2002. After recovering, the market entered one of the worst bear markets in history from 2007 through 2009 as the markets experienced the impact of the global financial crisis. This graph shows how the value of a $10,000 investment changed between 1999 and mid-2009.

**Market Segment**
— NASDAQ Composite price return
— DJ Industrial Average price return

stockholders, but not all of them have publicly traded shares. The stocks of interest to us in this book are the so-called *publicly traded issues*—the shares that are readily available to the general public and that are bought and sold in the open market. Aside from the initial distribution of common stock when the corporation is formed, subsequent sales of additional shares may be made through a procedure known as a *public offering*. In a public offering, the corporation, working with its underwriter, simply offers the investing public a certain number of shares of its stock at a certain price. Exhibit 12.4 depicts the announcement for such an offering. Note in this case that Advanced Micro Devices (AMD) is offering 14,096,000 shares of stock at a price of $35.20 per share. The new issue of common stock provided this NYSE-traded company with nearly $500 million in new capital. When issued, the new shares are commingled with the outstanding shares and the net result will be an increase in the number of shares outstanding. In case you're

wondering, since these stocks were issued in 2006, the market price of AMD shares also fell victim to the 2007–08 bear market, as its shares dropped to about $4.00 a share by mid-year, 2009. That's a loss of 88%—ouch!

## Voting Rights

The holders of common stock normally receive *voting rights*, which means that for each share of stock held they receive one vote. In some cases, common stock may be designated as nonvoting at the time of issue, but this is the exception rather than the rule. Although different voting systems exist, small stockholders need not concern themselves with them because, regardless of the system used, their chances of affecting corporate control with their votes are quite slim.

Corporations have annual stockholders' meetings, at which time new directors are elected and special issues are voted on. Because most small stockholders

---

### Exhibit 12.4   An Announcement of a New Common Stock Issue

Here the company—Advanced Micro Devices—is issuing over 14 million shares of stock at a price of $35.20 per share. For this manufacturer of microprocessors and memory chips, the new issue will mean nearly *half a billion dollars* in fresh capital. Unfortunately, the price of the stock had fallen to a fraction of its offering price by mid-2009.

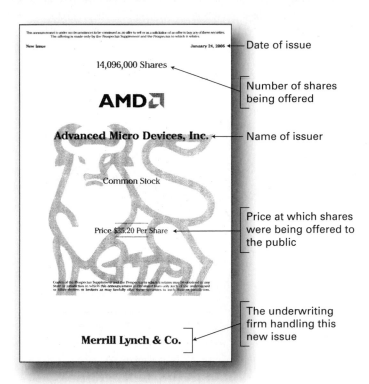

*Source: The Wall Street Journal,* February 2, 2006. Used by permission of AMD and Merril Lynch.

can't attend these meetings, they can use a proxy to assign their votes to another person, who will vote for them. A **proxy** is a written statement assigning voting rights to another party.

### Basic Tax Considerations

Common stocks provide income in the form of dividends, usually paid quarterly, and/or capital gains, which occur when the price of the stock goes up over time. From a tax *rate* perspective, it really makes no difference whether the investment return comes in the form of dividends or long-term capital gains— today, they're both taxed at the same rate of 15%, or less (it's 5% for those filers in the 10% and 15% tax brackets). There's one slight difference between the taxes due on dividends and those due on capital gains: namely, there is no tax liability on any capital gains until the stock is actually sold (*paper gains*— that is, any price appreciation occurring on stock that you still own—accumulate tax free). *Bottom line: taxes are due on any dividends and capital gains in the year in which the dividends are received or the stock is actually sold.*

Here's how it works: Assume that you just sold 100 shares of common stock for $50 per share. Also assume that the stock was originally purchased 2 years ago for $20 per share and that during each of the past 2 years, you received $1.25 per share in cash dividends. Thus, for tax purposes, you would have received cash dividends of $125 (i.e., $1.25/ share × 100 shares) *both* this year and last, plus you would have generated a capital gain, which is taxable this year, of $3,000 ($50/share − $20/ share × 100 shares). Suppose you're in the 33% tax bracket. Even though you're in one of the higher brackets, both the dividends and capital gains earned on this investment qualify for the lower 15% tax rate. Therefore, on the dividends, you'll pay taxes of $125 × 0.15 = $18.75 (for each of the past 2 years), and on the capital gains, you'll owe $3,000 × 0.15 = $450 (for this year only). Therefore, last year, your tax liability would have been $18.75 (for the dividends), and this year, it will be $468.75 (for the dividends and capital gains). Bottom line: out of the $3,250 you earned on this investment over the past 2 years, you keep $2,762.50 after taxes.

## Dividends

Corporations pay dividends to their common stockholders in the form of cash and/or additional stock. *Cash dividends* are the most common. Cash dividends are normally distributed quarterly in an amount determined by the firm's board of directors. For example, if the directors declared a quarterly cash dividend of 50 cents a share and if you

owned 200 shares of stock, then you'd receive a check for $100.

A popular way of assessing the amount of dividends received is to measure the stock's dividend yield. **Dividend yield** is a measure of common stock dividends on a relative (percentage) basis—that is, the dollar amount of dividends received is compared to the market price of the stock. Dividend yield is an indication of the rate of current income being earned on the investment. It's computed as follows:

$$\text{Dividend yield} = \frac{\text{Annual dividend received per share}}{\text{Market price per share of stock}}$$

For example, a company that pays $2 per share in annual dividends and whose stock is trading at $50 a share will have a dividend yield of 4% ($2/$50 = 0.04). Dividend yield is widely used by income-oriented investors looking for (reasonably priced) stocks with a long and sustained record of regularly paying higher-than-average dividends.

Occasionally, the directors may declare a stock dividend as a supplement to or in place of cash dividends. **Stock dividends** are paid in the form of additional shares of stock. That is, rather than receiving cash, shareholders receive additional shares of the company's stock—say, 1/10 of a share of new stock for each share owned (as in a *10% stock dividend*). Although they often satisfy the needs of some investors, stock dividends really have no value because they represent the receipt of something already owned. For example, if you owned 100 shares of stock in a company that declared a 10% stock dividend, you'd receive 10 new shares of stock. Unfortunately, you'll be no better off after the stock dividend than you were before. That's because the total market value of the shares owned would be roughly the same after the stock dividend as before.

## Some Key Measures of Performance

Seasoned investors use a variety of financial ratios and measures when making common stock investment decisions. They look at such things as dividend yield (mentioned above), book value, return on equity, and earnings per share to get a feel for the investment merits of a particular stock. Fortunately, most of the widely followed ratios can be found in published reports—like those produced by *Value*

**proxy** A written statement used to assign a stockholder's voting rights to another person, typically one of the directors.

**dividend yield** The percentage return provided by the dividends paid on common stock.

**stock dividends** New shares of stock distributed to existing stockholders as a supplement to or substitute for cash dividends.

*Line* or Standard & Poor's (see Exhibit 11.5 in Chapter 11 for an example of an S&P stock report)—so you don't have to compute them yourself. Even so, if you're thinking about buying a stock or already have some stocks, there are a few measures of performance you'll want to keep track of: like book value (or book value per share), net profit margin, and the like.

### Book Value
The amount of stockholders' equity in a firm is measured by **book value**. This accounting measure is found by subtracting the firm's liabilities and preferred stocks from the value of its assets. Book value indicates the amount of stockholder funds used to finance the firm. For instance, assume that our example company (TAC) had assets of $5 million, liabilities of $2 million, and preferred stock valued at $1 million. The book value of the firm's common stock would be $2 million ($5 million − $2 million − $1 million). If the book value is divided by the number of shares outstanding, then the result is *book value per share.* So if TAC had 100,000 shares of common stock outstanding, then its book value per share would be $20 ($2,000,000/100,000 shares). Because of the impact it can have on the firm's growth, you'd like to see book value per share steadily increasing over time. Also look for stocks whose market prices are comfortably above their book values.

### Net Profit Margin
As a yardstick of profitability, **net profit margin** is one of the most widely followed measures of corporate performance. This ratio relates the firm's net profits to its sales, providing an indication of how well the company is controlling its cost structure. The higher the net profit margin, the more money the company earns. Look for a relatively stable—or even better, an increasing—net profit margin.

### Return on Equity
Another important and widely followed measure, **return on equity (or ROE)** reflects the firm's overall profitability from the equityholders' perspective. It captures, in a single ratio, the amount of success the firm is having in managing its assets, operations, and capital structure. ROE is important because it is significantly related to the profits, growth, and dividends of the firm. As long as a firm is not borrowing too much money, the better the ROE the better the company's financial condition and competitive position. Look for a stable or increasing ROE; watch out for a falling ROE because that could spell trouble.

### Earnings per Share
With stocks, the firm's annual earnings are usually measured and reported in terms of **earnings per share (EPS)**. EPS translates total corporate profits into profits on a per-share basis and provides a convenient measure of the amount of earnings available to stockholders. Earnings per share is found by using this simple formula:

$$EPS = \frac{\text{Net profit after taxes} - \text{Preferred dividends paid}}{\text{Number of shares of common stock outstanding}}$$

For example, if TAC reported a net profit of $350,000, paid $100,000 in dividends to preferred stockholders, and had 100,000 shares of common outstanding, then it would have an EPS of $2.50 [($350,000 − $100,000)/100,000]. Note that preferred dividends are *subtracted* from profits because they must be paid before any monies can be made available to common stockholders. Stockholders follow EPS closely because it represents the amount the firm has earned on behalf of each outstanding share of common stock. Here, too, look for steady growth in EPS.

### Price/Earnings Ratio
When the prevailing market price of a share of common stock is divided by the annual earnings per share, the result is the **price/earnings (P/E) ratio**, a measure that's viewed as an indication of investor confidence and expectations. The higher the price/earnings multiple, the more confidence investors are presumed to have in a given security. In the case of TAC, whose shares are currently selling for $30, the price/earnings ratio is 12 ($30 per share/$2.50 per share). In other words, TAC stock is selling for 12 times its earnings. Price/earnings ratios are important to investors because they reveal how aggressively the stock is being priced in the market. Watch out for very high P/Es—that is, P/Es that are way out of line with the market—because that could indicate the stock is overpriced (and thus might be headed for a big drop in price). Price/earnings ratios tend to

# MONEY IN ACTION

## Investing Lessons from the Financial Crisis

Although the financial crisis did enormous economic damage, it also provided some valuable lessons on how to—and how not to—invest. The key lessons are as follows.

- *Moderate portfolio risk by mixing high-grade bonds and stocks.* Stocks and high-grade bonds are different asset classes, which tend to perform quite differently. Mixing them can provide helpful diversification in a down market.

- *Stay away from complex investment products.* Examples include Booster-Plus Notes, Reverse Convertibles, and Super-Track Notes. Sound exotic? Yes, and they are hard to understand, which means you can really do without them.

- *Only include easy-to-understand investments in your portfolio.* Most individual investors can create excellent portfolios by combining plain-vanilla stocks, bonds, mutual funds, and exchange-traded funds (ETFs).

- *Avoid leveraged investments.* There's no need to invest in products that rely on a lot of borrowed money. While leverage increases potential returns, it brings a lot of risk, too. The failures of Fannie Mae, Freddie Mac, and Bear Stearns resulted in large part from their use of high leverage.

- *Use low-cost, tax-efficient investments.* A key part of your portfolio should be passively managed, low-cost, and tax-efficient index funds and ETFs.

- *Rebalance your portfolio periodically and don't try to time the market.* Look over your portfolio at least once a year and reassess whether you have the right mix of stocks and bonds. Invest consistently and don't try to time the market. The evidence shows that few investors can time the market—and almost no one can do so consistently.

*Source:* Adapted from William Reichenstein and Larry Swedroe, "Bear Market Grads: What You Should Learn from the Financial Crisis," *AAII Journal,* July 2009, pp. 5–8. Adapted with permission.

---

move with the market. So when the market is soft, a stock's P/E will be low; when the market heats up, the stock's P/E will rise.

## Beta

A stock's **beta** is an indication of its *price volatility;* it shows how responsive the stock is to changes in the overall stock market. In recent years, using betas to measure the *market risk* of common stock has become widely accepted. As a result, published betas are now available from most brokerage firms and investment services. The beta for a given stock is determined by a statistical technique that relates the stock's historical returns to the market. The market (as measured by something like the S&P index of 500 stocks) is used as a benchmark of performance, and always has a beta of 1.0. From there, everything is relative: low-beta stocks—those with betas of less than 1.0—have low price volatility, whereas high-beta stocks—those with betas of more than 1.0—are considered to be highly volatile. In short, the higher a stock's beta, the riskier it's considered to be. Beta is an *index* of relative price performance. So, if TAC has a beta of, say, 0.8, then it should rise (or fall) only 80% as fast as the market. In contrast, if the stock had a beta of 1.8, then it would go up or down 1.8 times as fast—the price of the stock would rise higher and fall harder than the market.

Other things being equal, if you're looking for a relatively conservative investment, then you should stick with low-beta stocks; on the other hand, if it's capital gains and price volatility you're after, go with high-beta securities.

**beta** An index of the price volatility for a share of common stock; a reflection of how the stock price responds to market forces.

**blue-chip stock** A stock generally issued by companies expected to provide an uninterrupted stream of dividends and good long-term growth prospects.

 **Go to Smart Sites**

Enter a stock's ticker symbol or the company name and 411 Stocks pulls together a complete page of stock data: price, news, discussion groups, charts, and fundamentals. ●

## Types of Common Stock

Common stocks are often classified on the basis of their dividends or their rate of growth in EPS. Some popular types of common stock are blue-chip, growth, tech stocks, income, speculative, cyclical, defensive, large-cap, mid-cap, and small-cap stocks.

### Blue-Chip Stocks

**Blue-chip stocks** are the cream of the common stock crop; these stocks are unsurpassed in quality and have a long and stable record of earnings and dividends. They're issued by large, well-established firms that have impeccable financial credentials—firms like Wal-Mart, IBM, Microsoft, and ExxonMobil. These companies hold important if not leading positions in their industries, and they often determine the standards by which other firms are measured. Blue chips are particularly attractive to investors who seek high-quality investment outlets offering decent dividend yields and respectable growth potential.

## Growth Stocks

Stocks that have experienced—and are expected to continue experiencing—consistently high rates of growth in operations and earnings are known as **growth stocks**. A good growth stock might exhibit a *sustained* rate of growth in earnings of 15% to 20% over a period when common stocks are averaging only 6%–8%. In mid-2009, prime examples of growth stocks include Netflix, eBay, Gamestop, Electronic Arts, and Weyerhaeuser. These stocks often pay little or nothing in dividends, as these firms tend to plow back all or most of their earnings. Because of their potential for dramatic price appreciation, they appeal mostly to investors who are seeking capital gains rather than dividend income.

## Tech Stocks

**Tech stocks** represent the technology sector of the market and include all those companies that produce or provide technology-based products and services such as computers, semiconductors, computer software and hardware, peripherals, Internet services, and wireless communications. There are literally thousands of companies that fall into the tech stock category, including everything from very small firms providing some service on the Internet to huge multinational companies. Tech stocks may offer the potential for attractive, even phenomenal returns, but they also involve considerable risk and so are probably most suitable for investors with high tolerance for such risk. Included in the tech stock category are some big names—Microsoft, Cisco Systems, Google, and Dell—as well as many not-so-big-names, such as iRobot, Techwell, Cbeyond, and Red Hat.

## Income Stocks versus Speculative Stocks

Stocks whose appeal is based primarily on the dividends they pay are known as **income stocks**. They have a fairly stable stream of earnings, a large portion of which is distributed in the form of dividends. Income shares have relatively high dividend yields and thus are ideally suited for investors seeking a relatively safe and high level of current income from their investment capital. An added (and often overlooked) feature of these stocks is that, unlike bonds and preferred stock, holders of income stock can expect *the amount of dividends paid to increase over time*. Examples of income stocks include Consolidated Edison, PPG Industries, Johnson & Johnson, and Southern Company.

Rather than basing their investment decisions on a proven record of earnings, investors in **speculative stocks** gamble that some new information, discovery, or production technique will favorably affect the firm's growth and inflate its stock price. The value of speculative stocks and their P/E ratios tend to fluctuate widely as additional information about the firm's future is received. Investors in speculative stocks should be prepared to experience losses as well as gains because *these are high-risk securities*. In mid-2009, they include companies like Broadcom, Dendreon, Western Lithium, and Tesla Motors.

### Cyclical Stocks or Defensive Stocks

Stocks whose price movements tend to follow the business cycle are called **cyclical stocks**. This means that when the economy is in an expansionary stage, the prices of cyclical stocks tend to increase; during a contractionary stage (recession), they decline. Most cyclical stocks are found in the basic industries—automobiles, steel, and lumber, for example—which are generally sensitive to changes in economic activity. Caterpillar, Alcoa, Dow Chemical, and Ford Motor are all examples of cyclical stocks.

The prices and returns from **defensive stocks**, unlike those of cyclical stocks, are expected to remain stable during periods of contraction in business activity. For this reason, they're often called *countercyclical*. The shares of consumer goods companies, certain public utilities, and gold mining companies are good examples of defensive stocks. Because they're basically income stocks, their earnings and dividends tend to hold their market prices up during periods of economic decline. Coca-Cola, McDonald's, Safeway, Wal-Mart, and Merck are all examples of defensive stocks.

### Large-Caps, Mid-Caps, and Small-Caps

In the stock market, a stock's size is based on its market value—or, more commonly, on what's known as its *market capitalization* or *market cap*. A stock's market cap is found by multiplying its market price by the number of shares outstanding. The market can generally be broken into three major segments, as measured by a stock's market "cap":

**Large-cap—Market caps of more than $10 billion**

**Mid-cap—Market caps of $2 to $10 billion**

**Small-cap—Stocks with market caps of less than $2 billion**

Of the three major categories, the **large-cap stocks** are the real biggies—the Wal-Marts, GEs, and Microsofts of the world. Just because they're big, however, doesn't mean they're better. Indeed, both the small- and mid-cap segments of the market tend to hold their own with, or even outperform, large stocks over time.

**Mid-cap stocks** offer investors some attractive return opportunities, as they provide much of the sizzle of small-stock returns but without all the price volatility. At the same time, because these are fairly good-sized companies, and many of them have been around for a long time, they offer some of the safety of the big, established stocks. Among the ranks of the mid-caps are Tootsie Roll, PetSmart, and Sirius XM Radio. These securities offer a nice alternative to large stocks without all the drawbacks and uncertainties of small-caps, although they're probably most appropriate for investors who are willing to tolerate a bit more risk and price volatility.

Some investors consider small companies to be in a class by themselves. They believe these firms hold especially attractive return opportunities, and in many cases this has turned out to be true. Known as **small-cap stocks**, these companies generally have annual revenues of less than $250 million; because of their size, spurts of growth can dramatically affect their earnings and stock prices. Liz Claiborne, Palm, Tupperware, E*Trade Financial, K-Swiss, and Jos. A. Bank Clothiers are just some of the better-known small-cap stocks. Although some small-caps are solid companies with equally solid financials, that's definitely not the case with most of them! Because many of these companies are so small, they don't have a lot of stock outstanding, and their shares aren't widely traded. These stocks may hold the potential for high returns, but investors should also be aware of the high-risk exposure associated with them.

## Market Globalization and Foreign Stocks

Besides investing in many of the different types of stocks already mentioned, a growing number of American investors are turning to foreign markets as a way to earn attractive returns. Ironically, as our world is becoming smaller, our universe of investment opportunities is growing by leaps and bounds! Consider, for example, that in 1970 the U.S. stock market accounted for fully *two-thirds of the world*

**cyclical stock** Stock whose price movements tend to parallel the various stages of the business cycle.

**defensive stock** Stock whose price movements are usually contrary to movements in the business cycle.

**large-cap stock** A stock with a total market value of more than $10 billion.

**mid-cap stock** A stock whose total market value falls somewhere between $2 billion and $10 billion.

**small-cap stock** A stock with a total market value of less than $2 billion.

*market*. In essence, our stock market was twice as big as the rest of the world's stock markets *combined*. That's no longer true. The U.S. share of the world equity market is now more like 35%. Among the various ways of investing in foreign shares, two stand out: mutual funds and American Depositary Receipts (ADRs). Without a doubt, the best and easiest way to invest in foreign markets is through *international mutual funds* (we'll discuss such funds in Chapter 13). An alternative to mutual funds is to buy ADRs, which are *denominated in dollars and are traded directly on U.S. markets* (such as the NYSE). They're just like common stock, except that each ADR represents a specific number of shares in a specific foreign company. The shares of more than 1,000 companies from some 50 foreign countries are traded on U.S. exchanges as ADRs; these companies include Honda Motor Co., Nestlé, Nokia, Ericsson, Tata Motors, and Vodafone. ADRs are a great way to invest in foreign stocks because their prices are quoted in dollars, not in British pounds, Swiss francs, or euros. What's more, all dividends are paid in dollars.

## Investing in Common Stock

There are three basic reasons for investing in common stock: (1) to use the stock as a warehouse of value, (2) to accumulate capital, and (3) to provide a source of income. Storage of value is important to all investors because nobody likes to lose money. However, some investors are more concerned about it than others, and they put safety of principal first in their stock selection process. These investors are more quality conscious and tend to gravitate toward blue chips and other low-risk securities. Accumulation of capital generally is an important goal to individuals with long-term investment horizons. These investors use the capital gains and dividends that stocks provide to build up their wealth. Some use growth stocks for such purposes; others do it with income shares; still others use a little of both. Finally, some people use stocks as a source of income; to them, a dependable flow of dividends is essential. High-yielding, good-quality income shares are usually their preferred investment vehicle.

© BENDAO/SHUTTERSTOCK

### Advantages and Disadvantages of Stock Ownership

Ownership of common stock has both advantages and disadvantages. Its advantages are threefold. First, the potential returns, in the form of both dividend income and price appreciation, can be substantial. Second, many stocks are actively traded and so are a highly liquid form of investment. Finally, market and company information about literally thousands of common stocks is widely published and readily available.

The disadvantages of owning common stock include risk, the problem of timing purchases and sales, and the uncertainty of dividends. Although potential common stock returns may be high, the risk and uncertainty associated with the actual receipt of that return is also great. Even though the careful selection of stocks may reduce the amount of risk to which the investor is exposed, a significant risk–return trade-off still exists. When it comes to common stock, not even dividends are guaranteed. If things turn bad, the company can always shut off the stream of dividends and suffer no legal ramifications. Finally, there's the timing of purchases and sales; human nature being what it is, we don't always do it right. Take a common stock that's loaded with uncertainty, add in our lack of accurate foresight, and you have the perfect recipe for making mistakes.

### Making the Investment Decision

The first step in investing is to know *where* to put your money; the second is to know *when* to make your moves. The first question basically involves matching your risk and return objectives with the available investment vehicles. *A stock (or any other investment vehicle) should be considered a viable investment candidate as long as it promises to generate a sufficiently attractive rate of return* and, in particular, one that fully compensates you for any risks you must take. Indeed, if you can't get enough return from the security to offset the risk, then you shouldn't invest in the stock!

## Putting a Value on Stock

No matter what kind of investor you are or what your investment objectives happen to be, sooner or later you'll have to face one of the most difficult questions in the field of investments: *How much are you willing to pay for the stock?* To answer this question, you must place a value on the stock. As noted earlier, we know that the value of a stock depends on its expected stream of future earnings. Once you have a handle on the expected stream of future earnings, you can use that information to find the *expected rate of return on the investment.* If the expected return from the investment exceeds your desired or minimum rate of return, then you should make the investment. If the expected return is less than your desired rate of return, then you should not buy the stock now because it's currently "overpriced," and thus you won't be able to earn your desired rate of return.

So, how do you go about finding a stock that's right for you? The answer is by doing a little digging and crunching a few numbers. Here's what you'd want to do. First, find a company you like and then take a look at how it has performed *over the past 3 to 5 years.* Find out what kind of growth rate (in sales) it has experienced, if it has a strong ROE and has been able to maintain or improve its profit margin, how much it has been paying out to stockholders in the form of dividends, and so forth. This kind of information is readily available in publications like *Value Line* and *S&P Stock Reports,* or from a number of Web sites. The idea is to find stocks that are financially strong, have done well in the past, and continue to hold prominent positions in a given industry or market segment. But looking at the past is only the beginning; what's really important to stock valuation is the *future!*

Therefore, let's turn our attention to the expected future performance of a stock. Of particular concern are future dividends and share price behavior. As a rule, it doesn't make much sense to go out more than 2 or 3 years (5 at the most) because the accuracy of most forecasts begins to deteriorate rapidly after that. Thus, using a 3-year investment horizon, you'd want to forecast annual dividends per share for each of the next 3 years, *plus* the future price of the stock at the end of the 3-year holding period. You can try to generate these forecasts yourself or you can check such publications as *Value Line* to obtain projections (*Value Line* projects dividends and share prices 3–5 years into the future). After projecting dividends and share price, you can use the approximate yield equation, or a handheld calculator, to determine the expected return from the investment.

Consider the common shares of Nike, Inc., the world's leading designer and marketer of high-quality athletic footwear, apparel, and accessories. According to several financial reporting services, the company has strong financials; its sales have been growing at a bit more than 9% per year for the past 5 years, its recent net profit margin is more than 7%, and its ROE is around 18%. Thus, historically, the company has performed well and is definitely a market leader in its field. In August of 2009, the stock was trading at around $55 a share and was paying annual dividends at the rate of about $1.00 a share. One major financial service was projecting dividends to grow by about 13% over the next 3 to 5 years; it was also estimating that the price of the stock could rise to as high as $100 a share over that period.

Using these projections together with current (2009) dividends of $1.00 a share, we could expect dividends of about $1.13 a share next year (2010), $1.28 a share the year after (2011), and $1.44 a share in 2012—assuming that dividends do in fact grow as forecast. Now, because the approximate yield equation uses "average annual current income" as one of the inputs, let's use the midpoint of our projected dividends ($1.28 a share) as a proxy for average annual dividends. Because this stock is currently trading at $55 a share and has a projected future price of $100 a share, we can find the expected return (for our 3-year investment horizon) as follows:

$$\text{Approximate yield (Expected return)} = \frac{\$1.28 + \left[\dfrac{\$100 - \$55}{3}\right]}{\left[\dfrac{\$100 + \$55}{2}\right]}$$

$$= \frac{\$1.28 + \$15}{\$77.50} = \underline{\underline{21.00\%}}$$

## Calculator Keystrokes

You can use a handheld financial calculator—set in the *annual compounding mode*—to find the expected return on a stock that you purchase at $55 a share, hold for 3 years (during which time you receive average annual dividends of $1.28 a share), and then sell at $100 per share. Simply use the keystrokes shown in the margin, where

$N$ = number of *years* you hold the stock

$PV$ = the price you pay for the stock (entered as a *negative* value)

$PMT$ = average amount of dividends received each *year*

$FV$ = the price you expect to receive when you sell the stock (in 3 years)

The expected return (of 23.99%) is a bit higher here, but even so, it's still reasonably close to the return (of 21%) we computed using the approximate yield method.

**dividend reinvestment plan (DRP)** A program whereby stockholders can choose to take their cash dividends in the form of more shares of the company's stock.

| Inputs | Functions |
|--------|-----------|
| 3 | N |
| −55 | PV |
| 1.28 | PMT |
| 100.00 | FV |
| | CPT |
| | I/Y |
| | **Solution** |
| | 23.99 |

SEE APPENDIX E FOR DETAILS.

Thus, if Nike's stocks performs as expected, it should give us a return of around 21%–24%. In today's market, that would be a very attractive return and one that likely will *exceed* our required rate of return (which probably should be around 12%–15%). If that's the case, then this stock *should* be considered a viable investment candidate.

### Timing Your Investments

Once you find a stock that you think will give you the kind of return you're looking for, then you're ready to deal with the matter of timing your investment. As long as the prospects for the market and the economy are positive, the time may be right to invest in stocks. Sometimes, however, investing in stocks makes no sense—in particular, *don't* invest in stocks under the following conditions.

- You feel *strongly* that the market is headed down in the short run. If you're absolutely certain the market's in for a big fall (or will continue to fall,

if it's already doing so), then wait until the market drops and buy the stock when it's cheaper.

- You feel uncomfortable with the general tone of the market—it lacks direction, or there's way too much price volatility to suit you. Once again, wait for the market to settle down before buying stocks.

### Be Sure to Plow Back Your Earnings

Unless you're living off the income, the basic investment objective with stocks is the same as it is with any other security: to earn an attractive, fully compounded rate of return. This requires regular reinvestment of dividend income. And there's no better way to accomplish such reinvestment than through a **dividend reinvestment plan (DRP)**. In a dividend reinvestment plan, shareholders can sign up to have their cash dividends automatically reinvested in additional shares of the company's common stock—in essence, it's like taking your cash dividends in the form of more shares of common stock. Such an approach can have a tremendous impact on your investment position over time, as seen in Exhibit 12.5.

Today, over 1,000 companies have DRPs, and each one gives investors a convenient and inexpensive way to accumulate capital. Stocks in most DRPs are acquired free of any brokerage commissions, and most plans allow *partial participation*. That is, rather than committing all of their cash dividends to these plans, participants may specify a portion of their shares for dividend reinvestment and receive cash dividends on the rest. Some plans even sell their shares in their DRP programs at discounts of 3% to 5%. Most plans also credit fractional shares to the investors' accounts. There is a catch, however: even though these dividends take the form of additional shares of stock, *reinvested dividends are taxable, in the year they're received, just as if they had been received in cash.*

## LG5, LG6 Investing in Bonds

In contrast to stocks, *bonds are liabilities*—they're publicly traded IOUs where the bondholders are actually *lending money* to the issuer. Bonds are often referred to as *fixed-income securities* because the debt service obligations of the issuer are fixed—that is, the issuing organization agrees to pay a *fixed amount of interest periodically and to repay a fixed amount of principal at or before maturity*. Bonds normally have face values of $1,000 or $5,000 and have maturities of 10 to 30 years or more.

## Why Invest in Bonds?

Bonds provide investors with two kinds of income: (1) They provide a generous amount of current income, and (2) they can often be used to generate

## Exhibit 12.5  Cash or Reinvested Dividends

Participating in a dividend reinvestment plan is a simple yet highly effective way of building up capital over time. Over the long haul, it can prove to be a great way of earning a fully compounded rate of return on your money.

*Situation:* Buy 100 shares of stock at $25 a share (total investment $2,500); stock currently pays $1 a share in annual dividends. Price of the stock increases at 8% per year; dividends grow at 5% per year.

| Investment Period | Number of Shares Held | Market Value of Stock Holdings | Total Cash Dividends Received |
|---|---|---|---|
| **Take Dividends in Cash** | | | |
| 5 years | 100 | $ 3,672 | $ 552 |
| 10 years | 100 | $ 5,397 | $1,258 |
| 15 years | 100 | $ 7,930 | $2,158 |
| 20 years | 100 | $11,652 | $3,307 |
| **Participate in a DRP** | | | |
| 5 years | 115.59 | $ 4,245 | $0 |
| 10 years | 135.66 | $ 7,322 | $0 |
| 15 years | 155.92 | $12,364 | $0 |
| 20 years | 176.00 | $20,508 | $0 |

substantial amounts of capital gains. The current income, of course, is derived from the interest payments received periodically over the life of the issue. Indeed, this regular and highly predictable source of income is a key factor that draws investors to bonds. But these securities can also produce capital gains, which occurs whenever market interest rates fall. A basic trading rule in the bond market is that *interest rates and bond prices move in opposite directions:* when interest rates rise, bond prices fall; conversely, when interest rates fall, bond prices rise. Thus, it's possible to buy bonds at one price and, if interest rate conditions are right, to sell them sometime later at a higher price. Taken together, the current income and capital gains earned from bonds can lead to highly competitive investor returns. In addition, because of the general high quality of many bonds, they can also be used for the preservation and long-term accumulation of capital. In fact, some individuals commit all or a good deal of their investment funds to bonds because of this single attribute.

## Bonds versus Stocks

Although bonds definitely do have their good points—low risk and high levels of current income, along with *desirable diversification properties*—they also have a significant downside: their *comparative* returns. The fact is, *relative to stocks*, there's

**coupon** Bond feature that defines the annual interest income the issuer will pay the bondholder.

usually a big sacrifice in returns when investing in bonds—which, of course, is the price you pay for the even bigger reduction in risk! But just because there's a deficit in long-term returns, it doesn't mean that bonds are always the under-achievers. Consider, for example, what's happened over the past 20 years or so. Starting in the 1980s, fixed-income securities held their own and continued to do so through the early 1990s, only to fall far behind for the rest of the decade. But then along came a couple of nasty bear markets in stocks (2000–2002 and 2007–2009). The net results of all this can be seen in Exhibit 12.6, which tracks the comparative returns of stocks (via the S&P 500) and bonds (using the Merrill Lynch U.S.Treasuries 15+ year maturity total return index) from 1989 through mid-2009.

As can be seen in the exhibit, the bear markets of 2000–2002 and 2007–2009 had devastating effects on stocks. Indeed, over the roughly 20-year period from 1989 to mid-2009, the S&P 500 underperformed long-term Treasury bonds by 0.19 percentage points (8.73% versus 8.92%). The net result was that a $10,000 investment in 1989 would have generated a terminal value in mid-2009 of about $55,961 for stocks, compared to about $58,093 for bonds. While historically the long-term performance of stocks typically outstrips that of bonds, there have been times when that just wasn't so.

## Basic Issue Characteristics

A bond is a negotiable, long-term debt instrument that carries certain obligations on the part of the issuer. Unlike the holders of common stock, bondholders have no ownership or equity position in the issuing firm or organization. This is so because bonds are debt, and thus the bondholders, in a roundabout way, are only lending money to the issuer.

As a rule, bonds pay interest every 6 months. The amount of interest paid depends on the **coupon**, which defines the annual interest that the issuer will pay to the bondholder. For instance, a $1,000 bond with an 8% coupon would pay $80 in interest

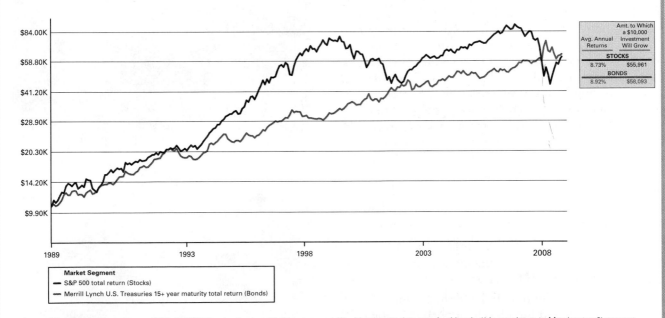

**Exhibit 12.6   Comparative Performance of Stocks and Bonds: 1989–mid-2009**

This graph shows what happened to $10,000 invested in bonds over the (roughly) 20-year period from January 1989 through mid-2009, versus the same amount invested in stocks. It is clear that, although stocks held a commanding lead through early 2000 and then again in 2003–2006, the bear markets of 2000–2002 and 2007–2009 largely erased all of that. As a result, stocks and bonds finished the period at ending (or "terminal") values that were a mere $2,100 apart—with *bonds actually performing better than stocks!*

Market Segment
— S&P 500 total return (Stocks)
— Merrill Lynch U.S. Treasuries 15+ year maturity total return (Bonds)

| | Avg. Annual Returns | Amt. to Which a $10,000 Investment Will Grow |
|---|---|---|
| **STOCKS** | | |
| | 8.73% | $55,961 |
| **BONDS** | | |
| | 8.92% | $58,093 |

*Source:* Morningstar Direct, August, 2009. © 2009 Morningstar, Inc. All rights reserved. The Morningstar data contained herein 1) is proprietary to Morningstar; 2) may not be copied or distributed without written permission; and 3) is not warranted to be accurate, complete or timely. Morningstar is not responsible for any damages or losses arising from any use of this information and has not granted its consent to be considered or deemed an"expert" under the Securities Act of 1933.

every year ($1,000 × 0.08 = $80), generally in the form of two $40 semi-annual payments. The principal amount of a bond, also known as its *par value*, specifies the amount of capital that must be repaid at maturity—there's $1,000 of principal in a $1,000 bond.

Of course, debt securities regularly trade at market prices that differ from their principal (or par) values. This occurs whenever an issue's coupon differs from the prevailing market rate of interest; in essence, the price of an issue will change until its yield is compatible with prevailing market yields. Such behavior explains why a 7% issue will carry a market price of only $825 when the market yield is 9%; the drop in price is necessary to raise the yield on this bond from 7% to 9%. Issues with market values lower than par are known as *discount bonds* and carry coupons that are less than those on new issues. In contrast, issues with market values above par are called *premium bonds* and have coupons greater than those currently being offered on new issues.

## Types of Issues

In addition to their coupons and maturities, bonds can be differentiated from one another by the type of collateral behind them. In this regard, the issues can be viewed as having either junior or senior standing. *Senior bonds are secured obligations* because they're backed by a legal claim on some specific property of the issuer that acts as *collateral* for the bonds. Such issues include **mortgage bonds**, which are secured by real estate, and **equipment trust certificates**, which are backed by certain types of equipment and are popular with railroads and airlines. *Junior bonds*, on the other hand, are backed only with a promise by the issuer to pay interest and principal on a timely basis. There are several classes of *unsecured* bonds, the most popular of which is known as a **debenture**. Issued as either notes (with maturities of 2 to 10 years) or bonds (maturities of more than 10 years), debentures are totally unsecured in the sense that there's no collateral backing them up—other than the issuer's good name.

## Sinking Fund

Another provision that's important to investors is the **sinking fund**, which describes how a bond will be paid off over time. Not all bonds have these requirements; but for those that do, a sinking fund specifies the annual repayment schedule to be used in paying off the issue and indicates how much principal will be retired each year. Sinking fund requirements generally begin 1 to 5 years after the date of issue and continue annually thereafter until all or most of the issue has been paid off. Any

amount not repaid by maturity is then retired with a single balloon payment.

## Call Feature

Every bond has a **call feature**, which stipulates whether a bond can be called (that is, retired) before its regularly scheduled maturity date and, if so, under what conditions. Basically, there are three types of call features.

- A bond can be *freely callable*, which means the issuer can prematurely retire the bond at any time.

- A bond can be *noncallable*, which means the issuer is prohibited from retiring the bond prior to maturity.

- The issue could carry a *deferred call*, which means the issue cannot be called until after a certain length of time has passed from the date of issue. In essence, the issue is noncallable during the deferment period and then becomes freely callable thereafter.

Call features are normally used to prematurely retire a bond and replace it with one that carries a lower coupon; in this way, the issuer benefits by being able to realize a reduction in annual interest cost. In an attempt to compensate investors who have their bonds called out from under them, a *call premium* (usually equal to about 6 months to 1 year of interest) is tacked onto the par value of the bond and paid to investors, along with the issue's par value, at the time the bond is called. For example, if a company decides to call its 7% bonds some 15 years before they mature, then it might have to pay $1,052.50 for every

©JUSTASC/SHUTTERSTOCK

**Treasury bond** A bond issued by and backed up by the full faith and credit of the U.S. government.

**Treasury inflation-indexed bond (TIPS)** A bond issued by the U.S. government that has principal payments that are adjusted to provide protection again inflation, as measured by the Consumer Price Index (CPI).

**agency bond** An obligation of a political subdivision of the U.S. government.

**mortgage-backed securities** Securities that are a claim on the cash flows generated by mortgage loans; bonds backed by mortgages as collateral.

**municipal bond** A bond issued by state or local governments; interest income is usually exempt from federal taxes.

$1,000 bond outstanding (in this case, a call premium equal to 9 months' interest—$70 × 0.75 = $52.50—would be added to the par value of $1,000). Although this might sound like a good deal, it's really not for the investor. The bondholder may indeed get a few extra bucks when the bond is called; but in turn, she loses a source of high current income. For example, the investor may have a 7% bond called away at a time when the best she can do in the market is may be 4% or 5%.

## The Bond Market

One thing that really stands out about the bond market is its size—the U.S. bond market is huge and getting bigger almost daily. Indeed, in 2007, the dollar value of bonds outstanding in this country exceeded $27 *trillion*! Given such size, it's not surprising that today's bond market offers securities to meet just about any type of investment objective and suit virtually any type of investor, no matter how conservative or aggressive.

of $1,000, and although interest income is subject to normal federal income tax, *it is exempt from state and local taxes.*

The newest type of Treasury issue is the **Treasury inflation-indexed bond**, or **TIPS** (which stands for "Treasury Inflation-Protected Securities"). These securities—which are issued with maturities, of 5, 10, or 20 years—give the investor the opportunity to keep up with inflation by periodically adjusting their returns for any inflation that has occurred. For instance, if inflation is running at an annual rate of 3%, then, at the end of the year, the par (or maturity) value of your bond will increase by 3%. Unfortunately, the coupons on these securities are set very low because they're meant to provide investors with *real (inflation-adjusted) returns.* So one of these bonds might carry a coupon of only 3.5 % (when regular T-bonds are paying, say, 6.5% or 7%). But there's an upside even to this: the actual *size of the coupon payment will increase over time as the par value on the bond increases.*

### Agency and Mortgage-Backed Bonds

**Agency bonds** are an important segment of the U.S. bond market. Although issued by political subdivisions of the U.S. government, *these securities are not obligations of the U.S. Treasury.* An important feature of these securities is that they customarily provide yields that are comfortably above the market rates for Treasuries and thus offer investors a way to increase returns with little or no real difference in

 *Today's bond market offers securities to meet just about any type of investment objective and suit virtually any type of investor.*

### Treasury Bonds

**Treasury bonds** (sometimes called *Treasuries* or *governments*) are a dominant force in the bond market and, if not the most popular, are certainly the best known. The U.S. Treasury issues bonds, notes, and other types of debt securities (such as the Treasury bills discussed in Chapter 4) as a means of meeting the federal government's ever-increasing needs. All Treasury obligations are of the highest quality (backed by the full faith and credit of the U.S. government), a feature that, along with their liquidity, makes them extremely popular with individual and institutional investors, both domestically and abroad.

*Treasury notes* are issued with maturities of 2, 3, 5, and 10 years, whereas *Treasury bonds* carry 20- and 30-year maturities. The Treasury issues its securities at regularly scheduled auctions, and it's through this process that the Treasury establishes the initial yields and coupons on the securities it issues. All Treasury notes and bonds are sold in minimum denominations

risk. Some actively traded and widely quoted agency issues include those sold by the Federal Farm Credit Bank, the Federal National Mortgage Association (or Fannie Mae), the Student Loan Marketing Association, and the Federal Home Loan Mortgage Corporation (FHLMC or Freddie Mac). Although the various agencies issue traditional unsecured notes and bonds, they are perhaps best known for their **mortgage-backed securities**. Two of the biggest issuers of such securities are Fannie Mae and Freddie Mac, who package and issue bonds backed by mortgages that have no government guarantee. The Government National Mortgage Association (or Ginnie Mae) is also active in the mortgage market. Owned by the U.S. government, it insures bonds that are backed by VA and FHA home loans.

### Municipal Bonds

**Municipal bonds** are the issues of states, counties, cities, and other political subdivisions, such as school districts and water and sewer districts. They're unlike other bonds in that their interest income is usually free from federal income tax (which is why they're known as *tax-free bonds*). Note, however, that this tax-free status does not apply to any capital gains that may be earned on these securities as such gains are subject to the usual federal taxes. A tax-free yield is probably the most important feature of municipal bonds and is certainly a major reason why individuals invest in them.

As a rule, the yields on municipal bonds are (usually, but not always) lower than the returns available from fully taxable issues. So unless the tax effect is sufficient to raise the yield on a municipal to a level that equals or exceeds the yields on taxable issues, it obviously doesn't make sense to buy municipal bonds. You can determine the return that a fully taxable bond must provide in order to match the after-tax return on a lower-yielding tax-free issue by computing the *fully taxable equivalent yield*:

$$\text{Fully taxable equivalent yield} = \frac{\text{Yield on municipal bond}}{1 - \text{Tax rate}}$$

For example, if a certain municipal bond offered a yield of 6%, then an individual in the 35% federal tax bracket would have to find a fully taxable bond with a yield of more than 9% to reap the same after-tax return—that is: $6\% \div (1 - 0.35) = 6\% \div 0.65 = 9.23\%$. The Bonus Exhibit, "Table of Taxable Equivalent Yields" (available at 4ltrpress.cengage .com), shows what a taxable bond (such as a Treasury issue) would have to yield to equal the take-home yield of a tax-free municipal bond. It demonstrates how the yield attractiveness of municipal bonds varies with an investor's income level; clearly, the higher the individual's tax bracket, the more attractive municipal bonds become.

Municipal bonds are generally issued as **serial obligations**, meaning that the issue is broken into a series of smaller bonds, each with its own maturity date and coupon rate. Thus, instead of the bond having just one maturity date 20 years from now, it will have a series of (say) 20 maturity dates over the 20-year time frame. Although it may not seem that municipal issuers would default on either interest or principal payments, it does occur! Investors should be especially cautious when investing in **revenue bonds**, which are municipal bonds serviced from the income generated by specific income-producing projects, such as toll roads. Unlike issuers of so-called **general obligation bonds**—which are backed by the full faith and credit of the municipality—the issuer of a revenue bond is obligated to pay principal and

interest *only if a sufficient level of revenue* is generated. General obligation municipal bonds, in contrast, are required to be serviced in a prompt and timely fashion regardless of the level of tax income generated by the municipality.

### Corporate Bonds

The major nongovernmental issuers of bonds are corporations. The market for **corporate bonds** is customarily subdivided into several segments, which include *industrials* (the most diverse of the group), *public utilities* (the dominant group in terms of volume of new issues), *rail and transportation bonds*, and *financial issues* (banks, finance companies, etc.). In this market, you'll find the widest range of different types of issues, from first mortgage and convertible bonds (discussed below) to debentures, subordinated debentures, and income bonds. Interest on corporate bonds is paid semi-annually, and sinking funds are common. The bonds usually come in $1,000 denominations and maturities usually range from 5 to 10 years but can be up to 30 years or more. Many of the issues carry call provisions that prohibit prepayment of the issue during the first 5 to 10 years. Corporate issues are popular with individuals because of their relatively high yields.

### Convertible Bonds

Another popular type of specialty issue, convertible bonds are found only in the corporate market. They are a type of *hybrid security* because they possess the features of both corporate bonds and common stocks. That is, while they are initially issued as debentures (unsecured debt), they carry a provision that enables them to be converted into a certain number of shares of the issuing company's common stock.

The key element of any convertible issue is its **conversion privilege**, which stipulates the conditions and specific nature of the conversion feature. First, it states exactly when the bond can be converted. Sometimes there'll be an initial waiting period of 6 months to perhaps 2 years after the date of issue, during which time the issue cannot be converted. The *conversion period* then begins, after which the issue can be converted at any time. From the investor's point of view, the most important item of information

**serial obligation** An issue that is broken down into a series of smaller bonds, each with its own maturity date and coupon rate.

**revenue bond** A municipal bond serviced from the income generated by a specific project.

**general obligation bond** A municipal bond backed by the full faith and credit of the issuing municipality.

**corporate bond** A bond issued by a corporation.

**conversion privilege** The provision in a convertible issue that stipulates the conditions of the conversion feature, such as the conversion period and conversion ratio.

**conversion ratio** A ratio specifying the number of shares of common stock into which a convertible bond can be converted.

**conversion value** A measure of what a convertible issue would trade for if it were priced to sell based on its stock value.

**conversion premium** The difference between a convertible security's market price and its conversion value.

**junk bond** Also known as *high-yield bonds*, these are highly speculative securities that have received low ratings from Moody's or Standard & Poor's.

is the **conversion ratio**, which specifies the number of shares of common stock into which the bond can be converted. For example, one of these bonds might carry a conversion ratio of 20, meaning you can "cash in" one convertible bond for 20 shares of stock.

Given the significance of the price behavior of the underlying common stock to the value of a convertible security, one of the most important measures to a convertible bond investor is conversion value. In essence, **conversion value** is an indication of what a convertible issue would trade for *if it were priced to sell based on its stock value*. Conversion value is easy to find: simply multiply the conversion ratio of the issue by the current market price of the underlying common stock. For example, a convertible that carried a conversion ratio of 20 would have a conversion value of $1,200 if the firm's stock traded at $60 per share (20 × $60 = $1,200). But convertibles seldom trade precisely at their conversion value; instead, they usually trade at **conversion premiums**, which means the convertibles are priced in the market at more than their conversion values. For example, a convertible that traded at $1,400 and had a conversion value of $1,200 would have a conversion premium of $200 (i.e., $1,400 – $1,200 = $200). Convertible securities appeal to investors who want *the price potential of a common stock along with the downside risk protection of a corporate bond*.

## Bond Ratings

Bond ratings are like grades: A letter grade is assigned to a bond, which designates its investment quality. Ratings are widely used and are an important part of the municipal and corporate bond markets. The two largest and best-known rating agencies are Moody's and Standard & Poor's. Every time a large, new corporate or municipal issue comes to the market, a staff of professional bond analysts determine its default risk exposure and investment quality. The financial records of the issuing organization are thoroughly examined and its future prospects assessed. The result of all this is the assignment of a bond rating at the time of issue that indicates *the ability of the issuing organization to service its debt in a prompt and timely manner*. Exhibit 12.7 lists the various ratings assigned to bonds by each of the two major agencies. Note that the top four

ratings (Aaa through Baa; or AAA through BBB) designate *investment-grade bonds*—such ratings are highly coveted by issuers because they indicate financially strong, well-run companies or municipalities. The next two ratings (Ba/B; or BB/B) are where you'll find most **junk bonds**; these ratings indicate that although the principal and interest payments on the bonds are still being met, the risk of default is relatively high because the issuers lack the financial strength found with investment-grade issues.

### Go to Smart Sites

If bonds are still a mystery to you, then check out the wealth of practical and educational tools and useful links available at the Bond Market Association's "Investing in Bonds" Web site. ●

Once a new issue is rated, the process doesn't stop there. Older, outstanding bonds are also regularly reviewed to ensure that their assigned ratings are still valid. While most issues will carry a single rating to maturity, ratings can change over time as new information becomes available. Finally, although it may appear that the issuing firm or municipality is receiving the rating, it's actually the individual issue that is being rated. As a result, a firm (or municipality) can have different ratings assigned to its issues. Most investors pay careful attention to ratings because they affect comparative market yields: other things being equal, *the higher the rating, the lower the yield of an obligation*. Thus, whereas an A-rated bond might offer a 5% yield, a comparable AAA-rated issue would probably yield something like 4.25 or 4.50%.

---

### FINANCIAL ROAD SIGN

$$$

**NO-NAME JUNK?**
Junk bonds are low-rated debt securities that carry relatively high risk of default. You'd expect to find a bunch of no-name companies residing in this neighborhood, but that's not always the case. Here's a list of some well-known companies whose bonds were rated as junk in mid-2009:

- Liz Claiborne (B– / B3)*
- Sirius XM Radio (B+ / Caa2)
- Brunswick (B– / Ba3)
- Dish Network (BB– / Ba3–)
- Sprint Nextel (BB./ Ba2)
- Ford Motor (BB+ / Ba2)

These issues carried low ratings because their operating earnings lacked the quality and consistency of high-grade bonds. So why invest in them? For their high returns!

*The first rating is by Standard & Poor's and the second is by Moody's.

**Exhibit 12.7   Moody's and Standard & Poor's Bond Ratings**

Agencies like Moody's and Standard & Poor's rate corporate and municipal bonds; these ratings provide an indication of the bonds' investment quality (particularly regarding an issue's default risk exposure).

| Bond Ratings* | | |
|---|---|---|
| Moody's | S&P | Description |
| Aaa | AAA | *Prime-Quality Investment Bonds*—This is the highest rating assigned, denoting extremely strong capacity to pay. |
| Aa<br>A | AA<br>A | *High-Grade Investment Bonds*—These are also considered very safe bonds, though they're not quite as safe as Aaa/AAA issues; double-A-rated bonds (Aa/AA) are safer (have less risk of default) than single-A-rated issues. |
| Baa | BBB | *Medium-Grade Investment Bonds*—These are the lowest of the investment-grade issues; they're felt to lack certain protective elements against adverse economic conditions. |
| Ba<br>B | BB<br>B | *Junk Bonds*—With little protection against default, these are viewed as highly speculative securities. |
| Caa<br>Ca<br>C<br>D | CCC<br>CC<br>C<br>D | *Poor-Quality Bonds*—These are either in default or very close to it; they're often referred to as "Zombie Bonds." |

*Some ratings may be modified to show relative standing within a major rating category; for example, Moody's uses numerical modifiers (1, 2, 3) whereas S&P uses plus (+) or minus (−) signs.

## Pricing a Bond

Unlike stocks, bonds aren't widely quoted in the financial press, not even in the *Wall Street Journal*. So, rather than looking at how bonds are quoted, let's look at how they're priced in the marketplace. Regardless of the type, *all bonds are priced as a percentage of par*, meaning that a quote of, say, 85 translates into a price of 85% of the bond's par value. In the bond market, 1 point = $10, so a quote of 85 does not mean $85 but rather $850. This is so because market convention assumes that bonds carry par values of $1,000. Also keep in mind that the price of any bond is always related to the issue's coupon and maturity—those two features are always a part of any listed price because of their effect on the price of a bond. (We'll talk more about the impact of coupons and maturities on bond price behavior in the section on "Bond Prices and Yields.")

In the corporate and municipal markets, bonds are priced in decimals, using three places to the right of the decimal point. Thus a quote of 87.562, as a percentage of a $1,000 par bond, converts to a price of $875.62; similarly, a quote of 121.683 translates into a price of 1.21683 × $1,000 = $1,216.83. In contrast, U.S. Treasury and agency bond quotes are stated in *thirty-seconds of a point* (where, again, 1 point = $10). For example, you might see the price of a T-bond listed at, "94:16." Translated, this means that

the bond is being priced at $94^{16}/_{32}$, or 94.5% of par—in other words, it's being priced at $945.00. With government bonds, the figures to the right of the colon (:) show the number of thirty-seconds embedded in the price.

## Bond Prices and Yields

The price of a bond depends on its coupon, maturity, and the movement of market interest rates. *When interest rates go down, bond prices go up, and vice versa.* The relationship of bond prices to market rates is captured in Exhibit 12.8. The graph serves to reinforce the *inverse* relationship between bond prices and market interest rates; note that *lower* rates lead to *higher* bond prices. The exhibit also shows the difference between premium and discount bonds. A **premium bond** is one that sells for more than its par value, which occurs whenever market interest rates drop below the coupon rate on the bond; a **discount bond**, in contrast, sells for less than par and is the result of market rates being greater than the issue's coupon rate. So the 10% bond in our illustration traded as a premium bond when market rates were at 8%, but as a discount bond when rates stood at 12%.

**premium bond** A bond whose market value is higher than par.

**discount bond** A bond whose market value is lower than par.

Exhibit 12.8    Price Behavior of a Bond with a 10% Coupon

A bond sells at its par value as long as the prevailing market interest rate remains the same as the bond's coupon (for example, when both coupon and market rates equal 10%). But if market rates drop then bond prices rise, and vice versa; moreover, as a bond approaches its maturity, the issue price always moves toward its par value no matter what happens to interest rates.

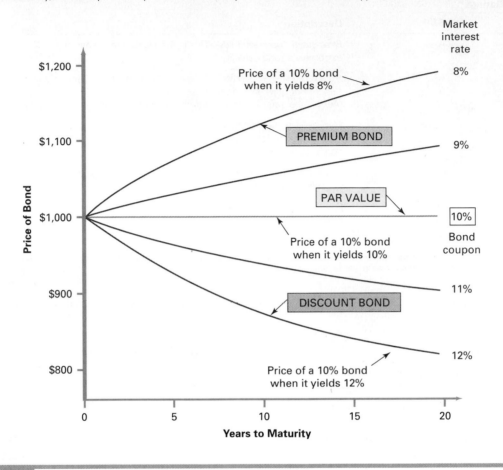

**current yield** The amount of current income a bond provides relative to its market price.

What happens to the price of the bond over time is of considerable interest to most bond investors. We know that how much bond prices move depends not only on the *direction* of interest rates changes but also on the *magnitude* of such changes; for the greater the moves in interest rates, the greater the swings in bond prices. But there's more, for bond prices will also vary according to the coupon and maturity of the issue—that is, bonds with *lower coupons* and/or *longer maturities* will respond more vigorously to changes in market rates and undergo *greater price swings*. Thus, if interest rates are moving up, then the investor should seek high coupon bonds with short maturities because this will cause minimal price variation and *preserve as much capital as possible*. In contrast, if rates are heading down, that's the time to be in long-term bonds: if you're a speculator

looking for a lot of capital gains, then go with long-term, *low coupon bonds*; but if you're trying to lock in a high level of coupon (interest) income, then stick with long-term, *high coupon* bonds that offer plenty of call protection.

### Current Yield and Yield to Maturity

The two most commonly cited bond yields are current yield and yield to maturity. **Current yield** reflects the amount of annual interest income the bond provides relative to its current market price. Here's the formula for current yield:

$$\text{Current yield} = \frac{\text{Annual interest income}}{\text{Market price of bond}}$$

As you can see, the current yield on a bond is basically the same as the dividend yield on a stock.

Assume, for example, that a 6% bond with a $1,000 par value is currently selling for $910. Because annual interest income would amount to $60 and because the current market price of the bond is $910, its current yield would be 6.59% ($60/$910). This measure would be of interest to *investors seeking current income*; other things being equal, the higher the current yield, the more attractive the bond would be.

The annual rate of return a bondholder would receive *if she held the issue to its maturity* is captured in the bond's **yield to maturity**. This measure captures both the annual interest income and the recovery of principal at maturity; it also includes the impact of interest on interest and therefore provides a fully compounded rate of return. If a bond is purchased at its face value, then its yield to maturity will equal the coupon, or stated, rate of interest. On the other hand, if the bond is purchased at a discount or premium, then its yield to maturity will vary according to the prevailing level of market yields.

You can find the yield to maturity on discount or premium bonds by using the *approximate yield* formula introduced earlier in this chapter. Or you can use a handheld financial calculator (which we'll demonstrate soon) to obtain a yield to maturity that's a bit more accurate and is, in fact, very close to the measure used in the market; the only difference is that market participants normally use semi-annual compounding in their calculations whereas we use annual compounding.

By setting the future price (FP) of the investment equal to the bond's face value ($1,000), you can use the following version of the equation to find the *approximate yield to maturity on a bond*:

$$\text{Approximate yield to maturity} = \frac{CI + \left[\dfrac{\$1,000 - CP}{N}\right]}{\left[\dfrac{CP + \$1,000}{2}\right]}$$

Recall, CI equals annual current income (or in this case, annual interest income), CP is the current price of the bond, and N is the investment period (number of years to maturity).

## Crunching the Numbers

Now, assume that you're contemplating the purchase of a $1,000, 6% bond with 15 years remaining to maturity, and that the bond is trading at a price of $910. Given CI = $60, CP = $910, and N = 15, the approximate yield to maturity on this bond will be:

$$\text{Approximate yield to maturity} = \frac{\$60 + \left[\dfrac{\$1,000 - \$910}{15}\right]}{\left[\dfrac{\$910 + \$1,000}{2}\right]}$$

$$= \frac{\$60 + \left[\dfrac{\$90}{15}\right]}{\left[\dfrac{\$1,910}{2}\right]} = \underline{6.91\%}$$

Note that because this bond was purchased at a discount, its computed yield to maturity is above both the 6% stated coupon rate, and the 6.59% current yield.

## Calculator Keystrokes

You can also *find the yield to maturity on a bond* by using a financial calculator; here's what you'd do. With the calculator in the *annual mode*, to find the yield to maturity on our 6% (annual pay), 15-year bond that's currently trading at $910, use the keystrokes shown here, where:

N = number of *years* to maturity
PV = the current market price of the bond [entered as a *negative*]
PMT = the size of the annual coupon payments [in *dollars*]
FV = the par value of the bond

A value of 6.99 should appear in the calculator display, which is the bond's yield to maturity using annual compounding; note that it's very close to the approximate yield of 6.91% we just computed.

Measures of yield to maturity are used by investors to assess the attractiveness of a bond investment. The higher the yield to maturity, the more attractive the investment, other things being equal. *If a bond provided a yield to maturity that equaled or exceeded an investor's desired rate of return, then it would be considered a worthwhile investment candidate* because it would promise a yield that should adequately compensate the investor for the perceived amount of risk involved.

**Yield to maturity**
The fully compounded rate of return that a bond would yield if it were held to maturity.

| CALCULATOR | |
|---|---|
| Inputs | Functions |
| 15 | N |
| −910 | PV |
| 60 | PMT |
| 1000 | FV |
| | CPT |
| | I/Y |
| | **Solution** |
| | 6.99 |

SEE APPENDIX E FOR DETAILS.

# FINANCIAL PLANNING EXERCISES

**LG1, 2**
1. **What makes for a good investment?** Use the approximate yield formula or a financial calculator to rank the following investments according to their expected returns:
   a. Buy a stock for $45 a share, hold it for 3 years, and then sell it for $75 a share (the stock pays annual dividends of $3 a share).
   b. Buy a security for $25, hold it for 2 years, and then sell it for $60 (current income on this security is zero).
   c. Buy a 1-year, 12% note for $950 (assume that the note has a $1,000 par value and that it will be held to maturity).

**LG3, 4**
2. An investor is thinking about buying some shares of Financial Concepts, Inc., at $60 a share. She expects the price of the stock to rise to $100 a share over the next 3 years. During that time, she also expects to receive annual dividends of $3 per share. Given that the investor's expectations (about the future price of the stock and the dividends it pays) hold up, what rate of return can the investor expect to earn on this investment? (*Hint:* Use either the approximate yield formula or a financial calculator to solve this problem.)

**LG3, 4**
3. The price of YouRus is now $65. The company pays no dividends. Mr. Milton Rapier expects the price 4 years from now to be $105 a share. Should Mr. Rapier buy YouRus if he desires a 15% rate of return? Explain.

**LG5, 6**
4. An investor in the 28% tax bracket is trying to decide which of two bonds to select: one is a 6.5% U.S. Treasury bond selling at par; the other is a municipal bond with a 5.25% coupon, which is also selling at par. Which of these two bonds should the investor select? Why?

**LG5, 6**
5. Describe and differentiate between a bond's (a) current yield and (b) yield to maturity. Why are these yield measures important to the bond investor? Find the yield to maturity of a 20-year, 9%, $1,000 par value bond trading at a price of $850. What's the current yield on this bond?

# 13

# INVESTING IN MUTUAL FUNDS AND REAL ESTATE

© DIGITAL VISION GETTY IMAGES FROM DV1080 MONEY MATTERS

## LEARNING GOALS

**LG1** Describe the basic features and operating characteristics of a mutual fund. (p. 290)

**LG2** Differentiate between open- and closed-end funds as well as exchange-traded funds, and discuss the various types of fund loads and charges. (p. 290)

**LG3** Discuss the types of funds available to investors and the different kinds of investor services offered by mutual funds. (p. 296)

**LG4** Gain an understanding of the variables that should be considered when selecting funds for investment purposes. (p. 302)

**LG5** Identify the sources of return and calculate the rate of return earned on an investment in a mutual fund. (p. 302)

**LG6** Understand the role that real estate plays in a diversified investment portfolio, along with the basics of investing in real estate, either directly or indirectly. (p. 306)

# FINANCIAL PLANNING EXERCISES

**LG4** 1. For *each pair* of funds listed below, select the fund that would be the *least* risky and briefly explain your answer.
a. Growth versus growth-and-income
b. Equity-income versus high-grade corporate bonds
c. Intermediate-term bonds versus high-yield municipals
d. International versus balanced

**LG5** 2. About a year ago, Chris Beattie bought some shares in the Stratosphere Mutual Fund. He bought the stock at $24.50 a share, and it now trades at $26.00. Last year, the fund paid dividends of 40 cents a share and had capital gains distributions of $1.83 a share. Using the approximate yield formula, what rate of return did Chris earn on his investment? Repeat the calculation using a handheld financial calculator. Would he have made a 20% rate of return if the stock had risen to $30 a share?

**LG2, 3** 3. Describe an ETF and explain how these funds combine the characteristics of open- and closed-end funds. In the Vanguard family of funds, which would most closely resemble a "Spider" (SPDR)? In what respects are the Vanguard fund (that you selected) and Spiders the same and how are they different? If you could invest in only one of them, which would it be? Explain.

**LG5** 4. A year ago, the Everlast Growth Fund was being quoted at an NAV of $21.50 and an offer price of $23.35; today, it's being quoted at $23.04 (NAV) and $25.04 (offer). Use the approximate yield formula, or a handheld financial calculator, to find the rate of return on this load fund; it was purchased a year ago, and its dividends and capital gains distributions over the year totaled $1.05 a share. (*Hint:* As an investor, you buy fund shares at the offer price and sell at the NAV.)

**LG6** 5. Paloma Ortiz is thinking about investing in some residential income-producing property that she can purchase for $200,000. Paloma can either pay cash for the full amount of the property or put up $50,000 of her own money and borrow the remaining $150,000 at 8% interest. The property is expected to generate $30,000 per year after all expenses but *before* interest and income taxes. Assume that Paloma is in the 28% tax bracket. Calculate her annual profit and return on investment assuming that she (a) pays the full $200,000 from her own funds or (b) borrows $150,000 at 8%. Then discuss the effect, if any, of leverage on her rate of return. (HINT: Earnings before interest & taxes *minus* Interest expenses (if any) *equals* Earnings before taxes *minus* Income taxes (@28%) *equals* Profit after taxes.)

# Retirement Plan

©FENG YU/SHUTTERSTOCK

# 14

# PLANNING FOR RETIREMENT

## LEARNING GOALS

**LG1** Recognize the importance of retirement planning, and identify the three biggest pitfalls to good planning. (p. 313)

**LG2** Estimate your income needs in retirement and your retirement income. (p. 313)

**LG3** Explain the eligibility requirements and benefits of the Social Security program. (p. 318)

**LG4** Differentiate among the types of basic and supplemental employer-sponsored pension plans. (p. 321)

**LG5** Describe the various types of self-directed retirement plans. (p. 321)

**LG6** Choose the right type of annuity for your retirement plan. (p. 328)

## An Overview of Retirement Planning

Retiring is easy. What's difficult is retiring in style, and that's where retirement planning comes into play! But to enjoy a comfortable retirement, you must *start now*—for one of the biggest mistakes people make in retirement planning is waiting too long to begin. Accumulating adequate retirement funds is a daunting task that takes careful planning. Like budgets, taxes, and investments, retirement planning is vital to your financial well-being and is a critical link in your personal financial plans.

{ *Retiring is easy. What's difficult is retiring in style.* }

### Role of Retirement Planning in Personal Financial Planning

The financial planning process would be incomplete without retirement planning. Certainly no financial goal is more important than achieving a comfortable standard of living in retirement. In many respects, retirement planning captures the very essence of financial planning. It is forward looking, affects both your current and future standard of living, and can be highly rewarding and contribute significantly to your net worth.

The first step in retirement planning is to set *retirement goals* for yourself. Take some time to describe the things you want to do in retirement, the standard of living you hope to maintain, the level of income you'd like to receive, and any special retirement goals you may have (like buying a retirement home in Arizona). Such goals are important because *they give direction to your retirement planning*. Of course, like all goals, they're subject to change over time as the situations and conditions in your life change.

Once you know what you want out of retirement, the next step is to establish the *size of the nest egg* you're going to need to achieve your retirement goals. And while you're at it, you'll also want to formulate an *investment program* that'll enable you to build up your required nest egg. This usually involves (1) creating some type of systematic savings plan in which you put away a certain amount of money each year and (2) identifying the types of investment vehicles that will best meet your retirement needs.

Investments and investment planning are the vehicles for building up your retirement funds. They're the active, ongoing part of retirement planning in which you invest and manage the funds you've set aside for retirement. It's no coincidence that a major portion of most individual investor portfolios is devoted to building up a pool of funds for retirement. Tax planning is also important because a major objective of sound retirement planning is to legitimately shield as much income as possible from taxes and, in so doing, maximize the accumulation of retirement funds.

### The Three Biggest Pitfalls to Sound Retirement Planning

Human nature being what it is, people often get a little carried away with the amount of money they want to build up for retirement. Having a nest egg of $4 million or $5 million would be great, but it's really beyond the reach of most people. Besides, you don't need that much to live comfortably in retirement. So set a more realistic goal. But when you set that goal, remember: it's not going to happen by itself; you'll have to do something to bring it about. And this is precisely where things start to fall apart. Why? Because when it comes to retirement planning, people tend to make three big mistakes:

- They start too late.
- They put away too little.
- They invest too conservatively.

Many people in their 20s, or even 30s, find it hard to put money away for retirement. Most often that's because they have other, more pressing financial concerns—such as buying a house, retiring a student loan, or paying for child care. The net result is that they *put off retirement planning until later in life*—in many cases, until they're in their late 30s or 40s. Unfortunately, the longer people put it off, the less they're going to have in retirement. Or they won't to be able to retire as early as they'd hoped. Even worse, once people start a retirement program, *they tend to put away too little*. Although this may also be due to pressing financial needs, all too often it boils down to lifestyle choices. They'd rather spend for today than save for tomorrow.

On top of all this, many *people tend to be far too conservative* in the way they invest their retirement money. The fact is, they place way too much of their retirement money into *low-yielding*, fixed-income securities such as CDs and Treasury notes. Although you should *never speculate* with something as important as your retirement plan, there's no need to totally avoid risk. There's nothing wrong with following an investment program that involves a reasonable amount of risk, provided it results in a correspondingly higher level of expected return. Being overly cautious can be costly in the long run. Indeed, a low rate of return can have an enormous impact on the long-term accumulation of capital and, in many cases, may mean the difference between just getting by or enjoying a comfortable retirement.

### Compounding the Errors

All three of these pitfalls become even more important when we introduce *compound interest*. That's because *compounding essentially magnifies the impact of these mistakes*. As an illustration, consider the first variable—starting too late. If you were to start a retirement program at age 35 by putting away $2,000 a year, it would grow to almost $160,000 by the time you're 65, if invested at an average rate of return of 6%. Not a bad deal. But look at what you end up with if you start this investment program just 10 years earlier, at age 25: that same $2,000 a year will grow to over $309,000 by the time you're 65. Think of it—for another $20,000 ($2,000 a year for an extra 10 years), you can nearly double the terminal value of your investment! Of course, it's not the extra $20,000 that's doubling your money; rather, it's *compound interest* that's doing most of the work.

And the same holds true for the rate of return you earn on the investments in your retirement account. Take the second situation just described—starting a retirement program at age 25. Earning 6% yields a retirement nest egg of over $309,000; increase that rate of return to 8% (a reasonable investment objective), and your retirement nest egg will be worth just over $518,000! *You're still putting in the same amount of money*, but because your money is working harder, you end up with a much bigger nest egg. Of course, when you seek higher returns, that generally means you also have to take on more risks. But not everyone can tolerate higher levels of risk. And if that applies to you, then simply stay away from the higher-risk investments. Rather, stick to safer, lower-yielding securities and find some other way to build up your nest egg. For instance, contribute more each year to your plan or extend the length of your investment period. The only other option—and not a particularly appealing one—is to accept the possibility that you won't be able to build up as big a nest egg as you had thought and therefore will have to accept a lower standard of living in retirement.

## Estimating Income Needs

Retirement planning would be much simpler if we lived in a static economy. Unfortunately (or perhaps fortunately), we don't, so you'll have to live with the fact that both your personal budget and the general state of the economy will change over time. This makes accurate forecasting of retirement needs difficult at best. Even so you'll have to live with the fact that it's a necessary task, and you can handle it in one of two ways. One strategy is to plan for retirement over *a series of short-run time frames*. A good way to do this is to state your retirement income objectives as a percentage of your present earnings. Then, every 3 to 5 years, you can revise and update your plan.

Alternatively, you can follow *a long-term approach* in which you formulate the level of income you'd like to receive in retirement along with the amount of funds you must amass to achieve that desired standard of living. Rather than addressing the problem in a series of short-run plans, this approach goes 20 or 30 years into the future—to the time when you'll retire—in determining how much saving and investing you must do today in order to achieve your long-run retirement goals. Of course, if conditions or expectations should happen to change dramatically in the future, then it may be necessary to make corresponding alterations to your long-run retirement goals and strategies.

### Determining Future Retirement Needs

To illustrate how future retirement needs and income requirements can be formulated, let's consider the case of Jim and Agnes Mitchem. In their mid-30s, they have two children and an annual income of about $80,000 before taxes. Even though it's still some 30 years away, Jim and Agnes recognize it's now time to seriously consider their situation to see if they'll be able to pursue the kind of retirement lifestyle that appeals to them. Worksheet 14.1 provides the basic steps to follow in determining retirement needs. It shows how the Mitchems have estimated their retirement income and determined the amount of investment assets they must accumulate to meet their retirement objectives.

Jim and Agnes began by determining what their *household expenditures* will likely be in retirement. A simple way to derive an estimate of expected household expenditures is to base it on the current level of such expenses. Assume that the Mitchems'

A worksheet like this one will help you define your income requirements in retirement, the size of your retirement nest egg, and the amount you must save annually to achieve your retirement goals.

### PROJECTING RETIREMENT INCOME AND INVESTMENT NEEDS

Name(s) _Jim & Agnes Mitchem_  Date _8/31/2010_

#### I. Estimated Household Expenditures in Retirement:

| | |
|---|---:|
| A. Approximate number of years to retirement | 30 |
| B. Current level of annual household expenditures, excluding savings | $ 56,000 |
| C. Estimated household expenses in retirement as a *percent* of current *expenses* | 70 % |
| D. Estimated annual household expenditures in retirement (B × C) | $ 39,200 |

#### II. Estimated Income in Retirement:

| | |
|---|---:|
| E. Social Security, annual income | $ 24,000 |
| F. Company/employer pension plans, annual amounts | $ 9,000 |
| G. Other sources, annual amounts | $ 0 |
| H. Total annual income (E + F + G) | $ 33,000 |
| I. Additional required income, or annual shortfall (D − H) | $ 6,200 |

#### III. Inflation Factor:

| | |
|---|---:|
| J. Expected average annual rate of inflation over the period to retirement | 5 % |
| K. Inflation factor (in Appendix A):  Based on _30_ years to retirement (A) and an expected average annual rate of inflation (J) of _5%_ | 4.32 |
| L. Size of inflation-adjusted annual shortfall (I × K) | $ 26,784 |

#### IV. Funding the Shortfall:

| | |
|---|---:|
| M. Anticipated return on assets held *after* retirement | 8 % |
| N. Amount of retirement funds required—size of nest egg (L ÷ M) | $ 334,800 |
| O. Expected rate of return on investments *prior* to retirement | 6 % |
| P. Compound interest factor (in Appendix B): Based on _30_ years to retirement (A) and an expected rate of return on investments of _6%_ | 79.1 |
| Q. Annual savings required to fund retirement nest egg (N ÷ P) | $ 4,235 |

*Note:* Parts I and II are prepared in terms of current (today's) dollars. Parts III and IV can be computed with a handheld calculator that has a time-value function.

annual household expenditures (*excluding savings*) currently run about $56,000 a year (this information can be readily obtained by referring to their most recent income and expenditures statement). After making some obvious adjustments for the different lifestyle they'll have in retirement—e.g., their children will no longer be living at home, their home will be paid for, and so on—the Mitchems estimate that they should be able to achieve the standard of living they'd like in retirement at an annual level of household expenses equal to about 70% of the current

amount. Thus, *based on today's dollars*, their estimated household expenditures in retirement will be $56,000 × 0.70 = $39,200. (This process is summarized in steps A through D in Worksheet 14.1.)

### Estimating Retirement Income

The next question is: Where will the Mitchems get the money to meet their projected household expenses of $39,200 a year? They've addressed this problem by estimating what their *income* will be in retirement—again *based on today's dollars*. Their two basic sources

# MONEY IN ACTION

## IS YOUR PENSION PLAN AT RISK?

In 2005, a financially troubled United Airlines terminated its pension plan, leaving workers with significantly reduced benefits. The pilot who was promised $140,000 a year instead earns $28,000 a year in retirement. Delta and Northwest Airlines would have followed suit but for the **Pension Protection Act** of 2006, which gave the airlines more time to fund their troubled plans. It's not just underfunded plans that are in jeopardy; companies such as Verizon, Sears, IBM, and Hewlett-Packard have also moved to freeze their pension plans. In such situations, how do you avoid losing your retirement savings?

First, it's important to distinguish between plans that are frozen and those that are terminated. Plans that are terminated are typically taken over by the Pension Benefit Guaranty Corporation (PBGC), a government-run insurer that guarantees private-sector pensions up to certain limits. PBGC took over United's pension plan when executives proved that the airline couldn't remain in business unless the plan was terminated. To find out if your pension plan is covered by PBGC, check your company's Summary Plan Description. Although cases such as United attract a lot of media attention, the odds of a company defaulting on a pension plan are pretty low. What seems increasingly more likely is that a pension plan will be frozen. In mid-2009, Watson Wyatt, a human resources firm, estimated that 31% of Fortune 1000 companies had frozen pensions. Many companies are freezing

pension plans to eliminate this large liability from their books and stay competitive with companies that don't have pension plans to fund. If a plan is frozen, employees may collect any benefits earned up to that point; but the size of the pension won't grow. Many companies that freeze pension plans will instead contribute a percentage of an employee's salary to the firm's 401(k) plan in compensation.

If you do retire with a pension, you need to be careful that the choices you make don't lead to reduced benefits. The amount of your yearly payout could vary by thousands of dollars depending on retirement age and the number of years on the job. The combination of a higher salary and more years of service can significantly boost your pension. In one scenario, a person who retires at age 58 might draw a pension of $21,000 a year; but if this same person had waited until age 60 to retire, the payout would have been about $39,000 a year. In this case it certainly pays to work 2 more years. The human resources department at your company or your retirement benefits manager can help you with projections to determine the right scenario for you.

*Sources:* Lynn Cowan, "Rate of Frozen Pension Plans Rising," *The Wall Street Journal*, July 22, 2009, http://online.wsj.com/article/BT-CO-20090722-711858.html, accessed August 2009. Ellen E. Schultz and Theo Francis, "How Safe Is Your Pension?" *The Wall Street Journal*, January 12, 2006, p. D1.

---

**Pension Protection Act** A federal law passed in 2006 intended to shore up the financial integrity of private traditional (defined benefit) plans and, at the same time, to encourage employees to make greater use of salary reduction (defined contribution) plans.

**thrift and savings plan** A plan to supplement pension and other fringe benefits; the firm contributes an amount equal to a set proportion of the employee's contribution.

Some big companies offer *voluntary profit-sharing plans* that invest heavily (almost exclusively) in their own stock. It's common in many of these cases for long-term career employees to accumulate several hundred thousand dollars worth of the company's stock. And we're not talking about highly paid corporate executives here; rather, these are just average employees who had the discipline to consistently divert a portion of their salary to the company's profit-sharing plan. However, *there is a real and significant downside to this practice:* if the company should hit hard times, then not only could you face salary cuts (or even worse, the loss of a job), but also the value of your profit-sharing account will likely tumble. Just look at what happened to employees in the technology sector during the 2000–2002 bear market.

### Thrift and Savings Plans

**Thrift and savings plans** were established to supplement pension and other fringe benefits. Most plans require the employer to make contributions to the

© SANDRA G/SHUTTERSTOCK

savings plan in an amount equal to a set proportion of the amount contributed by the employee. For example, an employer might match an employee's contributions at the rate of 50 cents on the dollar up to, say, 6% of salary. These contributions are then deposited with a trustee, who invests the money in various types of securities, including stocks and bonds of the employing firm. With IRS-qualified thrift and savings plans, the *employer's* contributions and earnings on the savings aren't included in the *employee's* taxable income until he or she withdraws the money. Unfortunately, this attractive tax feature doesn't extend to the *employee's contributions*, so any money put into one of these savings plans is still considered part of the employee's taxable income and subject to regular income taxes. An employee who has the option should seriously consider participating in a thrift plan. The returns are usually pretty favorable, especially when you factor in the *employer's* contributions.

 **Go to Smart Sites**

You'll find several useful retirement calculators, tools, and an asset-allocation worksheet at Fidelity Investments' 401(k) site. ●

## Salary Reduction Plans

Another type of supplemental retirement program— and certainly the most popular judging by employee response—is the **salary reduction plan**, or the **401(k) plan** as it's more commonly known. Our discussion here centers on 401(k) plans, but similar programs are available for employees of public, nonprofit organizations, including public schools, colleges, hospitals, and state and local governments. Known as *403(b) plans* or *457 plans*, they offer many of the same features and tax shelter provisions as 401(k) plans.

Today, more and more companies are cutting back on their contributions to traditional (defined benefit) retirement plans. They're turning instead to 401(k) plans, a type of defined contribution plan. A 401(k) plan basically gives employees the option to divert part of their salary to a company-sponsored, tax-sheltered savings account. In this way, the earnings diverted to the savings plan accumulate tax free. Taxes must be paid eventually, but not until the employee starts drawing down the account at retirement. In 2009, an individual employee could put as much as $16,500 into a tax-deferred 401(k) plan. (Contribution limits for 403(b) and 457 plans are the same as those for 401(k) plans.)

To see how such tax-deferred plans work, consider an individual with taxable income of $75,000 in 2009 who would like to contribute the maximum allowable—$16,500—to the 401(k) plan where she works. Doing so will reduce her taxable income to $58,500

and, assuming she's in the 25% tax bracket, will lower her federal tax bill by some $4,125 (i.e., $16,500 × 0.25). Such tax savings will offset a big chunk of her 401(k) contribution, as she'll add $16,500 to her retirement program with only $12,375 of her own money; the rest will come from the IRS via a reduced tax bill.

**salary reduction, or 401(k), plan** An agreement by which part of a covered employee's pay is withheld and invested in some form of investment; taxes on the contributions and the account earnings are deferred until the funds are withdrawn.

These plans are generally viewed as attractive *tax shelters* that offer not only substantial tax savings but also a way to save for retirement. As long as you can afford to put the money aside, *you should seriously consider joining a 401(k)/403(b)/457 plan if one is offered at your place of employment*. This is especially true when one considers the matching features offered by many of these plans. Most companies that offer 401(k) plans have some type of matching contributions program, often putting up 50 cents (or more) for every dollar contributed by the employee. Such matching plans give both tax and savings incentives to individuals and clearly enhance the appeal of 401(k) plans.

Now, another kind of 401(k) plan is being offered by a growing number of firms. This new retirement savings option, which first became available in January 2006, is the so-called *Roth 401(k)*. It's just like a traditional 401(k) except for one important difference: *All contributions to Roth 401(k) plans are made in after-tax dollars*. That means there are no tax savings to be derived from the annual employee contributions; if you earn, say, $75,000 a year and want to put $15,000 into your Roth 401(k), you'll end up paying taxes on the full $75,000. That's the bad news; now the good news. Because all contributions are made in after-tax dollars, *there are no taxes to be paid on plan withdrawals (in other words, they're tax free)*, provided you're at least 59½ and have held the account for 5 years or more. Like traditional 401(k) plans, Roth 401(k)s also have a contribution cap of $16,500 (in 2009). And that limit applies to *total contributions to both types of 401(k) plans combined*, so you can't put $15,000 into a traditional 401(k) plan and then put another $15,000 into a Roth 401(k). You can also have employer matches with the Roth plans, although technically those matches will accumulate in a separate account that will be taxed as ordinary income at withdrawal. Essentially, *employer* contributions represent tax-free income to employees, so they'll pay taxes on that income, and on any account earnings, when the funds are withdrawn—as is done with a traditional 401(k).

Both Roth and traditional 401(k) plans typically offer their participants various investment options, including equity and fixed-income mutual funds, company stock, and a variety of interest-bearing vehicles

**Keogh plan** An account to which self-employed persons may make specified payments that may be deducted from taxable income; earnings also accrue on a tax-deferred basis.

such as bank CDs. Indeed, the typical 401(k) has about 10 choices, and some plans have as many as 20 or more. Today, the trend is toward giving plan participants more options and providing seminars and other educational tools to help employees make informed retirement plan decisions.

## Evaluating Employer-Sponsored Pension Plans

When participating in a company-sponsored pension plan, you're entitled to certain benefits in return for meeting certain conditions of membership—which may or may not include making contributions to the plan. Whether your participation is limited to the firm's basic plan or includes one or more of the supplemental programs, *it's vital that you take the time to acquaint yourself with the various benefits and provisions* of these plans. And be sure to familiarize yourself not only with the basic plans but also with any (voluntary) supplemental plans you may be eligible to join.

So, how should you evaluate these plans? Most experts agree that you can get a pretty good handle on essential plan provisions and retirement benefits by taking a close look at the following features.

- **Eligibility requirements.** Precisely what are they?
- **Defined benefits or contributions.** Which one is defined? If it's the benefits, exactly what formula is used to define them? Pay particular attention to how Social Security benefits are treated in the formula. If it's a defined contribution program, do you have any control over how the money is invested? If so, what are your options?
- **Vesting procedures.** Does the company use a cliff or graded procedure?
- **Contributory or noncontributory.** If the plan is contributory, how much comes from you and how much from the company? If it's noncontributory, what is the company's contribution as a percentage of your salary?
- **Retirement age.** What's the normal retirement age, and what provisions are there for *early retirement*? Are the pension benefits *portable*—that is, can you take them with you if you change jobs?
- **Voluntary supplemental programs.** How much of your salary can you put into one or more of these plans, and what—if anything—is matched by the company?

Finding answers to these questions will help you determine where you stand and what improvements are needed to be made in your retirement plans. As part of this evaluation process, try to determine, as best as you can, *what your benefits are likely to be at retirement*—before you start cranking out the numbers, check with the people who handle employee benefits at your workplace; they'll usually give you the help you need. Then, using a procedure similar to that followed in Worksheet 14.1, you can estimate what portion of your retirement needs will be met from your company's basic pension plan. If there's a shortfall—*and it's likely there will be*—it will indicate the extent to which you need to participate in some type of company-sponsored supplemental program, such as a 401(k) plan, or (alternatively) how much you'll need to rely on your own savings and investments to reach the standard of living you're looking for in retirement.

## Self-Directed Retirement Programs

In addition to participating in company-sponsored retirement programs, individuals can set up their own tax-sheltered retirement plans. There are two basic types of self-directed retirement programs: *Keogh* and *SEP plans*, which are for self-employed individuals, and *individual retirement arrangements (IRAs)*, which can be set up by almost anyone.

### Keogh and SEP Plans

**Keogh plans** were introduced in 1962 as part of the Self-Employed Individuals Retirement Act, or simply the Keogh Act. Keogh plans allow self-employed individuals to set up tax-deferred retirement plans for themselves and their employees. Like contributions to 401(k) plans, payments to Keogh accounts may be taken as deductions from taxable income. As a result, they reduce the tax bills of self-employed individuals. The maximum contribution to this tax-deferred retirement plan in 2009 was $49,000 per year, or 25% of earned income, whichever is less. Any individual who is self-employed, either full- or part-time, is eligible to set up a Keogh account. These accounts can also be used by individuals who hold full-time jobs and moonlight part-time—for instance, the accountant who does tax returns at night and on weekends. And note that even though he has a Keogh account, this individual is still eligible to receive full retirement benefits from his full-time job and to have his own IRA. (SEP Plans are just like Keogh plans, except they're aimed at small business owners, particularly those with no employees, who want a plan that's simple and easy to administer. Except for some administrative details, they have the same features and limitations as standard Keogh accounts.)

Keogh accounts can be opened at banks, mutual funds, and other financial institutions. Annual contributions must be made at the time the respective tax return is filed or by April 15th of the following calendar year (for example, you have until April 15, 2010, to contribute to your Keogh for 2009). Although a designated financial institution acts as custodian of all the funds held in a Keogh account, *actual investments held in the account are directed completely by the individual contributor*. These are self-directed retirement programs; the *individual* decides which investments to buy and sell.

Income earned from the investments must be reinvested in the account. This income also accrues tax free. All Keogh contributions and investment earnings must remain in the account until the individual turns 59½, unless he or she becomes seriously ill or disabled. Early withdrawals for any other reason are subject to 10% tax penalties. However, the individual is *not required* to start withdrawing the funds at age 59½; the funds can stay in the account (and continue earning tax-free income) until the individual is 70½. The individual *must* then begin withdrawing funds from the account—unless he or she continues to be gainfully employed past the age of 70½. Of course, once an individual starts withdrawing funds (upon or after turning 59½), all such withdrawals are treated as ordinary income and subject to normal income taxes.

### Individual Retirement Arrangements (IRAs)

Some people mistakenly believe that an IRA is a specialized type of investment. It's not. An **individual retirement arrangement (IRA)**, or individual retirement *account*, as it's more commonly known, is virtually the same as any other investment account you open with a bank, stockbroker, or mutual fund, except that it's clearly designated as an IRA. That is, the form you complete designates the account as an IRA and makes the institution its trustee. That's all there is to it. Any gainfully employed person (and spouse) can have an IRA account, although the type of accounts a person can have and the tax status of those accounts depend on several variables. All IRAs, however, have one thing in common: they're designed to encourage retirement savings for individuals. Today, an individual has three IRA types to choose from, as follows.

- **Traditional (deductible) IRAs,** which can be opened by anyone without a retirement plan at his or her place of employment, *regardless of income level*, or by couples filing jointly who—even if

they are covered by retirement plans at their places of employment—have adjusted gross incomes of less than $85,000 (or single tax payers with AGIs of less than $53,000). In 2009, individuals who qualify may make tax-deductible contributions of up to $5,000 a year to their accounts (an equal tax-deductible amount can be contributed by a nonworking spouse). All account earnings grow tax free until withdrawn, when ordinary tax rates apply (though a 10% penalty normally applies to withdrawals made before age 59½).

- **Nondeductible (after-tax) IRA,** which is open to anyone regardless of their income level or whether they're covered by a retirement plan at their workplace. In 2009, contributions of up to $5,000 a year can be made to this account, but they're *made with after-tax dollars* (that is, the contributions are not tax deductible). However, *the earnings do accrue tax free and are not subject to tax until they are withdrawn*, after the individual reaches age 59½ (funds withdrawn before age 59½ may be subject to the 10% penalty).

- **Roth IRAs** are the newest kid on the block (available only since 1998); they can be opened by couples filing jointly with adjusted gross incomes of up to $166,000 (singles up to $105,000), whether or not they have other retirement or pension plans. But the best part of the Roth IRA is its tax features—although the annual contributions of up to $6,000 a person in 2009 are made with nondeductible/after-tax dollars, all earnings in the account grow tax free. And *all withdrawals from the account are also tax free,* as long as the account has been open for at least 5 years and the individual is past the age of 59½. In other words, as long as these conditions are met, you won't have to pay taxes on any withdrawals you make from your Roth IRA!

Key features and provisions of all three of these IRAs are outlined in the Bonus Exhibit, "Qualifying for an IRA" (available at 4ltrpress.cengage.com).

Regardless of the type and notwithstanding the conditions just described, penalty-free withdrawals are generally allowed from an IRA as long as the funds are being used for first-time home purchases (up to $10,000), qualifying educational costs, certain major medical expenses, or other qualified emergencies. Also, with both the traditional/deductible and nondeductible IRAs, you must start making withdrawals from your account once you reach age 70½—although *this requirement does not apply to Roth IRAs*.

> **individual retirement arrangement (IRA)** A retirement plan, open to any working American, to which a person may contribute a specified amount each year.

the annuity is distributed, you can take a lump-sum payment or, as is more often the case, you can *annuitize* the distribution by systematically parceling out the money into regular payments over a defined or open-ended period. Because most people choose to annuitize their proceeds (which is how an annuity is intended to be used), let's look at the most common annuity disbursement options.

- **Life annuity with no refund (pure life).** The annuitant receives a specified amount of income for life, whether the disbursement period turns out to be 1 year or 50 years. The estate or family receives no refunds when the annuitant dies. This results in the largest monthly payments of any of the distribution methods.

- **Guaranteed-minimum annuity (life annuity, period certain).** In this type of contract, the benefits (future cash flows) aren't limited to the annuitant only and may extend to named beneficiaries. With a **life annuity, period certain,** the annuitant gets a guaranteed monthly income for life with the added provision that the insurance company will pay the monthly benefits for a minimum number of years (5 or 10, for example). If the annuitant dies soon after the distribution begins, then his or her beneficiaries receive the monthly benefits for the balance of the "period certain."

- **Annuity certain.** This type of annuity pays a set amount of monthly income for a specified number of years, thereby filling a need for monthly income that will expire after a certain length of time. An annuitant selecting a 10-year annuity certain receives payments for 10 years, regardless of whether he or she lives for 2 or 20 more years.

### Fixed versus Variable Annuity

When you put your money into an annuity, the premium is invested on your behalf by the insurance company, much as a mutual fund invests the money you put into it. From the time you pay the first (or only) annuity premium until it's paid back to you as a lump sum or as an annuitized monthly benefit, you'll earn a rate of return on your investment. How that rate of return is figured determines whether you own a fixed or variable annuity. In a **fixed-rate annuity**, the insurance company safeguards your principal and agrees to pay a guaranteed minimum rate of interest over the life of the contract. These are conservative, very low-risk annuity products that essentially promise to return *the original investment plus interest* when the money is paid out to the annuitant (or any designated beneficiaries). Unlike bond mutual funds, fixed annuities don't fluctuate in value when interest rates rise or fall; so your principal is always secure.

Imagine an investment vehicle that lets you move between stocks, bonds, and money funds and, at the same time, accumulate profits tax free. That, in a nutshell, is a variable annuity. With a **variable annuity**, the amount that's ultimately paid out to the annuitant varies with the investment results obtained by the insurance company—*nothing is guaranteed, not even the principal!* When you buy a variable annuity, *you decide* where your money will be invested, based on your investment objectives and tolerance for risk; you can usually choose from stocks, bonds, money market securities, real estate, alternative investments, or some combination thereof. As an annuity holder, you can stay put with a single investment for the long haul; or, as with most variable annuities, you can more aggressively play the market by switching from one fund to another. Obviously, when the market goes up, investors in variable annuities do well; but when the market falters, the returns on these policies will likewise be reduced.

 **Go to Smart Sites**

How large of an annuity do you need to buy to receive a $1,300 monthly payment? The annuities calculator at ImmediateAnnuities.com gives quick answers as well as names of companies offering the product in your state. ●

## Sources and Costs of Annuities

Annuities are administered by life insurance companies, so it's no surprise that they're also the leading sellers of these financial products. Annuities can also be purchased from stock brokers, mutual fund organizations, banks, and financial planners. When you buy an annuity, the cost will vary with the annuitant's age at issue, the annuitant's age when payments begin, the method used to distribute benefits, the number of lives covered, and the annuitant's gender.

As with mutual funds, there are some annual fees that you should be aware of. In particular, be prepared to pay insurance fees of 1% or more—in addition to the annual management fees of perhaps 1% to 2% paid on variable annuities. That's a total of 2% to 3% or more taken right off the top, year after year. There is also a *contract charge* (or maintenance fee) that's deducted annually to cover various contract-related expenses; these fees usually run from about $30 to $60 per year. Obviously, these fees can drag down returns and reduce the advantage of tax-deferred income. Finally, most annuities charge hefty *penalties for early withdrawal*. This means that, in order to get out of a poorly performing annuity, you'll have to forfeit a chunk of your money.

## Investment and Income Properties of Annuities

A major attribute of most types of annuities is that they're a source of income that can't be outlived. Although individuals might be able to create a similar arrangement by simply living off the interest or dividends from their investments, they'd find it difficult to systematically liquidate their principal so that the last payment would coincide closely (or exactly) with their death. Another advantage is that the income earned in an annuity is allowed to accumulate tax free, so it's a form of *tax-sheltered investment*. Actually, the income from an annuity is *tax deferred*, meaning that taxes on

the earnings will have to be paid when the annuity is liquidated.

Shelter from taxes is an attractive investment attribute, but there's a hitch. You may be faced with a big tax penalty if you close out or withdraw money from an annuity before it's time. Specifically, the IRS treats annuity withdrawals like withdrawals from an individual retirement account: that is, except in cases of serious illness, *anyone who takes money out before reaching age 59½ will incur a 10% tax penalty*. All of which only reinforces the notion that *an annuity should always be considered a long-term investment*. Assume that it's a part of your retirement program (that's the way the IRS looks at it) and that you're getting in for the long haul.

From an investment perspective, the returns generated from an annuity can be, in some cases, a bit disappointing. For instance, as we discussed earlier, the returns on *variable annuities* are tied to returns in the money and capital markets; even so, they're still no better than what you can get from other investment vehicles—indeed, they're often lower, due in part to higher annuity fees. Keep in mind that these differential returns aren't due to tax features because in both cases, returns are measured on a before-tax basis. But *returns from annuities are tax sheltered*, so that makes those lower returns a lot more attractive.

If you're considering a variable annuity, go over it much like you would a traditional mutual fund: look for superior past performance, proven management talents, and the availability of attractive investment alternatives that you can switch in and out of. And *pay particular attention to an annuity's total expense rate*. These products have a reputation of being heavily loaded with fees and charges, but it's possible to find annuities with both above-average performance and relatively low fee structures. That's the combination you're looking for.

One final point: If you're seriously considering buying an annuity, be sure to read the contract carefully and see what the guaranteed rates are, how long the initial rate applies, and if there's a bailout provision. (A *bailout provision* allows you to withdraw your money free of any surrender fees, if the rate of return on your annuity falls below a specified minimum level. Of course, even if you exercise a bailout provision, you may still have to face a tax penalty for early withdrawal—unless you transfer the funds to another annuity through what's known as a *1035 exchange*.) Just as important, because *the annuity is only as good as the insurance company that stands behind it*, check to see how the company is rated by Best's, Standard & Poor's, or Moody's. It's important to make sure that the insurance company itself is financially sound before buying one of its annuity products. See Chapter 8 for more discussion on these insurance ratings and how they work.

**LG2**

1. Shawn Burton, a 25-year-old personal loan officer at Second State Bank, understands the importance of starting early when it comes to saving for retirement. She has committed $3,000 per year for her retirement fund and assumes she'll retire at age 65.
   a. How much will she have when she turns 65 if she invests in equities and earns 8% on average?
   b. Shawn is urging her friend, Richard Sheperd, to start his plan right away, too, because he's 35. What would his nest egg amount to if he invested in the same manner as Shawn and he, too, retires at age 65? Comment on your findings.

**LG4**

2. Mike Gibson has just graduated from college and is considering job offers from two companies. Although the salary and insurance benefits are similar, the retirement programs are not. One firm offers a 401(k) plan that matches employee contributions with 25 cents for every dollar contributed by the employee, up to a $10,000 limit. The other has a contributory plan that allows employees to contribute up to 10% of their annual salary through payroll deduction and matches it dollar for dollar; this plan vests fully after 5 years. Because Mike is unfamiliar with these plans, he turns to you for help. So, explain the features of each plan so that he can make an informed decision.

**LG4, 5**

3. Describe the three basic types of IRAs, including their respective tax features and what it takes to qualify for each. Which is most appealing to you personally? Explain.

**LG6**

4. Explain how buying a variable annuity is much like investing in a mutual fund. Do you, as a buyer, have any control over the amount of investment risk to which you're exposed in a variable annuity contract? Explain.

# 15

# PRESERVING YOUR ESTATE

## LEARNING GOALS

**LG1** Describe the role of estate planning in personal financial planning, and identify the seven steps involved in the process. (p. 334)

**LG2** Recognize the importance of preparing a will and other documents to protect you and your estate. (p. 337)

**LG3** Explain how trusts are used in estate planning. (p. 345)

**LG4** Determine whether a gift will be taxable and use planned gifts to reduce estate taxes. (p. 348)

**LG5** Calculate federal taxes due on an estate. (p. 351)

**LG6** Use effective estate planning techniques to minimize estate taxes. (p. 352)

333

## LG1 Principles of Estate Planning

Like it or not, no one lives forever. Although this thought may depress you, safeguarding the future of the people you care about is one of the most important aspects of financial planning. Unless you develop plans and take steps during your lifetime to accumulate, preserve, and distribute your wealth on your death, chances are that your heirs and beneficiaries will receive only part of your estate. The rest will go (often unnecessarily) to taxes and various administrative costs. This process, called *estate planning*, requires knowledge of wills, trusts, and taxes.

## Who Needs Estate Planning?

Estate planning should be part of everyone's financial plan, whether they're married or single and have five children or none. For example, married couples who own many assets jointly and have designated beneficiaries for them need to name an executor to administer the estate, specify a guardian for children, clarify how estate taxes will be paid, and direct the distribution of property that doesn't go directly to a joint owner. Unmarried partners and single persons also need estate planning , particularly if they own a home or other assets that they want to leave to a partner, a specific individual, or to a charity. Estate planning involves both *people planning* and *asset planning*.

### People Planning

*People planning* means anticipating the psychological and financial needs of those you love, and

> { *Unless you develop plans and take steps during your lifetime to accumulate, preserve, and distribute your wealth on your death, chances are that your heirs and beneficiaries will receive only part of your estate.* }

**Estate planning** is the process of developing a plan to administer and distribute your assets after death in a manner consistent with your wishes and the needs of your survivors, while minimizing taxes. It includes plans to manage your affairs if you become disabled and a statement of your personal wishes for medical care should you become unable to clearly state them. A key focus of estate planning is to eliminate or minimize taxes, and thereby maximize the amount of your estate that ultimately passes to your heirs and beneficiaries. Estate planning is closely related to insurance and retirement planning because both focus on retaining and preserving your accumulated wealth, which can be passed on to your heirs and designated beneficiaries according to your wishes.

If an individual fails to plan, then state and federal laws will control the disposition of their assets at death and determine who bears the burden of expenses and taxes, which may be higher because of the lack of planning. People who wish to plan their estates must systematically uncover problems in several important areas and solve them. Exhibit 15.1 lists the major types of problems and their associated causes or indicators.

providing adequate resources to ensure continuation of their way of life. It involves keeping Mother's cameo brooch in the family or preserving the business that Granddad started 75 years ago. People planning is especially important for individuals with children who are minors; children who are exceptionally artistic or intellectually gifted; children or other dependents who are emotionally, mentally, or physically handicapped; and spouses who can't or don't want to handle money, securities, or a business.

 ### Go to Smart Sites

What should you do first when someone close to you dies? Download the University of Pittsburgh Medical Center's comprehensive guide, "When a Loved One Dies," to help you through these difficult times. Whenever you see *"Go to Smart Sites"* in this chapter, visit 4ltrpress.cengage.com for help finding answers online. ●

How many of us have handled hundreds of thousands of dollars? Clearly, minor children can't legally handle large sums of money or deal directly

Careful estate planning can prevent many problems that arise when settling an estate. The first step toward preventing problems is an awareness and understanding of their major causes or indicators.

| Problem | Major Cause or Indicator |
| --- | --- |
| Excessive transfer costs | Taxes and estate administrative expenses higher than necessary. |
| Lack of liquidity | Insufficient cash; not enough assets that are quickly and inexpensively convertible to cash within a short period of time to meet tax demands and other costs. |
| Improper disposition of assets | Beneficiaries receive the wrong asset, or the proper asset in the wrong manner or at the wrong time. |
| Inadequate income at retirement | Capital insufficient or not readily convertible to income-producing status. |
| Inadequate income, if disabled | High medical costs; capital insufficient or not readily convertible to income-producing status; difficulty in reducing living standards. |
| Inadequate income for family at estate owner's death | Any of the above causes. |
| Insufficient capital | Excessive taxes, inflation, improper investment planning. |
| Special problems | A family member with a serious illness or physical or emotional problem; children of a prior marriage; beneficiaries who have extraordinary medical or financial needs; beneficiaries who can't agree on how to handle various estate matters, business problems, or opportunities. |

with real estate or securities. Think of the burden we place on others when we expect those who can't—or don't want to—handle such large sums of money or securities to do so. Engaging in people planning demonstrates a high degree of caring. People planning also involves talking about estate planning with your loved ones, as the nearby *Money in Action* box explains.

## Asset Planning

From the standpoint of wealth alone, estate planning is essential for anyone—single, widowed, married, or divorced—with an estate exceeding $1,000,000 in 2011 under current law. Most estate planning professionals expect a comprehensive overhaul of estate tax laws in the next few years. When an estate involves a closely-held business, estate planning is essential to stabilize and maximize value, both during the owner's lifetime and at the owner's death or disability. Likewise, estate planning is essential to avoid the special problems that occur when an estate owner holds title to property in more than one state. The estate planning process is more complicated for blended families or those with special requests. Careful planning is needed to make sure that your assets will go to the desired beneficiaries.

## Why Does an Estate Break Up?

Quite often, when people die their estates die with them—not because they've done anything wrong,

but because they haven't done anything. There are numerous forces that, if unchecked, tend to shrink an estate, reduce the usefulness of its assets, and frustrate the objectives of the person who built it. These include death-related costs, inflation, lack of liquidity, improper use of vehicles of transfer, and disabilities.

1. **Death-related costs.** When someone dies, their estate incurs certain types of death-related costs. For example, medical bills for a final illness and funeral expenses are good examples of *first-level death-related costs. Second-level death-related costs* consist of fees for attorneys, appraisers, and accountants, along with probate expenses— so-called administrative costs, federal estate taxes, and state death taxes. Most people also die with some current bills unpaid, outstanding long-term obligations (such as mortgages, business loans, and installment contracts), and unpaid income taxes and property taxes.

2. **Inflation.** Failure to continuously reappraise and rearrange an estate plan to counter the effects of inflation can impair the ability of assets—personal property and investments—to provide steady and adequate levels of financial security.

3. **Lack of liquidity.** Insufficient cash to cover death costs and other estate obligations has always been a major factor in estate impairment. Sale of the choicest parcel of farmland or a business that's

# MONEY IN ACTION

HAVING "THE TALK" WITH PARENTS—ABOUT ESTATE PLANNING, THAT IS

Did your grandmother ever threaten that if you didn't behave, you'd be "out of her will?" While she was (probably) just joking, it's unlikely you asked her what was in her will. Because few adult children discuss estate planning issues with their family, they typically don't know what to do with their parents' wealth if they become incapacitated. So how do you have "the talk" with your parents?

The first issue is whether a talk is really necessary. If your parents have saved and invested wisely, your role in their estate planning is minimal. If they have not and you're concerned that they haven't planned for the distribution of their assets, it's time to consider "the talk."

Here are some constructive ways to approach your parents about estate planning. Begin by expressing your desire to understand what your parents want—not with what you want. So start with questions like: "Mom, I want to carry out your wishes, but I need to understand them better. Do you want to use your assets to provide income that supports you and Dad? Have you arranged to avoid high taxes and costly probate?" Acknowledge that you understand these are their assets and that discussion is about their needs and preferences.

A subtle way to get the talk started is to share your own experience writing a will or doing estate planning. This can create an opportunity to discuss how your parents have (or have not) handled these issues. You could also share a true story of how someone who didn't have a will or do adequate estate planning caused the children to lose much of their parents' estate to taxes and probate. If your parents remain uncomfortable talking with you about estate planning, recommend that they see a financial planner.

If the talk gets moving, the following questions would be helpful to pursue.

- Where do you keep your important documents? You may well have to locate birth and marriage certificates, insurance policies, bank and investment accounts, online account passwords, and will and trust documents.
- Do you expect to have enough money to live on in retirement? This should include some discussion of their asset allocation, risk exposure, planning horizon, and how their portfolio accommodates inflation.
- How do you plan to handle an illness? Does this include durable powers of attorney to handle financial decisions and paying the bills? Do you have living wills that describe your wishes concerning hospital care and life-prolonging procedures? Do you prefer to remain at home as long as possible or is an assisted living facility an option? Is your health insurance coverage adequate?
- Have you written wills or established any trusts? If so, where are they kept and how often are they reviewed? Wills should be reviewed at least every 3 years or when there are major life changes.

*Source:* Adapted from "Talking to Your Parents about Estate Planning," *The Complete Idiot's Guide to Caring for Aging Parents,* by Linda Colvin Rhodes. Penguin Group (USA) Inc. 2001. http://life.familyeducation.com/estate-planning/aging-parents/50442.html, accessed September 2009.

---

**probate estate** The real and personal property owned by a person that can be transferred at death.

**gross estate** All property that might be subject to federal estate taxes on a person's death.

been in the family for generations, for instance, often has undesirable financial and psychological effects on the heirs.

4. **Improper use of vehicles of transfer.** Improper use of vehicles of transfer may pass property to unintended beneficiaries or to the proper beneficiaries in an improper manner or at an incorrect time. For example, spendthrift spouses or minors may be left large sums of money outright in the form of life insurance, through joint ownership of a savings account, or as the beneficiaries of an employee fringe benefit plan.

5. **Disabilities.** A prolonged and expensive disability of a family wage earner that results in loss of income is often called a *living death*. This financial situation is further complicated by inadequate management of currently owned assets. This can not only threaten a family's financial security, but can also quickly diminish the value of the estate.

## What Is Your Estate?

Your **probate estate** consists of the real and personal property you own in your own name that can be transferred at death according to the terms of a will or, if you have no valid will, under *intestate* laws. The probate estate is distinct from the **gross estate**, which includes all the property—both probate and nonprobate—that might be subject to federal estate taxes at your death. Life insurance, jointly held property with rights of survivorship, and property passing under certain employee benefit plans are common examples of nonprobate assets that might be subject to federal (and state) estate taxes.

You also can provide for property that's not probate property and won't be part of your estate for federal estate tax purposes yet will pass to your family and form part of their financial security program.

There are two types of such assets. One is *properly arranged* life insurance. For example, you could give assets to your daughter to allow her to purchase, pay the premiums for, and be the beneficiary of a policy on your life. At your death, the proceeds wouldn't be included as part of your estate. The other type of financial asset that falls into this category is *Social Security*. Social Security payments to a surviving spouse and minor children generally are not probate assets and are not subject to any federal (or state) estate taxes. This category of assets provides unique and substantial estate Planning opportunities.

## The Estate Planning Process

The estate planning process consists of seven important steps, as summarized in Exhibit 15.2. First, you must assess your family situation, evaluating its strengths and weaknesses, and set estate planning goals. Next, gather comprehensive and accurate data on all aspects of the family. The Bonus Exhibit, "Data Needed for Estate Planning" (available at 4ltrpress.cengage.com), summarizes the data that professionals require to prepare detailed estate plans. Then, you should take inventory and determine the value of your estate. Next, you must designate beneficiaries of your estate's assets, estimate estate transfer costs, and formulate and implement your plan. The final step is ongoing: review your estate plan periodically—at least every 3 to 5 years, and revise it as circumstances dictate.

The objective of estate plans, of course, is to maximize the usefulness of people's assets during their lives and to achieve their personal objectives after their deaths. As the needs, desires, and circumstances of the parties involved change, you must modify your estate plan. Key events that should trigger an estate plan review include the death or disability of a spouse or other family member, moving to another state, changing jobs, getting married or divorced, having children, acquiring new assets, and substantial changes in income, health, or living standards. Because of the general complexity of the laws relating to estate transfer, professional assistance from an attorney, accountant, and/or financial planner is often necessary to develop an effective estate plan.

**will** A written and legally enforceable document expressing how a person's property should be distributed on his or her death.

## LG2 Thy Will Be Done...

A **will** is a written, legally enforceable expression or declaration of a person's wishes concerning the disposition of his or her property on death. Unfortunately, about 70% of all Americans do not have valid wills. The importance of a valid will is apparent when you consider what happens when someone dies without one.

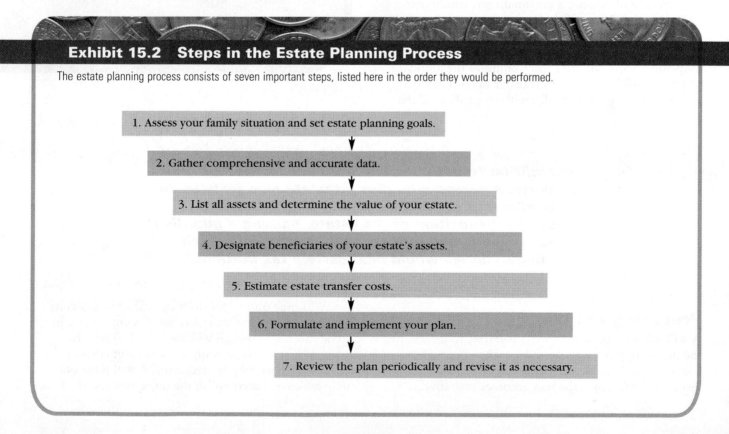

**Exhibit 15.2    Steps in the Estate Planning Process**

The estate planning process consists of seven important steps, listed here in the order they would be performed.

1. Assess your family situation and set estate planning goals.
2. Gather comprehensive and accurate data.
3. List all assets and determine the value of your estate.
4. Designate beneficiaries of your estate's assets.
5. Estimate estate transfer costs.
6. Formulate and implement your plan.
7. Review the plan periodically and revise it as necessary.

**intestacy** The situation that exists when a person dies without a valid will.

**testator** The person who makes a will that provides for the disposition of property at his or her death.

## Absence of a Valid Will: Intestacy

Suppose that Trevor Powers died without a valid will, a situation called **intestacy**. State intestacy laws "draw the will the decedent failed to make" in order to determine the disposition of the probate property of those who have died intestate. Generally, under these statutes, the decedent's spouse is favored, followed by the children and then other offspring. If the spouse and children or other offspring (e.g., grandchildren or great-grandchildren) survive, then they will divide the estate, and other relatives will receive nothing. If no spouse, children, or other offspring survive, then the deceased's parents, brothers, and sisters will receive a share of the estate.

The Bonus Exhibit, "Distribution of a Typical Intestate Estate" (available at 4ltrpress.cengage.com) gives an example of how a typical intestate estate is distributed. After paying debts and taxes and deducting state-defined family exemptions, that individual's separately owned property would be distributed as shown. Where property goes to the state due to the absence of a will, the property is said to *escheat to the state.*

In addition to not controlling the disposition of their property, a person who dies intestate also forfeits the privilege of naming a personal representative to guide the disposition of the estate, naming a guardian for persons and property, and specifying which beneficiaries would bear certain tax burdens. Estate planning and a valid will may also minimize the amount of estate shrinkage through transfer taxes. Clearly, it's important to have a valid will—regardless of the estate size.

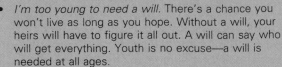

### FINANCIAL ROAD SIGN

**WRITE A WILL—NO EXCUSES**
Two out of three people don't have a will! Consider the following common excuses, and why they fall apart.

- *I'm too young to need a will.* There's a chance you won't live as long as you hope. Without a will, your heirs will have to figure it all out. A will can say who will get everything. Youth is no excuse—a will is needed at all ages.
- *My family knows how to distribute my assets.* That may be true, but without a will, it's the state that decides who gets what. For example, even if you want your spouse to inherit your assets, your children will still be given a piece of your estate.
- *I don't have enough assets to need a will.* It's not just how much you have, it's who gets whatever you own. It's best to provide detailed instructions about who gets what and to update them often.
- *My mother would take care of the kids.* Perhaps she would, but what if your mother-in-law decides *she* wants the kids? If there is no will, then a judge will decide who gets your children. So choose guardians carefully and put your choices in a will.
- *Writing a will is too expensive.* Not true. It doesn't cost much to write a will. Many state bar associations make available forms for a simple will. There's even software to do it.
- *I have no kids and I'm single, so there is no one to protect.* Single or married, if you have no will, the state will leave everything to your relatives. And if you have no relatives, the state gets it all. A will can assure that your friends and preferred charities get something.

*Source*: Adapted from Ginita Wall, "There's No Excuse Not to Write a Will," http://home.ivillage.com/homeoffice/insurance/0,,nwmg,00.html, accessed September 2009.

> In addition to not controlling the disposition of their property, a person who dies intestate also forfeits the privilege of naming a personal representative to guide the disposition of the estate, naming a guardian for persons and property, and specifying which beneficiaries would bear certain tax burdens.

## Preparing the Will

A will allows a person, called a **testator**, to direct the disposition of property at his or her death. The testator can change or revoke a will at any time; on the death of the testator, the will becomes operative.

Will preparation (or drafting) varies in difficulty and cost, depending on individual circumstances. In some cases, a two-page will costing $150 may be adequate; in others, a complex document costing $1,500 or more may be necessary. A will must not only effectively accomplish the objectives specified for distributing assets but also take into consideration income, gift, and estate tax laws. Will preparation also requires a knowledge of corporate, trust, real estate, and securities laws.

A properly prepared will should meet these three important requirements:

- Provide a plan for distributing the testator's assets according to his or her wishes, the beneficiaries' needs, and federal and state dispositive and tax laws

- Consider the changes in family circumstances that might occur after its execution

- Be concise and complete in describing the testator's desires

*Will drafting, no matter how modest the estate size, should not be attempted by a layperson.* The complexity and interrelationships of tax, property, domestic relations, and other laws make the home-made will a potentially dangerous document. Few things may turn out more disastrous in the long run than the do-it-yourself will.

## Common Features of the Will

There's no absolute format that must be followed when preparing a will, but most wills contain similar distinct sections. Exhibit 15.3, which presents the will of Raymond James Ferrell, includes generalized examples of each of these clauses. Refer to the exhibit as you read these descriptions of the clauses.

- **Introductory clause.** An introductory clause, or preamble, normally states the testator's name and residence; this determines the county that will have legal jurisdiction and be considered the testator's domicile for tax purposes. The revocation statement nullifies old and forgotten wills and *codicils*—legally binding modifications of an existing will.

- **Direction of payments.** This clause directs the estate to make certain payments of expenses. As a general rule, however, the rights of creditors are protected by law, and therefore this clause might be left out of a professionally drafted will.

- **Disposition of property.** Raymond's will has three examples of clauses dealing with disposition of property:

  1. *Disposition of personal effects:* A testator may also make a separate detailed and specific list of personal property and carefully identify each item, and to whom it is given, as an informal guide to help the executor divide the property. (This list generally should not appear in the will itself because it's likely to be changed frequently.)

  2. *Giving money to a specifically named party:* Be sure to use the correct legal title of a charity.

  3. *Distribution of residual assets after specific gifts have been made:* Bequests to close relatives (as defined in the statute) who die before the testator will go to the relative's heirs unless the will includes other directions. Bequests to nonrelatives who predecease the testator will go to the other residual beneficiaries.

- **Appointment clause.** Appointment clauses name the *executors* (the decedent's personal representatives who administer the estate), guardians for minor children, and trustees and their successors.

- **Tax clause.** In the absence of a specified provision in the will, the *apportionment statutes* of the testator's state will allocate the burden of taxes among the beneficiaries. The result may be an inappropriate and unintended reduction of certain beneficiaries' shares or adverse estate tax effects. Because the spouse's share and the portion going to a charity are deducted from the gross estate before arriving at the taxable estate, neither is charged with taxes.

- **Simultaneous death clause.** The assumption that the spouse survives in the event of simultaneous death is used mainly to permit the marital deduction, which offers a tax advantage. Other types of clauses are similarly designed to avoid double probate of the same assets—duplication of administrative and probate costs. Such clauses require that the survivor live for a certain period, such as 30 or 60 days, to be a beneficiary under the will.

- **Execution and attestation clause.** Every will should be in writing and signed by the testator at its end as a precaution against fraud. Many attorneys suggest that the testator also initial each page after the last line or sign in a corner of each page.

- **Witness clause.** The final clause helps to affirm that the will in question is really that of the deceased. All states require two witnesses to the testator's signing of the will. Most states require witnesses to sign in the presence of one another after they witness the signing by the testator. Their addresses should be noted on the will. If the testator is unable to sign his or her name for any reason, most states allow the testator to make a mark and to have another person (properly witnessed) sign for him or her.

**Exhibit 15.3    A Representative Will for Raymond James Ferrell**

Raymond James Ferrell's will illustrates the eight distinct sections of most wills.

### The Last Will and Testament of Raymond James Ferrell

#### Section 1 — Introductory Clause

I, Raymond James Ferrell, of the city of Chicago, state of Illinois, do hereby make my last will and revoke all wills and codicils made prior to this will.

#### Section 2 — Direction of Payments

*Article 1: Payment of Debts and Expenses*

I direct payment out of my estate of all just debts and the expenses of my last illness and funeral.

#### Section 3 — Disposition of Property

*Article 2: Disposition of Property*

I give and bequeath to my wife, Gretchen Smyth Ferrell, all my jewelry, automobiles, books, and photography equipment, as well as all other articles of personal and household use.

I give to the Chicago Historical Society the sum of $100,000.

All the rest, residue, and remainder of my estate, real and personal, wherever located, I give in equal one-half shares to my children, Richard James and Lara Sue, their heirs and assigns forever.

#### Section 4 — Appointment Clause

*Article 3: Nomination of Executor and Guardian*

I hereby nominate as the Executor of this Will my beloved wife, Gretchen Smyth Ferrell, but if she is unable or unwilling to serve then I nominate my brother, William Dean Ferrell. In the event both persons named predecease me, or shall cease or fail to act, then I nominate as Executor in the place of said persons, the Southern Trust Bank of Atlanta, Georgia.

If my wife does not survive me, I appoint my brother, Robert Lambert Ferrell, Guardian of the person and property of my son, Richard James, during his minority.

#### Section 5 — Tax Clause

*Article 4: Payment of Taxes*

I direct that there shall be paid out of my residuary estate (from that portion which does not qualify for the marital deduction) all estate, inheritance, and similar taxes imposed by a government in respect to property includable in my estate for tax purposes, whether the property passes under this will or otherwise.

#### Section 6 — Simultaneous Death Clause

*Article 5: Simultaneous Death*

If my wife and I shall die under such circumstances that there is not sufficient evidence to determine the order of our deaths, then it shall be presumed that she survived me. My estate shall be administered and distributed in all respects in accordance with such assumption.

#### Section 7 — Execution and Attestation Clause

In witness thereof, I have affixed my signature to this, my last will and testament, which consists of five (5) pages, each of which I have initialed, this 15th day of September, 2010.

*Raymond James Ferrell*

#### Section 8 — Witness Clause

Signed, sealed, and published by Raymond James Ferrell, the testator, as his last will, in the presence of us, who, at his request, and in the presence of each other, all being present at the same time, have written our names as witnesses.

(Note: Normally the witness signatures and addresses would follow this clause.)

## Requirements of a Valid Will

To be valid, a will must be the product of a person with a sound mind, there must have been no *undue influence* (influence that would remove the testator's freedom of choice), the will itself must have been properly executed, and its execution must be free from fraud.

1.  **Mental capacity.** You must be of "sound mind" to make a valid will. This means that you:

a. Know what a will is and are aware that you are making and signing one.

b. Understand your relationship with persons for whom you would normally provide, such as a spouse or children, and who would generally be expected to receive your estate (even though you might not be required to leave anything to them).

c. Understand what you own.

d. Are able to decide how to distribute your property.

Generally, mental capacity is presumed. Setting aside a will requires clear and convincing proof of mental incapacity, and the burden of proof is on the person contesting the will.

2. **Freedom of choice.** When you prepare and execute your will, you must not be under the undue influence of another person. Threats, misrepresentations, inordinate flattery, or some physical or mental coercion employed to destroy the testator's freedom of choice are all types of undue influence.

3. **Proper execution.** To be considered properly executed, a will must meet the requirements of the state's wills act or its equivalent. It must also be demonstrable that it is in fact the will of the testator. Most states have statutes that spell out who may make a will (generally any person of sound mind, age 18 or older but 14 in Georgia and 16 in Louisiana), the form and execution the will must have (most states require a will to be in writing and to be signed by the testator at the logical end), and requirements for witnesses. Generally, a beneficiary should not serve as a witness.

## Changing or Revoking the Will: Codicils

Because a will is inoperative until the testator's death, the testator (only) can change it at any time, as long as he or she has the mental capacity. In fact, periodic revisions should occur, especially on these events:

- His or her (or the beneficiaries') health or financial circumstances change significantly
- Births, deaths, marriages, or divorces alter the operative circumstances
- The testator moves to a state other than where the will was executed
- An executor, trustee, or guardian can no longer serve
- Substantial changes occur in the tax law

### Changing the Will

A **codicil** is a simple, often single-page document that provides a convenient legal means of making minor changes in a will. It reaffirms all the existing provisions in the will except the one to be changed, and should be executed and witnessed in the same formal manner as a will.

When a will requires substantial changes, a new will is usually preferable to a codicil. In addition, if a gift in the original will is removed, it may be best to make a new will and destroy the old, to avoid

offending the omitted beneficiary. Sometimes, however, the prior will should not be destroyed even after the new will has been made and signed. If the new will fails for some reason (because of the testator's mental incapacity, for example), then the prior will may qualify. Also, a prior will could help to prove a "continuity of testamentary purpose"—in other words, that the latest will (which may have provided a substantial gift to charity) continued an earlier intent and wasn't an afterthought or the result of an unduly influenced mind.

**codicil** A document that legally modifies a will without revoking it.

### Revoking the Will

A will may be revoked either by the testator or automatically by the law. A testator can revoke a will in one of four ways:

1. Making a later will that expressly revokes prior wills
2. Making a codicil that expressly revokes all wills earlier than the one being modified
3. Making a later will that is inconsistent with a former will
4. Physically mutilating, burning, tearing, or defacing the will with the intention of revoking it

## FINANCIAL ROAD SIGN

### WRITING YOUR WILL

Here are some tips to help you write your will in a way that will prevent problems later:

- *Take inventory.* Compile lists of your assets, outstanding debts, and family members and other beneficiaries.
- *Decide who gets what.* Take your time considering how to distribute your assets equitably.
- *Consider taxes.* A carefully designed estate plan and will can reduce the taxes your heirs will owe.
- *Talk about your will and your intentions.* Let family members know what you're leaving them, and why, to avoid hard feelings afterward.
- *Create a trust.* Evaluate whether trusts make sense for estate administration and to reduce estate taxes.
- *Be reasonable.* You don't have to divide everything equally among your children, but strive for fairness in asset distribution. Again, explain the rationale behind your decisions.
- *Spread the wealth.* Try to bequeath something to all those with a valid interest in your estate. Otherwise, they might try to contest the will.
- *Review and update regularly.* Life circumstances change, and your will may no longer be appropriate.
- *Leave more than money.* An ethical will that discusses the values you hope to have left your survivors can be a wonderful gift in addition to one that deals with possessions.

**letter of last instructions** An informal memorandum that is separate from a will and contains suggestions or recommendations for carrying out a decedent's wishes.

**probate process** The court-supervised disposition of a decedent's estate.

**executor** The personal representative of an estate designated in the decedent's will.

**administrator** The personal representative of the estate appointed by the court if the decedent died intestate.

The law automatically modifies a will under certain circumstances, which vary from state to state but generally center on divorce, marriage, birth or adoption, and murder. In many states, if a testator becomes divorced after making a will, all provisions in the will relating to the spouse become ineffective. If a testator marries after making a will, the spouse receives that portion of the estate that would have been received had the testator died without a valid will. If a testator did not provide for a child born or adopted after the will was made (unless it appears that such lack of provision was intentional), the child receives that share of the estate not passing to the testator's spouse that would have been given to him or her had the deceased not had a will. Finally, almost all states have some type of slayer's statute forbidding a person who commits murder from acquiring property as the result of the deed.

© COMSTOCK/GETTY IMAGES FROM CD WALL ST. WORLD KCD 159 COM

## Safeguarding the Will

In most cases, you should keep your original will in a safe-deposit box, with copies in a safe and accessible place at home and with the attorney who drafted it. Worksheet 15.1 contains an executor's checklist of documents and information that should be kept in a safe-deposit box. If each spouse has a separate safe-deposit box, then the couple may want to keep their wills in each other's boxes. Some states provide for *lodging* of the will, a mechanism for filing and safe-keeping it in the office of the probate court (also called *orphan's* or *surrogate's court*), which satisfies the need to safeguard the will.

## Letter of Last Instructions

A **letter of last instructions** is the best way to communicate to others to carry out thoughts and instructions that aren't appropriate to include in your will. It's typically an informal memorandum separate from the will. (The letter of last instructions should contain no bequests because it has no legal standing.) It's best to make several copies of the letter, keeping one at home and the others with the estate's executor or attorney, who can deliver it to beneficiaries at the appropriate time.

A letter of last instructions might provide directions regarding such items as:

1. Location of the will and other documents
2. Funeral and burial instructions (often a will is not opened until after the funeral)
3. Suggestions or recommendations as to the continuation, sale, or liquidation of a business.
4. Personal matters that the testator might prefer not be made public in the will, such as statements (e.g., comments about a spendthrift spouse or a reckless son) that might sound unkind or inconsiderate but would be valuable to the executor.
5. Recommended legal and accounting services
6. An explanation of the actions taken in the will, which may help avoid litigation (for instance, "I left only $5,000 to my son, Stephen, because..." or "I made no provisions for my oldest daughter, Vanessa, because...")
7. Suggestions on how to divide the personal property

## Administration of an Estate

When people die, they usually own property and owe debts, and may be owed money by other persons. The **probate process**, similar to that used in liquidating a business, is often required to settle an estate. A local court generally supervises the probate process through the *decedent's personal representative*—either an **executor** named in the decedent's will or, if the decedent died without a valid will, through a court-appointed **administrator**.

## Worksheet 15.1 A Checklist of Items to Keep in a Safe-Deposit Box

This checklist itemizes the various documents and information that the executor may need to effectively carry out the terms of the will. These items should be kept in a safe-deposit box.

**CHECKLIST FOR EXECUTORS**

**Name (Testator)** ______________________ **Date** ______________

| | |
|---|---|
| ____ 1. Marriage certificates (including prior marriages) | ____ 6. Bonds, stocks, and securities |
| ____ 2. Your will and trust agreements | ____ 7. Real estate deeds |
| ____ 3. Life insurance policies or certificates | ____ 8. Business agreements |
| ____ 4. Your Social Security number | ____ 9. Automobile titles and insurance policies |
| ____ 5. Military discharge papers | ____ 10. Property insurance policies |
| | ____ 11. Tax information |
| | ____ 12. Letter of last instructions |

**List** all checking and savings account numbers, bank addresses, and locations of safe-deposit boxes:

______________ ______________ ______________

______________ ______________ ______________

**List** names, addresses, and phone numbers of property and life insurance agents:

______________ ______________ ______________

______________ ______________ ______________

**List** names, addresses, and phone numbers of attorney and accountant:

______________ ______________ ______________

______________ ______________ ______________

**List** names, addresses, and phone numbers of (current or last) employer. State retirement date, if applicable. Include employee benefits booklets:

______________ ______________ ______________

______________ ______________ ______________

**List** all debts owed to *and* by you, including names and account numbers:

______________ ______________ ______________

______________ ______________ ______________

**List** the names, addresses, telephone numbers, and birth dates of your children and other beneficiaries (including charities):

______________ ______________ ______________

______________ ______________ ______________

*Source*: Based on Stephan R. Leimberg, Stephen N. Kandell, Ralph Gano Miller, Morey S. Rosenbloom, and Timothy C. Polacek, *The Tools & Techniques of Estate Planning*, 14th ed. (Upper Saddle River, NJ: Prentice Hall, 2006); http://law.enotes.com/everyday-law-encyclopedia/wills; Metropolitan Life Insurance Company, The Executor's Checklist, http://www.metlife.com.

The executor or administrator becomes the decedent's legal representative, taking care of such matters as collecting bank accounts and money owed the decedent, paying off debts, creating clear title to make real estate marketable, and distributing what's left to those entitled to it by will or the state's intestate laws. Clearly, an executor should not only be familiar with the testator's affairs but also be able to effectively handle the responsibilities of being an executor.

## Other Important Estate Planning Documents

Several other documents that are useful in protecting your family and you include a durable power of attorney

**durable power of attorney for financial matters** Legal document that authorizes another person to take over someone's financial affairs and act on his or her behalf.

**living will** A document that precisely states the treatments a person wants if he or she becomes terminally ill.

**durable power of attorney for health care** A written power of attorney authorizing an individual to make health care decisions on behalf of the principal when the principal is unable to make such decisions. Also called *advanced directive for health care.*

**ethical will** A personal statement left for family, friends, and community that shares your values, blessings, life's lessons, and hopes and dreams for the future. Also called *legacy statement.*

**right of survivorship** The right of surviving joint owners of property to receive title to the deceased joint owner's interest in the property.

**joint tenancy** A type of ownership by two or more parties, with the survivor(s) continuing to hold all such property on the death of one or more of the owners.

**tenancy by the entirety** A form of ownership by husband and wife, recognized in certain states, in which property automatically passes to the surviving spouse.

for financial matters, a living will, a durable power of attorney for health care, and an ethical will.

### Power of Attorney

A **durable power of attorney for financial matters** allows you to name the person, perhaps a spouse or other relative, you wish to take over your financial affairs in the event of a serious illness. Because this simple document transfers enormous power to your designated appointee, it is important to name a qualified, trustworthy person. To make it durable—that is, effective even when you are incapacitated—the document must clearly state that your agent's authority to act on your behalf will continue during your incapacity. It is also a good idea to clear your power of attorney with all brokerage firms and mutual funds where you have accounts.

### Living Will and Durable Power of Attorney for Health Care

If a person falls into a coma with little or no hope of recovery, without a *living will* or *durable power of attorney for health care* to guide them, his family could face difficult decisions regarding his medical care. These documents specify the medical care a person wishes to receive, or *not* receive, if he becomes seriously ill and unable to give informed consent. The **living will** states, precisely, the desired treatments and the degree to which they are to be continued. The document must specifically state your wishes or risk being put aside because it is too vague.

Many experts recommend a **durable power of attorney for health care**, often called *advanced directives for health care*, instead of a living will. The durable power of attorney for health care authorizes an individual (your *agent*) to make health care decisions for you if you're unable to do so either temporarily or permanently. Unlike a living will, it applies in any case where you cannot communicate your wishes, not just

when you're terminally ill. You should spend some time specifying the scope of the power and instructions for medical treatment, and then review your thinking with your family and the person you designate as your agent. These documents, held by your designated agent and your doctor, should make it easier for your family to deal with these difficult issues.

### Ethical Wills

In addition to a traditional will, many people also prepare an **ethical will**, sometimes called a *legacy statement*. They are informal documents that are usually added to formal wills and read at the same time, that allow the deceased to share their morals, business ethics, life experiences, family stories and history, and more with future generations. They can be in the form of handwritten letters or essays, computer files, or digitally recorded media. It's a good idea to have your lawyer review your ethical will because its interpretation could lead to a challenge of your formal will.

## What About Joint Ownership?

The two forms of joint ownership—*joint tenancy* or *tenants by the entirety*—share the following characteristics.

1. Under the **right of survivorship**, the interest of a decedent passes directly to the surviving joint tenant(s)—that is, to the other joint owner(s)—by operation of the law and is free from the claims of the decedent's creditors, heirs, or personal representatives.
2. A **joint tenancy** may consist of any number of persons, who don't have to be related. A **tenancy by the entirety** can exist only between husband and wife.
3. In a *joint tenancy*, each joint tenant can unilaterally sever the tenancy, whereas a *tenancy by the entirety* can be severed only by mutual agreement, divorce, or conveyance by both spouses to a third party.
4. The co-owners must have equal interests.

Joint tenancy, the more common form of joint ownership, offers a sense of family security, quick and easy transfer to the spouse at death, exemption of jointly owned property from the claims of the deceased's creditors, and avoidance of delays and publicity in the estate settlement process. The key disadvantage of joint tenancy is the inability to control jointly owned property by a will, so that the first joint owner to die cannot control the property's disposition and management on his or her death.

For example, a father who has two unmarried children—a daughter with whom he has a good relationship and an estranged son—purchases property and places it in his own and his daughter's name as joint tenants. The father has a will that leaves everything he has to his daughter and specifically disinherits his son. The daughter has no estate planning documents. While traveling together, the father is killed outright in a car accident and the daughter is severely injured; indeed, she never fully recovers and dies two months later. At her death, intestate, her estate will likely pass to her brother. Had her father taken the property in his name only, then he could have stipulated in his will a longer survivorship requirement (say, 6 months) with a provision that in the event his daughter did not survive that period, there would be an alternative disposition (e.g., to a charity or to friends).

You should also be familiar with two other forms of ownership: *tenancy in common* and *community property*.

### Tenancy in Common

Under a **tenancy in common**, there is *no right of survivorship*, and each co-owner can leave his or her share to whomever he or she desires. Thus, the decedent owner's will controls the disposition of the decedent's partial interest in the asset. Unlike joint tenancy where all interests must be equal, tenancy in common interests can be unequal; hence, a property owned by three co-owners could be apportioned such that their respective shares are 50%, 30%, and 20% of the property.

### Community Property

**Community property**, a form of marital ownership found primarily in Southwestern states, is all property acquired by the effort of either or both spouses during marriage while they reside in a community property state. For example, wages and commissions earned and property acquired by either spouse while living in a community property state are automatically owned

© IOFOTO/SHUTTERSTOCK

equally by both spouses, even if only one was directly involved in acquiring the additional wealth. Property acquired before marriage or by gift or inheritance can be maintained as the acquiring spouse's separate property. Each spouse can leave his or her half of the community property to whomever he or she chooses, so there's *no right of survivorship* inherent in this form of ownership.

## LG3 Trusts

Trusts, which are another important estate planning tool, facilitate the transfer of property and the income from that property to another party. A **trust** is a legal relationship created when one party, the **grantor** (also called the *settlor*, *trustor*, or *creator*), transfers property to a second party, the **trustee** (an organization or individual), for the benefit of third parties, the **beneficiaries**, who may or may not include the grantor. The property placed in the trust is called *trust principal* or *res* (pronounced "race"). The trustee holds the legal title to the property in the trust and must use the property and any income it produces solely for the benefit of trust beneficiaries as specified by the grantor.

A trust may be *living* (funded during the grantor's life) or *testamentary* (created in a will and funded by the probate process). It may be *revocable* or *irrevocable*. The grantor can regain property placed into a revocable trust and alter or amend the terms of the trust. The grantor cannot recover property placed into an irrevocable trust during its term.

### Why Use a Trust?

Trusts are designed for various purposes. The most common motives are to attain income and estate tax savings and to manage and conserve property over a long period.

### Income and Estate Tax Savings

Under certain circumstances, a grantor who is a high-bracket taxpayer can shift the burden of paying taxes

**tenancy in common** A form of co-ownership under which there *is no right of survivorship* and each co-owner can leave his or her share to whomever he or she desires.

**community property** All marital property co-owned equally by both spouses while living in a community property state.

**trust** A legal relationship created when one party transfers property to a second party for the benefit of third parties.

**grantor** A person who creates a trust and whose property is transferred into it. Also called *settlor, trustor, or creator*.

**trustee** An organization or individual selected by a *grantor* to manage and conserve property placed in trust for the benefit of the *beneficiaries*.

**beneficiaries** Those who receive benefits—property or income—from a trust or from the estate of a decedent. A grantor can be a beneficary of his own trust.

on the income produced by securities, real estate, and other investments to a trust itself or to its beneficiary, both of whom are typically subject to lower income tax rates than the grantor is. Impressive *estate tax* savings are possible because the appreciation in the value of property placed into such a trust can be entirely removed from the grantor's estate and possibly benefit several generations of family members without incurring adverse federal estate tax consequences.

## FINANCIAL ROAD SIGN

**TIPS ON USING A TRUST**
The following tips will help you use trusts to protect assets and save taxes:

1. Avoid unneeded trusts. If none of your heirs is a minor, you may not need a trust.
2. Make sure to name the trust correctly.
3. Verify that title to the assets you want to place in the trust have been transferred properly
4. Be sure that the trustee of an insurance trust purchases the policy and takes title to it in his or her name as trustee of the trust.
5. If you name the trust's beneficiary as trustee, you can avoid having the trust's assets become part of the beneficiary's estate by limiting the use of proceeds to education, support, health, and maintenance.
6. Be aware that retaining control of spending decisions for a minor's trust may result in a tax liability for parents.
7. Consider co-trustees and create a way for beneficiaries to replace poorly performing trustees.

### Managing and Conserving Property

The trustee assumes the responsibility for managing and conserving the property on behalf of the beneficiaries. Management by the trustee is sometimes held in reserve in case a healthy and vigorous individual is unexpectedly incapacitated and becomes unable or unwilling to manage his or her assets.

## Selecting a Trustee

Five qualities are essential in a trustee. He or she must

1. Possess sound business knowledge and judgment
2. Have an intimate knowledge of the beneficiary's needs and financial situation
3. Be skilled in investment and trust management
4. Be available to beneficiaries (specifically, the trustee should be young enough to survive the trust term)
5. Be able to make decisions impartially

A corporate trustee, such as a trust company or bank that has been authorized to perform trust duties, may be best able to meet these requirements. On the other hand, a corporate trustee may charge high fees or be overly conservative in investments, be impersonal, or lack familiarity with and understanding of family problems and needs. Often a compromise involves appointing one or more individuals and a corporate trustee as co-trustees.

## Common Types and Characteristics of Trusts

Although there are various types of trusts, the most common ones are the *living trust*, the *testamentary trust*, and the *irrevocable life insurance trust*, each of which is described in the following sections. Exhibit 15.4 describes seven other popular trusts.

### Living Trusts

A **living (inter vivos) trust** is one created and funded during the grantor's lifetime. It can be either revocable or irrevocable and can last for a limited period or continue long after the grantor's death.

**REVOCABLE LIVING TRUST.** The grantor reserves the right to revoke the trust and regain trust property in a **revocable living trust**. For federal income tax purposes, grantors of these trusts are treated as owners of the property in the trust and are therefore taxed on any income produced by the trust.

Revocable living trusts have three basic advantages:

1. Management continuity and income flow are ensured even after the grantor's death. No probate is necessary because the trust continues to operate after the death of the grantor just as it did while he or she was alive.
2. The trustee assumes the burdens of investment decisions and management responsibility. For example, an individual may want to control investment decisions and management policy as long as he or she is alive and healthy but sets up a trust to provide backup help in case he or she becomes unable or unwilling to continue managing the assets.
3. The details of the estate plan and the value of assets placed into the trust do not become public knowledge, as they would during the probate process.

The principal disadvantages of these trusts include the fees charged by the trustee for managing the property placed into the trust and the legal fees charged for drafting the trust instruments.

**Exhibit 15.4   Seven Popular Trusts**

Trusts shift assets (and thus appreciation) out of one's estate while retaining some say in the future use of the assets. The drawback is that trusts can be cumbersome and expensive to arrange and administer. Here are brief descriptions of seven popular trusts:

- **Credit shelter trust.** The most common tax-saving trust for estate planning; couples with combined assets worth more than the "applicable exclusion amount" (AEA) can gain full use of each partner's exclusion by having that amount placed in a bypass trust—that is, one that bypasses the surviving spouse's taxable estate. It's called a *credit shelter trust* because, when one spouse dies, the trust receives assets from the decedent's estate equal in value to the estate AEA ($3.5 million in 2009).

- **Qualified terminable interest property (QTIP) trust.** Usually set up in addition to a *credit shelter trust* to ensure that money stays in the family; it receives some or all of the estate assets over the applicable exclusion amount ($3,500,000 in 2009). The survivor receives all income from the property until death, when the assets go to the persons chosen by the first spouse to die. Estate taxes on QTIP trust assets can be delayed until the second spouse dies. It is also useful for couples with children from prior marriages, because the QTIP property can be distributed to the children of the grantor-spouse only after the death of the surviving spouse.

- **Special needs trust.** An irrevocable trust established for the benefit of a person with disabilities. It is designed to provide extra help and life enrichment without reducing state and federal government help to the beneficiary.

- **Minor's section 2503(c) trust.** Set up for a minor, often to receive tax-free gifts. However, assets must be distributed to the minor before he or she turns 21.

- **Crummey trust.** Used to make tax-free gifts up to the annual exclusion amounts to children; unlike a *minor's section 2503(c) trust,* these funds need not be distributed before age 21. However, the beneficiary can withdraw the funds placed into the trust for a limited time (e.g., for up to 30 days), after which the right to make a withdrawal ceases.

- **Charitable lead (or income) trust.** Pays some or all of its income to a charity for a period of time, after which the property is distributed to noncharitable beneficiaries. The grantor receives an immediate income tax deduction based on expected future payout to charity. If the grantor's children are the so-called remaindermen of the trust, then the value of the gift for gift or estate tax purposes is greatly reduced because their possession and enjoyment of the trust assets is delayed until the charitable interest terminates.

- **Charitable remainder trust.** Similar to a *charitable lead trust,* except that income goes to taxable beneficiaries (e.g., the grantor or the grantor's children) and the principal goes to a charity when the trust ends. The grantor gets an immediate income tax deduction based upon the value of the remainder interest that is promised to the charity.

**IRREVOCABLE LIVING TRUST.** Grantors who establish an **irrevocable living trust** relinquish title to the property they place in it and give up the right to revoke or terminate the trust. Such trusts have all the advantages of revocable trusts plus the potential for reducing taxes. Disadvantages of such a trust relate to the fees charged by trustees for managing assets placed into it, possible gift taxes on assets placed into it, and the grantor's forfeiture of the right to alter the terms of the trust as circumstances change.

**LIVING TRUSTS AND POUR-OVER WILLS.** A will can be written so that it "pours over" designated assets into a previously established revocable or irrevocable living trust. The trust may also be named the beneficiary of the grantor's insurance policies. The **pour-over will** generally contains a provision passing the estate—after debts, expenses, taxes, and specific bequests—to an existing living trust, ensuring that property left out of the living trust will make its way into the trust (that is, "pour over" into it). Such an arrangement provides for easily coordinated and well-administered management of estate assets.

**Testamentary Trust**

A trust created by a decedent's will is called a **testamentary trust.** Such a trust comes into existence only after the will is probated and a court order directs the executor to transfer the property to the trustee in order to fund the trust. The revocable living trust and the testamentary trust can have pretty much the same terms and long-range functions, for example, providing for asset management for the trustor's family long after the trustor has died. Indeed, the two main differences are: (1) only the living trust provides for management

**irrevocable living trust** A trust in which the grantor gives up the right to revoke or terminate the trust.

**pour-over will** A provision in a will that provides for the passing of the estate—after debts, expenses, taxes, and specific bequests—to an existing living trust.

**testamentary trust** A trust created by a decedent's will and funded through the probate process.

when and if the trustor becomes incapacitated and (2) the living trust is funded by transfers to the trustee by assignment or deed during the trustors life, whereas the funding mechanism for the testamentary trust is a court order distributing the property to the trustee at the end of the probate process.

### Irrevocable Life Insurance Trust

A wealthy individual might want to establish an **irrevocable life insurance trust** in which the major asset of the trust is life insurance on the grantor's life. To avoid having the proceeds of the policy included in the grantor's estate, the independent trustee usually acquires the policy on the life of the wealthy person and names the trustee as the beneficiary. The terms of the trust enable the trustee to use the proceeds to pay the grantor's estate taxes and to take care of the grantor's spouse and children, and probably eventually to distribute the remainder of the proceeds to the children or other beneficiaries as specified in the trust document.

### LG4 Federal Unified Transfer Taxes

Federal tax law establishes a **gift tax** on the value of certain gifts made during one's lifetime and an **estate tax** on "deathtime" gifts. While the tax rate is the same for gifts and estates and is known as the **unified rate schedule** (see the graduated table of rates in Exhibit 15.5), the amount that can pass tax free, called the **applicable exclusion amount (AEA)**, is lower for gifts than it is for estates, which means that large gifts will result in more tax paid than on a comparable estate transfer.

Consider these two examples:

1.  Robert gives his daughter a $6,000,000 taxable gift in 2009. Gift taxes equal $2,235,000.
2.  Sarah dies in 2009 and leaves her son a $6,000,000 taxable estate. The estate tax equals $1,125,000.

Because of the difference in the respective applicable exclusion amounts (see Exhibit 15.6), in the

previous examples, the gift tax is $1,110,000 higher than the estate tax—even though the transferred amount is the same.

The *Economic Growth and Tax Relief Reconciliation Act of 2001* (EGTRRA) greatly complicated estate planning for wealthy families. As we have just demonstrated, EGTRRA makes gift taxes more costly than estate taxes. In 2009, the AEA for gifts was frozen at $1 million but increased for estates in increments of $3.5 million, but the estate tax (not the gift tax) is scheduled to be eliminated altogether for the year 2010 and then in 2011 return to what it would have been had the act never been passed. Congress is likely to act in 2010 to extend, for at least the next several years, the $3.5 million estate AEA, perhaps even increase it to $4 million or $5 million. At whatever value the AEA is reset, it is likely to be indexed for inflation and may once again be the same for gifts and estates.

## Gifts and Taxes

Gifting can be a good way to transfer property to a beneficiary before you die. However, very large transfers might be subject to gift taxes. There's no gift tax on services that one person performs for another, nor is the rent-free use of property a taxable transfer. A tax may be payable on cash gifts, gifts of

## Exhibit 15.5    Federal Unified Transfer Tax Rates

This *unified rate schedule* defines the amount of federal gift and estate taxes that estates of various sizes would have to pay; it incorporates the rates passed in the *Economic Growth and Tax Relief Reconciliation Act of 2001*. Estates under the exclusion amount pay no federal tax. The estate exclusion amount increased annually from $2,000,000 in 2006 to $3,500,000 in 2009 (see Exhibit 15.6). From 2007 to 2009, the top tax rates for estates worth more than $2,000,000 decreased slightly from 46% to 45%. *(Reminder:* Congress will probably not allow the repeal of estate taxes slated for 2010 to go into effect; expect a change in this area of the tax law by the end of 2010.)

| Taxable Estate Value | | Tentative Tax | | |
|---|---|---|---|---|
| More Than | But Not More Than | Base Amount | + Percent | On Excess Over |
| $ 0 | $ 10,000 | $ 0 | | |
| 10,000 | 20,000 | 1,800 | 20% | $ 10,000 |
| 20,000 | 40,000 | 3,800 | 22 | 20,000 |
| 40,000 | 60,000 | 8,200 | 24 | 40,000 |
| 60,000 | 80,000 | 13,000 | 26 | 60,000 |
| 80,000 | 100,000 | 18,200 | 28 | 80,000 |
| 100,000 | 150,000 | 23,800 | 30 | 100,000 |
| 150,000 | 250,000 | 38,800 | 32 | 150,000 |
| 250,000 | 500,000 | 70,800 | 34 | 250,000 |
| 500,000 | 750,000 | 155,800 | 37 | 500,000 |
| 750,000 | 1,000,000 | 248,300 | 39 | 750,000 |
| 1,000,000 | 1,250,000 | 345,800 | 41 | 1,000,000 |
| 1,250,000 | 1,500,000 | 448,300 | 43 | 1,250,000 |
| 1,500,000 | 2,000,000 | 555,800 | 45 | 1,500,000 |
| Top rate, 2009 2,000,000 | | 780,800 | 45 | 2,000,000 |
| 2010 | Repealed for estates. The maximum rate for gifts is 35% starting at $500,000. | | | |
| 2011 and beyond | Returns to pre-2001 tax law levels unless otherwise modified by Congress. | | | |

*Source:* Adapted from material in John C. Bost, *Estate Planning and Taxation*, 14th ed. (Dubuque, IA: Kendall Hunt, 2006).

personal or real property, and even indirect gifts. For example, if a father makes the mortgage payments on his adult son's home, then the payment is an indirect gift from father to son. In fact, almost any shifting of financial advantage in which the recipient does not provide full consideration in money or money's worth may be considered a gift.

Usually a gift is considered to be made *when the donor relinquishes dominion and control over the property or property interest transferred*. For example, if a mother places cash in a bank account held jointly with her son, no gift is made until the son makes a withdrawal. Until then, the mother can completely recover the entire amount placed in the account. So, when parents place property into a revocable trust

for their children, no gift occurs because they haven't relinquished control over the assets placed in it. But if they later make the trust irrevocable and thereby relinquish their right to control the gift, the transfer will be considered a completed gift.

## Is It Taxable?

Not everything that's transferred by an individual is subject to a gift tax. **Annual exclusions, gift splitting,** charitable deductions,

**annual exclusion**
Under the federal gift tax law, the amount that can be given each year without being subject to gift tax—for example, $13,000 in 2009. This amount is indexed for inflation and is likely to increase to $14,000 in 2012 or 2013.

**gift splitting** A method of reducing gift taxes; a gift given by one spouse, with the consent of the other spouse, can be treated as if each had given one-half of it.

## Exhibit 15.6 Unified Credits and Applicable Exclusion Amounts for Estates and Gifts

The *Economic Growth and Tax Relief Reconciliation Act of 2001* increased the applicable exclusion amount on a scheduled basis over the period from 2002 to 2009, with a complete repeal of the estate tax in 2010. This table shows the step-up in the exclusion amount from 2009 through repeal in 2010. Also shown are the unified tax credit amounts over the 2009–2011 period. (*Reminder:* The exclusion and credit amounts for 2010 and beyond are likely to change before the end of 2010.)

| Year | Unified Tax Credit—Estates | Applicable Exclusion Amount—Estates | Unified Tax Credit—Gifts | Applicable Exclusion Amount—Gifts |
|------|---------------------------|-------------------------------------|--------------------------|-----------------------------------|
| 2006 | $780,800 | $2,000,000 | $345,800 | $1,000,000 |
| 2007 | $780,800 | $2,000,000 | $345,800 | $1,000,000 |
| 2008 | $780,800 | $2,000,000 | $345,800 | $1,000,000 |
| 2009 | $1,455,800 | $3,500,000 | $345,800 | $1,000,000 |
| 2010 | Estate tax repealed for 2010 | | $330,800 | $1,000,000 |
| 2011 | $345,800 | $1,000,000 | $345,800 | $1,000,000 |

and marital deductions are all means of reducing the total amount for tax purposes.

- **Annual exclusions.** The gift tax law allows a person to give gifts—present interests with no strings attached—up to a specified annual amount per calendar year—$13,000 in 2009—to any number of recipients. For example, a person could give gifts of $13,000 each to 30 individuals, for a total of $390,000, without using up any of the recipient's applicable exclusion amount (and, of course, not paying any gift tax). Furthermore, the ability to give tax-free gifts of $13,000 per recipient renews annually. It is important to understand that a gift is not considered income to the recipients, so most gifts are income-tax-neutral. Of course, the donor doesn't get to claim an income tax deduction for making the gift.

- **Gift splitting.** In this method of reducing gift taxes, a gift given by one spouse can, with the consent of his or her spouse, be treated as if each had given one-half of it. Here's an example. From investments in her own name, Mary gives her son Charlie stock worth $480,000. Mary's husband Roberto agrees to split the gift. They each must file gift tax returns showing a gift worth $240,000, where the taxable amount is $227,000, after applying the $13,000 annual exclusion. Assuming no prior taxable gifts, they would each still have an AEA for gifts of $773,000 (i.e., $1,000,000 AEA for gifts less the $227,000 taxable gift amount). No gift taxes are

actually paid until the donor, who makes gifts, uses up all of his or her AEA.

- **Charitable deductions.** There's no limit on the amount that can be given—with no gift tax—to a qualified charity (one to which deductible gifts can be made for income tax purposes). Therefore, people could give their entire estates to charity and receive gift tax deductions for the total amount, and there would be no federal gift taxes.

- **Marital deductions.** Federal law permits an unlimited deduction for gift tax and estate tax purposes on property given or left to a spouse who is a U.S. citizen. Special rules apply for transfers to a spouse who is not a U.S. citizen.

## Reasons for Making Lifetime Gifts

Estate planners recommend gift giving for these tax-related reasons:

- **Gift tax annual exclusion.** As noted earlier, a single individual can give any number of donees up to $13,000 each year with no tax costs to either the donees or the donor.

- **Gift tax exclusion escapes estate tax.** Fortunately, property that qualifies for the annual exclusion is not taxable and is thus free from gift and estate taxes. Regardless of a gift's size, it's typically not treated as part of the donor's gross estate. However, the taxable portion of lifetime gifts, i.e., the amounts above the annual exclusion, are called *adjusted taxable* *gifts* and these may push the donor's estate into a higher tax bracket.

- **Appreciation in value.** Generally, a gift's increase in value after it was given is excluded from the donor's estate. Suppose that Harvey gives his son, Jason, a gift of stock worth $35,000 in 2007. When Harvey dies 2 years later, the stock is worth $60,000. The amount subject to transfer taxes will be $22,000 ($35,000 − $13,000)—the adjusted taxable gift amount. None of the appreciation is subject to gift or estate tax.

- **Credit limit.** Because of the credit that's used to offset otherwise taxable gifts, gift taxes don't have to be paid on cumulative lifetime gifts up to the applicable gift exclusion amount of $1,000,000 (remember the AEA for gifts doesn't increase over the years); see Exhibit 15.6. To the extent that the credit is used against lifetime gift taxes, it's not available to offset estate taxes.

- **Impact of marital deduction.** The transfer tax marital deduction allows one spouse to give the other spouse (a U.S. citizen) an unlimited amount of property entirely transfer tax free without reducing the donor-spouse's AEA (i.e., the amount that can be transferred to others tax free).

© SUPRI SUHARJOTO/SHUTTERSTOCK

## LG5 Calculating Estate Taxes

**unified tax credit** The credit that can be applied against the tentative tax on estate tax base.

Federal estate taxes are levied on the transfer of property at death, so one goal of effective estate planning is to minimize the amount of estate taxes paid. The tax is measured by the value of the property that the deceased transfers (or is deemed to transfer) to others. The phrase "deemed to transfer" is important because the estate tax applies not only to transfers that a deceased actually makes at death but also to certain transfers made during the person's lifetime—called *lifetime gifts*. For example, if the owner-insured gives away his or her life insurance policy within 3 years of his or her death, the proceeds will be included in the insured's gross estate.

### Computing the Federal Estate Tax

The computation of federal estate taxes involves six steps.

1. Determine the *gross estate*, the total of all property in which the decedent had an interest and that is required to be included in the estate.
2. Find the *adjusted gross estate* by subtracting from the gross estate any allowable funeral and administrative expenses, debts, and other expenses incurred during administration.
3. Calculate the *taxable estate* by subtracting any allowable marital deduction or charitable deduction from the adjusted gross estate.
4. Compute the *estate tax base*. After determining the value of the taxable estate, any "adjusted taxable gifts" (i.e., gifts above the annual exclusion) made after 1976 are added to the taxable estate. The unified tax rate schedule, shown in Exhibit 15.5, is used to determine a *tentative tax* on the estate tax base.
5. After finding the tentative tax, subtract both the gift taxes the decedent paid on the adjusted taxable gifts and the **unified tax credit** (described below). The result is the total death taxes.
6. Determine the *federal estate tax due*. Some estates will qualify for additional credits, which are fairly rare but when available result in a dollar-for-dollar reduction of the tax. After reducing the total death taxes by any eligible credits, the federal estate tax due is payable by the decedent's executor, generally within 9 months of the decedent's death.

You can use Worksheet 15.2 to estimate federal estate taxes. The worksheet depicts the computations for a hypothetical situation involving a death in 2009, when the $3.5 million estate AEA applies. Note that the AEA is not subtracted from the gross estate. The worksheet is useful in following the flow of dollars from the gross estate to the federal estate tax due. Note that the worksheet factors the unified credit

This worksheet is useful in determining federal estate tax due. Note that taxes are payable at the marginal tax rate applicable to the estate tax base (line 7), which is the amount that exists before the tax-free exclusion is factored in by application of the unified credit.

### COMPUTING FEDERAL ESTATE TAX DUE

Name _Jim Levitt_  Date _9/5/2009_

| Line | Computation | Item | Amount | Total Amount |
|------|-------------|------|--------|--------------|
| 1 | | Gross estate | | $ 5,850,000 |
| 2 | Subtract sum of: | (a) Funeral expenses | $ 6,800 | |
| | | (b) Administrative expenses | 75,000 | |
| | | (c) Debts | 125,000 | |
| | | (d) Other expenses | 0 | |
| | | Total | | ( 206,800 ) |
| 3 | Result: | Adjusted gross estate | | $ 5,643,200 |
| 4 | Subtract sum of: | (a) Marital deduction | 0 | |
| | | (b) Charitable deduction | 180,000 | |
| | | Total | | ( 180,000 ) |
| 5 | Result: | Taxable estate | | $ 5,463,200 |
| 6 | Add: | Adjusted taxable gifts (post-1976) | | $ 0 |
| 7 | Result: | Estate tax base | | $ 5,463,200 |
| 8 | Compute: | Tentative tax on estate tax base[a] | | $ 2,339,240 |
| 9 | Subtract sum of: | (a) Gift tax payable on post-1976 gifts | $ 0 | |
| | | (b) Unified tax credit[b] | 1,455,800 | |
| | | Total | | ($ 1,455,800 ) |
| 10 | Result: | Total estate taxes[c] | | 883,440 |
| 11 | Subtract: | Other credits | | ($ 0 ) |
| 12 | Result: | Federal estate tax due | | $ 883,440 |

[a]Use Exhibit 15.5 to calculate the tentative tax.

[b]Use Exhibit 15.6 to determine the appropriate unified credit.

[c]Note that the tax amount shown on line 10 is the significant number because most states are "pickup tax" states, meaning that the state simply collects the state death tax credit, a dollar-for-dollar credit.

for the year 2009 into the calculation at line 9b. The $1,455,800 shown on that line is equal to the tentative tax on an estate tax base of $3.5 million. If the tentative tax shown on line 8 is *less* than the unified credit available for the decedent's year of death, then no federal estate tax is due.

## LG6 Estate Planning Techniques

Judicious use of certain tax-oriented estate planning strategies will minimize estate shrinkage and maximize financial security. Two basic estate planning techniques

are dividing the estate and deferring income. Life insurance is another estate planning tool.

{ *Judicious use of certain tax-oriented estate planning strategies will minimize estate shrinkage and maximize financial security.* }

## Dividing

Each time you create a new taxpaying entity, you'll save income taxes and stimulate estate accumulation. Here are some popular techniques.

1. **Giving income-producing property to children, either outright or in trust.** Because each child can receive a specified amount of unearned income each year, some income tax savings may be realized even by persons who are not in high tax brackets.

2. **Establishing a corporation.** Incorporation may permit individuals in high tax brackets, such as doctors or other professionals, to save taxes by accumulating income in a manner subject to relatively lower income tax rates.

3. **Properly qualifying for the federal estate tax marital deduction.** This marital deduction allows an individual to pass—estate tax free—unlimited amounts to a spouse, taking full advantage of both spouses' unified credits.

© SKIEMINE KIRILL/SHUTTERSTOCK

## Deferring

Techniques for minimizing the total tax burden by spreading income over more than one tax year or deferring the tax to a later period—so the taxpayer can invest the tax money for a longer time—apply to estate planning as well as income tax planning. Here are some examples.

1. **Nonqualified deferred-compensation plans** for selected individuals in corporate businesses and private contractors.

2. **Making installment sales** instead of cash sales to spread the taxable gain over several years.

3. **Private annuities,** which are arrangements whereby one person transfers property to another, usually a younger family member. This recipient promises in return to pay an annuity to the original owner for as long as he or she lives. The income tax attributable to such an annuity can thereby be spread over several years.

4. **Qualified pension and profit-sharing plans** that allow tax deferral on the income and gains from investments.

5. **Government Series EE bonds**—because their earnings can be treated as taxable income at maturity rather than yearly as earned.

6. **Stocks that pay no or low dividends** but have high price appreciation because they invest retained earnings in profitable projects.

7. **Life insurance policies** in which lifetime growth in value is not subject to income tax and the death proceeds are income tax free. If the insured converts the policy into an annuity then the earnings inherent in the policy become taxable only as received, so the tax on any gain can be deferred over a lifetime.

8. **Depreciable real estate** that yields high write-offs in years when the estate owner is earning high levels of taxable passive income.

9. **Installment payment of federal estate taxes** applicable to a business interest that equals or exceeds 35% of the adjusted gross estate. Payments can be spread over as many as 14 years with only the interest being paid on the unpaid tax during the first 4 years.

10. **Likely decrease in the estate tax** in the near future, or at least additional significant increases in the AEA that would reduce the estate tax on large estates and eliminate it completely for more modest estates.

## Life Insurance as an Estate Planning Tool

*Life insurance* can be a valuable component of your estate plan. A policy can be purchased for an annual premium of from 3% to 6% of the face (death) value of the policy. If someone other than the insured owns the policy, then the proceeds of such insurance can pass to the decedent's beneficiaries free of income tax, estate tax, inheritance tax, and probate costs. In addition, whole life and universal life insurance policies are an attractive form of loan collateral.

## Future of the Estate Tax

As we've learned in this chapter, estate planning goes beyond minimizing taxes. It is the best way to take care of the people you love, help charitable organizations, transfer property, and spell out your wishes if you die or become disabled. Regardless of what happens to the estate tax in the future, estate planning will continue to be a key component of personal financial planning.

# FINANCIAL PLANNING EXERCISES

**LG1**

1. Chris and James Simon are in their mid-30s and have two children, ages 8 and 5. They have combined annual income of $95,000 and own a house in joint tenancy with a market value of $310,000, on which they have a mortgage of $250,000. James has $100,000 in group term life insurance and an individual universal life policy for $150,000. However, the Simons haven't prepared their wills. James plans to do one soon, but they think that Chris doesn't need one because the house is jointly owned. As their financial planner, explain why it's important for both James and Chris to draft wills as soon as possible.

**LG2**

2. Your best friend has asked you to be executor of his estate. What qualifications do you need, and would you accept the responsibility?

**LG2, 3, 5**

3. Michael Singleton, 48 and a widower, and Nicole Whitt, 44 and divorced, were married 5 years ago. They have children from their prior marriages, two children for Michael and one child for Nicole. The couple's estate is valued at $1.4 million, including a house valued at $475,000, a vacation home in the mountains, investments, antique furniture that has been in Nicole's family for many years, and jewelry belonging to Michael's first wife. Discuss how they could use trusts as part of their estate planning, and suggest some other ideas for them to consider when preparing their wills and related documents.

**LG4, 5**

4. *Use Worksheet 15.2.* When Harvey Smitham died in 2009, he left an estate valued at $5,850,000. His trust directed distribution as follows: $20,000 to the local hospital, $160,000 to his alma mater, and the remainder to his three adult children. Death-related costs were $6,800 for funeral expenses, $40,000 paid to attorneys, $5,000 paid to accountants, and $30,000 paid to the trustee of his living trust. In addition, there were debts of $125,000. Use Worksheet 15.2 and Exhibits 15.5 and 15.6 to calculate the federal estate tax due on his estate.

# APPENDICES

## APPENDIX A
### Table of Future Value Factors

Instructions: To use this table, find the future value factor that corresponds to both a given time period (year) and an interest rate. For example, if you want the future value factor for 6 years and 10%, move across from year 6 and down from 10% to the point at which the row and column intersect: 1.772. Other illustrations: for 3 years and 15%, the proper future value factor is 1.521; for 30 years and 8%, it is 10.062.

INTEREST RATE

| Year | 2% | 3% | 5% | 6% | 8% | 9% | 10% | 12% | 15% | 20% | 25% | 30% |
|------|------|------|------|------|------|------|------|------|------|------|------|------|
| 1 | 1.020 | 1.030 | 1.050 | 1.060 | 1.080 | 1.090 | 1.100 | 1.120 | 1.150 | 1.120 | 1.250 | 1.300 |
| 2 | 1.040 | 1.060 | 1.102 | 1.120 | 1.166 | 1.190 | 1.210 | 1.254 | 1.322 | 1.440 | 1.562 | 1.690 |
| 3 | 1.061 | 1.090 | 1.158 | 1.190 | 1.260 | 1.290 | 1.331 | 1.405 | 1.521 | 1.728 | 1.953 | 2.197 |
| 4 | 1.082 | 1.130 | 1.216 | 1.260 | 1.360 | 1.410 | 1.464 | 1.574 | 1.749 | 2.074 | 2.441 | 2.856 |
| 5 | 1.104 | 1.160 | 1.276 | 1.340 | 1.469 | 1.540 | 1.611 | 1.762 | 2.011 | 2.488 | 3.052 | 3.713 |
| 6 | 1.126 | 1.190 | 1.340 | 1.420 | 1.587 | 1.670 | 1.772 | 1.974 | 2.313 | 2.986 | 3.815 | 4.827 |
| 8 | 1.172 | 1.260 | 1.477 | 1.590 | 1.851 | 1.990 | 2.144 | 2.476 | 3.059 | 4.300 | 5.960 | 8.157 |
| 10 | 1.219 | 1.340 | 1.629 | 1.790 | 2.159 | 2.360 | 2.594 | 3.106 | 4.046 | 6.192 | 9.313 | 13.786 |
| 12 | 1.268 | 1.420 | 1.796 | 2.010 | 2.518 | 2.810 | 3.138 | 3.896 | 5.350 | 8.916 | 14.552 | 23.298 |
| 15 | 1.346 | 1.560 | 2.079 | 2.390 | 3.172 | 3.640 | 4.177 | 5.474 | 8.137 | 15.407 | 28.422 | 51.185 |
| 20 | 1.486 | 1.810 | 2.653 | 3.210 | 4.661 | 5.600 | 6.727 | 9.646 | 16.366 | 38.337 | 86.736 | 190.047 |
| 25 | 1.641 | 2.090 | 3.386 | 4.290 | 6.848 | 8.620 | 10.834 | 17.000 | 32.918 | 95.395 | 264.698 | 705.627 |
| 30 | 1.811 | 2.420 | 4.322 | 5.740 | 10.062 | 13.260 | 17.449 | 29.960 | 66.210 | 237.373 | 807.793 | 2619.936 |
| 35 | 2.000 | 2.810 | 5.516 | 7.690 | 14.785 | 20.410 | 28.102 | 52.799 | 133.172 | 590.657 | 2465.189 | 9727.598 |
| 40 | 2.208 | 3.260 | 7.040 | 10.280 | 21.724 | 31.410 | 45.258 | 93.049 | 267.856 | 1469.740 | 7523.156 | 36117.754 |

Note: All factors are rounded to the nearest 1/1000 in order to agree with values used in the text.

## APPENDIX B
### Table of Future Value Annuity Factors

Instructions: To use this table, find the future value of annuity factor that corresponds to both a given time period (year) and an interest rate. For example, if you want the future value of annuity factor for 6 years and 10%, move across from year 6 and down from 10% to the point at which the row and column intersect: 7.716. Other illustrations: for 3 years and 15%, the proper future value of annuity factor is 3.472; for 30 years and 6%, it is 79.060.

INTEREST RATE

| Year | 2% | 3% | 5% | 6% | 8% | 9% | 10% | 12% | 15% | 20% | 25% | 30% |
|------|------|------|------|------|------|------|------|------|------|------|------|------|
| 1 | 1.000 | 1.000 | 1.000 | 1.000 | 1.000 | 1.000 | 1.000 | 1.000 | 1.000 | 1.000 | 1.000 | 1.000 |
| 2 | 2.020 | 2.030 | 2.050 | 2.060 | 2.080 | 2.090 | 2.100 | 2.120 | 2.150 | 2.200 | 2.250 | 2.300 |
| 3 | 3.060 | 3.090 | 3.152 | 3.180 | 3.246 | 3.270 | 3.310 | 3.374 | 3.472 | 3.640 | 3.813 | 3.990 |
| 4 | 4.122 | 4.180 | 4.310 | 4.380 | 4.506 | 4.570 | 4.641 | 4.779 | 7.993 | 5.368 | 5.766 | 6.187 |
| 5 | 5.204 | 5.310 | 5.526 | 5.630 | 5.867 | 5.980 | 6.105 | 6.353 | 6.742 | 7.442 | 8.207 | 9.043 |
| 6 | 6.308 | 6.460 | 6.802 | 6.970 | 7.336 | 7.520 | 7.716 | 8.115 | 8.754 | 9.930 | 11.259 | 12.756 |
| 8 | 8.583 | 8.890 | 9.549 | 9.890 | 10.637 | 11.030 | 11.436 | 12.300 | 13.727 | 16.499 | 19.842 | 23.858 |
| 10 | 10.950 | 11.460 | 12.578 | 13.180 | 14.487 | 15.190 | 15.937 | 17.549 | 20.304 | 25.959 | 33.253 | 42.619 |
| 12 | 13.412 | 14.190 | 15.917 | 16.870 | 18.977 | 20.140 | 21.384 | 24.133 | 29.001 | 39.580 | 54.208 | 74.326 |
| 15 | 17.293 | 18.600 | 21.578 | 23.270 | 27.152 | 29.360 | 31.772 | 37.280 | 47.580 | 72.035 | 109.687 | 167.285 |
| 20 | 24.297 | 26.870 | 33.066 | 36.780 | 45.762 | 51.160 | 57.274 | 72.052 | 102.443 | 186.687 | 342.945 | 630.157 |
| 25 | 32.030 | 36.460 | 47.726 | 54.860 | 73.105 | 84.700 | 98.346 | 133.333 | 212.790 | 471.976 | 1054.791 | 2348.765 |
| 30 | 40.567 | 47.570 | 66.438 | 79.060 | 113.282 | 136.300 | 164.491 | 241.330 | 434.738 | 1181.865 | 3227.172 | 8729.805 |
| 35 | 49.994 | 60.460 | 90.318 | 111.430 | 172.314 | 215.700 | 271.018 | 431.658 | 881.152 | 2948.294 | 9856.746 | 32422.090 |
| 40 | 60.401 | 75.400 | 120.797 | 154.760 | 259.052 | 337.870 | 442.580 | 767.080 | 1779.048 | 7343.715 | 30088.621 | 120389.375 |

Note: All factors are rounded to the nearest 1/1000 in order to agree with values used in the text.

# APPENDIX C
## Table of Present Value Factors

Instructions: To use this table, find the present value factor that corresponds to both a given time period (year) and an interest rate. For example, if you want the present value factor for 25 years and 7%, move across from year 25 and down from 7% to the point at which the row and column intersect: .184. Other illustrations: for 3 years and 15%, the proper present value factor is .658; for 30 years and 8%, it is .099.

INTEREST RATE

| Year | 2% | 3% | 5% | 7% | 8% | 9% | 10% | 12% | 15% | 20% | 25% | 30% |
|---|---|---|---|---|---|---|---|---|---|---|---|---|
| 1 | .980 | .971 | .952 | .935 | .926 | .917 | .909 | .833 | .870 | .893 | .800 | .769 |
| 2 | .961 | .943 | .907 | .873 | .857 | .842 | .826 | .797 | .756 | .694 | .640 | .592 |
| 3 | .942 | .915 | .864 | .816 | .794 | .772 | .751 | .712 | .658 | .579 | .512 | .455 |
| 4 | .924 | .888 | .823 | .763 | .735 | .708 | .683 | .636 | .572 | .482 | .410 | .350 |
| 5 | .906 | .863 | .784 | .713 | .681 | .650 | .621 | .567 | .497 | .402 | .328 | .269 |
| 6 | .888 | .837 | .746 | .666 | .630 | .596 | .564 | .507 | .432 | .335 | .262 | .207 |
| 8 | .853 | .789 | .677 | .582 | .540 | .502 | .467 | .404 | .327 | .233 | .168 | .123 |
| 10 | .820 | .744 | .614 | .508 | .463 | .422 | .386 | .322 | .247 | .162 | .107 | .073 |
| 12 | .789 | .701 | .557 | .444 | .397 | .356 | .319 | .257 | .187 | .112 | .069 | .043 |
| 15 | .743 | .642 | .481 | .362 | .315 | .275 | .239 | .183 | .123 | .065 | .035 | .020 |
| 20 | .673 | .554 | .377 | .258 | .215 | .178 | .149 | .104 | .061 | .026 | .012 | .005 |
| 25 | .610 | .478 | .295 | .184 | .146 | .116 | .092 | .059 | .030 | .010 | .004 | .001 |
| 30 | .552 | .412 | .231 | .131 | .099 | .075 | .057 | .033 | .015 | .004 | .001 | * |
| 35 | .500 | .355 | .181 | .094 | .068 | .049 | .036 | .019 | .008 | .002 | * | * |
| 40 | .453 | .307 | .142 | .067 | .046 | .032 | .022 | .011 | .004 | .001 | * | * |

*Present value factor is zero to three decimal places.

Note: All factors are rounded to the nearest 1/1000 in order to agree with values used in the text.

# APPENDIX D
## Table of Present Value Annuity Factors

Instructions: To use this table, find the present value of annuity factor that corresponds to both a given time period (year) and an interest rate. For example, if you want the present value of annuity factor for 30 years and 7%, move across from year 30 and down from 7% to the point at which the row and column intersect: 12.409. Other illustrations: for 3 years and 15%, the proper present value of annuity factor is 2.283; for 30 years and 8%, it is 11.258.

INTEREST RATE

| Year | 2% | 3% | 5% | 7% | 8% | 9% | 10% | 12% | 15% | 20% | 25% | 30% |
|---|---|---|---|---|---|---|---|---|---|---|---|---|
| 1 | .980 | .971 | .952 | .935 | .926 | .917 | .909 | .893 | .870 | .833 | .800 | .769 |
| 2 | 1.942 | 1.913 | 1.859 | 1.808 | 1.783 | 1.759 | 1.736 | 1.690 | 1.626 | 1.528 | 1.440 | 1.361 |
| 3 | 2.884 | 2.829 | 2.723 | 2.624 | 2.577 | 2.531 | 2.487 | 2.402 | 2.283 | 2.106 | 1.952 | 1.816 |
| 4 | 3.808 | 3.717 | 3.546 | 3.387 | 3.312 | 3.240 | 3.170 | 3.037 | 2.855 | 2.589 | 2.362 | 2.166 |
| 5 | 4.713 | 4.580 | 4.329 | 4.100 | 3.993 | 3.890 | 3.791 | 3.605 | 3.352 | 2.991 | 2.689 | 2.436 |
| 6 | 5.601 | 5.417 | 5.076 | 4.767 | 4.623 | 4.486 | 4.355 | 4.111 | 3.784 | 3.326 | 2.951 | 2.643 |
| 8 | 7.326 | 7.020 | 6.463 | 5.971 | 5.747 | 5.535 | 5.335 | 4.968 | 4.487 | 3.837 | 3.329 | 2.925 |
| 10 | 8.983 | 8.530 | 7.722 | 7.024 | 6.710 | 6.418 | 6.145 | 5.650 | 5.019 | 4.192 | 3.570 | 3.092 |
| 12 | 10.575 | 9.954 | 8.863 | 7.943 | 7.536 | 7.161 | 6.814 | 6.194 | 5.421 | 4.439 | 3.725 | 3.190 |
| 15 | 12.849 | 11.938 | 10.380 | 9.108 | 8.560 | 8.061 | 7.606 | 6.811 | 5.847 | 4.675 | 3.859 | 3.268 |
| 20 | 16.352 | 14.878 | 12.462 | 10.594 | 9.818 | 9.129 | 8.514 | 7.469 | 6.259 | 4.870 | 3.954 | 3.316 |
| 25 | 19.524 | 17.413 | 14.094 | 11.654 | 10.675 | 9.823 | 9.077 | 7.843 | 6.464 | 4.948 | 3.985 | 3.329 |
| 30 | 22.396 | 19.601 | 15.373 | 12.409 | 11.258 | 10.274 | 9.427 | 8.055 | 6.566 | 4.979 | 3.995 | 3.332 |
| 35 | 24.999 | 21.487 | 16.378 | 12.948 | 11.655 | 10.567 | 9.844 | 8.176 | 6.617 | 4.992 | 3.998 | 3.333 |
| 40 | 27.356 | 23.115 | 17.159 | 13.332 | 11.925 | 10.757 | 9.779 | 8.244 | 6.642 | 4.997 | 3.999 | 3.333 |

Note: All factors are rounded to the nearest 1/1000 in order to agree with values used in the text.

# APPENDIX E
## Using a Financial Calculator

**Important Financial Keys on the Typical Financial Calculator**
The important financial keys on a typical financial calculator are depicted and defined below. On some calculators, the keys may be labeled using lowercase characters for "N" and "I". Also, "I/Y" may be used in place of the "I" key.

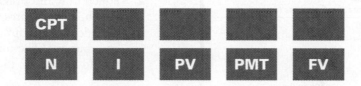

| **CPT** | Compute key; used to initiate financial calculation once all values are input |
| **N** | Number of periods |
| **I** | Interest rate per period |
| **PV** | Present value |
| **PMT** | Amount of payment; used only for annuities |
| **FV** | Future value |

The handheld financial calculator makes it easy to calculate time value. Once you have mastered the time value of money concepts using tables, we suggest you use such a calculator. For one thing, it becomes cumbersome to use tables when calculating anything other than annual compounding. For another, calculators rather than tables are used almost exclusively in the business of personal financial planning.

You don't want to become overly dependent on calculators, however, because you may not be able to recognize a nonsensical answer in the event that you accidentally push the wrong button. The important calculator keys are shown and labeled above. Before using your calculator to make the financial computations described in this text, be aware of the following points.

1. The keystrokes on some of the more sophisticated and expensive calculators are menu-driven: after you select the appropriate routine, the calculator prompts you to input each value; a compute key (CPT) is not needed to obtain a solution.

2. Many calculators allow the user to set the number of payments per year. Most of these calculators are preset for monthly payments, or 12 payments per year. Because we work primarily with *annual* payments—one payment per year—it is important to make sure that your calculator is set for one payment per year. Although most calculators are preset to recognize that all payments occur at the end of the period, it is also important to make sure your calculator is actually in the END mode. Consult the reference guide that accompanies your calculator for instructions on these settings.

3. To avoid including previous data in current calculations, always clear all registers of your calculator before inputting values and making a new computation.

4. The known values can be punched into the calculator in any order; the order specified here and in the text simply reflects the authors' personal preference.

## Calculator Keystrokes

Let's go back to the future value calculation on page 42, where we are trying to calculate the future value of $5,000 at the end of 6 years if invested at 5%. Here are the steps for solving the problem with a calculator:

1. Punch in 5000 and press PV.
2. Punch in 6 and press N.
3. Punch in 5 and press I.
4. To calculate the future value, press CPT and then FV. The future value of 6700.48 should appear on the calculator display.

On many calculators, this value will be preceded by a minus sign, which is a way of distinguishing between cash inflows and cash outflows. For our purposes, this sign can be ignored.

To calculate the yearly savings (the amount of an annuity), let's continue with the example on page 42. For this example, the interest rate is 5%, the number of periods is 6, and the future value is $38,300. Your task is to solve the equation for the annuity. The steps using the calculator are:

1. Punch in 6 and press N.
2. Punch in 5 and press I.
3. Punch in 38300 and press FV.
4. To calculate the yearly payment or annuity, press CPT and then PMT.

The annuity of 5,630.77 should appear on the calculator display. Again, a negative sign can be ignored.

A similar procedure is used to find present value of a future sum or an annuity, except you would first input the FV or PMT before pressing CPT and then PV to calculate the desired result. To find the equal annual future withdrawals from an initial deposit, the PV would be input first; you solve for the PMT by pressing CPT and then PMT.

---

**CALCULATOR**

| Inputs | Functions |
|--------|-----------|
| 5000   | PV        |
| 6      | N         |
| 5      | I         |
|        | CPT       |
|        | FV        |
|        | *Solution* |
|        | 6700.48   |

SEE APPENDIX E FOR DETAILS.

---

**CALCULATOR**

| Inputs | Functions |
|--------|-----------|
| 6      | N         |
| 5      | I         |
| 38300  | FV        |
|        | CPT       |
|        | PMT       |
|        | *Solution* |
|        | 5630.77   |

SEE APPENDIX E FOR DETAILS.

# INDEX

## A

abortion, health insurance coverage for, 203–204
accelerated benefits, 188
accident policies, 201
**account executives.** *See* **stockbrokers**
**account reconciliation,** 84, 85
**accumulation period, 328**
active income, 50
**actual cash value, 216**
**add-on method, 161–162**
**adjustable-rate mortgage (ARM), 115–116**
**adjusted gross income (AGI), 52,** 53, 61
adjusted taxable gifts, 351
**adjustment period, 115**
**adjustments to (gross) income, 52**
**administrator,** estate, 342
advisory services, 253
**affinity card, 131**
affordability, of homeownership, 107–110
age, income and, 21
**agency bonds, 282**
aggressive growth funds, 297
alternative minimum tax (AMT), 54–55
**amended returns, 63.** *See also* **taxes**
American Depositary Receipts (ADRs), 275–276
American Stock Exchange (AMEX), 241
amortization schedules, 161
**annual exclusions, 349,** 350
**annual percentage rate (APR)**
calculation of, 158, 159
explanation of, **138,** 152, 156
**annual stockholders' report, 250**
**annuities**
classification of, 328–329
deposition of proceeds for, 329–330
explanation of, **42, 328**
future value of, 41–43
investment and income properties of, 331
present value of, 43–44
sources and costs of, 330–331
**annuity certain, 330**
**applicable exclusion amount (AEA), 348**
apportionment statutes, 339
**arbitration, 247**
**ask price, 242**
asset acquisition, 12
asset allocation, 299
**asset allocation, 258**
asset allocation funds, 299
**asset management account (AMA),** 76–77
asset planning, 335
**assets**
explanation of, 12, **25**
types of, 26–27
**automated teller machines (ATMs)**
cash advances from, 130
explanation of, 77
**automatic investment plans, 300**
**automatic reinvestment plans, 300**
automobile insurance
comprehensive, 227
explanation of, 223
financial responsibility laws and, 229

medical payments coverage by, 198, 225–226
no-fault, 227
premiums for, 227–229
types of, 223–227
automobile leases
decisions at end of, 99–100
explanation of, 98
process related to, 98–99
purchases vs., 99, 100
automobile loans, 146
automobile purchases
accepting offers for, 98
affordability issues related to, 94–96
brand, model, and feature choices for, 93–96
guidelines for, 93
leases vs., 99, 100
price negotiations for, 96–98
**average daily balance (ADB), 138,** 139
**average propensity to consume, 4**
**average tax rate, 48**

## B

**back-end load, 294**
bailout provision, 331
balanced budget, 37
balanced funds, 297
balance sheet equation, 25
balance sheet ratios, 34–35
**balance sheets**
example of, 28–30
explanation of, **25**
format for, 29
bank-by-phone accounts, 78
**bank credit cards.** *See also* credit cards
cash advances on, 130
explanation of, **129**

fees related to, 130–131
interest charges on, 130
line of credit on, 129
special types of, 131–132
bankruptcy
credit abuse and, 140
personal, 143
straight, 143
banks
checking and saving accounts offered by, 75–84
deposit insurance programs and, 73–74
electronic services offered by, 77–79
explanation of, 72
factors to consider when choosing, 81
safe-deposit boxes at, 79–80
as source of consumer loans, 149–150
as source of mortgage loans, 113
**base rate, 130**
**bear market, 244**
**beneficiaries, 345**
**beneficiary, 185**
**beta, 273**
**bid price, 242**
**biweekly mortgages, 117**
**blue-chip stock, 273–274**
**Blue Cross/Blue Shield plans, 194**
**bodily injury liability losses, 223–224**
bond funds, 297–298
bond rating agencies, 284, 285
bonds
agency and mortgage-backed, 282
call feature for, 281–282
convertible, 283–284
corporate, 283

shopping around
for, 141
wise use of, 140
credit bureau report,
135–137
**credit bureaus, 135, 137**
Credit Card Act of 2009,
130–131
credit card fraud,
142–143
credit cards
bank, 129–131
payments for, 139–140
retail, 132
special types of bank,
131–132
statements for, 139,
140
credit crisis of 2007–2009,
123–124. *See also*
financial crisis of
2008–2009
**credit investigation, 135**
**credit life insurance,**
**182**
**credit limit, 129**
**credit scoring, 137, 154**
**credit unions, 149, 150**
**current (short-term)**
**liabilities, 27, 29**
**current yield, 286–287**
**cyclical stock, 275**

**D**

dealer markets, 242–243
**debenture, 281**
**debit card, 132**
**debit cards, 77–78**
**debt, 153, 154**
**debt safety ratio,**
**126–128**
**debt service ratio, 35**
**decreasing term policy,**
**175–176**
**deductibles, 201–202,**
**222**
**defensive stock, 275**
**deferred annuity, 329**
deficits, 37–38
**defined benefit plans,**
**322–323**
**defined contribution**
**plans, 322**
**demand deposit, 75**
dental insurance, 201
**deposit insurance,**
**73–74**

depository financial
institutions, 72, 73
**depreciation, 95**
**depression, 19**
**desired rate of return,**
**268**
diesel cars, 95
**disability clause, 188**
**disability income**
**insurance**
estimating need for,
209–210
explanation of,
208–209
provisions and costs of,
210–211
**discount bonds, 281, 285,**
**286**
**discount brokers, 246,**
**248**
**discount method,**
**158, 159**
**distribution period,**
**328**
diversification, 290, 291
**dividend reinvestment**
**plan (DRP), 278**
**dividend yield, 271**
**Dow Jones Industrial**
**Average (DJIA), 242,**
**250–251, 268–269**
**Dow Jones Wilshire 5000**
**index, 251**
**down payment, 104–105**
dread disease policies,
201
**durable power of**
**attorney for financial**
**matters, 344**
**durable power of**
**attorney for health**
**care, 344**

**E**

**earnest money deposit,**
**112**
**earnings per share (EPS),**
**272**
earthquake insurance,
229
economic cycles, 18–20
economic environment.
*See also* financial
planning environment
elements of, 17–20
financial management
in difficult, 16

Economic Growth
and Tax Relief
Reconciliation Act
of 2001 (EGTRRA),
348
education
income and, 21
investor, 253
electronic banking
services, 77–78
**electronic funds transfer**
**system (EFTS)**
explanation of, 77–78
regulation of, 78–79
Electronic Fund Transfer
Act of 1978, 78
employee benefits,
14–16
**Employee Retirement**
**Income Security Act**
**of 1974 (ERISA), 321**
employee-sponsored
retirement plans. *See*
*also* retirement plans
contributions to, 322
defined contribution
or defined benefit,
322–323
evaluation of, 326
explanation of, 321
participation
requirements for,
321–322
profit-sharing,
323–324
qualified, 323
salary reduction,
325–326
thrift and savings,
324–325
enrolled agents (EAs), 64
**equipment trust**
**certificate, 281**
**equity, 27**
equity-income funds, 297
**estate planning**
documents related to,
343–344
explanation of,
334–335
function of, 15
joint ownership and,
344–345
letter of last
instructions and,
342
life insurance as
element of, 353

lifetime gifts and,
350-351
steps in, 337
taxes and, 348–353
techniques for, 352–353
trusts and, 345–438
wills and, 337–342
estates
administration of,
342–343
break-up of, 335–336
determining your,
336–337
estate taxes
calculation of, 351–352
explanation of, 346,
348
future of, 353
methods to deal with,
352–353
**estimated taxes, 49,**
**62–63**
**ethical will, 344**
**event risk, 264**
**exchange-traded funds**
**(ETFs)**
commissions to buy or
sell, 294
explanation of, 240,
293–294
mutual funds vs., 293
**exclusive provider**
**organization (EPO),**
**194**
executors, 339, 342, 343
**exemptions, 53–54**
**expansion, 19**
expenses
on cash budget, 37
estimation of, 37
explanation of, 30, 32
exposure
liability, 215–216
to property loss,
214–215
extended term insurance,
186–187

**F**

**fair market value, 27**
federal deposit insurance
programs, 73–74
federal income tax. *See*
**income taxes**
**Federal Insurance**
**Contributions Act**
**(FICA), 49**

tax issues related to, 52

**homeowner's insurance**
explanation of, **109,** 217
limitations on payment coverage in, 221–222
locations covered in, 220–221
medical expense coverage by, 198
perils covered in, 217–220
personal property floater in, 219
persons covered in, 220
premiums for, 222, 225
property covered in, 219, 220
renter's policies as, 219–220
HomePath Mortgage Financing program, 105
HomePath Renovation Mortgage Financing program, 105
home purchases
affordability analysis for, 103–104, 109–110
financing issues related to, 113–118
overview of, 101
price trends and, 101
process of, 110–112
renting vs., 101, 102–103
type of, 101
home remodeling, 111
**home service life insurance, 182**
hospital income policies, 201
hospitalization insurance policy, 199
hybrid cars, 95
hybrid securities, 240

**I**

**immediate annuity, 329**
income
allocation of, 32
on cash budget, 36
categories of, 50
determinants of, 20–22
explanation of, **30**
gross, **50**
investments to supplement, 239
for retirement, 317–318
taxable, 49, **50,** 51, 54–56
tax-free and tax deferred, 67
**income and expense statements**
example of, 31
explanation of, **25,** 30, 32
preparation of, 32–33
ratios for, 35
**income shifting, 67**
**income stock, 274**
**income taxes.** *See also* **taxes**
explanation of, **48**
function of, 47
state and local, 50
indemnity, principles of, 216–217
**indemnity plans, 192,** 193
**independent agent, 230**
index funds, 298
**index rate, 115**
**individual practice association (IPA), 194**
**individual retirement arrangement (IRA),** 301, **327,** 328
**industrial life insurance, 182**
inflation
explanation of, 20
homeownership as hedge against, 104
**insolvency, 27–28**
**installment loans (ILs)**
explanation of, 146, **149,** 159–160
finance charges on, 160–162
prepayment penalties on, 162–164
**installment premium annuity contract, 329**
insurance. *See also* health insurance; life insurance; **property insurance**
earthquake, 229
explanation of, 169
flood, 229–230
function of, 13
long-term care, 205–208
personal liability umbrella, 230
risk and, 169–170
workers' compensation, 196–197
insurance agents
life, 184–185
property and liability, 230
insurance companies
explanation of, 150–151
property and liability, 230–231
selection of, 184–185
underwriting by, 170
**insurance policies, 170**
interest
add-on, 161–162
compound, 87–88
credit card, 130
earning interest on, 265–266
explanation of, 86
factors that determine, 89
mortgage payment, 106–107
mortgage points and, 105
simple, 87, 160–161
**interest-only mortgages, 116**
**interest rate cap, 115**
**interest rate risk, 264**
**interim financing, 149**
intermediate goals, 9–11
**internal limits, 202**
Internal Revenue Service (IRS), 47, 49, 62–64
**international funds, 299**
**intestacy, 338**
inventories, property, 214–215
investing
determining amount of capital for, 236–238
getting started in, 13–14, 235–236
objectives of, 235, 238–239, 257
online, 253
risks and rewards of, 263–267
Investment Company Act of 1940, 244
**investments.** *See also specific types of investments*
explanation of, 12, **26**
features of good, 267–268
making informed, 249–255
managing your, 256–260
present value to analyze, 44
securities markets and, 240–249
types of, 239–240
investor education, 253
**irrevocable life insurance trust, 348**
**irrevocable living trust, 347**
**I savings bonds, 90**
**itemized deductions**
examples of, 61
explanation of, 52, 53

**J**

**joint tenancy, 344–345**
**junk bonds, 284**

**K**

**Keogh plans,** 301, 321, 326–328

**L**

**large-cap stock, 275**
**lease, 98**
**legacy statement, 344**
**letter of last instructions, 342**
**liabilities, 12, 27**
liability exposures, 215–216
**liability insurance**
automobile, 223–225
explanation of, **214**
liability planning, 12–13
**lien, 156**

national health care,
194–195
National Labor Relations
Board (NLRB), 321
needs analysis method,
171–173
negative amortization,
116
negligence, 216
negotiable order of
withdrawal (NOW)
account, 76
net asset value (NAV),
292
net profit margin, 272
net worth, 27, 29
New York Stock
Exchange (NYSE),
241–242, 247
no-load funds, 294, 304
noncontributory pension
plans, 322
nondeductible IRA, 327
nondepository financial
institutions, 72
nonforfeiture right, 177,
186–187
NYSE Euronext,
241–242
NYSE index, 251

O

odd lot, 247
old-age benefits, Social
Security, 319
Old Age Survivor's
Disability, and
Health Insurance
(OASDHI)
program, 318
OMB AB, 243
online banking, 78, 79
online brokers, 246
online investor
services, 253
open account credit, 129
open account credit
obligations, 27
open-end investment
company, 292
open-end lease, 98
optional renewability,
207
OTC Bulletin Board
(OTCBB), 243
other-insurance clause,
216–217

overdraft protection, 82
overdraft protection line,
133
overdrafts, 82
over-the-counter (OTC)
market, 242, 243

P

paid-up insurance,
186–188
participating policy, 188
participation
(coinsurance) clause,
202
par value, 281
passive income, 50
pay-as-you-go system, 49
payment cap, 115
Pension Protection Act of
2006, 324
people planning,
334–335
perils
covered in property and
liability policies,
217–219
explanation of, 214
identification of, 215
Perkins loans, 147, 148
personal automobile
policy (POP), 223,
224
personal bankruptcy,
143
personal financial
planning. See also
financial planning
explanation of, 5–6
function of, 3
life cycle of, 11–12
role of investing in,
236–238
personal financial
statements, 25, 33.
See also financial
statements
personal liability umbrella
policy, 230
personal loans, 147. See
also loans
personal property,
12, 27
personal property floater
(PPF), 219
personal relationships, 8
physical expense
insurance, 201

Pink Sheets, 243
PITI, 108
PLUS loans, 147–149
point-of-service (POS)
plan, 194
policy loans, 186
pooled diversification,
290–292
portfolio income, 50
portfolios
asset allocation for,
257–258
development of,
256–257, 259
explanation of, 256
model, 259
pour-over will, 347
preauthorized
deposits, 78
predatory lenders, 152
preexisting conditions
clause, 203
preferred provider
organization (PPO),
194
preferred securities, 240
pregnancy, health
insurance coverage
for, 203–204
premium bonds,
285, 286
prepayment penalty
explanation of, 156
for installment loans,
162
prequalification, 112
prescription drug
coverage, 196
present value, 43–44
present value annuity
factor, 44
price/earnings (P/E) ratio,
272–273
prices, negotiation of
automobile, 96–98
primary markets,
240–241
principles of indemnity,
216–217
private mortgage
insurance (PMI),
105
probate estate, 336
probate process, 342
profit-sharing plans,
323–324
progressive tax
structure, 48

property
inventories of, 214–215
personal, 12, 27
real, 12, 27
property damage liability
losses, 225
property insurance
automobile insurance
and, 223–229
explanation of, 214
guidelines for
purchasing,
230–231
homeowner's insurance
as, 217–222
indemnity principles
and, 216–217
personal liability
umbrella, 230
supplemental,
229–230
types of exposure and,
214–216
property taxes
explanation of,
108–109
as tax deduction, 104
proxy, 271
publicly traded issues
of common stock,
270
public offering, 270
purchase option, 99
purchasing power, 20
purchasing power risk,
263–264
qualified pension plans,
323

Q

Quicken, 65
QuickenOnline.com, 38

R

rate of return
desired, 268
risk-free, 266–267
ratio analysis, 34–35
real estate agents,
111–112
real estate investment
explanation of, 240,
306–308
in income property, 308
speculation in raw land
as, 308

**WHAT'S INSIDE** An introduction to t... the impact that the f... environment, age, geographic location, pers...

What's a Prep Card?
To help you prepare, we've developed a Prep Card for each chapter. Each card starts with a short list of key concepts covered in the chapter.

## LEARNING GOALS

**LG1** Identify the benefits of using personal financial planning techniques to manage your finances. (p. 3)

**LG2** Describe the personal financial planning process and define your goals. (p. 5)

**LG3** Explain the life cycle of financial plans, the role they play in achieving your financial goals, how to deal with special planning concerns, and the use of professional financial planners. (p. 11)

**LG4** Examine the economic environment's influence on personal financial

Chapter Elements
This column contains a list of learning goals, key terms with page references, chapter exhibits and worksheets.

of career choic... and their relationship t... ersonal financial plar...ing. (p. 20)

## KEY TERMS

**average propensity to consume** *4*
**consumer price index (CPI)** *20*
**depression** *19*
**expansion** *19*
**financial assets** *5*
**financial goals** *7*
**flexible-benefit (cafeteria) plans** *15*
**goal dates** *9*
**inflation** *20*
**money** *7*
**personal financial planning** *5*
**purchasing power** *20*
**recession** *19*

## CHAPTER OUTLINE

Chapter at a Glance
The outline with page references gives you a quick snapshot of the content covered in the chapter.

PowerPoints and video topics with sample questions are provided for all applicable chapters.

## MULTIMEDIA

### PowerPoints
See the PFIN PowerPoints for Chapter 1 at 4LTRpress.cengage.com.

## CHAPTER EXHIBITS & WORKSHEETS

### Kiplinger Videos

Available at the PFIN section c ___ Tips" videos offer quick mone ___ Ask your students to answe ___

**Video: "The Profitable** ___

● What key topics ___ esse ___ map of your fin ___ cial goals?

**Online Assignment**

These recommended assignments help students apply what they've learned to their personal lives as well as to sample cases.

### Applying Personal Finance

Go to PFIN's the "Applying Personal ___ ance" section of **4ltrpress .cengage.com.** Assign students to ___ ad the online exercise about attitudes toward money. Through a ___ eries of questions, this exercise helps students examine thei ___ attitude toward money and wealth so that they can formula ___ e realistic goals and plans.

### Critical Thinking Cases

Go to PFIN's Critical Thinking Cases section of **4ltrpress.cengage .com** and assign students the online cases about personal financial planning and finding a new job. Answers to Critical Thinking Questions are supplied for instructors only in the *Instructor's Manual.*

**WHAT'S INSIDE** An introduction to the life cycle of personal financial planning and the impact that the following has on personal finances: economic environment, age, geographic location, personal income, and career choice.

## LEARNING GOALS

**LG1** Identify the benefits of using personal financial planning techniques to manage your finances. (p. 3)

**LG2** Describe the personal financial planning process and define your goals. (p. 5)

**LG3** Explain the life cycle of financial plans, the role they play in achieving your financial goals, how to deal with special planning concerns, and the use of professional financial planners. (p. 11)

**LG4** Examine the economic environment's influence on personal financial planning. (p. 17)

**LG5** Evaluate the impact of age, education, and geographic location on personal income. (p. 20)

**LG6** Understand the importance of career choices and their relationship to personal financial planning. (p. 20)

## KEY TERMS

average propensity to consume *4*
consumer price index (CPI) *20*
depression *19*
expansion *19*
financial assets *5*
financial goals *7*
flexible-benefit (cafeteria) plans *15*
goal dates *9*
inflation *20*
money *7*
personal financial planning *5*
purchasing power *20*
recession *19*

## CHAPTER OUTLINE

## MULTIMEDIA

### PowerPoints

See the PFIN PowerPoints for Chapter 1 at 4ltrpress.cengage.com.

## Kiplinger Videos

Available at the PFIN section of 4ltrpress.cengage.com. "Kip Tips" videos offer quick money management and investing advice. Ask your students to answer the corresponding questions.

**Video: "The Profitable Payoff of Financial Planning"**

- What key topics are essential to study when creating a road-map of your financial goals?

## Applying Personal Finance

Go to PFIN's "Applying Personal Finance" section of **4ltrpress .cengage.com.** Assign students to read the online exercise about attitudes toward money. Through a series of questions, this exercise helps students examine their attitude toward money and wealth so that they can formulate realistic goals and plans.

## Critical Thinking Cases

Go to PFIN's "Critical Thinking Cases" section of **4ltrpress.cengage .com** and assign students the online cases about personal financial planning and finding a new job. Answers to Critical Thinking Questions are supplied for instructors only in the *Instructor's Manual.*

**WHAT'S INSIDE** Understanding income statements, creating personal balance sheets, income and expense statements, developing budgets to monitor spending, and learning the time value of money.

# LEARNING GOALS

**LG1** Understand the interlocking network of financial plans and statements. (p. 25)

**LG2** Prepare a personal balance sheet. (p. 25)

**LG3** Generate a personal income and expense statement. (p. 30)

**LG4** Develop a good recordkeeping system and use ratios to interpret personal financial statements. (p. 33)

**LG5** Construct a cash budget and use it to monitor and control spending. (p. 35)

**LG6** Describe the use of *time value of money* concepts to put a monetary value on financial goals. (p. 41)

## KEY TERMS

## CHAPTER OUTLINE

## MULTIMEDIA

### PowerPoints

See the PFIN PowerPoints for Chapter 2 at 4ltrpress.cengage.com.

### Kiplinger Video

Available at the PFIN section of 4ltrpress.cengage.com. "Kip Tips" videos offer quick money management and investing advice. Ask your students to answer the corresponding questions.

## CHAPTER EXHIBITS & WORKSHEETS

### Video: "The B-Word: Budget"

- What is the first thing you should do when deciding how to create a budget?
- What is a budget leak and what can you do when you identify one?

### Applying Personal Finance

Go to PFIN's "Applying Personal Finance" section of **4ltrpress .cengage.com.** Assign students to read the exercise on assessing their financial condition. This exercise guides them to create their own balance sheet of income and expenses and challenges them to assess whether they like where they are and what they can do to change their financial condition.

### Critical Thinking Cases

Go to PFIN's "Critical Thinking Cases" section of **4ltrpress .cengage.com** and assign students Case 2.2 about recent graduate Jim Pavlov's budget. Answers to Critical Thinking Questions are supplied for instructors only in the *Instructor's Manual.*

**WHAT'S INSIDE** The basic principles of income taxes, how to prepare a basic tax return, where to get help with your taxes, and how to implement an effective tax-planning strategy.

## LEARNING GOALS

**LG1** Discuss the basic principles of income taxes and determine your filing status. (p. 47)

**LG2** Describe the sources of gross income and adjustments to income, differentiate between standard and itemized deductions and exemptions, and calculate taxable income. (p. 50)

**LG3** Prepare a basic tax return using the appropriate tax forms and rate schedules. (p. 54)

**LG4** Explain who needs to pay estimated taxes, when to file or amend your return, and how to handle an audit. (p. 62)

**LG5** Know where to get help with your taxes and how software can streamline tax return preparation. (p. 62)

**LG6** Implement an effective tax planning strategy. (p. 66)

## KEY TERMS

## CHAPTER OUTLINE

## MULTIMEDIA

### PowerPoints

See the PFIN PowerPoints for Chapter 3 at 4ltrpress.cengage.com.

### Kiplinger Videos

Available at the PFIN section of 4ltrpress.cengage.com. "Kip Tips" videos offer quick money management and investing advice. Ask your students to answer the corresponding questions.

## CHAPTER EXHIBITS & WORKSHEETS

**Video: "Get Your Tax Refund Your Way"**

● Name two ways you can get your tax refund faster from the IRS.

**Video: "Two Key Tax Tips: Don't Hide and Don't Overwithhold"**

● What should you do if you can't pay what you owe to the IRS by April 15th?

● Receiving a substantially large tax refund indicates what kind of withholding blunder? How could you remedy it?

**Video: "Pay As You Earn"**

● Employers are required to withhold what kind of taxes for each paycheck?

● How often must a self-employed person pay taxes? What are the exceptions?

**Video: "The Power of Tax Planning"**

● What do you need to know about your finances to prepare for the amount of taxes you might owe?

### Applying Personal Finance

Go to PFIN's "Applying Personal Finance" section of **4ltrpress .cengage.com.** Assign students to read the exercise on tax relief. This exercise will help the students learn about any tax shelters currently allowed by law.

### Critical Thinking Cases

Go to PFIN's "Critical Thinking Cases" section of **4ltrpress .cengage.com** and assign students Case 3.1 about Raj and Kavitha Rao and their tax return. Answers to Critical Thinking Questions are supplied for instructors only in the *Instructor's Manual.*

## PREP CARD 4 Managing Your Cash and Savings

WHAT'S INSIDE Understanding cash management, using a checking account, calculating interest, and developing savings strategies.

## LEARNING GOALS

**LG1** Understand the role of cash management in the personal financial planning process. (p. 71)

**LG2** Describe today's financial services marketplace, both depository and nondepository financial institutions. (p. 72)

**LG3** Select the checking, savings, electronic banking, and other bank services that meet your needs. (p. 74)

**LG4** Open and use a checking account. (p. 80)

**LG5** Calculate the interest earned on your money using compound interest and future value techniques. (p. 84)

**LG6** Develop a savings strategy that incorporates a variety of savings plans. (p. 84)

## KEY TERMS

account reconciliation *84*
asset management account (AMA) *76*
automated teller machine (ATM) *77*
cashier's check *84*
cash management *71*
certificate of deposit (CD) *88*
certified check *84*
checkbook ledger *81*
compound interest *87*
debit cards *77*
demand deposit *75*
deposit insurance *73*
effective rate of interest *87*
electronic funds transfer systems (EFTSs) *77*
Internet bank *73*
I Savings bond *90*
money market deposit account (MMDA) *76*
money market mutual fund (MMMF) *76*
negotiable order of withdrawal (NOW) account *76*

## CHAPTER OUTLINE

## MULTIMEDIA

### PowerPoints

See the PFIN PowerPoints for Chapter 4 at 4ltrpress.cengage.com.

### Kiplinger Videos

Available at the PFIN section of 4ltrpress.cengage.com. "Kip Tips" videos offer quick money management and investing advice. Ask your students to answer the corresponding questions.

## CHAPTER EXHIBITS & WORKSHEETS

### Video: "Cyber Banking"

- List several advantages of using an online bank rather than a traditional brick and mortar bank.

### Applying Personal Finance

Go to PFIN's "Applying Personal Finance" section of **4ltrpress.cengage.com**. Assign students to read the exercise on managing their cash. This exercise will help the students evaluate their cash management needs and the various financial services available, allowing them to select the one best suited for their needs.

### Critical Thinking Cases

Go to PFIN's "Critical Thinking Cases" section of **4ltrpress.cengage.com** and assign students Case 4.1 about Deborah Tan's Savings and Banking plans. Answers to Critical Thinking Questions are supplied for instructors only in the *Instructor's Manual*.

**WHAT'S INSIDE** Deciding whether to lease or buy an automobile, identifying housing alternatives, evaluating the benefits and costs of purchasing a home, and choosing appropriate mortgage financing.

## LEARNING GOALS

**LG1** Implement a plan to research and select a new or used automobile. (p. 93)

**LG2** Decide whether to buy or lease a car. (p. 98)

**LG3** Identify housing alternatives, assess the rental option, and perform a rent-or-buy analysis. (p. 101)

**LG4** Evaluate the benefits and costs of home ownership and estimate how much you can afford for a home. (p. 104)

**LG5** Describe the home-buying process. (p. 110)

**LG6** Choose mortgage financing that meets your needs. (p. 113)

## KEY TERMS

## CHAPTER OUTLINE

## MULTIMEDIA

### PowerPoints

See the PFIN PowerPoints for Chapter 5 at 4ltrpress.cengage.com.

## CHAPTER EXHIBITS & WORKSHEETS

## Kiplinger Videos

Available at the PFIN section of 4ltrpress.cengage.com. "Kip Tips" videos offer quick money management and investing advice. Ask your students to answer the corresponding questions.

### Video: "How Much House Can You Afford?"

- What guidelines do lenders typically follow when deciding whether to approve you for a loan to buy a house?

- How does your credit score affect your interest rate on a home loan?

### Video: "Should You Prepay Your Mortgage?"

- Describe how making extra payments on your mortgage could help you save money.

- How might you be better off investing extra monthly money rather than putting it toward prepaying your mortgage?

### Video: "Fixed Rate vs. Adjustable Rate Mortgage"

- What are the risks and advantages of an adjustable rate mortgage (ARM)?

### Video: "Haggle-Free Car Buying"

- Describe car buying services and how they are able to haggle the price of a car for you.

### Video: "Buy or Lease a Car?"

- What is the major determinate of whether you should buy or lease a car?

- What do the leasing terms "money factor" and "residual value" mean?

## Applying Personal Finance

Go to PFIN's "Applying Personal Finance" section of **4ltrpress .cengage.com**. Assign students to read the exercise on the housing market. For this exercise, the students will gather information on their local housing markets by reading recent issues of area newspapers and then describing the market for purchased and rental homes.

## Critical Thinking Cases

Go to PFIN's "Critical Thinking Cases" section of **4ltrpress .cengage.com** and assign students Case 5.2 about evaluating a mortgage loan for Michelle and Ken Dun. Answers to Critical Thinking Questions are supplied for instructors only in the *Instructor's Manual*.

# PREP CARD 6 Using Credit

**WHAT'S INSIDE** Developing a plan to create a strong credit history, different forms of open account credit, choosing the right credit cards, and avoiding credit problems.

## LEARNING GOALS

**LG1** Describe the reasons for using consumer credit and identify its benefits and problems. (p. 123)

**LG2** Develop a plan to establish a strong credit history. (p. 123)

**LG3** Distinguish among the different forms of open account credit. (p. 129)

**LG4** Apply for, obtain, and manage open forms of credit. (p. 134)

**LG5** Choose the right credit cards and recognize their advantages and disadvantages. (p. 140)

**LG6** Avoid credit problems, protect yourself against credit card fraud, and understand the personal bankruptcy process. (p. 140)

## KEY TERMS

affinity cards *131*
annual percentage rate (APR) *138*
average daily balance (ADB) method *138*
bank credit card *129*
base rate *130*
cash advance *130*
credit bureau *135*
credit investigation *135*
credit limit *129*
credit scoring *137*
debit card *132*
debt safety ratio *126*
grace period *130*
home equity credit line *133*
line of credit *129*
minimum monthly payment *139*
open account credit *129*
overdraft protection line *133*
personal bankruptcy *143*
retail charge card *132*

## CHAPTER OUTLINE

## MULTIMEDIA

### PowerPoints

See the PFIN PowerPoints for Chapter 6 at 4ltrpress.cengage.com.

## CHAPTER EXHIBITS & WORKSHEETS

## Kiplinger Videos

Available at the PFIN section of 4ltrpress.cengage.com. "Kip Tips" videos offer quick money management and investing advice. Ask your students to answer the corresponding questions.

### Video: "How to Pick the Right Credit Card"

- What kind of credit card is better for you if you pay off your balance every month? If you carry a balance each month?
- What negatives should you watch out for in a rewards card?

### Video: "Protecting Your Credit Score"

- List several measures you can take to ensure your credit score doesn't decline.

### Video: "Get Out of Debt Now"

- What are some of the first steps to take to pay off your debts?
- What can you do about repaying student loans?

## Applying Personal Finance

Go to PFIN's "Applying Personal Finance" section of **4ltrpress .cengage.com**. Assign students to read the exercise on credit. This exercise asks the student to obtain a copy of his or her credit report and examine it for any inaccuracies. Should the student need to improve his or her credit, what steps should be taken?

## Critical Thinking Cases

Go to PFIN's "Critical Thinking Cases" section of **4ltrpress .cengage.com** and assign students Case 6.2 about Patricia's new start after bankruptcy. Answers to Critical Thinking Questions are supplied for Instructors only in the *Instructor's Manual*.

**WHAT'S INSIDE** When to use consumer loans and identify various sources. How to calculate the finance charges of single-payment loans and determine the costs of installment loans.

## LEARNING GOALS

**LG1** Know when to use consumer loans and be able to differentiate between the major types. (p. 146)

**LG2** Identify the various sources of consumer loans. (p. 146)

**LG3** Choose the best loans by comparing finance charges, maturity, collateral, and other loan terms. (p. 151)

**LG4** Describe the features of, and calculate the finance charges on, single-payment loans. (p. 153)

**LG5** Evaluate the benefits of an installment loan. (p. 159)

**LG6** Determine the costs of installment loans and analyze whether it is better to pay cash or take out a loan. (p. 159)

## KEY TERMS

**add-on method** *161*

**captive finance company** *150*

**cash value (of life insurance)** *150*

**chattel mortgage** *156*

**collateral** *146*

**collateral note** *156*

**consumer finance company** *150*

**consumer loans** *146*

**discount method** *159*

**installment loan** *149*

**interim financing** *149*

**lien** *156*

**loan application** *153*

**loan disclosure statement** *156*

**loan rollover** *156*

**prepayment penalty** *156*

## CHAPTER OUTLINE

## MULTIMEDIA

### PowerPoints

See the PFIN PowerPoints for Chapter 7 at 4ltrpress.cengage.com.

### Applying Personal Finance

Go to PFIN's "Applying Personal Finance" section of **4ltrpress**.cengage.com. Assign students to read the exercise on making new car payments. This exercise will help the students learn about how loan payments are determined and the obligation they take on as a borrower.

## Critical Thinking Cases

Go to PFIN's "Critical Thinking Cases" section of **4ltrpress.cengage .com** and assign students Case 7.2 about Aaron Woods and his decision to buy a new car. Answers to Critical Thinking Questions are supplied for instructors only in the *Instructor's Manual*.

## WHAT'S INSIDE
The concept of risk, the basics of underwriting, how to calculate the amount of insurance one needs, and how to become familiar with life insurance policies.

# LEARNING GOALS

**LG1** Explain the concept of risk and the basics of insurance underwriting. (p. 169)

**LG2** Discuss the primary reasons for life insurance and identify those who need coverage. (p. 170)

**LG3** Calculate how much life insurance you need. (p. 171)

**LG4** Distinguish among the various types of life insurance policies and describe their advantages and disadvantages. (p. 175)

**LG5** Choose the best life insurance policy for your needs at the lowest cost. (p. 182)

**LG6** Become familiar with the key features of life insurance policies. (p. 185)

## KEY TERMS

## CHAPTER OUTLINE

## CHAPTER EXHIBITS & WORKSHEETS

## MULTIMEDIA

### PowerPoints

See the PFIN PowerPoints for Chapter 8 at 4ltrpress.cengage.com.

### Kiplinger Videos

Available at the PFIN section of 4ltrpress.cengage.com. "Kip Tips" videos offer quick money management and investing advice. Ask your students to answer the corresponding questions.

#### Video: "Life Insurance—How Much and How Long?"

- What basic calculations do you need to make to estimate how much life insurance you need?
- Why would a stay-at-home parent require life insurance in addition to the employed parent?

### Applying Personal Finance

Go to PFIN's "Applying Personal Finance" section of **4ltrpress .cengage.com**. Assign students to read the exercise on insuring their lives. This exercise will help the students determine current and future life insurance needs.

### Critical Thinking Cases

Go to PFIN's "Critical Thinking Cases" section of **4ltrpress .cengage.com** and assign students Case 8.1 about Chunhua Zua, who is trying to determine a life insurance policy for herself. Answers to Critical Thinking Questions are supplied for instructors only in the *Instructor's Manual*.

**WHAT'S INSIDE** The importance of health insurance and the types of medical expenses covered, how to analyze health insurance needs, and the features of disability income insurance.

## LEARNING GOALS

**LG1** Discuss why having adequate health insurance is important and identify the factors contributing to the growing cost of health insurance. (p. 191)

**LG2** Differentiate among the major types of health insurance plans and identify major private and public health insurance providers and their programs. (p. 192)

**LG3** Analyze your own health insurance needs and explain how to shop for appropriate coverage. (p. 197)

**LG4** Explain the basic types of medical expenses covered by the policy provisions of health insurance plans. (p. 199)

**LG5** Assess the need for, and features of, long-term care insurance. (p. 205)

**LG6** Discuss the features of disability income insurance and how to determine your need for it. (p. 208)

## KEY TERMS

## CHAPTER OUTLINE

## MULTIMEDIA

### Powerpoints

See the PFIN PowerPoints for Chapter 9 at 4ltrpress.cengage.com.

## CHAPTER EXHIBITS & WORKSHEETS

## Kiplinger Videos

Available at the PFIN section of 4ltrpress.cengage.com. "Kip Tips" videos offer quick money management and investing advice. Ask your students to answer the corresponding questions.

### Video: "Hold Down Health Insurance Costs"

● What kind of personal calculations should you make prior to choosing a health plan?

● What are some benefits to choosing a high deductible plan?

### Video: "Make the Most of Health Care Flex Plans"

● What are the financial advantages of a Flex Plan?

● Why shouldn't you be too scared of the "use it or lose it" rule?

### Video: "Long-Term Care Insurance"

● What are the options for paying for long-term care?

● Why is it best to consider long-term care insurance in one's 40s, 50s, and 60s?

## Applying Personal Finance

Go to PFIN's "Applying Personal Finance" section of **4ltrpress** **.cengage.com**. Assign students to read the exercise on insuring their health. This exercise will help the students examine their health insurance needs and determine the appropriate coverage for them.

## Critical Thinking Cases

Go to PFIN's "Critical Thinking Cases" section of **4ltrpress** **.cengage.com** and assign students Case 9.1 about self-employed window washer Brad Rowe. Answers to Critical Thinking Questions are supplied for instructors only in the *Instructor's Manual*.

**WHAT'S INSIDE** The importance of property insurance and coverage, how to analyze and choose cost effective policies, and other types of liability and property insurance.

# LEARNING GOALS

**LG1** Discuss the importance and basic principles of property insurance, including types of exposure, indemnity, and co-insurance. (p. 214)

**LG2** Identify the types of coverage provided by homeowner's insurance. (p. 217)

**LG3** Select the right homeowner's insurance policy for your needs. (p. 217)

**LG4** Analyze the coverage in a personal automobile policy (PAP) and choose the most cost-effective policy. (p. 223)

**LG5** Describe other types of property and liability insurance. (p. 229)

**LG6** Choose a property and liability insurance agent and company, and settle claims. (p. 230)

## KEY TERMS

**actual cash value** *216*
**bodily injury liability losses** *223*
**captive agent** *230*
**claims adjustor** *231*
**co-insurance** *217*
**collision insurance** *227*
**comprehensive automobile insurance** *227*
**comprehensive policy** *217*
**financial responsibility laws** *229*
**independent agent** *230*
**liability insurance** *214*
**named peril policy** *217*
**negligence** *216*
**no-fault automobile insurance** *227*
**peril** *214*
**personal automobile policy (PAP)** *223*
**personal liability umbrella policy** *230*
**personal property floater (PPF)** *219*
**principle of indemnity** *216*

## CHAPTER OUTLINE

## CHAPTER EXHIBITS & WORKSHEETS

## MULTIMEDIA

### PowerPoints

See the PFIN PowerPoints for Chapter 10 at 4ltrpress.cengage.com.

### Kiplinger Videos

Available at the PFIN section of 4ltrpress.cengage.com. "Kip Tips" videos offer quick money management and investing advice. Ask your students to answer the corresponding questions.

**Video: "Insuring Your Car"**

● List three things you can do to lower your auto insurance premium.

**Video: "Control the Cost of Homeowner's Insurance"**

● List several ways that you can cut your costs on homeowner's insurance.

● What is a C.L.U.E. report?

### Applying Personal Finance

Go to PFIN's "Applying Personal Finance" section of **4ltrpress .cengage.com.** Assign students to read the exercise on insuring property. This exercise will help the students determine property insurance needs.

### Critical Thinking Cases

Go to PFIN's "Critical Thinking Cases" section of **4ltrpress.cengage .com** and assign students Case 10.2 about Rob Worley and his insurance needs for a new car. Answers to Critical Thinking Questions are supplied for instructors only in the *Instructor's Manual.*

**WHAT'S INSIDE** Investments in the financial planning process, broker and dealer markets, buying and selling securities, and developing a securities portfolio.

## LEARNING GOALS

**LG1** Discuss the role that investing plays in the personal financial planning process and identify several different investment objectives. (p. 235)

**LG2** Distinguish between primary and secondary markets as well as between broker and dealer markets. (p. 240)

**LG3** Explain the process of buying and selling securities and recognize the different types of orders. (p. 244)

**LG4** Develop an appreciation of how various forms of investment information can lead to better investing skills and returns. (p. 249)

**LG5** Gain a basic understanding of the growing impact of the computer and the Internet on the field of investments. (p. 253)

**LG6** Describe an investment portfolio and how you'd go about developing and managing a portfolio of securities. (p. 256)

## KEY TERMS

## CHAPTER OUTLINE

## CHAPTER EXHIBITS & WORKSHEETS

## MULTIMEDIA

### PowerPoints

See the PFIN PowerPoints for Chapter 11 at 4ltrpress.cengage.com.

### Kiplinger Videos

Available at the PFIN section of 4ltrpress.cengage.com. "Kip Tips" videos offer quick money management and investing advice. Ask your students to answer the corresponding questions.

### Video: "The Time Value of Money"

- What does the "time value of money" mean?
- What is the "rule of 72"?

### Applying Personal Finance

Go to PFIN's "Applying Personal Finance" section of **4ltrpress .cengage.com.** Assign students to read the exercise on researching your investments. This exercise will help students learn about the annual stockholders' report of a company they've selected.

### Critical Thinking Cases

Go to PFIN's "Critical Thinking Cases" section of **4ltrpress .cengage.com** and assign students Case 11.1 about Eric and Stephanie Erikson and their investment goals. Answers to Critical Thinking Questions are supplied for instructors only in the *Instructor's Manual.*

WHAT'S INSIDE Types of investor risk, the merits of investing in common stock, issue characteristics of bonds, and the different types of bonds.

# LEARNING GOALS

**LG1** Describe the various types of risks to which investors are exposed, as well as the sources of return. (p. 263)

**LG2** Know how to search for an acceptable investment on the basis of risk, return, and yield. (p. 263)

**LG3** Discuss the merits of investing in common stock and be able to distinguish among the different types of stocks. (p. 268)

**LG4** Become familiar with the various measures of performance and how to use them in placing a value on stocks. (p. 268)

**LG5** Describe the basic issue characteristics of bonds as well as how these securities are used as investment vehicles. (p. 278)

**LG6** Distinguish between the different types of bonds, gain an understanding of how bond prices behave, and know how to compute different measures of yield. (p. 278)

## KEY TERMS

## CHAPTER OUTLINE

## CHAPTER EXHIBITS & WORKSHEETS

## MULTIMEDIA

### PowerPoints

See the PFIN PowerPoints for Chapter 12 at 4ltrpress.cengage.com.

### Kiplinger Videos

Available at the PFIN section of 4ltrpress.cengage.com. "Kip Tips" videos offer quick money management and investing advice. Ask your students to answer the corresponding questions.

#### Video: "What to Do When the Market Drops"

- What is an alternative to trying to "time the market"?
- What does it mean to "rebalance" your portfolio?

#### Video: "The Dow and Other Stock Indexes"

- How are the Dow Jones and S&P indexes different from one another?
- Why do professional investors pay more attention to the S&P index?
- Name and describe several other indexes besides the Dow Jones and S&P.

#### Video: "Investing in Bonds"

- What factors determine a bond's interest rate?
- What are the risks of bond investments?

### Applying Personal Finance

Go to PFIN's "Applying Personal Finance" section of **4ltrpress .cengage.com**. Assign students to read the "What's Your Type?" exercise. This exercise will help students examine the returns on various types of common stock.

### Critical Thinking Cases

Go to PFIN's "Critical Thinking Cases" section of **4ltrpress .cengage.com** and assign students Case 12.2 about Kristin Earhardt and her decision to invest. Answers to Critical Thinking Questions are supplied for instructors only in the *Instructor's Manual*.

**WHAT'S INSIDE** Mutual funds, open- and closed-end funds, funds available to investors, sources of return, and how to calculate the rate of return earned on an investment in a mutual fund.

## LEARNING GOALS

**LG1** Describe the basic features and operating characteristics of a mutual fund. (p. 290)

**LG2** Differentiate between open- and closed-end funds as well as exchange-traded funds, and discuss the various types of fund loads and charges. (p. 290)

**LG3** Discuss the types of funds available to investors and the different kinds of investor services offered by mutual funds. (p. 296)

**LG4** Gain an understanding of the variables that should be considered when selecting funds for investment purposes. (p. 302)

**LG5** Identify the sources of return and calculate the rate of return earned on an investment in a mutual fund. (p. 302)

**LG6** Understand the role that real estate plays in a diversified investment portfolio along with the basics of investing in real estate, either directly or indirectly. (p. 306)

## KEY TERMS

**12(b)-1 fee** *294*
**automatic investment plan** *300*
**automatic reinvestment plan** *300*
**back-end load** *294*
**closed-end investment company** *292*
**conversion (exchange) privileges** *300*
**exchange-traded fund (ETF)** *293*
**general-purpose money fund** *298*
**government securities money fund** *298*
**income (income-producing) property** *308*
**international fund** *299*

## CHAPTER OUTLINE

## CHAPTER EXHIBITS & WORKSHEETS

## MULTIMEDIA

### PowerPoints

See the PFIN PowerPoints for Chapter 13 at 4ltrpress.cengage.com.

### Kiplinger Videos

Available at the PFIN section of 4ltrpress.cengage.com. "Kip Tips" videos offer quick money management and investing advice. Ask your students to answer the corresponding questions.

**Video: "Mutual Fund Basics"**

- What is a mutual fund?
- How is an index fund different than other managed mutual funds?
- What is the difference between a "no-load" and "load" fund?

**Video: "Be a Better Fund Investor"**

- Why is a fund's past performance important yet limiting?
- What should you know about a fund's manager when assessing risk?
- Why are fast-growing assets a red flag for popular, well-performing funds?

**Video: "The Right Way to Invest in Real Estate"**

- What is the definition of a REIT?
- What makes a REIT a potentially attractive investment?

### Applying Personal Finance

Go to PFIN's "Applying Personal Finance" section of **4ltrpress .cengage.com.** Assign students to read the exercise on mutual funds. This exercise will help students learn about the types of mutual funds and how to pick based on investment needs.

### Critical Thinking Cases

Go to PFIN's "Critical Thinking Cases" section of **4ltrpress .cengage.com** and assign students Case 13.1 about Ray Sutton and his dilemma. Answers to Critical Thinking Questions are supplied for instructors only in the *Instructor's Manual.*

**WHAT'S INSIDE** Retirement planning, estimating income needs for retirement, types of employer-sponsored pension plans, and self-directed retirement plans.

## LEARNING GOALS

**LG1** Recognize the importance of retirement planning, and identify the three biggest pitfalls to good planning. (p. 313)

**LG2** Estimate your income needs in retirement and your retirement income. (p. 313)

**LG3** Explain the eligibility requirements and benefits of the Social Security program. (p. 318)

**LG4** Differentiate among the types of basic and supplemental employer-sponsored pension plans. (p. 321)

**LG5** Describe the various types of self-directed retirement plans. (p. 321)

**LG6** Choose the right type of annuity for your retirement plan. (p. 328)

## KEY TERMS

## CHAPTER OUTLINE

## MULTIMEDIA

### PowerPoints

See the PFIN PowerPoints for Chapter 14 at 4ltrpress.cengage.com.

### Kiplinger Videos

Available at the PFIN section of 4ltrpress.cengage.com. "Kip Tips" videos offer quick money management and investing advice. Ask your students to answer the corresponding questions.

## CHAPTER EXHIBITS & WORKSHEETS

### Video: "The Power of the IRA"
- Why invest in an IRA?
- Why is it better to make your yearly IRA contribution at the beginning of the calendar year?

### Video: "Paying for Retirement"
- Describe how you can estimate the amount of money you'll need to retire.

### Video: "Roth or Traditional IRA?"
- What are the tax benefits for each type of IRA?
- Why is a Roth IRA generally considered a better bet?

### Video: "The Roth Idea Comes to the 401(k)"
- What is a Roth 401(k)?
- Why might it be a better choice than a traditional 401(k)?

## Applying Personal Finance

Go to PFIN's "Applying Personal Finance" section of **4ltrpress .cengage.com.** Assign students to read the exercise on planning an ideal retirement plan. This exercise will help students learn about the retirement program that would best meet their needs.

## Critical Thinking Cases

Go to PFIN's "Critical Thinking Cases" section of **4ltrpress .cengage.com** and assign students Case 14.1 about neighbors Barbara Worrell and Rita Young. Answers to Critical Thinking Questions are supplied for instructors only in the *Instructor's Manual.*

# PREP CARD 15    Preserving Your Estate

**WHAT'S INSIDE** The role of estate planning, preparing a will, trusts, calculating federal taxes on an estate, and estate planning techniques.

## LEARNING GOALS

**LG1** Describe the role of estate planning in personal financial planning, and identify the seven steps involved in the process. (p. 334)

**LG2** Recognize the importance of preparing a will and other documents to protect you and your estate. (p. 337)

**LG3** Explain how trusts are used in estate planning. (p. 345)

**LG4** Determine whether a gift will be taxable and use planned gifts to reduce estate taxes. (p. 348)

**LG5** Calculate federal taxes due on an estate. (p. 351)

**LG6** Use effective estate planning techniques to minimize estate taxes. (p. 352)

## KEY TERMS

## CHAPTER OUTLINE

## MULTIMEDIA

### PowerPoints

See the PFIN PowerPoints for Chapter 15 at 4ltrpress.cengage.com.

## CHAPTER EXHIBITS & WORKSHEETS

### Kiplinger Videos

Available at the PFIN section of 4ltrpress.cengage.com. "Kip Tips" videos offer quick money management and investing advice. Ask your students to answer the corresponding questions.

**Video: "Why You Need a Will"**

● List three reasons why it is important to have a will.

● How do you create a will?

### Applying Personal Finance

Go to PFIN's "Applying Personal Finance" section of **4ltrpress** **.cengage.com.** Assign students to read the exercise on preparing a will. This exercise will help students learn what their will should contain and how it can be changed based on future circumstances.

### Critical Thinking Cases

Go to PFIN's "Critical Thinking Cases" section of **4ltrpress** **.cengage.com** and assign students Case 15.2 about Edward Thorpe and his wife's will. Answers to Critical Thinking Questions are supplied for instructors only in the *Instructor's Manual*.